PATTERNS IN ACTION

Robert A. Schwegler

University of Rhode Island

LITTLE, BROWN and COMPANY

Boston   Toronto

Library of Congress Cataloging in Publication Data

Schwegler, Robert A.
  Patterns in action.

  Includes index.
  1. College readers. 2. English language—Rhetoric.
I. Title.
PE1417.S366 1985   808'.0427   84-25054
ISBN 0-316-77577-0

Copyright © 1985 by Robert A. Schwegler

Library of Congress Catalog Card No. 84-25054

ISBN 0-316-77577-0

9 8 7 6 5 4 3 2 1

MV

Published simultaneously in Canada
by Little, Brown & Company (Canada) Limited
Printed in the United States of America

Acknowledgments

Page 489: Margaret Bourke-White, *Life* Magazine, © 1936 Time Inc.
Edward Abbey, "The Damnation of a Canyon." From *Beyond the Wall* by
Edward Abbey. Copyright © 1971, 1976, 1977, 1979, 1984 by Edward Abbey. Re-
printed by permission of Holt, Rinehart and Winston, Publishers.
A. Alvarez, "A Test of Will." Copyright © 1983 by The New York Times
Company. Reprinted by permission.
Michael J. Arlen, "Ode to Thanksgiving." From *The Camera Age* by Michael J.
Arlen. Copyright © 1978, 1981 by Michael J. Arlen. Reprinted by permission of
Farrar, Straus and Giroux, Inc.

(continued on page 585)

PREFACE

Successful writers know how to make good use of their skills and knowledge. They know how to draw on experiences, facts, and ideas and can blend them to create an essay whose content is worth sharing with readers. They are able to employ a variety of forms of written expression, using different sentence, paragraph, and essay patterns as ways of sharing information, arguments, and feelings. They shape and revise their writing to take into account the demands of the subject, the purpose for which they are writing, and the expectations and attitudes of their audience.

Above all, successful writers have mastered the skills of exploring a subject and organizing, drafting, and revising an essay—skills we often refer to collectively as "the writing process." It makes sense to talk of writing as a process because the act of writing calls for using these skills not individually but in combination. In probing a subject to discover ideas for an essay, a writer may recognize ways to arrange the finished product. Or in revising, the writer may decide to go beyond changes in wording and style to alter the purpose of the essay or to add new information and ideas. Thus much writing instruction today is properly directed at acquainting students with the elements and interrelationships of the writing process, often by observing a piece of writing in various stages of development or by describing the practices characteristic of experienced writers.

Yet though we speak of the writing process, we might with even more justification refer to it as "the writing/reading process" because reading plays an essential role in all the stages of writing. It is through reading that developing and experienced writers alike gather material for their writing and build a repertoire of stylistic and rhetorical patterns to draw on as they compose. Reading gives writers a chance to understand their audience's needs and expectations because it allows them to see what kinds of expression have succeeded (or failed) when addressed to similar audiences. And reading teaches us how to explore our own experience and the world around us by sharing the questions, arguments, and ideas that other people have used as guides.

The essays, discussions, questions, and activities in *Patterns in Action* are all directed toward helping developing writers make reading a useful and indispensable part of their writing. The essays provide models of effective writing and subjects for lively discussion; they also suggest perspectives that can provide a fresh view of experience. The discussion that opens each chapter shows how various patterns of expression can be used to promote thinking and to aid communication. The questions and activities following the selection encourage students to respond with ideas and feelings that might in turn be developed into essays, and they also direct attention to strategies of style and structure that students can use in their own work. The opening chapter ("Reading and Writing") and Chapter 11 ("Writers on Writing") speak directly of the many connections between reading and writing and suggest how the skills of critical reading stressed elsewhere in the text can help students organize and revise what they have to say. (The structure of this text is discussed in detail at the end of Chapter 1—"How This Book Is Arranged," pp. 13–15.)

The text throughout emphasizes the aims of writing (to express feelings, to inform and explain, to persuade, to re-create experience) as well as the forms. In addition, it is built around discussion of ideal rhetorical patterns, such as comparison and classification. The text recognizes that in real writing—in action—these forms are shaped by audience and occasions and that good writing mixes the patterns in many different ways. The instructor's manual for this text, written with the aid of Judith Stanford and with a bibliography on reading and writing by Chris Anson, explores some of the many interactions of form and purpose and suggests a variety of activities to explore these relationships.

For their help in preparing this book I would like to thank Carolyn Potts of Little, Brown who nurtured and guided it; Virginia Pye and Elizabeth Schaaf (also of Little, Brown) who made sure that ideas turned into chapters, and Adrienne Weiss and Carolyn Woznick, who helped in the final stage. Most of all, I would like to thank Nancy Newman Schwegler, who is responsible for whatever good the text contains but none of its miscues. Sylvan Barnet, Harvey Wiener, and Judith Stanford provided help and counsel throughout the project. Chris Anson, Sam Watson, Pat Murray, Marie Secor, Janice Neuleib, and Susan Pratt helped me in many ways with their comments on the readings and on the design of the content, and William Kelly read large portions of the manuscript and acted as a sounding board. Three students provided papers for this text: Greg Glovach, Margi Ganucci (Chapter 9), and Heather Kaye. Finally, I am greatly indebted to Sylvan Barnet and Mike Rose for sharing their experiences as writers and their advice as teachers through the essays they prepared for Chapter 11.

CONTENTS

7 CAUSE AND EFFECT

Asking Why It Happened and What Will Happen Next   263

8 DEFINITION

Identifying and Probing the Meaning   317

FURTHER READINGS

PATTERNS
IN ACTION

1

&. INTRODUCTION

Reading and Writing

"To learn to write you need to read both widely and well." This often-repeated advice springs from the reasonable assumption that the work of accomplished writers can introduce us to ways of improving our own writing. Published essays—finished products—cannot, of course, tell us much about what goes on during the act of writing. They cannot show us the false starts, the mistakes, and the frequent revisions that are an inevitable part of the efforts of even the best writers. Nor do they reveal the ways writers discover interesting ideas or decide which of two or three possible methods will best convey these ideas to readers. However, published essays can do some equally important things. As models for effective writing, they help us set goals for our own essays. They suggest ideas, strategies, and styles of writing that we can draw on in our work. Finally, they help us become aware of the ways an essay affects its audience, readers like ourselves.

Not all reading contributes equally to the development of writing skills, however. To read essays or books only for the facts they present is of little benefit to writing because such reading calls for no attention to the ideas behind the facts or to the ways that both information and ideas are shared with readers.

For your writing to benefit, you must read with a critical eye—that is, with an awareness both of what an author is saying and how it is being said. Critical reading operates at three levels, each of which can make a different contribution to your writing. At one level it involves reading for meaning—going beyond the facts presented

1

in an essay to identify the ideas that link them. By examining an essay carefully to make sure you understand its generalizations and arguments as well as the evidence that supports them, and by responding to its conclusions with opinions of your own, you can develop insights and ideas worth sharing through your own writing.

At a second level, critical reading means being aware of the strategies a writer uses to introduce and organize an essay, to support an argument, and to structure paragraphs. It means paying attention to the ways a writer uses words to emphasize ideas, to create tone and convey attitudes, or to communicate emotions and paint vivid pictures. Writing strategies can be as broad as the patterns used to organize entire essays or sections of essays, like those illustrated in the chapters of this text (including comparison, description, analysis, and narration), and they can be as limited as the brief examples used to support a generalization. Stylistic strategies—the words an author chooses and the way they are combined in sentences—may involve the creation of images that allow a reader to visualize a scene or share the author's feelings, or they may involve variations in sentence structure to achieve clarity and emphasis.

To help understand reading for strategy and style, you might try this brief experiment. Write a set of directions for something you can do well, such as baking a souffle, waterskiing on one ski, or playing handball. Assume that your audience does not share your level of expertise. As you write, notice the many decisions you make: "Should I abbreviate teaspoons?" "Will I have to explain what kind of shoes to wear when playing handball, or tell people where to find a handball court?" "How can I begin talking about waterskiing?" After you have finished, look at similar directions in a cookbook, a pamphlet on the rules for handball, or a book about water sports. As you read, see how many details you notice that you did not notice when you read similar things in the past. You may find yourself remarking, "That's a good way to get people interested in waterskiing!" "Yes, I thought writing out *teaspoons* was a waste of space, but I didn't know whether to put a period after the abbreviation." "I had trouble explaining that complicated way of hitting the ball; the way this writer does it is really clear." As you read, you will be collecting strategies to use the next time in your own writing.

At a third level, critical reading calls for an awareness of how well a work meets the needs of an audience. It means developing the ability to judge how most readers would respond to an essay, knowing whether they would be convinced by the author's arguments and supporting evidence, knowing when they would require more information and explanation, and recognizing when the writer has presented more detail than most readers will need. It also means judging the merit of an author's ideas (Are her arguments for gun control sensible? Are they workable? Has she taken account of the major objections to gun control?) and of the way the ideas are presented (Is her analysis of the problem of rapidly rising health care costs easy to follow? Does she identify the major causes? Is her outlook made clear in a thesis statement?). Finally, it means being able to judge the appropriateness of the strategies an author has chosen (Is cause-and-effect the best pattern for talking about this subject? Would the author be able to shed more light on it by comparing it with similar predicaments our society faced fifty years ago?).

To interpret and evaluate as you read and to recognize the strategies a piece of writing employs, you must draw on your experiences and values and also on what you have learned about forms of expression through many different kinds of reading, both fiction and nonfiction. Just as your outlook and the awareness of writing strategies you bring to an essay will differ from those of other readers, so you can expect your responses to differ, too, both in important and unimportant ways. To someone who has always lived in a city, for example, an informative article on beekeeping may seem interesting and authoritative. A beekeeper, however, may respond in irritation because the article's information may be inaccurate or its advice potentially harmful either to the novice beekeeper or the bees themselves. Your response to an essay may also change from the first time you read it to the second or third.

Variety in response is, of course, one of the pleasures of rereading and of talking with others about an essay or story. Some kinds of writing, mostly stories and novels, but nonfiction essays and books as well, even seem to encourage differing interpretations and to invite controversy. In most essays, though, the writer tries to limit the range of responses in order to make sure the meaning is clear to most members of the audience. One of the most effective ways a writer can do this is by employing forms of expression—such as the patterns illustrated in this text—whose meaning and purpose should be clear to most readers. Yet critical reading is never simply a matter of recognizing such patterns and extracting the meaning from an essay.

It is an active response to what an essay says (and how it says it), an activity as creative and challenging in its own way as is the writing of an essay.

PATTERNS IN ACTION

This text emphasizes the role patterns of thought and expression play in both reading and writing. The basic patterns of thought are ways our minds can explore a subject, looking at it from different perspectives and isolating different aspects. The patterns include narration, description, example, comparison, process, cause-effect, definition, division, and classification.[1] Perhaps the easiest way to understand the patterns is to regard them as questions one might ask about a subject. In thinking about a computer, for example, you might view it as a process, asking "What happens inside a computer between the time I ask it to perform a complicated mathematical operation and the time the answer is printed out on the screen?" or "How do the chips that make up computers actually operate?" You might look at it as a cause or an effect, asking "What major changes in business and industry are computers likely to cause in the next decade?" or "What technological discoveries made small, high-speed, low-cost computers possible?"

In the following list, each pattern of thought is accompanied by questions of the type it enables us to ask about a subject. As you prepare to write, you may wish to use these or similar questions to probe a topic and to develop ideas or interpretations. Notice, too, that the questions for each pattern of thought will encourage you to take a different perspective on the topic.

Narration
> What happened?
> To whom did it happen?
> When? Where?

Description
> What are the physical features?
> How is it organized in space?

---

1. The patterns of argument, discussed in Chapter 10, are combinations of these basic patterns.

Example
    What are some reasonable illustrations?
    What are some representative examples or instances?
Comparison
    Is it similar to other things?
    Is it different from other things?
Process
    How does it work?
    How can it be done?
Cause-Effect
    Why did it happen?
    What is likely to happen in the future?
Definition
    To what class of things does it belong?
    What features characterize it and set it off from other things?
Division
    What are the parts?
    How are they related to each other and to the whole?
Classification
    Into what categories does it fall?
    What are the characteristics of each category?

The basic ways of thinking about a subject correspond, in turn, to writing strategies, to patterns of development that can be used to organize whole essays or paragraphs and other sections of an essay. For example, in asking what steps a computer follows to estimate a company's future sales and profits or to predict population growth in a region, you have already begun to divide its operation into a series of logical stages that make the whole process easier to understand. This arrangement would help readers understand the process too, and you would probably choose to use it in organizing a written explanation, perhaps following a general outline like this:

Step 1 (description and discussion)
Step 2 (description and discussion)
Steps 3, 4, 5, etc. (description and discussion)

Likewise, in sharing your speculations about the causes (or effects) of a recent fad in clothes or entertainment, you might choose to arrange and develop your conclusions in a pattern similar to that you followed arriving at them, beginning by isolating the probable causes then moving on to discuss the possible effects as in this outline:

Cause 1 (description and discussion)
Causes 2, 3, 4, etc. (description and discussion)
Effect 1 (description and discussion)
Effects 2, 3, 4, etc. (description and discussion)

(The relationship between ways of thinking and ways of developing and arranging an essay is explored in depth in Chapters 2–10 of this book.)

These basic patterns of thought and expression can be used for a variety of purposes in writing: to inform or explain, to argue, to explore or speculate, to express feelings, or to amuse and entertain. The specific purposes they serve will depend on both the subject and the point an author is trying to make. A writer might, for instance, use comparison as a pattern of development in arguing that a new highway is a better solution for traffic congestion in a particular city than is a new mass transit system. Another writer might explore the effects of each solution and conclude that neither will do much to relieve the current problem. A third might use classification to explain the solutions that have been adopted in other cities. A fourth might use narration or description to express the feelings of a commuter caught in a traffic jam.

Sometimes, moreover, the patterns appear in a more precise form as adaptations to the needs of the occasion. When addressing the causes of a problem or the possible solutions, for example, cause-and-effect often takes the form of a problem analysis or a problem-solution essay. Process turns up frequently as a set of directions; comparison appears in evaluations as a way of deciding which of two or more options (products or courses of action, for instance) is preferable.

These more specific patterns represent ways our culture has chosen to respond to specific subjects and situations and to communicate about them. Once you have been alerted to these "patterns in action," you will find it relatively easy to identify them in your reading and to recognize writing situations that call for them because you have probably encountered and used them many times before—

without consciously recognizing them as patterns of thought and expression. Your experience will also tell you that they are not rigid rules governing the way people communicate but loose and useful agreements among writers and readers about the most effective ways to share ideas, information, and feelings. The patterns can and should be adapted to meet the needs of different purposes, topics, and occasions.

THE READING PROCESS

To understand how the basic patterns of development and the more specific ones derived from them can form an important link between writers and readers, let us look briefly at some of the things that happen as we read.

As we begin reading an essay, we look for signs of its purpose and of the pattern it will follow. Sometimes a title makes these clear: "How to Build Your Own Airplane for Less than $4000" (purpose: to inform; pattern: process). At other times words and phrases provide adequate clues: *acid rain, problem causing all sorts of trouble, have not yet taken any effective action* (purpose: to argue for immediate action; pattern: cause-effect). Often a direct statement (thesis statement) indicates the conclusion or interpretation an essay will support: "In a surprising number of cases, however, a healthful activity like running, weightlifting, or bicycling becomes an obsession or an addiction, harming physical and mental well-being rather than improving it" (purpose: explain and defend a point of view; pattern: example). In a well-written essay, these and other signs allow us to predict with some certainty the pattern an essay will follow and at the same time to recognize its purpose, to understand why the author is writing it and what he or she expects us to understand and feel when we have finished reading.

Developing the ability to recognize almost automatically the pattern and purpose of an essay is important for two reasons: (1) Readers who have a sense of the arrangement and direction of an essay can spend their time trying to understand and respond to the ideas and information and to the language through which they are presented rather than worrying about what point the author is trying to make, how the parts of the essay fit together, and whether the piece is worth the energy needed to finish reading it. (2) Readers who understand the aim of an essay are free to evaluate how it accomplishes that aim, to judge how well the essay's strategies, evidence, and arguments deal with the subject and meet the needs of readers.

As a writer, you need to be aware that your readers will expect you to follow a clear and consistent pattern in your writing and to convey a clear sense of your purpose so they can understand what you have to say and be able to respond to it fully and critically. This means using patterns of expression your readers will be able to recognize and providing your audience with indications of purpose through such devices as thesis statements, transitions (cue words), and topic sentences. These strategies and others are discussed in detail in the Glossary (pp. 569–584) and in the introductions to individual chapters.

To write clearly does not mean that you should follow slavishly any of the patterns discussed in this text or that you should assume that the way professional writers use patterns in the readings are the only ways the patterns can be used. On the contrary, the patterns are simply flexible frameworks for thought and expression; the readings and discussions in this text indicate some of the many ways the patterns can be adapted to a variety of subjects, purposes, and occasions.

Almost all good writing mixes patterns, arranging them in whatever combination best serves the point the author wants to make. As long as the patterns being mixed are familiar and their arrangement is clearly announced through transition words and topic sentences or statements that summarize the author's aim, readers should have no more trouble understanding the arrangement of an essay that mixes patterns to serve a clear purpose than they would have following a straightforward narrative or a set of directions. Successful writers develop a kind of tact, too, that helps them recognize when an audience will need guidance to understand the structure of an essay and when readers will be able to recognize the arrangement with little help. The general rule is that the more complicated the structure or the more involved an essay's conclusions and the evidence that supports them, the more guidance readers will need. Observing the strategies experienced writers follow is a good way to develop this tact in your own writing.

THE WRITING PROCESS

While the main focus of this text is on the contributions reading can make to writing, it also pays attention to the many decisions a writer has to make in moving from initial idea to finished essay. These decisions are often referred to collectively as the writing process or the stages of writing. Learning about them from the example and advice of successful writers can be an excellent way to develop your own writing skills.

It is useful to think of the writing process as a series of stages: finding a topic and deciding on a pattern, gathering material and refining purpose, organizing, writing, and revising. Yet experience indicates that writing usually does not follow such a simple pattern. While revising the sentences in a paragraph, a writer may discover a new and interesting point to make or may alter his or her view of an essay's purpose. A writer may sometimes complete the second half of a paper while the first half is still in rough draft. In your own case, the way you write may depend in part on the composing process that works best for you and in part on the demands of your subject. Good writers frequently move backwards and forwards in the writing process, inventing, organizing, and revising. Nonetheless, there is a general movement in the way most people write, from ideas and feelings through various rough drafts to a polished essay. Among the activities useful at each stage, three contribute the most to successful writing: probing a topic, choosing a plan, and revising.

There are many ways to probe a topic in order to discover insights and ideas for writing. Some writers just sit and think about the topic; others employ questions that reflect one of the basic patterns of thought (like the questions listed on pp. 4–5). Most people use a variation of either *freewriting* or *brainstorming and clustering.* Freewriting means putting down on paper every idea that comes into your head without stopping to decide if it is good or bad and without caring how closely related it is to the particular topic. Freewriting gets ideas flowing; it unfreezes your creativity and helps you explore a topic from fresh perspectives. Though freewriting needs no specific topic, the kind you do to get started on a paper or to come up with ideas for a difficult point in an essay you are writing will generally be directed to a specific subject. Here is how student Susan Andrade started a ten-minute in-class assignment in freewriting following the instruction, "Write about something that really bothers you."

> Bothers? The only thing that really bothers me is this assignment—and maybe the water, yeah the water. Last time I was home it was even browner, and smellier, and disgustinger, and yukkier, and chemically-er than I ever remembered. Mom says the Bristol water company can't afford new pipes—I'll bet they can't, sooner or later someone will die or come up with permanent brain damage from the water and then they'll have to spend the money or give up and start getting the water from some other reservoirs and not their own—that might make a difference *if* they do something about the pipes too. . . .

As you can see, Susan soon discovered something that was bothering her, and she was even able to be reasonably specific about the source of her discontent. Of course, this freewriting is far from being a final piece of writing, but at least it suggests both a topic (the water) and some possible purposes (to explain why the water is so bad; to explore ways of solving the problem). Freewriting like this can get the whole writing process off to a good start by giving the writer a glimpse not only of the possibilities of a subject but of the reasons for sharing thoughts about it with an audience.

Brainstorming is similar in intent to freewriting, but it calls simply for a listing of ideas, facts, arguments, and counterarguments about a topic and can be done over several days as well as in one sitting. Clustering is the second half of brainstorming. It involves circling or underlining the elements in the list to discover relationships and to suggest ways of writing about a topic. Here is how some of Susan Andrade's thoughts about the water might have looked in the form of brainstorming and clustering:

Water—

- the smell
- the taste
- the brownish color
- how it looks coming out of the faucet

- Is it unhealthy?
- Has anyone died from Bristol County water?
- What if someone did die?
- Could it hurt a fetus? How many retarded children or kids with birth defects each year in the area?

Water authority people—
　　Not really competent?
　　　　Why not do something?
　　　　Money?
　　　　Laziness?
Big scandal in newspapers
Water shortage—smelled and looked even worse
Reservoirs too small
Pipes too old

Like the freewriting, this exercise suggests a topic and some possible purposes for writing, but the clustering also helps identify subtopics—the appearance of the water, the causes of the problem, the effects on health—that might become sections within an essay. The technique you choose to use may depend on which works best for you or which seems most likely to provide you with the kind of help you need. Both help you generate ideas and probe a topic, however, and both can be used anytime in the writing process.

Although a few people can sit down with only a few ideas in mind and write a draft of a paper, most people find writing virtually impossible without some sort of plan. Plans can take all sorts of forms. They can be lists of ideas, formal or informal outlines (see Glossary: Outlines), or tentative thesis statements followed by a series of supporting generalizations. Another effective kind of plan is to have in mind a general pattern for an essay and to divide up your material according to the pattern before you begin writing. The first sections of Chapters 2–10 suggest some general patterns for essays that you may find useful in organizing your writing. Another pattern useful for much of the writing you will do in college (essays, term papers, essay exams) is the standard essay pattern. This pattern consists of an introduction, the body, and a conclusion:

Introduction—introduces the topic and indicates why it is worth reading about; states the author's point, generally in the form of a thesis statement; focuses the readers' attention on the most important parts of the topic and on the author's reasons for writing about it.

Body—paragraphs that explain and support the thesis through illustrations and examples, explanations, arguments, and facts and figures; to maintain unity in the essay, the supporting paragraphs are usually linked explicitly or implicitly to the thesis they support.

Conclusion—reminds readers of the thesis and may restate it; summarizes the supporting arguments and evidence briefly and reinforces the essay's overall purpose.

Before she wrote the essay that developed out of her freewriting, Susan Andrade prepared the following plan based on the standard essay pattern:

Introduction—describe the smell, taste, and appearance of the water that comes out of faucets in Bristol County homes; then give thesis: "The condition of water in Bristol County has become so bad that it is time to start looking for solutions."

Body—Paragraph 1: Tell about the way the water stains porcelain sinks, stainless steel and aluminum pans, tea and coffee cups, and teeth; say what an irritation and waste this is.

Paragraph 2: Tell how people often feel ill after drinking the water, and about how the county health officer has started to investigate cases of diarrhea and skin irritation that may be linked to the water.

Paragraph 3: Tell how Bristol County has the highest rate of birth defects and infectious diseases in the state; suggest that even though no one has been able to link these to the water they are serious enough effects to need further research into their relationship with the water.

Conclusion—summarize the evidence and remind people that looking into the effects of the water is better than letting real problems creep up on us.

This plan helped Susan write a good rough draft even though she realized as she wrote it that the effects she planned to describe in the third supporting paragraph were so speculative that they pro-. vided weak support for her thesis and would need further development. Before she revised the essay, Susan did some research and found that the links to disease were much stronger than she had thought, and in the final form the third supporting paragraph turned into two paragraphs that helped make the essay quite convincing.

The difference between a good essay and an average essay is often simply a matter of revision. Effective revising calls for critical reading, for the ability to look at one's work from the outside and judge its effectiveness. Effective revision is also usually more than a matter of superficial changes in wording. It requires whatever changes in strategy and style are necessary to help the essay fulfill its purpose and to meet the needs and expectations of readers. In your own revision, the knowledge of writing strategies you have gained through critical reading and the ability you have developed to judge the effectiveness of an essay come together to help you evaluate and improve your own work.

Critical reading is thus linked to writing in a number of important ways. It is the purpose of this text to help you develop your reading and writing skills at the same time so that they can work together to help you share your ideas and feelings effectively with your readers.

HOW THIS BOOK IS ARRANGED

Each of the main chapters in this text (Chapters 2–10) focuses on one or more of the chief patterns of thought and expression that appear frequently in professional writing and that are important strategies for all writers to master: narration, description, example, comparison, process, cause-and-effect, definition, division, classification, and argument.[2] The essays in each chapter not only illustrate the patterns and provide models for student writing, they are also worth reading and discussing in their own right. The selections in each chapter are arranged in increasing order of complexity and usually of length. Moreover, they range from those that embody a pattern in a relatively straightforward manner (usually the early selections in a chapter) to those that mix patterns in various ways.

The introduction to each reading provides background information on the author and the selection, calls attention to the essay's most important strategies, and often invites students to respond to

2. Argument is both a pattern of development and a purpose for writing (see Chapter 10, pp. 419–436).

what the author has to say. The questions following each essay encourage critical reading by directing attention to the essay's meaning, to its probable effect on readers, to the strategies it employs, and to its language and style. In addition, each essay is followed by topics for further study, discussion, or writing, and each chapter concludes with a variety of writing suggestions.

The discussions that open Chapters 2–10 have three parts: "What the Pattern Does," "The Process," and "The Pattern in Action." "What the Pattern Does" defines a pattern and explores its roles in thought and expression, providing an illustration in the form of a paragraph taken from the work of a professional writer. "The Process" contains detailed suggestions for writing essays making use of the strategy as well as examples of student writing representing different stages of planning, writing, and revision. "The Pattern in Action" shows how the basic pattern of development appears frequently in forms adapted to the needs of particular situations or audiences. In addition, following the opening essay in each chapter is a "Commentary" discussing how the writer has adapted the basic strategy to the needs of a specific subject, audience, and purpose and pointing out the essay's usefulness as a model for student writing.

Because the strategies of thought and expression illustrated in this text are based on the ways our minds naturally view experience, they can be found in writing for all occasions and from all historical periods. The way writers choose to combine the patterns, however, and the commonly used forms of writing based on them (problem analysis and evaluation, for example) vary from century to century, reflecting changes in the aims of writing and in taste. The essays in "Further Readings: Classic Essays" illustrate some of the structures and purposes for writing authors have employed in the past. The essays in "Further Readings: Contemporary Essays" show how current writers have begun to stretch and reshape the ways we express ourselves. The essays in both sections may suggest ways student writers can experiment in their own work. The selections are presented without extensive comment to encourage free-ranging discussion and response.

The essays in Chapter 11, "Writers on Writing," were written by professional writers who are themselves teachers of writing. The selections offer detailed, practical advice for mastering the elements of the writing process and for overcoming difficulties that all writers, including professionals, must face. Two of these essays, Sylvan Barnet's "Writing and Reading: Some Concrete Observations" and Mike Rose's "Writing Around Rules" were written especially for this collection and speak directly to readers of this book about choosing a subject, developing ideas, and avoiding writer's block. The other essays, Eudora Welty's "Listening," Donald M. Murray's "The Maker's Eye: Revising Your Own Manuscripts," and William Zinsser's "Writing With a Word Processor" suggest ways to develop skills of observation and revision and describe techniques for achieving a clear, concise style.

The text concludes with a glossary of terms and concepts that provides practical advice in addition to definitions and explanations.

2

❧ NARRATIVE

Writing About Yourself and Others

WHAT NARRATIVE DOES

You begin the story this way: "Last night I got home from work late, about 8:15, because I had to pick up my car from the repair shop and get some groceries. The apartment was dark, and as I opened the door I heard a dull thump; a low, rasping noise; then suddenly. . . ." As you speak you hope that your friends and co-workers will look up from writing, from drinking coffee, or from conversation to listen attentively. You re-create the events in detail so that listeners will share the surprise and fear you felt. Though you often tell stories simply to amuse or to share an experience, this time your purpose is more specific: you want to convince your audience that there are good reasons for your not having quite finished the project you promised to have done for today.

Stories like this—personal narratives that make a point—are familiar elements of everyday conversation, and they appear almost as often in written form in letters and diaries, in newspaper columns, magazine articles, and books. Narrative appears in other places, too, though we may fail to recognize it at first. Accident reports, news items, records of experiments, and history texts are all narratives; so are the anecdotes (accounts of a single event) we use as evidence in an argument or as illustrations to help explain a difficult concept. With the possible exception of description, no pattern of expression turns up as frequently as narrative does, either as a pattern for entire essays or as a source of examples and illustrations.

17

Novels and short stories, are, of course, narratives, but unlike these invented stories, narrative essays do not invite us to enter a fictional world created by the author. Instead, they may present events drawn from the writer's personal experience: childhood memories of a divorce, the day fellow employees got revenge on a dishonest boss, or an act of courage by a handicapped person. Or they may present events gathered through a variety of means: by direct observation (a case study of activities in an elementary classroom), through interviews (a narrative of an election campaign), from written sources (an account of an important historical event).

As writers we can use narrative to share a personal view of events: to tell what it is like to be the victim of a tornado, robbery, or fire, or to share anger over the discovery of corruption and dishonesty among fellow employees ("I had heard about the 'shrinkage' of profits caused by employees taking a dollar or two from the cash register, but what happened during my second week of work was far more than petty theft. . . ."). We can use it to inform: to retrace the steps in human evolution, perhaps, or the development of Impressionistic painting in France during the nineteenth century ("Soon after Manet's paintings appeared in the gallery, crowds of laughing, jeering viewers surrounded them, and the critics, too, were hostile. . . ."). We can use it to support or convince: to argue in favor of stricter enforcement of drunk-driving laws by telling how a high school classmate was killed in an automobile accident.

Having a specific purpose in mind as you prepare a narrative is important, of course, but you also need to be aware of what readers expect from a narrative essay so you can take these expectations into account as you write and revise.

To begin with, readers expect a narrative essay to help them understand *what happened*. They expect a writer to put events in some reasonable order (usually chronological) and to tell what happened, when, where, and to whom. They expect him or her to indicate what events led to others and to distinguish between important events and less important ones. As anyone who has tried to write even a simple accident report or the minutes of a meeting realizes, getting a narrative to make plain the relationships between events can be a challenging task. Rearranging those relationships to emphasize the most important points without at the same time creating confusion can be even more difficult.

Next and most important, readers expect an essay to help them see the *significance* of events. They look for the point the author is making, for what he or she has to say about an episode or for how the events are used to support a thesis. So strong is this expectation that unless the point is made clear either directly, through comments on the events or a thesis statement, or indirectly, through an arrangement that calls attention to the most important happenings, readers will complain that they "don't know what the essay is about."

Too often, inexperienced writers assume that if the significance is clear to them—even if they discovered it only after writing several drafts—then it ought to be apparent, more or less automatically, to an audience. Or they hesitate to "break the spell" with direct comments on the meaning of a story. Yet commentary can be interesting itself, as in "The Angry Winter," in which Loren Eiseley takes a small incident (his dog's refusal to part with a fossil bone) and meditates on what it reveals about the survival of primitive attitudes in both animals and humans.

Finally, readers expect a narrative essay to *re-create* events so that they can share the experience, at least to the extent this is possible through writing. Because we rely heavily on the authority of our own experience or the experience of others that we have shared in some way, narrative can be a particularly effective means of support. But the events should not be portrayed so vividly that they call attention only to themselves or presented in such detail that they obscure the point of an essay.

Even incidents as remote as those from the medieval period can be made accessible through narrative. For example, in this passage taken from *A Distant Mirror: The Calamitous 14th Century,* Barbara Tuchman tells how the Black Death, the bubonic plague, came to Europe. Though this narrative paragraph (from the opening of a chapter) contains no explicit thesis, its purpose is clearly to set forth the theme to be developed in the rest of the discussion: The Black Death was gruesome, sudden, and beyond control; little wonder that many in the fourteenth century believed that "This is the end of the world."

> In October 1347, two months after the fall of Calais, Genoese trading ships put into the harbor of Messina in Sicily with dead and dying men at the oars. The ships had come from the Black Sea port of Caffa (now Feodosiya) in the Crimea, where the Genoese maintained

a trading post. The diseased sailors showed strange black swellings about the size of an egg or an apple in the armpits and groin. The swellings oozed blood and pus and were followed by spreading boils and black blotches on the skin from internal bleeding. The sick suffered severe pain and died quickly within five days of the first symptoms. As the disease spread, other symptoms of continuous fever and spitting of blood appeared instead of the swellings or buboes. These victims coughed and sweated heavily and died even more quickly, within three days or less, sometimes in 24 hours. In both types everything that issued from the body—breath, sweat, blood from the buboes and lungs, bloody urine, and blood-blackened excrement—smelled foul. Depression and despair accompanied the physical symptoms, and before the end "death is seen seated on the face" (Barbara Tuchman, *A Distant Mirror: The Calamitous 14th Century*, 1978).

Tuchman manages to weave the facts that have survived into a brief but powerful historical narrative. She identifies the time, the place, and the initial events and shows how rapidly the disease spread. Beyond this she conveys a sense of the horror and foulness of the disease: the suddenness with which it began, "sometimes in 24 hours," and its horrifying effect both on those who observed its advance and on those who suffered its symptoms. In re-creating the events so vividly she points also to their significance, indicating why the plague had such a devastating effect on European civilization in the fourteenth century.

THE PROCESS

If you choose to write a personal narrative or to use examples drawn from your experience, the place to begin is with your memories. Look especially for funny, painful, or frightening events and incidents that revealed the character of other people or taught you something about yourself. Use techniques like freewriting, brainstorming, and clustering (see Chapter 1, pp. 9–11) to help you explore the experiences and gather details for a well-developed essay. If, however, your narrative calls for observation, interviewing, or reading, as with a case study for a sociology class or a history paper, you might wish to start by writing down ideas for possible topics in order to give your research clear direction. Once you decide on a topic, make use of question systems like the five W's (Who, What, When, Where, and Why) to ensure that your note-taking covers all the information you will need.

Even a simple narrative, the story of your first day at work, for example, contains many small events—meeting your fellow workers, dealing with your first rude customer, realizing just how tired you can get standing up for eight hours—far more than can be included in a narrative without causing confusion and obscuring the point of the essay. Yet if the focus and point of a narrative essay you are preparing is not clear to you from the start, an abundance of material can be a good thing. It will allow you to look at the incidents from many perspectives and allow you to select the most telling details. The more information you accumulate, however, the more difficult it may be to decide what point to make or how to make it clear to an audience. You need to develop ways to discover a potential focus for your writing and to discover or refine your point.

You will have time as you write and revise, of course, to give focus to your essay by directing attention to important events rather than unimportant ones. You should also have a plan in mind as you begin writing, one that is firm enough to give direction to a first draft but can be adapted to ideas you discover as you write. Informal and formal planning techniques (idea clusters, scratch outlines, detailed outlines) can come in handy at this time, as can focus statements. A *focus statement* is a note to yourself about events or details that seem most important or about ideas and emotions you most want to share with readers. As you take notes for a paper on the incidents that led to the discovery of DNA, or as you jot down ideas for a personal narrative, stop occasionally to note your answers to these three questions:

1.   What events seem most important?
2.   What ideas and emotions are most worth sharing with readers?
3.   What point do I want to make?

Here is a sample of how one student, Patricia Ahearn, brainstormed a topic for a personal narrative and made use of focus statements:

Graduation Day!!!
At breakfast Dad says, "*We* never thought you would make it
        this far." *He* didn't, but I know *Mom* did!
Nerves—hot—waiting for the principal to announce my name
Looking at Mom—she says "I love you."

Jean comes over at 10 and we laugh a lot.
Remember when I told Mom and Dad I wanted to drop out of
    school—get a job
Every morning Mom made me feel I was worthwhile—some-
    thing my teachers never did—made me popcorn the night
    Jim and I broke up—told me how she felt when she quit
    school; the fun but the really bad times on her first job
Dad yelled a lot—didn't help.

Focus:

Mom made the difference; she did things that helped me
    believe in myself.
I knew it at the moment I looked at her on graduation day.
Want to focus on my feelings for Mom.

In a history paper about the Black Death, you might create focus statements like these: "What is most shocking is how many people died (a third of the population of Europe). The Black Death must have been horrifying to people who had no knowledge of germs or infectious diseases—and I want my readers to share a little of the terror the plague created."

When you begin writing, you may decide to set events down in the simplest form: x leads to y leads to z. As you revise, however, keep in mind one of the following approaches, either to solve specific problems a topic poses or to provide a fresh and interesting perspective.

1. *Limit the time frame.* Many writers are gripped by a compulsion to get all the details of a story down whether they are relevant to the point of the essay or not. Radical surgery is often the best solution. Instead of recounting a whole week or a whole day, try covering in detail only the single most important incident, the four or five minutes when all the forces at work during the day came together. In telling the story of a car crash as a way of warning against drinking and driving, you might focus on your reactions in the few moments just before, during, and right after the crash to show the effect of alcohol on your behavior. Necessary background information could come in a brief summary: "One night I had been out drinking with four of my friends, . . ." or in a flashback: "As I

negotiated the turns, ever more sloppily, I could barely feel the wheel because my hands were so numb. I thought back to when I had a clear sense of touch as I picked up the first cool, wet mug of beer. . . ."

Your choice, then, is between a *summary presentation* (useful for background information or less-important events) and a *detailed presentation* that explores in depth the events relevant most directly to the point you want to make.

If your topic is a broad one, like the development of the early Mormon community in Utah, for instance, you can still be selective. Pick only those episodes that are the most important and that support your interpretation of the subject.

2. *Arrange the events.* In its basic form, a narrative essay (like any other story) starts by setting the scene and introducing the characters. It then presents, sometimes in summary form, events that introduce a conflict or prepare for the central event. Finally, it explores in detail the most important incident (the climax), in which the conflict is resolved or the writer's outlook is made plain. Of the essays in this chapter, Sharon Curtin's "Garbage Man" most clearly follows this pattern.

The traditional, chronological approach can make it difficult to emphasize the most important aspects of a story. You may want instead to start in the middle of things, perhaps at the climactic episode, and fill in prior occurrences through flashbacks. Or you might adopt the strategy Ira Berkow uses in "At Nineteen, Thomas Makes His Decision." To give a sense of the multitude of events in Isiah Thomas's life that led him to leave college early for a professional basketball career, Berkow presents brief episodes from Thomas's life, many of which are not in chronological order, and intersperses quotations from family and friends.

3. *Choose a point of view.* Most often a personal narrative is told in the first person (named after the first-person pronouns *I, we,* and *they*). The writer presents events from the point of view of a participant ("I saw . . . I thought . . ."). Historical narratives, biographies, news accounts, and similar narratives are often presented in the third person (named after the third-person pronouns *he, she, it,* and *they*). This strategy allows for a point of view broader than that of any single participant and lends itself to reporting simultaneous events and the thoughts of all the people involved.

You need not limit yourself to the first person for personal narratives or to the third person for other kinds of narratives. You might, for example, write in the third person about events that happened to you in order to create a sense of objectivity and give yourself an opportunity to comment harshly on your actions: "Then, foolishly, Kimberley started chattering about how much money she was making on her summer job, paying no attention to the horrified reactions of her friends. . . ."

4. *Decide how much commentary to include.* How clearly to announce your point to readers is a decision you will have to make and remake as you write. In its simplest form, this can come down to deciding whether or not to use an explicit thesis statement. On a more complicated level, it involves deciding whether to comment on the meaning of an incident, to let it speak for itself, or to develop it in detail as a way of calling attention to it.

Deciding how much commentary to include is often a balancing act involving, on one hand, a desire to let the narrative do its own work and, on the other hand, a realization that narratives can permit many interpretations and that the author may need to provide some guidance. Unless you are confident that the point will be clear, give your readers some direction.

Don't be surprised if your final draft turns out to be quite different from the first draft. In the initial version of her essay on high school graduation, Patricia Ahearn began with an explicit thesis statement, "I realized only on graduation day how much of who I am and what I achieved I owed to my mother." She covered the events of the day leading up to the graduation ceremony in summary form, and then shifted to a detailed presentation ending at the moment she received her diploma. Her final version was quite different:

> "And the graduating class of '84 . . ." started Mr. Dunn, our school principal.
> "So this is it," I whispered to myself, "I am finally graduating."
> The air hung thick and heavy around me as several speakers alternately approached the brown wooden podium to give dull speeches. I was facing over three hundred people, watching their heads staring steadfastly at the speaker, but all I could think about was Mom. I kept thinking about how she just smiled at me and held my hand when Dad was yelling, "You can't quit school. You can't throw away the fine life we have given you on some stupid rebellion." I remembered

the many ways she helped me feel good about myself on days when the teachers told me how lazy I was and how I would never graduate if I didn't work harder.

My white gown clung to me as my skin became clammy from nervousness. In about two minutes I would rise out of my chair to receive my diploma. The thought of it made me want to cry. I thought of how Mom almost cried when she told me how hard a time she had on her first job just after she left school. I also remembered how we shared the popcorn she made on the night Jim and I broke up.

The air was silent and still as the speaker's voice echoed over hundreds of heads which looked like a mass of different colored balloons tied to chairs. In the background I could hear birds singing while overhead flew an orange-breasted robin with autumn brown wings. My throat was dry like a piece of parchment paper, causing pain every time I swallowed.

"Patricia Ahearn!" blared the microphone. I slowly arose and walked towards Mr. Latos, the awards presenter. As my hands closed around the rough brown envelope I happened to glance up. Through the thick mass of people I caught my mother's eyes and noticed a tear cascading down her cheek. I saw her lips form "I love you."

In revising this short essay, Patricia considered using the third person but rejected the idea because she wanted to emphasize the emotional meaning of the day. She then rearranged the presentation to focus on what to her were the most important parts of the day and to emphasize her relationship with her mother, which she correctly recognized as the real point of the narrative. Though the essay could still use more work, including greater emphasis on the scenes from the past and less on the details of the graduation, it does illustrate how using some different strategies can make a narrative interesting and effective.

THE PATTERN IN ACTION

Pick up some magazines at the drugstore or library and see how many of their articles are narratives. Look at your college textbooks to see how often they present information in narrative form or use brief narratives as examples. This should give you some idea of the popularity of narrative as a writing strategy as well as an idea of the many forms it can take.

Narration is such a widely used pattern that it makes little sense to try to list all the situations for which it is appropriate. Yet an awareness of some of its most common uses can help you recognize when it would be a useful vehicle for sharing ideas or feelings or when a particular task calls for it, as these do:

> Write up a report on the explosion at our Doylestown plant. (assigned by a vice president in charge of manufacturing)
> Discuss the development of Native American civilization in Arizona and New Mexico. (assigned by a college instructor)
> Give me a report on what our opponent has been doing. (assigned by a director of a political campaign)

Most narrative essays you encounter in your reading or writing will fall into one of three categories: personal narrative, reportorial narrative, or analytical narrative.

Personal narratives are essays based on personal experience or records of events that include the writer as observer rather than as full participant. Personal narratives are familiar to us from the autobiographies of movie stars and politicians, from memoirs of childhood (like Sharon Curtin's "Garbage Man" and Alice Walker's "Beauty: When the Other Dancer Is the Self" in this chapter), and from many other works written from a personal perspective in order to draw on the author's insights or experience: travel guides, cookbooks, and fashion or fitness books. Such is our belief in the value and reliability of personal experience that many writers mix personal examples with other writing patterns to add authority and vitality to what they say. Jim Vilas does this in his directions for preparing *real* southern fried chicken (Jim Vilas, "Fried Chicken," Chapter 6) as does Susan Brownmiller in "The Contrived Postures of Femininity" (Chapter 8). The realization that the observer's attitudes can shape reporting has meant that many journalists and other contemporary writers have begun to make their own reactions part of the events they record. The essays in the present chapter illustrate the prevalence of personal narrative in modern writing.

A *reportorial narrative* focuses on the events themselves, usually presenting the incidents in chronological order in the third person with little or no commentary on their meaning or significance. News reports are generally reportorial narratives as are lab reports and records of observations by physicians, psychologists, and anthropologists (see Sissela Bok, "Placebos," Chapter 7, for an example of such a report). Even a summary of the events in a novel or drama presented as part of a critical essay on literature is a reportorial narrative.

Because they are presented in the third person and because they concentrate on telling readers what happened, reportorial narratives often given an impression of objectivity, as if the writer were a videotape machine recording all that was done and said. This is not the case. The clinical psychologist who takes notes on a session with a patient, the chemist who records the progress of an experiment, and the journalist jotting down details at the scene of an accident are all engaged in understanding as well as recording. In fact, their recording is selective. They determine which of the many small actions that make up an event are worth preserving and which can be ignored. A reportorial narrative is useful not because it is fully objective—a narrative is inevitably selective and therefore subjective—but because it presents essential information in a clear and easily accessible form. Outside of newspapers, therefore, reportorial narratives seldom stand alone. They are usually combined with some other pattern of writing (as in the analytical narratives discussed below), and their job is to provide the facts for discussion and interpretation.

Analytical narratives make the events themselves the subject of commentary and analysis. Most often they alternate between reportorial narrative and analytical comment in the manner of this news analysis:

> Last month senior Soviet officials made state visits to India and Syria. In each case, the state-controlled press in Moscow reported that the officials conveyed greetings not only from Prime Minister Constantin Chernenko and Premier Nicolai Tikhonov but also from Foreign Minister Gromyko. What was not reported is that including the foreign minister's name in such communications is a recent development and is not required by protocol.
>
> Because it represents a break with past practice, the inclusion of Gromyko's name would seem to be an indication of his growing power. Diplomats familiar with Soviet affairs see it as one more indication that Gromyko's role has expanded greatly in recent months even though his title remains the same.

or of this student literature paper:

> The folktale known as "The Small-Tooth Dog" revolves around an act of hospitality and the moral obligation it imposes. In this story a traveling merchant is rescued from thieves by a large dog, then taken to the dog's house and nursed back to health. Placed in the dog's debt,

the merchant offers him precious gifts, but the dog refuses them all and requests the merchant's daughter. The merchant is distressed, but he cannot deny the dog his wish, for the dog saved his life. The daughter goes to live at the dog's house but is soon very unhappy and asks to see her father. The dog complies with her wish only when she speaks sweetly to him; when they finally reach her father's house, however, the dog is transformed into "the handsomest young man in the world." Of course, he and the daughter marry and live happily ever after.

In the tale, both the dog's kindness and the merchant's willingness to repay the debt despite the hardship it imposes on him emphasize the importance of hospitality. In addition, the happy ending reinforces the "lesson" about hospitality and suggests that such acts have an impact not only on the individuals involved but on the many other kinds of relationships that make up a society.

Academic papers and business and professional reports often contain long passages of analytical narrative; some are even organized entirely around the pattern. Indeed, any situation in which a person's interpretation of the events is as important or more important than the events themselves is an appropriate time for using the mix of narrative and commentary characteristic of analytical narrative.

The essays in this chapter illustrate some of the possible uses of narrative as well as the frequency with which techniques of personal narrative are used in contemporary writing. Sharon Curtin in "Garbage Man" uses personal narrative to make a point about the way our society treats old people. Loren Eiseley in "The Angry Winter" mingles personal and analytical narrative to suggest that ancient motivations still remain within us despite the civilization we have developed. In "A Crime of Compassion," Barbara Huttman uses a personal experience to argue against prolonging life needlessly with medical technology. Ira Berkow expands what might otherwise be a brief note on the sports page into a report on the events that motivate a major sports figure. Alice Walker's "Beauty: When the Other Dancer Is the Self" mixes reporting, analysis, and personal narrative as she explores her life and tells us also about the nature of beauty and the need for self-acceptance.

❧ SHARON CURTIN

Sharon Curtin was born in Douglas, Wyoming, and was raised in a family of ranchers and craftspeople. She has operated a small farm in Virginia and has worked as a nurse in New York and California. Her book, *Nobody Ever Died of Old Age* (1972), is based on her experiences of growing up in a large family, working as a visiting nurse, and living among elderly urban poor people in a transient hotel in New York City. It is an investigation of our attitudes towards elderly people, an attack on government policies and social forces that condemn them to lives without meaningful activity filled often with poverty and suffering, and an account of their independence and nobility. Much of the book's considerable power comes from Curtin's portraits of old people: some living on social security in the hills of Kentucky, others stuffing their baggy clothes full of items stolen from drug and department stores in New York City or sitting day after day with nothing to do on the front porches of boarding houses in small midwestern towns.

Garbage Man

This essay is drawn from *Nobody Ever Died of Old Age: In Praise of Old People; In Outrage at Their Loneliness,* and its story of a confrontation between a young girl and an old man reflects both the anger and the compassion indicated by the book's subtitle. Like most personal narratives, the essay assumes that readers will be able to understand, perhaps even sympathize with, the author's experiences. As you read the essay, try to decide whether your experiences are in any way similar to the author's and whether you believe that her implied criticism of our society is justified.

An old man I remember from my childhood was called the "Garbage Man" because he used to scavenge through all the garbage cans in town looking for scraps for his chickens. He was a mother's nightmare of a dirty old man; dressed in tattered stained clothing, an old stocking cap pulled over his head, he shuffled through the alleys of the town pulling a gunny sack. One of his legs was crippled and he wore some sort of heavy shoe, so his step had a special sound. You could hear him coming down the block, step and clump and slide, step and clump! and slide, as he pulled his burdens down the graveled alleys of the town.

29

Children and dogs teased him. We had a strange mongrel called   2
"Waggles" who would attack anything that was crippled (my mother
said he was like a lot of people; he couldn't bear imperfection or
any sign of weakness) and someone would always have to hold the
dog until the Garbage Man had passed. There was some kind of
jingle we used to sing about him:

> *Garbage man, garbage man*
> *Drinks his piss from an old tin can*
> *Had a wife, away she ran*
> *When she smelled the*
> *Garbage man, garbage man . . .*

The summer I was eight was a drought year. I remember the   3
leaves of the cottonwood trees were dull with dust and the young
trees died. They closed the town swimming pool because of a polio
scare; so we all swam in the river. That year I developed a consuming
curiosity about the Garbage Man. At first I just became aware I had
no idea what his face looked like. I knew him by his step, and by
the jingle that accompanied him down the alleys, but I had never
seen his face. I knew he was pretty old because my father said he
had been collecting garbage ever since *he* could remember. The
Garbage Man collected garbage, fed it to his chickens, and sold the
eggs back to the people who provided the garbage.

We weren't allowed to swim in the river, and my sister told my   4
mother that I had, which resulted in the hiding of my bathing suit
and my restriction to the yard. So I didn't have much else to do but
sit and stare at the cottonwood trees and wonder about the Garbage
Man.

I developed an elaborate plan of action. I decided to follow him   5
on his route, run around the block in order to reach the end of the
alley before he did, and get a look at his face before he knew what
was happening. If that failed, I would have to climb a tree, yell at
him, and solve the mystery when he looked up to see what was in
the tree. (I had achieved some minor fame as a spy earlier in the
summer by discovering a group of older kids trading peeks at various
anatomical details, and charging them a quarter each to keep my
mouth shut.)

The plan was simple, and a failure. Both times I found myself   6
unable to look at his face. I was frightened. I decided that if no one

knew what he looked like, there must be a reason. Either he was so horribly ugly and deformed that my heart would stop or there was something so secret and so sinister about his past that he was hiding his face from all men, and if I saw him he would kill me. I think this was the period I read a good many Nancy Drew, Girl Detective books. Whatever the reason, I didn't look at his face. But I came close enough to realize that he didn't smell bad at all; he smelled sort of like clove chewing gum and chicken feathers.

I began to follow the Garbage Man around town. Sometimes I would stalk him like a real detective, sometimes I would just run around and pop up at the end of alleys until I got bored. Sometimes I would follow him home, and watch him feed his chickens. I decided the chickens were pretty ordinary, and had nothing to do with the main plot. They were part of his masquerade. His house was fairly mysterious, an old two-story frame house which hadn't been painted in years. But why did an old man living alone have such a large house? Was someone held prisoner? Was the treasure so vast that it required a building bigger than the Converse County National Bank?

After weeks of skulking around after the Garbage Man I still hadn't seen his face. But careful questioning of a certain source (my father) had revealed the fact that he had been in town since before World War I, and that there had been "some trouble" because the Garbage Man had a German surname. In fact, his wife had left him, taking their son, and the old man had been a little queer ever since. My informant also stated that some fools had gotten drunk one night and tried to burn down the old man's house, because he "wasn't American." But it all cleared up, and now no one minded that he stole their garbage to feed his chickens, and sold them the eggs.

The Garbage Man began to look for me but because of his posture (his shoulders were on a level with the top of his head and he had a sort of hunchback, not really, but the kind of humpback people get when they are old; not the kind you rub for good luck) I still never saw his face. He would stop suddenly in the middle of an alley, and stare up at the trees, looking for me; or turn around at the sound of running footsteps. Since I never taunted him with the Garbage Man jingle my motives for following him around must have remained totally mysterious. He began to vary his route, something that had never happened in all those years and was enough of a happening to cause talk around town. People talked about the Garbage Man who hadn't thought about him in years, because they were made uncomfortable by his changing his routine.

It became a game, the rules developed without any communication between us, for me to be at the end of an alley before he could stop me and change his direction. Or he would not appear on his rounds at the regular time, but would suddenly turn up in the alley (step, clump! and slide) at twilight or dawn when I was inside. This elaborate hide-and-seek went on long enough for my sisters to begin teasing me about my "Garbage Man boyfriend." At first I was so embarrassed I decided to stop my investigation, but when my mother expressed concern about the amount of time I spent following the man around, and questioned me very closely about my motives, I decided that there must be something going on if the adults were worried and suspicious. My mother came close to ordering me to stop, but I quickly evaded the issue.

I finally had to tell my oldest sister that my reason for following the Garbage Man around was because I wanted to see what his face looked like. She hooted and made faces for a few minutes, while I carefully kept my face innocent and clear. I didn't want her to know the real reason was that I suspected him of being a secret millionaire, with thousands of dollars hidden in that old firetrap of a house. The money, I figured, had to be in gold bars so he wouldn't have to worry about a fire. And he only scrambled through town garbage cans so that people wouldn't know he had so much money; he wasn't a real miser, just careful. And if I could get to be his friend, maybe, well, maybe he would let me see the hidden network of tunnels he had under his house to get the gold inside without anyone knowing . . . but first I had to see his face, so he would know he could trust me because I wouldn't tell anyone what he looked like. It was very hard to keep my face straight and not reveal what a fantastic secret I had.

Mickey soon tired of teasing me and decided to take my problem seriously. Since she was six years older, she had that much more experience fooling and evading adults, and came up with the perfect plan: All I had to do was hide inside one of the garbage cans—and when he lifted the lid, I would have the perfect chance to see his face. Mickey thought he would probably be so ugly that I should have a backup team, in case I fainted from fright and risked being picked up and thrown in the town dump. So she did a little recruiting; two of the Dixon boys for scouts, to let me know when to duck down in the garbage can; my sister Carol to run and tell my mother in case of attack or fainting spells; and herself to direct all operations. I was a little uncomfortable about all the extra troops; somehow, it made the Garbage Man less real, and it seemed to break the rules of my game. But by this time things had gone so far that I had to go along with the plan; Mickey *was* six years older.

> *Garbage Man, Garbage Man*
> *He ain't got no pension plan*
> *Steals his meals from my ash can . . .*

That was the Dixon boys warning me that the old man was approaching. Mickey stuffed my head down in the can and slammed down the lid. I could hear her running over to join Carol near the box elder hedge in the McKibben yard. 13

It was the McKibben garbage can; I had known the family for years, never been close to them, and there I was alone with the smell of their garbage. It just smelled like regular garbage. Sometimes we went up to the town dump with our .22 rifles and shot rats; the garbage can smelled the same as the dump when it wasn't burning. It was fairly dark inside the can, just a little light from around the lid where it didn't fit tight. This was the first year we had to have lids on our garbage cans, because of the polio scare. 14

Step, clump! and slide. Step, clump! and slide. Here he came. I would of rather been at High Mass on a blistering July day than inside that can. He was too close for me to run, too close for me to want to hurt him, too close for me to sneak away without being labeled chicken, too close for me . . . what if I scared *him* to death? No one would miss him but me, I'd have to bury him and wear black, and everything, if he left me the money. 15

The sun came sliding in so fast I didn't have time to blink. And the Garbage Man reached inside to rummage through the Mc-Kibbens' garbage before he took a look. Old dry skin, calloused fingers, like chicken talons, touched my arm. 16

Before I had time to scream, or he had time to know it was me, we both hollered and jumped. The garbage can fell over, The Garbage Man began to run. The Dixon boys ran after him, and back again to ask if they ought to tackle him and hold him for the sheriff. Mickey and Carol ran out from behind the box elder and tried to separate me from the garbage enough to tell whether or not I was 17 killed. And Mrs. McKibben ran out of her house with a broom, yelling at us all to clean up the mess we had made in her alley. The Garbage Man disappeared.

By the time all the uproar had settled, I had run away to hide 18 in a secret tree house in the tree behind the garage. High up in the green and blue world, with the tiny beginnings of apples on the branches around me, I cried. He hadn't been ugly or mysterious— just a regular old face, with bags and wrinkles and interesting bumps and spots. His eyes were bad; all red and runny, one of them half closed and the other popping out in compensation. It was just an old man's face. No mystery, no secret; just an old man's face.

COMMENTARY

"Garbage Man" is a good example of how personal experience can be used in an essay to make a point that applies to readers as individuals and to society as a whole. The impact of this narrative may depend in part on what a reader brings to it. The reader who has had an experience similar to one of the incidents in the story will probably feel a stronger emotional effect from it than from other incidents. Whatever their reactions, most readers would agree that the last episode in the story when the author (as a young girl) looks into the Garbage Man's face is clearly the climax of the narrative. The other episodes are all either part of the young girl's pursuit of the old man or provide background information for it. The presentation moves from summary to a detailed treatment of the events, thus emphasizing the importance of the final scene.

The incidents in the essay raise a number of important matters: peer pressure among children, the differences in attitude between children and adults, and the pressure within a community to exclude all who do not behave in a "normal" manner. Yet the attention paid throughout to the young girl's distorted view of the garbage man and the cruel behavior that springs from it, combined with the emphasis given to her discovery that he is merely an old man, suggests that the central purpose of the essay is to criticize the way she, and the rest of us by implication, treat old people. The author might have chosen to state her criticism directly in a thesis statement, and in doing so she would have eliminated any uncertainty about the purpose of the narrative. But an explicit thesis might also have limited the ability of readers to respond to other issues raised in the essay, especially if it came at the beginning of the essay where it would shape a reader's reaction to the entire essay. As with many decisions a writer must face, the choice of whether to include a thesis statement in an essay like "Garbage Man" is not a clear one.

The detailed presentation of events in "Garbage Man" accounts for much of the essay's emotional power. The children's rhymes in paragraphs 2 and 12 bring to mind memories of how cruel children can be. The heat, darkness, and smell of the garbage can emphasize the seriousness of what the little girl has set out to do, and when combined with the "Step, clump! and slide" of the Garbage Man, they create much suspense. The old man's face, "with bags and wrinkles and interesting bumps and spots" is a fittingly precise and final reward for the end of her search and at the same time a symbol of what she has learned. Finally, the first person point of view, which limits our knowledge to the little girl's experience and tells us nothing of what the old man is thinking, adds to the suspense and also makes a point about how little she (or we) know about old people.

RESPONSES AND IDEAS

1. In response to this essay, freewrite for five minutes about an old person whose character or actions you admire, focusing, if possible, on a single incident. Then freewrite about a person who irritates or angers you. When you have finished, summarize your attitude towards each person in a single sentence. If you changed your attitude while you were writing, your summary sentence should reflect the change.

2. State briefly how you felt about the children in the story when you read about their song (par. 2). Were you amused? Angered? Explain why. Did you feel that their parents should have forbidden such behavior? How did you react to the author as she kept pursuing the Garbage Man? Did you become irritated? Did you sympathize with her curiosity? Explain why.

3. Why did the author cry after seeing the Garbage Man's face (par. 18)? Was she disappointed? Scared?

PURPOSE, AUDIENCE, AND STRATEGIES

1. What does the statement about the dog "Waggles" suggest about the ways people often respond to the elderly in our society? Do you think

the author intended this statement to give readers an idea of her purpose
in this essay? Explain why. What do you think her purpose is, and
would your estimate of it change if the sentence about Waggles were
eliminated? (See Glossary: Purpose.)

2.   Which incidents in this narrative are similar to experiences you had as
     a child? Do you find it difficult to understand any of the episodes that
     are not similar to your experiences? If so, which ones? Why do you
     think it is difficult for you to understand them? Has the author taken
     any steps to help readers understand the incidents? What are the steps,
     if any?

3.   Elsewhere in the book from which this essay is taken, Curtin makes
     this comment:

     Attitudes. That used to be what my teachers told me I had Plenty of.
     All wrong. But the kind of culturally, socially enforced attitude I want
     to talk about makes me bigoted against old people; it makes me think
     young is best; it makes me treat old people like outcasts.

     What interpretation of the story does this passage suggest? Are other
     interpretations possible?

4.   What connection, if any, is there between the events of the summer
     (par. 3) and the author's interest in the old man? Besides details of the
     setting (the dry summer), what other background information does the
     author provide in the first four paragraphs? How is this information
     important for an understanding of the events in the story? Could it have
     been presented elsewhere in the essay? Where? Would it be as effective
     in some other place? Explain.

5.   Which of the author's actions in the story might have been motivated
     by her fascination with "Nancy Drew, Girl Detective books" (par. 6)?
     Is there any irony in the contradiction between what she hopes to
     discover about the old man and the discovery she finally makes? Ex-
     plain. (See Glossary: Irony.)

LANGUAGE AND STYLE

1.   What sections of this essay are particularly rich in concrete detail? Tell
     why you think the author chose to include so much specific detail in
     these places. To what extent does the author's choice of words (diction)
     make the details concrete? Explain and give examples. (See Glossary:
     Abstract/Concrete, Diction.)

2.   Is the style of this essay formal, informal, or somewhere in between?
     Cite specific evidence to support your answer. (See Glossary: Style.)

3.   If you do not know the meaning of some of the following words, look
     them up in a dictionary: *polio* (par. 3), *anatomical* (5), *skulking* (8),
     talons (16), *box elder* (17).

WRITING ACTIVITIES

1. Write about an incident that changed your attitudes towards an unpopular person or a social outcast. Attempt to describe what made the person a misfit. Physical appearance? Social background? Be aware of what the incident reveals about the values of our society and, if appropriate, criticize the values.

2. How often are people's mistaken perceptions of each other the cause of unhappiness? Conflict? Do conflicts between social groups, even nations, often stem from mistaken perceptions? Develop your ideas in an essay that uses one or more brief narratives to support your conclusions. Or write an essay making the opposite point—that mistaken perceptions can often turn into deeper understanding. You may wish to emphasize the humorous aspects of the incidents you present.

❧ LOREN EISELEY

Loren Eiseley (1907–1977) was born in Lincoln, Nebraska, and was educated at the University of Nebraska and the University of Pennsylvania. He taught anthropology, sociology, and the history of science at the University of Kansas, Oberlin College, Columbia, Berkeley, Harvard, and the University of Pennsylvania. Eiseley was both a poet and a scientist, and his writing combines a scientific interest in the development of various forms of life with a concern for the growth of the human imagination and spirit. Besides numerous articles in scientific journals, Eiseley published many books on the natural world that demonstrate his ability to write about scientific subjects in a clear, often poetic style accessible to a wide variety of readers. These books include *The Immense Journey* (1957), *Darwin's Century* (1958), *The Firmament of Time* (1960), *The Mind as Nature* (1962), *The Unexpected Universe* (1969), *The Invisible Pyramid* (1970), and *The Night Country* (1971).

The Angry Winter

In this brief essay, the opening section of a chapter from *The Unexpected Universe,* Loren Eiseley demonstrates how small events can reveal much about personality and culture. Like many anthropologists and biologists, he suggests that our actions preserve features of earlier stages in human development—in the same way our brains contain structures characteristic of the reptile brain and the rodent brain, prior stages in our physical evolution. The essay also reveals Eiseley's ability to use language and imagination to explore human experience.

A time comes when creatures whose destinies have crossed   1
somewhere in the remote past are forced to appraise each other as though they were total strangers. I had been huddled beside the fire one winter night, with the wind prowling outside and shaking the windows. The big shepherd dog on the hearth before me occasionally glanced up affectionately, sighed, and slept. I was working, actually, amidst the debris of a far greater winter. On my desk lay the lance point of ice age hunters and the heavy leg bone of a fossil bison. No remnants of flesh attached to these relics. The deed lay more than

ten thousand years remote. It was represented here by naked flint and by bone so mineralized it rang when struck. As I worked in my little circle of light, I absently laid the bone beside me on the floor. The hour had crept toward midnight. A grating noise, a heavy rasping of big teeth diverted me. I looked down.

The dog had risen. That rock-hard fragment of a vanished beast was in his jaws and he was mouthing it with a fierce intensity I had never seen exhibited by him before.   2

"Wolf," I exclaimed, and stretched out my hand. The dog backed up but did not yield. A low and steady rumbling began to rise in his chest, something out of a long-gone midnight. There was nothing in that bone to taste, but ancient shapes were moving in his mind and determining his utterance. Only fools gave up bones. He was warning me.   3

"Wolf," I chided again.   4

As I advanced, his teeth showed and his mouth wrinkled to strike. The rumbling rose to a direct snarl. His flat head swayed low and wickedly as a reptile's above the floor. I was the most loved object in his universe, but the past was fully alive in him now. Its shadows were whispering in his mind. I knew he was not bluffing. If I made another step he would strike.   5

Yet his eyes were strained and desperate. "Do not," something pleaded in the back of them, some affectionate thing that had followed at my heel all the days of his mortal life, "do not force me. I am what I am and cannot be otherwise because of the shadows. Do not reach out. You are a man, and my very god. I love you, but do not put out your hand. It is midnight. We are in another time, in the snow."   6

"The *other* time," the steady rumbling continued while I paused, "the other time in the snow, the big, the final, the terrible snow, when the shape of this thing I hold spelled life. I will not give it up. I cannot. The shadows will not permit me. Do not put out your hand."   7

I stood silent, looking into his eyes, and heard his whisper through. Slowly I drew back in understanding. The snarl diminished, ceased. As I retreated, the bone slumped to the floor. He placed a paw upon it, warningly.   8

And were there no shadows in my own mind, I wondered. Had I not for a moment, in the grip of that savage utterance, been about   9

to respond, to hurl myself upon him over an invisible haunch ten
thousand years removed? Even to me the shadows had whispered—
to me, the scholar in his study.

"Wolf," I said, but this time, holding a familiar leash, I spoke   10
from the door indifferently. "A walk in the snow." Instantly from his
eyes that other visitant receded. The bone was left lying. He came
eagerly to my side, accepting the leash and taking it in his mouth as
always.

A blizzard was raging when we went out, but he paid no heed.   11
On his thick fur the driving snow was soon clinging heavily. He
frolicked a little—though usually he was a grave dog—making up
to me for something still receding in his mind. I felt the snowflakes
fall upon my face, and stood thinking of another time, and another
time still, until I was moving from midnight to midnight under ever
more remote and vaster snows. Wolf came to my side with a little
whimper. It was he who was civilized now. "Come back to the fire,"
he nudged gently, "or you will be lost." Automatically I took the
leash he offered. He led me safely home and into the house.

"We have been very far away," I told him solemnly. "I think   12
there is something in us that we had both better try to forget."
Sprawled on the rug, Wolf made no response except to thump his
tail feebly out of courtesy. Already he was mostly asleep and dream-
ing. By the movement of his feet I could see he was running far
upon some errand in which I played no part.

Softly I picked up his bone—our bone, rather—and replaced it   13
high on a shelf in my cabinet. As I snapped off the light the white
glow from the window seemed to augment itself and shine with a
deep, glacial blue. As far as I could see, nothing moved in the long
aisles of my neighbor's woods. There was no visible track, and
certainly no sound from the living. The snow continued to fall
steadily, but the wind, and the shadows it had brought, had vanished.

RESPONSES AND IDEAS

1.   Respond to this essay in either of these ways: (a) Write a paragraph-
     length narrative of an event that prompted you to think about human
     relationships, human history, or patterns of human behavior; (b) Write
     a paragraph explaining why you think Eiseley's meditations are the
     product of his imagination, with little basis in reality.

2. Explain the meaning of the following passages: "something out of a long-gone midnight" (par. 3); "Its shadows were whispering in his mind" (5); "the other time in the snow, the big, the final, the terrible snow, when the shape of this thing I hold spelled life" (7); "until I was moving from midnight to midnight under ever more remote and vaster snows" (11).

3. Does the snow mentioned at several places in the essay function as a symbol? If so, what does it symbolize? (See Glossary: Symbol.)

PURPOSE, AUDIENCE, AND STRATEGIES

1. Is there an explicit thesis statement in this essay? If so, what is it? (See Glossary: Thesis.) State in your own words the point or points Eiseley makes in this essay. Does the narrative provide adequate support for what he says?

2. At what points in the essay is specialized knowledge of anthropology, geology, or some other field needed in order to understand Eiseley's meditations? Be specific. Are most readers likely to have this knowledge, or is the audience for this essay restricted to people who are well-acquainted with the fields of study on which Eiseley draws? Is it possible to follow what Eiseley says in this essay without having any special knowledge? Explain.

3. Instead of opening the essay by describing the scene or moving directly into the action, Eiseley begins with a sentence that makes a general statement. Why do you think he chose to do this? Would the essay be weakened or changed in any substantial way if the first sentence were dropped entirely? (See Glossary: Introductions.)

4. Which paragraphs are devoted entirely to narrating events? To commentary? Would the essay be more effective if it contained less commentary? Indicate specifically what commentary, if any, could be cut without harming the essay.

5. Identify the kinds of transitions the author uses between paragraphs 2 and 3; 5 and 6; 6 and 7; 8 and 9.

LANGUAGE AND STYLE

1. Cite specific examples in the essay to show whether the language Eiseley uses to narrate events is more or less abstract than the language he uses to comment on them. Are the levels of abstraction used in narrating and commenting consistent throughout the essay? Where, if anywhere, do they vary? (See Glossary: Abstract/Concrete.)

2. What figures of speech are represented in these passages: "the wind prowling outside" (par. 1); "His flat head swayed low and wickedly as a reptile's above the floor" (5)? (See Glossary: Figures of Speech.)

3. If you do not know the meaning of some of the following words, look them up in a dictionary: *appraise, mineralized* (par. 1); *strained* (6); *haunch, removed* (9); *indifferently, visitant* (10); *grave* (11); *augment, glacial* (13).

WRITING ACTIVITIES

1. Unlike Eiseley, few of us are likely to discover in some brief incident a reminder of humanity's early history. Yet we have all had brief experiences that, on further reflection, revealed interesting, humorous, or even profound insights into the reasons behind human behavior. Choose one such incident, a glimpse of an old person playing with a young child, for example, or a jealous response to seeing a girlfriend or boyfriend talking to your rival, and develop it into an essay. Try to make sure your essay strikes a balance between your retelling of the incident and your commentary on its significance.

2. Public figures like politicians, movie stars, sports heroes, and even community leaders often do things that tell us a lot about the way they really think and feel as opposed to the public image they have created. Write about one such incident—humorous or otherwise—and explain what it revealed about the person in question.

❧ BARBARA HUTTMAN

After members of her family had been hospitalized seventeen times, Barbara Huttman decided to become a nurse at age forty-one, in part to combat what she called her "hospital phobia." She received her nursing degree in 1976 and worked as a staff nurse, a coordinating nurse supervisor, and a clinical coordinator in various major metropolitan hospitals. In 1980, Huttman was one of the founders of Professional Health Care Consultants, a consulting service for hospitals, nursing groups, and consumers of health care. She currently serves as its director.

Barbara Huttman has received several awards for her writing on issues of nursing and health care, and her articles have appeared in numerous periodicals, including *American Journal of Nursing*, *RN Magazine*, and *Nursing Life*. Her first book, *The Patient's Advocate* (1981), is a consumer's guide to health care. Her second book, *Code Blue* (1982), is an autobiographical account of her training as a nurse and her often unsettling encounters with current medical practices.

A Crime of Compassion

"A Crime of Compassion," first published in *Newsweek*, reflects Huttman's concern with the way our hospitals treat the sick and dying. In it she uses a brief introductory anecdote about her appearance on the "Phil Donahue Show" and a longer narrative drawn from her experience as a nurse to argue forcefully for a change in the way we treat terminally ill patients. Issues of life and death are not restricted to people in medical fields, however; we face them directly in our personal lives and indirectly when we elect politicians who take stands on euthanasia, medical research, and abortion. This essay asks us to consider the practical impact of abstract moral positions.

"Murderer," a man shouted. "God help patients who get *you* for 1 a nurse."

"What gives you the right to play God?" another one asked. 2

It was the Phil Donahue show where the guest is a fatted calf 3 and the audience a 200-strong flock of vultures hungering to pick at the bones. I had told them about Mac, one of my favorite cancer patients. "We resuscitated him 52 times in just one month. I refused

43

to resuscitate him again. I simply sat there and held his hand while he died."

There wasn't time to explain that Mac was a young, witty, macho   4
cop who walked into the hospital with 32 pounds of attack equipment, looking as if he could single-handedly protect the whole city,
if not the entire state. "Can't get rid of this cough," he said. Otherwise,
he felt great.

Before the day was over, tests confirmed that he had lung cancer.   5
And before the year was over, I loved him, his wife, Maura, and
their three kids as if they were my own. All the nurses loved him.
And we all battled his disease for six months without ever giving
death a thought. Six months isn't such a long time in the whole
scheme of things, but it was long enough to see him lose his youth,
his wit, his macho, his hair, his bowel and bladder control, his sense
of taste and smell and his ability to do the slightest thing for himself.
It was also long enough to watch Maura's transformation from a
young woman into a haggard, beaten old lady.

When Mac had wasted away to a 60-pound skeleton kept alive   6
by liquid food we poured down a tube, i.v. solutions we dripped
into his veins and oxygen we piped to a mask on his face, he begged
us: "Mercy . . . for God's sake, please just let me go."

Miracles: The first time he stopped breathing, the nurse pushed   7
the button that calls a "code blue" throughout the hospital and sends
a team rushing to resuscitate the patient. Each time he stopped
breathing, sometimes two or three times in one day, the code team
came again. The doctors and technicians worked their miracles and
walked away. The nurses stayed to wipe the saliva that drooled from
his mouth, irrigate the big craters of bedsores that covered his hips,
suction the lung fluids that threatened to drown him, clean the feces
that burned his skin like lye, pour the liquid food down the tube
attached to his stomach, put pillows between his knees to ease the
bone-on-bone pain, turn him every hour to keep the bedsores from
getting worse and change his gown and linen every two hours to
keep him from being soaked in perspiration.

At night I went home and tried to scrub away the smell of   8
decaying flesh that seemed woven into the fabric of my uniform. It
was in my hair, the upholstery of my car—there was no washing it
away. And every night I prayed that Mac would die, that his agonized
eyes would never again plead with me to let him die.

Every morning I asked his doctor for a "no-code" order. Without   9
that order, we had to resuscitate every patient who stopped breathing. His doctor was one of several who believe we must extend life
as long as we have the means and knowledge to do it. To not do it
is to be liable for negligence, at least in the eyes of many people,
including some nurses. I thought about what it would be like to
stand before a judge, accused of murder, if Mac stopped breathing
and I didn't call a code.

And after the 52nd code, when Mac was still lucid enough to   10
beg for death again, and Maura was crumbled in my arms again,
and when no amount of pain medication stilled his moaning and
agony, I wondered about a spiritual judge. Was all this misery and
suffering supposed to be building character or infusing us all with
the sense of humility that comes from impotence?

Had we, the whole medical community, become so arrogant that   11
we believed in the illusion of salvation through science? Had we
become so self-righteous that we thought meddling in God's work
was our duty, our moral imperative and our legal obligation? Did
we really believe that we had the right to force "life" on a suffering
man who had begged for the right to die?

Such questions haunted me more than ever early one morning   12
when Maura went home to change her clothes and I was bathing
Mac. He had been still for so long, I thought he at last had the
blessed relief of coma. Then he opened his eyes and moaned, "Pain
. . . no more . . . Barbara . . . do something . . . God, let me go."

Death: The desperation in his eyes and voice riddled me with   13
guilt. "I'll stop," I told him as I injected the pain medication.

I sat on the bed and held Mac's hands in mine. He pressed his   14
bony fingers against my hand and muttered, "Thanks." Then there
was one soft sigh and I felt his hands go cold in mine. "Mac?" I
whispered, as I waited for his chest to rise and fall again.

A clutch of panic banded my chest, drew my finger to the code   15
button, urged me to do something, anything . . . but sit there alone
with death. I kept one finger on the button, without pressing it, as
a waxen pallor slowly transformed his face from person to empty
shell. Nothing I've ever done in my 47 years has taken so much effort
as it took *not* to press that code button.

Eventually, when I was as sure as I could be that the code team   16
would fail to bring him back, I entered the legal twilight zone and

pushed the button. The team tried. And while they were trying, Maura walked into the room and shrieked, "No . . . don't let them do this to him . . . for God's sake . . . please, no more."

Cradling her in my arms was like cradling myself, Mac and all   17
those patients and nurses who had been in this place before who do the best they can in a death-denying society.

So a TV audience accused me of murder. Perhaps I am guilty.   18
If a doctor had written a no-code order, which is the only *legal* alternative, would he have felt any less guilty? Until there is legislation making it a criminal act to code a patient who has requested the right to die, we will all of us risk the same fate as Mac. For whatever reason, we developed the means to prolong life, and now we are forced to use it. We do not have the right to die.

RESPONSES AND IDEAS

1. Respond to this essay by looking at the author's actions in an unfavorable light, perhaps from the perspective of the people in the television show audience who attacked Huttman's actions. Write down reasons that her actions could be considered wrong, and suggest how she might have dealt with the problem in different ways.

2. Is the title, "A Crime of Compassion," appropriate for this essay? Explain. Is it ironic in any way? In what way or ways? (See Glossary: Irony.)

3. In paragraphs 10 and 11 Huttman raises some serious moral and religious questions. State the answers you believe most people would give to the questions. If your answers would differ from theirs in any way, indicate your response, too.

PURPOSE, AUDIENCE, AND STRATEGIES

1. Are the details in paragraphs 7 and 8 likely to offend or disgust most readers? Explain why or why not. What role do they play in helping convince the audience to agree with the author's point? Would the essay be less effective if the details were toned down or eliminated? Explain.

2. Most people are outraged by a person who admits to refusing to help a dying human being. What does the author do in the first three paragraphs to keep readers from reacting hostilely and to encourage them to listen to her story with an open mind? (See Glossary: Introductions, Argument.)

3. Is Huttman's purpose to defend her actions? To express her anger over the doctor's refusal to write a "no-code" order? To make us pity Mac?

List all the specific purposes you think the essay serves, and then decide which are the most important. Compare your list of the most important with those of your classmates. To what extent are the purposes you consider important determined by what Huttman emphasizes in the essay (see Glossary: Emphasis), and to what extent are they determined by the values you bring with you to the essay?

4. What does the author gain by waiting until paragraph 18 to announce her thesis directly? What is the thesis? What steps does Huttman take to make sure readers will understand her point of view and the focus of the essay before they arrive at the direct statement of thesis?

5. List the specific arguments and evidence Huttman uses to support her thesis. (See Glossary: Argument.) Do they provide enough support to justify her conclusions? If not, do you still find the essay persuasive? Why?

LANGUAGE AND STYLE

1. What elements in Huttman's diction appear to be chosen for their emotional impact? List specific examples from each third of the essay and describe their impact. Check to see if your classmates' responses to any passages differ from yours and try to account for the differences.

2. If you do not know the meaning of some of the following words, look them up in the dictionary: *fatted, resuscitate* (par. 3); *macho* (4); *haggard* (5); *bedsores* (7); *liable, negligence* (9); *lucid* (10); *waxen, pallor* (15).

WRITING ACTIVITIES

1. Do you know of an incident (or incidents) that offers a different perspective on sickness and death than Barbara Huttman's essay provides? Use it (or them) as the basis for a narrative essay. Make your opinion clear, of course, but for the most part let the narrative do the arguing for you.

2. Narrative essays frequently use dialogue to help present events directly and vividly. Prepare a narrative essay in which the central event—the conflict that most clearly reveals the significance of the incident—is presented through dialogue. Your narrative might be about a conflict between parent and child, friends or lovers, employer and employee, or, perhaps, between two strangers.

❧ IRA BERKOW

Ira Berkow, born 1940 in Chicago, Illinois, is a sports and general columnist for the *New York Times*. He studied at Miami University in Oxford, Ohio (B.A.) and at Northwestern University (M.A. in journalism). He has worked as a sports writer and book reviewer for the *Minneapolis Tribune* as well as a writer for the Newspaper Enterprise Association and Scripps-Howard newspapers. In addition to his newspaper work, Berkow has published *Beyond the Dream* (1975) and *Maxwell Street* (1975), a portrait of a colorful inner-city neighborhood in Chicago. His favorite book is *Rocking Steady: A Guide to Basketball & Cool* (1974), written with the former basketball player Walt Frazier.

At Nineteen, Thomas Makes His Decision

When Ira Berkow interviewed Isiah Thomas in order to write this article for a column in the *New York Times,* Thomas was surprised to learn that Berkow had grown up some years before in the same neighborhood on Chicago's West Side and that despite their differences they had many experiences in common. This essay enables us to view Thomas not as just a distant sports figure but as a person with a family, with a past, and with conflicts and burdens as well as rewards.

It was Draft Day in the ghetto. That's what everyone there called 1 it. On a few days each year, chieftains of the notorious Vice Lords street gang appeared at certain homes on the West Side of Chicago to take recruits.

On this summer night in 1966 about twenty-five Vice Lord chiefs 2 stopped in front of the home of Mary Thomas. She had nine children, seven of them boys, ranging from Lord Henry, fifteen years old, to Isiah, five. The Thomases lived on the first floor of a two-story red brick building on Congress Street, facing the Eisenhower Expressway.

One of the Lords rang the bell. Mary Thomas, wearing glasses, 3 answered the door. She saw behind him the rest of his gang, all wearing gold tams and black capes and some had guns in their waist bands that glinted under the street lamps.

"We want your boys," the gang leader told her. "They can't walk   4
around here and not be in no gang."

She looked him in the eye. "There's only one gang around here,   5
and that's the Thomas gang," she said, "and I lead that."

"If you don't bring those boys out, we'll get 'em in the street,"   6
he said.

She shut the door. The gang members waited. She walked   7
through the living room where the rest of the family sat. Isiah, frightened, watched her go into the bedroom and return with a sawed-off shotgun. She opened the front door.

She pointed the gun at the caped figure before her. "Get off my   8
porch," she said, "or I'll blow you 'cross the Expressway."

He stepped back, and slowly he and his gang disappeared into   9
the night.

Isiah Thomas never joined a gang, and was protected from the   10
ravages of street life—the dope, the drinking, the stealing, the killings—by his mother and his brothers, even those who eventually succumbed to the streets. Two of his brothers became heroin addicts, one was a pimp, a couple would be jailed, and one would become a Vice Lords chief.

Isiah, though, was the baby of the family, and its hope.   11

He became an honor student in grade school and high school,   12
an All-American basketball player in high school and college, and, as a six-foot one-inch point guard, led Indiana University to the National Collegiate Athletic Association championship last month. After only a few weeks out of high school, he was a standout on the United States team that won the gold medal in the 1979 Pan-American Games, and was a starter on the 1980 United States Olympic team.

The pros liked what they saw. "He's a terrific talent," said Rod   13
Thorn, general manager of the Chicago Bulls. "Not only physically— and he seems adept at every phase of the game—but he has a charisma, an ability to inspire confidence in his teammates that only a few players have, like Larry Bird and Magic Johnson and Julius Erving."

Last weekend, Isiah Thomas, a nineteen-year-old sophomore   14
and B student majoring in forensics, with an eye toward law school,

made an important decision. He passed up his last two years of
college basketball to declare his eligibility for the National Basketball
Association's draft on June 9. Thomas said that three teams—New
Jersey, Detroit and Chicago—had been told he could expect an offer
of at least $1 million to sign.

Thomas had wrestled with his decision all season.   15

"Don't do it," said Bobby Knight, the Indiana basketball coach.   16
"You can still improve in basketball. You could be worth more."

"Stay in school," said Quinn Buckner, a former Indiana player   17
and now with the Milwaukee Bucks. "The college experience at your
age is valuable and can't ever be repeated."

"What's left for you to prove in college?" said his brother,   18
Gregory.

"Go only if the price is right," said his former high school coach,   19
Gene Pingatore. "Don't sell yourself short."

"Son," said Mary Thomas, "do what makes you happy."   20

The idea of turning pro had been with Isiah for as long as he   21
can remember, instilled by his brothers who had their own basketball dreams squashed.

"There was a lot to consider," said Thomas. He sat on the arm   22
of a couch in his small apartment in the Fountain Park complex on
the Indiana campus in Bloomington. He wore a red baseball cap, a
blue U.S.A. Olympic jacket, jeans, and yellow sneakers. He speaks
softly, thoughtfully, with careful articulation. Sometimes he'll flash
that warm, dimpled smile that has become familiar from newspaper
photos and national magazine covers. Behind that smile is also a
toughness and intensity—twice last season he was involved in fights
in games.

"I know I'm a role model for a lot of people back in the ghetto,"   23
said Thomas. "Not too many of us get the chance to get out, to go
to college. If I quit school, what effect would that have on them?

"And I had said I wanted to be a lawyer, and one day return   24
there and help the people. They need it. I've seen kids who stole a
pair of pants and they get a five-year prison sentence. Literally.
Because there was no adequate help for them. I know that I'll get
my law degree. I know you can only play basketball for so many
years. Then you've got the rest of your life ahead of you.

"And I have to think of my family. My mother worked hard all   25
her life and for not much money. My father left when I was three
years old, and my mom kept us together by herself. She worked in

the community center, she worked in the church, she did whatever she could. She's got a job with the housing authority in Chicago now, and she shouldn't be working. Her eyes are bad, and her heart's not good. I'd like her to quit."

He feels that with the connections he makes in basketball he can help his brothers. He has already opened a few doors. Larry has a job with city housing and Mark is with the police department. 26

"I can always go back to school," Isiah said. "But I can't always make a million dollars. I won't always have a chance to provide stability for my family. And I'm doing it at basketball, a game I love." 27

He was a prodigy in basketball the way Mozart was in music. At age three, Amadeus was composing on a harpsichord; at three, Isiah could dribble and shoot baskets. He was the halftime entertainment at the neighborhood Catholic Youth Organization games. "We gave Isiah an old jersey that fell like a dress on him, and he wore black Oxfords and tossed up shots with a high arc," said Ted Kalinowski, who was called Brother Alexis before he left the order. "Isiah was amazing." 28

By the time Thomas was in the fourth grade, he was a standout on the eighth-grade team at Our Lady of Sorrows. 29

His mother and brothers watched him closely. Mary Thomas made sure that he went straight home from school, and did not dawdle in the streets. "If I did," he said, "my brothers would kick my butt." 30

From the time he was in grade school, his brothers lectured him. The seven of them sat in a bedroom and closed the door so that their mother and two sisters would not hear the horror stories of the street. They would take him for a walking tour and point out dangers. "They told me about the mistakes they had made, so that I wouldn't have to make them," said Thomas. 31

Lord Henry, for one, had been an all-city basketball player at St. Phillips; people in the neighborhood contend that he was the best basketball player in the family. He still holds the Catholic League single-season scoring record. But he had problems with discipline and grades and was thrown out of school. He went into the streets, and became a junkie. Isiah could see for himself the tortures his brother went through and the suffering it caused his mother. 32

As an eighth-grader, Isiah sought a scholarship to Weber High School, a Catholic League basketball power. The coach turned him 33

down—too short. He was five-six. "Look, I'm six-four," Larry
Thomas argued to the coach. "My brother will grow just as tall."

Gene Pingatore, the coach at St. Joseph's in Westchester, a Chi-   34
cago suburb, was convinced. "He was a winner," said Pingatore.
"He had that special aura."

At Westchester, a predominantly white school in a white middle-   35
class neighborhood, Thomas endeavored to learn textbook English.
At one point his brother Gregory was confused. Isiah recalls his
brother saying: "You done forgot to talk like a nigger. Better not
come around here like no sissy white boy."

"Hey," Isiah said, laughing, "pull up on that jive."   36

But the brothers, like Isiah, understood the importance of lan-   37
guage, and the handle it could provide in helping to escape the
ghetto, a dream they shared.

"What I was doing," said Isiah, "was becoming fluent in two   38
languages."

Isiah would rise at 5:30 in the morning to begin the one-and-a-   39
half-hour journey by elevated train and bus to Westchester.

"Sometimes I'd look out the window and see Isiah going to   40
school in the dark and I'd cry," said Mary Thomas. "I'd give him
grits with honey and butter for breakfast. And felt bad that I couldn't
afford eggs and bacon for him, too. He sure did like to eat."

Although he excelled in basketball, Isiah neglected his studies   41
and nearly flunked out of high school after his freshman year.

"You're a screwed up kid," said Larry. "You can go one of two   42
ways from here. I had a choice like this once. I chose hustlin'. It's a
disgustin' kind of life. You got the chance of a lifetime."

Pingatore emphasized that without a C average he could not get   43
a college scholarship, under NCAA rules.

"From that point on," recalls Isiah's sister, Ruby, "he was a   44
changed kid." He made the St. Joseph's honor roll in each of his
next three years.

He also led his team to second place in the Illinois state high   45
school tournament, and was chosen All-American. He had his pick
of hundreds of college scholarships. He chose Indiana because it
was close and because Bobby Knight played it straight. "He didn't
try to bribe me," said Mary Thomas. "Other schools offered hundreds
of thousands of dollars. One coach promised to buy me a beautiful
house. Another one said that there'd be a Lear jet so I could go to
all Isiah's games. All Bobby Knight promised was he'd try to get

Isiah a good education and give him a good opportunity to get better in basketball. He said that I might not even be able to get a ticket for a basketball game. I liked that." She also got tickets, and went to all of Isiah's games, sometimes traveling to Bloomington by bus.

He made all-Big Ten as a freshman. Last season he was a 46 consensus All-American. Despite this, he and Coach Knight had conflicts. Thomas appreciated Knight's basketball mind, and knew that the coach relied on his ability as a floor leader, but Thomas had trouble swallowing what he considered Knight's sometimes insulting behavior.

Once, Thomas, who had been appointed team captain, decided 47 to talk with Knight about the team's poor morale. Thomas believed that Indiana—going poorly at the beginning of the season—had some of the best players in the country, and could win the championship if they could pull together and not fight the coach. "There's a problem here, coach," said Isiah.

"There's no problem here," replied Knight. 48

Indiana, however, did improve and made it to the final of the 49 NCAA tournament against North Carolina at the Spectrum in Philadelphia on the night of March 30.

Amid the blaring of the school bands and the waving of pom- 50 poms and the screams from the crowd—the Indiana rooters were sectioned on one side of the court in red and white, the school colors, and the North Carolina fans on the other side wearing blue and white—the game was tightly played. North Carolina led by 26–25 as Isiah Thomas took the ball from under the Tar Heels' basket, and dribbled slowly upcourt. There were only twelve seconds to go in the half and tense Indiana fans wondered if the Hoosiers would get another shot off, especially with Thomas's casualness.

"I didn't want the team to press, I wanted them to relax, and if 51 they saw I wasn't rushing I hoped they wouldn't rush either," Thomas said later. With two seconds to go he hit Randy Wittman with a pass in the corner, and Wittman connected, giving Indiana its first lead of the game, and a terrific lift as it went to the locker room.

Starting the second half, Thomas stole two straight passes from 52 North Carolina and scored. Indiana went ahead by 31–26 and went on to a 63–50 victory. "Those two steals," said Dean Smith, the North Carolina coach, "were the turning point of the game." Thomas scored a game-high twenty-three points, and had five assists and four steals.

He was named the outstanding player of the championship tournament.

As soon as the game ended, Indiana fans rushed on the court.   53
One of them, Thomas saw, was a black woman in a red suit jacket
with a button on her lapel. The button read, "Isiah Thomas's Mom.
Mrs. Mary Thomas." Near the center of the court, they embraced.
She was crying and it looked as if Isiah was holding back tears.

"Thanks, Mom, thanks for everything you've gone through for   54
me. I hope I can do something for you."

"You done enough, honey," she said.   55

Reporters and cameramen were all around them. And Isiah   56
whispered in his mother's ear, "Well, you can do one more thing for
me," he said.

"What's that, baby?"   57

"I heard you in the first half when I threw a bad pass. You   58
hollered, 'What the hell are you doin'?' Don't cuss at me on the
court. I was fixin' to get it together."

Then Isiah was scooted off to receive the winner's trophy. And   59
the woman who wore the button proudly saying she was Isiah
Thomas's mom took out a handkerchief and wiped her eyes.

RESPONSES AND IDEAS

1. Respond to this essay by listing the advantages and disadvantages of
   leaving college early to play professional sports.

2. Are the sports figures quoted in the essay familiar to you? If so, what
   do the quotations add to the essay? If not, do you find the essay hard
   to understand as a result? Explain.

3. The title of this essay was probably added by an editor working for the
   newspaper in which it appeared. Is it an appropriate title? If so, why?
   If not, suggest a better one.

PURPOSE, AUDIENCE, AND STRATEGIES

1. This essay was originally published in the sports pages of the *New York
   Times*. Does Berkow assume that most of his readers will be familiar
   with the conditions in which Thomas grew up? Does he assume they
   will already be familiar with the pressures on Thomas to turn professional? Are his assumptions reasonable? Support your answer with
   specific evidence from the essay.

2. For what purpose or purposes does Berkow include in the essay so many quotations from Thomas's family and from people associated with his basketball career? Choose three quotations and tell what they contribute specifically to our knowledge of Thomas and his career.

3. State in your own words the purpose of this essay and say whether or not you believe Berkow is trying to make a particular point about Thomas or about his decision to become a professional athlete.

4. Are the events in this essay presented in chronological order? If not, in what order are they presented, and why? Be specific.

5. Is this narrative presented primarily in summary form or in detailed form (use evidence from the essay to support your answer)? Is the method of presentation appropriate for the purpose of the essay? When and why does Berkow use concrete sensory detail in this essay?

LANGUAGE AND STYLE

1. Identify those places in the essay where Berkow quotes speakers who use slang or speak in a nonstandard dialect. What do these quotations add to the essay? Would the effect of the essay (or of specific sections of the piece) be changed in any way if Berkow had chosen to report what the speakers had to say in standard English rather than in their own words?

2. Does Berkow provide adequate transition between the events that make up the essay, or do the shifts seem abrupt? Do the sentences have adequate variety, or do they seem excessively short and choppy? Use specific examples to support your answers. (See Glossary: Style, Transitions, Evaluation.)

3. If you had difficulty understanding any of the following words, look them up in the dictionary: *ravages* (par. 10); *charisma* (13); *forensics* (14); *articulation* (22); *aura* (34); *consensus* (46).

WRITING ACTIVITIES

1. Narrative essays often focus on the events leading up to a decision and comment on the significance of the decision. Write an essay in which you tell how you, a friend, a parent, a brother, a sister, or even someone you do not know well reached a decision. As you write, describe what the decision reveals about the person's character and values. The decision might be about a variety of matters ranging from personal to public (a divorce, whether or not to attend college, how to deal with a friend's dishonesty, or how to respond to a college instructor's unfairness in grading).

2. Berkow's narrative of Isiah Thomas is a reminder that talented athletes often face conflicts that less talented people do not. They frequently have to decide, for example, how much time to put into studies and how much into sports, or they have to choose between activities that lead to personal development and those that make for athletic success. Drawing on your experience or on what you have read and seen on television, explore such a conflict in a narrative essay.

3. Sports can sometimes become an obsession, crowding out other important parts of life. Explore a problem like this in a narrative essay.

⟨⟩ ALICE WALKER

Alice Walker, born in Georgia in 1944, was the youngest in a family of eight children. Her parents were sharecroppers, and Walker attended rural schools as a child. She studied at Spelman College and Sarah Lawrence College, from which she graduated. Walker has taught at a number of colleges and worked as an editor at *Ms.* magazine. Currently she lives in the San Francisco Bay area and teaches at the University of California at Berkeley.

A poet and novelist as well as an essayist, Alice Walker has published a number of highly-acclaimed books, including *Revolutionary Petunias and Other Poems* (1973); *In Love & Trouble* (1973), a collection of short stories; *Meridian* (1976), a novel; *The Color Purple* (1982), a novel awarded both a Pulitzer Prize and the American Book Award for fiction; and *In Search of Our Mothers' Gardens,* (1983), a collection of her essays.

Beauty: When the Other Dancer Is the Self

This essay, first published in *Ms.* magazine in 1983, uses a variety of writing techniques—including a brief poem—and is as much concerned with why things happened (cause-and-effect) as with what happened (narrative). Along with its personal subject matter, it takes up some of the broader concerns of feminist thought, including the definition of feminine strength and identity, as well as the effects of racism. Yet despite its complexity and breadth, the narrative is relatively easy to read and understand.

It is a bright summer day in 1947. My father, a fat, funny man   1
with beautiful eyes and a subversive wit, is trying to decide which of his eight children he will take with him to the county fair. My mother, of course, will not go. She is knocked out from getting most of us ready: I hold my neck stiff against the pressure of her knuckles as she hastily completes the braiding and then beribboning of my hair.

My father is the driver for the rich old white lady up the road.   2
Her name is Miss Mey. She owns all the land for miles around, as well as the house in which we live. All I remember about her is that she once offered to pay my mother thirty-five cents for cleaning her

house, raking up piles of her magnolia leaves, and washing her family's clothes, and that my mother—she of no money, eight children, and a chronic earache—refused it. But I do not think of this in 1947. I am two and a half years old. I want to go everywhere my daddy goes. I am excited at the prospect of riding in a car. Someone has told me fairs are fun. That there is room in the car for only three of us doesn't faze me at all. Whirling happily in my starchy frock, showing off my biscuit-polished patent-leather shoes and lavender socks, tossing my head in a way that makes my ribbons bounce, I stand, hands on hips, before my father. "Take me, Daddy," I say with assurance; "I'm the prettiest!"

Later, it does not surprise me to find myself in Miss Mey's shiny   3
black car, sharing the back seat with the other lucky ones. Does not surprise me that I thoroughly enjoy the fair. At home that night I tell the unlucky ones all I can remember about the merry-go-round, the man who eats live chickens, and the teddy bears, until they say: that's enough baby Alice. Shut up now, and go to sleep.

It is Easter Sunday, 1950. I am dressed in a green, flocked,   4
scalloped-hem dress (handmade by my adoring sister, Ruth) that has its own smooth satin petticoat and tiny hot-pink roses tucked into each scallop. My shoes, new T-strap patent leather, again highly biscuit-polished. I am six years old and have learned one of the longest Easter speeches to be heard that day, totally unlike the speech I said when I was two: "Easter lilies / pure and white / blossom in / the morning light." When I rise to give my speech I do so on a great wave of love and pride and expectation. People in the church stop rustling their new crinolines. They seem to hold their breath. I can tell they admire my dress, but it is my spirit, bordering on sassiness (womanishness), they secretly applaud.

"That girl's a little *mess*," they whisper to each other, pleased.   5

Naturally I say my speech without stammer or pause, unlike   6
those who stutter, stammer, or, worst of all, forget. This is before the word "beautiful" exists in people's vocabulary, but "Oh, isn't she the *cutest* thing!" frequently floats my way. "And got so much sense!" they gratefully add . . . for which thoughtful addition I thank them to this day.

It was great fun being cute. But then, one day, it ended.   7

I am eight years old and a tomboy. I have a cowboy hat, cowboy   8
boots, checkered shirt and pants, all red. My playmates are my

brothers, two and four years older than I. Their colors are black and green, the only difference in the way we are dressed. On Saturday nights we all go to the picture show, even my mother; Westerns are her favorite kind of movie. Back home, "on the ranch," we pretend we are Tom Mix, Hopalong Cassidy, Lash LaRue (we've even named one of our dogs Lash LaRue); we chase each other for hours rustling cattle, being outlaws, delivering damsels from distress. Then my parents decide to buy my brothers guns. These are not "real" guns. They shoot "BBs," copper pellets my brothers say will kill birds. Because I am a girl, I do not get a gun. Instantly I am relegated to the position of Indian. Now there appears a great distance between us. They shoot and shoot at everything with their new guns. I try to keep up with my bow and arrows.

One day while I am standing on top of our makeshift "garage"— 9 pieces of tin nailed across some poles—holding my bow and arrow and looking out toward the fields, I feel an incredible blow in my right eye. I look down just in time to see my brother lower his gun.

Both brothers rush to my side. My eye stings, and I cover it with 10 my hand. "If you tell," they say, "we will get a whipping. You don't want that to happen, do you?" I do not. "Here is a piece of wire," says the older brother, picking it up from the roof; "say you stepped on one end of it and the other flew up and hit you." The pain is beginning to start. "Yes," I say. "Yes, I will say that is what happened." If I do not say this is what happened, I know my brothers will find ways to make me wish I had. But now I will say anything that gets me to my mother.

Confronted by our parents we stick to the lie agreed upon. They 11 place me on a bench on the porch and I close my left eye while they examine the right. There is a tree growing from underneath the porch that climbs past the railing to the roof. It is the last thing my right eye sees. I watch as its trunk, its branches, and then its leaves are blotted out by the rising blood.

I am in shock. First there is intense fever, which my father tries 12 to break using lily leaves bound around my head. Then there are chills: my mother tries to get me to eat soup. Eventually, I do not know how, my parents learn what has happened. A week after the "accident" they take me to see a doctor. "Why did you wait so long to come?" he asks, looking into my eye and shaking his head. "Eyes are sympathetic," he says. "If one is blind, the other will likely become blind too."

This comment of the doctor's terrifies me. But it is really how I 13
look that bothers me most. Where the BB pellet struck there is a glob
of whitish scar tissue, a hideous cataract, on my eye. Now when I
stare at people—a favorite pastime, up to now—they will stare back.
Not at the "cute" little girl, but at her scar. For six years I do not
stare at anyone, because I do not raise my head.

Years later, in the throes of a mid-life crisis, I ask my mother 14
and sister whether I changed after the "accident." "No," they say,
puzzled. "What do you mean?"

What do I mean? 15

I am eight, and, for the first time, doing poorly in school, where 16
I have been something of a whiz since I was four. We have just
moved to the place where the "accident" occurred. We do not know
any of the people around us because this is a different county. The
only time I see the friends I knew is when we go back to our old
church. The new school is the former state penitentiary. It is a large
stone building, cold and drafty, crammed to overflowing with boisterous, ill-disciplined children. On the third floor there is a huge
circular imprint of some partition that has been torn out.

"What used to be here?" I ask a sullen girl next to me on our 17
way past it to lunch.

"The electric chair," says she. 18

At night I have nightmares about the electric chair, and about 19
all the people reputedly "fried" in it. I am afraid of the school, where
all the students seem to be budding criminals.

"What's the matter with your eye?" they ask, critically. 20

When I don't answer (I cannot decide whether it was an "ac- 21
cident" or not), they shove me, insist on a fight.

My brother, the one who created the story about the wire, comes 22
to my rescue. But then brags so much about "protecting" me, I
become sick.

After months of torture at the school, my parents decide to send 23
me back to our old community, to my old school. I live with my
grandparents and the teacher they board. But there is no room for
Phoebe, my cat. By the time my grandparents decide there *is* room,
and I ask for my cat, she cannot be found. Miss Yarborough, the
boarding teacher, takes me under her wing, and begins to teach me
to play the piano. But soon she marries an African—a "prince," she
says—and is whisked away to his continent.

At my old school there is at least one teacher who loves me. She 24
is the teacher who "knew me before I was born" and bought my
first baby clothes. It is she who makes life bearable. It is her presence
that finally helps me turn on the one child at the school who continually calls me "one-eyed bitch." One day I simply grab him by his
coat and beat him until I am satisfied. It is my teacher who tells me
my mother is ill.

My mother is lying in bed in the middle of the day, something 25
I have never seen. She is in too much pain to speak. She has an
abscess in her ear. I stand looking down on her, knowing that if she
dies, I cannot live. She is being treated with warm oils and hot bricks
held against her cheek. Finally a doctor comes. But I must go back
to my grandparents' house. The weeks pass but I am hardly aware
of it. All I know is that my mother might die, my father is not so
jolly, my brothers still have their guns, and I am the one sent away
from home.

"You did not change," they say. 26
Did I imagine the anguish of never looking up? 27

I am twelve. When relatives come to visit I hide in my room. 28
My cousin Brenda, just my age, whose father works in the post office
and whose mother is a nurse, comes to find me. "Hello," she says.
And then she asks, looking at my recent school picture, which I did
not want taken, and on which the "glob," as I think of it, is clearly
visible, "You still can't see out of that eye?"

"No," I say, and flop back on the bed over my book. 29

That night, as I do almost every night, I abuse my eye. I rant 30
and rave at it, in front of the mirror. I plead with it to clear up
before morning. I tell it I hate and despise it. I do not pray for sight.
I pray for beauty.

"You did not change," they say. 31

I am fourteen and baby-sitting for my brother Bill, who lives in 32
Boston. He is my favorite brother and there is a strong bond between
us. Understanding my feelings of shame and ugliness he and his
wife take me to a local hospital, where the "glob" is removed by a
doctor named O. Henry. There is still a small bluish crater where
the scar tissue was, but the ugly white stuff is gone. Almost immediately I become a different person from the girl who does not raise

her head. Or so I think. Now that I've raised my head I win the
boyfriend of my dreams. Now that I've raised my head I have plenty
of friends. Now that I've raised my head classwork comes from my
lips as faultlessly as Easter speeches did, and I leave high school as
valedictorian, most popular student, and *queen,* hardly believing my
luck. Ironically, the girl who was voted most beautiful in our class
(and was) was later shot twice through the chest by a male companion, using a "real" gun, while she was pregnant. But that's
another story in itself. Or is it?

"You did not change," they say.   33

It is now thirty years since the "accident." A beautiful journalist   34
comes to visit and to interview me. She is going to write a cover story
for her magazine that focuses on my latest book. "Decide how you
want to look on the cover," she says. "Glamorous, or whatever."

Never mind "glamorous," it is the "whatever" that I hear. Sud-   35
denly all I can think of is whether I will get enough sleep the night
before the photography session: if I don't, my eye will be tired and
wander, as blind eyes will.

At night in bed with my lover I think up reasons why I should   36
not appear on the cover of a magazine. "My meanest critics will say
I've sold out," I say. "My family will now realize I write scandalous
books."

"But what's the real reason you don't want to do this?" he asks.   37

"Because in all probability," I say in a rush, "my eye won't be   38
straight."

"It will be straight enough," he says. Then, "Besides, I thought   39
you'd made your peace with that."

And I suddenly remember that I have.   40

I remember: 41

I am talking to my brother Jimmy, asking if he remembers   42
anything unusual about the day I was shot. He does not know I
consider that day the last time my father, with his sweet home remedy
of cool lily leaves, chose me, and that I suffered and raged inside
because of this. "Well," he says, "all I remember is standing by the
side of the highway with Daddy, trying to flag down a car. A white
man stopped, but when Daddy said he needed somebody to take his
little girl to the doctor, he drove off."

I remember: 43

I am in the desert for the first time. I fall totally in love with it. 44

I am so overwhelmed by its beauty, I confront for the first time, consciously, the meaning of the doctor's words years ago: "Eyes are sympathetic. If one is blind, the other will likely become blind too." I realize I have dashed about the world madly, looking at this, looking at that, storing up images against the fading of the light. *But I might have missed seeing the desert!* The shock of that possibility—and gratitude for over twenty-five years of sight—sends me literally to my knees. Poem after poem comes—which is perhaps how poets pray.

On Sight   45

I am so thankful I have seen
The Desert
And the creatures in the desert
And the desert Itself.

The desert has its own moon
Which I have seen
With my own eye.
There is no flag on it.

Trees of the desert have arms
All of which are always up
That is because the moon is up
The sun is up
Also the sky
The stars
Clouds
None with flags.

If there *were* flags, I doubt
the trees would point.
Would you?

But mostly, I remember this: 46

I am twenty-seven, and my baby daughter is almost three. Since   47
her birth I have worried about her discovery that her mother's eyes are different from other people's. Will she be embarrassed? I think. What will she say? Every day she watches a television program called "Big Blue Marble." It begins with a picture of the earth as it appears from the moon. It is bluish, a little battered-looking, but full of light, with whitish clouds swirling around it. Every time I see it I weep with love, as if it is a picture of Grandma's house. One day when I am putting Rebecca down for her nap, she suddenly focuses

on my eye. Something inside me cringes, gets ready to try to protect myself. All children are cruel about physical differences, I know from experience, and that they don't always mean to be is another matter. I assume Rebecca will be the same.

But no-o-o-o. She studies my face intently as we stand, her inside   48
and me outside the crib. She even holds my face maternally between her dimpled little hands. Then, looking every bit as serious and lawyerlike as her father, she says, as if it may just possibly have slipped my attention: "Mommy, there's a *world* in your eye." (As in, "Don't be alarmed, or do anything crazy.") And then, gently, but with great interest: "Mommy, where did you *get* that world in your eye?"

For the most part, the pain left then. (So what, if my brothers   49
grew up to buy even more powerful pellet guns for their sons and to carry real guns themselves. So what, if a young "Morehouse man" once nearly fell off the steps of Trevor Arnett Library because he thought my eyes were blue.) Crying and laughing I ran to the bathroom, while Rebecca mumbled and sang herself off to sleep. Yes indeed, I realized, looking into the mirror. There *was* a world in my eye. And I saw that it was possible to love it: that in fact, for all it had taught me of shame and anger and inner vision, I *did* love it. Even to see it drifting out of orbit in boredom, or rolling up out of fatigue, not to mention floating back at attention in excitement (bearing witness, a friend has called it), deeply suitable to my personality, and even characteristic of me.

That night I dream I am dancing to Stevie Wonder's song "Al-   50
ways" (the name of the song is really "As," but I hear it as "Always"). As I dance, whirling and joyous, happier than I've ever been in my life, another bright-faced dancer joins me. We dance and kiss each other and hold each other through the night. The other dancer has obviously come through all right, as I have done. She is beautiful, whole and free. And she is also me.

RESPONSES AND IDEAS

1.   In paragraph 32, Walker tells of a young woman who was shot by a boyfriend. She then comments, "But that's another story in itself. Or is it?" Respond to the essay by exploring in writing the similarities and differences between the events in Walker's life and the story of the other young woman.

2. Explain what this phrase means: "Mommy, there's a *world* in your eye" (par. 48). In what ways does Walker see her blind eye as a symbol in this essay? (See Glossary: Symbol.)

3. What does the title of this essay mean? Is it appropriate for the essay, or is it misleading? Suggest an alternative.

PURPOSE, AUDIENCE, AND STRATEGIES

1. Are most readers likely to have had experiences similar to the author's? Choose three of the events presented in the narrative, and describe experiences of your own that are similar.

2. Using the repeated phrase, "I remember," as an introduction, Walker presents in the form of flashbacks the events that helped her come to terms with the injury to her eye (pars. 41–48). Explain how these events represent ways we can come to terms with our own lives.

3. Is the purpose of this essay to explain events in the author's life? To teach us how to deal with problems in our lives? Explain what you believe are the main purposes of the essay, and support your answer with evidence. (See Glossary: Purpose.)

4. This narrative contains many sudden leaps backward and forward in time. Identify each of the leaps in time, indicate whether each is a movement backward or forward, and tell what kind of transition Walker uses to signal the change. (See Glossary: Transitions, Setting.)

5. Why do you think Walker chose the rather puzzling title "Beauty: When the Other Dancer Is the Self" for her essay? Is the meaning of the title adequately explained by the essay (particularly paragraph 50)? In your own words state the title's meaning. Does the title add to or detract from the effectiveness of the essay? Explain.

LANGUAGE AND STYLE

1. What special devices of sentence structure and style does Walker use to emphasize differences between the way she views herself and the events in her life and the way other people view them? (See Glossary: Style, Emphasis.) Use specific examples to support your answer.

2. In what specific ways does the diction Walker uses to present events before the accident differ from the diction she uses after the accident? (See Glossary: Diction.)

3. If you do not know the meaning of some of the following words, look them up in a dictionary: *subversive* (par. 1); *biscuit-polished* (2); *flocked, crinolines, sassiness* (4); *cataract* (13); *throes* (14); *boisterous* (16); *abscess* (25).

WRITING ACTIVITIES

1. Was there an event in your childhood which, like the shot that blinded Walker's eye, greatly affected your view of yourself? Have you come to terms with the event? Have you been able to accept yourself as Walker does at the end of the essay? Write about the event and your attempts to deal with and overcome its impact.

2. Seeing ourselves as others see us is always difficult, but sometimes an incident gives us a chance to look at the way we appear to others, rather like a mirror allows us to view our bodies from the outside. Write about one such episode and indicate what it revealed or what lessons it taught.

3. Write three short narrative paragraphs about incidents that frightened you or that placed you or someone else in physical or psychological danger. Then either develop one of the paragraphs into a full-length essay or combine them to create an essay that makes a point through narration.

Writing Suggestions

EXPLORATIONS

1. Make a list of issues people frequently argue about (gun control, welfare, abortion). Choose three of the issues, and for each summarize an experience you had or an event you know about that could be used in an argument essay on the topic. If one of the narratives is particularly powerful, consider building an essay around it.

2. Identify three strong emotions (fear, anger, and so on) and freewrite for five minutes on each, beginning with this statement "[Anger] is like the time when I. . . ." If one of the freewritings starts turning into an essay, keep going.

3. Write five opening sentences for different narrative essays recounting an auto accident, at least one of which should be for a personal narrative and one for an analytical narrative. If one or more of the opening sentences suggests an arrangement of events different from the normal chronological pattern, describe the arrangement(s) briefly.

4. Look for a story of an accident in a newspaper and rewrite it in the first person. Then describe the changes you made as you rewrote it.

ACTIVITIES

1. Get a copy of one of these magazines: *Sports Illustrated, Glamour, Mademoiselle, Vogue,* the *New Yorker,* or *Esquire.* Skim the articles and columns it contains and decide how many are narrative essays or make extensive use of narrative examples. Decide whether each of the narratives is a personal, reportorial, or analytical narrative, or, if a narrative does not fit into one of these categories, describe its features. Write briefly your reasons for placing each essay in a particular category. Short stories (fiction) are not essays, of course, though they are narratives.

2. Watch a television program like *60 Minutes* or *20/20.* Decide whether the reports it presents can be classified as personal, reportorial, or analytical narratives, or some mixture, and make a list of the evidence that supports your answers.

3. As you watch *60 Minutes, 20/20,* or a regular television news program, try to decide whether the narratives they present are designed chiefly to amuse, to inform, to interpret and analyze, or to persuade. Write in brief form the reasons for your conclusions and be aware that the segments of the broadcast may have different purposes. Or look at five articles from *Time, Newsweek,* or *U.S. News and World Report* and identify their purposes.

4. Take a notebook with you to a busy place (a laundromat, the middle
    of campus, a noisy restaurant) and take notes on the events for a five-
    or ten-minute period. Then turn them into a narrative that presents the
    events, indicating those that happened at the same time and those that
    led to other events. Trade narratives with a classmate to see whether
    you conveyed the events without confusion.

MODELS

1. Taking "Garbage Man" as a model, write about an incident in which
    your view of a person (or an institution, such as a church or school)
    was abruptly shattered.

2. With "The Angry Winter" as a guide, meditate in writing on a brief
    event that reveals some element in human nature we often hide or deny,
    such as greed, jealousy, or a desire for revenge.

3. Follow Barbara Huttman's example in "A Crime of Compassion" and
    use a personal experience to argue that institutional rules, bureaucratic
    procedures, or restrictive laws often cause great pain.

4. Use many of the strategies employed by Ira Berkow in "At Nineteen,
    Thomas Makes His Decision," and present the events that led up to
    some important decision in your life.

5. Break a personal narrative into segments similar to the ones created by
    Alice Walker in "Beauty: When the Other Dancer Is the Self," and use
    it to explain how you came to terms with some element in your per-
    sonality or problem in your life.

3

❧ DESCRIPTION

Creating Details Through the Senses

WHAT DESCRIPTION DOES

How effective would a narrative be without details of the setting and a description of the participants? Would you be able to understand how a microscope works without a description of its parts? Or could you grasp the power of a tornado without knowing that homes have been blown apart, trees torn to bits, and cars flipped upside down and deposited hundreds of yards away? Think how hard it would be to argue for stricter drunk driving laws if you could not use descriptive detail to tell about accidents caused by drunk drivers. To understand the importance of description in each of these settings is to recognize what familiar and essential roles description plays in reading and writing, either on its own, or, as is frequently the case, in combination with some other pattern of expression.

By using sensory detail—the evidence of sight, hearing, touch, taste, and smell—descriptive writing presents (or re-creates) scenes, moments frozen in time. It calls up from memory the aroma of suntan lotion on a beach in summer or the stinging pain of fingers and toes slowly warming after time spent in the winter's cold. It creates in words a portrait of the steamy closeness of the Brazilian jungle or the jostling crowds and neon signs of Tokyo's nightclub district, the Ginza.

Description also conveys things not directly accessible to the senses. It brings back the feeling of being hopelessly in love with the most handsome boy or the most beautiful girl in the ninth-grade class, or it explores tangled, painful emotions like anger and jealousy. It reveals the character of a kind but eccentric uncle, or it illuminates the degrees of despair: that of a drunk slumped against a building in a filthy alley or of a child crying for her puppy just killed by a car.

Descriptive writing also arranges facts and details, making them easier to understand and remember. It specifies the shape and location of cells in the human brain or in the leaf of a tree. It indicates the relationships among the layers of sedimentary rock making up the wall of a canyon or among the architectural elements in a building:

> On the ground floor it is a sombre room, painted with rocks in the rustic manner of Italian grotto imitations. The staircase itself then unfolded between two curved walls, the outside wall solid, that on the inside opened in arcades through which one looked down into the semi-darkness of the oval grotto (Nikolaus Pevsner, *An Outline of European Architecture*, 1963).

As readers we look for the detail that description can provide before we consider a piece of writing convincing, whatever its aim: to inform or explain ("Tell me about it in concrete terms so I can understand what you are saying"); to share an experience ("I want to be able to see, hear, and feel what happened"), or to persuade ("In precisely what ways will I feel healthier if I sign up for this program?").

The basis for a successful description, then, is concrete detail—specific things or qualities, the evidence of our senses ("The floodwater turned the carpet into a slippery mess smelling like dead fish and covered the electronic insides of the TV with a thin coat of black mud") rather than abstract, general impressions ("the flood soaked everything in the living room"). By gathering and organizing concrete detail that represents the essential qualities of a subject, writers can enable readers to create in their own minds a lively image of the scene being described.

Specific detail is important even when the subject is something accessible to the senses only indirectly, like a person's character or intelligence, for we construct our understanding of such matters to a great extent from external evidence. We can arrive at an understanding of a person by observing how he or she talks, walks, and dresses, and what he or she does or says. Figures of speech like simile and metaphor use concrete detail to aid understanding by comparing something we cannot grasp directly to something we can easily understand ("The tornado sounded like a train rushing by"—simile; "The tornado, a hell-bent train, rushed by"—metaphor). These devices of language can also give us a more imaginative look at a subject through unusual comparisons: "His long, thin fingers twitched nervously as he talked, flickering back and forth like a snake's tongue." (See Glossary: Figures of Speech for a fuller discussion of simile, metaphor, and other devices of language.)

No writer can hope to include in an essay all the tiny details that make up a scene and still keep the piece a reasonable length. Moreover, even a brief descriptive passage composed almost entirely of concrete detail would be unreadable because it would provide too much information for a reader to take in at once:

> In this part of the forest the flickering light played on the black, foul-smelling pools of water, covered in part with a grey scum of dead algae that smelled like burnt rubber and on the dark-brown, twisted, scarred roots of the trees, themselves covered by a pale-green, sponge-like moss that was soft to the touch, but sticky, too, clinging to clothes, hair, fingers, and elbows like gritty cotton candy, only wetter; and the air, heavy with moisture, and filled with a metallic blue haze, smelling like coal smoke or car exhaust, stung the nostrils and lungs like cigar smoke inhaled deeply, and bit at the skin till it turned a dull red and began itching. . . .

Still, writers can expect their readers to do some of the work. When you present significant details from a relatively familiar scene (the feel of hot sand on a beach, the sound of children playing in the water), you can expect readers to fill in the rest of the details by drawing on their memories of similar experiences. This process goes on, though to a lesser extent, even when the subject is unfamiliar. Notice, for example, how the writer of the following passage draws directly on our experience of other scenes to help create in our imaginations a scene most of us have never encountered before, the clumps of trees along a path in the Himalaya mountains:

> To the north, high on the mountain's face, has come in view the village called Rohagaon. The track passes along beneath wild walnut trees. The last leaves are yellowed and stiff on the gaunt branches, and the nuts are fallen; the dry scratch and whisper of sere leaves bring on the vague melancholy of some other autumn, half-remembered. Cracked nutshells litter big flat stones along the path, and among the shells lie fresh feathers of a hoopoe, perhaps killed in the act of gleaning by the

accipiter that darts out of the bush ahead and down over the void of the Suli Gorge. In a copse below Rohagaon, maple, sumac, locust, and wild grape evoke the woods of home, but the trees differ just enough from the familiar ones to make the wood seem dreamlike, a wildwood of children's tales, found again in a soft autumn haze. The wildwood brings on mild nostalgia, not for home or place, but for lost innocence— the paradise lost that, as Proust said, is the only paradise (Peter Matthiessen, *The Snow Leopard*, 1978).

The scene Matthiessen describes is an exotic one, and some of the terms he uses are probably just as unfamiliar (*sere*—dry, withered; *accipiter*—a hawk; *hoopoe*—a European and Asian bird with fancy plumage). Yet the scene should not be difficult for most readers to imagine because he constructs it from familiar sights and sounds ("The last leaves are yellowed and stiff on the gaunt branches") and because he connects these details of the scene directly to the readers' memories, inviting readers to complete the picture ("the dry scratch and whisper of sere leaves bring on the vague melancholy of some other autumn, half-remembered"). Thus even if readers have never walked under a nut tree, they can imagine what the crushed nuts must look like on the ground. Although they probably have no idea what a hoopoe is, readers can guess from the feathers that it is some kind of bird and that the accipiter that flies from the bush over the gorge is a predator like an owl or an eagle.

Finally, though the scene is not a familiar one, Matthiessen avoids overloading the description with detail and sketches out only its most important features to create a basis for the emotional response to which the whole passage is directed, the sense of lost innocence. In trying to elicit this emotion, he also draws on the readers' memories, this time of the strange forest filled with unusual animals and adventures that are a frequent feature of children's books.

Descriptions are often put into two categories, objective and subjective. An objective description tries to convey the details of the subject thoroughly and accurately without suggesting the writer's feelings or bias and without trying to evoke an emotional response from the reader. Newspaper reports, technical manuals, field reports from a biologist or geologist, records of experiments, and other kinds of informative, historical, or scientific writing rely heavily on objective description. They use description to help an audience understand a subject and to provide a basis for any judgments that need to be made. Thus an oil geologist looks to an objective description of rock structures to decide where to drill; a financial analyst depends on a description of a company's new products in order to decide whether to buy stock in the firm.

A subjective description, on the other hand, makes plain the author's values and feelings and often encourages readers to respond emotionally. While attitudes may be conveyed by direct statement, writers indicate them more often through choice of detail or the connotations of words (*connotations:* the feelings or set of associations that accompany a word as opposed to its dictionary meaning). Note, for example, the slightly different meanings created by the connotations in these sentences:

> Her views on the matter were clear (firm/determined/unyielding/ rigid).
> He spoke unfavorably (negatively/harshly/bitterly) of his experience working for ACM Corporation.

Subjective description is appropriate in those instances when you wish to convey your feelings, as Andrew Malcolm does in "Dad," a character sketch of his father, or E. B. White does in his account of a summer visit to a rural lake, "Once More to the Lake." It is also useful when you wish to encourage a specific emotional response. In arguing for stricter controls on acid rain, for example, a writer might describe in unlimited detail the death of thousands of young fish in a stream whose waters have turned acidic—in part to support a thesis, but at the same time hoping to horrify readers and get them to take whatever action they can.

Descriptive writing is seldom purely subjective or purely objective; in practice you may find that a blend of the two is appropriate or that in one part of an essay your writing is objective and in another part subjective.

As you work on descriptive writing, you need to keep in mind the active role that readers play. The decisions you make while you write and revise—particularly about how much specific detail to include and how to arrange it—need to be directed by an awareness of how much your readers already know about the subject and what attitudes toward it they bring with them.

THE PROCESS

Descriptive writing starts with the subject. As you begin to write, look through your memories to find a place or person that still has a strong emotional meaning for you (the place you used to hide when everyone was angry with you; the aunt or sister who was always more kind and understanding than your mother), a scene that sums up a point you wish to make (an accident scene that demonstrates the value of seat belts or the danger of drinking and driving), or a setting that is so remarkable in some way that you wish to share it with others. Or if you keep a journal, as many writers do, focus some of the entries on a place, person, or emotion in order to discover potential topics for an essay.

After you have identified a tentative topic, explore it using the techniques for probing a topic outlined in Chapter 1 in the section "The Writing Process" or use one of the following sets of questions:

For scenes or objects:

1. What does it look like (colors, shapes, height, depth)?
2. What does it sound like (loud, soft, rasping, soothing, musical, like a chain saw)?
3. What does it smell like (smoky, acrid, like gasoline, like soap, like a wood fire)?
4. What does it feel like (smooth, sticky, like a fish, like a spider's web, like mashed potatoes)?
5. What does it taste like (bitter, salty, like grass, like feathers)?

For emotions (excitement, fear) or ideas (freedom, oppression):

1. What effect does it have on behavior (anger: red face, abrupt gestures)?
2. What is it like (freedom is like taking a deep breath of air after leaving a smoky room)?

For people:

1. What does the person look like (hair uncombed, dandruff, shirt hanging out)?
2. What are some characteristic aspects of the person's behavior (rubs hands on skirt, picks ear)?

3. What characteristic things has the person done or said (cheated on a chemistry test; stole from roommate; called a friend "a real jerk")?

4. How do others act towards the person; what do they say (turn to him for advice, call him a slob)?

You may also be able to develop your own set of questions that will reflect the purposes for which you are writing. If you are on a field trip for botany class, for instance, you probably know what features of the trees and bushes you observe are most important and can turn the features into a set of questions to guide note-taking.

As you probe a topic, try to recognize the dominant impression you want to convey, the emotional reaction you want to encourage, or the point you intend the description to support. If you are writing about Times Square in New York City, the Loop in Chicago, Fishermen's Wharf in San Francisco, or a similar crowded, hectic spot in a large city, you might make this note to yourself: "The dominant impression I want readers to carry with them after reading my essay is of the vitality of the place. I know this comes through in the way the people talk, act, and dress." Or you might write, "I want people to understand the cruelty of my fourth-grade teacher. I want them to sense it from her pinched cheeks and cold eyes and from the chopping motions her hands made as she talked."

Having gathered material and decided on your purpose, in a general way at least, the only thing left for you to do before starting to draft your essay is to decide on a tentative arrangement for it. The impression you wish to convey or the thesis you intend to support should be reflected in the organization of your description; otherwise, readers may have to plow through a shapeless mass of detail without any idea of its purpose. Depending on your subject and aim, you may wish to choose one of the following kinds of organization, each of which can be adapted to the demands of a particular essay.

Spatial Organization   A clear spatial organization will help your readers understand a visually complex subject. If you wish to describe a complicated scene (a three-ring circus, for example), you might begin with the left and move to the right, or from the bottom to the top (clowns, jugglers, and dog acts on the ground; trapeze artists and a sway pole above), or use some other spatial pattern that readers can easily follow. In describing a person, you might begin with the shoes (scuffed, heels run down), move to the shirt (unpressed, cuffs frayed), and end with the face (blotched, unshaven).

Chronological Organization   If you wish to have your audience look at a scene from several perspectives, you might decide to organize the description around a change in time, beginning perhaps with early morning, moving to midday, and ending at night. Such a strategy allows you to make a point by contrasting the scenes and provides variety and interest. Time organization is effective in character description because it allows a person to be viewed at different stages of life (see Andrew H. Malcolm's essay, "Dad," in this chapter). Time and spatial organization can also be combined effectively by presenting a scene through the eyes of an observer moving through it.

Thematic Organization   A thematic organization places emphasis on the dominant impression or the thesis by means of repetition. It may involve emphasizing the dominant impression by repeating clusters of key words (*grim, grasping, hard, short-tempered*) or images (pink ribbons, the scent of violets). It may mean arranging the segments of the description in increasing order of importance or building the entire essay around a thesis and using a variety of descriptive details to support it. (Michael Arlen uses a variation on this last strategy in "Ode to Thanksgiving.")

As you write and revise, the purpose and plan for your essay should become clearer to you, and you will be able to shift your attention away from such matters as choice of subject and arrangement of detail to decisions about perspective (including point of view) and the need to give more emphasis to some details and less to others.

Perspective means in part the point of view used in a description, either first-person point of view ("I looked . . .") or third-person ("He stretched and sighed. . . .") (See Glossary: Point of View.) It also includes such matters as the location of the observer and any limitations on the observer's ability to see and understand. You might wish to change the perspective from that of an observer looking at the scene from a distance ("I could see the trees swaying . . ." to that of a person moving through the scene or participating in it ("I bumped against the small tree, and the water from the leaves fell on me"). For a special effect you might limit the outlook of your observer in some way. William Faulkner does this in an unusual manner in the novel *The Sound and the Fury* by having the character Benji, a 33-year-old idiot, describe a golf game:

> Through the fence, between the curling flower spaces, I could see them hitting. They were coming toward where the flag was and I went along the fence. Luster was hunting in the grass by the flower tree. They took the flag out, and they were hitting. Then they put the flag back and they went to the table, and he hit and the other hit. Then they went on, and I went along the fence. Luster came away from the flower tree and we went along the fence and they stopped and we stopped and I looked through the fence while Luster was hunting in the grass.
>
> "Here, caddie." He hit. They went away across the pasture. I held to the fence and watched them going away.

If you are writing in the third person, you might decide to adopt a specific angle of vision—from a cliff above the scene, for example.

As you revise you should check to see that details unessential to the dominant impression or those details readers can easily understand from their own experience have been presented in *summary form*. Others essential to the point or containing information likely to be new to the audience should be presented in *expanded form*.

To illustrate how you might deal with perspective and emphasis in revising a description, here is a passage from a student essay showing the changes made between an early draft and the final one:

Early draft:

> The water in the stream was so clear that the bottom was visible. The sunlight reflected here and there off the surface of the water showing the spot where a quiet eddy broke the surface or a large water skimmer stirred it up. Though the day was hot, the air around the stream was cold; this reflected the temperature of the water. The blue tinge of the water was either a reflection from the clear sky or of the blue-gray rocks in the stream.

Final draft:

> As I got close to the stream, I could feel its coolness despite the heat of the day. When I finally looked down into it the impression of icy coldness was reinforced by the bluish tinge of the water, picked up either from the tint of the sky or the reflection of the blue-gray stones on the stream bed. Even the occasional gleam of sun on the surface did nothing to lessen the sense of numbing cold.

The revised version of this passage puts emphasis on the feature of the scene the writer wanted to emphasize most—the coldness of the water—and subordinates other details, like the sun gleaming on the surface of the stream, to the dominant impression of coldness. In fact, even the image of the sun becomes a way of indicating just how cold the water was. By shifting to first person and indicating how he moved towards the stream, the writer limits the focus of the passage, too, making the water the center of attention.

THE PATTERN IN ACTION

In our reading we encounter description so often in combination with some other pattern of expression that we may fail to recognize the ways it can be used as a pattern for entire essays except in the extended description of a natural scene, its most obvious form. Yet description can be the main pattern for several types of essays or the primary method for developing and supporting a thesis; it can also play a central role in an essay that combines several patterns of expression. The essays in this chapter illustrate some of the many uses of description and suggest ways you can use it to share ideas and perceptions.

The *descriptive meditation* is probably the most familiar use of the pattern. In simple form, a descriptive meditation consists of a description of a place accompanied by the writer's thoughts, or meditations, about it. Often, however, it appears in more complex forms as in John Haines's "The Yard," a detailed description of a section of a city. In this selection the author focuses on the social structure of the area and the effect of the place on children who grew up there. A description of a typical family apartment in Cairo that opens a study of family structure in Egypt or the detailed layout of a fishing village in the middle of a study of island cultures in the Pacific are also meditations in an extended form. Such writing goes beyond simply recording details to explore the effects a place has on those who live in it. Even journalists writing about Jamaica and Puerto Vallarta for a travel magazine or recent Paris fashion shows for *Vogue* try to go beyond simple presentation of the scene to provide information for the person making travel plans or fashion decisions. Though it may be tempting to write about a favorite place in the hope that your readers will share your appreciation of it, a meditation is most likely to be successful when your subject is itself a source of special interest or when you have something fresh or useful to say about it.

The *character sketch* is a form of description sometimes found on its own, as in Andrew H. Malcolm's "Dad" in this chapter, but more often it is part of a longer work. A character sketch creates a sense of a personality, of an individual's outlook and motivation, of his or her influence on others. To do this it combines description with narrative detail, usually in the form of brief but representative incidents (anecdotes that are not linked to form a story). Character sketches are regular features of biographies and autobiographies. They are also common in historical works of all kinds, in national history, the history of science, military history, and political science. Writers often use sketches to show how the personality of a scientist like Einstein, Madame Curie, Newton, or Darwin helps to explain his or her work or how exploring the motivation of politicians like Roosevelt or Stalin can help us understand their actions. Articles about prominent people in magazines often take the form of character sketches, lengthy ones in magazines like the *New Yorker* or *Atlantic* and in brief form in *People*.

Technical descriptions are part of almost every field of research and of business as well. They usually reflect the methods, needs, and values of a field. Art historians have a particular way of describing a painting, focusing on color, line, shape, and brushstroke; biologists look for those features of a frog that are marks of evolution or function. Although most technical descriptions are objective, they are also selective. We would not expect a biologist to spend much time describing the appearance of a frog except perhaps for an article in a magazine with a wide and varied readership, like *National Geographic.* Nor would we expect an art historian to dwell on the anatomy of a horse that appears in a landscape painting.

Technical descriptions appear most often in business and research reports where they provide information on which to base conclusions, strategies, or plans of action, and in scholarly articles where they provide evidence to support the author's conclusions. Despite their objective tone, such descriptions usually present details carefully selected to support the writer's outlook.

As a *pattern of development and support*, description appears most frequently either in examples or in introductions where it highlights the most interesting features of a subject. (See Glossary:

Introductions.) However, Andrea Lee's "Mayakovsky Square," one of the selections in this chapter, uses description as a primary means of supporting a point. In addition, Michael Arlen uses description ironically and satirically to convey his feelings about Thanksgiving in "Ode to Thanksgiving"; he also casts the entire essay in the form of an argument, using descriptive passages for evidence.

In essays with *mixed patterns,* description is most often combined with narration; it provides background for events and a chance to comment on their significance. In E. B. White's "Once More to the Lake," for example, long meditations on scenes at the lake combine with brief character sketches to do most of the work of conveying the author's point, though they fit at all times within a narrative framework that in turn dictates a comparison of scenes from two periods of time.

The essays in this chapter thus call attention to some of the ways description can be used to shape entire essays, not just to the ways it can be used to add vivid detail to other kinds of writing.

♆ JOHN HAINES

John Haines was born in 1924 in Norfolk, Virginia, the son of a naval officer. After serving in the United States Navy, he attended the National Art School and American University. Though trained as a sculptor, Haines has worked primarily as a poet, and has been a poet-in-residence or teacher at the Universities of Alaska, Washington, Montana, Michigan, and Idaho State as well as Oberlin College. In the mid-1950's Haines moved to Alaska as a homesteader and has lived and worked there ever since. Haines's poetry is influenced heavily by his meditations on the natural world and reflects the experiences and culture of the Alaskan frontier. He has published many volumes of poetry, including *Winter News* (1966), *Cicada* (1977), and *In A Dusty Light* (1977).

The Yard

This description of the naval yard in which Haines spent a portion of his childhood is part of a set of character sketches, descriptions, and brief narratives of his early years published under the title "The Yard" in the *Ohio Review* (1979). The ending of this excerpt is rather abrupt—a reflection of the way one section of the "notes" flows into another; but in most other respects it is a tightly organized essay and an interesting example of a descriptive meditation. "The Yard" shows that a meditation can focus on urban as well as rural subjects and can deal with social events as well as places. Haines's work also shows how descriptive writing can be a way to understand our experiences as well as a way to share images of a place.

Much of my childhood was spent around naval bases. Our family   1
was hauled from one coast to another, to Hawaii and back again, as my father's station changed from year to year, or as sometimes happened, changed twice within the year. It was a restless, unsettled life, of changing schools and environments, and of brief relationships, a pattern that continues to influence my life.

. . . . .

A constancy of a kind in so much unsettledness lay in the fact   2
that we were always coming back to the same places, picking up again a life left behind six months or a year before. We lived longest in one place when my father was ordered to shore duty. He himself

81

disliked this, preferring to be at sea in his beloved submarines; but when he finally came in from the ships and was ordered east, we knew we were going to stay in one place for a while. And that place, more often than not, turned out to be the old naval gun factory in Washington, D.C.—the Yard. For nearly six years in the 1930s we lived there, enduring the oppressive and electrical summers, and the winters that came late and damp, with snow and occasional hard frost.

Those were the years of the Great Depression. The Yard was in   3
a rundown section of Washington, near the car barn at the end of the trolley line. Here the trollies were put to bed late at night, and in the daytime were turned around and headed back uptown. A Sunday drive through that section revealed block after block of decaying brick row houses, boarded shops, and idle factories. Men out of work sat on the front steps of the houses, staring at the cars going by. Trash and old newspapers blew on the gritty, brick-paved streets. It was not considered safe in that part of Washington, and we children were not allowed to go out into the city streets alone. We were told scare stories about what might happen to us if we did.

The Yard itself occupied several blocks along the Anacostia   4
River, crowded in by the city and with no room to grow. Within those cramped limits, the Yard was defined by its areas and functions. A small area on high ground near the north or main gate included the marine barracks and the officers' quarters. The quarters were set along a tree-shaded street that ran a short distance east and west from the gate. They were sprawling houses of brick and wood, many of them dating from the Civil War, and needing constant repair and a raft of servants to run properly. Downhill were the offices and administration buildings, below these, the machine shops and the foundries, and finally the river docks. Across the river lay Virginia, humid and vaguely threatening.

Just inside the main gate stood the bandstand, an aging wooden   5
structure rather like a gazebo, with slender columns supporting its roof, and painted a pale yellow with white trim. Below it, the parade ground, a sloping green field surrounded by tall hedges. On Saturday evenings in the summer, concerts were held there for the people in the Yard and the general public. The members of the band sweated and performed in their white uniforms, the brass of the trumpets and horns gleaming in the dusk under lights. We children lay in the grass below the stand, sometimes listening, but more often chattering

among ourselves. Becoming restless, we got up and horsed around behind the audience, chasing fireflies. The girls, and there were always a few girls, sat apart from us boys in a small group, whispering, and giggling in the darkness.

The Yard fire station stood across the street from the bandstand. 6 The crew, who were marines, were always polishing and tinkering with a great red machine that never seemed to run right, no matter what they did. It came roaring and coughing out of the stationhouse on a fire call, with its bell ringing and the crew clinging half-dressed to the running boards and rear platform. The firehouse, so near to the quarters, was a place to which we were naturally attracted. On any summer afternoon a few of us might be found there, talking to some of the crew, hoping to hear again one of their numerous dirty stories. When we were older we learned to smoke behind the firehouse, encouraged by one or two of the crew. We were officers' brats, not ordinary people, but with the natural democracy of youth we made friends with the enlisted men, sailors and marines, everywhere.

Down the street from the bandstand and the firehouse, at one 7 end of Quarters Row, stood the big sail loft where we played badminton on winter evenings. And there we were sometimes allowed to attend one of the grand balls put on at Christmas or New Year's, and at other times in honor of some visiting official. We might circulate among the adults, clutching a glass of lemonade or root beer, gaping at the uniformed dancers, admiring the backs and shoulders of the young women in their evening gowns, until we were sent home at midnight. At one end of that enormous room for a time the painter, Howard Christie, worked on "The Signing of the Constitution," a mural-sized patriotic work that now hangs somewhere in the United States Capitol. He allowed us to watch him, as long as we were quiet and did not disturb him. I can see him clearly now, standing beside his huge, unfinished canvas: a small, white-haired man in a paint-smeared smock, who smoked Rum & Maple tobacco in his pipe as he worked.

Closed off in this compound, we were in the city and yet not of 8 it. We kids, my brother and I, and the other officers' children, went to school uptown. We were driven there in a special bus or station wagon, and were picked up at the end of the day and brought home. Our close friendships were with each other, and seldom included those we went to school with. Though we sometimes complained of the confinement, many kids would have envied us. Where else could you climb around on actual cannons, naval guns, and other equipment left over from all the wars? From the river docks we could watch the tugs and barges, the destroyers, the cruisers, and the other ships that came and went on some mission or other. And there were sometimes grand and exciting events. Roosevelt himself would come to the Yard, flying through the main gate in a big open car to board the presidential yacht, "Sequoia," and sail down the Potomac for a few days fishing on Chesapeake Bay.

COMMENTARY

John Haines's description of the Yard has a dual focus, the Yard itself and the people who lived there. The relationships between the people and the setting are complex, and the author often leaves us to discover them for ourselves through careful reading and consideration of the descriptive detail he presents.

While the essay makes a complex point about the linking of people to their environment, its structure and the arrangement of the descriptive detail are quite easy to follow. Each paragraph after the first two takes up a different aspect of the Yard, and each describes both the setting and the way people lived within and responded to it.

The harshness, loneliness, and social pressures Haines conveys through the language of his description and the choice of detail support what he says in the opening paragraphs about the isolation and uncertainty of his life as a child. But at the same time, the descriptions of the way the children of the Yard amused themselves indicate that the Yard had its special pleasures, just as Haines suggests in the last paragraph.

The geography of the Yard and of its social relationships is likely to be unfamiliar to most readers, and Haines provides considerable detail to describe them. Throughout the essay, however, he prefers to use a single highly-specific detail, like the "Rum & Maple tobacco" (par. 7) or the "pale yellow" roof (par. 5), rather than a cluster of details. Since the Yard is likely to be an unfamiliar scene to most readers, this strategy allows him to give a sense of its reality without burdening readers with too much information.

RESPONSES AND IDEAS

1. Respond to this essay with a brief description of a feature of the town
    or neighborhood in which you grew up (the grade school yard, the
    shopping center, the movie theaters).

2. Did Haines enjoy living in the Yard? To support your answer, use
    evidence drawn from the author's statements, the connotations of words,
    and the repetition of phrases or images. (See Glossary: Connotation.)

3. What parallels, if any, are there between the relationship of the Yard
    to the rest of the city and the relationship of the military society in the
    essay to the society at large?

PURPOSE, AUDIENCE, AND STRATEGIES

1. In paragraph 3, how much knowledge of the Great Depression does
    Haines assume his readers possess? What details in the essay describe
    effects of the Great Depression? Be specific.

2. Where would you place this essay on a continuum with objective
    description on one end and subjective description on the other? Support
    your answer with references to specific words and phrases.

3. What dominant impression of the Yard and of the society it contains
    does Haines want to convey? Where in the essay does he use repetition
    of words and images to convey that impression?

4. Does this essay follow a spatial, chronological, or thematic arrange-
    ment? Does it combine patterns of arrangement in some way? Cite
    evidence to support your answers.

5. What are the point of view and the perspective in this essay? (See
    Glossary: Point of View for a discussion of perspective; also see pp. 76–
    77.) How does the perspective reflect and support the purpose of the
    essay?

LANGUAGE AND STYLE

1. Underline those sentences in the essay that add concrete details to the
    end of a complete statement in the manner of this sentence: "It came
    roaring and coughing out of the stationhouse on a fire call, *with its
    bell ringing and the crew clinging half-dressed to the running boards
    and rear platform*" (par. 6). What do these sentences contribute to the
    overall impact of the essay?

2. Identify the verbs Haines uses in the descriptions in paragraphs 6 and
    7. Which of them seem to contribute most to the vividness of the
    descriptions? Explain why they are particularly effective.

3. If you had difficulty understanding any of the words in this essay, look them up in the dictionary.

WRITING ACTIVITIES

1. Write a description of some object or scene that calls to mind childhood memories and emotions. In your description, try to convey these same feelings and memories to readers.

2. Create a description of an imaginary scene that will call up a strong emotional reaction from readers. You may wish to evoke several emotional responses in the course of the essay. Though the scene is imaginary, make the description both detailed and realistic.

&❧ANDREA LEE

Andrea Lee (born in Philadelphia in 1953) is a journalist who spent ten months living in Russia in 1978–79, part of the time in Moscow, the rest in Leningrad. At the time, both she and her husband were graduate students participating in an exchange program. Because they lived in student dormitories, spoke Russian, and shopped in regular stores rather than in the special shops for foreigners, they had extensive contact with ordinary Russians and the daily realities of Soviet life. *Russian Journal* (1981) is a record of her experiences—"a set of photographs," she calls it. The journal takes into account the political and social system of the Soviet Union but makes no attempt to explain it. Instead, Lee attempts to provide a personal glimpse of the way Russians live. To explain her own perspective, she says of the journal, "Each entry presents a small piece of Russian reality as seen by an American whose vision, if not refined by study, was at least not much distorted by prejudice for or against Communism."

Mayakovsky Square

In "Mayakovsky Square," the November 3 entry from *Russian Journal,* description (or perception) is at once the subject of the essay and, along with comparison, the method by which the author develops her ideas. As is appropriate for a journal, Lee spends much of the essay describing her own perceptions. Her larger purpose, however, is to explore the links between perception and culture, or between political systems and ideas of beauty. For this purpose, description is an appropriate method of development because it enables her to deal directly with the way she and other people view reality.

In Mayakovsky Square, not far from the Tchaikovsky Concert   1
Hall, a big computerized electric sign sends various messages flashing out into the night. An outline of a taxi in green dots is accompanied by the words: "Take Taxis—All Streets Are Near." This is replaced by multicolored human figures and a sentence urging Soviet citizens to save in State banks. The bright patterns and messages come and go, making this one of the most sophisticated examples of advertising in Moscow. Even on chilly nights when I pass through the square, there is often a little group of Russians standing in front

of the sign, watching in fascination for five and ten minutes as the colored dots go through their magical changes. The first few times I saw this, I chuckled and recalled an old joke about an American town so boring that people went out on weekends to watch the Esso sign. With each month I live here, however, I'm more and more tempted to join the spectators in Mayakovsky Square.

Tourists I've met here invariably refer to Moscow as a "gray" 2 city: this impression, when I examine it, does not come entirely from the weather—I've lived through grayer Novembers in Paris—or from the color of the buildings, a surprising number of which are painted in charming pastels. It springs more from the unbeautiful aspect of the crowds (Russian bodies and faces are heavy; Russian clothes, when not actually hideous, are monotone and forgettable), and most of all, from the lack of Western-style advertising. Advertising, of course, is the glamorous offspring of capitalism and art: why advertise in a country where there is only one brand, the State brand, of anything, and often not enough even of that? There is nothing here comparable to the glittering overlay of commercialism that Americans, at least, take for granted as part of our cities; nothing like the myriad small seductions of the marketplace, which have led us to expect to be enticed. The Soviet political propaganda posters that fill up a small part of the Moscow landscape with their uniformly cold red color schemes and monumental robot-faced figures are so unappealing that they are dismissable. (It's interesting to try to figure out exactly whom these posters are aimed at. Every Russian I know, even the most conservative, finds them dreadful; perhaps they're intended for a future race of titans.)

I realize now, looking back, that for at least my first month in 3 Moscow, I was filled with an unconscious and devastating disappointment. Hardly realizing it, as I walked around the city, I was looking for the constant sensory distractions I was accustomed to in America. Like many others my age, I grew up reading billboards and singing advertising jingles; my idea of beauty was shaped—perniciously, I think—by the models with painted eyes and pounds of shining hair whose beauty was accessible on every television set and street corner. In Moscow, I found none of this easy stimulation—only the rarer, more demanding pleasures of nature and architecture: rain on the gold domes inside the Kremlin walls; yellow leaves stuck to a wet pavement; a decayed stone grotesque on the peeling front of a mansion in the Arbat; a face in a subway crowd.

Living in these comparatively simple surroundings has made my   4
inner life more intense. Tom and I have found that our dreams have
gained color and our memories have become sharper; we are both
more attentive to beauty. I finally understand in part the Russian
phenomenon of staring: now, when I see a well-cut dress (terribly
rare), a handsomely bound book (still rarer), or an attractive face,
I stare with amazing persistence, until my ravenous eyes are satisfied.
Tom and I have found that we can sit for an hour looking—just
looking—with lingering pleasure at the most banal American magazine—*Good Housekeeping,* for example—stunned by the attractive-
ness of its layout and photographs. Last week I received a tiresome
dunning letter from the alumni office of my university; I was about
to throw it away when my Russian friend Olga snatched it, stared
at the elaborate graphics of the letterhead, and said, "It's so beautiful
. . . may I have it?" Later I found she'd pinned it up beside her bed.

Everywhere we go in Moscow, we find a frantic enthusiasm for   5
any kind of natural or man-made beauty. At parties, pretty girls are
feted with an innocent, extravagant adulation from men and women
alike; ordinary people show a passion for art and literature which
might be suspect as a pose in America. The deepest roots of this
quality of Russian life are hard to discern, and I am setting aside
the ugly fact of government censorship of the arts, which obviously
plays its own perverse role in intensifying enthusiasm for beauty. I
mean to observe here only that a more austere environment seems
to favor sensitivity. This isn't a new idea at all, of course. People on
islands, in prisons, in monasteries have all discovered the same thing.
But it's a remarkable feeling to have my mind clearing up week by
week, like a lens that was filmed and dim, until, just as the year
goes dark with winter, I've started to see the subtle points of light in
this gray city.

RESPONSES AND IDEAS

1. Respond to this essay in one of these two ways: (a) go to a busy spot,
   like a shopping center, a city business district, or a student union, and
   take notes on how much of what you see is the product of advertising
   or commercial art; (b) go to a natural spot, such as an open meadow
   or a wooded area, and take notes on whatever sources of beauty you
   find in your surroundings.

2. Explain the connection Lee makes between capitalism and visual beauty
   (or glamour) (pars. 2–3). Does she make any connection between

communism and the lack of such visual displays? If so, explain the connection. What does Lee mean in the phrase "a more austere environment seems to favor sensitivity" (5)?

3.   What positive qualities does Lee find in the absence of advertising and commercial art in the Soviet Union? What negative qualities does she find? Be specific. Are her attitudes conveyed through the connotations of the words she uses? If so, identify the words and their connotations. (See Glossary: Connotation and Denotation.)

PURPOSE, AUDIENCE, AND STRATEGIES

1.   Underline the words and phrases that most clearly reveal the author's purpose in this essay. (See Glossary: Purpose.)

2.   By using general rather than specific detail in paragraph 2, the author seems to assume that her readers are already familiar with certain aspects of Soviet life and culture. What specific knowledge does she assume? Are her assumptions likely to be correct?

3.   In the opening paragraph, the author compares the people watching the sign in Mayakovsky Square to people in a small American town watching an Esso sign. How is this comparison likely to make readers feel about the people in the square? About themselves? By reporting her own response to the people, does the author attempt to influence the reader's response in any way? Explain.

4.   Underline the most important descriptive passages in this selection. How are they related to the point of the essay?

5.   How much of this essay is devoted to comparison rather than to description? Why is it appropriate to say that description is the primary, or most important, method of development?

LANGUAGE AND STYLE

1.   Lee uses the Mayakovsky billboard as a symbol of Russian culture and attitudes. What other symbols does she create, and what do they represent? (See Glossary: Symbol.)

2.   In the last sentence of the essay the author uses a figure of speech. What figure is it (see Glossary: Figures of Speech), and what does the sentence as a whole mean?

3.   If you do not know the meaning of some of the following words, look them up in the dictionary: *myriad, titans* (par. 2); *perniciously, grotesque* (3); *ravenous, banal, graphics* (4); *feted, adulation, austere* (5).

WRITING ACTIVITIES

1. Do people with different personalities from different social backgrounds or ethnic groups perceive the world in different ways? Prepare a description that looks at one scene from the perspective of two or more people, each with a different personal or cultural outlook.

2. Write an essay in which you use description as a way of supporting a thesis. To argue for an increase in government and private aid, for example, you might choose to present several scenes that reveal the devastation and despair caused by unemployment and poverty. You might describe several scenes in a public school to show that it is a much better and happier place than most people think (or that it is even more grim and unhappy than many suppose).

❧ ANDREW H. MALCOLM

Andrew H. Malcolm was born in Cleveland in 1943. He received a journalism degree from Northwestern University before working for several newspapers and United Press International. In 1967 he began working for the *New York Times* and was soon assigned as a reporter in New York, Chicago, and San Francisco and as a foreign correspondent in the Far East and Toronto. As a foreign correspondent he covered the end of the Vietnam War in 1975 and the refugee evacuations that followed; he was then a correspondent in Tokyo and Korea for three years and later was chief of the *Times* bureau in Toronto. He is currently bureau chief for the *Times* in Chicago.

Mr. Malcolm has won several major awards for his reporting and has published one book, *Unknown America* (1975). He is currently writing a book on Canada.

Dad

This character sketch was originally published as a magazine article in 1983. It talks about a personal subject but does so in a way that seems designed to bring to mind similar experiences readers may have had. Ask yourself as you read this essay whether the links it describes between father and son can apply also to the relationship between father and daughter or mother and daughter. Like most character sketches, this essay reports what its subject did and said as a way of revealing his character, but because these events are not linked to form a single story, the pattern of the selection is primarily description, not narration.

The first memory I have of him—of anything, really—is his   1
strength. It was in the late afternoon in a house under construction near ours. The unfinished wood floor had large, terrifying holes whose yawning darkness I knew led to nowhere good. His powerful hands, then age 33, wrapped all the way around my tiny arms, then age 4, and easily swung me up to his shoulders to command all I surveyed.

The relationship between a son and his father changes over   2
time. It may grow and flourish in mutual maturity. It may sour in resented dependence or independence. With many children living in single-parent homes today, it may not even exist.

92

But to a little boy right after World War II, a father seemed a god with strange strengths and uncanny powers enabling him to do and know things that no mortal could do or know. Amazing things, like putting a bicycle chain back on, just like that. Or building a hamster cage. Or guiding a jigsaw so it formed the letter F; I learned the alphabet that way in those pretelevision days, one letter or number every other evening plus a review of the collection. (The vowels we painted red because they were special somehow.) 3

He seemed to know what I thought before I did. "You look like you could use a cheeseburger and chocolate shake," he would say on hot Sunday afternoons. When, at the age of 5, I broke a neighbor's garage window with a wild curve ball and waited in fear for 10 days to make the announcement, he seemed to know about it already and to have been waiting for something. 4

There were, of course, rules to learn. First came the handshake. None of those fishy little finger grips, but a good firm squeeze accompanied by an equally strong gaze into the other's eyes. "The first thing anyone knows about you is your handshake," he would say. And we'd practice it each night on his return from work, the serious toddler in the battered Cleveland Indians cap running up to the giant father to shake hands again and again until it was firm enough. 5

When my cat killed a bird, he defused the anger of a 9-year-old with a little chat about something called "instinked." The next year, when my dog got run over and the weight of sorrow was just too immense to stand, he was there, too, with his big arms and his own tears and some thoughts on the natural order of life and death, although what was natural about a speeding car that didn't stop always escaped me. 6

As time passed, there were other rules to learn. "Always do your best." "Do it now." "NEVER LIE!" And, most importantly, "You can do whatever you have to do." By my teens, he wasn't telling me what to do anymore, which was scary and heady at the same time. He provided perspective, not telling me what was around the great corner of life but letting me know there was a lot more than just today and the next, which I hadn't thought of. 7

When the most important girl in the world—I forget her name now—turned down a movie date, he just happened to walk by the kitchen phone. "This may be hard to believe right now," he said, "but someday you won't even remember her name." 8

One day, I realize now, there was a change. I wasn't trying to   9
please him so much as I was trying to impress him. I never asked
him to come to my football games. He had a high-pressure career,
and it meant driving through most of Friday night. But for all the
big games, when I looked over at the sideline, there was that familiar
fedora. And, by God, did the opposing team captain ever get a firm
handshake and a gaze he would remember.

Then, a school fact contradicted something he said. Impossible   10
that he could be wrong, but there it was in the book. These accumulated over time, along with personal experiences, to buttress my
own developing sense of values. And I could tell we had each taken
our own, perfectly normal paths.

I began to see, too, his blind spots, his prejudices and his   11
weaknesses. I never threw these up at him. He hadn't to me, and,
anyway, he seemed to need protection. I stopped asking his advice;
the experiences he drew from no longer seemed relevant to the
decisions I had to make. On the phone, he would go on about
politics at times, why he would vote the way he did or why some
incumbent was a jerk. And I would roll my eyes to the ceiling and
smile a little, though I hid it in my voice.

He volunteered advice for a while. But then, in more recent   12
years, politics and issues gave way to talk of empty errands and,
always, to ailments—his friends', my mother's and his own, which
were serious and included heart disease. He had a bedside oxygen
tank, and he would ostentatiously retire there during my visits, asking
my help in easing his body onto the mattress. "You have very strong
arms," he once noted.

From his bed, he showed me the many sores and scars on his   13
misshapen body and all the bottles for medicine. He talked of the
pain and craved much sympathy. He got some. But the scene was
not attractive. He told me, as the doctor had, that his condition
would only deteriorate. "Sometimes," he confided, "I would just like
to lie down and go to sleep and not wake up."

After much thought and practice ("You can do whatever you   14
have to do."), one night last winter, I sat down by his bed and
remembered for an instant those terrifying dark holes in another
house 35 years before. I told my father how much I loved him. I
described all the things people were doing for him. But, I said, he
kept eating poorly, hiding in his room and violating other doctor's

orders. No amount of love could make someone else care about life, I said; it was a two-way street. He wasn't doing his best. The decision was his.

He said he knew how hard my words had been to say and how   15 proud he was of me. "I had the best teacher," I said. "You can do whatever you have to do." He smiled a little. And we shook hands, firmly, for the last time.

Several days later, at about 4 A.M., my mother heard Dad   16 shuffling about their dark room. "I have some things I have to do," he said. He paid a bundle of bills. He composed for my mother a long list of legal and financial what-to-do's "in case of emergency." And he wrote me a note.

Then he walked back to his bed and laid himself down. He   17 went to sleep, naturally. And he did not wake up.

RESPONSES AND IDEAS

1. Respond to this essay by making a list of ten people in your life who would be good subjects for a character sketch and include with each name a brief statement of what you would want readers to know about the person. Then choose three of the people listed and write down five details to support and explain your brief statements about them.

2. What does the phrase "there was that familiar fedora" mean (par. 8)? Use a dictionary if necessary. What figure of speech is used in the phrase? (See Glossary: Figures of Speech.) What does it say about the father's character?

3. At what points in this essay does the author's view of his father change? In what ways?

PURPOSE, AUDIENCE, AND STRATEGIES

1. Does the author seem to find any special significance in his father's actions just before he died? If so, what is it, and why doesn't he state it directly?

2. What emotional effect is this essay likely to have on readers? To what extent will the effect depend on how the essay is written and to what extent on memories readers bring with them?

3. Is the main purpose of this essay to reveal Dad's character, or is it to explore how differences in the son's outlook affect the way he views his father? Use evidence from the essay to explain and support your answer.

4. What strategy does Malcolm use to open the essay? (See Glossary: Introductions.) Does it effectively indicate the purpose of the essay?

5. What means of describing his father's character does Malcolm rely on most heavily in this essay? On what he says? Does? Looks like? In what ways might the essay benefit from a greater variety in the techniques of description?

LANGUAGE AND STYLE

1. Identify the words, phrases, and details in the essay that echo in one way or another the idea of the father's strength presented in paragraph 1. What other strategies of style and diction does the author use to emphasize the traits of his father's character? (See Glossary: Style, Diction.)

2. Identify the most important words and phrases (particularly transitions) that Malcolm uses in this essay to indicate the passing of time and to call attention to changes in his father and in their relationship. In what ways do these words and phrases make the essay easier to understand? (See Glossary: Transitions.)

3. If you do not know the meaning of some of the following words, look them up in the dictionary: *yawning* (par. 1); *uncanny* (3); *fedora* (9); *incumbent* (11); *ostentatiously* (12).

WRITING ACTIVITIES

1. From what you know about some public figure through television, newspapers, radio, and books, create a character sketch of him or her. Make sure the description clearly conveys your judgment of the person but at the same time try to make your portrait balanced and reasonable enough so most readers will respect your conclusions even if they do not agree with you entirely. You might consider drawing the portrait of a historical figure (Queen Victoria, Jesse Owens, or Mao Tse Tung) as well as someone who is currently in the news.

2. In the seventeenth century people often wrote "characters," portraits of a type of person, like a milkmaid, a tailor, a merchant, a noble lady, or a soldier. Write a "character" describing some contemporary type, a college professor, for example, an athletic coach, a stockbroker, or a rock musician. The key to writing a successful character is to include enough specific detail to make the subject of your description seem like a real person while including those qualities that people with the same occupation or role often have in common.

❧ MICHAEL J. ARLEN

Michael Arlen was born in England in 1930 and raised in the United States. He has written numerous books, including *Passage to Ararat* (1975), an account of his Armenian heritage; *Exiles* (1970), the story of his parents' lives; *An American Verdict* (1973); *Living Room War* (1969); and *Thirty Seconds* (1980), about the making of a television commercial. His criticism of television, which appears in the *New Yorker,* has been collected in *The View from Highway 1* (1976) and *The Camera Age: Essays on Television* (1981).

Ode to Thanksgiving

This essay, which first appeared as a magazine article in 1978 and was reprinted in *The Camera Age,* is designed to irritate, to amuse, and perhaps even convince. The essay is arranged as an argument with a variety of evidence and even a refutation of the opposing point of view (see Chapter 10, "Argument"). A special feature of this argument, though, is that the evidence consists for the most part of descriptive detail rather than facts and figures. As a result, the essay is also a sharp-eyed portrait of the American family at an important gathering.

It is time, at last, to speak the truth about Thanksgiving, and the truth is this. Thanksgiving is really not such a terrific holiday. Consider the traditional symbols of the event: Dried cornhusks hanging on the door! Terrible wine! Cranberry jelly in little bowls of extremely doubtful provenance which everyone is required to handle with the greatest of care! Consider the participants, the merrymakers: men and women (also children) who have survived passably well throughout the years, mainly as a result of living at considerable distances from their dear parents and beloved siblings, who on this feast of feasts must apparently forgather (as if beckoned by an aberrant Fairy Godmother), usually by circuitous routes, through heavy traffic, at a common meeting place, where the very moods, distempers, and obtrusive personal habits that have kept them all happily apart since adulthood are then and there encouraged to slowly ferment beneath the cornhusks, and gradually rise with the aid of the terrible wine, and finally burst forth out of control under the

1

stimulus of the cranberry jelly! No, it is a mockery of a holiday. For instance: *Thank you, O Lord, for what we are about to receive.* This is surely not a gala concept. There are no presents, unless one counts Aunt Bertha's sweet rolls a present, which no one does. There is precious little in the way of costumery: miniature plastic turkeys and those witless Pilgrim hats. There is no sex. Indeed, Thanksgiving is the one day of the year (a fact known to everybody) when all thoughts of sex completely vanish, evaporating from apartments, houses, condominiums, and mobile homes like steam from a bathroom mirror.

Consider also the nowhereness of the time of year: the last week 2 or so in November. It is obviously not yet winter: winter, with its death-dealing blizzards and its girls in tiny skirts pirouetting on the ice. On the other hand, it is certainly not much use to anyone as fall: no golden leaves or Oktoberfests, and so forth. Instead, it is a no-man's-land between the seasons. In the cold and sobersides northern half of the country, it is a vaguely unsettling interregnum of long, mournful walks beneath leafless trees: the long, mournful walks following the midday repast with the dread inevitability of pie following turkey, and the leafless trees looming or standing about like eyesores, and the ground either as hard as iron or slightly mushy, and the light snow always beginning to fall when one is halfway to the old green gate—flecks of cold, watery stuff plopping between neck and collar, for the reason that, it being not yet winter, one has forgotten or not chosen to bring along a muffler. It is a corollary to the long, mournful Thanksgiving walk that the absence of this muffler is quickly noticed and that four weeks or so later, at Christmastime, instead of the Sony Betamax one had secretly hoped the children might have chipped in to purchase, one receives another muffler: by then the thirty-third. Thirty-three mufflers! Some walk! Of course, things are more fun in the warm and loony southern part of the country. No snow there of any kind. No need of mufflers. Also, no long, mournful walks, because in the warm and loony southern part of the country everybody drives. So everybody drives over to Uncle Jasper's house to watch the Cougars play the Gators, a not entirely unimportant conflict which will determine whether the Gators get a Bowl bid or must take another post-season exhibition tour of North Korea. But no sooner do the Cougars kick off (an astonishing end-over-end squiggly thing that floats lazily above the arena before plummeting down toward K. C. McCoy and catching him on the helmet) than Auntie Em starts hustling turkey. Soon Cousin May is slamming around the bowls and platters, and Cousin Bernice is oohing and ahing about "all the fixin's," and Uncle Bob is making low, insincere sounds of appreciation: "Yummy, yummy Auntie Em, I'll have me some more of these delicious yams!" Delicious yams? Uncle Bob's eyes roll wildly in his head. Billy Joe Quaglino throws his long bomb in the middle of Grandpa Morris saying grace, Grandpa Morris speaking so low nobody can hear him, which is just as well, since he is reciting what he can remember of his last union contract. And then, just as J. B. (Speedy) Snood begins his ninety-two-yard punt return, Auntie Em starts dealing everyone second helpings of her famous stuffing, as if she were pushing a controlled substance, which it well might be, since there are no easily recognizable ingredients visible to the naked eye.

Consider for a moment the Thanksgiving meal itself. It has   3 become a sort of refuge for endangered species of starch: cauliflower, turnips, pumpkin, mince (whatever "mince" is), those blessed yams. Bowls of luridly colored yams, with no taste at all, lying torpid under a lava flow of marshmallow! And then the sacred turkey. One might as well try to construct a holiday repast around a fish—say, a nice piece of boiled haddock. After all, turkey tastes very similar to haddock: same consistency, same quite remarkable absence of flavor. But then, if the Thanksgiving *pièce de résistance* were a nice piece of boiled haddock instead of turkey, there wouldn't be all that fun for Dad when Mom hands him the sterling-silver, bone-handled carving set (a wedding present from her parents and not sharpened since) and then everyone sits around pretending not to watch while he saws and tears away at the bird as if he were trying to burrow his way into or out of some grotesque, fowl-like prison.

What of the good side to Thanksgiving, you ask. There is always   4 a good side to everything. Not to Thanksgiving. There is only a bad side and then a worse side. For instance, Grandmother's best linen tablecloth is a bad side: the fact that it is produced each year, in the manner of a red flag being produced before a bull, and then is always spilled upon by whichever child is doing poorest at school that term and so is in need of greatest reassurance. Thus: "Oh, my God, *Veronica*, you just spilled grape juice [or plum wine or tar] on Grandmother's best linen tablecloth!" But now comes worse. For at this point Cousin Bill, the one who lost all Cousin Edwina's money on the car dealership three years ago and has apparently been drinking steadily since Halloween, bizarrely chooses to say: "Seems to me those old glasses are always falling over." To which Auntie Meg is heard to add: "Somehow I don't remember receivin' any of those old glasses." To which Uncle Fred replies: "That's because you and George decided to go on vacation to Hawaii the summer Grandpa Sam was dying." Now Grandmother is sobbing, though not so uncontrollably that she can refrain from murmuring: "I think that volcano painting I threw away by mistake got sent me from Hawaii, heaven knows why." But the gods are merciful, even the Pilgrim-hatted god of cornhusks and soggy stuffing, and there is an end to everything, even to Thanksgiving. Indeed, there is a grandeur to the feelings of finality and doom which usually settle on a house after the Thanksgiving celebration is over, for with the completion of Thanksgiving Day the year itself has been properly terminated: shot through the cranium with a high-velocity candied yam. At this cal-endrical nadir, all energy on the planet has gone, all fun has fled, all the terrible wine has been drunk.

But then, overnight, life once again begins to stir, emerging, even   5
by the next morning, in the form of Japanese window displays and Taiwanese Christmas lighting, from the primeval ooze of the nation's department stores. Thus, a new year dawns, bringing with it im-mediate and cheering possibilities of extended consumer debt, office-party flirtations, good—or, at least, mediocre—wine, and visions of Supersaver excursion fares to Montego Bay. It is worth noting, per-haps, that this true new year always starts with the same mute, powerful mythic ceremony: the surreptitious tossing out, in the early morning, of all those horrid aluminum-foil packages of yams and cauliflower and stuffing and red, gummy cranberry substance which have been squeezed into the refrigerator as if a reenactment of the siege of Paris were shortly expected. Soon afterward, the phoenix of Christmas can be observed as it slowly rises, beating its drumsticks, once again goggle-eyed with hope and unrealistic expectations.

RESPONSES AND IDEAS

1.   Respond to this essay either with a brief description of Thanksgiving that portrays it positively or with a portrait of some other holiday that takes an approach similar to the one in this essay.

2. What is the significance of the title "Ode to Thanksgiving"? (Look up *ode* in the dictionary if you do not know what it means.) Is the title ironic in any way? Explain. (See Glossary: Irony.)

3. Explain the meaning of the following phrases (use the dictionary if necessary): "bowls of extremely doubtful provenance" (par. 1); "it is a vaguely unsettling interregnum of long, mournful walks beneath leafless trees" (2); "a not entirely unimportant conflict" (2).

PURPOSE, AUDIENCE, AND STRATEGIES

1. Does this essay contain a thesis statement? If so, what is it, and is the purpose of the essay clearly indicated by it? (See Glossary: Thesis, Purpose.)

2. Are most readers likely to find Arlen's descriptions of Thanksgiving greatly exaggerated or only moderately so? Explain.

3. Is Arlen's real purpose to attack Thanksgiving, or does he have another purpose? If so, what is it? Does he, for example, wish to criticize our attitude toward family or holidays in general? (See Glossary: Purpose.)

4. What repeated phrase does Arlen use to introduce the major sections of his argument, except for the refutation of opposing points of view? In what ways, if any, does the repetition add to the impact of the essay?

5. What kind of evidence or descriptive detail does Arlen cover in each major section? Summarize in your own words the main point or points he makes in each section.

LANGUAGE AND STYLE

1. What is the effect of the long sentences in the essay? Are they difficult to understand? What devices of syntax does Arlen use to construct them? (See Glossary: Syntax.)

2. Identify an example of each of these figures of speech in the essay: metaphor, simile, allusion. (See Glossary: Figures of Speech.) Then explain how the figure is more effective than a literal expression would be in the same sentence.

3. If you do not know the meaning of some of the following words, look them up in the dictionary: *provenance, forgather, aberrant, gala* (par. 1); *pirouetting, Oktoberfests, sobersides, interregnum* (2); *mince, luridly, torpid, repast, pièce de résistance* (3); *grandeur, cranium, velocity, calendrical, nadir* (4); *primeval, surreptitious, phoenix* (5).

WRITING ACTIVITIES

1. Prepare a description that either reinforces or calls into question some widely held belief. You might, for example, take either a positive or a

negative view of a religious service, a family picnic, or a sports event. You could even combine the approaches in your essay by presenting two scenes, each with a different viewpoint.

2. Prepare a descriptive essay poking fun at clothing styles or common behavior among a particular group of people such as politicians, golf or tennis players, video game addicts, or college students.

❧ E. B. WHITE

E. B. White was born in Mount Vernon, New York, in 1899. He attended Cornell University and worked as a reporter and advertising copywriter. In 1926 he joined the staff of the *New Yorker* magazine and has also written on a regular basis for *Harper's* magazine. Since 1938 he has done most of his writing at his farm in Maine. Among his many works are three books for children, including *Charlotte's Web* (1952), and several collections of his essays: *One Man's Meat* (1944), *The Second Tree from the Corner* (1953), *The Points of My Compass* (1962), *Essays of E. B. White* (1977), and *Poems and Sketches* (1981).

Once More to the Lake

This essay was written in 1941 and collected in *One Man's Meat* (1944). The descriptive passages in this selection are particularly powerful and vivid. They present White's memories of earlier visits to the lake mingled with his meditation on the scenes of a later visit accompanied by his son. Though the essay has strong narrative elements and makes use of comparison in many passages, it is in the descriptive sections that White's concerns are most fully developed.

August 1941

One summer, along about 1904, my father rented a camp on a lake in Maine and took us all there for the month of August. We all got ringworm from some kittens and had to rub Pond's Extract on our arms and legs night and morning, and my father rolled over in a canoe with all his clothes on; but outside of that the vacation was a success and from then on none of us ever thought there was any place in the world like that lake in Maine. We returned summer after summer—always on August 1 for one month. I have since become a salt-water man, but sometimes in summer there are days when the restlessness of the tides and the fearful cold of the sea water and the incessant wind that blows across the afternoon and into the evening make me wish for the placidity of a lake in the woods. A few weeks ago this feeling got so strong I bought myself a

1

couple of bass hooks and a spinner and returned to the lake where we used to go, for a week's fishing and to revisit old haunts.

I took along my son, who had never had any fresh water up his   2
nose and who had seen lily pads only from train windows. On the journey over to the lake I began to wonder what it would be like. I wondered how time would have marred this unique, this holy spot— the coves and streams, the hills that the sun set behind, the camps and the paths behind the camps. I was sure that the tarred road would have found it out, and I wondered in what other ways it would be desolated. It is strange how much you can remember about places like that once you allow your mind to return into the grooves that lead back. You remember one thing, and that suddenly reminds you of another thing. I guess I remembered clearest of all the early mornings, when the lake was cool and motionless, remembered how the bedroom smelled of the lumber it was made of and of the wet woods whose scent entered through the screen. The partitions in the camp were thin and did not extend clear to the top of the rooms, and as I was always the first up I would dress softly so as not to wake the others, and sneak out into the sweet outdoors and start out in the canoe, keeping close along the shore in the long shadows of the pines. I remembered being very careful never to rub my paddle against the gunwale for fear of disturbing the stillness of the cathedral.

The lake had never been what you would call a wild lake. There   3
were cottages sprinkled around the shores, and it was in farming country although the shores of the lake were quite heavily wooded. Some of the cottages were owned by nearby farmers, and you would live at the shore and eat your meals at the farmhouse. That's what our family did. But although it wasn't wild, it was a fairly large and undisturbed lake and there were places in it that, to a child at least, seemed infinitely remote and primeval.

I was right about the tar: it led to within half a mile of the shore.   4
But when I got back there, with my boy, and we settled into a camp near a farmhouse and into the kind of summertime I had known, I could tell that it was going to be pretty much the same as it had been before—I knew it, lying in bed the first morning, smelling the bedroom and hearing the boy sneak quietly out and go off along the shore in a boat. I began to sustain the illusion that he was I, and therefore, by simple transposition, that I was my father. This sensation persisted, kept cropping up all the time we were there. It was

not an entirely new feeling, but in this setting it grew much stronger. I seemed to be living a dual existence. I would be in the middle of some simple act, I would be picking up a bait box or laying down a table fork, or I would be saying something, and suddenly it would be not I but my father who was saying the words or making the gesture. It gave me a creepy sensation.

We went fishing the first morning. I felt the same damp moss 5 covering the worms in the bait can, and saw the dragonfly alight on the tip of my rod as it hovered a few inches from the surface of the water. It was the arrival of this fly that convinced me beyond any doubt that everything was as it always had been, that the years were a mirage and that there had been no years. The small waves were the same, chucking the rowboat under the chin as we fished at anchor, and the boat was the same boat, the same color green and the ribs broken in the same places, and under the floorboards the same fresh-water leavings and débris—the dead helgramite, the wisps of moss, the rusty discarded fishhook, the dried blood from yesterday's catch. We stared silently at the tips of our rods, at the dragonflies that came and went. I lowered the tip of mine into the water, tentatively, pensively dislodging the fly, which darted two feet away, poised, darted two feet back, and came to rest again a little farther up the rod. There had been no years between the ducking of this dragonfly and the other one—the one that was part of memory. I looked at the boy, who was silently watching his fly, and it was my hands that held his rod, my eyes watching. I felt dizzy and didn't know which rod I was at the end of.

We caught two bass, hauling them in briskly as though they 6 were mackerel, pulling them over the side of the boat in a business-like manner without any landing net, and stunning them with a blow on the back of the head. When we got back for a swim before lunch, the lake was exactly where we had left it, the same number of inches from the dock, and there was only the merest suggestion of a breeze. This seemed an utterly enchanted sea, this lake you could leave to its own devices for a few hours and come back to, and find that it had not stirred, this constant and trustworthy body of water. In the shallows, the dark, water-soaked sticks and twigs, smooth and old, were undulating in clusters on the bottom against the clean ribbed sand, and the track of the mussel was plain. A school of minnows swam by, each minnow with its small individual shadow, doubling the attendance, so clear and sharp in the sunlight.

Some of the other campers were in swimming, along the shore, one of them with a cake of soap, and the water felt thin and clear and unsubstantial. Over the years there had been this person with the cake of soap, this cultist, and here he was. There had been no years.

Up to the farmhouse to dinner through the teeming, dusty field, 7 the road under our sneakers was only a two-track road. The middle track was missing, the one with the marks of the hooves and the splotches of dried, flaky manure. There had always been three tracks to choose from in choosing which track to walk in; now the choice was narrowed down to two. For a moment I missed terribly the middle alternative. But the way led past the tennis court, and something about the way it lay there in the sun reassured me; the tape had loosened along the backline, the alleys were green with plantains and other weeds, and the net (installed in June and removed in September) sagged in the dry noon, and the whole place steamed with midday heat and hunger and emptiness. There was a choice of pie for dessert, and one was blueberry and one was apple, and the waitresses were the same country girls, there having been no passage of time, only the illusion of it as in a dropped curtain—the waitresses were still fifteen; their hair had been washed, that was the only difference—they had been to the movies and seen the pretty girls with the clean hair.

Summertime, oh, summertime, pattern of life indelible, the fade- 8 proof lake, the woods unshatterable, the pasture with the sweetfern and the juniper forever and ever, summer without end; this was the background, and the life along the shore was the design, the cottagers with their innocent and tranquil design, their tiny docks with the flagpole and the American flag floating against the white clouds in the blue sky, the little paths over the roots of the trees leading from camp to camp and the paths leading back to the outhouses and the can of lime for sprinkling, and at the souvenir counters at the store the miniature birch-bark canoes and the postcards that showed things looking a little better than they looked. This was the American family at play, escaping the city heat, wondering whether the new-comers in the camp at the head of the cove were "common" or "nice," wondering whether it was true that the people who drove up for Sunday dinner at the farmhouse were turned away because there wasn't enough chicken.

It seemed to me, as I kept remembering all this, that those times 9 and those summers had been infinitely precious and worth saving.

There had been jollity and peace and goodness. The arriving (at the beginning of August) had been so big a business in itself, at the railway station the farm wagon drawn up, the first smell of the pine-laden air, the first glimpse of the smiling farmer, and the great importance of the trunks and your father's enormous authority in such matters, and the feel of the wagon under you for the long ten-mile haul, and at the top of the last long hill catching the first view of the lake after eleven months of not seeing this cherished body of water. The shouts and cries of the other campers when they saw you, and the trunks to be unpacked, to give up their rich burden. (Arriving was less exciting nowadays, when you sneaked up in your car and parked it under a tree near the camp and took out the bags and in five minutes it was all over, no fuss, no loud wonderful fuss about trunks.)

Peace and goodness and jollity. The only thing that was wrong   10
now, really, was the sound of the place, an unfamiliar nervous sound of the outboard motors. This was the note that jarred, the one thing that would sometimes break the illusion and set the years moving. In those other summertimes all motors were inboard; and when they were at a little distance, the noise they made was a sedative, an ingredient of summer sleep. They were one-cylinder and two-cylinder engines, and some were make-and-break and some were jump-spark, but they all made a sleepy sound across the lake. The one-lungers throbbed and fluttered, and the twin-cylinder ones purred and purred, and that was a quiet sound, too. But now the campers all had outboards. In the daytime, in the hot mornings, these motors made a petulant, irritable sound; at night, in the still evening when the afterglow lit the water, they whined about one's ears like mosquitoes. My boy loved our rented outboard, and his great desire was to achieve single-handed mastery over it, and authority, and he soon learned the trick of choking it a little (but not too much), and the adjustment of the needle valve. Watching him I would remember the things you could do with the old one-cylinder engine with the heavy flywheel, how you could have it eating out of your hand if you got really close to it spiritually. Motorboats in those days didn't have clutches, and you would make a landing by shutting off the motor at the proper time and coasting in with a dead rudder. But there was a way of reversing them, if you learned the trick, by cutting the switch and putting it on again exactly on the final dying revolution of the flywheel, so that it would kick back against compression and

begin reversing. Approaching a dock in a strong following breeze, it was difficult to slow up sufficiently by the ordinary coasting method, and if a boy felt he had complete mastery over his motor, he was tempted to keep it running beyond its time and then reverse it a few feet from the dock. It took a cool nerve, because if you threw the switch a twentieth of a second too soon you would catch the flywheel when it still had speed enough to go up past center, and the boat would leap ahead, charging bull-fashion at the dock.

We had a good week at the camp. The bass were biting well 11 and the sun shone endlessly, day after day. We would be tired at night and lie down in the accumulated heat of the little bedrooms after the long hot day and the breeze would stir almost imperceptibly outside and the smell of the swamp drift in through the rusty screens. Sleep would come easily and in the morning the red squirrel would be on the roof, tapping out his gay routine. I kept remembering everything, lying in bed in the mornings—the small steamboat that had a long rounded stern like the lip of a Ubangi, and how quietly she ran on the moonlight sails, when the older boys played their mandolins and the girls sang and we ate doughnuts dipped in sugar, and how sweet the music was on the water in the shining night, and what it had felt like to think about girls then. After breakfast we would go up to the store and the things were in the same place— the minnows in a bottle, the plugs and spinners disarranged and pawed over by the youngsters from the boys' camp, the Fig Newtons and the Beeman's gum. Outside, the road was tarred and cars stood in front of the store. Inside, all was just as it had always been, except there was more Coca-Cola and not so much Moxie and root beer and birch beer and sarsaparilla. We would walk out with the bottle of pop apiece and sometimes the pop would backfire up our noses and hurt. We explored the streams, quietly, where the turtles slid off the sunny logs and dug their way into the soft bottom; and we lay on the town wharf and fed worms to the tame bass. Everywhere we went I had trouble making out which was I, the one walking at my side, the one walking in my pants.

One afternoon while we were there at that lake a thunderstorm 12 came up. It was like the revival of an old melodrama that I had seen long ago with childish awe. The second-act climax of the drama of the electrical disturbance over a lake in America had not changed in any important respect. This was the big scene, still the big scene.

The whole thing was so familiar, the first feeling of oppression and heat and a general air around camp of not wanting to go very far away. In mid-afternoon (it was all the same) a curious darkening of the sky, and a lull in everything that had made life tick; and then the way the boats suddenly swung the other way at their moorings with the coming of a breeze out of the new quarter, and the pre-monitory rumble. Then the kettle drum, then the snare, then the bass drum and cymbals, then crackling light against the dark, and the gods grinning and licking their chops in the hills. Afterward the calm, the rain steadily rustling in the calm lake, the return of light and hope and spirits, and the campers running out in joy and relief to go swimming in the rain, their bright cries perpetuating the deathless joke about how they were getting simply drenched, and the children screaming with delight at the new sensation of bathing in the rain, and the joke about getting drenched linking the gener-ations in a strong indestructible chain. And the comedian who waded in carrying an umbrella.

When the others went swimming, my son said he was going in, 13
too. He pulled his dripping trunks from the line where they had hung all through the shower and wrung them out. Languidly, and with no thought of going in, I watched him, his hard little body, skinny and bare, saw him wince slightly as he pulled up around his vitals the small, soggy, icy garment. As he buckled the swollen belt, suddenly my groin felt the chill of death.

RESPONSES AND IDEAS

1. Respond to this essay by describing a setting from two perspectives, that of a child and that of an adult. If you can adopt a perspective similar to that of E. B. White's in this essay, do so.

2. Much of the point of this essay is summed up in the phrase, "suddenly my groin felt the chill of death" (par. 13). What does the phrase mean? What causes White to feel the way he does?

3. What does the lake symbolize for White? (See Glossary: Symbol.) In-dicate specific passages in the essay that support your answer.

PURPOSE, AUDIENCE, AND STRATEGIES

1. How would you describe the tone of the essay? Does it remain the same throughout? If not, in what ways does it change?

2. If you have not had a vacation experience like White's and if you do not have children, do you have any trouble understanding or sympathizing with what he has to say about his experience? Identify some points in the essay where he uses expanded rather than summary description to make sure readers will understand him.

3. At what point in the essay does White's attitude towards the passage of time begin to change? How does he signal the change to the reader?

4. Identify those places in the essay where White comments directly on the passing of time and on permanence and change. Are we to take all these statements literally? Which, if any, are ironic or are the product of self-deception? (See Glossary: Irony.) Some of the statements are seemingly contradictory. Why do you think White included them in the essay?

5. Choose a descriptive passage from the essay and identify the pattern (or patterns) of arrangement it follows. Discuss how the arrangement reinforces the essay's dominant impression.

LANGUAGE AND STYLE

1. In what ways do the connotations of words in paragraphs 8 and 10 contribute to the dominant impression? Identify two other places in the essay where connotations are important.

2. Identify the figures of speech in paragraphs 7 and 8 and indicate the purposes for which they are used. Then discuss how these figures are particularly appropriate for the impression White is creating.

3. If you do not know the meaning of some of the following words, look them up in the dictionary: *incessant, placidity* (par. 1); *gunwale* (2); *primeval* (3); *transposition* (4); *helgramite, pensively* (5); *petulant* (10); *premonitory* (12); *languidly* (13).

WRITING ACTIVITIES

1. Choose a favorite place and write a descriptive essay in which you present it from two perspectives—one objective, the other subjective. Your aim in the essay might be to show how the world around us seems to change according to the values and feelings that color our perceptions, or it might be to show that no single kind of description can fully capture the essence of a scene. Whatever your purpose, try to make sure it is clear to your readers, but at the same time follow E. B. White's lead in letting the description do most of the work of conveying your thesis.

2. Prepare a description of an object or building whose appearance contrasts with its surroundings. You might focus on a well-maintained house or store in a run-down neighborhood or on a large piece of

antique furniture in a room otherwise filled with modern furnishings. In your description, emphasize how the values implied by one of the subjects compare with those implied by the other. The well-maintained building, for example, might imply pride in one's self, energy, thrift; the rest of the neighborhood might radiate frustration, anger, and loss of hope.

Writing Suggestions

EXPLORATIONS

1. Go to a place you like either very much or not at all, and take notes of your sense impressions, one sense at a time, trying to record the impact of the place. If your notes point towards an essay, keep writing.

2. Go to a place where you can observe people and take notes on one individual at a time, trying to produce a brief sketch of his or her personality from what he or she does, looks like, and says to others. Use your imagination, but try to be realistic in your speculations. If your brief sketch looks as if it would make a good essay, keep writing.

3. Describe a single scene (real or imaginary), using a variety of organizations including spatial patterns and dominant impression. If one of these approaches seems particularly promising, consider turning it into an essay.

4. Describe a scene or person from an unlikely viewpoint, that of a tree, a cat, or an old woman, for example. If you like the results, or if you get even more interesting ideas for a description, keep writing.

ACTIVITIES

1. Look through a textbook in the natural sciences or engineering, or a copy of the periodical *Science* or *Scientific American,* and locate a descriptive passage that seems typical of the ones it contains. How does it differ in diction, organization, point of view, emotional impact, and purpose from the descriptive essays in this chapter? Write a brief report comparing it to a passage similar in content drawn from one of the essays in this chapter.

2. Take notes during the day on the conversations, speeches, lectures, and discussions you listen to or participate in. How often do they use descriptive detail, what kind of detail do they use, and what do they use it for?

3. Collect a newspaper report of an accident or incident and an article from a news magazine on a similar subject. Compare their use of detail. Which presents more detail or makes greater use of sense impressions? Which uses descriptive detail to reinforce a thesis, either stated or implied? Which has the greater emotional impact, and why? How do the descriptions appear to differ in purpose?

4. Look through some favorite magazines for an example of the following kinds of descriptions, and tell how each is used: meditation, character sketch, technical description.

MODELS

1. Using John Haines's "The Yard" as a model, describe a neighborhood or community in which you lived, showing how the social structure was reflected in the layout of the community and how the environment shaped your personality and those of other residents.

2. Drawing ideas from the approach used in "Mayakovsky Square," write an essay commenting on the visual, oral, or other stimulation offered by the American environment, also commenting on this stimulation as a product of the American political or economic systems.

3. Borrowing techniques and approach from "Dad," create a character sketch of someone you dislike or of someone with an unusual personality. The subject need not die at the end of the sketch.

4. Using Michael Arlen's approach in "Ode to Thanksgiving," argue against some common gatherings. Your subject could be lectures, cafeteria lunches, football games, or some meetings you frequently attend.

5. Modeling your approach on E. B. White's in "Once More to the Lake," describe a real or imagined return to a scene from your childhood, and use descriptive detail to comment on the passage of time.

4

❧ EXAMPLE

Illustrating and Supporting

WHAT EXAMPLES DO

Suppose you came across this statement in an essay: "No popular form of exercise seems quite as strange as yoga." Even if you know something about yoga, you would probably expect the author to provide examples of those features that make it seem "strange." If you consider yoga a healthful physical and mental discipline, you would surely want to know what grounds the author has for considering it more unusual than, say, lifting steel bars with weights at each end, or running for miles in all kinds of weather. The examples in this version of the sentence might be what you would look for:

> No popular form of exercise seems quite as strange as yoga *with its inverted lotus position, its tree posture, and its lion routine (kneel, breathe out sharply, extending tongue until it touches chin, open eyes wide, extend arms stiffly with fingers spread).*

Examples—specific instances that reveal the qualities of a subject or that represent a group—help us understand and accept what we read. Examples clarify because they enable us to view a general statement in terms of individual events, people, objects, or ideas. They provide support by allowing us to share the information and ideas that shaped a writer's conclusions. A writer explaining the features of standardized tests, for instance, might give examples from the SAT (or ACT), thus using the reader's experience of a specific test to illuminate the larger subject. Donna Woolfolk Cross, in the essay "Sin, Suffer, and Repent," backs up her rather surprising generalization, "Dedicated watchers of soap operas often confuse fact

115

with fiction," by telling how the actress who plays the villainous Lisa in a soap opera called "Days of Our Lives" once had a container of milk poured over her by a woman in a supermarket.

The linking of broad statements (generalizations) and specific illustrations is a basic pattern in writing. It reflects what is in effect an unspoken agreement among writers and readers that general statements presenting new or unusual information or challenging our normal way of looking at things will be accompanied by— supported by—examples and explanations.

Not every general statement needs examples, of course. The writer who says, "It hurts to lose," can count on readers to remember the many times they have lost in sports, at cards or Monopoly, at love, or in their schoolwork, and these painful memories will enable them to appreciate the author's point. Yet if the subject of your essay is likely to be unfamiliar, if the discussion is complicated or technical, or if your perspective on a topic may be hard for readers to share at first, then you had better be ready to provide examples.

Frequent and well-chosen illustrations are a key feature of good writing: they give abstract ideas interest and substance. Prose that fails to interest or enlighten us, on the other hand, often does so not because it lacks worthwhile ideas but because it fails to be specific. Bad writers follow up an abstract statement not with details but with another statement and another, puzzling us or boring us, forcing us to provide our own instances—if we can. They write about sports without mentioning a single team or athlete; they criticize television but fail to cite specific programs: "Television schedules are crowded with 'soft news' shows. These programs provide little important or useful information. Their popularity reflects our desire for escapist entertainment."

Good writers know that examples can be as important as generalizations, sometimes even more important. The blunt opening sentence of the paragraph below presents a conclusion so startling that without substantial support, most readers are unlikely to take it seriously, much less agree with it. The supporting examples are in themselves so interesting that the value of the paragraph lies as much in the quality of the information the author presents as in the generalization he intends it to support:

> Foreigners are buying America. It's no longer just the smart money or the tax evasion money. It's the savings of a Bavarian innkeeper who can earn only 3.5 per cent a year at his bank at home; it's the British

Airways pension fund which owns a shopping center in Houston. It's the oil money of Iranians, among them a sister of the Shah, who have bought so many of the million-dollar homes in the Truesdale Estates section of Beverly Hills that the natives call it "the Persian Gulf." And it's the Eurodollars in the coffers of polyglot multi-nationals in Stockholm and Stuttgart using the profits from their exports to the U.S. to build and buy factories here. The Germans make Volkswagen Rabbits in a Pennsylvania factory that Chrysler had to abandon. The Japanese bottle Coca-Cola in New Hampshire, raise cattle in Utah and make soy sauce in rural Wisconsin ("The Buying of America," *Newsweek,* 27 Nov. 1978).

The examples in this paragraph are varied and concrete: some factual detail ("3.5 per cent a year"), a hint of a story ("bought so many of the million-dollar homes"), a quotation ("the Persian Gulf"), and some surprising occurrences ("soy sauce in rural Wisconsin"). The power of examples in writing arises from these qualities: variety makes reading enjoyable, and concreteness makes the author's point memorable.

THE PROCESS

Whether they appear as brief illustrations in a sentence, as the body of a paragraph, or as the primary method for developing an entire essay (as with the selections in this chapter), examples can make your writing readable, informative, and convincing. But in order to use them effectively, you must first know where to find good illustrations and how to develop them. Almost any aspect of a subject can offer you potential examples. Depending on your purpose for writing, you might want to look for representative people, events, or quotations; typical attitudes, beliefs, or ideas; revealing stories, statistics, or physical details; even a hypothetical situation that has been thought out it detail.

Sometimes you can find promising material simply by letting your mind run over a subject. In considering the importance of sports in our society, for instance, you might think of the amount of space that sports news occupies in newspapers, or of the percentage of your friends who are fans of a sport or a team, or of what a friend usually says to justify watching a game on TV rather than studying. You could try to recall events and physical details that indicate the high status of sports (or of a particular athlete) in your high school;

you could think of the many different ways people say "sport builds character"; or you could relive an event, perhaps only a brief anecdote, that demonstrates the impact Little League (or figure skating, or basketball) had on you as a child. Finally, you might imagine a hypothetical situation like the banning of sports in a high school or college, and then speculate—offering detailed conjectures—about its impact.

As you probe a topic, try to keep a dual perspective: guide your search with a sense of what you want the examples to do, but remain open to new ideas and changes of direction. The push and pull between your original idea (tentative thesis) and the examples you discover can be one of the most creative stages in writing. The generalization you start with, "Sports are important in our society," may end up being modified into something more interesting for you and your readers: "Women's college sports are finally beginning to draw crowds, attention, and money."

The freewheeling approach to discovering examples does not always work, however. How often have you tried to think of an example and gotten . . . nothing? Or shaken your head like a cookie jar to find only a single bare example rattling around ("The day contact football was banned at Rahman H.S., gloom descended. Students were depressed"), unaccompanied by the descriptive or narrative details necessary to make it convincing and informative: "Athletes walked around in a black fog; band members hit only sour notes; even the strongest cheerleader wept." Perhaps you need to explore the topic with a pen in hand. Try using some of the pump-priming techniques described in Chapter 1 under the heading "The Writing Process." Take a scratch pad and freewrite for a minute or two with your generalization in mind. Brainstorm by listing or clustering possible illustrations, focusing on concrete detail as much as you can.

Or in searching for examples, you might focus your attention on one of these rich sources:

1. *Personal experience.* Think of your involvement with the topic. For an essay on technology in medicine, your experiences with physicians or emergency rooms can be a good starting place. Routine events like blood tests from a family doctor or X-rays for a broken bone show how much our health depends on machines. For that matter, you even use a machine of sorts (a thermometer) to take your

temperature. Look especially for experiences that directly support the point you want to make: "How do I know that academic standards in many secondary schools are low? Well, in one science course I took. . . ." Your personal involvement with the subject will lend credibility to your writing, particularly if you use your narrative and descriptive skills to make the supporting incidents believable and also show that they are typical, not idiosyncratic. Fox Butterfield uses this source very effectively in the opening of "Foreign Devils" when he tells of the Chinese man who walked into a tree while staring at the author and his young son. William F. Buckley's essay, "Why Don't We Complain?" devotes twelve of its twenty-three paragraphs to five personal examples.

2. *Other people.* Think of people whose experiences or personalities are consistent with your assertions. If you claim that career changes are quite common, you can speak of a neighbor who at age thirty-five sold a successful plumbing business to attend law school; of your Aunt Janet, who went from teaching to work as a stock broker; and of Ronald Reagan, the radio announcer turned actor turned President. Donna Woolfolk Cross supports her conclusions about soap operas by describing the personalities and activities of well-known characters, including Erica Kane of "All My Children" and Lisa Anderson of "Days of Our Lives."

When you draw on this source, try not to assume that readers already know something about the people and events you are describing or that your audience will immediately view the illustrations in the same light you do. Even if you cite TV personalities or politicians, provide enough detail to allow readers to share your perspective.

3. *One from a group.* When a subject is so broad that you can think of several possible examples, but none very distinct or effective, try focusing on one element of the whole, or on a single member of a group. Think how learning about this element will help your readers, and then look for details they will need to know. If in a business course you are told to write a paper on the American response to efficient Japanese manufacturing, you probably already have in mind several industries that have been modernizing factories and streamlining procedures, including automobiles, steel, home appliances, and electronics. Focus on a representative company, or even one plant (the main plant of General Motors' Buick division, for instance), and develop informative detail that helps readers see

why this is a good example (changes in the operation of the assembly line, in the use of robots, in building layout, in the responsibility of workers for quality control, in parts inventory, and in worker-management relations).

Chances are that as you concentrate on a single instance, you will remember details that did not come to mind at first; or perhaps you will decide that you need to do research in order to create a truly effective illustration. One of the purposes of writing is, after all, to teach yourself as well as your readers; when you hunt for examples, you will find that you get a deeper view of your subject.

Examples from this source are often relatively long. They work well either as paragraph-length illustrations supporting a thesis (like those Lewis Thomas uses in "Clever Animals") or as a source of multiple examples used throughout an essay.

4. *Statistics.* Usually we think of statistics as technical details in someone else's writing, or as a strategy that deceives as often as it enlightens ("Figures don't lie, but liars can figure"). Yet at their best, statistics sum up and highlight the meaning of many instances. By taking a mathematical perspective, you can turn a vague example, "In recent years, most presidents have been in office for one term," into a precise and revealing illustration: "In the past four decades 71 percent, or five out of seven presidents, have been elected for only one term—less, in Ford's case."

5. *Turn to others for help.* If you are reading or interviewing in preparation for writing, be on the alert for useful details and quotations. Many of the funniest and most effective passages in the essay "Sin, Suffer, and Repent" come from the author's reading and television viewing and make good use of quotation.

Deciding when and how to use examples can be difficult. No simple rule will tell you if a concept is understood easily on its own or needs illustration; no easy rule of thumb will tell you whether to employ a single brief example; an extended example in one or more paragraphs; or multiple examples, perhaps varying in length. Yet keeping aware of your reader's needs and of your essay's purpose can help you make appropriate decisions.

When writing to a group of people you know—fellow students or people you work with—you should have little trouble deciding what your readers already know or agree with and what things in your essay will need either illustration or support. Most often, however, we write to people we know only slightly, if at all.

One way to understand the needs of this so-called general audience is to look at a draft of your work from a reader's perspective, trying to imagine what it would be like to encounter the essay if you knew nothing about the topic. Another useful though indirect method for learning about an audience's expectations is to study the work of experienced, professional writers, looking at places they feel an example is necessary and observing the strategies they use in choosing and introducing illustrations. Each of the essays in this chapter is addressed to a general audience, and each makes slightly different assumptions about the nature and needs of this audience, a variety that adds to their usefulness as models. (The questions that follow the essays call attention to the assumptions the authors seem to make about their various audiences.)

Developing a *for-example* habit will help you remember to add a brief illustration or explanation whenever you present an unusual concept, a controversial statement, or a technical term. Remember, there are many ways to introduce examples:

> Some recent Nobel Prize winners have been women; for example, (for instance/including/among them). . . .
> Animals nearing extinction, like the California condor and the giant panda, are often the subject of intensive study.
> Dolly Parton, Willie Nelson, Kenny Rogers, Bing Crosby, Elvis Presley, and David Bowie are all examples of singers who turned to acting, though not always successfully.

If you are writing an essay on Nobel Prize winners, or endangered species, or singers who have become actors, and cannot come up with such a list, you have homework to do before you can complete your essay. Do not give up; make the necessary effort.

The aim of an essay, too, should affect your choice of examples. Informative writing often contains illustrations of several sentences or a whole paragraph either following or leading up to a general statement. In such paragraphs the examples may constitute the real substance of the essay, and the general statement may simply be a device for organizing and introducing them.

Essays whose main purpose is to justify the author's interpretation of the topic generally present multiple examples, often paragraph-length, designed to support part or all of the thesis. The more controversial or unusual your thesis, the more attention you will have to pay to providing a variety of fully developed examples to help readers agree with your assertion. If you are preparing an argumentative essay, you will need to pay even more attention to the logical relationship of thesis and examples as well as to the ways other people might view the evidence you consider favorable to your case (See Chapter 10, "Argument and Persuasion").

Though it is possible to put too many examples in a piece of writing, we most often do the opposite: we underestimate the number and length of the illustrations needed. One student, Susan Clark, submitted an essay containing this brief paragraph:

> The actual cost of that economy car whose nationally advertised price fits, just barely, into your budget can also end up being more than you expect. After the dealer gets through adding on all the extras that you have to take unless you want to wait six months for a specially ordered model, you may pay almost fifty percent more than you wanted to.

In a conference, Susan's instructor pointed out that this paragraph was a lot less effective than the other paragraphs in the essay, which covered in considerable detail the unexpected costs of college, of dining out, and of buying clothes. This was the case, he said, because the paragraph presented too little information to clarify the problem she wanted to describe or to convince the reader to accept her position. He suggested that she explore in greater detail the extras she mentioned.

As she looked over her paper to revise it, Susan realized that the paragraph on buying a car was underdeveloped because she had assumed her readers had experiences with car dealers similar to one she recently had. To revise the essay, she visited a local car dealership, took notes on what she discovered, and produced this detailed paragraph:

> That economy car whose price on TV fits just barely within your budget can also end up costing a lot more than you expect. To begin with, you probably won't find the basic economy model in the showroom. The dealer will tell you, "The company doesn't send us any of those—only the more expensive models," and "I can order one for you, but it may take up to six months." Even if you find a model starting at no more than a thousand dollars above what you wanted to pay plus

another thousand for popular but not essential accessories the dealer ordered with the car, you can't just pay the sticker price plus taxes and drive the car away. On the window of the car you want, next to the large price sticker, you will find a smaller sticker entitled, "Dealer Supplemental Price label." This piece of paper will probably tell you that the dealer has added rust protection ($249). This is certainly a worthwhile feature, but you can get it elsewhere for a hundred dollars less. The cost might also include a Paint Protection System ($169). This is basically a coat of deluxe wax. The extra Fabric Protection System ($69) is similar to the treatment you can give the upholstery with a $4.95 can of Scotchgard. You may even find a charge for an item that doesn't even pretend to be practical, a custom stripe ($89). Finally, if you want to buy a popular imported car, you may find yourself paying anywhere from an extra one hundred to one thousand dollars for a "competitive market adjustment," just a fancy name for the old practice of "charging what the market will bear."

Susan Clark's revision is clearly stronger than her original paragraph. How can you decide, as she did, what kind of examples will be convincing? An example is a *sample,* a representative member of a group. First of all, therefore, it must accurately represent the group from which it comes. Cadillac and Mercedes are good examples of luxury cars, but they are really unrepresentative of cars in general, and their distinctive features are even less appropriate as illustrations of the qualities of family cars. Next, to be convincing, an example must also be long enough and detailed enough to be easily understood. Making something clearer by making it longer may seem contrary to common sense; if the details you add are ones your audience will readily understand, however, they can create a bridge between your meaning and your readers.

For many situations, of course, one brief example will be enough because no one will question the truth or accuracy of the illustration. Yet when you think that your audience may view an illustration in a different way from the way you do, you will need to develop it more fully. If, for instance, you want to use the tennis player John McEnroe to typify ill-behaved professional athletes, you will have to take into account the view that his actions are simply the result of youthful energy and love of competition, perhaps in this way: ". . . ill-behaved athletes, like John McEnroe, whose outbursts are not, as some claim, a sign of energy and 'competitive involvement,' but a mark of his boorishness." Finally, if the example you present is particularly appropriate, let your reader know. Lewis Thomas does this when he introduces the first main example in his essay "Clever

Animals" by saying, "The most famous case in point is that of Clever Hans. . . ."

THE PATTERN IN ACTION

Professional writers don't set out to compose something called an example essay, but they do recognize that the *exemplification pattern* offers useful strategies for developing and organizing essays, strategies that serve many common writing situations and can be adapted easily for others. Whenever writers think, "I'd better use examples here to help my readers," or, "Perhaps I can get my point across by stating it briefly and following up with several paragraphs of examples," they are drawing on a knowledge of the options the exemplification pattern provides them. By studying the pattern in action in essays like the ones in this chapter, you develop your ability to recognize situations that call for the pattern and learn ways to modify it to suit your needs. As you read the selections you will notice, too, that although it can be used to organize entire essays, the exemplification pattern is less a rigid form than it is a general framework that helps readers understand your ideas and that encourages you to move your thinking about a subject away from vague generalizations toward the specifics that provide both depth and insight.

Examples appear so frequently in essays of all kinds—explanatory, argumentative, informative, expressive—that it is easy to think of them simply as a technique that makes writing more effective, or as a habit of mind that good writers develop. To a certain extent this point of view is accurate, and we can expect to encounter examples frequently in essays that follow other patterns of development. Essays that concentrate on process or definition use illustrations to clarify technical terms. Classifications use them to explore and explain the various categories. Arguments use them both as a means of support and as a way of making other kinds of support more vivid and convincing. Yet exemplification frequently turns up as a pattern for organizing whole essays or sections of long essays.

The most important conventional essay pattern based on the linking of statement and example is the *thesis-and-support* essay. In its basic form this pattern consists of a generalization (thesis) followed by several paragraphs of examples (support); alternatively, it can consist of a description of the topic followed by paragraphs of examples and a conclusion that sums up their meaning. A table illustrating these two patterns follows.

Introduction (including thesis)	Introduction (statement of topic)
Example 1	Example 1
Example 2	Example 2
Example 3	Example 3
Example 4	Example 4
Conclusion (summary)	Conclusion (including thesis)

The thesis-and-support strategy is particularly useful for three kinds of writing: academic papers, brief memoranda, and presentations of a fresh or unusual point of view. College instructors often ask their students to reach a conclusion about a subject (a poem, a historical event, a social phenomenon) and to provide support for the interpretation. The thesis-and-support pattern is helpful in two ways. It reminds the writer to reach a specific conclusion (thesis) and to back it up with evidence; and it highlights for instructors both the interpretation and the evidence on which it rests. In a literature class, for instance, you could use the pattern to present your interpretation of the role symbolism plays in a specific poem, like Robert Frost's "Mending Wall." Your paper might open with some background information on the work, move to a statement of your view of the importance of symbolism in it, and then provide support for your generalization in the form of examples from different parts of the poem.

The brief memorandum is often used in business and public affairs to share judgments about recent events. Because each example represents a large group of instances, you can use examples to demonstrate in a brief space that your judgment is well founded. A memorandum presenting your conclusion about the success of a sales campaign (or the progress of a mayoral campaign) could present as evidence one or two short but revealing events, some quotations from people affected by the events, and a statistical summary.

When you have a new, unusual, or startling point of view, the thesis-and-support pattern allows you to state it and demonstrate that your outlook is based on reasonable evidence. (In reverse order, the pattern allows you to show how the conclusion flows out of the evidence and contains the implicit message that, given the chance, readers will come to view the subject in the same way you do.) Occasions of this sort are so common and the form so widely used that it is often referred to as the "standard essay form" (see Chapter 1, under "The Writing Process"). It can also be adapted easily for argument because it provides a strategy for dealing with audiences whose point of view differs sharply from the author's. (Lewis Thomas's "Clever Animals," a model of the thesis-and-support essay, is followed by a commentary that discusses how Thomas adapts the pattern to a particular subject, purpose, and audience.)

Another common essay form based on the linking of broad statement and specific example is the *representative example* paper. In essays of this sort the author tries to give a picture of an entire group by first generalizing about its qualities and then presenting an extended portrait of a particularly representative member of the group. In discussing religious groups that maintain a clear social identity, for instance, you might focus on a single group like the Mennonites, Mormons, or Black Muslims. In a long paper, for a sociology class perhaps, you could expand the representative example pattern by discussing each of the groups in depth and in order. The pattern is also frequently used to organize parts of longer works, such as chapters in a book, because it allows authors to explore a subject in considerable detail.

Though exemplification frequently appears in conventional patterns like thesis-and-support or representative example, it turns up even more often in mixed forms serving a variety of purposes. The essays in this chapter provide evidence of its many uses. Fox Butterfield shows how examples can be clustered so as to provide understanding of a complex and puzzling cultural phenomenon. William F. Buckley combines the pattern with narrative to lead readers to an interesting perspective on our social and political behavior. Donna Woolfolk Cross shows how well-chosen examples can provide humor as well as insight.

➣ LEWIS THOMAS

Lewis Thomas was born in Flushing, New York, in 1913. He attended Princeton University and Harvard Medical School, and he has been a research pathologist and a medical administrator. He was president of Memorial Sloan-Kettering Cancer Center from 1973 to 1980 and is currently its chancellor. Thomas writes a regular column for the *New England Journal of Medicine* and has published three collections of essays, many of which are drawn from his columns: *The Lives of a Cell* (1974) (winner of the National Book Award), *The Medusa and the Snail* (1979), and *Late Night Thoughts on Listening to Mahler's Ninth Symphony* (1983). His memoir of his career as a physician and medical researcher, *The Youngest Science: Notes of a Medicine-Watcher* (1983), is at the same time a chronicle of the development of medical science in the twentieth century.

Clever Animals

"Clever Animals" first appeared as an essay in the *New England Journal of Medicine* and was reprinted later in *Night Thoughts on Listening to Mahler's Ninth Symphony*. The essay grows out of Thomas's professional interests and his curiosity about the ways human beings, particularly scientists, behave. Though the essay examines research in the behavioral sciences primarily, it comments by implication on our often undiscriminating acceptance of so-called scientific truth in general.

Both the opening of "Clever Animals" and the author's choice of supporting examples reflect an awareness of the attitudes towards research that readers—both scientists and non-scientists—are likely to bring with them to the essay. As you read the selection, you might try to be aware of the degree of success with which the author has anticipated your attitudes. You might also ask if, in addition to demonstrating the cleverness of animals, the essay shows that the very presence of a researcher can distort the results of an experiment.

Scientists who work on animal behavior are occupationally   1
obliged to live chancier lives than most of their colleagues, always at risk of being fooled by the animals they are studying or, worse, fooling themselves. Whether their experiments involve domesticated laboratory animals or wild creatures in the field, there is no end to

the surprises that an animal can think up in the presence of an investigator. Sometimes it seems as if animals are genetically programmed to puzzle human beings, especially psychologists.

The risks are especially high when the scientist is engaged in training the animal to do something or other and must bank his professional reputation on the integrity of his experimental subject. The most famous case in point is that of Clever Hans, the turn-of-the-century German horse now immortalized in the lexicon of behavioral science by the technical term, the "Clever Hans Error." The horse, owned and trained by Herr von Osten, could not only solve complex arithmetical problems, but even read the instructions on a blackboard and tap out infallibly, with one hoof, the right answer. What is more, he could perform the same computations when total strangers posed questions to him, with his trainer nowhere nearby. For several years Clever Hans was studied intensively by groups of puzzled scientists and taken seriously as a horse with something very like a human brain, quite possibly even better than human. But finally in 1911, it was discovered by Professor O. Pfungst that Hans was not really doing arithmetic at all; he was simply observing the behavior of the human experimenter. Subtle, unconscious gestures—nods of the head, the holding of breath, the cessation of nodding when the correct count was reached—were accurately read by the horse as cues to stop tapping.

2

Whenever I read about that phenomenon, usually recounted as the exposure of a sort of unconscious fraud on the part of either the experimenter or the horse or both, I wish Clever Hans would be given more credit than he generally gets. To be sure, the horse couldn't really do arithmetic, but the record shows that he was considerably better at observing human beings and interpreting their behavior than humans are at comprehending horses or, for that matter, other humans.

3

Cats are a standing rebuke to behavioral scientists wanting to know how the minds of animals work. The mind of a cat is an inscrutable mystery, beyond human reach, the least human of all creatures and at the same time, as any cat owner will attest, the most intelligent. In 1979, a paper was published in *Science* by B. R. Moore and S. Stuttard entitled "Dr. Guthrie and Felis domesticus or: tripping over the cat," a wonderful account of the kind of scientific mischief native to this species. Thirty-five years ago, E. R. Guthrie and G. P. Horton described an experiment in which cats were placed

4

in a glass-fronted puzzle box and trained to find their way out by jostling a slender vertical rod at the front of the box, thereby causing a door to open. What interested these investigators was not so much that the cats could learn to bump into the vertical rod, but that before doing so each animal performed a long ritual of highly stereotyped movements, rubbing their heads and backs against the front of the box, turning in circles, and finally touching the rod. The experiment has ranked as something of a classic in experimental psychology, even raising in some minds the notion of a ceremony of superstition on the part of cats: before the rod will open the door, it is necessary to go through a magical sequence of motions.

Moore and Stuttard repeated the Guthrie experiment, observed   5
the same complex "learning" behavior, but then discovered that it occurred only when a human being was visible to the cat. If no one was in the room with the box, the cat did nothing but take naps. The sight of a human being was all that was needed to lauunch the animal on the series of sinuous movements, rod or no rod, door or no door. It was not a learned pattern of behavior, it was a cat greeting a person.

The French investigator R. Chauvin was once engaged in a field   6
study of the boundaries of ant colonies and enlisted the help of some enthusiastic physicists equipped with radioactive compounds and Geiger counters. The ants of one anthill were labeled and then tracked to learn whether they entered the territory of a neighboring hill. In the middle of the work the physicists suddenly began leaping like ballet dancers, terminating the experiment, while hundreds of ants from both colonies swarmed over their shoes and up inside their pants. To Chauvin's ethological eye it looked like purposeful behavior on both sides.

Bees are filled with astonishments, confounding anyone who   7
studies them, producing volumes of anecdotes. A lady of our acquaintance visited her sister, who raised honeybees in northern California. They left their car on a side road, suited up in protective gear, and walked across the fields to have a look at the hives. For reasons unknown, the bees were in a furious mood that afternoon, attacking in platoons, settling on them from all sides. Let us walk away slowly, advised the beekeeper sister, they'll give it up sooner or later. They walked until bee-free, then circled the fields and went back to the car, and found the bees there, waiting for them.

There is a new bee anecdote for everyone to wonder about. It   8 was reported from Brazil that male bees of the plant-pollinating euglossine species are addicted to DDT. Houses that had been sprayed for mosquito control in the Amazonas region were promptly invaded by thousands of bees that gathered on the walls, collected the DDT in pouches on their hind legs, and flew off with it. Most of the houses were virtually stripped of DDT during the summer months, and the residents in the area complained bitterly of the noise. There is as yet no explanation for this behavior. They are not harmed by the substance; while a honeybee is quickly killed by as little as six micrograms of DDT, these bees can cart away two thousand micrograms without being discommoded. Possibly the euglossine bees like the taste of DDT or its smell, or maybe they are determined to protect other insect cousins. Nothing about bees, or other animals, seems beyond imagining.

COMMENTARY

Thomas's use of the thesis-and-support pattern (see pp. 124–126) in this essay illustrates how effective a strategy it can be for presenting an unusual or surprising point of view and encouraging readers to accept it. Since most of us, whether we are trained as scientists or not, have a high regard for the careful methods scientific research uses to reach conclusions, Thomas's viewpoint, expressed in his thesis statement, is likely to be a bit unsettling: "Sometimes it seems as if animals are genetically programmed to puzzle human beings, especially psychologists." The idea of such strange genetic programming is likely to make most of us say, "I'd like to see some evidence before I accept this."

Clearly, Thomas is aware of the assumptions his readers bring to the essay; he begins, therefore, by suggesting that we dissociate our view of researchers who work with animals from our normal view of scientists and the certainties of the scientific method: "Scientists who work on animal behavior are occupationally obliged to live chancier lives than most of their colleagues, always at risk of being fooled by the animals they are studying or, worse, fooling themselves." He then provides four paragraph-length examples of animal behavior that support his thesis. Each example is developed in detail and accompanied by a comment that shows how it supports Thomas's outlook. The number, variety, and detail of the examples helps make them convincing, and though they describe complicated experiments, they can be easily understood by non-scientists. Thomas's humor acts both as a gentle criticism of the experiments he describes and as a way of encouraging us to be cautious in our judgment of what people claim are advances in knowledge. At the end of the essay, most readers are likely to agree with Thomas's closing statement: "Nothing about bees, or other animals, seems beyond imagining."

Thomas does a good deal of arguing in this essay, at least in the sense that he provides reasoned, logical support for his point of view. The essay as a whole, however, is not an argument in a formal sense because Thomas spends more time explaining why his perspective is reasonable than in getting us to take his side in a conflict or to undertake a particular course of action (see Chapter 10, "Argument and Persuasion"). Many thesis-and-support essays are like Thomas's in that they come close to argument; in the end, though, their aim is simply to explain why the author's point of view is consistent with the facts of the matter.

The structure of Thomas's essay is close to the basic thesis-and-support pattern. Like much good writing, however, it avoids following the pattern slavishly by allotting one paragraph to each example; instead, Thomas takes time between the examples to comment on their significance. In developing the examples, moreover, the author draws on his skill in narrative and descriptive writing as well as on the kind of logical reasoning common to analysis and argument.

RESPONSES AND IDEAS

1. Even if you find what Thomas has to say convincing, you may still be able to think of explanations other than the cleverness of animals for the behavior described in the essay. For each of the examples list as many alternate explanations as you can. Do the alternate explanations undercut the value of the essay for you, or do they simply enrich the experience of reading it? Explain your response.

2. From what fields of study are the examples in this essay taken (for example, psychology, anthropology, biology)? For each example, write a brief explanation of why you assigned it to a specific category or categories. Are Thomas's conclusions limited to the fields from which the examples are taken or do they apply to natural, behavioral, and medical sciences in general? Be ready to defend your answer.

3. For what purpose is the example of Clever Hans usually used? In what way does Thomas interpret it? Is his interpretation convincing? If so, why? If not, how could he make it more convincing?

PURPOSE, AUDIENCE, AND STRATEGIES

1. Is the purpose of this essay to criticize scientific research, our attitudes towards it, or both? Explain. If you think the essay has some other purpose, what is it? (See Glossary: Purpose.)

2. Identify the places in the essay where the author comments directly on the meaning of the examples. Does the commentary increase or decrease the effectiveness of the examples? To what extent does the commentary repeat or reinforce points made in the opening paragraph of the essay?

3. Thomas first published this essay in the *New England Journal of Medicine.* Is there any indication in the opening, however, that he intended to address the essay only to physicians and scientists? If not, are there any indications at the beginning of the essay or throughout it that the essay is directed at a more general audience? Has he, for instance, avoided technical language? Complicated explanations? (See Glossary: Audience.)

4. In what order of importance are the examples in this essay arranged: ascending order, descending order, or mixed order? (See Glossary: Arrangement.) What is the effect of this order? Could the order be reversed and still effectively support the thesis and the conclusion? Explain. Identify each example and suggest what pattern of development (narration, description, and so on) Thomas uses in it.

5. Several times in the essay the author summarizes scientific research. How does he keep the summaries from being too lengthy or boring, yet still manage to provide all the necessary information?

LANGUAGE AND STYLE

1. The generally accepted guidelines for scientific writing call for a style that avoids use of the first person point of view ("I believe" "we observed") and employs instead either the third person point of view ("it grew larger") or passive constructions ("It was observed that . . ."). (See Glossary: Point of View, Syntax.) In two paragraphs, Thomas uses the first person: paragraph 3 ("I read"; "I wish") and paragraph 7 ("A lady of our acquaintance"). Explain the effect of these shifts in point of view. Do they make the essay seem unscientific? In what ways do they make the selection more (or less) effective? (See Glossary: Evaluation.)

2. Describe the tone of the essay. (See Glossary: Tone.) To what extent are both the tone and the humor in the essay a result of the diction? (See Glossary: Diction.)

3. If you do not know some of the following words, look them up in a dictionary: *domesticated, genetically* (par. 1); *lexicon, cessation* (2); *inscrutable* (4); *sinuous* (5); *ethological* (6); *discommoded* (8).

WRITING ACTIVITIES

1. Write an essay that uses examples to call into question some widely held assumption. You might wish to take a hard look at the belief that success in school leads to success in a career; that most men feel threatened by strong, aggressive women; or that technology has greatly improved the quality of life. In order to make your essay convincing, use at least three separate, well-developed examples.

2. Prepare an essay in which you offer an interpretation of a recent social trend or cultural phenomenon. Make sure your interpretation is surprising, unusual, or controversial enough so that most readers will accept it only if you provide support through reasonable examples. Be sure to develop the examples in sufficient detail so they are convincing.

❧ FOX BUTTERFIELD

Fox Butterfield has spent much of his life studying China and Chinese culture. Born in Lancaster, Pennsylvania, in 1939, he studied at Harvard, receiving a bachelor's degree in 1961 and a master's degree (in Chinese history) in 1964. He spent 1961–62 in Taiwan as a Fulbright Fellow and returned in 1967–69 as a Ford Foundation Fellow. Butterfield has worked as a reporter for the *Washington Post* and the *New York Times*. As a *Times* reporter, he was part of the team that prepared the Pulitzer-prize-winning *The Pentagon Papers* (1971). His understanding of Chinese culture and his ability to speak Chinese both came into play during his appointment as the first *New York Times* bureau chief in Peking, The People's Republic of China (1979–81). He is the author (with Kwang-Ching Liu) of *American Missionaries in China* (1965) and the author of *China: Alive in the Bitter Sea* (1982), which won the American Book Award for nonfiction. Currently he is Boston bureau chief of the *New York Times*.

Foreign Devils

"Foreign Devils" is the opening section of a chapter with the same name in *China: Alive in the Bitter Sea,* a work that draws on the author's talents as a journalist and as a historian. In the book as a whole, Butterfield attempts to create a realistic social and political portrait of contemporary China, cutting through the romantic myths that often distort our view of China as well as our "cultural condescension, an unwillingness to look at things from the Chinese perspective." "Foreign Devils" serves these larger purposes as well as a more restricted aim: to explain the Chinese attitude towards foreigners.

Though the selection contains several brief narratives, it is not in itself a narrative because the stories are linked not to each other but to the generalizations about Chinese culture (both explicit and implicit) that they support and develop. The emphasis throughout is on providing a variety of detail to help us consider the subject from many different angles and to view ourselves through others' eyes.

Is it not a pleasure to have friends come from afar?
Confucius, in the opening passage of the Analects

My four-year-old son, Ethan, and I were walking down the 1
Avenue of Eternal Tranquility outside the Peking Hotel on a blustery
fall afternoon when I noticed a bespectacled man in his fifties,
dressed in a shabby gray overcoat, staring at us. I had long since
become accustomed to the Chinese habit of gawking at foreigners.
They gathered in front of the Peking Hotel, where I lived and worked
for the first year I was stationed in China, and surrounded any
Westerner who emerged. It was always friendly, simple curiosity,
never menacing. And Ethan was a special marvel, with long blond
hair trimmed in a Buster Brown cut and the build of a miniature
fullback.

This spectator was so intense that he began to follow us, a few 2
steps off to the left, never taking his eyes off us. He was still staring
at us when, with a loud thwack, he walked straight into a tree. His
horn-rimmed glasses split neatly in two over the bridge of his nose,
the two halves dropping to the pavement and smashing. He was
stunned by the blow, bouncing off a few feet before falling to the
ground. A trickle of blood flowed from a gash on his forehead. I
went over to try to help him, but he looked up at me and smiled.
Where an American would have cursed or cried out in anger, he
smiled.

As much as any other during my twenty months in China, this 3
tragicomic encounter illustrated how bizarre foreigners seem to
Chinese, how exotic Westerners are in Chinese eyes. For in a land
of people who all have straight dark hair, our hair is not hair color
at all, but yellow, brown, even red, curly, not straight, like old
Chinese paintings of demons. Our bodies are too fat and covered
with horrible fuzz, like animals; Chinese have smooth, hairless skin.
In a country where history weighs heavily, we foreigners have too
much bouncing vitality and always try to get things accomplished
too quickly. Perhaps because of our richer diet, we have energy to
waste that Chinese prefer to conserve for the long haul. If we move
in allegro, Chinese are keyed in adagio. We are too frank; we can
quarrel in public and then make up later without fear of losing face
and causing permanent enmity.

The gap between Chinese and foreigners is almost unbridgeable. 4
Every Monday through Saturday I sat in *The Times*'s office—an

ordinary hotel room supplemented by three filing cabinets, a book-case, and a typewriter—with my Chinese assistant, Wu Qianwei. Lanky and angular, with an incorrigible cowlick and heavy Coke-bottle glasses, he was assigned to me by the Diplomatic Services Bureau, the government agency which provides foreign diplomats and journalists with everything from housing to maids and chauf-feurs. But despite our constant physical proximity and a certain slow warmth that developed between us, Wu still referred to me, when he was talking to other Chinese in the room or over the phone, as the *wai-guo-ren,* literally, the "external country person," the for-eigner. When I lived in Taiwan for three years as a graduate student and later as a part-time correspondent for *The Times,* the neighbor-hood children always shouted, *"Yang-gui-zi"* (Foreign devil), when I walked in and out of the house.

China's greatest twentieth-century writer, Lu Xun, observed,   5
"Throughout the ages, the Chinese have had only two ways of looking at foreigners, up to them as superior beings or down on them as wild animals. They have never been able to treat them as friends, to consider them as people like themselves."

This sense of separateness has a long history. For 4,000 years,   6
the Chinese rested secure in their superiority. The Chinese empire was unquestionably the greatest in the world, the "Central King-dom," its boundaries coterminous with civilization. Outside it were only barbarians. The Chinese Emperor was the "Sun of Heaven," mediator between heaven and earth; China had invented paper, gunpowder, and the compass; its poetry and art neared the sublime; its system of government by an elite of ethical bureaucrats had achieved perfect equipoise. Not even famines, floods, or conquest by alien nomads disturbed its serenity for long. In the early legends of the origin of the universe in China, there is an odd omission. There is no hint of any hero who led the Chinese to China from elsewhere. It was assumed that the Chinese originated in China.

The pride all this inspired among the Chinese is something   7
beyond Western experience and comprehension. "Nationalism" is too paltry a word to describe it, for to the Chinese, China was a synthesis of people, territory, language, history, art, and philosophy, more like a religion than simply another nation state. In the twentieth century Chinese xenophobia became a potent force contributing to the Communists' victory, as many frustrated middle-class Chinese intellectuals and hungry peasants threw in their lot with Mao when

they came to believe that only the Communists could expel the Japanese and make China strong again.

If nationalism has now gone out of style for many people in 8 Europe and America, it has not for Chinese. At a banquet my wife, Barbara, and I attended in the immense East Room of the Great Hall of the People given by Pan American World Airlines to mark the beginning of its flight from New York to Peking, several Chinese officials were discussing the news they had just heard that John Lennon had been shot in New York. The menu that evening included sharks' fin soup with crab meat, roast goose with plum sauce, candied white fungus, and giant sliced prawns with chillies. Pan Am had added to the festivities by giving each guest a battery-operated quartz alarm clock, a trinket the Chinese at our table had never seen before. But they were concerned about Lennon. He was a famous singer, wasn't he, with some British musical group? a stern-faced cadre in a black Mao suit asked. Yes, said another, he had been honored by the Queen for his services to England. The shooting was a real tragedy, the second man added.

"Lennon certainly earned a lot of foreign exchange for his coun- 9 try." For the Chinese, that was John Lennon's epitaph; not the member of the Beatles, or the singer who pioneered a new musical idiom, or the pacifist, but the patriot.

RESPONSES AND IDEAS

1. It is often easier to identify traits of other cultures than to recognize similar traits in our own culture. As part of your response to this essay, list common American attitudes about ourselves and about other cultures that might be considered elements of American nationalism. Then, after looking over Butterfield's discussion of the historical roots of Chinese nationalism, write a brief account of those features of our history that contributed substantially to our national outlook; take into account relatively recent events and forces as well as earlier ones.

2. To what extent is the title of this selection ironic? (See Glossary: "Irony.") Is the quotation from Confucius that opens the selection ironic? If so, in what way? What other elements of the piece, if any, are ironic? Using specific evidence from the essay, support or attack this statement: "Butterfield seems to see the Chinese as 'Foreign Devils' almost as much as they view Westerners in this way."

3. State in your own words what appears to be the Chinese definition of *patriot* (pars. 8–9). Then write a favorable definition of patriotism that

you think most Americans would find acceptable. If you think it is impossible to arrive at such a definition, explain why.

PURPOSE, AUDIENCE, AND STRATEGIES

1. In this piece, Butterfield discusses the sources of Chinese nationalism. Does this mean that the purpose of the selection is to isolate the causes and effects of nationalism? If not, what is the purpose? (See Glossary: Purpose.)

2. What assumptions does Butterfield make about his audience's knowledge of Chinese culture? Is he writing for fellow foreign correspondents? For professors of Chinese civilization? For a clearly hostile, anticommunist audience? For Americans of Chinese descent? Choose several of Butterfield's examples to illustrate your definition of his intended audience.

3. Is there an explicit thesis statement in this selection? If not, construct a thesis statement for it and then decide if the piece would benefit from such a statement. If the selection already contains an explicit thesis, indicate whether you think it might be improved in any way and suggest possible revisions. (See Glossary: Thesis.)

4. What strategy does the author use in the opening of this selection? (See Glossary: Introduction.) Is it effective? How many paragraphs in the selection contain direct or indirect references to the title? In what ways do these references help unify the selection? (See Glossary: Unity.)

5. What are the different sources for the examples Butterfield uses? Does he provide a single example in each paragraph, or does he use some other strategy? Indicate which of the examples in this selection are designed to shock or surprise readers, and explain why Butterfield might have chosen to use them.

LANGUAGE AND STYLE

1. Is the diction in this selection abstract or concrete? Does the degree of concreteness vary? If so, why? What do Butterfield's word choice (diction) and his choice of examples reveal about his attitude towards the Chinese? About his own relationships (or lack of them) with the Chinese people he knew? (See Glossary: Diction.)

2. What sentence patterns does Butterfield use in paragraph 3 to emphasize contrasts between Chinese and Westerners? (See Glossary: Syntax; Parallelism.) Explain how he keeps these strategies from seeming too repetitive.

3. If you do not understand some of the following terms, look them up in a dictionary: *bespectacled* (par. 1); *tragicomic, allegro, adagio, frank, enmity* (3); *proximity* (4); *coterminous, mediator, sublime, ethical, equipoise, nomads* (6); *synthesis, xenophobia* (7); *epitaph* (9).

WRITING ACTIVITIES

1. Write an essay in which you explain through examples the special qualities of life in a community (a small town, an inner-city neighborhood) or the outlook and values of a cultural, social, or religious group (recent immigrants from a foreign country, long-distance runners, Orthodox Jews or born-again Christians).

2. Why do you like junk food? What pleasures do comic books provide? What makes video games so interesting, even addictive? Explain to a potentially skeptical audience what it is that you find so attractive in junk food, comics, video games, or some other feature of contemporary culture. Use detailed examples to allow readers to understand and share your enjoyment.

❧ DONNA WOOLFOLK CROSS

Donna Woolfolk Cross, born in 1947 in New York, received a B.A. from the University of Pennsylvania and an M.A. from UCLA. She has been an advertising copywriter but now teaches at Onondaga Community College near Syracuse, New York. Among her publications are *Word Abuse* (1979); *Mediaspeak: How Television Makes Up Your Mind* (1983); *Daddy's Little Girl* (1983) (with her father, the novelist William Woolfolk); and a college textbook, *Speaking of Words* (with James McKillop). Most of Cross's writing focuses on ways language shapes the way we live, either helping us see reality clearly or distorting our vision. In *Mediaspeak* she describes the impact of television, one of the most important forces in our lives: "The language of television, which I call Mediaspeak, is the house we all live in. Mediaspeak is not merely a way of communicating: it is a way of *perceiving* reality. It provides us with our windows on the world."

Sin, Suffer, and Repent

"Sin, Suffer, and Repent" is the opening part of a chapter with the same title in *Mediaspeak*. Despite its humor, "Sin, Suffer, and Repent" has a serious purpose. In it, Cross explains some of the many ways soap operas present inaccurate portraits of life and tries to alert us to some of the potentially harmful effects of these shows. In the introduction to *Mediaspeak* Cross says, ". . . we seem oddly unaware that much of what we believe to be true derives from television." The many illustrations in "Sin, Suffer, and Repent" not only support her specific observations about soap operas but also serve the broader purpose of informing us. Still, we may well suspect that the relish with which the author describes episodes from the serials indicates that she enjoys watching them.

Soap operas reverse Tolstoy's famous assertion in *Anna Karenina* that "Happy families are all alike; every unhappy family is unhappy in its own way." On soaps, *every* family is unhappy, and each is unhappy in more or less the same way.

—*Marjorie Perloff*

It is the hope of every advertiser to habituate the housewife to an engrossing narrative whose optimum length is forever and at the same time to saturate all levels of her consciousness with the miracle of a given product, so she will be aware of it all the days of her life and mutter its name in her sleep.

—*James Thurber*

In July 1969, when the entire nation was glued to television sets 1
watching the first man walk on the moon, an irate woman called a
Wausau, Wisconsin, TV station to complain that her favorite soap
opera was not being shown that day and why was that. The station
manager replied, "This is probably the most important news story
of the century, something you may never again see the equal of."
Unimpressed, the lady replied, "Well, I hope they crash."

One can hardly blame her. For weeks, she had been worrying 2
that Audrey might be going blind, that Alice would marry that
scoundrel Michael, and that Dr. Hardy might not discover his patient
Peter to be his long-lost natural son before the boy died of a brain
tumor. Suddenly, in the heat of all these crises, she was cut off from
all information about these people and forced to watch the comings
and goings of men in rubber suits whom she had never met. It was
enough to unhinge anybody.

Dedicated watchers of soap operas often confuse fact with fic- 3
tion.[1] Sometimes this can be endearing, sometimes ludicrous. During
the Senate Watergate hearings (which were broadcast on daytime
television), viewers whose favorite soap operas were preempted simply adopted the hearings as substitute soaps. Daniel Shorr reports
that the listeners began "telephoning the networks to criticize slow-
moving sequences, suggesting script changes and asking for the
return of favorite witnesses, like 'that nice John Dean.'"

Stars of soap operas tell hair-raising stories of their encounters 4
with fans suffering from this affliction. Susan Lucci, who plays the
promiscuous Erica Kane on "All My Children," tells of a time she
was riding in a parade: "We were in a crowd of about 250,000,
traveling in an antique open car moving ver-r-ry slowly. At that time
in the series I was involved with a character named Nick. Some man
broke through, came right up to the car and said to me, 'Why don't
you give *me* a little bit of what you've been giving Nick?'" The man
hung onto the car, menacingly, until she was rescued by the police.
Another time, when she was in church, the reverent silence was
broken by a woman's astonished remark, "Oh my god, Erica prays!"

---

1. Contrary to popular belief, soap operas are not the harmless pastime of lonely
housewives only. Recent surveys show that many high school and college students, as
well as many working and professional people, are addicted to soaps. A sizable chunk
of the audience is men. Such well-known people as Sammy Davis, Jr., Van Cliburn,
John Connally, and Supreme Court Justice Thurgood Marshall admit to being fans of
one or more soap operas.

Margaret Mason, who plays the villainous Lisa Anderson in "Days of Our Lives," was accosted by a woman who poured a carton of milk all over her in the supermarket. And once a woman actually tried to force her car off the Ventura Freeway.

Just as viewers come to confuse the actors with their roles, so too they see the soap image of life in America as real. The National Institute of Mental Health reported that a majority of Americans actually adopt what they see in soap operas to handle their own life problems. The images are not only "true to life"; they are a guide for living. 5

What, then, is the image of life on soap operas? For one thing, marriage is touted as the *ne plus ultra* of a woman's existence. Living together is not a respectable condition and is tolerated only as long as one of the partners (usually the woman) is bucking for eventual marriage. Casual sex is out; only the most despicable villains engage in it: "Diane has no respect for marriage or any of the values we were brought up with. She's a vicious, immoral woman." Occasionally, a woman will speak out against marriage, but it's clear that in her heart of hearts she really wants it. Women who are genuinely not interested in marriage do not appear on soap operas except as occasional caricatures, misguided and immature in their thinking. Reporter Martha McGee appeared on "Ryan's Hope" just long enough to titillate the leading man with remarks like, "I don't know if you're my heart's desire, but you're sexy as hell." Punished for this kind of heretical remark, she was last seen sobbing brokenly in a telephone booth. 6

No, love and marriage still go together like a horse and carriage in soap operas, though many marriages don't last long enough for the couple to put away all the wedding gifts. As Cornell professor Rose Goldsen says, this is a world of "fly-apart marriages, throwaway husbands, throwaway wives." There is rarely any clear logic behind the dissolution of these relationships; indeed, the TV formula seems to be: the happier the marriage, the more perilous the couple's future. A blissful marriage is the kiss of death: "I just can't believe it about Alice and Steve. I mean, they were the *perfect* couple, the absolute *perfect* couple!" 7

Most marriages are not pulled apart by internal flaws but by external tampering—often by a jealous rival: "C'mon, Peter. Stay for just one more drink. Jan won't mind. And anyway, the night's still young. Isn't it nice to be together all nice and cozy like this?" 8

Often the wife has willfully brought this state of affairs on herself   9
by committing that most heinous of all offenses: neglecting her man.
"NHM" almost always occurs when the woman becomes too
wrapped up in her career. Every time Rachel Corey went to New
York City for a weekend to further her career as a sculptress, her
marriage tottered. At this writing, Ellen Dalton's marriage to Mark
appears to be headed for big trouble as a result of her business trip
to Chicago:

> Erica: I warned you, Ellen, not to let your job interfere with your
> marriage.
> Ellen: I have tried to do my best for my marriage *and* my job . . . Mark
> had no right to stomp out of here just now.
> Erica: Don't you understand? He just couldn't take anymore.
> Ellen: What do you mean?
> Erica: It's not just the trip to Chicago that Mark resents. It's your putting
> your job before having a family.
> Ellen: I demand the right to be treated as an equal. I don't have to
> apologize because I don't agree to have a child the minute my
> husband snaps his fingers. I'm going to Chicago like a big girl and
> I'm going to do the job I was hired to do. (stalks out the door)
> Erica: (musing to herself) Well, I may be old-fashioned, but that's no
> way to hold onto your man.

Career women do appear frequently on soap operas, but the   10
ones who are romantically successful treat their careers as a kind of
sideline. Female cardiologists devote fifteen years of their lives to
advanced medical training, then spend most of their time in the
hospital coffee shop. One man remarked to a career woman who
was about to leave her job, "Oh Kate, you'll miss working. Those
long lunches, those intimate cocktail hours!" Women residents apparently schedule all their medical emergencies before dinnertime,
because if they should have to stay late at the hospital, it's the
beginning of the end for their marriages. It's interesting to speculate
how they might work this out:

> Nurse: Oh my God, Dr. Peterson, the patient's hemorrhaging!
> Dr. Peterson: Sorry, nurse, it'll have to wait. If I don't get my meat loaf
> in by a quarter to six, it'll never be ready before my husband gets
> home.

Husbands, weak-minded souls, cannot be expected to hold out   11
against the advances of any attractive woman, even one for whom
they have contempt, if their wives aren't around. Meatloafless, they

are very easily seduced. The clear suggestion is that they could hardly have been expected to do otherwise:

> "Well, after all, Karen, you weren't around very much during that time. It's not surprising that Michael turned to Pat for a little comfort and understanding."

If, in the brief span of time allotted to them, a couple manage to have intercourse, the woman is certain to become pregnant. Contraception on soap operas is such a sometime thing that even the Pope could scarcely object to it. The birth rate on soaps is eight times as high as the United States birthrate; indeed it's higher than the birthrate of any underdeveloped nation in the world. This rabbitlike reproduction is fraught with peril. One recent study revealed that out of nineteen soap opera pregnancies, eight resulted in miscarriages and three in death for the mother. Rose Goldsen has estimated that the odds are 7 to 10 against any fetus making it to full term, worse if you include getting through the birth canal. Women on soap operas miscarry at the drop of a pin. And of course, miscarriages are rarely caused by any defect with mother or baby: again, external forces are to blame. Often, miscarriage is brought on by an unappreciative or unfaithful mate. For example, on "Another World," Alice, the heroine, suffered a miscarriage when her husband visited his ex-wife Rachel. One woman lost her baby because her husband came home drunk. This plot twist is no doubt particularly appealing to women viewers because of the instant revenge visited upon the transgressing mate. They can fantasize about similar punishment for husbandly malfeasance in their own lives—and about his inevitable guilt and repentance:

> Husband: (stonily) Jennifer, these potatoes are too gluey. I can't eat this!
> Wife: (clutches her belly) Oh no!
> Husband: What? What is it?
> Wife: It's the baby! Something's wrong—call the doctor!
> Husband: Oh my God, what have I done?
> *Later, at the hospital:*
> Doctor: I'm sorry, Mr. Henson, but your wife has lost the baby.
> Husband: (brokenly) I didn't know, I didn't know. How could I have attacked her potatoes so viciously with her in such a delicate condition!
> Doctor: Now, now. You mustn't blame yourself. We still don't know exactly what causes miscarriages except that they happen for a complicated set of physical and emotional reasons.
> Husband: Oh, thank you, Doctor.
> Doctor: Of course, carping about the potatoes couldn't have *helped.*

Miscarriage is effective as a punishment because it is one of the 13 very worst things that can happen to a woman on a soap opera. In the world of soaps, the one thing every good and worthwhile woman wants is a baby. Soap operas never depict childless women as admirable. These "real people" do not include women like Katharine Hepburn, who once announced that she never wanted to have children because "the first time the kid said no to me, I'd kill it!" Childless women are either to be pitied, if there are physical reasons that prevent them from getting pregnant, or condemned, if they are childless by choice.

Second only to neglecting her man in her hierarchy of female 14 crime is having an abortion. No admirable character *ever* gets an abortion on a soap opera. Occasionally, however, a virtuous woman will consider it, usually for one of two reasons: she doesn't want the man she loves to feel "trapped" into marrying her; or she has been "violated" by her husband's best friend, a member of the underworld, or her delivery boy, who may also be her long-lost half brother. But she always "comes around" in the end, her love for "the new life growing inside me" conquering her misgivings. If the baby should happen to survive the perilous journey through the birth canal (illegitimate babies get miscarried at a far higher rate than legitimate ones), she never has any regrets. Why should she? Babies on soap operas never drool, spit up, or throw scrambled eggs in their mothers' faces. Babyhood (and its inevitable counterpart, motherhood) is "sold" to American women as slickly as soap. Kimberly, of "Ryan's Hope," is so distressed when she finds out she is pregnant that she runs away from home. She has the baby, prematurely, while alone and unattended on a deserted houseboat. It is a difficult and dangerous birth. But once the baby is born, Kimberly is all maternal affection. "Where is she?" she shouts. "Why won't they let me see my little girl?" By the end of the day, she announces, "If anything happens to this baby, I don't know what I'll do!"

Mothers are never tired, sleepless, or discouraged. Radiant, they 15 boast about the baby's virtues:

Well, he's just the smartest, best little baby in the whole wide world!

He looks just like his daddy—those big blue eyes, that enchanting smile!

Look at her little hands and feet. Have you ever seen anything more adorable! And she's good as gold—really, no trouble at all. She's Mommy's precious little princess, aren't you, darling?

One producer of a (now defunct) soap opera actually wanted, 16
as a promotion gimmick for one of the plotlines, to give away one
baby a week as a prize! The idea was abandoned only because of
the lack of cooperation from adoption agencies.

After the age of about ten months, children are of no interest in 17
soap operas unless they are hit by a car or contract a fever of
unknown origin, in which case they occasion a lot of hand-wringing
and pious sentiments from all the adults. If the producers cannot
arrange any such misfortune, the rule is that children are not to be
seen or heard. Having a young child around would interrupt the
endless raveling of the sleeve of romance. It won't do to have little
Bobby need to go on the potty or have his nose blown in the middle
of the adults' complicated lives, which have, as one critic says, "all
the immediacy of a toothache and the urgency of a telegram."

You may hear a good deal of pious talk about a young child's 18
need for stability and love, but usually only when a couple's marriage
is on the rocks. Children on soap operas still go to sleep at night
having no idea whether one or both of their parents will be around
in the morning—a situation which brings to mind Lady Bracknell's
remark in *The Importance of Being Earnest:* "Losing one parent
might be regarded as a misfortune; losing two seems like careless-
ness."

Children on soap operas are secondary. Because they serve 19
largely as foils for the adult characters, their development does not
follow the slow, steady pattern of the rest of the action.[2] Their growth
is marked by a series of sudden and unsettling metamorphoses as
new and older juvenile actors assume the role. On Tuesday, little
Terence is cooing in his cradle. On Monday next, he is the terror of
the Little League. By Thursday, his voice begins to change. Friday
night is his first date. He wakes up on Monday a drug-crazed

2. The pace of many soap operas has picked up considerably in the last few
years, as audience surveys have revealed a strong viewer interest in action-and-
adventure stories. Before 1980, however, plot movement on the soaps was glacierlike,
and on the earliest soaps, almost imperceptible. James Thurber claimed that it took
one male character in a soap three days to get an answer to the simple question,
"Where have you been?" He wrote, "If . . . you missed an automobile accident that
occurred on a Monday broadcast, you could pick it up the following Thursday and
find the leading woman character still unconscious and her husband still moaning
over her beside the wrecked car. In one program . . . [a character] said, 'It doesn't
seem possible to me that Ralph Wilde arrived here only yesterday.' It should not have
seemed possible to anyone else, either, since Ralph Wilde had arrived, as mortal time
goes, thirteen days before."

teenager, ready to be put to use creating heartbreak and grief for his devoted mother and her new husband. He stays fifteen years old for about two to five years (more if he managed to get into lots of scrapes), and then one day he again emerges from the off-camera cocoon transformed into a full-fledged adult, with all the rights, privileges, pain, and perfidy of that elite corps. And so the cycle continues.

Under the surface of romantic complications, soap operas sell a   20 vision of morality and American family life, of a society where marriage is the highest good, sex the greatest evil, where babies are worshiped and abortion condemned, where motherhood is exalted and children ignored. It is a vision of a world devoid of social conflict. There are hardly any short-order cooks, bus drivers, mechanics, construction workers, or farmers on soap operas. Bue-collar problems do not enter these immaculate homes. No one suffers from flat feet or derrière spread from long hours spent at an unrewarding or frustrating job. The upwardly mobile professionals who populate soap operas love their work, probably because they are hardly ever at it—one lawyer clocked in at his office exactly once in three months. Their problems are those of people with time on their hands to covet the neighbor's wife, track down villains, betray friends, and enjoy what one observer has called "the perils of Country Club Place."

RESPONSES AND IDEAS

1. In a single paragraph summarize Cross's criticism of the portrayal of reality in soap operas in such a way that someone who has not read the essay will be able to understand her point of view.

2. "Sin, Suffer, and Repent" contains a number of generalizations about soap operas, many of them at the beginning of paragraphs. Identify as many as you can, and indicate how many are supported by evidence (examples).

3. If you watch daytime soap operas or similar prime-time shows, discuss Cross's description of their contents, indicating whether what she says applies to current shows or whether their content has changed in substantial ways since this selection was published in 1983.

PURPOSE, AUDIENCE, AND STRATEGIES

1. Is Cross addressing regular soap opera watchers with this essay? If so, why does she provide so many examples? Is the essay addressed to

people who seldom, if ever, watch the programs? To people who read fan magazines and plot summaries in the newspaper? How would you define the intended audience for the essay?

2.   In your own words state Cross's specific purpose in this essay. Is her general purpose expository, argumentative, or a mixture of the two? (See Glossary: Purpose, Argument, Exposition.)

3.   What favorable things can you say about the portrayal of life in soap operas and the impact of the shows on our own lives? If you can think of favorable things to say about the shows, why do you think Cross ignores such a point of view in her comments?

4.   How frequently does the author use quotations from television programs or from other writers? In what different ways does she present them in the text? Does she use any hypothetical examples? What role do the two opening quotations play in the selection? Would it be changed in any significant way if they were omitted?

5.   Many of the paragraphs in this essay consist of an opening generaliza- tion followed by supporting examples. Identify the paragraphs that follow this pattern. (See Glossary: Paragraphs.) Does the lack of variety in paragraph structure help or hurt the piece? In what ways?

LANGUAGE AND STYLE

1.   At times, the words Cross uses to describe scenes from television pro- grams seem as vivid and startling as the events themselves. Analyze a paragraph from the essay to isolate the words that add liveliness and color to the examples. (See Glossary: Diction.) Does the tone of this essay display consistent disapproval of the television shows? If not, is there an ambivalence in the tone that affects the impact of the essay? (See Glossary: Tone.)

2.   What statements in paragraphs 12–19 contain hyperbole (obvious ex- aggeration)? (See Glossary: Figures of Speech.) Explain why the exag- geration either increases or undermines the effectiveness of the exam- ples. Does it increase or decrease your willingness to believe her conclusions? Why?

3.   If you do not know what some of the following words mean, look them up in a dictionary: *irate* (par. 1); *ludicrous, preempted* (3); *promis- cuous, accosted* (4); *ne plus ultra, despicable, titillate, heretical* (6); *dissolution* (7); *cardiologists, hemorrhaging* (10); *contraception, fraught, malfeasance* (10); *hierarchy* (11); *defunct* (13); *derrière* (17).

WRITING ACTIVITIES

1.   In an essay of your own, take issue with Cross's interpretation of soap operas and use examples to support your thesis. You might wish to

argue that the portrait of life offered by soap operas is quite realistic, especially when compared to that offered by other kinds of television shows. You might argue that, as in cowboy movies, mystery novels, and other forms of romantic melodrama, the way soap operas reshape events to make a moral point is perfectly acceptable. Or you might offer one of many other possible defenses of this perenially popular and frequently criticized form of entertainment.

2. In an essay, offer your judgment of the accuracy or inaccuracy of events portrayed by television news programs, newspapers, or newsmagazines. In supporting your thesis, choose examples that are clearly representative of the medium you are criticizing and develop them fully so that they are convincing.

🐚 WILLIAM F. BUCKLEY, JR.

William F. Buckley, Jr., is an essayist, editor, political commentator, and novelist whose energy and productivity are chronicled in *Overdrive* (1983), an autobiographical record of one week in 1982. The consistent themes in all of Buckley's activities and writings are his political conservatism and his belief that the combination of capitalism and democracy represents the true spirit and strength of our society. His conservative outlook, which often places principles above pragmatism, is evident in his many volumes of political and social commentary, beginning with *God and Man at Yale: The Superstitions of Academic Freedom* (1951). His entertaining series of spy novels built around the dashing CIA agent Blackford Oakes provides a conservative perspective on major political events of the 1950's and 1960's. The series includes *Saving the Queen* (1976), *Who's on First?* (1980), *Marco Polo, If You Can* (1982), and *The Story of Henri Tod* (1983).

Buckley's ideas and influence reach many people through his work as editor-in-chief of *National Review* and as host of Public Television's "Firing Line." His writings also appear frequently in general circulation magazines and in newspapers. Buckley was born in 1925 in New York where he currently lives with his wife and son.

Why Don't We Complain?

This essay illustrates how a number of patterns can work together within the framework of the exemplification pattern. The essay contains elements of the cause-and-effect pattern in its search for the causes of reputed American passivity and in its warning about the potential effects of this trait. In the episodes from Buckley's experience that make up much of the essay, it uses narration and description effectively. It also mingles purposes, sometimes explaining our behavior, at other times arguing in a general way that we should change the way we act. The primary pattern here, however, is exemplification. The essay consists of a series of examples, accompanied by a commentary on their meaning, that state and reinforce Buckley's point, ending in an attempt to connect our country's political policies to the ideas presented earlier through the examples of personal behavior.

Buckley's political and social outlook is evident in this essay, as it is in the rest of his work. Even if you disagree with him, you should take note of the way the personal examples make his opinions easy to understand and enjoyable to read. In this selection, as in much of his writing, Buckley's personality and the everyday events in his life are the center of much attention. The hint of self-mockery in his self-portraits and the liveliness of his prose style usually keep Buckley's talk of himself from being boring or ego-tistical. Whether he manages to avoid these negative qualities in this essay is a matter for you to decide.

It was the very last coach and the only empty seat on the entire train, so there was no turning back. The problem was to breathe. Outside, the temperature was below freezing. Inside the railroad car the temperature must have been about 85 degrees. I took off my overcoat, and a few minutes later my jacket, and noticed that the car was flecked with the white shirts of the passengers. I soon found my hand moving to loosen my tie. From one end of the car to the other, as we rattled through Westchester County, we sweated; but we did not moan. 1

I watched the train conductor appear at the head of the car. "Tickets, all tickets, please!" In a more virile age, I thought, the passengers would seize the conductor and strap him down on a seat over the radiator to share the fate of his patrons. He shuffled down the aisle picking up tickets, punching commutation cards. *No one addressed a word to him.* He approached my seat, and I drew a deep breath of resolution. "Conductor," I began with a considerable edge to my voice. . . . Instantly the doleful eyes of my seatmate turned tiredly from his newspaper to fix me with a resentful stare: what question could be so important as to justify my sibilant intrusion into his stupor? I was shaken by those eyes. I am incapable of making a discreet fuss, so I mumbled a question about what time were we due in Stamford (I didn't even ask whether it would be before or after dehydration could be expected to set in), got my reply, and went back to my newspaper and to wiping my brow. 2

The conductor had nonchalantly walked down the gauntlet of eighty sweating American freemen, and not one of them had asked him to explain why the passengers in that car had been consigned to suffer. There is nothing to be done when the temperature *outdoors* is 85 degrees, and indoors the air conditioner has broken down; obviously when that happens there is nothing to do, except perhaps curse the day that one was born. But when the temperature outdoors is below freezing, it takes a positive act of will on somebody's part 3 to set the temperature *indoors* at 85. Somewhere a valve was turned too far, a furnace overstocked, a thermostat maladjusted: something that could easily be remedied by turning off the heat and allowing the great outdoors to come indoors. All this is so obvious. What is not obvious is what has happened to the American people.

It isn't just the commuters, whom we have come to visualize as   4
a supine breed who have got on to the trick of suspending their sensory faculties twice a day while they submit to the creeping dissolution of the railroad industry. It isn't just they who have given up trying to rectify irrational vexations. It is the American people everywhere.

A few weeks ago at a large movie theater I turned to my wife   5
and said, "The picture is out of focus." "Be quiet," she answered. I obeyed. But a few minutes later I raised the point, again, with mounting impatience. "It will be all right in a minute," she said apprehensively. (She would rather lose her eyesight than be around when I make one of my infrequent scenes.) I waited. It was *just* out of focus—not glaringly out, but out. My vision is 20-20, and I assume that is the vision, adjusted, of most people in the movie house. So, after hectoring my wife throughout the first reel, I finally prevailed upon her to admit that it *was* off, and very annoying. We then settled down, coming to rest on the presumption that: (a) someone connected with the management of the theater must soon notice the blur and make the correction; or (b) that someone seated near the rear of the house would make the complaint in behalf of those of us up front; or (c) that—any minute now—the entire house would explode into catcalls and foot stamping, calling dramatic attention to the irksome distortion.

What happened was nothing. The movie ended, as it had begun,   6
just out of focus, and as we trooped out, we stretched our faces in a variety of contortions to accustom the eye to the shock of normal focus.

I think it is safe to say that everybody suffered on that occasion.   7
And I think it is safe to assume that everyone was expecting someone else to take the initiative in going back to speak to the manager. And it is probably true even that if we had supposed the movie would run right through the blurred image, someone surely would have summoned up the purposive indignation to get up out of his seat and file his complaint.

But notice that no one did. And the reason no one did is because   8
we are all increasingly anxious in America to be unobtrusive, we
are reluctant to make our voices heard, hesitant about claiming our
rights; we are afraid that our cause is unjust, or that if it is not
unjust, that it is ambiguous, or if not even that, that it is too trivial
to justify the horrors of a confrontation with Authority; we will sit
in an oven or endure a racking headache before undertaking a head-
on, I'm-here-to-tell-you complaint. That tendency to passive compliance, to a heedless endurance, is something to keep one's eyes on—
in sharp focus.

I myself can occasionally summon the courage to complain, but   9
I cannot, as I have intimated, complain softly. My own instinct is so
strong to let the thing ride, to forget about it—to expect that someone
will take the matter up, when the grievance is collective, in my
behalf—that it is only when the provocation is at a very special key,
whose vibrations touch simultaneously a complexus of nerves, aller-
gies, and passions, that I catch fire and find the reserves of courage
and assertiveness to speak up. When that happens, I get quite carried
away. My blood gets hot, my brow wet, I become unbearably and
unconscionably sarcastic and bellicose; I am girded for a total show-
down.

Why should that be? Why could not I (or anyone else) on that   10
railroad coach have said simply to the conductor, "Sir"—I take that
back: that sounds sarcastic—"Conductor, would you be good enough
to turn down the heat? I am extremely hot. In fact, I tend to get hot
every time the temperature reaches 85 degr—" Strike that last sentence. Just end it with the simple statement that you are extremely
hot, and let the conductor infer the cause.

Every New Year's Eve I resolve to do something about the   11
Milquetoast in me and vow to speak up, calmly, for my rights, and
for the betterment of our society, on every appropriate occasion.
Entering last New Year's Eve, I was fortified in my resolve because
that morning at breakfast I had had to ask the waitress three times
for a glass of milk. She finally brought it—after I had finished my
eggs, which is when I don't want it any more. I did not have the
manliness to order her to take the milk back, but settled instead for
a cowardly sulk, and ostentatiously refused to drink the milk—
though I later paid for it—rather than state plainly to the hostess, as
I should have, why I had not drunk it, and would not pay for it.

So by the time the New Year ushered out the Old, riding in on   12
my morning's indignation and stimulated by the gastric juices of
resolution that flow so faithfully on New Year's Eve, I rendered my
vow. Henceforward I would conquer my shyness, my despicable
disposition to supineness. I would speak out like a man against the
unnecessary annoyances of our time.

Forty-eight hours later, I was standing in line at the ski repair   13
store in Pico Peak, Vermont. All I needed, to get on with my skiing,
was the loan, for one minute, of a small screwdriver, to tighten a
loose binding. Behind the counter in the workshop were two men.
One was industriously engaged in servicing the complicated requirements of a young lady at the head of the line, and obviously he
would be tied up for quite a while. The other—"Jiggs," his workmate
called him—was a middle-aged man, who sat in a chair puffing a
pipe, exchanging small talk with his working partner. My pulse
began its telltale acceleration. The minutes ticked on. I stared at the
idle shopkeeper, hoping to shame him into action, but he was impervious to my telepathic reproof and continued his small talk with
his friend, brazenly insensitive to the nervous demands of six good
men who were raring to ski.

Suddenly my New Year's Eve resolution struck me. It was now   14
or never. I broke from my place in line and marched to the counter.
I was going to control myself. I dug my nails into my palms. My
effort was only partially successful:

"If you are not too busy," I said icily, "would you mind handing   15
me a screwdriver?"

Work stopped and everyone turned his eyes on me, and I ex-   16
perienced that mortification I always feel when I am the center of
centripetal shafts of curiosity, resentment, perplexity.

But the worst was yet to come. "I am sorry, sir," said Jiggs   17
deferentially, moving the pipe from his mouth. "I am not supposed
to move. I have just had a heart attack." That was the signal for a
great whirring noise that descended from heaven. We looked,
stricken, out the window, and it appeared as though a cyclone had
suddenly focused on the snowy courtyard between the shop and the
ski lift. Suddenly a gigantic army helicopter materialized, and hovered down to a landing. Two men jumped out of the plane carrying
a stretcher, tore into the ski shop, and lifted the shopkeeper onto the
stretcher. Jiggs bade his companion good-by, was whisked out the
door, into the plane, up to the heavens, down—we learned—to a

nearby army hospital. I looked up manfully—into a score of man-eating eyes. I put the experience down as a reversal.

As I write this, on an airplane, I have run out of paper and need 18 to reach into my briefcase under my legs for more. I cannot do this until my empty lunch tray is removed from my lap. I arrested the stewardess as she passed empty-handed down the aisle on the way to the kitchen to fetch the lunch trays for the passengers up forward who haven't been served yet. "Would you please take my tray?" "Just a *moment*, sir!" she said, and marched on sternly. Shall I tell her that since she is headed for the kitchen *anyway*, it could not delay the feeding of the other passengers by more than two seconds nec-essary to stash away my empty tray? Or remind her that not fifteen minutes ago she spoke unctuously into the loudspeaker the words undoubtedly devised by the airline's highly paid public relations counselor: "If there is anything I or Miss French can do for you to make your trip more enjoyable, *please* let us—" I have run out of paper.

I think the observable reluctance of the majority of Americans 19 to assert themselves in minor matters is related to our increased sense of helplessness in an age of technology and centralized political and economic power. For generations, Americans who were too hot, or too cold, got up and did something about it. Now we call the plumber, or the electrician, or the furnace man. The habit of looking after our own needs obviously had something to do with the asser-tiveness that characterized the American family familiar to readers of American literature. With the technification of life goes our direct responsibility for our material environment, and we are conditioned to adopt a position of helplessness not only as regards the broken air conditioner, but as regards the overheated train. It takes an expert to fix the former, but not the latter; yet these distinctions, as we withdraw into helplessness, tend to fade away.

Our notorious political apathy is a related phenomenon. Every 20 year, whether the Republican or the Democratic Party is in office, more and more power drains away from the individual to feed vast reservoirs in far-off places; and we have less and less say about the shape of events which shape our future. From this alienation of personal power comes the sense of resignation with which we accept the political dispensations of a powerful government whose hold upon us continues to increase.

An editor of a national weekly news magazine told me a few 21 years ago that as few as a dozen letters of protest against an editorial stance of his magazine was enough to convene a plenipotentiary meeting of the board of editors to review policy. "So few people complain, or make their voices heard," he explained to me, "that we assume a dozen letters represent the inarticulated views of thousands of readers." In the past ten years, he said, the volume of mail has noticeably decreased, even though the circulation of his magazine has risen.

When our voices are finally mute, when we have finally sup- 22
pressed the natural instinct to complain, whether the vexation is trivial or grave, we shall have become automatons, incapable of feeling. When Premier Khrushchev first came to this country late in 1959, he was primed, we are informed, to experience the bitter resentment of the American people against his tyranny, against his persecutions, against the movement which is responsible for the great number of American deaths in Korea, for billions in taxes every year, and for life everlasting on the brink of disaster; but Khrushchev was pleasantly surprised, and reported back to the Russian people that he had been met with overwhelming cordiality (read: apathy), except, to be sure, for "a few fascists who followed me around with their wretched posters, and should be horse-whipped."

I may be crazy, but I say there would have been lots more 23
posters in a society where train temperatures in the dead of winter are not allowed to climb to 85 degrees without complaint.

RESPONSES AND IDEAS

1. Buckley is well known for his conservative political and social outlook; do his views in this essay reflect a specifically conservative outlook? To provide a basis for your response, list five political issues and five broad social issues (for example, relations with communist countries, abortion) about which conservatives and liberals generally disagree. Then describe the positions each group would hold on the various issues. Next, look at the essay to see if Buckley takes a clearly conservative position on any of the various issues he raises, and decide if the essay as a whole has a conservative perspective.

2. Does the episode in the ski shop support or contradict Buckley's point about complaining? Explain. If it seems to contradict his point, why did he include it in the essay?

3. What is the thesis of this essay? If it is unstated, summarize Buckley's main idea in a single sentence. (See Glossary: Thesis.)

PURPOSE, AUDIENCE, AND STRATEGIES

1. Does Buckley believe that readers will find the examples drawn from his experience representative of their experiences? If so, is he correct in assuming this, and does he take any steps to select and present the examples in a way that will make them seem representative? What steps does he take?

2. How does Buckley expect his readers to respond to the extended examples in the essay? Does he expect different responses to each example? For instance, are there some examples readers will identify with easily and others that may evoke hostility?

3. Do you believe Buckley expects that his audience already shares his political views or is hostile to his views? Or does he assume some attitude in between? Cite specific passages to support your definition of his intended audience.

4. What examples other than those based on personal experience does Buckley use? Is their placement significant in any way? Would the essay be more effective with fewer personal examples, and if so, what might be used in their place?

5. Identify the paragraphs that follow a pattern other than exemplification. If you can state what pattern they follow, do so. How does Buckley keep the mixture of patterns in the essay from creating confusion? (See Glossary: Unity.)

LANGUAGE AND STYLE

1. Many of the sentences in paragraphs 3, 9, 13, and 22 are longer than those we usually encounter in essays. What resources of syntax does Buckley employ to keep them from becoming too confusing? (See Glossary: Syntax.) Do you find them easy to understand despite their length? Why, or why not?

2. Many of the words Buckley uses in this essay are not in the regular vocabulary of even highly-educated people. Take several representative passages from the essay and analyze them to determine whether the diction can be regarded as sophisticated, as pretentious, or in some other way. (See Glossary Diction.) What is the likely effect of the diction on the average reader? Does it mean that the essay is addressed only to highly-educated readers?

3. If you do not know the meaning of some of the following words, look them up in a dictionary: *virile, doleful, sibilant, discreet* (par. 2); *gauntlet, consigned* (3); *supine, faculties, dissolution, rectify* (4); *hectoring* (5); *purposive* (7); *unobtrusive, ambiguous* (8); *provocation, complexus, unconscionably, bellicose, girded* (9); *infer* (10); *ostentatiously* (11); *impervious, reproof* (13); *centripetal* (16); *deferentially*

(17); *unctuously* (18); *technification* (19); *apathy, phenomenon, dispensations* (20); *stance, plenipotentiary, inarticulated* (21); *automatons* (22).

WRITING ACTIVITIES

1. What do our favorite sports (football, baseball, basketball), our pastimes (hunting and fishing, camping, running and exercising), or our favorite kinds of entertainment (rock music, movies about outlaws and adventurers) reveal about our attitudes and values? Write an essay explaining what a sport, form of entertainment, or other activity reveals about those who enjoy it and use examples to explain and support your conclusions.

2. Is it true that people often buy a product not because they need it but because of the status it confers on them? Write an essay that uses examples to support this or a similar generalization.

Writing Suggestions

EXPLORATIONS

1. Think back over the last few days to an event, person, or idea that angered you. Then make a list of examples of similar things that have angered you in the past. When you are finished with the list, look it over to see if the examples suggest a conclusion worth sharing with your readers. If they do, use the list as a starting point for writing an essay.

2. Glance through a newspaper or a magazine looking for articles about fashions, fads, popular hobbies and sports, or celebrities. See if these items suggest any generalizations about our society that might be the basis for an essay, and if they do, begin your search for useful examples with the items you have already found. Imagine as your audience a person your age emigrating from an isolated Iron Curtain country to this country.

3. Write a paragraph-length example to support or illustrate one (or more) of the following general statements. Include as much vivid descriptive detail as you can without making the example difficult to read or understand:

    Sport builds muscles, not character.
    Television presents a distorted view of life.
    Learning how to take a test is as important as understanding the material covered in courses.
    Physical appearance often is (*or* is not) a key to a person's character.
    Failure can often be a source of wisdom.
    Drug and alcohol abuse is (*or* is not) a serious problem in many high schools.
    Guilt is a healthy (*or* unhealthy) emotion.
    Americans are in love with cars.

4. Medical researchers have recently begun to argue that our habits rather than infectious diseases are the worst enemies of our health. Make a list of examples of at least ten unhealthy habits and ten healthy ones. If these examples suggest any insights or advice worth sharing, use them as the basis for an essay.

ACTIVITIES

1. Writing can use examples in many different ways—to explain a difficult concept, to provide a touch of humor, to help convince readers to take action on a problem, among other uses. Try to identify at least five different uses by looking at some of the sources listed below, or others

you find, and then in two or three sentences describe each different use you have identified:

a technology magazine like *Science Digest*
a college textbook
a glossy magazine like *Cosmopolitan* or *GQ*
a sports magazine
a travel guide
a scholarly book on anthropology, history, or literature
a how-to book or article
a news magazine
a newspaper editorial

2. What writing situations or kinds of topics would be well suited for a thesis-and-support essay? Give a minimum of four examples and explain briefly why one particular kind of topic or situation would be well suited. (For a start, think of the kinds of papers you have been assigned in college classes, or the kind of tests you have taken.)

3. Choose an essay from this collection following one of the other patterns (with the exception of narration and description). Identify some of the long and short examples it contains, if any, and indicate why and how it uses them. You might begin by looking at the essays on "Division and Classification" (Chapter 9), "Comparison" (Chapter 5), and "Argument and Persuasion" (Chapter 10).

4. Look through a general interest magazine for articles that use numerous examples, for articles that are organized around a series of examples, and for articles, if any, that use the thesis-and-support or representative-example patterns. Choose one that has a clear organization and outline it, identifying, for example, the introduction and thesis, extended examples used for support, other supporting materials, and the conclusion. (Your instructor may wish to have the entire class look at a particular magazine or specific issues to furnish the basis for class discussion.)

MODELS

1. Using "Clever Animals" as a model, write an essay in which you contradict a widely accepted interpretation of the way people act. You might, for example, try to show that politicians are caring people; that physicians make less money than people think; that plumbers solve complex problems, not just repair leaky faucets; or that women at home with their families face substantial intellectual challenges in their work.

2. Taking "Foreign Devils" as a model, use examples to explain a cultural phenomenon or the outlook of a particular group: how hunters view people who oppose their sport, for example; how conservatives (or liberals) view their political opponents; or the outlook of the average high school student on drug use.

3. Building your strategies on those used in "Sin, Suffer, and Repent," discuss the distortion of reality in television shows other than the kind discussed by Cross, or in other media, such as paperback adventure stories, romance novels, or films.

4. Using William F. Buckley's approach, present examples of everyday behavior (they need not be personal) that reflect national attitudes; if you think we should change these attitudes, say so. You could explore attitudes towards sports, fair play, the opposite sex, money, people on welfare, competition, or the government, among many others.

5

🪶 COMPARISON

Exploring Similarities and Differences

WHAT COMPARISON DOES

A customer in a department store is examining two cameras, trying to decide which one to buy. She considers their similarities (both take good pictures, are easy to use, and have interchangeable lenses) as well as their differences (one costs seventy-five dollars more because it focuses automatically). Reasoning that an automatic rangefinder will make taking pictures a lot more fun, she picks the more expensive model, even though it will stretch her budget a bit.

We go through similar steps every time we choose the bargain-priced cola over the nationally advertised brand or turn the TV dial to the movie rather than the basketball game or the adventure show. At the heart of each of these decisions is the process of *comparison,* involving both the examination of similarities (comparison) and of differences (contrast). By helping us look closely enough at the alternatives to understand how they are alike and how they differ, the use of comparison enables us to see each more clearly than we might if we viewed it alone. Comparison, moreover, gives us standards on which to base a decision: because the bargain product is as good or almost as good as the national brand, we have a reason for choosing it.

As a writing strategy, comparison can be a means to evaluate the merits of each alternative or to argue for a particular choice. A pamphlet on eye care might compare the features of glasses, hard contact lenses, and soft contact lenses, pointing out their advantages and disadvantages, but recommending only that people choose the

163

product most appropriate for their pocketbooks or work and recreational habits. In contrast, a newspaper editorial evaluating proposals for solving a toxic waste problem would probably argue for one of the solutions, contrasting its effectiveness, cost, and safety with those of the alternatives.

Not every comparison leads to a choice, however. Some comparisons add to our understanding and knowledge, helping explain one subject by measuring it against another or examining their connections and contrasts. A brief, relaxing vacation helps us understand stresses on the job or at school that we did not fully appreciate before. Reading about child-raising techniques in the South Pacific or in nineteenth-century England alerts us to special features of the parent-child relationship in contemporary America as well as to the experiences common to childhood regardless of time or place.

In written form, such comparisons need to be more than simple lists of similarities and differences. They should offer fresh interpretations and insights as well as evidence for their conclusions, with the appropriate amount of support depending on both the subject and the audience. Thus a comparison whose significance is already clear to readers can concentrate on providing useful or interesting information. When new Medicaid or Social Security disability regulations are announced, for example, most elderly people will already understand the need to compare them with the previous rules: They know the new regulations may affect their participation in the programs. What they will need and expect from an essay on the changes will be an indication of any substantial ways the rules have been altered along with a quick summary of the changes to allow them to verify their continued eligibility.

Yet explanations and supporting detail are necessary when a comparison offers readers a novel or controversial perspective or when it reveals surprising relationships. For instance, to be convincing, a comparison suggesting that supposedly dangerous sports like stock car racing and skydiving are in many ways safer than activities like boating, swimming, or running would need to present detailed evidence for its assertions. It might show, perhaps, that participants in the supposedly riskier activities generally pay better attention to their physical preparation and the safety of their equipment.

Comparison is a favorite tool of researchers in all fields, and in their hands explanation often becomes exploration as well. Archaeologists trying to understand why the ancient Mayans abandoned their cities in the forests of southern Mexico might look to parallel behavior in other jungle civilizations in order to find a reasonable explanation. Or a specialist in children's literature might compare the style and moral outlook of children's books of the 1880s with those of the 1970s and 1980s in order to highlight the significant features of each and at the same time to point out some of the enduring qualities of good children's literature. We compare things, then, not simply as a mechanical task but as a way of learning about them.

Because comparison is such a powerful tool for discovery, college instructors often assign papers or projects calling for it as a pattern of thought and expression: "Compare family structures typical of middle-class suburban communities to those typical of economically depressed inner-city communities" [sociology class], "Compare current American policies toward intervention in Central and South America to those of the early nineteenth century (Monroe Doctrine) and the late nineteenth and early twentieth centuries (including the Big Stick policies)" [American history class].

Comparison is a way of evaluating, explaining, and exploring, not an end in itself. Readers, therefore, expect a written comparison to serve some purpose: evaluate alternatives, make a point that is interesting or surprising, or share insights arrived at through the process of comparison itself. In the paragraph below, for example, the anthropologist Edward Hall puts comparison to work explaining why an English student at an American university felt that his roommate and other Americans never allowed him any privacy. As he put it, "I'm walking around the apartment and it seems that whenever I want to be alone my roommate starts talking to me. Pretty soon he's asking 'What's the matter?' and wants to know if I'm angry. By then I am angry and say something." Hall discusses the phenomenon this way:

> It took some time but finally we were able to identify most of the contrasting features of the American and British problems that were in conflict in this case. When the American wants to be alone he goes into a room and shuts the door—he depends on architectural features for screening. For an American to refuse to talk to someone else present in the same room, to give them the "silent treatment," is the ultimate form of rejection and a sure sign of great displeasure. The English, on the other hand, lacking rooms of their own since childhood, never developed the practice of using space as a refuge from others. They have in

effect internalized a set of barriers, which they erect and which others are supposed to recognize. Therefore, the more the Englishman shuts himself off when he is with an American the more likely the American is to break in to assure himself that all is well. Tension lasts until the two get to know each other. The important point is that the spatial and architectural needs of each are not the same at all (*The Hidden Dimension*, 1966).

Comparison is essential to Hall's investigation and explanation. By comparing the behavior of the two cultural groups he identifies the unique characteristics of each. Without comparison, it would be impossible to tell whether a particular type of behavior is restricted to the group or is typical of other societies as well. Moreover, by viewing the behavior of the Englishman and his roommate as similar to that of other members of their cultural groups, Hall is able to explain the difficulties of their relationship in terms of the broader conflicts between the values and behavior of their respective cultures.

If the two people involved in this case were an American and a Russian, or an Italian and an Australian, the cultural differences would be so clear that the detailed explanation Hall gives might be unnecessary. But most people assume that English and American cultures are quite similar; in this paragraph, therefore, Hall uses comparison as a pattern of expression to highlight the differences and to show how they support his interpretation of the phenomenon. The paragraph opens by stating the subject—that is, the contrasting features that the case displays—and by indicating that the writer will view the case as a matter of cultural conflict. It then presents the contrasts between the cultures in a modified subject-by-subject comparison (see p. 174) and concludes with a direct statement of the author's interpretation (his thesis): "the spatial and architectural needs of each [culture] are not the same at all."

To be effective, a comparison needs to deal with subjects that are similar enough to make it worthwhile. When the subjects belong to the same general class or when they share important traits, then a comparison may highlight common elements and help identify unique characteristics. When the subjects of a comparison have little in common, the process will do little to shed light on either one or on their relationship. It might be interesting to compare the habits of wolves and foxes, for example, since both are predators and behave in broadly similar ways, though with some intriguing and revealing differences. It would not make sense, however, to compare either to the giraffe because the extensive and obvious differences would overwhelm the relatively few similarities.

Yet one special use of comparison, *analogy,* calls for subjects that are different in all but a few significant ways. Although people have few traits in common with sheep, for instance, both people and sheep sometimes blindly follow a leader, and this similarity can be used to make a point about human behavior. Analogy may be used to explain a complex, abstract, or unusual subject in familiar and easy-to-understand terms. To explain, for example, how an electromagnetic field transmits radio signals from a station's transmitter to the radio in a listener's home, the physicist Richard Feynman asks his readers to imagine two corks floating in a pool of water. If we jiggle one cork, he points out, the waves in the water transmit the influence of our action and the second cork begins to jiggle too. Like the water, an electromagnetic field transmits energy from sender to receiver in the form of waves—electromagnetic waves—conveying radio signals, a television picture, a radar image, or even plain light.

Analogy may also be used to explore a controversy or problem, arguing for a fresh perspective or for new approaches and solutions. The comparison of earth to a self-contained spaceship is often used to argue that we must abandon our view that once pollutants have been dispersed into the air they are gone for good. The analogy points out that pollutants do not disappear into the universe but are carried along inside the blanket of air that forms the outer skin of "Spaceship Earth" as it travels through the cosmos.

An analogy is therefore a limited form of comparison that focuses on one rather than both of the elements in a comparison, explaining or exploring the difficult or unfamiliar element by means of the familiar or more easily understood one. In writing, analogies commonly are only brief comparisons, metaphors designed to illuminate a specific point or to suggest ideas for further speculation ("The Japanese corporation is like a family, with the workers and the managers each responsible for keeping the social unit together, and with each group willing to sacrifice for the good of the whole in the same way Japanese parents and children are willing to sacrifice for their families").

Occasionally a writer develops an analogy at greater length in order to encourage readers to explore a new outlook (as does Barry

Lopez in "My Horse") or to explain a difficult or interesting concept. In the following passages from his book *Basin and Range* (1981), John McPhee uses several analogies to explain why geologists like the places where roads have been cut through hills and ridges and what they see when they stare at the rocks exposed by roadbuilding:

> Geologists on the whole are inconsistent drivers. When a roadcut presents itself, they tend to lurch and weave. To them, the roadcut is a portal, a fragment of a regional story, a proscenium arch that leads their imaginations into the earth and through the surrounding terrain. In the rock itself are the essential clues to the scenes in which the rock began to form—a lake in Wyoming, about as large as Huron; a shallow ocean reaching westward from Washington Crossing; big rivers that rose in Nevada and fell through California to the sea. Unfortunately, highway departments tend to obscure such scenes. They scatter seed wherever they think it will grow. They "hair everything over"—as geologists around the country will typically complain.

Each of the analogies McPhee uses presents a slightly different perspective: the roadcut is a doorway to the past ("a portal"), part of the geological history of an area ("fragment of a regional story"), and the framework surrounding a stage ("proscenium arch") on which the play of geologic events can be observed. Once readers come to view roadcuts in these ways they can understand why geologists value them so highly as "clues to the scenes" of past ages of the earth and why they get so upset when highway departments cover the scenes with grass.

Extended analogies often ask readers to adopt a speculative, *as if* perspective. They may suggest creative ways of viewing a problem ("Look at the conflicts within an organization as if they were arguments among the various members of a family, and see whether the conflicts can be resolved in ways similar to those that work successfully in families"). They may also be used to argue for a particular point of view. People who argue that international organizations should make birth control rather than an increase in the food supply their top priority in dealing with overpopulation often use the so-called lifeboat analogy: the world is like a lifeboat in danger of sinking because too many people are in it; we must reduce the number of people through birth control, not add to the number of people struggling to get in by providing enough food to encourage them to keep on reproducing at the present rate. This latter form of analogy might be termed *argumentative* even though it does not offer direct logical proof; instead, it encourages readers to view a controversy in a fresh way, hoping thereby to make them more receptive to the arguments and evidence the writer has to offer in support of a position.

Comparisons longer than a sentence or two make great demands. They ask readers to keep in mind two (or more) subjects, the various similarities and differences among them, and the relationships of all these to the point the author is trying to make.

Readers in turn expect their attention to be rewarded by new information, by a fresh interpretation or insight, or by evidence that clearly supports the author's arguments. To say that readers look for the specific purpose behind a comparison is to repeat what is true of any essay, of course, but this point deserves special attention because the comparison pattern can set a trap for writers. The danger for anyone writing a comparison is that the process itself, the examining and arranging of detail, may be so involving that the larger purpose of the writing is ignored, obscured, or forgotten, and the essay fails to make a clear point.

Lack of a clear point, or thesis, is seldom a problem in comparisons that evaluate or argue. The emphasis on relative merits of the alternatives reminds writers to tie the whole together with a judgment or recommendation. Too often, however, the only real purpose behind some other use of the pattern seems to be a desire to list all the details the writer has discovered: "Playing tennis on a clay court is different in many ways from playing on a grass or asphalt surface, yet it is also similar in some important respects." Perhaps because a subject like tennis (camping, scuba diving, astrology, or rock music) is interesting to them personally or because the process of comparison is complicated and involving, many writers fail to consider whether the information they present will be interesting to readers, too. Or they forget that comparison should help readers look at events in fresh ways: "The next time you hear that one of the world's top tennis players has lost to an unknown in a major tournament, ask if the match was played on clay courts. A clay court can turn tennis into a very different game from the one played on grass or asphalt."

Admittedly, a paper written for a college course may not furnish insights and interpretations that an instructor will regard as new.

College instructors, however, assign comparison papers not because they expect students to come up with original insights (though they certainly reward fresh ideas) but because they want students to investigate a subject on their own and to go beyond the level of understanding reached in class discussion. The following section suggests some ways to take a comparison beyond the obvious so that it becomes a way of discovering and sharing insights.

THE PROCESS

As with the other patterns of expression, the decision to use comparison should be based on your purpose and subject ("When I worked in a hospital, I was amazed by how much more nurses seemed to know about the condition of the patients than the doctors did. Maybe I can develop this contrast into a paper that will change the way my readers view both doctors and nurses"), or on the demands of particular occasions ("We need to decide whether to put our resources as a company into research, marketing, or improving manufacturing productivity. Write up your evaluation of these alternatives"). In college, the comparison pattern is often part of a writing assignment, probably because instructors see it as an essential pattern of thought and expression and want to give their students practice using it. Sometimes the assignment leaves the topic more or less open ("Write a comparison-contrast essay about some aspect of campus life, a comparison of campus and national politics, for instance" or "Compare contemporary American attitudes towards marriage to those in one of the other cultures we have studied this semester"). At other times the assignment specifies a topic ("Compare the campaign strategies of Mondale and Reagan in the 1984 presidential election").

Topics appropriate for a comparison can come from personal experience (including work, school, and leisure activities), reading and television (including world and national issues, current forms of entertainment), or the classroom (any field of study can suggest a number of possible topics). Techniques like brainstorming and freewriting (see Chapter 1, "Reading and Writing") can also be used to uncover possible subjects for comparison or to suggest ideas and interpretations worth sharing.

Another way to investigate possible topics is to ask questions based on features that are commonly the focus of comparisons, including:

Physical aspects (shape, color, size, texture)
Historical period (Middle Ages, Renaissance, 1780s, 1950s)
Uses (to amuse, to heal, to make money)
Costs (financial, emotional, political, social)
Benefits (individual, social, political, environmental)
Context (cultural, social, economic)
Consequences (immediate and future effects)
Relationships (with other ideas, objects, people, organizations)
Structure (parts and their relationships; organization)
Processes (method of operation, instructions)

Each feature can suggest a variety of questions. Questions focusing on a historical period, for example, can uncover subjects ("What currently popular activity [sport, hobby, handicraft] was popular two hundred years ago and how much has it changed since then?"), or they can help explore and develop topics ("Golf was played in sixteenth-century Scotland. Has the game changed in significant ways since then? What elements have remained constant?"). In general, the more specific the questions, the more useful they are. You should also feel free to create questions that reflect your own interests and attitudes: What does it feel like to ride on a motorcycle in comparison to riding in a car? How much do students learn from different teaching methods? Is the work involved in an engineering degree greater than that called for by a liberal arts major?

As soon as you have selected a possible topic and have begun to explore it, you should start thinking about points of comparison around which to build an essay. A *point of comparison* is a feature of the group or class to which the subjects belong. Doctors and nurses, for example, are health professionals, and like all members of this group (also including pharmacists and dentists), they can be compared on the basis of their training; their attitude towards patients; their contributions to the healing process; their responsibilities; their views on the respective roles of diet, medication, and therapy in the treatment of illness; and the size of their salaries.

Not all possible points of comparison are worth talking about, however. Most readers will be unsurprised to learn that cats, dogs, and birds make different kinds of pets, nor will they want to spend time reading about how much care a bird takes compared to the care of a cat or dog. Yet information about how much each species contributes to the psychological health of its owner or an evaluation of the pets based on the kinds of diseases they can transmit to humans would get the attention of many people.

A college assignment frequently identifies points that would make a good basis for comparison or, on the other hand, those that are too obvious to be worth talking about, as does this assignment from a world literature course:

> Aside from the differences in the forms of the *Odyssey* (epic poem) and *Huckleberry Finn* (comic novel), there are differences in the presentation of the hero and his character in each work that express the philosophies of life of each author. *Choose and compare some aspect of these heroes in order to come to some conclusions about the philosophies of life of each author.* (Be sure to choose the same aspect of each to compare—for example, response to danger or relationship to society. The fact that they are both on a journey is not enough; you would have to analyze the type and purpose of the journey.)

By listing possible points of comparison along with details that might be used to explain or explore them, you can begin to see which points are most worth covering, and you can come up with some tentative statements of purpose to guide the rest of the composing process, perhaps even a possible thesis statement for the final essay (see Glossary: Purpose, Thesis). Purpose statements should identify the major points of comparison and the specific impact the essay is to have on an audience:

> I want to convince my readers that moving mentally retarded citizens out of institutions into group homes is a very good idea because the homes provide better care at lower cost and help residents develop social skills.

> At the end of this essay I want readers to understand the most important differences between investing their money in a mutual fund (slower growth but safer; professional stock analysts do the work of selecting the stocks the fund invests in) and in common stocks (more risk but chances for bigger gains; much of the work of choosing the stock falls to the individual investor even when the broker provides help).

Thesis statements should be more specific than purpose statements and should indicate the particular judgment or interpretation the essay will support: "For all but the most sophisticated investors, mutual funds are a better buy than common stocks because they are safer and are also likely to provide a substantial return on the initial investment."

A list of points of comparison along with a purpose statement or thesis statement can be the basis of a plan to guide the writing of an essay. Such a plan may be anything from an informal list of points to a formal outline. The kind of plan you choose should depend on what works best for you and the complexity of the essay you are writing. Other planning strategies can be helpful too, including freewriting or clustering ideas developed through brainstorming. Whatever method you choose, some form of planning and preparation is usually very important because of the need to consider at length an audience's possible response and the need to construct a complex but clear organization for the finished essay. A list or other planning technique will also help you ascertain if the points of comparison around which you want to build an essay are too few or too insignificant to deserve extended discussion.

To avoid producing a comparison that presents little new or interesting information or that fails to make a clear point, you should use your plan in order to suggest questions about the possible responses of readers to the essay you have in mind: "How many of my readers are likely to know about this similarity (difference) already, and how much are they likely to know?" "In what ways will readers benefit from my explanation?" and "Will readers already know about or agree with my thesis, or will it be interesting and controversial enough to get and hold their attention?"

By putting your plan on paper, you will also be able to share it with classmates, friends, or a teacher to get responses that will help find potential strengths and weaknesses in what you plan to say. Here is part of the planning sheet one student, Jim Rivera, prepared for the assignment calling for a comparison of the heroes in the *Odyssey* and *Huckleberry Finn*:

Odyssey

   Odysseus—an epic hero, represents his society's values and traditions and is admired and respected (at end of poem defeats the suitors and restores order; participates in games at Nausicaa's palace and is shown to be superior)
   Deals with giants, gods, and other supernatural forces
   Lives out the fate determined by the gods (on trip to underworld Tiresias tells him his fate and he accepts it)

Huck Finn

Huck—a comic hero, is an outcast from society and is in conflict
    with his society's values (doesn't like wearing shoes and
    going to school and church so he eventually runs away;
    he accepts Jim, an escaped slave)
  Deals with various aspects of human society
  Huck struggles to define his fate (at the end of the novel he
    refuses to go back to civilization)

In organizing a comparison essay or paragraph, you need to
pay attention to presenting the different points of comparison and at
the same time to making clear the relationships among them. To do
both these things, most comparisons, short or long, follow a variation
of one of these patterns:

Subject-by subject pattern:
Introduction (subjects of comparison, thesis)
    Subject 1 (*Odyssey,* for instance)
        Feature 1 (character)
        Feature 2 (plot)
        Features 3, 4, 5, and so on
    Subject 2 (*Huckleberry Finn,* for instance)
        Feature 1 (character)
        Feature 2 (plot)
        Features 3, 4, 5, and so on
Conclusion (summary)

Point-by-point pattern:
Introduction (subjects of comparison, thesis)
    Feature 1 (character)
        Subject 1 (Odysseus)
        Subject 2 (Huck)
    Feature 2 (plot)
        Subject 1 (*Odyssey*)
        Subject 2 (*Huckleberry Finn*)
    Features 3, 4, 5, and so on
        Subject 1
        Subject 2
Conclusion (summary)

Although these patterns can be combined, the results tend to be confusing. The best approach is usually to choose a pattern appropriate to your subject and purpose and develop it consistently. The subject-by-subject pattern is useful when you wish to emphasize broad differences and similarities between the subjects. It is also most effective in shorter essays; longer essays following the pattern often seem to fall into two distinct parts, and it is usually difficult for readers to keep in mind the features of the first subject while they are reading the second half of a long essay. The point-by-point pattern works best for long papers and allows writers to emphasize that the subjects are different in some aspects but not in others. Yet the movement back and forth between the subjects can be confusing unless the relationships are signalled clearly, and in a long paper the pattern usually needs to be varied to keep readers from being bored by its repetitiveness.

Because it emphasizes similarities rather than differences, an analogy often follows a different pattern:

Basic analogy pattern:
Introduction (subject being compared, purpose of comparison)
    Main point of similarity
    Second point of similarity
    Third, fourth, and fifth points, and so on
Conclusion (limitations of the comparison, summary)

An extended analogy usually stops after covering the major points of similarity because extending the comparison to minor points often calls to mind the major differences between the subjects and thereby threatens the effectiveness of the entire analogy. An analogy used in an argument, however, may openly acknowledge the differences between the subjects in order to anticipate criticism.

Transitions signaling relationships among the elements in a comparison are an important guide to readers, as are topic sentences and other statements that provide reminders of the purpose of an essay (see Glossary: Topic Sentences). In revising a comparison essay, it is important to check that each section provides enough detail to give readers adequate information or to support the essay's thesis, that the role each section plays in accomplishing the overall purpose of the essay is indicated clearly, and that the elements of the subjects and their relationships are indicated by words like these:

> Words identifying aspects of a subject: *trait, characteristic, element part, segment, unit, feature*
>
> Words indicating relationships among subjects: *in comparison, in contrast, on the other side, on the other hand, likewise, moreover, similarly, in the same (different) manner, in addition, then, further, yet, but, however, nonetheless, first, second, third, although, still*

This paragraph from the final draft of Jim Rivera's paper comparing the *Odyssey* and *Huckleberry Finn* illustrates a number of strategies that can help readers understand and agree with the point being made in a comparison essay:

> In contrast with Odysseus's action of setting his house and community in order, Huck at the end of the novel rejects the values of home and civilization. At the end of the novel, Huck is offered a place in Aunt Polly's home as well as the money Judge Thatcher had been investing for him. Home and money represent to him all the values he has encountered and rejected along the journey, so he looks at them as a kind of prison. His friend Tom, too, now seems to him representative of the civilizing forces he cannot accept. Therefore he chooses to resume his quest alone, and he "lights out for the territory."

This paragraph opens with a transition that indicates its relationship to the discussion immediately preceding: "In contrast with Odysseus's action." The opening sentence then finishes by revealing the point of the paragraph in a phrase that also echos an interpretation of Huck that Rivera has been advancing throughout his paper (compare his planning sheet on pp. 173–174): "Huck . . . rejects the values of home and civilization." The three sentences in the body of the paragraph support the writer's interpretation of Huck. In their emphasis on Huck's rejection of "home" and "civilizing forces" they also provide a strong contrast with Odysseus's commitment to "his house and community" mentioned in the opening sentence. The final sentence reinforces the point of the paragraph. At all points in this paragraph, Jim Rivera thus makes his interpretation of Huck clear, and at the same time reminds readers of the overall structure and purpose of his comparison essay.

THE PATTERN IN ACTION

As a pattern of expression, comparison appears frequently in evaluations and comparison-contrast papers. It is also an important strategy in argument (see Chapter 10, "Argument and Persuasion"), and when combined with analysis it forms the issue analysis pattern (see Chapter 9, "Division and Classification"). Used along with other patterns, comparison (including analogy) can help the writer view alternatives, explore ideas, and clarify ideas. Indeed, most essays of medium length or longer contain comparisons ranging from a single sentence to several paragraphs or more.

Evaluation as a writing strategy calls for a comparison of the qualities of two or more alternatives—products, procedures, or courses of action—and a recommendation based on their relative merits. Probably the most familiar use of evaluation is in product reviews in magazines like *Consumer's Guide, Consumer Reports,* and *Car and Driver.* In addition, business, industry, government, and such large institutions as universities use evaluation in so-called recommendation reports whenever there is a need to choose among competing products ("Which computer system should we install?"), policies ("Should we award scholarships on the basis of need or merit?"), or courses of action ("Which system of quality control should we adopt in our newly automated factory?).

The standards or goals for a decision determine which features of the competing products or policies need to be examined. Products like computers are frequently compared on the basis of cost, durability, ease of use, and capacity. Policies are often judged according to their consistency with a company's objectives and other policies, their likelihood of success, and their cost to implement.

In most evaluations, the opening section announces the purpose. A product review, for example, commonly points out when and where the item is used and reminds readers of the importance of making a correct decision when they buy it. A recommendation report for a potential plant site might remind readers briefly that the new facility is needed to boost production capacity and to speed up distribution of finished goods. In most cases, the opening section then goes on to review the criteria (goals, standards) by which the alternatives will be judged.

The body of an evaluation usually follows a subject-by-subject pattern if the comparison is relatively simple, or a point-by-point pattern if the comparison involves more than two alternatives. Though the body may indicate some preliminary judgments, it is usually the closing that sums up the findings of the evaluation and makes a specific recommendation.

College writing assignments and essay examinations often call for comparison-contrast papers, either directly ("Compare and contrast mitosis and meiosis") or indirectly by asking students to "discuss" or "explore" the features of two or more comparable subjects. Typical subjects for a comparison include the styles of several painters, the structure of two poems, or the aims of different political movements.

A satisfactory response to such an assignment generally demonstrates (1) the student's knowledge of significant points of comparison between the subjects (determined to a great extent by the approach used in the class) and (2) the student's special insight into either of the two subjects or into their relationships. In writing a comparison-contrast paper, therefore, you should begin by identifying those features thought to be most important according to the method of analysis used in a particular class or the approach of a particular discipline. In writing a comparison paper for a literature course, for example, you would be expected to identify the features of works (symbolism, setting, characterization, and so on) that contributed most to its impact. In writing an essay examination for a sociology class stressing the role of conflict in society, you would need to pay attention to evidence of social conflict in your subjects. Having identified the basic features for comparison, you can look for other features worth mentioning and begin developing your own insights and interpretations.

The opening of a comparison-contrast paper should usually state the subjects to be compared and the major features to be examined. The thesis statement should point clearly to the author's interpretations and conclusions. The opening should also indicate why the subjects are worth investigating or what special perspective the writer believes comparison will provide. (This element is unnecessary in an examination essay because the motivation for the comparison arises from the examination itself.)

The body of a comparison-contrast essay generally follows either a simple subject-by-subject pattern or a point-by-point pattern. Each stage of the comparison, however, should examine the subjects in detail and show how the detail supports the writer's thesis. The conclusion should summarize the points covered (if the essay is relatively long) and restate the thesis in order to emphasize it.

Comparison can take many other forms in writing, some of which are illustrated by the readings in this chapter. Robert Jastrow's "Brains and Computers" uses comparison to explain the operation of both mechanical and natural thinking machines and to point out their many similarities. Bruce Catton's "Grant and Lee: A Study in Contrasts" presents and supports an interpretation of two important historical figures and the social and political forces they represent. Ellen Goodman's "The Challenge to Keep Family Together" uses comparison to explore and suggest new perspectives as well as to explain. Barry Lopez's "My Horse" combines comparison, analogy, and a number of other patterns in an imaginative excursion into the relationships among humans, animals, and machines.

❧ ROBERT JASTROW

Robert Jastrow was born in 1925 in New York City and studied at Columbia University, from which he received a Ph.D. He has taught at Dartmouth College and Columbia University and was formerly director of the Goddard Institute for Space Studies. He has written a textbook, *Astronomy: Fundamentals and Frontiers* (1972) (with Malcolm H. Thompson) and a trilogy of books describing the development of the universe and of human life: *Red Giants and White Dwarfs* (1967), *Until the Sun Dies* (1977), and *The Enchanted Loom* (1981).

Brains and Computers

In "Brains and Computers," a chapter from *The Enchanted Loom*, Jastrow explains the operation of both brains and computers by identifying the basic principles that govern them both. Readers who usually find computers confusing will discover that the carefully organized comparison and the simple definitions and examples in the essay make the essay quite readable and keep even the most technical parts of the explanation relatively easy to follow.

Circuits, wires and computing are strange terms to use for a   1
biological organ like the brain, made largely of water, and without electronic parts. Nonetheless, they are accurate terms because brains work in very much the same way as computers. Brains think; computers add and subtract; but both devices seem to work on the basis of the same fundamental steps in logical reasoning.

All arithmetic and mathematics can be broken down into these   2
fundamental steps. Most kinds of thinking can also be broken down into such steps. Only the highest realms of creative activity seem to defy this analysis, but it is possible that even creative thinking could be broken down in this way, if the subconscious mind could be penetrated to examine the processes that appear at the conscious level as the flash of insight, or the stroke of genius.

The basic logical steps that underlie all mathematics and all   3
reasoning are surprisingly simple. The most important ones are called AND and OR. AND is a code name for the reasoning that

180

says, "If 'a' is true *and* 'b' is true, then 'c' is true." OR is a code name for the reasoning that says, "IF 'a' is true *or* 'b' is true, then 'c' is true." These lines of reasoning are converted into electrical circuits by means of devices called "gates." In a computer the gates are made out of electronic parts—diodes or transistors. In the brain of an animal or a human, the gates are neurons or nerve cells. A gate—in a computer or in a brain—is an electrical pathway that opens up and allows electricity to pass through when certain conditions are satisfied. Normally, two wires go into one side of the gate, and another wire emerges from the other side of the gate. The two wires coming into the gate on one side represent the two ideas "a" *and* "b." The wire going out the other side of the gate represents the conclusion "c" based on these ideas. When a gate is wired up to be an AND gate, it works in such a way that if electrical signals flow into it from both the "a" and "b" wires, an electrical signal then flows out the other side through the "c" wire. From an electrical point of view, this is the same as saying, "If 'a' *and* 'b' are true, then 'c' is true."

When the gate is wired as an OR gate, on the other hand, it 4 permits electricity to pass through the outgoing, or "c," wire if an electrical signal comes into the other side through either the "a" wire *or* the "b" wire. Electrically, this is the same as saying, "If 'a' *or* 'b' is true, then 'c' is true."

How do these two kinds of gates do arithmetic? How do they 5 carry on a line of reasoning? Suppose a computer is about to add "1" and "1" to make "2"; this means that inside the computer a gate has two wires coming into it on one side, representing "1" and "1," and a wire coming out on the other side, representing "2". If the gate is wired as an AND gate, then, when electrical signals come into it through both of the "1" wires, it sends a signal out the other side through the "2" wire. This gate has added "1" and "1" electrically to make "2."

Slightly different kinds of gates, but based on the same idea, can 6 subtract, multiply and divide. Thousands of such gates, wired together in different combinations, can do income tax returns, algebra problems and higher mathematics. They can also be connected together to do the kinds of thinking and reasoning that enter into everyday life. Suppose, for example, that a company distributes several different lines of goods, and its management assigns a computer the task of keeping a continuous check on the inventories in these various product lines. Inside that computer, certain gates will be wired as AND gates to work in the following way: two wires coming into one side of the gate carry signals that indicate "stock depleted" and "sales volume heavy." If the stock is depleted *and* the sales are brisk, the gate opens, and a decision comes through: Order more goods!

OR gates are just as important in reasoning. Suppose that the   7
same company also relies on its computer for guidance in setting prices. That means that a certain gate inside the computers is wired as an OR gate; coming into one side of this gate is a wire that indicates cash flow, another wire that indicates prices charged by a competitor for similar products, and a third wire that indicates the inventory in this particular product. If the company needs cash, *or* it is being undersold by its competitors, *or* it has an excess inventory, then the decision gate opens and a command comes through: Cut prices!

In a simple computer, the gates are wired together permanently,   8
so that the computer can only do the same tasks over and over again. This kind of computer comes into the world wired to do one set of things, and can never depart from its fixed repertoire. A computer that solves the same problems in the same way, over and over again, is like a frog that can only snap at dark, moving spots; if either kind of brain is presented with a novel situation, it will react stupidly, or not react at all, because it lacks the wiring necessary for a new response to a new challenge. Such brains are unintelligent.

Larger, more complex computers have greater flexibility. In these   9
computers, the connections between the gates can be changed, and they can be wired up to do different kinds of things at different times; their repertoire is variable. The instructions for connecting the gates to do each particular kind of problem are stored in the computer's memory banks. These instructions are called the computer's "program." When a computer expert wants his machine to stop one kind of task and start another, he inserts a new program into the computer's memory. The new program automatically erases the old one, takes command of the machine, and sets about doing its appointed task.

However, this computer is still not intelligent; it has no innate   10
flexibility. The flexibility and intelligence reside in its programmer.

But if the memory banks of the computer are extremely large a great advance in computer design becomes possible, that marks a highlight in the evolution of computers comparable to the first appearance of the mammals on the earth. A computer with a very large memory can store a set of instructions lengthy enough to permit it to learn by experience, just like an intelligent animal. Learning by experience requires a large memory and a very long set of instructions, i.e., a complicated program, because it is a much more elaborate way of solving problems than a stereotyped response would be. When a brain—electronic or animal—learns by experience, it goes through the following steps: first, it tries an approach; then it compares its result with the desired result, i.e., the goal; then, if it succeeds in achieving its goal, it sends an instruction to its memory to use the same approach next time; in the case of failure, it searches through its reasoning or computations to pinpoint the main source of error; finally, the brain adjusts the faulty part of its program to bring the result into line with its desires. Every time the same problem arises, the brain repeats the sequence and makes new adjustments to its program. A large computer has programs that work in just that fashion. Like a brain, it modifies its reasoning as its experience develops. In this way, the computer gradually improves its performance. It is learning.

A brain that can learn possesses the beginnings of intelligence. 11 The requirements for this invaluable trait are, first, a good-sized memory, and, second, a wiring inside the brain that permits the circuits connecting the gates to be changed by the experience of life. In fact, in the best brains—judging brain quality entirely by intelligence—many circuits are unwired initially; that is, the animal is born with a large number of the gates in its brain more or less unconnected with one another. The gates become connected gradually, as the animal learns the best strategies for its survival. In man, the part of the brain filled with blank circuits at birth is greater than in any other animal; that is what is meant by the plasticity of human behavior.

Large computers have some essential attributes of an intelligent 12 brain: they have large memories, and they have gates whose connections can be modified by experience. However, the thinking of these computers tends to be narrow. The richness of human thought depends to a considerable degree on the enormous number of wires, or nerve fibers coming into each gate in the human brain. A gate in a computer has two, or three, or at most four wires entering on one side, and one wire coming out the other side. In the brain of an animal, the gates may have thousands of wires entering one side, instead of two or three. In the human brain, a gate may have as many as 100,000 wires entering it. Each wire comes from another gate or nerve cell. This means that every gate in the human brain is connected to as many as 100,000 other gates in other parts of the brain. During the process of thinking innumerable gates open and close throughout the brain. When one of these gates "decides" to open, the decision is the result of a complicated assessment involving inputs from thousands of other gates. This circumstance explains much of the difference between human thinking and computer thinking.

Furthermore, the gates in the brains of an animal or a human   13 do not work on an "all-or-nothing" basis. The AND gate in a computer, for example, will only open if *all* wires coming into it carry electrical signals. If one wire entering a computer gate fails to carry a signal, the gate remains shut. If every one of the 100,000 pathways into a gate in a human brain had to transmit an electrical signal before that gate could open, the brain would be paralyzed. Instead, most gates in the brain work on the principle of ALMOST, rather than AND or OR. The ALMOST gate makes human thought so imprecise, but so powerful. Suppose that 50,000 wires enter one side of a gate in a human brain; if this were an AND gate in a computer, all 50,000 things would have to be true simultaneously before that gate opened and let a signal through. In real life, 50,000 things are rarely true at the same time, and any brain that waited for such a high degree of assurance before it acted would be an exceedingly slow brain. It would hardly ever reach a decision, and the possessor of a brain like that would not be likely to pass its genes on to the next generation.

Real brains work very differently. Wired largely out of ALMOST   14 gates, they only require that, say, 10,000 or 15,000 things out of 50,000 shall be true about a situation before they act, or perhaps an even smaller number than that. As a consequence, they are inaccurate; they make mistakes sometimes; but they are very fast. In the struggle for survival, the value to the individual of the speed of such a brain more than offsets the disadvantages in its imprecision.

COMMENTARY

Many people refer to computers as brains—of a sort, at least. Far fewer people, however, refer to brains as computers, perhaps because to do so would mean admitting that human brains are similar in many ways to machines and not necessarily superior, either. This attitude leads to curiosity about the kind of comparison Jastrow attempts in this essay. He builds indirectly on the curiosity in the opening paragraph of the essay by remarking that words drawn from the science of computers are "strange terms" to use for a brain. Although the introduction might have been more effective if it had contained a direct appeal to the audience's curiosity, most readers are likely to regard the subjects of comparison themselves (announced clearly in the title) as interesting and significant enough to warrant reading the essay. From paragraph 8 to the end of the selection, moreover, Jastrow addresses the question of comparative intelligence—brain vs. computer—directly. He suggests that although computers can actually learn on their own, the ability of brains to make decisions without requiring complete certainty makes them both faster and more adaptable, hence superior in aiding our survival as individuals and as a species.

The comparison in paragraphs 1–7 has explanation as its primary aim. Taking the logical steps of AND and OR as points of comparison, Jastrow discusses the broad similarities between the devices. From paragraph 8 on, however, the comparison evaluates as well as explains, focusing mainly on the ability to respond to new or uncertain situations. The conclusion of each comparison is clear: the two devices have similar logical operations, but brains are superior in some ways. The two halves of the essay, moreover, form a unified whole, with the explanation in the first part forming the basis for the discussion of relative merits in the second half.

Many of the paragraphs in this essay are quite technical, particularly paragraphs 3–7. Yet by describing the logical operations as gates—an analogy based on the two states in which a gate can exist, open and shut—and by providing easy-to-understand examples and frequent definitions, Jastrow keeps his explanation of the process by which the devices operate relatively easy to understand. Nor is the vocabulary at any point particularly technical or unusual. Jastrow's comparison essay, therefore, addresses his readers' concerns in a

direct, clear manner, providing them with both worthwhile information and an interesting opinion about a question of growing
importance.

RESPONSES AND IDEAS

1. Respond to this essay either with a paragraph describing what you like,
    dislike, fear, or envy most about computers or with a paragraph pre-
    dicting some of the new roles computers will play in the next decade.

2. List the similarities and differences between brains and computers
    presented in this essay. Then list any obvious similarities or differences
    the author omits. Which of these might he have covered without harm-
    ing the unity of the essay? (See Glossary: Unity.)

3. Define in your own words an AND gate, an OR gate, and an ALMOST
    gate. How do these gates help distinguish brains from computers?

PURPOSE, AUDIENCE, AND STRATEGIES

1. Is the essay addressed to people who already know something about
    computers or to people who know very little? What evidence in the
    essay indicates the audience for which it is intended?

2. Where in the essay does Jastrow move from explaining the way brains
    and computers operate to evaluating their relative strengths and weak-
    nesses? Is there any evidence in the essay that the evaluation is an
    important part of the essay rather than simply an added feature de-
    signed to make it more interesting? If so, what is the evidence? Does
    the writer blend explanation and evaluation without destroying the
    unity of the essay? Explain.

3. Are there any places in the essay where readers who are unfamiliar
    with computers might find the explanations difficult to follow? If so,
    where are they and how might they be improved?

4. Does this essay follow a subject-by-subject pattern or a point-by-point
    pattern? Could the essay be organized in a more effective manner?
    How? Consider both the subject matter and the purpose of the essay.
    (See Glossary: Evaluation.)

5. What strategy does the author use to conclude this selection? What
    other closing strategies might be appropriate? (See Glossary: Closings.)

LANGUAGE AND STYLE

1. Where in the essay does the author use parallel paragraphs, sentences,
    or parts of sentences to emphasize the comparison? In what ways do

they help make the explanation clearer? Does he use them in the evaluation? In what way? (See Glossary: Parallelism.)

2. How does Jastrow use diction and syntax in paragraphs 11, 13, and 14 to emphasize the superiority of the human brain? (See Glossary: Diction, Syntax, Emphasis.)

3. If you do not know the meaning of any of the following words, look them up in the dictionary: *circuits* (par. 1): *diodes, transistors, neurons* (3); *inventories, depleted* (6); *cash flow, excess* (7); *repertoire, novel* (8); *variable* (9); *innate, computations* (10); *plasticity* (11); *attributes, assessment* (12); *imprecise* (13).

WRITING ACTIVITIES

1. If riding in a car is such an improvement over walking, why do people spend their spare time running and jogging? If frozen foods and microwave ovens are such advances in food preparation, why do people still grow vegetables in their gardens or cook dinners over charcoal? If modern airplanes make flying fast and safe, why do people risk their lives in flimsy ultralight aircraft that resemble the planes used in the first years of flying? Write an essay about some advance in technology and through comparison explain why it has failed to replace entirely the product or activity it was supposed to make obsolete.

2. Some people think that movies are a better form of entertainment than television; other people believe each has different appeals and serves different purposes. Likewise, some people view live concerts as far superior to recorded music; others believe that each kind of performance provides its own pleasures. In an essay of your own, explore the similarities and differences between two related activities (sports, forms of entertainment, occupations), two similar organizations (public and private colleges, large corporations and small businesses), or two similar products (boats, running shoes, home computers). Then either explain why one of the two is superior or explore their different strengths and purposes.

❧ BRUCE CATTON

Bruce Catton, born in Petosky, Michigan, in 1899, was until his death in 1978 one of the foremost historians of the American Civil War. He worked as a reporter and as director of information for the United States Department of Commerce before becoming a full-time writer and editor of *American Heritage* magazine. His books include *Mr. Lincoln's Army* (1951), *Glory Road* (1952), *A Stillness at Appomattox* (1953) (awarded the Pulitzer Prize and the National Book Award), *America Goes to War* (1958), *The Coming Fury* (1961), *Terrible Swift Sword* (1963), *Never Call Retreat* (1966), *Waiting for the Morning Train: An American Boyhood* (1972) (an autobiography), and *Gettysburg: The Final Fury* (1974).

Grant and Lee: A Study in Contrasts

"Grant and Lee: A Study in Contrasts" first appeared in *The American Story* (1956), a collection of essays by noted historians. In the essay, Catton compares Grant and Lee not only as individuals but as representatives of different forces in American history. Though Catton presents a good deal of historical detail in "Grant and Lee," it never obscures the point of the essay because he subordinates the information to his conclusions about the contrast between the generals, and he organizes the information carefully within the comparison pattern that runs through the essay.

When Ulysses S. Grant and Robert E. Lee met in the parlor of a 1 modest house at Appomattox Court House, Virginia, on April 9, 1865, to work out the terms for the surrender of Lee's Army of Northern Virginia, a great chapter in American life came to a close, and a great new chapter began.

These men were bringing the Civil War to its virtual finish. To 2 be sure, other armies had yet to surrender, and for a few days the fugitive Confederate government would struggle desperately and vainly, trying to find some way to go on living now that its chief support was gone. But in effect it was all over when Grant and Lee signed the papers. And the little room where they wrote out the terms was the scene of one of the poignant, dramatic contrasts in American History.

188

They were two strong men these oddly different generals, and   3
they represented the strengths of two conflicting currents that,
through them, had come into final collision.

Back of Robert E. Lee was the notion that the old aristocratic   4
concept might somehow survive and be dominant in American life.

Lee was tidewater Virginia, and in his background were family,   5
culture, and tradition . . . the age of chivalry transplanted to a New
World which was making its own legends and its own myths. He
embodied a way of life that had come down through the age of
knighthood and the English country squire. America was a land that
was beginning all over again, dedicated to nothing much more
complicated than the rather hazy belief that all men had equal rights
and should have an equal chance in the world. In such a land Lee
stood for the feeling that it was somehow of advantage to human
society to have a pronounced inequality in the social structure. There
should be a leisure class, backed by ownership of land; in turn,
society itself should be keyed to the land as the chief source of wealth
and influence. It would bring forth (according to this ideal) a class
of men with a strong sense of obligation to the community; men who
lived not to gain advantage for themselves, but to meet the solemn
obligations which had been laid on them by the very fact that they
were privileged. From them the country would get its leadership; to
them it could look for the higher values—of thought, of conduct, or
personal deportment—to give it strength and virtue.

Lee embodied the noblest elements of this aristocratic ideal.   6
Through him, the landed nobility justified itself. For four years, the
Southern states had fought a desperate war to uphold the ideals for
which Lee stood. In the end, it almost seemed as if the Confederacy
fought for Lee; as if he himself was the Confederacy . . . the best
thing that the way of life for which the Confederacy stood could ever
have to offer. He had passed into legend before Appomattox. Thousands of tired, underfed, poorly clothed Confederate soldiers, long
since past the simple enthusiasm of the early days of the struggle,
somehow considered Lee the symbol of everything for which they
had been willing to die. But they could not quite put this feeling into
words. If the Lost Cause, sanctified by so much heroism and so many
deaths, had a living justification, its justification was General Lee.

Grant, the son of a tanner on the Western frontier, was everything   7
Lee was not. He had come up the hard way and embodied nothing
in particular except the eternal toughness and sinewy fiber of the

men who grew up beyond the mountains. He was one of a body of men who owed reverence and obeisance to no one, who were self-reliant to a fault, who cared hardly anything for the past but who had a sharp eye for the future.

These frontier men were the precise opposites of the tidewater aristocrats. Back of them, in the great surge that had taken people over the Alleghenies and into the opening Western country, there was a deep, implicit dissatisfaction with a past that had settled into grooves. They stood for democracy, not from any reasoned conclusion about the proper ordering of human society, but simply because they had grown up in the middle of democracy and knew how it worked. Their society might have privileges, but they would be privileges each man had won for himself. Forms and patterns meant nothing. No man was born to anything, except perhaps to a chance to show how far he could rise. Life was competition.

Yet along with this feeling had come a deep sense of belonging to a national community. The Westerner who developed a farm, opened a shop, or set up in business as a trader could hope to prosper only as his own community prospered—and his community ran from the Atlantic to the Pacific and from Canada down to Mexico. If the land was settled, with towns and highways and accessible markets, he could better himself. He saw his fate in terms of the nation's own destiny. As its horizons expanded, so did his. He had, in other words, an acute dollars-and-cents stake in the contin-ued growth and development of his country.

And that, perhaps, is where the contrast between Grant and Lee becomes most striking. The Virginia aristocrat, inevitably, saw him-self in relation to his own region. He lived in a static society which could endure almost anything except change. Instinctively, his first loyalty would go to the locality in which that society existed. He would fight to the limit of endurance to defend it, because in de-fending it he was defending everything that gave his own life its deepest meaning.

The Westerner, on the other hand, would fight with an equal tenacity for the broader concept of society. He fought so because everything he lived by was tied to growth, expansion, and a con-stantly widening horizon. What he lived by would survive or fall with the nation itself. He could not possibly stand by unmoved in the face of an attempt to destroy the Union. He would combat it with everything he had, because he could only see it as an effort to cut the ground out from under his feet.

So Grant and Lee were in complete contrast, representing two 12 diametrically opposed elements in American life. Grant was the modern man emerging; beyond him, ready to come on the stage, was the great age of steel and machinery, of crowded cities and a restless burgeoning vitality. Lee might have ridden down from the old age of chivalry, lance in hand, silken banner fluttering over his head. Each man was the perfect champion of his cause, drawing both his strengths and his weaknesses from the people he led.

Yet it was not all contrast, after all. Different as they were—in 13 background, in personality, in underlying aspiration—these two great soldiers had much in common. Under everything else, they were marvelous fighters. Furthermore, their fighting qualities were really very much alike.

Each man had, to begin with, the great virtue of utter tenacity 14 and fidelity. Grant fought his way down the Mississippi Valley in spite of acute personal discouragement and profound military handicaps. Lee hung on in the trenches at Petersburg after hope itself had died. In each man there was an indomitable quality . . . the born fighter's refusal to give up as long as he can still remain on his feet and lift his two fists.

Daring and resourcefulness they had, too: the ability to think 15 faster and move faster than the enemy. These were the qualities which gave Lee the dazzling campaigns of Second Manassas and Chancellorsville and won Vicksburg for Grant.

Lastly, and perhaps greatest of all, there was the ability, at the 16 end, to turn quickly from war to peace once the fighting was over. Out of the way these two men behaved at Appomattox came the possibility of a peace of reconciliation. It was a possibility not wholly realized, in the years to come, but which did, in the end, help the two sections to become one nation again . . . after a war whose bitterness might have seemed to make such a reunion wholly impossible. No part of either man's life became him more than the part he played in their brief meeting in the McLean house at Appomattox. Their behavior there put all succeeding generations of Americans in their debt. Two great Americans, Grant and Lee—very different, yet under everything very much alike. Their encounter at Appomattox was one of the great moments of American history.

RESPONSES AND IDEAS

1. Respond to this essay by writing a brief comparison of two recent political figures who you think sum up the qualities of the countries or political movements they represent. You might choose two recent presidents or presidential candidates, or you might choose leaders of two countries, of two social movements, or of two religious sects.

2. Catton says that Grant "embodied nothing in particular except the eternal toughness and sinewy fiber of the men who grew up beyond the mountains (par. 7)." Does this mean that Grant had no personality or values? What does it mean?

3. In contrast with Grant, what qualities and values did Lee represent?

PURPOSE, AUDIENCE, AND STRATEGIES

1. If you knew very little about the Civil War, would you still be able to understand what this essay has to say about Grant and Lee? About the social and economic backgrounds of the Civil War? Explain your responses. What steps, if any, does Catton take to help readers understand the historical detail presented in the essay?

2. State the thesis of this essay in your own words. Is the thesis the same as the purpose? What is the purpose? (See Glossary: Thesis, Purpose.)

3. Does Catton want readers to sympathize with either Lee or Grant? To admire either of them? What steps does he take to either encourage or discourage admiration and sympathy? Point out specific passages in the essay that support your conclusion.

4. Which paragraphs in the essay are devoted to Lee? Which to Grant? Which to both? To what extent does this distribution of emphasis reflect the purposes of the essay? Could the distribution be improved in any ways? How?

5. This essay contains a number of short paragraphs. Does Catton appear to use them for any special purposes? For what special purposes are they intended? (See Glossary: Paragraphs.)

LANGUAGE AND STYLE

1. What effect does Catton achieve in paragraph 2 by beginning one sentence with *and*, another with *but*? What is the effect of the short sentence that ends paragraph 8? The sentence which opens paragraph 10 begins this way: "And that. . . ." To what is the author referring with the word *that*? How effective is his strategy for opening the paragraph? Compose another opening for the paragraph that you believe will be as effective or more effective than the present opening sentence.

2. Identify the metaphors in paragraphs 1, 3, 5, 7–11, and 16. Describe the purposes for which they are used and indicate how effective they are. (See Glossary: Figures of Speech.)

3. If you are unfamiliar with any of the following words, look them up in the dictionary: *virtual, poignant* (par. 2); *concept* (4); *sinewy, obeisance* (7); *implicit* (8); *tenacity* (11); *diametrically, burgeoning* (12); *aspiration* (13); *fidelity, profound, indomitable* (14); *succeeding* (16).

WRITING ACTIVITIES

1. To what extent do sports teams resemble the cities from which they come (e.g., Los Angeles Rams and Dallas Cowboys; New York Yankees and San Diego Padres)? To what extent do products represent the cultures that produce them (e.g., Toyota and Mercedes Benz automobiles; hot dogs and Coca-Cola; the soufflé and champagne)? Write an essay comparing two countries, cultures, age groups, or organizations by examining their activities, products, or artistic achievements.

2. People approach problems in different ways, both effective and ineffective. Write an essay explaining contrasting approaches to a local problem (theft of materials from a college library; construction that threatens forests, wildlife, or wetlands), a national problem (acid rain, the role of religion in public schools), or a social or moral problem (drug use, medical treatment of infants with life-threatening birth defects). Evaluate the different approaches, and, if you wish, argue in favor of one.

❧ ELLEN GOODMAN

Ellen Goodman was born in 1941 in Boston and educated at
Radcliffe College. In 1967 she became a reporter for the *Boston
Globe* and has been a full-time columnist since 1974. Her columns
are nationally syndicated, appearing in more than two hundred
papers nationwide. In addition, her writing has appeared in
McCall's, the *Village Voice*, *Family Circle*, *Harper's Bazaar*, and
other publications. In 1980 she won the Pulitzer Prize for distinguished commentary. Her columns have been collected in *Close to
Home* (1979), *Turning Points* (1979), and *At Large* (1981).

The Challenge to Keep Family Together

"The Challenge to Keep Family Together" first appeared as a
newspaper column, and it reflects many of the ideas typical of
Goodman's writing: concern with the impact of current social and
economic forces on the family and on human relationships. Her
focus in this selection is not simply on contemporary behavior,
however, but on patterns and values that have been part of American culture for at least a hundred years, if not more. The historical
perspective that forms the basis for this comparison does not so
much explain as it suggests new ways of interpreting events, and
much of the essay consists of Goodman's exploration of those ideas.

Some weeks ago, I wrote about the new American migrants, the 1
economically uprooted who are once again choosing mobility over
unemployment, work over home.

In particular, I told the story of Anne, a woman whose unem- 2
ployed husband found a job a thousand miles away. Anne was torn
between her children, her aging mother and her job at home, and
her husband half-a-country away.

The mail I got was not unexpected. I received letters from wives 3
(mostly) who had made this sort of move and wives who had chosen
not to. I heard from people who were sympathetic with Anne's
situation, and people who were not.

But there was one curious theme in my mail. At least a third of 4
my correspondents and one irate caller reminded me that this was
not the first generation of Americans who had to vote with their feet.
Several told me of grandparents and great-grandparents who had

moved west in the last century. Two at least criticized Anne for not having the grit of her foremothers.

This comparison struck me, because I'd just begun Lillian Schlissel's "Women's Diaries of the Westward Journey." Her book is a record of the hardships and, yes, the grit of women who took the overland trail to Oregon and California in the middle of the 19th century.   5

The women's story is told in the understated words of their own journals. It's a story that had been virtually lost in the frontier history written by and about men. When, recently, women looked in American history textbooks for their own neglected sex they found themselves hidden in classic lines like this: "Pioneers pushed west over the mountains. Their wives and children went along."   6

But in Schlissel's book, women on the trail were far more than excess baggage riding comfortably in a covered wagon. They were essential partners along this hostile trail. Though one-fifth of them were pregnant at some point in the journey, though most had small children, they did ordinary drudgery under extraordinary conditions. They rolled out dough on the wagon seats, cooked with fires made out of buffalo chips, tended the sick, and marked the graves of their children, husbands and each other.   7

In comparison, our modern moves, made with a trailer truck along an interstate highway, pale. Yet there is a sense in which the wives and mothers of that migration and this migration—perhaps any migration—have much in common emotionally.   8

You see, at the moment of the original decision, most of our "gritty" foremothers didn't want to go.   9

The women who went were almost all married. But it was husbands who were captured by the glowing descriptions of the West; wives who were skeptical. Husbands who thought of what could be gained; wives who thought of what would be lost.   10

As Schlissel describes them: "Riding side by side, sitting in the very same wagons, crossing the continent in response to the call for free land, women did not always see the venture in the clear light of the expectation of success. There were often shadows in their minds, areas of dark reservation and opposition."   11

For every woman who saw this as an adventure, there were a hundred like Margaret Hereford Wilson, the grandmother of General George S. Patton, who wrote in 1850 to her mother, with typical anguish: "Dr. Wilson has determined to go to California. I am going   12

with him as there is no other alternative. . . . Oh my dear Mother. . . .
I thought that I felt bad when I wrote you . . . from Independence,
but it was nothing like this."

Schlissel suggests that for men breaking away and moving, the   13
frontier was a pursuit of masculinity, "an expression of testing and
reaching." The male pioneers were chasing what our life-cycle plot-
ters today like to call "The Dream."

But women saw themselves as caretakers, keepers of homes,   14
keepers of relationships. For them the separation from parents,
home, friends and environment was far more threatening. In fact,
they measured their accomplishment on the trail in terms of their
ability to keep the family together.

Unlike Margaret Wilson, wives today have different options and   15
responsibilities. More women now choose to test themselves against
some frontier; more men nurture their roots. Yet it is still more
common for men to embrace moves and women to dread them.

In this new season of migration, when the economy acts like a   16
centrifuge, it is equally challenging to keep a family together, especially when jobs and generations are a thousand miles apart. No
matter what my letter-writers say, I suspect that our foremothers in
the caravans of covered wagons would understand.

RESPONSES AND IDEAS

1. Respond to this essay by describing how your family or some other
   family you are acquainted with held together (or fell apart) under the
   pressure of some challenge or test. Indicate, if you can, the roles different
   members of the family played in choosing to respond to the challenge
   or in working to hold the family together.

2. What values and behavior does Goodman see as characteristic of American men? Of women? Does she see any differences in the way men
   and women displayed these qualities in 1850 and the way they do so
   now? What are the differences?

3. Tell why Goodman believes it is important "to keep the family together."
   Indicate where and how she explains her belief in the importance of
   this endeavor.

PURPOSE, AUDIENCE, AND STRATEGIES

1. According to paragraphs 3 and 4, what group of people make up at
   least a portion of Goodman's audience? Is there any evidence in the
   essay that she is aiming her writing primarily at this group? What is

it? Or is there evidence that she intends to address a wider audience? If so, what is the evidence?

2. How would you describe Goodman's purpose in this essay? Does the essay have a clear point? If so, what is it, and where in the essay does she announce it? (See Glossary: Purpose, Thesis.)

3. Do the references to the mail the author has received make this essay too informal for the serious matters it discusses, or do they add to its effectiveness? Explain. Would the essay be more effective if it were more formal? Why?

4. What unusual opening strategy does Goodman use in this essay, and how does it help her shape her readers' attitude towards the subject of the essay? Does the fact that you are encountering this essay outside its normal context in a newspaper harm the effectiveness of the opening in any way? Explain. (See Glossary: Introductions.)

5. The short paragraphs in this selection are characteristic of newspaper writing. Do they make the essay seem too choppy when it is encountered outside a newspaper? Which paragraphs could be combined without obscuring the organization of the essay? (See Glossary: Paragraphs.)

LANGUAGE AND STYLE

1. Where in the essay does the author use *but* in order to emphasize a contrast? What other transitions does she use to highlight the pattern of thought followed in the essay? To what extent does she use sentence structure (including parallelism) to emphasize comparisons and contrasts? (See Glossary: Syntax, Parallelism.) How might you rewrite the first sentence in paragraph 8 to make it easier to understand? Are there any other sentences in the essay that might benefit from revision? Which are they, and how could they be improved?

2. What connotations does the word *grit* hold for you? (See Glossary: Connotation.) Why is Goodman's use of the term in paragraphs 4, 5, and 9 appropriate to her subject and purpose? (You may wish to look the word up in the dictionary.)

3. If you do not know the meaning of some of the following words, look them up in the dictionary: *irate, grit* (par. 4); *overland* (5); *understated* (6); *drudgery* (7); *pale* (8); *reservation* (11); *nurture* (15).

WRITING ACTIVITIES

1. In an essay explore how your attitudes towards work, family, religion, friendship, sex, or similar matters differ from those of your parents, grandparents, or other people from previous generations whom you know. If you can account for the different attitudes on the basis of changes in the economic, social, and cultural forces that shaped each generation, then do so. Be sure also to examine those values that you

share with preceding generations and to explore the reasons these values have remained constant while other attitudes have changed.

2. Do you agree with Goodman's statement, "More women now choose to test themselves against some frontier; more men nurture their roots"? If so, use it as the basis for an essay of your own. If not, explore the contrasting (or similar) roles you believe that men and women play. (You may also wish to explore the roles played by other groups of people such as business people, entertainers, and professionals.)

3. One recurring theme in Goodman's writing is her belief that people who act as caretakers and nurturers (teachers, doctors, mothers and fathers) are essential to the health of families and the society as a whole. She also believes society does not provide adequate respect or monetary reward for caretakers and nurturers. Is she right? Do the high financial rewards we offer engineers and business people indicate that we value them as more important than teachers and nurses? If so, should we change our attitudes and the system of rewards? Or does the fact that we pay most politicians (including the president) less than we pay most corporate executives indicate that the value we place on an activity and its financial rewards are not linked? Prepare an essay explaining your stand on one or more of these issues.

❧ BARRY LOPEZ

Barry Lopez was born in 1945 in Port Chester, New York. He attended the University of Notre Dame and the University of Oregon. He now lives in Oregon and works as a writer and photographer specializing in natural subjects. His writing and photography has been published in *Audubon, National Wildlife,* and other magazines. His books are *Desert Notes: Reflections in the Eye of the Raven* (1976), *Of Wolves and Men* (1978), *River Notes: The Dance of the Herons* (1979), and *Winter Count* (1982).

My Horse

"My Horse" was first published in the *North American Review* in 1975. The subjects compared in this essay, a truck and a horse, are dissimilar enough so that the piece can be considered an extended analogy, yet at the same time the subjects are both methods of transportation and may be regarded as legitimate subjects for a comparison. Besides mixing analogy and comparison, the essay contains numerous descriptive passages and several short narratives. The opening, moreover, provides a glimpse of the past in its explanation of the important role horses played in Crow Indian culture. The result of this combination of strategies is an essay that explores from various perspectives the relationship between humans and the animals or machines with which they share their lives.

It is curious that Indian warriors on the northern plains in the   1
nineteenth century, who were almost entirely dependent on the horse for mobility and status, never gave their horses names. If you borrowed a man's horse and went off raiding for other horses, however, or if you lost your mount in battle and then jumped on mine and counted coup on an enemy—well, those horses would have to be shared with the man whose horse you borrowed, and that coup would be mine, not yours. Because even if I gave him no name, he was my horse.

If you were a Crow warrior and I a young Teton Sioux out after   2
a warrior's identity and we came over a small hill somewhere in the Montana prairie and surprised each other, I could tell a lot about you by looking at your horse.

199

Your horse might have feathers tied in his mane, or in his tail, 3
or a medicine bag tied around his neck. If I knew enough about the
Crow, and had looked at you closely, I might make some sense of
the decoration, even guess who you were if you were well-known.
If you had painted your horse I could tell even more, because we
both decorated our horses with signs that meant the same things.
Your white handprints high on his flanks would tell me you had
killed an enemy in a hand-to-hand fight. Small horizontal lines
stacked on your horse's foreleg, or across his nose, would tell me
how many times you had counted coup. Horse hoof marks on your
horse's rump, or three-sided boxes, would tell me how many times
you had stolen horses. If there was a bright red square on your
horse's neck I would know you were leading a war party and that
there were probably others out there in the coulees behind you.

You might be painted all over as blue as the sky and covered 4
with white dots, with your horse painted the same way. Maybe
hailstorms were your power—or if I chased you a hailstorm might
come down and hide you. There might be lightning bolts on the
horse's legs and flanks, and I would wonder if you had lightning
power, or a slow horse. There might be white circles around your
horse's eyes to help him see better.

Or you might be like Crazy Horse, with no decoration, no marks 5
on your horse to tell me anything, only a small lightning bolt on
your cheek, a piece of turquoise tied behind your ear.

You might have scalps dangling from your rein. 6

I could tell something about you by your horse. All this would 7
come to me in a few seconds. I might decide this was my moment
and shout my war cry—*Hoka hey!* Or I might decide you were like
the grizzly bear: I would raise my weapon to you in salute and go
my way, to see you again when I was older.

I do not own a horse. I am attached to a truck, however, and I 8
have come to think of it in a similar way. It has no name; it never
occurred to me to give it a name. It has little decoration; neither of
us is partial to decoration. I have a piece of turquoise in the truck
because I had heard once that some of the southwestern tribes tied
a small piece of turquoise in a horse's hock to keep him from
stumbling. I like the idea. I also hang sage in the truck when I go
on a long trip. But inside, the truck doesn't look much different from

others that look just like it on the outside. I like it that way. Because
I like my privacy.

For two years in Wyoming I worked on a ranch wrangling   9
horses. The horse I rode when I had to have a good horse was a
quarter horse and his name was Coke High. The name came with
him. At first I thought he'd been named for the soft drink. I'd known
stranger names given to horses by whites. Years later I wondered if
some deviate Wyoming cowboy wise to cocaine had not named him.
Now I think he was probably named after a rancher, an historical
figure of the region. I never asked the people who owned him for
fear of spoiling the spirit of my inquiry.

We were running over a hundred horses on this ranch. They all   10
had names. After a few weeks I knew all the horses and the names
too. You had to. No one knew how to talk about the animals or put
them in order or tell the wranglers what to do unless they were
using the names—Princess, Big Red, Shoshone, Clay.

My truck is named Dodge. The name came with it. I don't know   11
if it was named after the town or the verb or the man who invented
it. I like it for a name. Perfectly anonymous, like Rex for a dog, or
Old Paint. You can't tell anything with a name like that.

The truck is a van. I call it a truck because it's not a car and   12
because "van" is a suburban sort of consumer word, like "oxford
loafer," and I don't like the sound of it. On the outside it looks like
any other Dodge Sportsman 300. It's a dirty tan color. There are a
few body dents, but it's never been in a wreck. I tore the antenna
off against a tree on a pinched mountain road. A boy in Midland,
Texas, rocked one of my rear view mirrors off. A logging truck in
Oregon squeeze-fired a piece of debris off the road and shattered
my windshield. The oil pan and gas tank are pug-faced from high-
centering on bad roads. (I remember a horse I rode for a while
named Targhee whose hocks were scarred from tangles in barbed
wire when he was a colt and who spooked a lot in high grass, but
these were not like "dents." They were more like bad tires.)

I like to travel. I go mostly in the winter and mostly on two-lane   13
roads. I've driven the truck from Key West to Vancouver, British
Columbia, and from Yuma to Long Island over the past four years.
I used to ride Coke High only about five miles every morning when
we were rounding up horses. Hard miles of twisting and turning.
About six hundred miles a year. Then I'd turn him out and ride

another horse for the rest of the day. That's what was nice about having a remuda. You could do all you had to do and not take it all out on your best horse. Three car family.

My truck came with a lot of seats in it and I've never really   14
known what to do with them. Sometimes I put the seats in and go somewhere with a lot of people, but most of the time I leave them out. I like riding around with that empty cavern of space behind my head. I know it's something with a history to it, that there's truth in it, because I always rode a horse the same way—with empty saddle bags. In case I found something. The possibility of finding something is half the reason for being on the road.

The value of anything comes to me in its use. If I am not using   15
something it is of no value to me and I give it away. I wasn't always that way. I used to keep everything I owned—just in case. I feel good about the truck because it gets used. A lot. To haul hay and firewood and lumber and rocks and garbage and animals. Other people have used it to haul furniture and freezers and dirt and recycled news-papers. And to move from one house to another. When I lend it for things like that I don't look to get anything back but some gas (if we're going to be friends). But if you go way out in the country to a dump and pick up the things you can still find out there (once a load of cedar shingles we sold for $175 to an architect) I expect you to leave some of those things around my place when you come back—if I need them.

When I think back, maybe the nicest thing I ever put in that   16
truck was timber wolves. It was a long night's drive from Oregon up into British Columbia. We were all very quiet about it; it was like moving clouds across the desert.

Sometimes something won't fit in the truck and I think about   17
improving it—building a different door system, for example. I am forever going to add better gauges on the dash and a pair of driving lamps and a sunroof, but I never get around to doing any of it. I remember I wanted to improve Coke High once too, especially the way he bolted like a greyhound through patches of cottonwood on a river flat. But all I could do with him was to try to rein him out of it. Or hug his back.

Sometimes, road-stoned in a blur of country like southwestern   18
Wyoming or North Dakota, I talk to the truck. It's like wandering on the high plains under a summer sun, on plains where, George

Catlin wrote, you were "out of sight of land." I say what I am thinking out loud, or point at things along the road. It's a crazy, sun-stroked sort of activity, a sure sign it's time to pull over, to go for a walk, to make a fire and have some tea, to lie in the shade of the truck.

I've always wanted to pat the truck. It's basic to the relationship. 19 But it never works.

I remember when I was on the ranch, just at sunrise, after I'd 20 saddled Coke High, I'd be huddled down in my jacket smoking a cigarette and looking down into the valley, along the river where the other horses had spent the night. I'd turn to Coke and run my hand down his neck and slap-pat him on the shoulder to say I was coming up. It made a bond, an agreement we started the day with.

I've thought about that a lot with the truck, because we've gone 21 out together at sunrise on so many mornings. I've even fumbled around trying to do it. But metal won't give.

The truck's personality is mostly an expression of two ideas: 22 "with-you" and "alone." When Coke High was "with-you" he and I were the same animal. We could have cut a rooster out of a flock of chickens, we were so in tune. It's the same with the truck: rolling through Kentucky on a hilly two-lane road, three in the morning under a full moon and no traffic. Picture it. You roll like water.

There are other times when you are with each other but there's 23 no connection at all. Coke got that way when he was bored and we'd fight each other about which way to go around a tree. When the truck gets like that—"alone"—it's because it feels its Detroit fat-ass design dragging at its heart and making a fool out of it.

I can think back over more than a hundred nights I've slept in 24 the truck, sat in it with a lamp burning, bundled up in a parka, reading a book. It was always comfortable. A good place to wait out a storm. Like sleeping inside a buffalo.

The truck will go past 100,000 miles soon. I'll rebuild the engine 25 and put a different transmission in it. I can tell from magazine advertisements that I'll never get another one like it. Because every year they take more of the heart out of them. One thing that makes a farmer or a rancher go sour is a truck that isn't worth a shit. The reason you see so many old pickups in ranch country is because these are the only ones with any heart. You can count on them. The weekend rancher runs around in a new pickup with too much engine and not enough transmission and with the wrong sort of tires because he can afford anything, even the worst. A lot of them have names for their pickups too.

My truck has broken down, in out of the way places at the worst 26 of times. I've walked away and screamed the foulness out of my system and gotten the tools out. I had to fix a water pump in a blizzard in the Panamint Mountains in California once. It took all day with the Coleman stove burning under the engine block to keep my hands from freezing. We drifted into Beatty, Nevada, that night with it jury-rigged together with—I swear—baling wire, and we were melting snow as we went and pouring it in to compensate for the leaks.

There is a dent next to the door on the driver's side I put there 27 one sweltering night in Miami. I had gone to the airport to meet my wife, whom I hadn't seen in a month. My hands were so swollen with poison ivy blisters I had to drive with my wrists. I had shut the door and was locking it when the window fell off its runners and slid down inside the door. I couldn't leave the truck unlocked because I had too much inside I didn't want to lose. So I just kicked the truck a blow in the side and went to work on the window. I hate to admit kicking the truck. It's like kicking a dog, which I've never done.

Coke High and I had an accident once. We hit a badger hole at 28 a full gallop. I landed on my back and blacked out. When I came to, Coke High was about a hundred yards away. He stayed a hundred yards away for six miles, all the way back to the ranch.

I want to tell you about carrying those wolves, because it was a 29 fine thing. There were ten of them. We had four in the truck with us in crates and six in a trailer. It was a five hundred mile trip. We went at night for the cool air and because there wouldn't be as much traffic. I could feel from the way the truck rolled along that its heart was in the trip. It liked the wolves inside it, the sweet odor that came from the crates. I could feel that same tireless wolf-lope developing in its wheels; it was like you might never have to stop for gas, ever again.

The truck gets very self-focused when it works like this; its heart 30 is strong and it's good to be around it. It's good to be *with* it. You get the same feeling when you pull someone out of a ditch. Coke High and I pulled a Volkswagen out of the mud once, but Coke didn't like doing it very much. Speed, not strength, was his center.

When the guy who owned the car thanked us and tried to pat Coke, the horse snorted and swung away, trying to preserve his distance, which is something a horse spends a lot of time on.

So does the truck. 31

Being distant lets the truck get its heart up. The truck has been 32 cold and alone in Montana at 38 below zero. It's climbed horrible, eroded roads in Idaho. It's been burdened beyond overloading, and made it anyway. I've asked it to do these things because they build heart, and without heart all you have is a machine. You have nothing. I don't think people in Detroit know anything at all about heart. That's why everything they build dies so young.

One time in Arizona the truck and I came through one of the 33 worst storms I've ever been in, an outrageous, angry blizzard. But we went down the road, right through it. You couldn't explain our getting through by the sort of tires I had on the truck, or the fact that I had chains on, or was a good driver, or had a lot of weight over my drive wheels or a good engine, because it was more than this. It was a contest between the truck and the blizzard—and the truck wouldn't quit. I could have gone to sleep and the truck would have just torn a road down Interstate 40 on its own. It scared the hell out of me; but it gave me heart, too.

We came off the Mogollon Rim that night and out of the storm 34 and headed south for Phoenix. I pulled off the road to sleep for a few hours, but before I did I got out of the truck. It was raining. Warm rain. I tied a short piece of red avalanche cord into the grill. I left it there for a long time, like an eagle feather on a horse's tail. It flapped and spun in the wind. I could hear it ticking against the grill when I drove.

When I have to leave that truck I will just raise up my left arm— 35 *Hoka hey!*—and walk away.

RESPONSES AND IDEAS

1. Respond to this essay by telling how some machine plays a part in your life similar in importance to that of Lopez's truck in his. If no machine plays such a major role in your life, then choose a machine that plays a minor but still important part in your daily activities.

2. What does Lopez mean when he says, "The value of anything comes to me in its use"? What examples does he employ to explain the statement? How well does the statement apply to his truck?

3. What does the war cry *Hoka hey!* mean in paragraph 7? Does it mean something different in paragraph 35? Explain why Lopez uses it in paragraph 35.

PURPOSE, AUDIENCE, AND STRATEGIES

1. For what purpose does Lopez try to get readers to participate in the life of a Crow warrior in paragraphs 2–7? How does he unify this section with the rest of the essay? (See Glossary: Unity.)

2. Is it possible to state concisely the thesis of this essay? Why, or why not? What appear to be Lopez's purposes in writing the essay? (See Glossary: Thesis, Purpose.)

3. What feelings towards the events he describes in the essay is Lopez trying to evoke in his readers? Where in the essay are there indications of the responses he is aiming for?

4. How many different sections does this essay have, and how does Lopez identify them? Do all the sections follow the comparison pattern, or does some other pattern dominate in one or more of them? What other pattern or patterns does he use to organize the different sections?

5. Why does Lopez bring up the story of the wolves in paragraph 16, then abruptly drop it until paragraph 29? Do the frequent jumps from topic to topic (in paragraphs 16–28, for example) mean that the essay lacks unity, or do the shifts follow some internal logical order? What order, if any, do they follow? (See Glossary: Unity.)

LANGUAGE AND STYLE

1. Identify the places in this essay where Lopez uses personification, and state why he uses it. (See Glossary: Figures of Speech.)

2. What other figures of speech, if any, appear in this essay? Give an example of each and indicate its purpose.

3. If you do not know the meaning of some of the following words, look them up in the dictionary: *mobility, coup* (par. 1); *flanks, rump* (3); *turquoise* (5); *partial, hock, sage* (8); *wranglers* (10); *pug-faced, spooked* (12); *remuda* (13); *jury-rigged, compensate* (26); *badger* (28).

WRITING ACTIVITIES

1. Manufacturers and advertisers often try to give their products personalities, both to help them appeal to specific groups of consumers and to distinguish them from competing products. Automobiles, electronic equipment, cooking utensils and appliances, and lines of clothing often have such personalities. In an essay, describe and compare the person-

alities of two well-known competing products, indicating what purpose the personalities play and whether they reflect the actual qualities of the products.

2. Sports like baseball, football, and basketball are frequent sources for analogies, but others, like fishing or long distance running, can provide analogies too. A salesperson, for example, might compare making a sale to catching a fish; a teacher might compare planning a class to deciding on a strategy for a marathon. Write an essay in which you try to give readers a fresh perspective on some activity by comparing it to a sport. (If you cannot think of any appropriate sports, you might want to use as the source for your analogy a hobby, like building model airplanes, or a craft, like knitting.)

3. Choose a scientific or technical subject about which you know a good deal and explain some aspect of it to readers by means of analogy. Here are a few of the many subjects you might choose to illuminate through analogy: black holes, subatomic particles, nuclear fusion, lasers, viral infections, allergic reactions, earthquakes, volcanic eruptions, changes in weather or climate, schizophrenia, acute depression, video recorders, computer chips, DNA, radio telescopes, oil painting, sculpture, and songwriting.

Writing Suggestions

EXPLORATIONS

1. Write a list of as many opposites (man-woman; good-evil; capitalism-communism; work-play, and so on) as you can but no more than fifteen. Choose two pairs and write down why they are less the opposite of each other than most people assume or explore any surprising similarities you can discover. If your writing gives you some interesting ideas, try turning them into an essay.

2. State your standards for an ideal college class, instructor, or textbook, and then describe the qualities of a class, text, or instructor from the current semester, comparing its (his, her) qualities to the ideal. If you wish, you may compare more than one to the ideal and judge their relative merits. If your exploratory writing suggests ideas for a critique or a product review you could share with fellow students, try using it as the basis for a paper.

3. Choose two of these imaginative comparisons and write a brief paragraph about each; then make up a comparison of your own and explore it in a paragraph:

   Compare an idea (freedom, sexuality, justice, and so on) to a place.
   Compare an emotion to a shape.
   Compare a person to a color.
   Compare a college experience (including that of a class, but not including food) to an illness.
   Compare the arguments over a social issue (gun control, euthanasia, and so on) to a family argument.
   Compare a current political issue to a popular song, or to some other artistic work.

4. List some products and services you think are worth evaluating, and for five of them explain briefly why you think an evaluation would be a good idea. If this exercise gives you a good idea for a paper, feel free to start writing.

ACTIVITIES

1. Look up two product reviews in magazines like *Glamour, Popular Science, Car and Driver,* or *Popular Computing* and describe briefly the arrangement they follow. (You may wish to use an outline to describe the arrangement.)

2. Collect comparison-contrast assignments from classes you are currently taking, either exam questions or writing assignments. Choose one of the assignments and interview the instructor who gave it, asking what he or she would look for in the content and structure of an ideal

response and what standards will be used to grade such papers or exam questions.

3. Which of the essays you read in this chapter used the point-by-point structure and which used the subject-by-subject structure? Did any of them combine the structures? In what way? Would any of the essays have been improved if the author chose a different structure? Choose one of the essays and describe how it could be revised to follow an arrangement different from the one it has.

4. Look at the editorial pages of a local newspaper for arguments that make use of comparison, either as a primary pattern or as one form of support. Clip two or more articles you believe use the pattern and bring them to class. Exchange your articles with classmates in order to discover the ones you think make the best use of comparison as a writing strategy, and discuss why they are so effective.

MODELS

1. Borrowing the general arrangement of "Brains and Computers," write a comparison paper that begins as an explanation and then moves to evaluation. (You might compare political, economic, or social policies; institutions like colleges; or different kinds of diets or exercise programs.)

2. Using "Grant and Lee: A Study in Contrasts" as a model, compare two people whose personal qualities represent different political movements, cultural or national groups, social practices, or academic disciplines. You might compare recent presidents, national leaders, movie stars, college professors, or even two of your friends.

3. Basing your approach on "The Challenge to Keep Family Together," draw parallels between some difficult experiences you have had and those someone you know in a previous generation has had. You may wish to use the experience of parents, grandparents, other relatives, or friends as a point of comparison. Make sure you reach some conclusion about the meaning of the experience, no matter how tentative it is.

4. Drawing on "My Horse" as a model, compare some important machine in your life (a car, a typewriter, a computer, a microscope, a washing machine, and so on) to an animal (cat, dog, canary, fox) or to some other unusual subject (a relative, a game like baseball, a social event). Make sure that your essay offers a new, perhaps even a humorous way of looking at the machine.

6

ॐ PROCESS

Looking at Each Step

WHAT PROCESS DOES

On the front of the box is a picture of a two-layer yellow cake that looks delicious. Inside is a fine beige powder. Between the powder and the picture lie two additional ingredients, several baking pans, a hot oven, and some careful work—a process described in detail by the recipe on the back of the box.

A *process* consists of the actions and materials that lead to a specific result. It can be the whirring of a machine wrapping chocolate kisses in foil; the silent calculations of a computer examining income tax returns; the talk, plans, and charts that go into a sales campaign; or the ideas and decisions that end up as a poem or essay.

A *process analysis* slows down events so that we can understand how they happen. It freezes the magician's hand until we can see the egg about to be tucked into the sleeve, where before we only saw the egg suddenly disappear. It reveals how the simultaneous activities of hundreds of people with cameras, cables, and satellites combine to broadcast a live sports event from Los Angeles to Frankfort, Kentucky; Ocala, Florida; and Syracuse, New York.

Most often, we turn to a process analysis for advice about how to do something or for a textbook explanation of a complicated procedure. In our search for useful or enlightening information, however, we may fail to notice how often writers use the pattern to persuade as well as to inform, working to convince us to try a

211

particular procedure or to reject someone else's explanation, as in this passage on "The Right Way to Take a Shower":

> Take a look at yourself after a long, hard training session. Your heart is still pounding as the sweat forms on your skin—sure signs that your internal temperature remains high from the recent activity. Now ease under a stream of water slightly cooler than your body's temperature. Your touch is your thermometer. The water temperature nearly matches your body's, so there is no shock. As you feel your body cool, gradually cool the water until your body's temperature is normal.
>
> Why not just jump under the cold water? Because the sudden blast of coldness on the skin confuses the body's cooling system. Many heart attacks have been brought on by the Finnish custom of going from a sauna (a steamy, hot bath) into the snow and back into the sauna. You can imagine the shock to the heart and circulatory system caused by that routine (Ken Sprague and Joe Jares, *The Athlete's Body*, 1980).

Here, obviously, we are informed about a process, yet not merely what it is, buy *why* it should be followed.

An argumentative essay or a report proposing a specific action may turn to process analysis for support to show that a proposed solution is realistic and workable:

> The new highway will be constructed in the following ways to prevent petroleum residues and road salt from polluting the watershed of the Big Bend Reservoir. . . .

> The subcontractor has agreed to use the following installation procedure to ensure that the large panes of glass on the front of the building will not loosen or fall during windstorms. . . .

Process analysis can amuse, too, by analyzing with a critical eye some common aspects of human behavior.

Finally, process analysis can be applied to a subject we know little about. It can be a tool for exploring the creative process in writing, as with the essays in Chapter 11, "Writers on Writing," or a way of speculating about the events that could have formed our universe during the Big Bang.

A good process essay does more than merely present the author's explanations and speculations. It indicates why the subject is worth knowing about, and it anticipates both the kind of information readers will need in order to understand the process and any objections they may have to the explanation. It sorts out the detailed, often simultaneous steps and presents them in a clear, logical order, yet with enough detail so that readers can visualize each one and understand the complexity of their relationships.

A parent halfway through assembling a child's bicycle late in the evening before a birthday may struggle to finish the job even though the manufacturer's directions are incomplete and hard to understand. An effective process analysis, however, avoids assuming that readers are captives, committed to understanding or performing the process no matter how confusing the explanation. Instead, it keeps the reader's needs and expectations in sight at all times.

This brief essay, first published as a magazine column, illustrates how a lively sense of the reader's presence can shape a process analysis:

What to Do About Soap Ends

This is admittedly not a problem qualitatively on the order of what to do about the proliferation of nuclear weaponry, but quantitatively it disturbs a great deal of Mankind—all those millions, in fact, who've ever used a bar of soap—except, of course, me. I've solved the problem of what to do about those troublesome, wasteful, messy little soap ends, and I'm ready now to deliver my solution to a grateful world.

The solution depends on a fact not commonly known, which I discovered in the shower. Archimedes made his great discovery about displacement ("Eureka!" and all that) in the bathtub, but I made mine in the shower. It is not commonly known that if, when you soap yourself, you hold *the same side* of the bar of soap cupped in the palm of your hand, that side will, after a few days, become curved and rounded, while the side of the bar you're soaping yourself *with* will become flat. (In between showers or baths, leave the bar curved side down so it won't stick to whatever it's resting on.) When the bar diminishes sufficiently, the flat side can be pressed onto a new bar of soap and will adhere sufficiently overnight to become, with the next day's use, a just slightly oversized new bar, ready to be treated in the same way as the one that came before it, in perpetuity, one bar after another, down through the length of your days on earth, with never a nasty soap end to trouble you ever again. Eureka, and now on to those nuclear weapons. Man is at his best, I feel, when in his problem-solving mode (L. Rust Hills, *Esquire,* March 1984).

THE PROCESS

The steps in writing a process analysis often occur simultaneously rather than in a rigid sequence. While deciding on a subject, a writer may think of a strategy for convincing readers they need to know about the process, or may recognize points that will need to be explained at length in the essay. Because the structure of such a discussion is inevitably linear, however, it is necessary to discuss the writing of a process essay as a series of stages, making due allowance for overlap and for the tendency of good writers to move backwards and forwards in their work, creating, rethinking, and revising at the same time. Here, then, are some of the major stages in writing a process analysis.

Choose a Subject   Your experience and your reading can provide you with many subjects worth sharing through process analysis. You may have participated in a sport like lacrosse or free-style skiing that appeals to readers' curiosity ("How to Ski Free-style Without Breaking a Leg—or More"; "Lacrosse: How a Famous Indian Game Is Played Today"). You may know something about a new discovery that changes our understanding of the world or that has practical benefits ("How Writing on a Word Processor May Lead to Better Grades"). Or you may know something that can help people avoid accidents and problems ("How *Not* to Use Your Chainsaw"; "The Best Way to Begin Investing").

If you have a point to make, looking at your subject as a process may provide you with the kind of support you need. If you want to protest student loan regulations, you might write about "How Student Loans Go to the Wrong People." Your argument for the use of seatbelts might be entitled, "How Seatbelts Save Lives."

One good way to choose or limit a topic is to ask questions that take the audience into account: "What sort of things has the average person already heard many times about seatbelts?" "What bothers people most when they go out to buy a car (refrigerator, air conditioner), and what advice could I give that would make the task a lot easier?" By paying attention to your audience in an early stage of writing, you will be reminding yourself that process analysis needs a purpose. The information you present must be useful or intriguing to readers in some way, or it must support a particular point you want readers to grasp.

Analyze the Process   Before you begin to write, make sure you understand the process. Break the process down into its major steps, stages, or components. Then try to list as many of the smaller steps as you can, both to explore the subject thoroughly before you begin writing and to identify any aspects that need further research. In preparing for a paper to be entitled "What to Do If You Are Raped," for instance, you might discover that the pamphlets you picked up during your visit to the rape crisis center contain little information on some important things to do. Interviewing a staff member on the phone or in person can help fill gaps in your knowledge and may even provide you with details to use in developing your essay.

Of course, in writing about a process you may discover features that you failed to notice in your preliminary analysis, but this does not mean you should postpone examining the process until you are drafting your essay. Writing requires attention to so many other matters—overall structure, convincing detail, sentence style, and correctness—that postponing your examination means you will probably be unable to give adequate attention to it.

As you examine the major stages of the process, try also to sketch out the relationships among them, including causes and effects and simultaneous events. In addition, identify any resources or materials used in the process, especially those that readers will need to have on hand before following any directions.

Jotting notes on paper or freewriting as you analyze the process will help you prepare for writing the essay. Another method is to construct a flowchart showing the relationships among the elements. The illustration on the next page shows how one student, Bill Adair, constructed a flowchart for an essay in which he wanted to show how nuclear fusion can be a source of energy.

Create a Need   Unless your subject is particularly intriguing or unusual, do not expect readers to understand on their own why it is worth reading about. Be ready to show them why they need to know about the process. Indicate the practical benefits, if any, of learning about it. Explain how knowledge of the process can contribute to an understanding of the natural world or of the way people behave. If the process is amusing or intriguing, try appealing to your reader's curiosity or suggesting, indirectly of course, that your essay will be fun to read.

The best place to create a need is in the opening of an essay. Besides introducing the process to be analyzed, providing necessary background, specifying any materials required (if the essay provides a set of directions), and stating the point (thesis), the opening paragraph(s) of a process essay should create an interest in the information about to be presented.

You may find it tempting to state only briefly when and why the

Fusion Reaction

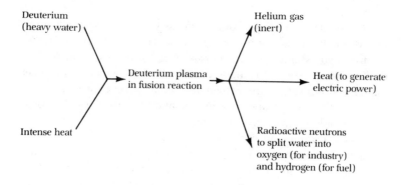

process will be useful, as did one student, Heather Kaye, in this short opening paragraph from the first draft of a set of directions:

> Bored? Grab a pad of paper, a pen, six dice, and a friend, and get ready to play Bones.

As Heather's instructor pointed out, however, this opening identifies a need that can be met by the information in the essay, but it fails to create that need in readers' minds by reminding them of how often they get bored and want something to help pass the time. In her revision, Heather added both details and explanation:

> When boredom strikes, what can you do if you don't own a video game, don't like chess, and don't have the money or time to go to a movie? Just collect a pad of paper, a pen, six dice, and a friend, and you are ready to play a game called "Bones." Bones provides fun and excitement, and you don't have to be Einstein to learn how to play. It is a game of chance and luck, laughter and friendship.

This new opening not only provides a brief description of the difficulty of finding a good, inexpensive cure for boredom, it also encourages the audience to read on by pointing out that Bones may be the perfect answer.

Set Up and Fill In an Outline   As you write, remember that a clear organization is important in process analysis as a way of helping readers keep track of the many steps they will need to follow ("Once you have filled the bottom third of the drywell with rocks ranging from three to five inches in diameter, you can begin to. . . .") or of the numerous stages in a complicated process ("In the next stage, the viral material, having penetrated the nucleus, begins attaching itself to the molecular chains carrying the genetic code. . . ."). Many process essays follow a simple linear pattern, presenting the steps or stages in chronological order while acknowledging, if necessary, that some of these elements may overlap or even occur simultaneously:

Process Pattern:
Introduction (thesis, background, materials, overview if appro-
        priate)
    Step (or stage) 1
    Step (or stage) 2
    Step (or stage) 3
    Step (or stage) 4
    Steps (or stages) 5, 6, 7
Conclusion

Yet even a simple process may have many small steps, and to help readers grasp the overall arrangement more quickly and easily, many essays divide a process into a few major sections, each of which consists of smaller steps:

Modified Process Pattern:
Introduction (thesis, background, materials, overview if appro-
        priate)
    Section 1
        Step (or stage) a
        Step (or stage) b
        Step (or stage) c
    Section 2
        Step (or stage) x
        Step (or stage) y
        Step (or stage) z
    Sections 3, 4, 5
Conclusion

Both of these patterns are abstractions, of course, strategies to be adapted to the demands of particular subjects, purposes, and audiences. The essays in this chapter illustrate some of the many different and imaginative forms the basic patterns can take, from the witty instructions Jim Villas presents in "Fried Chicken" to the complicated story of survival Roger Swain traces through thousands of years in "Avocados."

A process analysis also needs to provide enough detail to help people understand the subject and to keep them interested in it. Thus an extra example or a few more bits of descriptive detail are usually good additions, unless, of course, the process is complex enough without added detail. The major steps in a process should be described in greater detail, the smaller ones in less. For an audience that already knows something about the topic, it may even be possible to omit one or two minor steps or to mention them only in passing, adding instead information on refinements, the small details these readers do not yet know.

Pay Attention to the Audience   As you revise a process essay, pay special attention to the words you have used to signal the elements of the process to readers. These include:

> Words identifying the different stages—*step, event, element, component, phase, state, feature, occurrence*
>
> Words emphasizing relationships in time—*after, next, while, first, second, third, fourth, concurrently, the next week, later, preceding, following*
>
> Words indicating changes—*becomes, varies, transforms, causes, completes, alters, revises, uncovers, synthesizes, cures, builds.*

Check also whether you have included details that will allow readers to visualize the process, but not so many details that the analysis is confusing. If you have chosen to present the analysis in the second person (*you*) as in a set of directions ("You should then blend the ingredients"), make sure you have used this point of view consistently and have not shifted to the first person (*I* or *we*) or third person (*he, she, it,* or *they*) without good reason. Check for consistency, too, if you have chosen to present the analysis objectively in the third person or with the more personal impact of the first-person point of view.

Finally, decide whether your analysis would be more effective with visual aids like diagrams, flowcharts, or pictures (see Simon Woodroffe's "Staging Concerts" in this chapter). Should you decide to add these, however, make sure they supplement your written text, not substitute for it.

THE PATTERN IN ACTION

As a pattern for whole essays, process analysis generally takes one of two easy-to-recognize and widely used forms: instruction or explanation.

In almost every part of our lives we rely on *instructions.* They help us cook a meal, repair a car, get to a vacation spot, perform an experiment, and fill out a tax form. As how-to essays, instructions appear in newspapers, magazines, and books on a variety of topics, from fashion and makeup through sports and fitness, to computers, pets, and personal relationships. In a more complex form, sometimes combined with explanations of complex procedures, they constitute much of the substance of accounting, engineering, and nursing textbooks as well as of manuals for large corporations, government agencies, and the armed forces.

A set of instructions usually begins with a statement of the purpose and need for the procedure along with a list of the necessary materials. The steps of the process then follow in chronological order unless the complexity of the process calls for some other arrangement. A good set of instructions also contains frequent summaries to allow readers to check that they have followed the steps correctly. It takes account, too, of any special difficulties readers may encounter and any dangers the process entails ("Make sure you have put blocks under the front wheels; otherwise, as soon as you jack the car up, it may run away from you, or *over* you.")

If a procedure is long or difficult, the writer may take time to provide encouragement ("This may sound difficult, but it will work") or to give a reminder of the goal ("No pain, no gain; the only way to a flat tummy is through hard work"). In short, effective instructions keep the reader's needs, knowledge, and uncertainties in mind at all times.

We turn to *explanations* not when we want to do things but when we want to understand how things work. Explanations, therefore, are more likely to be found in encyclopedias and technical manuals than in more popular forms of writing, though magazines like *Omni, Science Digest, Popular Computing, Popular Photography,* and *Flying* regularly contain explanatory articles.

Explanations (and instructions, too) can focus on mechanical subjects (how an airplane engine works) or on social matters (how cliques form), psychological topics (how stress builds up), or natural subjects (how cancer cells take over from normal cells), among others. The arrangement of an explanation may depend on the subject. A process that takes place over a long period of time, like stress buildup, can be discussed as a set of relatively discrete stages. A process with many simultaneous events, like the functioning of a jet engine, would need to be divided into components, partly according to time sequence and partly according to the relationships within the machine. Such an explanation often requires visual aids to help explain the interaction of the components.

The audience to which an explanation is directed may determine the form it takes, too. Natural scientists and engineers have specific standards for reporting the process used in an experiment; social scientists like psychologists and sociologists have a different set of standards. Art historians and music historians, too, have particular ways of describing how a painting was created or a symphony composed. Less specialized explanations appearing in general interest books and magazines, however, usually begin by demonstrating why the process is of interest, and they pause frequently during the analysis to comment on its significance.

The essays in this chapter use process analysis in a number of ways. Jim Villas's "Fried Chicken" presents a set of instructions (several sets, actually) and at the same time comments on what it means to share knowledge of a process. Simon Woodroffe's "Staging Concerts" presents an inside view of a complex process most people take for granted: the preparation and staging of a rock concert. Alexander Petrunkevitch looks at a little-known subject, the relationship between wasp and tarantula, and in his essay "The Spider and the Wasp," explains the complicated process that intertwines their lives. In "Competing with Cool," Robert Brody uses a variety of patterns, including process, to give advice about ways to make our emotions work for us. Roger Swain also mixes patterns in the essay "Avocados," but his purpose is to explain the process by which avocados have survived and thrived.

?❧ JIM VILLAS

Jim Villas was born in 1938 in Charlotte, North Carolina ("I was bred in Charlotte," he says, "I'm very Southern."). He currently lives in New York City and is Wine and Food Editor for *Town and Country* magazine. Villas is a regular contributor to about twelve other magazines, usually on the subject of food. A champion of American cuisine, he has published one book, *American Taste* (1982), and is currently preparing the *Town and Country Cookbook*, to be published in 1985.

Fried Chicken

"Fried Chicken," first published in *Esquire* magazine, demonstrates how a set of directions can go beyond simple how-to writing and the listing of ingredients to engage an audience's interest and to display the author's feelings about his subject. Though this essay has almost as much to say about Villas and his sometimes quirky opinions as it does about cooking, it still provides exceptionally clear and thorough advice for preparing fried chicken.

When it comes to fried chicken, let's not beat around the bush   1
for one second. To know about fried chicken you have to have been weaned and reared on it in the South. Period. The French know absolutely nothing about it, and Julia Child and James Beard very little. Craig Claiborne knows plenty. He's from Mississippi. And to set the record straight before bringing on regional and possible national holocaust over the correct preparation of this classic dish, let me emphasize and reemphasize the fact that I'm a Southerner, born, bred, and chicken-fried for all times. Now, I don't know exactly why we Southerners love and eat at least ten times more fried chicken than anyone else, but we do and always have and always will. Maybe we have a hidden craw in our throats or oversize pulley bones or . . . oh, I don't know what we have, and it doesn't matter. What does matter is that we take our fried chicken very seriously, having singled it out years ago as not only the most important staple worthy of heated and complex debate but also as the dish that non-Southerners have never really had any knack for. Others just plain down don't *understand* fried chicken, and, to tell the truth, there're

lots of Southerners who don't know as much as they think they know. Naturally everybody everywhere in the country is convinced he or she can cook or identify great fried chicken as well as any ornery reb (including all the fancy cookbook writers), but the truth remains that once you've eaten real chicken fried by an expert chicken fryer in the South there are simply no grounds for contest.

As far as I'm concerned, all debate over how to prepare fried   2 chicken has ended forever, for recently I fried up exactly twenty-one and a half chickens (or 215 pieces) using every imaginable technique, piece of equipment, and type of oil for the sole purpose of establishing once and for all the right way to fix great fried chicken. In a minute I'll tell you what's wrong with most of the Kentucky-fried, Maryland-fried, oven-fried, deep-fried, creole-fried, and all those other classified varieties of Southern-fried chicken people like to go on about. But first *my* chicken, which I call simply Fried Chicken and which I guarantee will start you lapping:

Equipment (no substitutes):

> A sharp chef's or butcher's knife 12 to 13 in. long
> A large wooden cutting board
> A small stockpot half filled with water (for chicken soup)
> A large glass salad bowl
> A heavy 12-in. cast-iron skillet with lid
> Long-handled tweezer tongs
> 1 roll paper towels
> 2 brown paper bags
> 1 empty coffee can
> A serving platter
> A wire whisk
> A home fire extinguisher

Ingredients (to serve 4):

> 3 cups whole milk
> ½ fresh lemon
> 1½ lbs. (3 cups) top-quality shortening
> 4 tbsp. rendered bacon grease
> 1 whole freshly killed 3½- to 4-lb. chicken
> 1½ cups plus 2 tbsp. flour
> 3 tsp. salt
> Freshly ground black pepper

TO PREPARE CHICKEN FOR FRYING

Remove giblets and drop in stockpot with neck. (This is for a   3
good chicken soup to be eaten at another time.) Cut off and pull out
any undesirable fat at neck and tail. Placing whole chicken in center
of cutting board (breast-side up, neck toward you), grab leg on left
firmly, pull outward and down toward board, and begin slashing
down through skin toward thigh joint, keeping knife close to thigh.
Crack back thigh joint as far as possible, find joint with fingers, then
cut straight through to remove (taking care not to pull skin from
breast). Turn bird around and repeat procedure on other thigh. To
separate thigh from leg, grasp one end in each hand, pull against
tension of joint, find joint, and sever. Follow same procedure to
remove wings. Cut off wing tips and add to stockpot.

To remove pulley bone (or wishbone to non-Southerners), find   4
protruding knob toward neck end of breast, trace with fingers to
locate small indentation just forward of knob, slash horizontally
downward across indentation, then begin cutting carefully away
from indentation and downward toward neck till forked pulley-bone
piece is fully severed. Turn chicken backside up, locate two hidden
small pinbones on either side below neck toward middle of back,
and cut through skin to expose ends of bones. Put two fingers of
each hand into neck cavity and separate breast from back by pulling
forcefully till the two pry apart. (If necessary, sever stubborn tendons
and skin with knife.) Cut back in half, reserving lower portion (tail
end) for frying, and tossing upper portion (rib cage) into stockpot.
Place breast skin-side down, ram tip of knife down through center
cartilage, and cut breast in half.

(*Hint:* Level cutting edge of knife along cartilage, then slam   5
blade through with heel of hand.)

Rinse the ten pieces of chicken thoroughly under cold running   6
water, dry with paper towels, and salt and pepper lightly. Pour milk
into bowl, squeeze lemon into milk, add chicken to soak, cover, and
refrigerate at least two hours and preferably overnight.

TO FRY CHICKEN

Remove chicken from refrigerator and allow to return to room   7
temperature (about 70°). While melting the pound and a half of
shortening over high heat to measure ½ inch in skillet, pour flour,
remaining salt and pepper to taste into paper bag. Remove dark

pieces of chicken from milk, drain each momentarily over bowl, drop in paper bag, shake vigorously to coat, and add bacon grease to skillet. When small bubbles appear on surface, reduce heat slightly. Remove dark pieces of chicken from bag one by one, shake off excess flour, and, using tongs, lower gently into fat, skin-side down. Quickly repeat all procedures with white pieces; reserve milk, arrange chicken in skillet so it cooks evenly, reduce heat to medium, and cover. Fry exactly 17 minutes. Lower heat, turn pieces with tongs and fry 17 minutes longer uncovered. With paper towels wipe grease continuously from exposed surfaces as it spatters. Chicken should be almost mahogany brown.

Drain thoroughly on second brown paper bag, transfer to serving   8
platter *without* reheating in oven, and serve hot or at room temperature with any of the following items: mashed potatoes and cream gravy, potato salad, green beans, turnip greens, sliced home-grown tomatoes, stewed okra, fresh cornbread, iced tea, beer, homemade peach ice cream, or watermelon.

TO MAKE CREAM GRAVY

Discard in coffee can all but one tablespoon fat from skillet,   9
making sure not to pour off brown drippings. Over high heat, add two remaining tablespoons flour to fat and stir constantly with wire whisk till roux browns. Gradually pour 1¾ cups reserved milk from bowl and continue stirring till gravy comes to a boil, thickens slightly, and is smooth. Reduce heat, simmer two minutes, and check salt and pepper seasoning. Serve in gravy boat.

Now, that's the right way, the only way, to deal with fried   10
chicken. Crisp, juicy on the inside, full of flavor, not greasy and sloppy, fabulous. Of course one reason my recipe works so well is it's full of important subtleties that are rarely indicated in cookbooks but that help to make the difference between impeccable fried chicken and all the junk served up everywhere today. And just to illustrate this point, I cite a recipe for "Perfect Fried Chicken" that recently appeared in *Ladies' Home Journal*.

1. Rinse cut-up 2½- to 3-lb. broiler-fryer and pat dry.
2. Pour 1 in. vegetable oil in skillet, heat to 375°. Combine ½ cup flour, 2 tsp salt, dash of pepper in a bag. Coat a few pieces at a time.

3. Preheat oven to 250°. Place paper towels in shallow baking pan.
4. Fry thighs and drumsticks, turning occasionally, for 12 minutes until golden. Pierce with fork to see if juices run clear. Remove to baking pan and place in heated oven. Fry remaining pieces for 7 or 8 minutes. Serves four.

Snap! That's it. A real quicky. Fast fried chicken that promises 11 to be perfect. Bull! It tasted like hell, and if you don't believe me, try it yourself. The pitfalls of the recipe are staggering but typical. First of all, nobody in his right mind fries a skinny two-and-a-half-pound chicken for four people, not unless everyone's on some absurd diet or enjoys sucking bones. Second, the recipe takes for granted you're going to buy a plastic-wrapped chicken that's been so hacked and splintered by a meat cleaver that blood from the bones saturates the package. What help is offered if the chicken you happen to have on hand is whole or only partially cut up? Third, what type of skillet, and what size, for heaven's sake? If the pan's too light the chicken will burn on the bottom, and if you pour one full inch of oil in an eight-inch skillet, you'll end up with deep-fried chicken. And as for sticking forks in seared chicken to release those delicious juices, or putting fried chicken in the oven to get it disgustingly soggy, or serving a half-raw thick breast that's cooked only seven or eight minutes—well, I refuse to get overheated.

Without question the most important secret to any great fried 12 chicken is the quality of the chicken itself, and without question most of the three billion pullets marketed annually in the U.S. have about as much flavor as tennis balls. But, after all, what can you expect of battery birds whose feet never touch the dirty filthy earth, whose diet includes weight-building fats, fish flours, and factory-fresh chemicals, and whose life expectancy is a pitiful seven weeks? Tastelessness, that's what, the same disgraceful tastelessness that characterizes the eggs we're forced to consume. How many people in this country remember the rich flavor of a good old barnyard chicken, a nearly extinct species that pecked around the yard for a good fifteen weeks, digested plenty of barley-and-milk mash, bran, grain, and beer, got big and fat, and never sent one solitary soul to the hospital with contamination? I remember, believe you me, and how I pity the millions who, blissfully unconscious of what they missed and sadly addicted to the chicken passed out by Colonel Sanders, will never taste a truly luscious piece of fried chicken unless they're first shown how to get their hands on a real chicken. Of course, what you see in supermarkets are technically real chickens fit for consumption, but anyone who's sunk teeth into a gorgeous, plump barnyard variety (not to mention an inimitable French *poularde de Bresse*) would agree that to compare the scrawny, bland, mass-produced bird with the one God intended us to eat is something more than ludicrous.

I originally intended to tell you how to raise, kill, draw, and   13
prepare your own chickens. Then I came to my senses and faced the reality that unless you were brought up wringing chickens' necks, bleeding them, searching for the craws where food is stored, and pulling out their innards with your hands—well, it can be a pretty nauseating mess that makes you gag if you're not used to it. Besides, there's really no need to slaughter your own chickens, not, that is, if you're willing to take time and make the effort to locate either a good chicken raiser who feeds and exercises his chickens properly (on terra firma) or a reliable merchant who gets his chickens fresh from the farm. They do exist, still, be their number ever so dwindling. If you live in a rural area, simply get to know a farmer who raises chickens, start buying eggs from him and then tell him you'll pay him any amount to kill and prepare for you a nice 3½- to 4-pound pullet. He will, and probably with pride. If you're in a large city, the fastest method is to study the Yellow Pages of the phone book, search under "Poultry—Retail" for the words "Fresh poultry and eggs" or "Custom poultry" or "Strictly kosher poultry," and proceed from there.

Now, if you think I take my fried chicken a little too seriously,   14
you haven't seen anything till you attend the National Chicken Cooking Contest held annually in early summer at different locations throughout the country. Created in 1949, the festival has a Poultry Princess; vintage motorcar displays; a flea market; a ten-feet-by-eight-inch skillet that fries up to seven and a half tons of chicken; ten thousand chicken-loving contestants cooking for cash prizes amounting to over $25,000; and big-name judges who are chosen from among the nation's top newspaper, magazine, and television food editors. It's a big to-do. Of course, I personally have no intention whatsoever of ever entering any chicken contest that's not made up exclusively of Southerners, and of course you understand my principle. This, however, should not necessarily affect your now going to the National and showing the multitudes what real fried chicken

is all about. A few years back, a young lady irreverently dipped some chicken in oil flavored with soy sauce, rolled it in crushed chow mein noodles, fried it up, and walked away with top honors and a few grand for her Cock-a-Noodle-Do. Without doubt she was a sweetheart of a gal, but you know, the people who judged that fried chicken need help.

COMMENTARY

Most recipes are written in the third person with a calm, neutral tone, but not "Fried Chicken." From the first sentence on, Villas addresses his readers directly in his distinctive voice, attacking other food writers, telling his readers that they don't really understand how to make fried chicken even if they think they do, and talking about the connection between fried chicken and Southern culture. Far from being an act of self-indulgence, Villas's detailed introduction and his talk about matters not immediately related to the recipe he plans to present help the essay appeal to a variety of readers, including (1) people who like to read about cooking and about food experts—the audience for a magazine like *Cuisine,* (2) people who know little about cooking but might be interested in learning about a dish as famous as fried chicken if the writer's style is fresh and the essay promises to be more than a dull recipe, and (3) people who think they can cook good fried chicken but would be willing to look at an approach that promises to be genuinely different. Villas also uses the introduction to begin making a point that he emphasizes later in the essay as well: Food and the way we choose to prepare it reflect and shape our attitudes towards life.

The recipe itself is far longer and more detailed than most because it explains even simple operations at length. Instead of saying "Rinse, dry, salt and pepper lightly," as many cookbooks would, Villas describes the operations in detail, almost as if he were doing them while writing the information down: "Rinse the ten pieces of chicken thoroughly under cold running water, dry with paper towels, and salt and pepper lightly" (par. 6). In part, this description reflects his estimate that many readers of the essay will not be used to cooking (the essay was, after all, first published in *Esquire,* a magazine not noted for its treatment of food preparation). Yet it also emphasizes the contrast between his approach and that of the *Ladies' Home Journal* recipe, which he calls "a real quicky."

Villas's description of a process is also an argument for a certain approach towards the preparation and enjoyment of food. The comparison of his recipe to the one in the *Ladies' Home Journal* and his discussions of farming practices and cooking contests at the end of the essay (pars. 14–16) explore the connections between a culture and the food it produces, and they are an argument for changes in the way we live as well as the way we cook. "Fried Chicken" is thus not simply a discussion of the best way to prepare a favorite dish; it is an argument for honesty and quality in all our activities.

RESPONSES AND IDEAS

1. Respond to this essay by describing your favorite dish in detail, providing a recipe, if you can, and indicating what makes this dish better than other versions of the same kind of food.

2. List the cooking practices, recipes, and anything else that Villas attacks, and indicate what he dislikes about them.

3. Identify as many as you can of the "important subtleties" referred to in paragraph 10.

PURPOSE, AUDIENCE, AND STRATEGIES

1. Is this essay likely to be interesting to readers who do not like fried chicken and have no particular interest in cooking? What might they find interesting or enjoyable about it? What sections might they find especially interesting? Does Villas make any special attempts to appeal to such readers? If so, describe the strategies he uses.

2. Why does Villas talk about raising chickens (par. 13) if he admits that it will mean little to his readers? What purpose other than advising readers where to find good chickens does this entire paragraph serve?

3. In what ways would Villas have to change this essay if he wanted to publish it in *Ladies' Home Journal* or a similar magazine?

4. What evidence does Villas present in paragraphs 1 and 2 to establish that he is an authority on fried chicken? Is the evidence convincing? Does he present any other evidence in the course of the essay?

5. Identify the places in this essay where Villas provides definitions. Where else would you like to have seen definitions?

LANGUAGE AND STYLE

1. Describe the tone of the opening paragraph. (See Glossary: Tone.) What strategies of diction and syntax contribute to the tone? Be specific. How

does the tone allow Villas to say things about other food experts and other recipes that might be offensive if uttered in another tone?

2. Describe how Villas uses diction and figures of speech in paragraph 12 to influence readers' reactions to the different kinds of chickens he discusses. (See Glossary: Diction, Figures of Speech.)

3. If you do not know the meaning of any of the following words, look them up in the dictionary: *holocaust, craw, pulley, staple* (par. 1); *creole-fried* (2); *stockpot* (3); *rendered* (4); *cleaver* (11); *battery* (12); *wringing, innards, terra firma* (13).

WRITING ACTIVITIES

1. In an essay, explain the special ways your family or your friends celebrate a holiday or arrange a group activity like a picnic or a party. Emphasize the most important or intriguing elements of the gathering or activity, telling what they mean to the participants and indicating how they might enrich similar activities for your readers.

2. There is more than one way to catch a trout, prepare chili, or win at tennis. Choose an activity that will interest readers and explain two or more ways it can be done, highlighting the strengths and weaknesses of each approach.

❧ SIMON WOODROFFE

Simon Woodroffe trained in theater in London and then in the
early 1970s began providing lighting for rock shows. He ran a
lighting company in Europe for a number of years before deciding
to concentrate on stage and lighting design. Currently he designs
and produces shows for many major rock tours.

Staging Concerts

Usually the only glimpse we get of rock concerts is from the front
of the stage, or through publicity pictures that turn up in glossy
magazines. Simon Woodroffe's "Staging Concerts," published in
Making Music: The Guide to Writing, Performing, and Recording,
a collection of essays edited by George Martin (producer of the
Beatles' records), provides an insider's glimpse into the work of
presenting a concert. His description reveals that rock concerts
have a good deal in common with other theatrical productions,
although the scale and the style of performance are of course quite
different from those of more traditional fare.

The illustrations accompanying the essay demonstrate the kind
of detailed planning that goes into preparing and staging a rock
concert.

"Ladies and gentlemen, will you please welcome—The Rolling   1
Stones!" Backstage—Roy Lamb, stage manager: "Stand by all sta-
tions, go house curtains, go balloons." Fifteen thousand balloons
float heavenward and Balloon Crew 1's work is over. The Audito-
rium—Patrick Woodroffe, lighting designer: "Stand by stage lights,
bump to cue 1. Stand by spotlights 1, 4, 6 and 8. Colour to 4 to
pick up lead singer moving downstage. Go 1." Jagger moves stage
right. B. J. Schiller, sound: "Vocal monitor position 2. Local monitors
no feedback." Stage manager 1: "Stand by scrim reveal. Go!" The
singer rides a cherry picker 30 feet over the heads of the audience.
Backstage—the Ambience Crew have put the final touches to the
backstage decor, truck drivers relax before tonight's haul. The Box
Office—Bill Graham, tour promoter is settling up with the hall
manager: takings, production costs, local crew, transport, hotels,
entertainment—each item is checked against a budget.

Fifteen years ago, when they played Shea Stadium, The Beatles'   2
equipment arrived in a pick up truck; today The Rolling Stones use
a convoy of 32 trucks and a staff of 150. Shows have grown up and
an industry has evolved along with them. Not every act could or
would want to tour on this scale, but with more than 50,000 acts
competing for the audiences and stages of the world, shows are big
business.

To the average fan, a concert is a few hours of entertainment   3
provided by their favourite artist. The audience is unaware of the
months of work and planning that have gone into those few hours,
nor the number of people who are responsible for making or breaking a show.

THE PROMOTER

A successful group plans its activities up to a year ahead, the   4
time being divided into recording, promotion, touring and short
breaks for recuperating. To the promoter, a gambling man, every
group wants to play larger audiences, earn larger grosses and be
more successful. The promoter is responsible for filling the halls:
"bums on seats" is his game and, if a hall is too small, he has
underestimated the group's potential; if it is too large and there are
too many empty seats, it is demoralizing and unprofitable.

A promoter knows that a group's manager will want his band   5
to give concerts whenever an album is released. A touring itinerary
must be planned so that four or five shows can be played each week,
with travelling time allowed for. The promoter will block-book halls
even before booking the acts and will then juggle his clients to fit
his bookings. The promoters compete to offer acts the best deals and
venues, although in the case of a show such as Bill Graham's outdoor
"Day on the Green in San Francisco," the tides reverse as groups
clamour to play such a well presented and organized event.

STAGE PRODUCTION

As the touring date approaches, ideas for the stage show are   6
discussed, with inspiration likely to come from several directions: an
album cover, another show, or the manager producing an idea that
fits with his promotion of the group. A designer who specializes in
scenery and lighting liaises with the group's production manager

and a concept slowly emerges. It is the designer's job to realize the idea for final presentation, costing and approval; usually he produces a scale model, an artist's impression or a drawing. Designing for a touring rock stage is as much a feat of engineering as a creative process, because each piece must be able to withstand the rigours of being put up and taken down every day; a show that looks impressive at rehearsals must still look good six months later.

Eric Barrett is credited with having first used coloured lights— for Jimi Hendrix and The Beatles—but it was the flamboyant Californian Chip Monck who conceived the first rock show spectacle as we know it today. Monck didn't do things by halves; the story goes that his budget for The Rolling Stones' world tour was spent well before the entourage left rehearsals in Hawaii.   7

The 1970s was an age of mechanical shows: Electric Light Orchestra toured with a space ship that supported the lighting of the show; David Bowie floated over the audience in a mechanical hand; Alice Cooper magically stepped out of a movie screen (a trick invented by Walt Disney using a screen made of stretched elastic); Donny Osmond flew out over the audience (and nearly got stuck swinging over the 20,000 fans below); and Keith Emerson played a grand piano rotating through 360 degrees. All of this required planning, designing and engineering, and rock shows borrowed heavily from the mechanical expertise of theatre and film until by the 1980s rock stage production became a business in its own right.   8

THE TOUR MANAGER

Once the production of a show has been planned, two key personnel—the tour manager and the production manager—are hired.   9

The tour manager is responsible for the logistics of getting the entourage from one place to the next, and will work with a travel agent who specializes in the music industry. In the United States nearly all travelling is done in buses that are fitted with various degrees of luxury. All have sleeping bunks—an overnight run can be as far as 500 miles with a show at both ends—and cooking facilities, shower, video and hi-fi are all standard and necessary equipment because this will be home for up to ten people for three months.   10

Some groups charter aeroplanes, such as the Starship range, 11
which are equipped for a group's needs; in Europe flying is generally
the rule, whereas in Japan the bullet trains are more convenient.
Needless to say, checking in and out of airports can be strenuous if
done every day, especially for the tour manager. The tour manager
will also book hotels, and the larger shows will have a tour accoun-
tant to look after their finances.

And so the show goes on the road. Each hall will have what is 12
known as a technical rider which specifies all of the group's requirements from the amount of equipment to be hung from the roof, to
the food and drink needed in the band's dressing rooms.

THE PRODUCTION MANAGER

The production manager is in charge of the technical crew who 13
move independently of the band because they must arrive at a gig
early on the morning of the show. In the planning stages, the production manager will contract services such as lighting, sound, truck-
ing, rigging, bussing, and catering. There is stiff competition between
companies providing these services and decisions are made on the
quality of the equipment, management and crews, as well as the
prices bid.

When all of the major decisions have been made, a final pro- 14
duction meeting is held prior to rehearsals and it is here that, for
the first time, all key personnel meet. The tour manager presides; it
is an important time because the technical success of a tour is
dependent upon the crew working together efficiently and happily.

REHEARSALS

Rehearsals may be held in an unused theatre or film studio; Rod 15
Stewart once rehearsed a European tour in an RAF aircraft hangar,
much to the pleasure of the inhabitants. Two days are normally set
aside for technical rehearsals, although two weeks were allowed for
Pink Floyd's "The Wall" show. Rehearsals are the culmination of
many weeks' work, and preparation is essential because once the
show is on the road it is difficult to make changes. New equipment
can be extremely expensive to ship and so spare parts—from strings
and speakers to light bulbs and tiny electronic circuits—are essential.

Despite checking and rechecking, as in Murphy's Law, anything that can go wrong will; and as far as rock 'n' roll touring goes, Murphy was an optimist.

With all of the equipment finally set up, the group arrives for 16 the first day's rehearsal. By now the group should be together musically; these rehearsals are used mainly to integrate the group's performance with technicalities such as stage positions, and to give the sound and lighting crews an opportunity to test their plans in practice.

SETTING UP

Early in the morning on the day of the show, riggers will be in 17 the ceiling of the hall hanging cables from which to suspend sound and lighting equipment. The rigger's job developed in the early 1970s when rock shows moved out of theatres, with their sophisticated technical facilities, into halls and sports arenas which had not been built to house a stage and the technical equipment most shows require. The riggers borrowed heavily from techniques used for shows such as *Holiday on Ice* and *Disney on Parade,* adding their own innovations and setting high standards of technique and safety.

While the riggers are at work, local crews will have been split 18 into teams to work in various departments: truck unloading, lighting, sound and stage set up. Lighting will usually first be assembled on the ground in preparation for lifting by electric chain hoists. The tour electrician will tap into the mains of the building, since most shows require enough electricity to run a small town. For one show in South America the promoter of the group Queen arranged for part of the town in which they were playing to be blacked out for the duration of the concert to provide enough electricity for the 500 lights used in the show. To date, Van Halen holds the record, having carried more than 1,000 lights on tour, some million watts of electricity. Rock 'n' roll has always had a tendency towards the excessive and, of course, quality and quantity do not always go hand in hand.

The acoustics of every venue, unlike those of recording studios, 19 are different, and even with the best equipment in the world the sound mixer's task of using the acoustics to their fullest potential is crucial. Speakers must be angled to give even coverage to every seat and the engineer can then compensate for peaks and nulls in the frequency response of the room by using a graphic equalizer. Short of covering the walls and ceiling with deadening material, which

11. STAGE CALL
    8:00 a.m.   Rigging and power hook up
    10:00 a.m.   Lights and set
    12 Noon   Set and sound
    2 p.m.   Lunch (one hour)
    3 p.m.   Band equipment

12. LOCAL CREW CALL
    8:00 a.m.   2 house riggers
                  1 forklift operator
                  2 loaders
                  1 electrician
    At 8:00 a.m. only rigging and power supply to be unloaded
    from trucks and hooked up with a minimum crew.

    10:00 a.m.   12 working stage hands plus department heads
                  2 additional loaders

    Show Call 30 minutes before showtime
                  4 spot operators
                  4 stagehands/deckmen
                  1 electrician/houselights man
                  1 forklift operator

    After each act if possible will load out support acts.

    Out Call   16 working stagehands plus department heads
                  6 loaders (on out load two trucks at once)
                  2 house riggers
                  1 house electrician
                  1 forklift operator

13. SOUND CHECKS
    OZZY OSBOURNE sound check will begin at 4:30 p.m. until
    it is over. The auditorium must be kept clear of all
    non-working personnel.

14. SUPPORT ACT
    No support act will place any of their equipment on stage
    without checking with Ozzy Osbourne Production Manager.
    Any sound checks required by other act on the bill must
    be co-ordinated three (3) days in advance of day of show
    with Ozzy Osbourne Production Manager.

Production Checklist for an Ozzy Osbourne Concert

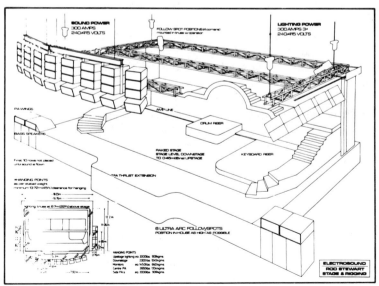

Stage and Rigging Diagram for a Rod Stewart Concert

has been done on occasion, the mixer has to cope with the natural echo of the room.

A musician obviously never sees or hears his own show and can only hear himself through his own speakers, and so monitors are of paramount importance. The performers rely upon the monitor mixer who is the most important person with regard to the performer's on-stage confidence.

THE ELEVENTH HOUR

By late afternoon everything should be up and working: sound equipment in position, lights focused and the stage made ready for a sound check which usually takes an hour or so to allow monitor levels to be adjusted and the sound engineer to set up his mixer. For the performers, this is a pre-show rehearsal and, if everything has gone smoothly, there may only be minor repairs or spare parts to be replaced. By six o'clock the technicians and crew can take a break until showtime.

During the few hours preceding the performance the house crew make final adjustments: barriers are placed in front of the stage, seats that have been removed for set-up are replaced, the security staff are briefed, spotlight and houselight operators meet the lighting designer, and stage hands are given the cues needed during the show.

Once the doors are opened, the show is rolling. The stage manager will organize the support acts until the final call to the band's dressing room. The houselights will then go down, and the show is on.

The moment the group leaves the stage after their final encore, the team that has been at work since 8 A.M. takes down all the equipment that has been up and working for only a few hours. Three hours later, the doors are closed on the last truck, and it is on to the next show.

RESPONSES AND IDEAS

1.   Respond to this essay by describing the kinds of arrangements necessary for a play, pageant, or similar activity you or someone you know has participated in. Did they follow any patterns similar to those Woodroffe describes?

2. From what sources are ideas for a stage show likely to come? What are the tour manager and the production manager responsible for?

3. Identify the major steps in the staging of a rock concert. What use does the author make of transitions and other devices in making the steps clear to readers? (See Glossary: Transitions.)

PURPOSE, AUDIENCE, AND STRATEGIES

1. Is this essay directed solely to fans of rock music? Support your answer with references to the text. Why might someone who prefers another kind of music be interested in reading "Staging Concerts"?

2. Is Woodroffe's purpose simply to explain how concerts are staged, or does he also have an opinion about them that he wants to share? If he does, what is his opinion, and how does he indicate it in the essay?

3. Where does Woodroffe reveal his feelings about any of the rock acts he uses as examples? Why does he reveal his feelings?

4. What strategy does Woodroffe use in the opening paragraph? (See Glossary: Introductions.) Does the opening paragraph announce in any way the point (thesis) of the essay? How? (See Glossary: Thesis.)

5. Where in the essay does Woodroffe use lists or clusters of details to explain or to support a point? How effective are the details?

LANGUAGE AND STYLE

1. At what points in the essay does Woodroffe's style become informal? Does this informality harm the effectiveness of the essay?

2. The word "bums" (par. 4) has a different meaning in Great Britain than it does in the United States. What does Woodroffe use it to mean? (You may want to look the word up in a dictionary.) What does "RAF" (par. 15) mean? Which words in the essay have British rather than American spellings?

3. If you do not know the meaning of any of the following words, look them up in the dictionary: *scrim, reveal, ambience* (par. 1); *grosses* (4); *itinerary, booking, venues, clamour* (5); *logistics, entourage* (10); *rider* (12); *gig* (13); *acoustics* (19).

WRITING ACTIVITIES

1. Have you ever prepared a flaming dessert in a restaurant, raced a hydroplane, or directed a play? If so, then you have an insider's view of events most people have seen only from the outside. Prepare an essay

that shares with readers your inside view of the process behind an interesting event or activity and that explains any differences between the way it appears to outsiders and to insiders.

2.   Though most people enjoy songs, paintings, movies, novels, and sculpture, few know how these works of art are created. In an essay, explain the process by which a work of art either big (a feature movie) or small (a crystal vase) comes into being. Do whatever research is necessary to get the information you need.

🐾 ALEXANDER PETRUNKEVITCH

Alexander Petrunkevitch (1875–1967) was born in Pliski, Russia, and educated in Europe. He came to the United States in 1903 and taught zoology at several leading American universities, including Yale. He was one of the world's foremost authorities on spiders. His publications include *Index Catalogue of Spiders of North, Central, and South America* (1911), *Principles of Classification* (1952), and *Choice and Responsibility* (1947), as well as translations of Russian poetry and poems of his own.

The Spider and the Wasp

"The Spider and the Wasp" was first published in *Scientific American* in 1952, and has since come to be regarded as a classic essay. It demonstrates the careful combination of several patterns, including process, to convey insight into a complex relationship between two insects. Though the subject is a technical one, Petrunkevitch manages to make it clear and understandable even for nonscientists.

In the feeding and safeguarding of their progeny insects and spiders exhibit some interesting analogies to reasoning and some crass examples of blind instinct. The case I propose to describe here is that of the tarantula spiders and their archenemy, the digger wasps of the genus *Pepsis*. It is a classic example of what looks like intelligence pitted against instinct—a strange situation in which the victim, though fully able to defend itself, submits unwittingly to its destruction.

Most tarantulas live in the tropics, but several species occur in the temperate zone and a few are common in the southern U.S. Some varieties are large and have powerful fangs with which they can inflict a deep wound. These formidable-looking spiders do not, however, attack man; you can hold one in your hand, if you are gentle, without being bitten. Their bite is dangerous only to insects and small mammals such as mice; for man it is no worse than a hornet's sting.

Tarantulas customarily live in deep cylindrical burrows, from which they emerge at dusk and into which they retire at dawn.

239

Mature males wander about after dark in search of females and occasionally stray into houses. After mating, the male dies in a few weeks, but a female lives much longer and can mate several years in succession. In a Paris museum is a tropical specimen which is said to have been living in captivity for 25 years.

A fertilized female tarantula lays from 200 to 400 eggs at a time; thus it is possible for a single tarantula to produce several thousand young. She takes no care of them beyond weaving a cocoon of silk to enclose the eggs. After they hatch, the young walk away, find convenient places in which to dig their burrows and spend the rest of their lives in solitude. The eyesight of tarantulas is poor, being limited to a sensing of change in the intensity of light and to the perception of moving objects. They apparently have little or no sense of hearing, for a hungry tarantula will pay no attention to a loudly chirping cricket placed in its cage unless the insect happens to touch one of its legs.

But all spiders, and especially hairy ones, have an extremely delicate sense of touch. Laboratory experiments prove that tarantulas can distinguish three types of touch: pressure against the body wall, stroking of the body hair, and riffling of certain very fine hairs on the legs called trichobothria. Pressure against the body, by the finger or the end of a pencil, causes the tarantula to move off slowly for a short distance. The touch excites no defensive response unless the approach is from above where the spider can see the motion, in which case it rises on its hind legs, lifts its front legs, opens its fangs and holds this threatening posture as long as the object continues to move.

The entire body of a tarantula, especially its legs, is thickly clothed with hair. Some of it is short and wooly, some long and stiff. Touching this body hair produces one of two distinct reactions. When the spider is hungry, it responds with an immediate and swift attack. At the touch of a cricket's antennae the tarantula seizes the insect so swiftly that a motion picture taken at the rate of 64 frames per second shows only the result and not the process of capture. But when the spider is not hungry, the stimulation of its hairs merely causes it to shake the touched limb. An insect can walk under its hairy belly unharmed.

The trichobothria, very fine hairs growing from disklike membranes on the legs, are sensitive only to air movement. A light breeze makes them vibrate slowly, without disturbing the common hair. When one blows gently on the trichobothria, the tarantula reacts with a quick jerk of its four front legs. If the front and hind legs are stimulated at the same time, the spider makes a sudden jump. This reaction is quite independent of the state of its appetite.

These three tactile responses—to pressure on the body wall, to moving of the common hair, and to flexing of the trichobothria—are so different from one another that there is no possibility of confusing them. They serve the tarantula adequately for most of its needs and enable it to avoid most annoyances and dangers. But they fail the spider completely when it meets its deadly enemy, the digger wasp *Pepsis.*   8

These solitary wasps are beautiful and formidable creatures. Most species are either a deep shiny blue all over, or deep blue with rusty wings. The largest have a wing span of about 4 inches. They live on nectar. When excited, they give off a pungent odor—a warning that they are ready to attack. The sting is much worse than that of a bee or common wasp, and the pain and swelling last longer. In the adult stage the wasp lives only a few months. The female produces but a few eggs, one at a time at intervals of two or three days. For each egg the mother must provide one adult tarantula, alive but paralyzed. The mother wasp attaches the egg to the paralyzed spider's abdomen. Upon hatching from the egg, the larva is many hundreds of times smaller than its living but helpless victim. It eats no other food and drinks no water. By the time it has finished its single Gargantuan meal and become ready for wasphood, nothing remains of the tarantula but its indigestible chitinous skeleton.   9

The mother wasp goes tarantula-hunting when the egg in her ovary is almost ready to be laid. Flying low over the ground late on a sunny afternoon, the wasp looks for its victim or for the mouth of a tarantula burrow, a round hole edged by a bit of silk. The sex of the spider makes no difference, but the mother is highly discriminating as to species. Each species of *Pepsis* requires a certain species of tarantula, and the wasp will not attack the wrong species. In a cage with a tarantula which is not its normal prey, the wasp avoids the spider and is usually killed by it in the night.   10

Yet when a wasp finds the correct species, it is the other way about. To identify the species the wasp apparently must explore the spider with her antennae. The tarantula shows an amazing tolerance   11 to this exploration. The wasp crawls under it and walks over it without evoking any hostile response. The molestation is so great and so persistent that the tarantula often rises on all eight legs, as if it were on stilts. It may stand this way for several minutes. Meanwhile the wasp, having satisfied itself that the victim is of the right species, moves off a few inches to dig the spider's grave. Working vigorously with legs and jaws, it excavates a hole 8 to 10 inches deep with a diameter slightly larger than the spider's girth. Now and again the wasp pops out of the hole to make sure that the spider is still there.

When the grave is finished, the wasp returns to the tarantula to 12 complete her ghastly enterprise. First she feels it all over once more with her antennae. Then her behavior becomes more aggressive. She bends her abdomen, protruding her sting, and searches for the soft membrane at the point where the spider's legs join its body—the only spot where she can penetrate the horny skeleton. From time to time, as the exasperated spider slowly shifts ground, the wasp turns on her back and slides along with the aid of her wings, trying to get under the tarantula for a shot at the vital spot. During all this maneuvering, which can last for several minutes, the tarantula makes no move to save itself. Finally the wasp corners it against some obstruction and grasps one of its legs in her powerful jaws. Now at last the harassed spider tries a desperate but vain defense. The two contestants roll over and over on the ground. It is a terrifying sight and the outcome is always the same. The wasp finally manages to thrust her sting into the soft spot and holds it there for a few seconds while she pumps in the poison. Almost immediately the tarantula falls paralyzed on its back. Its legs stop twitching; its heart stops beating. Yet it is not dead, as is shown by the fact that if taken from the wasp it can be restored to some sensitivity by being kept in a moist chamber for several months.

After paralyzing the tarantula, the wasp cleans herself by drag- 13 ging her body along the ground and rubbing her feet, sucks a drop of blood oozing from the wound in the spider's abdomen, then grabs a leg of the flabby, helpless animal in her jaws and drags it down to the bottom of the grave. She stays there for many minutes, some-times for several hours, and what she does all that time in the dark we do not know. Eventually she lays her egg and attaches it to the side of the sider's abdomen with a sticky secretion. Then she emerges, fills the grave with soil carried bit by bit in her jaws, and finally tramples the ground all around to hide any trace of the grave from prowlers. Then she flies away, leaving her descendant safely started in life.

In all this the behavior of the wasp evidently is qualitatively 14 different from that of the spider. The wasp acts like an intelligent animal. This is not to say that instinct plays no part or that she reasons as man does. But her actions are to the point; they are not automatic and can be modified to fit the situation. We do not know for certain how she identifies the tarantula—probably it is by some olfactory or chemo-tactile sense—but she does it purposefully and does not blindly tackle a wrong species.

On the other hand, the tarantula's behavior shows only confu- 15 sion. Evidently the wasp's pawing gives it no pleasure, for it tries to move away. That the wasp is not simulating sexual stimulation is certain because male and female tarantulas react in the same way to its advances. That the spider is not anesthetized by some odorless secretion is easily shown by blowing lightly at the tarantula and making it jump suddenly. What, then, makes the tarantula behave as stupidly as it does?

No clear, simple answer is available. Possibly the stimulation by 16 the wasp's antennae is masked by a heavier pressure on the spider's body, so that it reacts as when prodded by a pencil. But the explanation may be much more complex. Initiative in attack is not in the nature of tarantulas; most species fight only when cornered so that escape is impossible. Their inherited patterns of behavior apparently prompt them to avoid problems rather than attack them. For example, spiders always weave their webs in three dimensions, and when a spider finds that there is insufficient space to attach certain threads in the third dimension, it leaves the place and seeks another, instead of finishing the web in a single plane. This urge to escape seems to arise under all circumstances, in all phases of life, and to take the place of reasoning. For a spider to change the pattern of its web is as impossible as for an inexperienced man to build a bridge across a chasm obstructing his way.

In a way the instinctive urge to escape is not only easier but 17 often more efficient than reasoning. The tarantula does exactly what is most efficient in all cases except in an encounter with a ruthless and determined attacker dependent for the existence of her own species on killing as many tarantulas as she can lay eggs. Perhaps in this case the spider follows its usual pattern of trying to escape, instead of seizing and killing the wasp, because it is not aware of its danger. In any case, the survival of the tarantula species as a whole is protected by the fact that the spider is much more fertile than the wasp.

RESPONSES AND IDEAS

1. Summarize as briefly but as thoroughly as you can the relationship between the spider and the wasp.
2. What does Petrunkevitch mean when he describes the wasp's behavior as "intelligent" (par. 14)? Do you agree with his definition? Would you apply his definition to humans? Explain.
3. In paragraph 16 Petrunkevitch says, "For a spider to change the pattern of its web is as impossible as for an inexperienced man to build a bridge across a chasm obstructing his way." What reasonable objections might be raised to his view of human behavior?

PURPOSE, AUDIENCE, AND STRATEGIES

1. Where is the thesis of this essay stated, and what is it? (See Glossary: Thesis.)
2. What features of this essay indicate that it was originally addressed to an audience interested in scientific subjects?
3. Are most readers likely to draw comparisons between the behavior of the insects and the behavior of human beings? What in the essay would encourage or discourage such comparisons?
4. Identify the following patterns in the essay, and tell what they contribute to it: cause-and-effect, definition, and description.
5. How many paragraphs make up the conclusion of this essay, and what role do they play besides concluding the piece? (See Glossary: Closings.)

LANGUAGE AND STYLE

1. How do the verbs Petrunkevitch uses in paragraphs 9–13 make his account especially vivid? What other resources of diction does he use in these paragraphs? (See Glossary: Diction.)
2. Discuss how Petrunkevitch uses word choice (diction) and choice of examples in paragraphs 3 to 8 to make the spider's actions seem unintelligent, purely instinctive, sometimes almost passive. Contrast this portrait to his description of the wasp's activities in paragraphs 9 to 12. Pay particular attention to the verbs he uses in both sections and to the connotations of these and other words. (See Glossary: Diction, Connotation.) Explain why you believe that Petrunkevitch's method of com-

menting on his subjects' actions through the connotations of words is appropriate or inappropriate to writing about scientific subjects.

3. If you do not know the meaning of some of the following words, look them up in the dictionary: *progeny, archenemy, classic* (par. 1); *formidable* (2); *perception* (4); *riffling* (5); *disklike* (7); *tactile* (8); *pungent, chitinous* (9); *discriminating* (10); *evoking, molestation* (11); *harassed* (12); *secretion* (13); *qualitatively, olfactory, chemo-tactile* (14); *ruthless* (17).

WRITING ACTIVITIES

1. Have you spent much time in the outdoors hiking and camping or have you worked in some job that brought you in contact with nature (as a gardener or in the logging industry, for example)? If so, you may be aware of some unusual and interesting natural process or relationship. Make your experience the basis of an essay in which you share your knowledge with readers. (If necessary, substitute research for experience in preparing your essay.)

2. Read Sharon Curtin's "Garbage Man" (Chapter 2), then examine in an essay the ways in which the townspeople and the Garbage Man depend on each other and compare their relationship to that of the spider and the wasp.

❧ ROBERT BRODY

Robert Brody was born in 1952 in the Bronx, New York. He received a B.A. from Fairleigh Dickinson University and worked as a reporter for a community newspaper, the *Eastside Courier,* and as editor of *American Druggist* before becoming a free-lance writer. His articles on subjects of health, science, fitness, and medicine have appeared in *Esquire, GQ, Self, Science Digest,* and *American Health.*

Competing with Cool

In this essay, first published in *Esquire* magazine, Robert Brody combines a cause-effect (problem-solution) pattern with process to suggest ways of dealing with a problem that is not limited to sports, although it is perhaps most evident there. The interweaving of patterns in this essay is complicated, but the essay as a whole is easy enough to understand.

Even as a kid, I had a talent for getting ticked off in competition. 1
No occasion was too trivial for a tantrum, whether I was striking out, dropping a pass, or blowing a lay-up. In my more-reserved moments I had the decency to blame such failures on myself. But I also had a knack for discerning obscure causes that ranged from lucky curveballs and errant winds to lazy teammates and uncooperative backboards. In retrospect, it was uncanny how seldom I was at fault.

Of course, all my fuming and cursing were bad news when it 2
came to the caliber of my play. The more upset I became at my shortcomings, the worse I performed. I swung at bad pitches, forced jump shots from well beyond my range, double-faulted ad nauseam. Distracted from the business at hand, my concentration in smithereens, I could usually count on my game to self-destruct. In short, I had no cool.

Now that I'm an adult, poise is still not my specialty. Just a few 3
months back, a guy guarding me in basketball was hacking at my arms every time I took a shot and was climbing over my back for rebounds. After one especially nasty foul—I remember feeling to

make sure my head was still attached—I shoved him to the court. He laid off me from then on, but no matter—I was so ashamed of my violence that my game was hopelessly undermined for the night.

And so it has gone my whole life. Under competitive pressure I 4 have all the composure of an unfed Doberman. My anger gets so far out of hand that whatever skills I possess are seriously hampered. Only recently have I begun to realize that playing with poise is essential to a top-notch performance in any sport. Poise in this regard means a sense of emotional balance. Just about all the best athletes know that harnessing the emotions can spell the difference between the mediocre and the champion, that staying unruffled in the face of adversity is as much a sign of character as it is an act of sportsmanship.

For the weekend jock as well as the pro, keeping cool in the 5 heat of competition is more often a cultivated skill than an inborn trait. Even if you're the kind of hothead who snaps your 4 iron after a slice into the trees—so bent on excellence that you simply bear down too hard—you can still shed your reputation as a crybaby and salvage your game. Training yourself in techniques for self-control is really no sweat.

The key to keeping your feelings off your sleeve is to try stabiliz- 6 ing the degree to which you become aroused. The prevailing theory is that the simpler the athletic task, the more psyched you should become. For example, intense drive is conducive to producing the explosive strength called for in throwing the shot put, weight lifting, or blocking in football. But you can excel at foul shooting, golf, or archery only if you are calm enough to maintain precision, finesse, and a delicate touch. In other words, you can play well in the service of tension and anxiety—after all, nobody is immune to excitement— as long as you can set your flame at the right temperature for the sport in question.

Burning too hot in competition can lead to anger, an emotion 7 much overrated as an incentive in sports. If you go into conniptions after muffing a ground ball, you're probably draining away energy that you'd be better off conserving for the next play. The infantile rages of John McEnroe serve as proof that a hair-trigger temper is more likely to aggravate hostility than mollify it. "We're always our own worst enemy," says Bruce Ogilvie, a leading sports psychologist and consultant to professional athletes. "Some athletes have only a marginal capacity for adapting to stress, while others cannot function without some tension and anxiety. It's important to find the arousal level appropriate for each of us."

Anger can also be a serious strategic error. By swearing or 8 slamming your tennis racket into a fence after being aced, you're inviting opponents to exploit your deepest vulnerabilities.

My friend David often gets riled during tennis matches—always 9 at his own expense. He tries so hard to win that he swings his racket with unnecessary force, sacrificing accuracy for power. He thus has the distinction of belting the ball into the net or over the base line harder than anyone I know. What David is doing, more or less, is known as choking.

Choking is visible evidence that your body is a slave to your 10 mind—that, more specifically, your emotional state during competition dictates your neuromuscular actions. Let's say you're thinking too much and pushing too hard during a game. You become worried and self-conscious to the point of panic. Your left brain hemisphere shifts into overdrive for the emergency. Your pituitary gland lets loose more adrenaline than your central nervous system can comfortably handle. Nerve impulses give your muscles scrambled instructions.

Now your body starts to conk out. Your heart thumps faster, 11 your pores expand, your pupils dilate, your bronchial tubes tighten, your skin feels clammy. Your breathing is shallow, your mouth dry as sandpaper. Your digestive system shuts down to pump more blood into the muscles and, in so doing, touches off in your stomach the fluttering known as butterflies. Your sense of balance goes askew; your reflexes have no snap. Your jaw, neck, and back muscles knot with tension. Your arms and legs turn stiff and leaden, your movements jerky and uncoordinated.

The upshot is that you've psyched yourself out. You cannot 12 function, concentrate, or make strategy because your judgment has become suspect. You throw to the wrong base, run for a touchdown in the wrong direction.

"Everybody chokes in the clutch," says Gary Krahenbuhl, chair- 13 man of the physical education department at Arizona State University. "Some just choke less."

Some athletes are naturally blessed with glacial equanimity. The 14 best display of athletic self-control I ever witnessed took place about eleven years ago in an NBA play-off game. Walt Frazier of the New York Knicks was outclassing his opponent, Phil Chenier of the Baltimore Bullets. At one point, as Frazier was dribbling the ball up the court Chenier felt so stymied that he smacked him on the back of the head. Frazier never so much as flinched, much less cried foul. And, to cap it off, he went one-on-one with Chenier all through the second half, scoring on every shot. Say what you will, that man was *born* cool.

The trick is to make your anger an asset. To an extent, it's really 15 a matter of working the hydraulics of your body chemistry so that your neurotransmitters—the chemical couriers that deliver messages to your cells—behave appropriately. Ideally, exercise physiologists believe, high serotonin levels and low to moderate amounts of dopamine and adrenaline can keep you loose. "In the end," says Bruce Ogilvie, "you have no defense against getting ticked off. The key is how well and how fast you can handle your anger. You just have to program yourself to be in command of your emotions."

You can go far toward protecting yourself against stress in com- 16 petition if you shoot for sensible objectives. The tennis freak who is obsessive about beating everyone in straight sets, for instance, is not only bucking for disappointment but guaranteeing failure as well. Your next step is to identify what gets you peeved. You can free yourself from anger only after you've pinpointed its causes. Perhaps you sulk because your doubles partner hustles less than you'd like or because your handball adversary cheats. Reflect, if you will, on how you react to such anxieties. Do you ape the misbehavior, in turn hustling less or starting to cheat? Decide now how you'd *like* to adapt to those situations.

Another vital approach to competing with the right bearing is 17 to acknowledge that mistakes are inevitable and educational. Your best bet for capitalizing on mistakes is to figure out exactly what went wrong and, once you've resolved not to repeat it, forget it ever happened. "Assimilate every mistake without dwelling on it," says Dr. Richard M. Suinn, head of the Colorado State University psychology department and psychologist for three 1976 U.S. Winter Olympic teams. "By all means, you should do whatever you can to get off your own back."

Fix your attention on the task you're about to carry out, not on 18 its potential consequences. Think not about whether you're going to sink that eight-foot putt, but about how best to stroke the ball. That way, you'll do yourself the favor of playing with spontaneity. At the same time, try to screen out any peripheral thoughts. "The true champion," says Rainer Martens, physical education professor at the University of Illinois and a U.S. Olympic team consultant, "thinks only about his own performance, not about what his opponents are doing. He also comes to terms with factors he can't control, such as luck and the weather."

Let's assume that however hard you try to practice restraint your   19
frontal lobes still pulse with primal fury during competition. One rather unorthodox technique, if only because it would seem to make you a candidate for a straitjacket, is to talk to yourself. In carrying on a dialogue while you're playing, you can also be your own coach. You can, in effect, keep yourself in perspective, almost as if viewing yourself from outside. You can give yourself technical advice and pep talks, as Billie Jean King and Jimmy Connors frequently do. Derek Harper, now playing with the Dallas Mavericks in the NBA, improved his fieldgoal shooting percentage by 30 percent in college after experimenting with "selftalk." All you have to do is turn your negative thoughts into positive ones.

A more conventional method for keeping your emotions in check   20
is visualization—playing out in advance a mental scenario of how you'd like to perform. Picture yourself being as unflappable as Bjorn Borg in a Wimbledon tie breaker. The next time you're tempted to bellyache at being called for a foot fault, the odds are exponentially better that you'll take the decision in stride. You'll be programmed to behave like a gentleman.

Progressive muscle relaxation is also good therapy for anxiety.   21
Take a minute between innings or sets to tense each of your major muscles for five seconds, then relax, going in sequence from neck, shoulders, and arms to chest, abdomen, and legs. Thus stretched, your muscles cannot help but be more limber, putting you more at ease. This reaction is purely electrochemical—the squeezing out of calcium from your muscle fiber.

Perhaps your best safeguard is breathing regularly at all times,   22
says Dan Landers, physical education professor at Arizona State University. He advises that you breathe evenly and deeply, though not too deeply, lest you hyperventilate and become light-headed. Do so through your diaphragm, not your chest. Such steady breathing helps pump fresh oxygen into the blood cells and body tissues for the manufacture of energy and relays shipments of revitalized blood

to the brain. Arthur Ashe overcame his reputation as a "choke" in big matches after mastering breath control.

Once you find out which technique—or which combination— 23 works best for you, you'll be prepared at last to liberate your performance potential. My last tip is this: It's perfectly okay to get angry in competition as long as you can channel your anger in the right direction.

This I discovered in a recent two-on-two basketball game. The 24 guy I was covering drove for the basket, jumped straight into me, and clipped me in the jaw with his outstretched elbow, scoring on the shot. You can bet I was not tickled by this raw aggression. But to call an offensive foul in schoolyard basketball is to risk being branded a candy-ass. Besides, I decided retribution would be infinitely more rewarding. So I went into a fever of concentration. The next time he dribbled the ball toward me, I lunged forward, as if going for a steal. He was faked out by the move, forced to stop dribbling and clutch the ball. Then I pulled off a trick I had never done in twenty-three years of playing basketball. Like a pickpocket, I simply plucked the ball from his hands and scored on a lay-up. The guy was so flabbergasted that he quit the game and left the court with hardly a word. I guess he had no cool.

RESPONSES AND IDEAS

1. Respond to this essay by describing an incident from your experience that is similar to the one presented at the end of the essay (par. 24) where Brody gets the better of an opponent. The incident you describe need not involve sports. If you have never had such an experience, use your imagination to create one you would *like* to have.

2. Summarize the suggestions Brody provides for "competing with cool." Which seem most useful to you, and why?

3. Is Brody's advice limited to playing sports? Describe three other situations in which it might be useful. Do you disagree with any of Brody's advice or with any of his definitions? Explain.

PURPOSE, AUDIENCE, AND STRATEGIES

1. What is the problem Brody describes in the opening paragraph of the essay? Is it likely that most readers share this problem with Brody? Why does he describe it at such length?

2. Do any of the paragraphs in this essay seem needlessly repetitive? Which paragraphs, if any, could be eliminated without undermining the essay's purpose? State in your own words the purpose and the thesis of this essay. (See Glossary: Purpose, Thesis.)

3. How would you describe the tone of this essay? Are any readers likely to be offended by it? What kind of readers? (See Glossary: Tone.)

4. What pattern or patterns does Brody use in the opening paragraphs of the essay? Does the essay contain more than one process analysis? If so, identify each one.

5. Where does Brody use transitions to link the paragraphs in this essay? Point out any places in the essay that are lacking in effective transitions. (See Glossary: Transitions.)

LANGUAGE AND STYLE

1. What use does Brody make of irony in paragraph 4, and how effective is it? How does Brody use the words *cool* and *hot* and their synonyms to unify the essay? What other words does he use in a similar fashion? (See Glossary: Irony, Figures of Speech, Unity.)

2. Identify the metaphors in paragraphs 6, 7, 10, and 15. (See Glossary: Figures of Speech.) Explain what they contribute to the paragraphs in which they appear.

3. If you do not know the meaning of any of the following words, look them up in the dictionary: *knack, discerning, ranged, uncanny* (par. 1); *caliber, ad nauseam* (2); *poise, hacking, undermined* (3); *hampered, mediocre, unruffled, adversity* (4); *inborn* (5); *prevailing, conducive, finesse* (6); *aggravate, mollify* (7); *vulnerabilities* (8); *riled* (9); *neuromuscular, pituitary* (10); *stymied, flinched* (14); *hydraulics, neurotransmitters, physiologists, serotonin, dopamine, adrenaline* (15); *peripheral* (18); *frontal lobes* (19); *unflappable* (20); *electrochemical* (21); *hyperventilate, diaphragm* (22).

WRITING ACTIVITIES

1. Dating, dressing, talking, studying, and owning stereos (or cars) are just a few of the activities other than sports in which people compete. In an essay, explain a strategy or strategies that can help a person compete effectively in some activity.

2. Write an essay that tells how to lose ("How to Lose in Love," "How to Lose Friends," "A Guide for the Unsuccessful Student"). You may wish to make your essay either humorous or serious—or both.

❧ ROGER SWAIN

Roger Swain was born in 1949 in Cambridge, Massachusetts. He received his B.A., M.A., and Ph.D. from Harvard University and currently divides his time between Cambridge and a small farm in southern New Hampshire. Swain is science editor of *Horticulture* magazine and contributes a regular column to it. His articles have also appeared in the *New York Times Magazine*, *Discover*, and *Technology Illustrated*. His two books are *Earthly Pleasures: Tales from a Biologist's Garden* (1981) and *Field Days: Journal of an Itinerant Biologist* (1983).

Avocados

"Avocados" was first published in *Horticulture* magazine and reprinted in *Field Days*. In the essay, Swain speculates about the process by which avocado trees avoided extinction and ended up prospering, a process as curious and interesting as the fruit of the tree is unusual and delicious. In weighing alternative explanations of the process, Swain makes use of both cause-and-effect and narrative; in discussing the qualities of the avocado that ensured its survival he draws on definition and description. The result is an essay that mixes patterns effectively, both to explore its subject and to support the author's conclusion.

Under the abandoned avocado tree, pits cover the ground as 1 thickly as golf balls at a driving range. Some have rotted, some have sprouted, but none seem to have moved far from where the heavy fruits fell. The spreading limbs have cast a dark green shadow of seedlings on the forest floor, short whips growing too close to the coarsely fissured gray trunk ever to bear fruit of their own.

The largest avocado trees in this stand, their trunks 60 feet high 2 and 2 feet in diameter, were probably planted in the early years of Brazilian independence. At the time, this land on the southern bank of the Rio Ayayá, a tributary of the Amazon, belonged to the Baron of Santarem, who in 1825 built a forty-room *palacio* at the river's edge. With the labor of three hundred slaves, the forest was cleared for tobacco, sugarcane, and cacao. But slave traffic was banned in 1850, and even the possession of slaves was made illegal in 1888. In a few years, the forest had reclaimed the plantation.

Although other tropical trees now crowd in around them, the 3
avocado trees have not been forgotten. There is still a narrow trail
that follows the old oxcart track, and in season, the feet of José
Ceriaco and others who live nearby keep the mud freshly churned.
Because the lowest branch is well over his head, Ceriaco strips a
length of bark from a cacao shoot and hobbles his feet, binding his
ankles so that they are about eight inches apart. Then, embracing
the avocado trunk with his arms and with the splayed soles of his
bare feet, he hitches himself up the tree like an inchworm. Within
moments he is standing safely on a major limb, reaching for avocados and throwing them down to his son, who loads the fruit into
a palm-frond basket. Half a bushel later, Ceriaco descends, shoulders
his load, and the two of them head back toward the river single file.

Much of the weight in Ceriaco's basket is avocado pit. Domi- 4
nating the center of every avocado is a single spherical seed, 1½ to
2 inches in diameter, consisting of two large, fleshy cotyledons embracing a small embryo. A big pit is an advantage for a tropical tree
if it will be germinating on the shady forest floor. The nutrients
stored in the cotyledons will feed the seedling for weeks or months.
But once this inheritance is exhausted, the seedling is on its own. Its
survival will depend on whether or not the pit found transport. Those
pits that remain where they fall might as well not germinate, for
there are no competitors in the forest more overwhelming than one's
parents.

When it comes to getting away, big pits are a handicap. A 5
quarter-pound seed isn't going to be blown about by anything less
than a hurricane, and in water an avocado pit sinks. Yet the fat
seeds of *Persea americana* do get around—with the help of a fat
fruit.

Spherical, oblong, or pear-shaped, avocados come in many col- 6
ors: chartreuse, green, rust, maroon, purple, black. Skins may be
papery or leathery or woody, and of different thicknesses. But inside
every avocado is bright yellow flesh tinged with green and liberally
supplied with oil, oil that makes the avocado the richest of all fruits,
averaging a thousand calories per pound. This oil, which may account for up to 30 percent of the avocado's wet weight, is a staggering
investment on the part of the parent tree, for synthesizing oil takes
half again as much energy as synthesizing an equal amount of sugar.
Yet as costly as it may be, the oil is what makes the avocado so good
to eat.

"Four or five tortillas, an avocado, and a cup of coffee—this is   7
a good meal," say the Guatemalan Indians. The saying is an old
one. Avocados probably originated somewhere in southern Mexico
or Guatemala. Exactly where is problematic; wild avocados have
never been found. In 1916, the most primitive avocado that Wilson
Popenoe, agricultural explorer for the USDA's Office of Foreign Seed
and Plant Introduction, could locate was in the Verapaz Mountains
of northern Guatemala—a lime-sized fruit with a thin layer of oily,
fibrous flesh covering a seed that was nearly as large as the pits of
avocados sold in supermarkets today.

Even such skinny fruits must have had enough fat on them to   8
make them attractive, attractive enough to take home. When the
avocados had been eaten, their pits were thrown out into courtyards,
where some sprouted. The best avocados in the next generation were
the ones traded or sold, the avocados most likely to become trees in
other courtyards.

Century by century, casual selection improved the avocado, until   9
some of the fruits weighed three pounds. By the time of Columbus
all three horticultural races of avocados—the Mexican, Guatemalan,
and West Indian—were well established.

Since then avocado culture has spread to every country possess-   10
ing the tropical or subtropical climate that the trees require. In total
tonnage produced, avocados now rank fourteenth among fruit—right
behind apricots, strawberries, and papayas—and they are closing
fast. Every greengrocer on Broadway has them stacked under awn-
ings, and New Yorkers heading home six abreast along the concrete
sidewalk stop to pick out the softest and the heaviest, dropping them
into plastic bags. In Brazil avocados are dessert fruits; Ceriaco and
his family first fill the seed cavity with sugar. In the United States,
however, where indulgence in this fat fruit is perversely promoted
as a way to stay thin, avocados are served earlier in the meal. Some
are mashed with tomato, onion, and chile peppers to make guaca-
mole, or pureed with sour cream, sweet cream, and chicken broth
to make cold avocado soup. Others are simply cut in half and filled
with cooked lobster or crabmeat.

Outside of California and Florida, seedling avocados stand no   11
chance of surviving the winter, but the farther north one goes the
more likely one is to find avocado pits saved, impaled on three
toothpicks, suspended right-side-up in a tumbler of water, and left
to germinate safely on the kitchen windowsill.

As effective as humans have been at moving avocado pits around,   12
they are not the animal that avocado trees had in mind when they
evolved the big pit. After all, humans are only recent immigrants to
the New World, having crossed the Bering Strait a few tens of
thousands of years ago. But if man was not the first animal to seek
out these delicious fruits with their oversize seeds, what was?

In theory a fruit-eating animal is after the fruit, not the seeds,   13
accidentally ingesting the latter while it feeds. Once inside the animal, the seeds are carried some distance before they are regurgitated
or defecated. Some of the avocados in Ceriaco's basket have been
nibbled, but judging from the tooth marks, none of the animals were
capable of carrying an avocado very far, let alone swallowing the
pit.

What Central American animal is capable of accidentally swal-   14
lowing golf balls, and excreting them with impunity? The answer
may be none of them, at least none that are extant, for the tapir is
currently the only large animal in Central America. But in the Pleistocene, a geologic epoch extending from one million to ten thousand
years ago, it was another matter. Paleontologists point out that then
there were once as many different large animals in Central America
as there are in Africa today.

South America's sixty million years of isolation while the Isthmus   15
of Panama was submerged saw the evolution of several animals with
the appetite and bulk needed to disperse avocados. Giant ground
sloths, looking like a cross between a bear and a kangaroo, stood
upright on a tripod created by their massive hind legs and thick tail.
From this position they fed on treetops, pulling down branches with
their long-clawed front feet. The largest, *Eremotherium*, weighed 5
tons and stood 16 feet high, as high as the tallest giraffe. Another
Pleistocene browser was the large, loose-jointed *Macrauchenia*, a
camellike beast that was a forerunner of the guanaco.

While either of these animals could have eaten avocados straight   16
from the tree, it seems more likely that they preferred avocados on
the ground, for only after the avocado is separated from the tree does
the flesh soften to a buttery consistency. As long as the fruit remains
aloft it stays hard.

Grounded avocados could have been eaten by *Toxodon*, a rhi-   17
noceros-size animal (without the horn) that was probably semia-
quatic. Or they might have been eaten by glyptodonts. Glyptodonts,
weighing a ton or more, had a domed carapace, an armored tail

heavy enough to counterbalance the body as it moved and an armored head that could be withdrawn into the shell. These giant mammalian tortoises, rooting around in slimy avocado pits, could easily have swallowed a great many. So too could have gomphotheres, elephantlike beasts with tusks in both jaws. Or mammoths.

Which of these was the real avocado enthusiast must remain a 18 mystery. The last survivors died out about nine thousand years ago, victims of competition from North American species, or overspecialization, or changes in climate, or the weapons of early man. Until someone finds fossil avocado pits in the remains of giant sloths or glyptodonts, their role in the avocado tree's evolution can't be determined. All that we can say, looking at the avocado pit, is that whatever swallowed it must have been big. As big as those fossil skeletons staring out at us from behind the dusty glass of museum cases.

With the extinction of the large animals in Central America, it 19 is a wonder that the avocado trees didn't become extinct as well. Might they have been rescued by early man? We can imagine some primitive hunter-gatherer picking up fallen avocados. He moves quickly, glancing fearfully over his shoulder, listening for the slightest noise. He has heard that this tree is where dragons come. But he can relax now; the dragons are gone. The riches of the avocado are all his—and have been ever since.

RESPONSES AND IDEAS

1. Respond to this essay by listing as many other plants or animals as you can whose physical qualities or behavior patterns make their continued survival somewhat surprising. In your list include those species whose qualities have been so altered by humans that they depend on us for survival.

    or

    Respond to his essay by explaining why one or more of the currently popular ways that food is prepared and served (for example, frozen dinners, fast-food restaurants) is a response to social or economic forces.

2. Explain why the avocado might be extinct were it not for the intervention of animals and humans. Is Swain's explanation of the problems the avocado faces in propagating and surviving clear enough? (See Glossary: Evaluation.) If not, how might he make it clearer?

3. Who are the "dragons" mentioned in paragraph 19, and why does Swain use this term to refer to them?

PURPOSE, AUDIENCE, AND STRATEGIES

1. What kinds of information does Swain include in this essay to make it
    interesting to people who might not otherwise want to read about the
    process he describes? Is this essay directed at a general audience? How
    can you tell? If it is not intended for a general audience, describe the
    kind of reader to which it is directed, and support your answer with
    evidence from the essay.

2. Where and how does Swain first announce the purpose of this essay?
    In what ways elsewhere in the essay does he remind readers of its
    purpose? (See Glossary: Purpose.)

3. Does Swain's explanation convince you about the process by which
    avocado pits moved from place to place before humans appeared? If
    not, how might it be made more convincing?

4. Describe the strategies Swain uses to open and close the essay. How
    might they be improved, if at all? (See Glossary: Introductions, Clos-
    ings.)

5. Are any paragraphs in the essay not related directly to Swain's expla-
    nation of the processes by which avocados have survived as a species?
    If so, which paragraphs are they? Do they harm the unity of the essay?
    Why, or why not? (See Glossary: Unity.)

LANGUAGE AND STYLE

1. What role is played by the rhetorical questions in paragraphs 12 and
    14? (See Glossary: Figures of Speech.)

2. Examine the unusual sentence structures Swain uses in paragraph 6.
    Describe the structure of each sentence, and then discuss how it helps
    Swain convey his meaning and what effect it is likely to have on readers.

3. If you do not know the meaning of any of the following words, look
    them up in the dictionary: *seedlings, fissured* (par. 1); *tributary, cacao*
    (2); *hobbles, hitches, palm frond* (3); *cotyledons, germinating* (4);
    liberally (6); *problematic, fibrous* (7); *horticultural* (9); *impaled* (11);
    tapir, paleontologists (14); *browser, guanaco* (15); *carapace, rooting,
    mammoths* (17).

WRITING ACTIVITIES

1. Collect information on a local organization (student-run cooperative,
    historical society, camping or skiing club) or on a service agency (rape
    crisis center, career counseling office). Prepare an essay telling readers
    what the organization does, how it works, and what use they can make
    of it.

2. New exercise and health programs seem to appear every month, each making grand claims for its effectiveness and each claiming to be different from its competitors. Do some research on either a widely popular program or a heavily advertised new one and prepare an essay reporting on how it works and commenting (if possible) on its effectiveness.

Writing Suggestions

EXPLORATIONS

1. Write down five or more hobbies, sports, activities, or skills that you have but that relatively few other people in your audience know about. Choose one and list three things you could say about the topic that might interest readers in it. Then list the main steps in the activity. If you think the two lists might be the basis for a good explanation or set of directions, turn them into an essay.

2. Look up information on some well-known disaster (sinking of the *Titanic*, burning of the dirigible *Hindenburg*, eruption of Mt. St. Helens) or an event of more local interest (a large fire, a train derailment, a small-plane crash) and summarize the steps in the process. If you decide the information is worth sharing in an essay, remember that your writing has to have some point beyond merely describing the events in the process.

3. You would probably have no trouble telling an adult how to housebreak a puppy or teaching a ten-year-old to wash dishes. Yet you might find it more difficult to teach a recent immigrant from a European or Asian country to play baseball or football; it might, moreover, take a good deal of patience and tact to teach people who find machines confusing how to use a home computer. List ten more occasions when an explanation might call for verbal skill and an understanding of the audience's needs and outlook, and specify both the subject and the audience. Keep the occasions you describe realistic. If you find one of the occasions challenging, consider developing an essay response for it.

4. Think of some machines you use every day without fully understanding their operation (car, television, microwave oven, tape recorder, for instance). Look up an explanation of one of them, and write a paragraph about its basic principles of operation. If the subject interests you, turn the explanation into an essay.

ACTIVITIES

1. Television listings contain notices of a great many programs built around explanations of a process: how to repair old homes and cars, how cheetahs hunt, what happens when a volcano erupts. Watch one such program and prepare a report describing how it interests readers in the process, what the major stages in the process are, how viewers are alerted to the major stages, and how the program concludes.

2. Get a copy of any one of the many magazines that specialize in explaining how things work and how to do things. *Popular Science, Popular Computing, Gourmet,* and *Better Homes and Gardens* are just a few of the wide range of publications you can choose from. Look at

two process articles in the magazine you choose and write a brief report on the strategies they use to get readers interested in a topic and to hold that interest throughout the article.

3. Choose a topic for a process essay, but before you begin writing, interview three people with very different interests and backgrounds to determine what they already know about the topic and what they would like to learn about it. Use the information you gather to shape your essay, and submit a record of the interviews along with your final draft.

4. Read either Donald Murray's "The Maker's Eye: Revising Your Own Manuscripts" in Chapter 11 or John Houseman's "The Night the Martians Landed" in Chapter 7 and write a two- to three-paragraph explanation of the extent to which the essay you read depends on process as a pattern of thought and expression. Make sure your explanation makes direct reference to the essay.

MODELS

1. Following Jim Villas's lead in "Fried Chicken," present a set of directions in which you argue against other approaches and demonstrate that your approach embodies values that are either superior in themselves or more appropriate to the situation you are addressing. Possible topics include diets, forms of exercise, ways of choosing a career, studying methods, ways of maintaining a friendship, and strategies for raising children.

2. Taking Simon Woodroffe's "Staging Concerts" as a model, explain a complicated event in which you have taken part, such as staging a play, arranging a trip for a large group of people, or managing an athletic tournament. Make sure your explanation applies not only to your experience but to all other events of the same type.

3. Borrowing strategies from Alexander Petrunkevitch's "The Spider and the Wasp," describe a relationship among people that contains the same kind of complex interaction as the relationship of the spider and the wasp. You might want to look at relationships within a family, among friends, at work or school, or perhaps among corporations, political parties, or even nations.

4. Following Robert Brody's lead in "Competing with Cool," describe a process of behavior that commonly interferes with our happiness, success, or peace of mind, and suggest another process for overcoming the problem.

5. Using Roger Swain's "Avocados" as a model, present an explanation of a natural, technical, or artistic process whose steps are unclear to most people and that may call for some speculation on your part. You might talk about the creation of a painting or sculpture, the events surrounding the creation of the universe, or the process by which a fad takes hold of the imaginations of many people.

7

❧ CAUSE AND EFFECT

Asking Why It Happened and What Will Happen Next

WHAT CAUSE AND EFFECT DOES

"Talking about causes and effect is something only scientists and economists do," you might be tempted to say, "but not something that ordinary people worry a lot about." Yet popular magazines like *Glamour, Sports Illustrated,* and *Reader's Digest* are filled with articles asking why something happens (cause) and what is likely to happen in the future (effect):

"Does Dressing for Success Really Make a Difference?"
"Football All Year Long—The Next Step?"
"Why Teenagers Commit Suicide"

The suburban homeowner whose lawn is the worst in the neighborhood calls in a landscaping company to search for the source of the problem, and then wonders whether spending money improving his yard will increase the value of the property. A student planning to buy a camera or a computer turns to *Consumer Guide* or *Consumer Reports* to find the best buy in terms of expense and reliability.

Underlying these and all other searches for cause and effect, from the most rigorously scientific ("Researchers debate possible links between Agent Orange and cancer") to the most personal ("Why do I always end up arguing with my parents over things we all know are unimportant?") is the process of thought known as *causal analysis.* Causal analysis provides a basis for many decisions we make in our public or personal lives, and it is one of the primary means we have of understanding ourselves, other people, and the natural world. Most people believe, often correctly, that if they can identify causes, they can understand and control consequences. Many of the major issues of public debate—nuclear disarmament, prayer in the schools, the quality of teaching, national economic policy—are actually disagreements over causes and effects.

The key assumption of causal analysis is that no event can be fully understood on its own but must be viewed instead as part of a *causal chain.* The links in the chain are the *event* or *phenomenon* itself (the pollution of wells and drinking water); its causes, both *direct* (leaching of toxic chemicals from a landfill) and more *remote* (decision to locate the landfill near a populated area); *necessary conditions* that are not in themselves causes (porous soil that allows pollutants to enter the groundwater quickly); and the *results* of the event—that is, the *further effects* (illness of people who drink the water or use it in their homes).

A thorough causal analysis looks backward in time from an event, to identify its sources, and forward in time, to predict its consequences. In practice, however, most occasions call for more focused reasoning. The city planner studying the impact of a new shopping mall would be expected to report on its likely effect on employment, on traffic, and on other businesses in the area, but probably not on its consequences for housing development or the social behavior of high school students, though it may well have effects on both. Scientific researchers, too, are aware of the need to focus their work, to move step by step, investigating one aspect of a complicated problem at a time and looking at the larger relationships only later. The activities of modern cancer research, for example, focus on a variety of possible causes—environmental, hereditary, viral, immunological—whose relationships to each other are far from clear.

Even when time is not a factor, when we are looking into causal relationships not because of a problem we face but out of curiosity and a desire for understanding, the complexity of a subject and the need to provide detailed support for conclusions may require a narrowing of focus. One anthropologist studying the evolution of human intelligence may examine the remains of weapons or pottery, another may study diet or habits of hunting and gathering food, and still another may investigate the pressures of environment. And a writer may come along to synthesize their limited conclusions, thus disguising the piecemeal nature of their research: "Which factor played the most important role in the evolution of human intelligence? Was it the pressure of the Ice-Age climate? Or tools? Or language? No one can tell; all worked together, through Darwin's law of natural selection, to produce the dramatic increase in the size of the brain that has been recorded in the fossil record in the last million years" (Robert Jastrow, *Until the Sun Dies*, 1977).

Recognizing the occasions that call for cause and effect as a pattern of thought means becoming aware, too, of some of the many ways cause and effect can be used as a means of expression: in explanations and problem-solution essays, for example, or in arguments based on the effects of a particular action or policy (see "The Pattern in Action," below). Though these patterns are widely used, they are not the only forms cause and effect can take as a strategy for writing, either as a pattern for entire essays or in combination with other patterns. A newspaper account of the possible causes and solutions for a problem like acid rain may, for instance, simply try to inform readers. An editorial, however, may try to persuade business leaders and government officials to reduce the pollution from coal-burning plants that creates acid rain. A scientific paper may explore possible explanations, offering suggestions or hypotheses for further study; or it may support one interpretation and criticize others ("The emissions from coal-fired boilers and blast furnaces, not automobile emissions, are the primary cause of acid rain").

Because causal relationships are so complex and include both direct and remote causes as well as necessary conditions, it is often hard to prove in an absolute sense that X is the cause of Y, or that an action will always have the same desirable (or undesirable) result. What is often accepted as proof of a cause-effect relationship is actually a high correlation: ninety-five or ninety-eight percent of the time, X is followed by Y. In most instances a clear correlation is acceptable as proof of a causal relationship as long as it is accompanied by a qualifying word or phrase like *in most cases, usually,* or *there is a high correlation between X and Y.*

The audience and the occasion determine to a great extent the rigor of the causal analysis and the kind of support the writer must offer to make a convincing case. From politicians or international celebrities writing in an autobiography about the reasons for their actions, readers ask only that what the authors write be plausible and agree with the facts. Readers accept these writers' statements as personal outlook, not as proof. For a report or editorial arguing for a bottle bill, however, readers have a higher standard. They expect facts and figures, including data from states where such a bill is in effect, because the choice will have a personal impact as well as consequences for the local economy. The audience for a research paper in psychology submits writers to an even tougher test: the possibility that the results of an experiment occurred by chance must be less than one percent.

Although a scientific standard like the one followed in psychological research might seem in some ways the highest and best, it is often inappropriate. An essay that speculates about the impact of a new religious movement or explores the threat of nuclear war need only strive to pay careful attention to the facts and to be reasonable in its conclusions. To hold it to a more demanding level of proof might be to choke off the creativity needed to uncover new ideas and fresh solutions. Likewise, an informative article in a magazine based on widely accepted research need not bore us with extensive supporting evidence. The power of cause and effect as a pattern of expression does not come, then, simply from the demonstration of a strong likelihood of a causal relationship; in addition, this pattern allows writers to explore cause-effect relationships in a number of ways:

> to speculate about events
> to test a hypothesis
> to inquire into relationships
> as evidence to support arguments
> as a way to provide fresh information
> as a way to explain a subject

Writing that sheds light on cause-effect relationships can generate discussion and disagreement even when it is carefully researched and tightly reasoned. As a writer, try to regard an essay of causal analysis as the start of a discussion, even while you work to provide evidence for your conclusions and anticipate any possible objections readers may have to your thesis. The analysis you believe is reasonable and well-supported may leave your readers puzzled, even hostile, especially if your outlook is in any way controversial.

Here are two paragraphs from Robert H. Boyle's essay on the impact of acid rain on the Atlantic striped bass, "A Rain of Death on the Striper?" These paragraphs and the responses from readers in the weeks following publication of the essay give some idea of the difficulties writers face in sharing ideas with an audience:

The precipitation (rain, snow, even fog) that falls on Maryland is very acid, as acid as any in the world. Its pH ranges from 4.45 to 3.5; that is 15 to 110 times more acid than normal. A rainstorm in Baltimore three years ago had a pH of 2.9, more than 700 times more acid than normal. When a heavy rain hits this flat coastal plain, it's like throwing a bucket of water on a rubber sheet. What had been up in the sky a few hours before collects in the streams, and the streams can suffer sudden acid pulses. If the pH of a stream isn't being monitored daily, no one will notice the pulse. In a matter of hours, or a day, or two days, the pH can rebound to 7 or more, and the only witnesses to the destructive pulses are the larval fish that have been killed.

According to Dr. Serge Doroshov, who worked on the acclimatization of striped bass in Russia before he defected in 1975—he has taught animal science at the University of California at Davis since 1977—striped bass larvae have difficulty tolerating pH levels below 7. "Mortalities are higher in water with a low pH," he says. "I haven't seen the data [S[ports] I[llustrated] has for certain rivers], but with those pH levels I would speculate that striped bass larvae wouldn't survive. The larvae do best in water with a pH of 7.5 to 8.5. At Davis we raise them in water close to pH 8." Moreover, Doroshov adds, striped bass larvae are extremely sensitive to a sharp change of pH even within the favorable pH range. He cites two instances where a sudden change of pH by 0.8 to 1.0 caused 100% mortality (*Sports Illustrated*, April 23, 1984).

In these paragraphs Boyle attempts to isolate what to him are three of the most important parts of the causal chain. First he establishes that the rain falling in Maryland is highly acidic, then he shows that the rainwater changes drastically the acid content of the water in which the striped bass breed, and finally he shows that the striped bass cannot survive in such highly acidic water. He provides multiple pieces of evidence to support each of his conclusions, more than one would usually expect in an article in a popular magazine. He also speaks in two voices, the scientific voice that provides technical information and the journalist's voice that translates this information for the average reader. Despite his strong feelings about the subject, Boyle appears to have held himself to a high enough standard of proof to earn the respect even of those who disagree with his conclusions. Or so one would think.

Some readers were impressed with the presentation and wrote letters to the magazine voicing their approval: "Robert H. Boyle's striped bass piece is the most penetrating and provocative analysis of the topic that has been made." Others were not satisfied, perhaps because they believe that environmentalists usually overstate the danger of pollution: "Your special report sensationalizes what is already a national controversy. . . . Who made S[ports] I[llustrated] a scientific authority on striper fishery and/or the impact of acid rain?"

As these responses indicate, the expectations and beliefs of an audience can shape the way they read an essay. Although you cannot possibly please every reader, you should try to learn as much as you can about how your audience may respond.

THE PROCESS

Often the purpose, subject, and occasion for a cause-effect essay comes with the assignment:

Write a report on the reasons our sales campaign for Fresh'n Aerosol Soap was ineffective, and have it ready for the members of the Product Management Group by next Wednesday so that by Friday's meeting we will be ready to discuss ways of dealing with the problem.

To complete your application for admission to the graduate school, explain the experiences that have prepared you for graduate study in (chemistry, management, English), and indicate what you plan to do once you have finished your degree work.

If you are familiar with the kind of writing required by an assignment or if you know well the demands of the situation, jotting down a few ideas about your subject may be enough to help you define the task clearly so that you can begin writing or doing any necessary research. But if your supervisor tells you to prepare the report on Fresh'n Aerosol Soap and you have never written a report for the Product Management Group, or you know little about the sales campaign that failed, or you have never met the people you will be addressing, you need to focus on these aspects of the task (purpose, subject, and occasion) before you begin writing. Some thinking on paper might help:

> Product—Fresh'n was a disaster! Packaging was one obvious reason, but what were the others? Call up Jim, who looked into the problem while the sales campaign was going on, and Lisa from Sales Records, to get a printout of returns from retailers.
>
> Report form—They want me to focus on identifying the problems and at the end of the report to suggest some possible solutions to get the discussion going at Friday's meeting.
>
> Audience—Help! How comprehensive do I have to be? Do I have to mention every *possible* cause? Or only those that are clearly most important *and* within our control? What about the new aerosol soap from Ashton Pharmaceuticals? Will the members of the group know anything about it? Will they accept my word that the causes I have presented are correct, or will I need to offer pretty good support? Better check with someone who has done this before (Bill? Joann?) and maybe get a copy of a successful report.

Just as often, however, you have to decide on your own whether cause-and-effect is an appropriate pattern for thinking and writing about a subject. Your editor on a college newspaper might ask you to "Go over and check what's going on at the meeting on computer facilities for students." The personnel officer for a corporation may ask you to include a personal profile with your résumé. In cases like these you will have to decide whether the subject and the occasion are best served by an essay emphasizing cause and effect:

> Meeting on computer facilities—Is there a problem here that is worth exploring or telling my fellow students about? Will there be some proposed solutions to the shortage of terminals that my readers will be happy to learn about?
>
> Personal profile—Are there elements in my character that will make me particularly well-suited for this job? How can I suggest that I will do good work if I'm hired?

Occasionally you will get an assignment from a college instructor that calls for a cause-and-effect essay: "Write about the specific causes and effects of one of the major events we have studied this semester" (history exam); "Write a paper about a campus problem" (freshman English class). With such an assignment your chief concern should not be writing an essay that follows the proper form, but finding a subject about which cause-effect thinking can provide insight worth sharing with readers. Only then will the cause-effect writing pattern work as a way of communicating with an audience.

Here is how one student, Tony Lopez, responded to the assignment, "Write an essay based on this statement 'Why I never ––––––––––.'" He thought about completing the sentence with "never play basketball" and "never get an 'A' in math," but finally decided to explain "Why I never balance my checkbook." He chose this topic because he knew a lot of other people who put off balancing their checkbooks and felt that his readers might have fun exploring their motivations as he talked about his. After brainstorming for a few minutes, he came up with a list of causes that fell easily into an ascending order of importance, thus suggesting a way to arrange the essay: "Balancing the checkbook takes too much time; the record form in the checkbook is confusing and hard to use; I often don't fill in the record stub because I'm in a hurry; but, most important, I don't balance the checkbook because if I do, I'll find out how little money I really have."

Once you have selected a topic and a purpose for writing, you need to spend time with the subject, gathering information, identifying and sorting out causes and effects. For many topics, detailed research in printed sources will be necessary, with emphasis not only on what happened but on what came *before* (possible causes) and on what came *after* (possible effects). Other topics may call for extensive interviewing. To investigate why a chemical plant moved from your town you might interview the plant manager, the head of the local chamber of commerce, the mayor of the town, and the leader of the plant's union. They might be able to indicate, too, what the impact of the closing is likely to be.

Before you begin writing, you should have identified the direct and remote causes or the significant effects and their relationships to each other, although you may well change your mind about them as you write. Arranging causes and effects in a diagram like the one

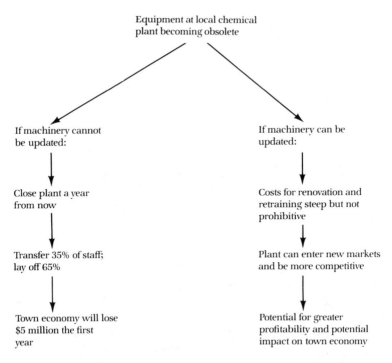

Equipment at local chemical
plant becoming obsolete

If machinery cannot
be updated:

Close plant a year
from now

Transfer 35% of staff;
lay off 65%

Town economy will lose
$5 million the first
year

If machinery can be
updated:

Costs for renovation and
retraining steep but not
prohibitive

Plant can enter new markets
and be more competitive

Potential for greater
profitability and potential
impact on town economy

above can help you understand their relationships and can suggest
ways of arranging an essay.

The organization of a cause-effect essay may be dictated by the
occasion for which it is written, in which case the patterns discussed
in the next section, "The Pattern in Action," will be helpful to you
as you write. On the other hand, you may discover that the point
you want to make—your thesis—is best served by a variation of one
of these basic patterns of organization:

Cause-to-Effect Patterns:
Introduction (including   Introduction (including
    thesis)   thesis)
    Cause 1   Effect 1
    Cause 2   Effect 2
    Cause 3   Effect 3
    Causes 4, 5, 6 . . .   Effects 4, 5, 6 . . .
Conclusion (summary)   Conclusion (summary)

Effect-to-Cause Patterns:

Introduction (including thesis)	Introduction (including thesis)
Cause	Effect
Effect 1	Cause 1
Effect 2	Cause 2
Effect 3	Cause 3
Effects 4, 5, 6 . . .	Causes 4, 5, 6 . . .
Conclusion (summary)	Conclusion (summary)

Besides introducing the topic and indicating why it is worth reading about, the introduction to a cause-effect essay generally presents the author's thesis. Most often, the thesis is a judgment about the relative importance of the causes and effects to be explored in the body of the essay, or an argumentative proposition that the discussion of causes and effects will support. During the course of an essay, most writers choose to acknowledge (and argue against) other ways of viewing the subject, reasoning that otherwise readers will raise the objections themselves, probably in a less sympathetic manner.

In revising a cause-effect essay, you should pay close attention to the way you alerted readers to the relationships among causes and effects and to the reasoning you followed in deciding how they are related. Because most causal relationships are complex and difficult to follow, a successful cause-and-effect essay usually relies on multiple signals to make sure readers understand the point being made and can follow the discussion easily. A concise statement, near the beginning of an essay, of the relationships you plan to examine can be helpful, as can statements in the body of the essay reminding readers of the point you are making. Likewise, terms like the following that identify causes and effects or that indicate their relationships can be useful guides:

result	effect	accomplishment	development
outcome	antecedent	source	first
cause	instrument	as a result	second
means	in contrast	motive	third
consequence	reason	agent	next

In checking over your reasoning, determine whether you have provided enough examples, statistics, or supporting arguments for your conclusions and make sure you have taken into account any alternate points of view that might undermine your thesis. Look to see that you have clearly distinguished major causes from minor ones, probable effects from less likely ones. Check also that you have missed no obvious factors. Finally, decide whether you have mistakenly assumed that because one thing follows another, they automatically stand in a cause-effect relationship (the *post hoc propter hoc* fallacy—see Chapter 10, p. 431) and make sure you have treated the subject fully and fairly, while not distorting the causal relationships simply to support your thesis.

THE PATTERN IN ACTION

The arrangement of cause-effect essays often reflects the expectations of an audience and the needs of an occasion. Though few, if any, writers set out to write a cause-effect essay, they often begin with a pattern like *problem analysis* or *explanation* because it provides a way to organize their thinking and a reminder of the goal for which they are writing. An awareness of these patterns in reading can help alert you to the author's purpose and to strategies that may be useful in your own writing.

One of the most widespread uses of cause and effect as a writing strategy is the *explanation pattern,* consisting of the description of a puzzling phenomenon followed by an explanation. In its simplest form, this strategy draws readers into an essay by appealing to their curiosity and then attempts to satisfy the curiosity with a detailed explanation.

The simplicity of the pattern gives it considerable power and flexibility. By isolating a phenomenon with intriguing or puzzling qualities, the opening section of the pattern gives focus and a clear purpose to the often complex task of causal analysis that makes up the rest of the essay. The explanation itself can be as complicated as necessary as long as it keeps in sight the purpose of the essay—that is, to explain the puzzling phenomenon. In writing designed to inform, the explanation pattern can help get readers interested in the information to be presented. Essays that speculate about social patterns and individual behavior often use this strategy to provide a theme around which to organize their speculations without having to announce a specific thesis or interpretation that would require detailed proof and extensive argument. For example, the essay "Our Rhythms Still Follow the African Sun," presented in this chapter, begins by pointing out that, like lions in Africa, people's alertness declines in the afternoon, and then uses the curiosity generated by this comparison to lead into a discussion of the cycles that govern our daily behavior.

The explanation pattern is widely used in academic and research writing. Scholars often look for a particularly puzzling element in a subject or a point over which there has been much disagreement and then build an essay around an attempt to explain the phenomenon: "Perhaps the most interesting feature of Donatello's early sculpture is . . ."; "Over the last decade researchers have argued over the role of aggressive behavior in the corporate society. . . ." Underlying college assignments like "Look for a particularly interesting aspect of Mennonite society and write about it" or "Discuss some special feature you noticed in your reading of this novel" is the expectation that your writing will follow an academic version of the explanation pattern. Keeping the strategy in mind as you begin writing a paper for a college class, therefore, can help focus your thinking as well as your writing: "One of the first things a reader of Faulkner's 'A Rose for Emily' notices is that the narrator is not 'I,' but 'we.' This unusual point of view has considerable impact on the way readers come to view the events in the story. . . ."

The *problem-solution pattern* reflects the roles causal analysis can play in helping understand and solve problems. A *problem analysis* essay, therefore, usually begins by reminding readers of the importance of the problem or creating a sense of its seriousness. In business writing or technical writing the tone of the introduction may be somewhat unemotional because the writer can assume that the audience for a report will consist only of those people who will be quickly able to recognize the importance of a problem. But writing addressed to a wider audience often needs to be more emotional and argumentative in order to create concern in readers who may have had little prior involvement with the subject:

> It is a brisk fall morning as I head north along the Mississippi River on Missouri Route 168, which runs from Hannibal to Palmyra. Coming around a sweeping curve in the road, I suddenly see clouds of white steam rising over stubbled cornfields into the cobalt-blue sky. This marks the home of the American Cyanamid Company's Agricultural Products Plant—one of three plants that make American Cy-

anamid the nation's largest producer of the antibiotic tetracycline for use in livestock feed. The particular form of tetracycline that Cyanamid produces is chlortetracycline (Aureomycin); it was the first of the tetracycline drugs to be discovered. As these and other antibiotics began to be manufactured in great quantities in the early fifties by American Cyanamid and other companies—both for human therapy and for use as a feed additive to promote growth and control subclinical disease in livestock—the bacterial world was assaulted with a barrage of bacteriostatic and bactericidal compounds. It was faced with an evolutionary challenge to respond or succumb. And respond it did, becoming resistant in increasing numbers by the transfer of R plasmids—genetic material that carries resistance to drugs—as if it were an army refitting itself for modern warfare (Orville Schell, "A Kind of Commons," *New Yorker*, April 30, 1984).

Although this paragraph is rather technical in places, its image of one of our main sources of food as a battlefield between germs and drugs is startling enough to call attention to the problem the writer is addressing and to make it seem like the reader's personal concern, too.

The rest of a problem analysis provides necessary background information and breaks the problem into parts for easier understanding and investigation. The analysis generally tries to identify major and minor causes and to indicate relationships among them as well as any contributing factors.

The *problem-solution* essay is concerned with effects as well as causes. It opens with an analysis of a problem, then proposes a solution based on the analysis. The extent to which a writer needs to argue in support of the solution depends on whether it flows clearly from the analysis or is likely to cause considerable disagreement. Written discussions of policy within a company or a government agency often follow either a problem analysis or a problem-solution pattern. Newspaper editorials and magazine articles on issues of public policy like capital punishment, the economy, or the environment often use a problem-solution strategy. Hartzel Lebed's "Who Will Take Care of the Children?" in this chapter is a newspaper editorial that proposes a solution for a common day-care problem and adopts a stance somewhere between simply presenting a possible solution and arguing strongly for it.

The *apology*, meaning not an expression of regret but a formal justification or defense, is a pattern that appears occasionally in magazine columns and collections of essays and quite frequently as an essential element in autobiographies and memoirs. In an apology, an author explores his or her own actions and motivations, usually in order to justify as well as explain them. Apologies follow no special arrangement but are characterized by attempts to draw the reader into the writer's experience to show why behavior that might from a distance seem unusual or deplorable (such as a celebrity's five marriages and many affairs or a financier's participation in a banking scandal) is understandable, almost proper, when seen from the point of view of the participant. A. Alvarez's "A Test of Will" is an apology for the often dangerous sport of mountain climbing.

In an *argument based on effects,* the writer looks to the real or hypothetical effects of a course of action to argue for or against it. Issues like changes in the drinking age and revisions of the income tax law are frequently discussed by means of this pattern, and it is particularly appropriate when present decisions must be made almost entirely on the basis of future events, as in the case of nuclear disarmament.

Evidence in an argument based on effects may be hypothetical, as in a discussion of the impact of global nuclear war, or may make use of detailed studies of results, as does Sissela Bok's "Placebos" in this chapter. Essays following this pattern move from describing the cause, usually the action or situation being argued about, to a presentation of the effects, frequently arranged in ascending order of importance to drive home the author's point at the end of the essay.

The last essay in this chapter, John Houseman's "The Night the Martians Landed," suggests some of the many other uses to which cause and effect can be put. Houseman mixes cause and effect with narration, description, and process to help re-create an event and explain it at the same time. His essay is a good reminder that the pattern of an essay should serve the purpose, and not the other way around.

❧ DAVID W. HARSHA AND MARCIA J. THOMPSON

David Harsha was born in 1949 in Kansas City, Kansas. He received a B.A. from the University of Kansas and a Ph.D. in physical anthropology from Tulane. He is currently assistant professor in the Department of Medicine at Louisiana State University Medical Center, New Orleans. He has published extensively in scholarly journals on topics of human growth development, body composition, and heart research.

Marcia Thompson was born in 1949 in Mobile, Alabama. She received a B.A. from Newcomb College and an M.A. in social anthropology. She has done field work in the Yucatan and other parts of Mexico, and she has worked as a medical editor. Currently Thompson is marketing director for DePaul Hospital in New Orleans. She is also applying her anthropological approach to business by studying how people choose to use their time.

Our Rhythms Still Follow the African Sun

"Our Rhythms Still Follow the African Sun," first published in *Psychology Today* and revised for this collection, shows how the explanation pattern can be used to bring sophisticated knowledge to bear on a common but puzzling phenomenon. Throughout the essay the authors draw parallels between the everyday experiences of their readers and the behavior they have observed through research in order to show that what may sometimes seem like cultural phenomena are actually part of the biological heritage of human beings.

By early afternoon, the hunt is over. A pride of lions, having 1 eaten their fill, gather in the shade of a thorn tree. Other animals drowse, play, or groom each other quietly. They have behaved this way in the early afternoon for millions of years, in a land where the heat of the sun rules all.

Far from the tropics, Scandinavian factory workers make more 2 mistakes on the job, German schoolchildren stumble over their arithmetic exercises, and Greek merchants close their shops. In offices everywhere, people have returned from lunch, but alertness flags and daydreams intrude. Some people tell themselves they must have eaten too heavily, while others begin to doubt that the hasty sandwich was enough and listen for the bell of the coffee cart. In truth, the post-lunch dip has little to do with food and much to do with our tropical heritage.

We have all experienced this fading sensation an hour or two   3
after the traditional noon meal. Yet by late afternoon, whether we've napped, drunk coffee, or just plugged along, alertness returns. We rally in time to wrap up our tasks, clear our desks, and head home.

There is an obvious temptation to attribute the phenomenon to   4
biochemical effects of eating, hence the "post-lunch" tag often attributed to circadian researcher M.J.F. Blake. But why is there no similar reaction after breakfast or supper, which in many cases are much heavier meals? In an unpublished study, Blake tested three groups of 12 subjects for efficiency in a range of tasks—vigilance, card-sorting, time estimation, and others—five times during the day. There were no significant differences between the group that ate lunch at 10 A.M., the one that ate at noon, and the one that ate at 2 P.M. Yet all three groups experienced a mid-afternoon drop in efficiency. Many other more recent studies have documented the same pattern among people in varied cultures and occupations all over the world.

For years, another popular explanation was body temperature: 5
As our temperature rises and falls, it was said, so does our efficiency. But in fact, body temperature rises steadily through the morning, reaching its high point in early or middle afternoon, just when our ability to do all but the simplest tasks declines markedly. And efficiency rises again later in the afternoon, as body temperature declines toward its low point at night when we sleep. If food isn't the answer, nor temperature, what does explain the post-lunch dip and the other variations we experience daily? Nearly every process in our bodies, from glandular secretions to our ability to memorize telephone numbers, fluctuates in a predictable 24-hour cycle. Researchers have plotted daily peaks and troughs of more than 100 physiological and performance variables, each with its own "natural" period, which may be longer or shorter than 24 hours. The periods are coaxed into synchrony by *zeitgebers,* or time cues, that mesh them with our patterns of sleeping and waking.

We believe that the explanation lies in the tropical environment   6
in which our species evolved. We have lived in temperate climates for less than a million years, and only in the last hundred thousand

years or so have we wandered into the sub-arctic latitudes. In evolutionary time, this was last week. Man is still fundamentally a tropical creature. Warm-blooded tropical animals exhibit a bigeminous, or two-peaked, daily rhythm of activity, with the late-morning peak more marked than the late-afternoon one. This rhythm, we suggest, stayed with us after we left the African plains and continues to thwart our efforts to live and work as if the hours of the day were as identical as sparkplugs off an assembly line.

Our primate relatives all generally observe a midday lull in   7 activity. Generally, monkeys and apes spend their mornings in active, noisy communal feeding. During the hottest part of the day, roughly from one to three hours after noon, activity subsides. This is not a mere rest period, but time for a different sort of activity. Older primates groom each other and their young, picking patiently through each other's fur rather than dozing; some use the time to build sleeping nests for the night to come. Jane Goodall's chimpanzees follow a similar pattern, sleeping for half an hour and spending the rest of the lull sprawling idly or grooming. Later in the afternoon, the animals resume active feeding until sunset.

The periods of high collective activity can be considered the   8 primates' working times, when they fulfill the most basic function of feeding themselves. By contrast, relaxed grooming and play may seem much less vital pursuits. But these are highly social species. During grooming and play, they reinforce the dominance and bonding relationships that establish social structure. Primates seem to seize the time when lions or elephants drowse as an opportunity to carry out activities which require less alertness but are just as necessary as eating.

Among humans, we find a rich and varied array of daily activity.   9 The most striking difference from other animals, of course, is that fire and electricity have stretched our day beyond the limits set by the sun, enabling us to add a new set of nighttime activities.

Let us sketch a simplified, world-wide human day. In the morn-   10 ing, a woman of the household arises and rekindles the fire, putting water on to boil. This occurs, with technological variations, among the Mbuti Pygmies, the Irish, the Monguors, and the Americans. Men and children often awaken a little later. Morning ablutions and other preparations for the day accompany breakfast.

After the morning meal, adults engage in the most important   11 work of the day, work connected with the group's subsistence. The

Shilluk and the Navajo herd their livestock. The Mixtecs, the Rajputs, the Maltese, the Yucatec Maya, and the Koreans work their fields. Samoyed men hunt wild reindeer and Arctic geese. Women may participate in this labor or do their own work, often in cooperation with other females.

The midday meal may occur any time between 11 A.M. and 2   12
P.M. In most societies, it is a family meal with the breadwinner returning from work. Less often, the women and children eat at home while the men eat at work.

Then comes the afternoon lull. In nonindustrial cultures, this   13
break is nearly universal. People retreat from the heat of the sun in warm climates, often choosing sedentary individual or small-group pursuits such as repairing tools or weaving mats, rather than those requiring large-group cooperation. Adults may visit and chat, while children play. Despite a common tendency to speak disparagingly of the "siesta," naps are not the usual activity, even in the tropics.

In late afternoon, people resume animated activity, at a pace   14
slower than the morning's. They continue until sunset, depending on the time of year and how long it takes to travel between work and home.

The end of the work day is a social time; strong drink is often   15
part of the ceremonial transition from work to the dinner hour. After dinner, early-rising groups usually end the day in sleep by 10 or 11 P.M. But the young, the strong, the enthusiastic (and even the early risers on ceremonial occasions) may enter a late-night, optional phase reserved for especially intense activities.

We have found such daily transitions in societies from equatorial   16
to polar latitudes, among nomadic hunter-gatherers and workers in modern industrial nations. No culture institutionalizes every phase, but when it doesn't, vestiges can often be found in casual behavior. This near-universality suggests that the transitions have a biological base. We believe they do, but the basis is complex, as the levels of hundreds of hormones, neurotransmitters, and other body chemicals rise and fall with their own circadian rhythms. Until we know much more about the interactions of such substances, we may learn more by looking carefully at cross-cultural patterns in daily activity.

Whether the human organism is examined from the cell out or   17
from the society in, it remains faithful to the rhythm of the tropical day that shaped its activities until very recently. Our ancestors learned

to avoid heat stress on their uniquely complex nervous systems. While both prey and predators slept, they did things they alone needed to do: manufacturing and caring for their tools, making the fabrics that came to replace other primates' fur, refining the symbolic connections that made them fully human.

The content of our workdays has changed, but our tropical 18 origins are still with us. Though we drill for oil beneath the ice caps and walk on the moon, though we shuffle our work routines to accommodate new production quotas and overseas conference calls, we remain subject to the dictates of the African sun.

COMMENTARY

"Our Rhythms Still Follow the African Sun" begins with an intriguing comparison between the behavior of lions and an experience we have all had, the "post-lunch dip." It then reviews common explanations of the mid-afternoon lull and rejects each one before stating what the authors believe to be the real cause, "the tropical environment in which our species evolved" (par. 6). In the rest of the essay the authors draw parallels between the behavior of animals that live in a tropical environment similar to that of early humans and the behavior of present-day humans. The aim of these parallels is to suggest that the body clocks of early humans were shaped by forces whose impact can also be traced in animals. The authors are careful throughout to draw examples of human behavior from multiple cultures to show that their conclusions reflect the basic biological nature of humans and not the habits of a particular civilization or culture.

In the course of an interview about the writing of this essay, the authors stated that their aim was to combine evolutionary biology (Harsha's field) and cultural anthropology (Thompson's field) in order to explain in as basic a way as possible a complex situation. They emphasized their desire to bring together research that has been done in diverse fields but which no one else seems to have correlated. The process they describe is similar to the one student writers use in preparing an informative or explanatory research paper, and "Our Rhythms Still Follow the African Sun" is a good model for students who are searching for a way to present the information and insights they have developed through research.

Thompson and Harsha's reliance on concrete examples combined with more technical explanations is a particularly good example of a strategy that allows writers to present complicated insights to a general audience without either oversimplifying the conclusions or confusing the reader.

The strength of this essay lies not simply in the clarity of its organization and reasoning, but also in the variety and detail of the examples of human and animal behavior. The explanations, too, are fascinating. They help us to see that many of our behaviors are dictated not by our rational minds but by our biological natures over which we have little control.

RESPONSES AND IDEAS

1. Respond to this essay by listing other behavior patterns (of eating, sleeping, social interaction, and so on) that you think may fit into the cyclical scheme proposed by the authors.

2. Explain why you consider the title of this essay either appropriate or inappropriate.

3. What is the thesis of this essay, and where is it stated? (See Glossary: Thesis.)

PURPOSE, AUDIENCE, AND STRATEGIES

1. Does the afternoon decline in alertness the authors describe in paragraph 3 ever affect you? How often, and in what ways? What effect does it have on other people you know? As you read the opening of the essay, did the author's discussion of the afternoon decline in alertness get your attention and make you want to read the essay? Explain why, or why not.

2. What explanations for the behavior pattern the authors describe did you have before you read the essay? Did the authors correctly anticipate the explanations you would have given for the way people feel after lunch? To what extent does the success of their explanation depend on having anticipated correctly the attitudes and ideas of the readers?

3. Do the authors anticipate that readers will find the attempt to explain complex human behavior in biological terms a bit far-fetched? If so, what steps do they take to make the explanation seem reasonable?

4. Identify any patterns other than cause-and-effect that are used in this essay, and indicate the purposes for which they are used. What strategy do the authors use to conclude the essay? Is it effective? How else might they have concluded? (See Glossary: Closings.)

5. Many of the examples in the essay are from unfamiliar cultures. Identify those examples drawn from cultures you know nothing about, and discuss whether the use of such examples makes it harder for you to accept the authors' thesis.

LANGUAGE AND STYLE

1. Look up the term *circadian* in the dictionary if you do not already know what it means. In what ways, if any, does learning the meaning of the term change your understanding of paragraph 4? Paragraph 16? Would either paragraph be more effective if the authors had chosen a less technical word or phrase? What, if anything, does the term contribute to the passages in which it occurs?

2. Describe how the authors use transitions in paragraphs 5 and 16 to add emphasis. (See Glossary: Transitions, Emphasis.)

3. If you do not know the meaning of some of the following words, look them up in the dictionary: *pride* (par. 1); *flags* (2); *rally* (3); *circadian, vigilance* (4); *glandular* (5); *bigeminous* (6); *communal, subsides* (7); *ablutions* (10); *vestiges, neurotransmitters* (16).

WRITING ACTIVITIES

1. People often do things that seem contrary to their best interests: They use alcohol and drugs in harmful ways; they drive unsafe cars; they put off doing an important job; they make risky or foolish investments; they smoke excessively; and they remain in destructive relationships. Choose one common but potentially harmful pattern of behavior, and, in an essay, explore the reasons why people continue to pursue that behavior despite what would seem to be clear evidence of its destructiveness.

2. Drawing on Thompson and Harsha's explanation of human behavior, suggest ways to improve the way we conduct our businesses, schools, or social activities. You might, for instance, suggest that colleges schedule lectures and lab sections in the morning and discussion groups in the afternoon in order to use the afternoon lull for communal activity.

❧ HARTZEL LEBED

Hartzel Lebed was born in 1928 in Columbia, Pennsylvania, and is a Phi Beta Kappa graduate of the University of North Carolina, Chapel Hill. In 1950 he joined the Connecticut General Life Insurance Company and over the next three decades served in a variety of positions with the company. In 1982 he became president of both Connecticut General Life Insurance and the Life Insurance Company of North America, as well as executive vice president of their parent company, CIGNA Corporation. Mr. Lebed is also a director of a variety of charities and business organizations.

Who Will Take Care of the Children?

"Who Will Take Care of the Children?" originally published as a newspaper editorial, grows out of the author's experience with a day-care program at his company. The problem he describes is widespread, however, and although the proposed solution may arouse some disagreement, it is worth taking seriously.

Eric, 3, is one of thousands of American pre-schoolers who 1 spend their days in child-care facilities. Each morning, his mother, an insurance company secretary, drops him off at a center on her way to the office.

Eric and his mother, however, are luckier than many parents 2 and children who follow the day-care routine each day. They can spend their lunch hours together every day; Eric's nursery school and his mother's office are at the same place—on company property.

Eric and his mother are part of a movement too small yet to be 3 called a trend: employer-sponsored child care. But if current trends in population and labor-force participation hold true, child care in the workplace will become increasingly necessary.

The 1980 census was the first in history to show that more than 4 half of all U.S. women—52 percent—work outside the home. Among women aged 18 to 34, some 67 percent are in the work force. Working women, in fact—including working mothers—have become such a commonplace phenomenon in America that we don't stop to reflect how swift and dramatic their movement into the work force has been. The statistics are striking: In 1960, fewer than 19 percent of the nation's mothers with children under six were working outside the home. By 1970, however, the figure had grown to 30 percent. Today, nearly half of all mothers with pre-school children are working outside the home.

Because of declining birth rates, the labor force will grow more 5 slowly over the next decade—which means that employers, increasingly, will recruit among women to fill their labor needs. As early as 1990, according to one estimate, women will comprise 60 percent of our more slowly expanding work force. Two out of three mothers will be working—80 percent of whom will have children under six. This works out to a total, in 1990, of more than 10 million pre-school children with mothers in the work force.

Who'll take care of the children? 6

Business, in my judgment, should help—and not just out of 7 altruism. If businesses don't help working mothers with child care, the result is likely to be high employee turnover or shortages of skilled workers: problems no employer wants.

Employers can help fulfill the need of their workers for com- 8 petent, affordable child care by teaming up with child-care professionals who can manage child-care centers on or near the work site.

In October, 1975, our Connecticut General subsidiary in Bloom- 9 field, Conn., became one of the first major companies in the nation to provide an on-site child-care facility for its employees and the neighboring community. We remodeled a former dairy building on our property and leased it to Kinder-Care Learning Centers, to operate a child-care center for 70 youngsters. The center has worked well: so well, in fact, that we recently completed a larger replacement center, this one for 100 children, which also is managed by Kinder-Care.

A good day-care program must provide more than baby-sitting; 10 it should offer not only supervised play, but a year-round program of pre-school learning, music, art and even drama. To be of maximum benefit to parents and children, the center must be close enough to the workplace to allow parents to visit their children at lunchtime or to reach them quickly in case of emergency. Employers who contemplate sponsoring a child-care program should do so, determined to give the project the priority it deserves—and to provide professional service to parents and children.

Where the idea has been tried, the results have been encour- 11
aging. Our managers express their belief that the company's child-
care program is yielding major benefits: reduced absenteeism and
job turnover, increased employee satisfaction and loyalty.

RESPONSES AND IDEAS

1. Respond to this essay by listing the problems parents, not just mothers,
   may face in caring for their children when both spouses have full-time
   jobs, or when a single parent has a full-time job.

2. In which paragraphs of the essay does the author identify a problem?
   In which does he explain its origins (causes)? What are they? What
   paragraphs present the proposed solution?

3. Do you think the problem Lebed describes is widespread? Do you agree
   with his analysis of its causes? Explain. What possible economic, technological, or social developments might affect the growing need for
   child care that he predicts?

PURPOSE, AUDIENCE, AND STRATEGIES

1. Is there evidence in the essay that the author intends his proposal to
   apply to government agencies and to small- to medium-sized businesses
   as well as large corporations? If so, what is it? If not, does the absence
   of such information weaken the essay? In what ways? Assume that at
   least part of the audience to which this essay is directed consists of
   corporate executives. What does the author say to convince them that
   child care is business's responsibility?

2. Is Lebed's purpose to explain a problem and one possible solution to
   it, or to argue that because the solution he proposes is the most effective
   and most workable, it is the one that should be adopted in most cases?
   Make sure that you support your answer with specific evidence from
   the essay, and if your view of its purpose differs in any way from the
   alternatives just stated, explain your outlook as part of your answer.
   (See Chapter 10, "Argument and Persuasion," and Glossary: Argument,
   Exposition.)

3. How might the assumptions of some readers about the need for child
   care, the importance of having it at the workplace, and the responsibilities of employers differ from Lebed's? Summarize briefly each of the
   possible points of disagreement. If you agree with most of Lebed's
   assumptions and conclusions, work extra hard to understand how
   someone might view them negatively.

4. This essay was originally written and published as a newspaper editorial, so it had to be relatively brief. Do you think it would be more

effective if it were developed more fully? If you were to expand it, precisely what would you add, and where would you add it?

5. Could paragraphs 1, 2, and 3 be combined without harming the effectiveness of the essay? 7 and 8? If so, why do you think the author chose to use such short paragraphs? If not, what do these short paragraphs add to the essay?

LANGUAGE AND STYLE

1. Explain how the author's word choice, including both denotation and connotation, helps emphasize any points he makes about the problem and the solution. (See Glossary: Diction.)

2. To what use does the author put the rhetorical question that makes up paragraph 6? (See Glossary: Figures of Speech.)

3. If you do not know the meaning of any of the following words, look them up in the dictionary: *altruism* (par. 7); *contemplate, priority* (10); *absenteeism* (11).

WRITING ACTIVITIES

1. Choose a social, environmental, economic, or political problem that has a number of possible causes and discuss them in an essay indicating how much you believe each cause contributes to the problem. You may wish to discuss a local problem such as the pollution of a town's water supply, a national problem such as a growing pattern of cheating on income tax, or an international problem such as a conflict between two or more nations.

2. Social and technological changes that seem at first to bring progress may at the same time create new problems. In an essay, discuss one such change and its expected or unexpected effects.

❧ A. ALVAREZ

A. Alvarez was born in 1929 in Hampstead, England, where he still lives. An essayist, social critic, literary critic, and novelist, Alvarez has published numerous articles in magazines and has written a wide range of books. Among his books are *The School of Donne* (1962), which is a volume of literary criticism; *The Savage God* (1982), a study of suicide; *Life after Marriage: Love in an Age of Divorce* (1982); and *The Biggest Game in Town* (1983), a novel. In his writings Alvarez explores the varieties—and extremes—of human behavior.

A Test of Will

"A Test of Will" was first published in the *New York Times Magazine*. Like many of Alvarez's other writings, it probes experiences that give meaning to our lives by showing us how fragile our existence is and by asking us to challenge our limitations. Some readers may question Alvarez's assumption that the meaning of life is plainest in such experiences; as you read, however, pay attention to the way Alvarez anticipates this response.

I started climbing in the summer of 1950, just before my 20th birthday, hit my peak at the sport about 15 years later and have been on a gradually accelerating decline ever since. Yet I still try to get onto the rocks any Sunday when the weather is halfway decent, although my stamina and flexibility are sharply diminishing, and the rocks I usually go to—a little sandstone outcrop south of London—would fit comfortably into the foyer of the new A.T.&T. Building. These days, I climb mostly with my son. At 15, he is too young to know any better. Yet the fact is, whenever work or rain deprives us of our weekly fix of climbing we exhibit identical withdrawal symptoms: restlessness, irritability, fretfulness, a glum conviction that our week has been spoiled. Climbing is an addictive sport that changes the psyche's chemistry as irredeemably as heroin changes the body's, and both of us are hooked.

When Mallory was asked why he wanted to climb Everest, he answered with a famous evasion: "Because it's there." I suspect that what he really meant was: "Because you're here"—"you" being not only his aggrieved and aggressive questioner but also the town, the

noise, the involvements, the problems, the routine. You climb to get
away from all that, to clear the head, to breathe free air. Yet most
weekend sportsmen—the fishermen and yachtsmen, golfers, even
Sunday painters—do what they do in order to get away, without
risking their necks in the process. Why, then, does climbing exert
such a curiously addictive power?

First, because it is one of the purest, least cluttered sports,   3
requiring a minimum of equipment: a pair of special boots, a rope,
a safety helmet, a few carabiners (snap links), nylon slings and
artificial steel chockstones or pitons for protection. The whole lot
costs very little, lasts for years and hangs easily around your neck
and from your waist. Unlike other sports, if something goes wrong,
the fault is nearly always in you, not in your gear. Conversely, the
reward, when a climb has gone well, is an intense sense of physical
well-being. On those rare occasions when mood, fitness and rock
all come together and everything goes perfectly, you experience an
extraordinary combination of elation and calm—tension dissolves,
movement becomes effortless, every risk is under control—a kind of
inner silence like that of the mountains themselves. No doubt every
athlete feels that on his best days, but in climbing that style of
contentment is attainable long after you pass, as I have, your physical
prime.

It is also not a competitive sport, however much the top climbers   4
vie among themselves for first ascents or ascents in the best style.
The competition is not even with the mountain or the rock face. You
are competing, instead, with yourself—with your protesting body,
your nerves and, when the going gets really tough, with your reserves
of character.

In 1964, for example, a companion and I spent a night belayed   5
to a small ledge—a couple of feet long and 18 inches wide—1,300
feet up an overhanging face in the Italian Dolomites. We had been
benighted on it by a sudden snowstorm and were soaked to the skin;
but because this was August in Italy, we were climbing light, which
meant we had neither protective clothing nor food. The route finished
up a thousand-foot vertical corner, down which a waterfall of melted
snow was pouring. It froze solid during the night, and privately both
of us assumed that we would do the same. But neither of us mentioned the possibility, because to have done so would not only have
undermined our confidence to complete the last 500 icy feet the next
morning—if there was a next morning for us—it would also have

been a violation of privacy. Our survival depended, as much as anything else, on tact. It was not just a question of being young enough and fit enough to withstand the cold, we also had to behave well and respect each other's feelings. Melodrama and self-pity would have done us in more surely than the freezing temperature.

I suspect that most men are secretly worried about how they will behave under pressure. Certainly, I emerged from that night on the bare mountain with frostbitten fingers and a good deal more self-confidence than I had had before—a confidence that was quite apart from the pleasure of having got up a difficult climb in bad conditions. I had learned that the ability to sit quiet in a crisis and not fuss was more valuable than physical strength. I also discovered in myself an unsuspected, obstinate ability to survive and that, in some devious way, seemed to absolve me from the youthful need continually to apologize and explain. As the poet, Thom Gunn, wrote, "I was myself: subject to no man's breath." Perhaps I should also add that I have not felt the need to repeat the experiment; the Via Comici on the north face of the Cima Grande di Lavaredo was the last serious climb I did without checking the weather forecast beforehand. 6

"Life loses in interest," wrote Freud, "when the highest stake in the game, life itself, may not be risked." Those who cultivate risk for its own sake, however, are probably emphasizing only their own inner torpor, just as the people who talk most fervently about the beautiful emotions induced by drugs are those who have most difficulty in feeling anything at all. The pleasure of risk is in the control needed to ride it with assurance so that what appears dangerous to the outsider is, to the participant, simply a matter of intelligence, skill, intuition, coordination—in a word, experience. Climbing, in particular, is a paradoxically intellectual pastime, but with this difference: You have to think with your body. Each pitch becomes a series of specific local problems: which holds to use, and in which combinations, in order to get up safely and with the least expense of energy. Every move has to be worked out by a kind of physical strategy, in terms of effort, balance and consequences. It is like playing chess with your body. 7

And that, for me, is the final satisfaction. To be a professional writer is, in the end, a sedentary, middle-class occupation, like accountancy or psychoanalysis, though more lonely. For five or six days each week, I sit at my desk and try to get sentences right. If I 8 make a mistake, I can rewrite it the following day or the next, or catch it in proof. And if I fail to do so, who cares? Who even notices?

On a climb, my concentration is no less, but I am thinking with 9 my body rather than my weary, addled head, and if I make a mistake, the consequences are immediate, obvious, embarrassing and possibly painful. For a brief period and on a small scale, I have to be directly responsible for my actions, without evasions, without excuses. In that beautiful, silent, useless world of the mountains, you can achieve at least a certain clarity, even seriousness of a wayward kind. It seems to me worth a little risk.

RESPONSES AND IDEAS

1. Respond to this essay by describing some activity that is an important part of your life, and tell why it is so important to you.

2. Explain in your own words what Alvarez means when he says, "climbing is an addictive sport that changes the psyche's chemistry as irredeemably as heroin changes the body's, and both of us are hooked" (par. 1). If Alvarez thinks climbing is a worthwhile activity, why does he compare it to heroin addiction? Explain what he means when he says, "Our survival depended, as much as anything else, on tact" (par. 5).

3. What specific answers does this essay give to the question, "Why do I climb mountains?"

PURPOSE, AUDIENCE, AND STRATEGIES

1. How would you describe the intended audience of this essay? Does Alvarez assume his audience is composed of people who like to skydive, to fly ultralight planes, or to race motorcycles? Does he assume his audience consists of business executives with high-powered jobs?

2. List the objections to mountain climbing as a sport for average people that most readers are likely to bring to the essay. To what extent is the essay organized as a response to such objections? To what extent is it framed as Alvarez's explanation of his actions? If you can account in some other way for the specific points the essay takes up and their order, do so. (See Glossary: Arrangement.)

3. Is Alvarez's general purpose in this essay to explain, to argue, to express feelings, to explore ideas, or some combination of these? Cite specific evidence from the essay to support your answer. If you think the essay has a combination of purposes, indicate which you believe are the most important, and explain your answer.

4.   What does the story of the night spent on the side of a mountain (par.
     5) contribute to the essay? Is this paragraph a narrative? If not, name
     the pattern it follows. What other patterns (besides cause-and-effect)
     does the essay contain?

5.   In what ways does Alvarez communicate the point of this essay? By
     means of direct statement including thesis statement? Through repeti-
     tion of words and images? With quotations from authorities? As you
     answer, be sure to indicate what you think the point of the essay is.
     (See Glossary: Thesis.)

LANGUAGE AND STYLE

1.   Identify an example of each of the following stylistic strategies in the
     essay, and tell what each contributes to the overall effect of the essay:
     parallelism, rhetorical question, paradox, irony. (See Glossary: Paral-
     lelism, Figures of Speech.)

2.   What use does Alvarez make of transitions in paragraphs 3–8 to identify
     what he believes are the various causes of the "curiously addictive
     power" (par. 2) of mountain climbing?

3.   If you do not know the meaning of some of the following words, look
     them up in the dictionary: *foyer, psyche* (par. 1); *evasion, aggrieved*
     (2); *chockstones, pitons, elation* (3); *belayed, benighted* (5); *torpor* (7);
     sedentary (8); *addled, wayward* (9).

WRITING ACTIVITIES

1.   Though they have been warned often about the lack of nutrition in fast
     food and the harmful effects of too much television, many people con-
     tinue to have a hamburger, shake, and french fries for dinner and to
     watch several hours of TV a day. In an essay, tell what you think are
     the causes of one of these habits or a similar pattern of behavior and
     explain why people continue it despite warnings about its effects.

2.   In an essay, argue that the possible harmful effects of a common
     practice, like working overtime or studying late at night, outweigh its
     benefits. To make your essay interesting, you might look at the negative
     side of activities most people consider enjoyable and beneficial, such
     as gardening, reading, or jogging.

❧ SISSELA BOK

Sissela Bok was born in Sweden and attended schools in Switzer-land, France, and the United States. She received a B.A. and M.A. in psychology from George Washington University and a Ph.D. in philosophy from Harvard University. She has published articles on medical ethics and has taught ethics and decision-making in med-icine at the Harvard Medical School and the John F. Kennedy School of Government. She is currently a lecturer at Harvard Uni-versity and has also taught at Tufts University. Her books are *Lying: Moral Choice in Public and Private Life* (1978) and *Secrets: On the Ethics of Concealment and Revelation* (1982). Her work as a philosopher represents a trend in current philosophic thinking away from abstract concerns of language and logic to the criticism and understanding of human action.

Placebos

In "Placebos," an essay included in her book *Lying,* Sissela Bok directly attacks our unquestioning assumption that the prescribing of little sugar pills, placebos, harms no one. In asking us to look at the consequences of what seems a simple white lie, Bok en-courages us to take moral responsibility for our actions and to apply to human affairs the kind of systematic thinking we often reserve for technical, scientific, financial, or academic matters.

The common practice of prescribing placebos to unwitting pa-   1
tients illustrates the two miscalculations so common to minor forms of deceit: ignoring possible harm and failing to see how gestures assumed to be trivial build up into collectively undesirable practices. Placebos have been used since the beginning of medicine. They can be sugar pills, salt-water injections—in fact, any medical procedure which has no specific effect on a patient's condition, but which can have powerful psychological effects leading to relief from symptoms such as pain or depression.

Placebos are prescribed with great frequency. Exactly how often   2
cannot be known, the less so as physicians do not ordinarily talk publicly about using them. At times, self-deception enters in on the part of physicians, so that they have unwarranted faith in the powers of what can work only as a placebo. As with salesmanship, medi-

cation often involves unjustified belief in the excellence of what is suggested to others. In the past, most remedies were of a kind that, unknown to the medical profession and their patients, could have only placebic benefits, if any.

The derivation of "placebo," from the Latin for "I shall please," gives the word a benevolent ring, somehow placing placebos beyond moral criticism and conjuring up images of hypochondriacs whose vague ailments are dispelled through adroit prescriptions of beneficent sugar pills. Physicians often give a humorous tinge to instructions for prescribing these substances, which helps to remove them from serious ethical concern. One authority wrote in a pharmacological journal that the placebo should be given a name previously unknown to the patient and preferably Latin and polysyllabic, and added:

> [I]t is wise if it be prescribed with some assurance and emphasis for psychotherapeutic effect. The older physicians each had his favorite placebic prescriptions—one chose tincture of Condurango, another the Fluidextract of *Cimicifuga nigra.*

After all, health professionals argue, are not placebos far less dangerous than some genuine drugs? And more likely to produce a cure than if nothing at all is prescribed? Such a view was expressed in a letter to *The Lancet:*

> Whenever pain can be relieved with a ml of saline, why should we inject an opiate? Do anxieties or discomforts that are allayed with starch capsules require administration of a barbiturate, diazepam, or propoxyphene?

Such a simplistic view conceals the real costs of placebos, both to individuals and to the practice of medicine. First, the resort to placebos may actually prevent the treatment of an underlying, undiagnosed problem. And even if the placebo "works," the effect is often short-lived; the symptoms may recur, or crop up in other forms. Very often, the symptoms of which the patient complains are bound to go away by themselves, sometimes even from the mere contact with a health professional. In those cases, the placebo itself is unnecessary; having recourse to it merely reinforces a tendency to depend upon pills or treatments where none is needed.

In the aggregate, the costs of placebos are immense. Many millions of dollars are expended on drugs, diagnostic tests, and psychotherapies of a placebic nature. Even operations can be of this nature—a hysterectomy may thus be performed, not because the condition of the patient requires such surgery, but because she goes from one doctor to another seeking to have the surgery performed, or because she is judged to have a great fear of cancer which might be alleviated by the very fact of the operation.

Even apart from financial and emotional costs and the squan- 7 dering of resources, the practice of giving placebos is wasteful of a very precious good: the trust on which so much in the medical relationship depends. The trust of those patients who find out they have been duped is lost, sometimes irretrievably. They may then lose confidence in physicians and even in bona fide medication which they may need in the future. They may obtain for themselves more harmful drugs or attach their hopes to debilitating fad cures.

The following description of a case where a placebo was pre- 8 scribed reflects a common approach:

A seventeen-year-old girl visited her pediatrician, who had been 9 taking care of her since infancy. She went to his office without her parents, although her mother had made the appointment for her over the telephone. She told the pediatrician that she was very healthy, but that she thought she had some emotional problems. She stated that she was having trouble sleeping at night, that she was very nervous most of the day. She was a senior in high school and claimed she was doing quite poorly in most of her subjects. She was worried about what she was going to do next year. She was somewhat overweight. This, she felt, was part of her problem. She claimed she was not very attractive to the opposite sex and could not seem to "get boys interested in me." She had a few close friends of the same sex.

Her life at home was quite chaotic and stressful. There were 10 frequent battles with her younger brother, who was fourteen, and with her parents. She claimed her parents were always "on my back." She described her mother as extremely rigid and her father as a discipli- narian, who was quite old-fashioned in his values.

In all, she spent about twenty minutes talking with her pediatri- 11 cian. She told him that what she thought she really needed was tran- quilizers, and that that was the reason she came. She felt that this was an extremely difficult year for her, and if she could have something to calm her nerves until she got over her current crises, everything would go better.

The pediatrician told her that he did not really believe in giving 12 tranquilizers to a girl of her age. He said he thought it would be a bad precedent for her to establish. She was very insistent, however, and claimed that if he did not give her tranquilizers, she would "get them somehow." Finally, he agreed to call her pharmacy and order medi- cation for her nerves. She accepted graciously. He suggested that she

call him in a few days to let him know how things were going. He also
called her parents to say that he had a talk with her and was giving
her some medicine that might help her nerves.

Five days later, the girl called the pediatrician back to say that the   13
pills were really working well. She claimed that she had calmed down
a great deal, that she was working things out better with her parents,
and had a new outlook on life. He suggested that she keep taking them
twice a day for the rest of the school year. She agreed.

A month later, the girl ran out of pills and called her pediatrician   14
for a refill. She found that he was away on vacation. She was quite
distraught at not having any medication left, so she called her uncle
who was a surgeon in the next town. He called the pharmacy to renew
her pills and, in speaking to the druggist, found out that they were only
vitamins. He told the girl that the pills were only vitamins and that she
could get them over the counter and didn't really need him to refill
them. The girl became very distraught, feeling that she had been de-
ceived and betrayed by her pediatrician. Her parents, when they heard,
commented that they thought the pediatrician was "very clever."

The patients who do *not* discover the deception and are left   15
believing that a placebic remedy has worked may continue to rely
on it under the wrong circumstances. This is especially true with
drugs such as antibiotics, which are sometimes used as placebos
and sometimes for their specific action. Many parents, for example,
come to believe that they must ask for the prescription of antibiotics
every time their child has a fever or a cold. The fact that so many
doctors accede to such requests perpetuates the dependence of these
families on medical care they do not need and weakens their ability
to cope with health problems. Worst of all, those children who cannot
tolerate antibiotics may have severe reactions, sometimes fatal, to
such unnecessary medication.

Such deceptive practices, by their very nature, tend to escape the   16
normal restraints of accountability and can therefore spread more
easily than others. There are many instances in which an innocuous-
seeming practice has grown to become a large-scale and more dangerous one. Although warnings against the "entering wedge" are
often rhetorical devices, they can at times express justifiable caution;
especially when there are great pressures to move along the undesirable path and when the safeguards are insufficient.

In this perspective, there is much reason for concern about   17
placebos. The safeguards against this practice are few or nonexis-
tent—both because it is secretive in nature and because it is condoned but rarely carefully discussed in the medical literature. And

the pressures are very great, and growing stronger, from drug companies, patients eager for cures, and busy physicians, for more medication, whether it is needed or not. Given this lack of safeguards and these strong pressures, the use of placebos can spread in a number of ways.

The clearest danger lies in the gradual shift from pharmacolog- 18 ically inert placebos to more active ones. It is not always easy to distinguish completely inert substances from somewhat active ones and these in turn from more active ones. It may be hard to distinguish between a quantity of an active substance so low that it has little or no effect and quantities that have some effect. It is not always clear to doctors whether patients require an inert placebo or possibly a more active one, and there can be the temptation to resort to an active one just in case it might also have a specific effect. It is also much easier to deceive a patient with a medication that is known to be "real" and to have power. One recent textbook in medicine goes so far as to advocate the use of small doses of effective compounds as placebos rather than inert substances—because it is important for both the doctor and the patient to believe in the treatment! This shift is made easier because the dangers and side effects of active agents are not always known or considered important by the physician.

Meanwhile, the number of patients receiving placebos increases 19 as more and more people seek and receive medical care and as their desire for instant, push-button alleviation of symptoms is stimulated by drug advertising and by rising expectations of what science can do. The use of placebos for children grows as well, and the temptations to manipulate the truth are less easily resisted once such great inroads have already been made.

Deception by placebo can also spread from therapy and diag- 20 nosis to experimentation. Much experimentation with placebos is honest and consented to by the experimental subjects, especially since the advent of strict rules governing such experimentation. But grievous abuses have taken place where placebos were given to unsuspecting subjects who believed they had received another substance. In 1971, for example, a number of Mexican-American women applied to a family-planning clinic for contraceptives. Some of them were given oral contraceptives and others were given placebos, or dummy pills that looked like the real thing. Without fully informed consent, the women were being used in an experiment to explore the side effects of various contraceptive pills. Some of those who were given placebos experienced a predictable side effect—they became pregnant. The investigators neither assumed financial responsibility for the babies nor indicated any concern about having bypassed the "informed consent" that is required in ethical experiments with human beings. One contented himself with the observation that if only the law had permitted it, he could have aborted the pregnant women!

The failure to think about the ethical problems in such a case   21 stems at least in part from the innocent-seeming white lies so often told in giving placebos. The spread from therapy to experimentation and from harmlessness to its opposite often goes unnoticed in part *because* of the triviality believed to be connected with placebos as white lies. This lack of foresight and concern is most frequent when the subjects in the experiment are least likely to object or defend themselves; as with the poor, the institutionalized, and the very young.

In view of all these ways in which placebo usage can spread, it   22 is not enough to look at each incident of manipulation in isolation, no matter how benevolent it may be. When the costs and benefits are weighed, not only the individual consequences must be considered, but also the cumulative ones. Reports of deceptive practices inevitably leak out, and the resulting suspicion is heightened by the anxiety which threats to health always create. And so even the health professionals who do not mislead their patients are injured by those who do; the entire institution of medicine is threatened by practices lacking in candor, however harmless the results may appear in some individual cases.

This is not to say that all placebos must be ruled out; merely   23 that they cannot be excused as innocuous. They should be prescribed but rarely, and only after a careful diagnosis and consideration of non-deceptive alternatives; they should be used in experimentation only after subjects have consented to their use.

RESPONSES AND IDEAS

1. Respond to this essay by describing the events that probably followed those described in the case study in paragraph 8. Make sure that the events you describe can be reasonably viewed as a result both of the prior events and of the character of the people involved.

2. How would you feel if you discovered that your physician had been giving you a placebo? Why?

3. Explain in your own words why regarding placebos humorously "remove[s] them from serious ethical concern" (par. 3). Is Bok justified in regarding certain kinds of operations as placebos (par. 6)? Discuss how the operations fit (or fail to fit) within the definition of *placebo*.

PURPOSE, AUDIENCE, AND STRATEGIES

1. List the positive effects of placebos and indicate the paragraphs in which Bok discusses them. List the negative effects and the paragraphs in which they are described. What does the way the discussion of positive and negative effects is arranged indicate about the structure of the essay? (See Glossary: Arrangement.)

2. In paragraph 2, Bok compares some of the actions of physicians to "salesmanship." Are most readers likely to agree with her implied negative attitude towards salesmanship? What point does she make by associating medical doctors with salesmen? Is the association of the two likely to conflict with readers' attitudes toward doctors, and if so, how are readers likely to respond to it?

3. Have you ever taken medications under the conditions described in paragraph 15—for instance, antibiotics to treat a cold? How did you regard the medicine at the time, and in what ways, if any, does this discussion change your attitude toward such use of medicine?

4. Is the purpose of this essay to explore and explain the effects of placebos? To argue against their use? To warn against careless prescribing of them? Does the purpose change from section to section of the essay? If so, identify each section and its purpose. To what extent does the essay suggest specific actions or changes in attitude? Identify the suggestions, if any.

5. At what point in the essay does Bok indicate she will be examining the effects of prescribing placebos? State in your own words the thesis of this essay. (See Glossary: Thesis.) Identify at least three paragraphs that consist of a topic sentence plus examples. (See Glossary: Paragraph.) Do the topic sentences reflect the thesis?

LANGUAGE AND STYLE

1. Identify the transitions in paragraph 5 and tell how the author uses them to help organize the paragraph and provide emphasis. (See Glossary: Transitions, Emphasis.) How does Bok use the word *costs* to organize the discussion in paragraphs 5–7?

2. How does the author use the connotation of words in paragraph 13 to convey her attitude? (See Glossary: Connotation.) How would you describe the tone of this paragraph? Of the essay as a whole? Where and in what way does the tone of the essay change? (See Glossary: Tone.)

3. If you do not know the meaning of any of the following words, look them up in the dictionary: *unwitting, deceit* (par. 1); *unwarranted* (2); *benevolent, hypochondriacs, adroit, beneficent, pharmacological, polysyllabic* (3); *simplistic* (5); *aggregate, psychotherapies, hysterectomy* (6); *squandering, irretrievably, bona fide, debilitating* (7); *disciplinarian* (10); *precedent* (12); *distraught* (14); *accede, antibiotics, perpetuates* (15); *accountability, innocuous, rhetorical, justifiable* (16); *condoned* (17); *inert* (18); *alleviation* (19); *ethical* (20); *triviality* (21); *cumulative, candor* (22).

WRITING ACTIVITIES

1. Choose another form of well-intentioned, seemingly harmless lie and in an essay explore its possible consequences in a manner similar to the approach Bok uses in "Placebos."

2. Take a stand on some local or national controversy over a policy or proposed course of action and draw much of the evidence to support the thesis of your essay from the probable effects of the action or policy.

❧ JOHN HOUSEMAN

John Houseman, born in Romania in 1902, was educated in England and came to the United States in 1925. Houseman is perhaps best known for his work as an actor, especially in the movie *The Paper Chase* (1974), for which he won an Academy Award; in a television series based on that movie; and in numerous television commercials. Yet he has also been a teacher, writer, movie and theatrical producer, and director. He has written three volumes of memoirs, *Run-through* (1972), *Front and Center* (1979), and *Final Dress* (1983).

The Night the Martians Landed

First published in *Harper's* magazine in 1948 and later in *Run-through*, "The Night the Martians Landed" mixes narration, example, and cause and effect. It re-creates the experience of the radio show, "The War of the Worlds," for those who have not heard it, and in describing the show's effects also explains the sources of the show's power over its audience.

On Sunday, October 30, 1938, at 8:00 P.M., E.S.T., in a studio littered with coffee cartons and sandwich paper, Orson Welles swallowed a second container of pineapple juice, put on his earphones, raised his long white fingers and threw the cue for the Mercury theme—the Tchaikovsky Piano Concerto in B Flat Minor #1. After the music dipped, there were routine introductions—then the announcement that a dramatization of H. G. Wells' famous novel, *The War of the Worlds*, was about to be performed. Around 8:01 Orson began to speak, as follows:

WELLES

We know now that in the early years of the twentieth century this world was being watched closely by intelligences greater than man's and yet as mortal as his own. We know now that as human beings busied themselves about their various concerns they were scrutinized and studied, perhaps almost as narrowly as a man with a microscope might scrutinize the transient creatures that swarm and multiply in a drop of water. With infinite complacence people went to and fro over the earth about their little affairs, serene in the assurance of their

301

dominion over this small spinning fragment of solar driftwood which by chance or design man has inherited out of the dark mystery of Time and Space. Yet across an immense ethereal gulf minds that are to our minds as ours are to the beasts in the jungle, intellects vast, cool, and unsympathetic regarded this earth with envious eyes and slowly and surely drew their plans against us. In the thirty-ninth year of the twentieth century came the great disillusionment.

It was near the end of October. Business was better. The war scare was over. More men were back at work. Sales were picking up. On this particular evening, October 30, the Crossley service estimated that thirty-two million people were listening in on their radios. . . .

Neatly, without perceptible transition, he was followed on the air by an anonymous announcer caught in a routine bulletin: 2

ANNOUNCER

. . . for the next twenty-four hours not much change in temperature. A slight atmospheric disturbance of undetermined origin is reported over Nova Scotia, causing a low pressure area to move down rather rapidly over the northeastern states, bringing a forecast of rain, accompanied by winds of light gale force. Maximum temperature 66; minimum 48. This weather report comes to you from the Government Weather Bureau. . . . We now take you to the Meridian Room in the Hotel Park Plaza in downtown New York, where you will be entertained by the music of Ramon Raquello and his orchestra.

At which cue, Bernard Herrmann led the massed men of the   3
CBS house orchestra in a thunderous rendition of "La Cumparsita." The entire hoax might well have exploded there and then—but for the fact that hardly anyone was listening. They were being entertained by Charlie McCarthy—then at the height of his success.

The Crossley census, taken about a week before the broadcast,   4
had given us 3.6 per cent of the listening audience to Edgar Bergen's 34.7 per cent. What the Crossley Institute (that hireling of the advertising agencies) deliberately ignored, was the healthy American habit of dial-twisting. On that particular evening, Edgar Bergen in the person of Charlie McCarthy temporarily left the air about 8:12 P.M., E.S.T., yielding place to a new and not very popular singer. At that point, and during the following minutes, a large number of listeners started twisting their dials in search of other entertainment. Many of them turned to us—and when they did, they stayed put! For by this time the mysterious meteorite had fallen at Grovers Mill in New Jersey, the Martians had begun to show their foul leathery

heads above the ground, and the New Jersey State Police were racing to the spot. Within a few minutes people all over the United States were praying, crying, fleeing frantically to escape death from the Martians. Some remembered to rescue loved ones, others telephoned farewells or warnings, hurried to inform neighbors, sought information from newspapers or radio stations, summoned ambulances and police cars.

The reaction was strongest at points nearest the tragedy—in   5 Newark, New Jersey, in a single block, more than twenty families rushed out of their houses with wet handkerchiefs and towels over their faces. Some began moving household furniture. Police switchboards were flooded with calls inquiring, "Shall I close my windows?" "Have the police any extra gas masks?" Police found one family waiting in the yard with wet cloths on faces contorted with hysteria. As one woman reported later:

> I was terribly frightened. I wanted to pack and take my child in my arms, gather up my friends and get in the car and just go north as far as we could. But what I did was just sit by one window, praying, listening, and scared stiff, and my husband by the other sniffling and looking out to see if people were running. . . .

In New York hundreds of people on Riverside Drive left their   6 homes ready for flight. Bus terminals were crowded. A woman calling up the Dixie Bus Terminal for information said impatiently, "Hurry please, the world is coming to an end and I have a lot to do."

In the parlor churches of Harlem evening service became "end   7 of the world" prayer meetings. Many turned to God in that moment:

> I held a crucifix in my hand and prayed while looking out of my open window for falling meteors. . . . When the monsters were wading across the Hudson River and coming into New York, I wanted to run up on my roof to see what they looked like, but I couldn't leave my radio while it was telling me of their whereabouts.
>
> Aunt Grace began to pray with Uncle Henry. Lily got sick to her stomach. I don't know what I did exactly but I know I prayed harder and more earnestly than ever before. Just as soon as we were convinced that this thing was real, how petty all things on this earth seemed; how soon we put our trust in God!

The panic moved upstate. One man called up the Mt. Vernon   8 Police Headquarters to find out "where the forty policemen were killed." Another took time out to philosophize:

I thought the whole human race was going to be wiped out—that seemed more important than the fact that we were going to die. It seemed awful that everything that had been worked on for years was going to be lost forever.

In Rhode Island weeping and hysterical women swamped the   9
switchboard of the Providence *Journal* for details of the massacre, and officials of the electric light company received a score of calls urging them to turn off all lights so that the city would be safe from the enemy. The Boston *Globe* received a call from one woman "who could see the fire." A man in Pittsburgh hurried home in the midst of the broadcast and found his wife in the bathroom, a bottle of poison in her hand screaming, "I'd rather die this way than that." In Minneapolis a woman ran into church screaming, "New York destroyed this is the end of the world. You might as well go home to die I just heard it on the radio."

The Kansas City Bureau of the AP received inquiries about the   10
"meteors" from Los Angeles; Salt Lake City; Beaumont, Texas; and St. Joseph, Missouri. In San Francisco the general impression of listeners seemed to be that an overwhelming force had invaded the United States from the air—was in process of destroying New York and threatening to move westward. "My God," roared an inquirer into a telephone, "where can I volunteer my services, we've got to stop this awful thing!"

As far south as Birmingham, Alabama, people gathered in   11
churches and prayed. On the campus of a Southeastern college—

> The girls in the sorority houses and dormitories huddled around their radios trembling and weeping in each other's arms. They separated themselves from their friends only to take their turn at the telephones to make long distance calls to their parents, saying goodbye for what they thought might be the last time. . . .

There are hundreds of such bits of testimony, gathered from coast to coast.

At least one book and quite a pile of sociological literature has   12
appeared on the subject of "The Invasion from Mars." Many theories have been put forward to explain the "tidal wave" of panic that swept the nation. I know of two factors that largely contributed to the broadcast's extraordinarily violent effect. First, its historical timing. It came within thirty-five days of the Munich crisis. For weeks, the American people had been hanging on their radios, getting most

of their news no longer from the press, but over the air. A new technique of "on-the-spot" reporting had been developed and eagerly accepted by an anxious and news-hungry world. The Mercury Theater on the Air by faithfully copying every detail of the new technique—including its imperfections—found an already enervated audience ready to accept its wildest fantasies. The second factor was the show's sheer technical brilliance. To this day it is impossible to sit in a room and hear the scratched, worn, off-the-air recording of the broadcast, without feeling in the back of your neck some slight draft left over from that great wind of terror that swept the nation. Even with the element of credibility totally removed it remains a surprisingly frightening show.

Radio drama was taken seriously in the thirties—before the Quiz   13
and the Giveaway became the lords of the air. In the work of such directors as Reis, Corwin, Fickett, Welles, Robson, Spier, and Oboler there was an eager, excited drive to get the most out of this new, all too rapidly freezing medium. But what happened that Sunday, up on the twentieth floor of the CBS building, was something quite special. Beginning around two, when the show started to take shape under Orson's hands, a strange fever seemed to invade the studio— part childish mischief, part professional zeal.

First to feel it were the actors. I remember Frank Readick (who   14
played the part of Carl Phillips, the network's special reporter) going down to the record library and digging up the Morrison recording of the explosion of the Hindenburg at Lakehurst. This is a classic reportage—one of those wonderful, unpredictable accidents of eyewitness description. The broadcaster is casually describing a routine landing of the giant gasbag. Suddenly he sees something. A flash of flame! An instant later the whole thing explodes. It takes him time— a full second—to react at all. Then seconds more of sputtering ejaculations before he can make the adjustment between brain and tongue. He starts to describe the terrible things he sees—the writhing human figures twisting and squirming as they fall from the white burning wreckage. He stops, fumbles, vomits, then quickly continues. Readick played the record to himself, over and over. Then, recreating the emotion in his own terms, he described the Martian meteorite as he saw it lying inert and harmless in a field at Grovers Mill, lit up by the headlights of a hundred cars—the coppery cylinder suddenly opening, revealing the leathery tentacles and the terrible pale-eyed faces of the Martians within. As they begin to emerge he freezes,

unable to translate his vision into words; he fumbles, retches—and then after a second continues.

A few moments later Carl Phillips lay dead, tumbling over the microphone in his fall—one of the first victims of the Martian Ray. There followed a moment of absolute silence—an eternity of waiting. Then, without warning, the network's emergency fill-in was heard— somewhere in a quiet studio, a piano, close on mike, playing "Clair de Lune," soft and sweet as honey, for many seconds, while the fate of the universe hung in the balance. Finally it was interrupted by the manly reassuring voice of Brigadier General Montgomery Smith, Commander of the New Jersey State Militia, speaking from Trenton, and placing "the counties of Mercer and Middlesex as far west as Princeton and east to Jamesburg" under Martial Law! Tension— release—then renewed tension. For soon after that came an eyewitness account of the fatal battle of the Watchung Hills; and then, once again, that lone piano was heard—now a symbol of terror, shattering the dead air with its ominous tinkle. As it played, on and on, its effect became increasingly sinister—a thin band of suspense stretched almost beyond endurance. | 15

That piano was the neatest trick of the show—a fine specimen of the theatrical "retard," boldly conceived and exploited to the full. It was one of the many devices with which Welles succeeded in compelling, not merely the attention, but also the belief of his invisible audience. *The War of the Worlds* was a magic act, one of the world's greatest, and Orson was just the man to bring it off. | 16

For Welles is at heart a magician whose particular talent lies not so much in his creative imagination (which is considerable) as in his proven ability to stretch the familiar elements of theatrical effect far beyond their normal point of tension. For this reason his productions require more elaborate preparation and more perfect execution than most. At that—like all complicated magic tricks— they remain, till the last moment, in a state of precarious balance. When they come off, they give—by virtue of their unusually high intensity—an impression of great brilliance and power; when they fail—when something in their balance goes wrong or the original structure proves to have been unsound—they provoke, among their audience, a particularly violent reaction of unease and revulsion. Welles' flops are louder than other men's. The Mars broadcast was one of his unqualified successes. | 17

Among the columnists and public figures who discussed the | 18 affair during the next few days (some praising us for the public service we had rendered, some condemning us as sinister scoundrels) the most general reaction was one of amazement at the "incredible stupidity" and "gullibility" of the American public, who had accepted as real, in this single broadcast, incidents which in actual fact would have taken days or even weeks to occur. "Nothing about the broadcast," wrote Dorothy Thompson with her usual aplomb, "was in the least credible." She was wrong. The first few minutes of our broadcast were, in point of fact, strictly realistic in time and perfectly credible, though somewhat boring, in content. Herein lay the great tensile strength of the show; it was the structural device that made the whole illusion possible. And it could have been carried off in no other medium than radio.

Our actual broadcasting time, from the first mention of the   19
meteorites to the fall of New York City, was less than forty minutes. During that time men traveled long distances, large bodies of troops were mobilized, cabinet meetings were held, savage battles fought on land and in the air. And millions of people accepted it—emotionally if not logically.

There is nothing so very strange about that. Most of us do the   20
same thing, to some degree, most days of our lives—every time we look at a movie or listen to a broadcast. Not even the realistic theater observes the literal unities; motion pictures and, particularly, radio (where neither place nor time exists save in the imagination of the listener) have no difficulty in getting their audiences to accept the telescoped reality of dramatic time. Our special hazard lay in the fact that we purported to be, not a play, but reality. In order to take advantage of the accepted convention, we had to slide swiftly and imperceptibly out of the "real" time of a news report into the "dramatic" time of a fictional broadcast. Once that was achieved—without losing the audience's attention or arousing their skepticism, if they could be sufficiently absorbed and bewitched not to notice the transition—then, we felt, there was no extreme of fantasy through which they would not follow us. We were keenly aware of our problem; we found what we believed was the key to its solution. And if, that night, the American public proved "gullible," it was because enormous pains and a great deal of thought had been spent to make it so.

In the script, *The War of the Worlds* started extremely slowly—   21
dull meteorological and astronomical bulletins alternating with mus-

ical interludes. These were followed by a colorless scientific interview and still another stretch of dance music. These first few minutes of routine broadcasting "within the existing standards of judgment of the listener" were intended to lull (or maybe bore) the audience into a false security and to furnish a solid base of realistic time from which to accelerate later. Orson, in making over the show, extended this slow movement far beyond our original conception. "La Cumparsita," rendered by "Ramon Raquello, from the Meridian Room of the Hotel Park Plaza in downtown New York," had been thought of as running only a few seconds; "Bobby Millette playing first 'Stardust' from the Hotel Martinet in Brooklyn," even less. At rehearsal Orson stretched both these numbers to what seemed to us, in the control room, an almost unbearable length. We objected. The interview in the Princeton Observatory—the clockwork ticking monotonously overhead, the woolly-minded professor mumbling vague replies to the reporters' uninformed questions—this, too, he dragged out to a point of tedium. Over our protests, lines were restored that had been cut at earlier rehearsals. We cried there would not be a listener left. Welles stretched them out even longer.

He was right. His sense of tempo, that night, was infallible.   22
When the flashed news of the cylinder's landing finally came—almost fifteen minutes after the beginning of a fairly dull show—he was able suddenly to spiral his action to a speed as wild and reckless as its base was solid. The appearance of the Martians; their first treacherous act; the death of Carl Phillips; the arrival of the militia; the battle of the Watchung Hills; the destruction of New Jersey—all these were telescoped into a space of twelve minutes without overstretching the listeners' emotional credulity. The broadcast, by then, had its own reality, the reality of emotionally felt time and space.

At the height of the crisis, around 8:31, the Secretary of the   23
Interior came on the air with an exhortation to the American people. His words, as you read them now, ten years later, have a Voltairean ring. (They were admirably spoken—in a voice just faintly reminiscent of the President's—by a young man named Kenneth Delmar, who has since grown rich and famous as Senator Claghorn.)

THE SECRETARY

Citizens of the nation: I shall not try to conceal the gravity of the situation that confronts the country, nor the concern of your Government in protecting the lives and property of its people. However, I wish to impress upon you—private citizens and public officials, all of you—the urgent need of calm and resourceful action. Fortunately, this formidable enemy is still confined to a comparatively small area, and we may place our faith in the military forces to keep them there. In the meantime placing our trust in God, we must continue the performance of our duties, each and every one of us, so that we may confront this destructive adversary with a nation united, courageous, and consecrated to the preservation of human supremacy on this earth. I thank you.

Toward the end of this speech (*circa* 8:30 E.S.T.), Davidson 24 Taylor, supervisor of the broadcast for the Columbia Broadcasting System, received a phone call in the control room, creased his lips, and hurriedly left the studio. By the time he returned, a few moments later—pale as death—clouds of heavy smoke were rising from Newark, New Jersey, and the Martians, tall as skyscrapers, were astride the Pulaski Highway preparatory to wading the Hudson River. To us in the studio the show seemed to be progressing splendidly—how splendidly Davidson Taylor had just learned outside. For several minutes now, a kind of madness had seemed to be sweeping the continent—somehow connected with our show. The CBS switchboards had been swamped into uselessness but from outside sources vague rumors were coming in of deaths and suicides and panic injuries.

Taylor had requests to interrupt the show immediately with an 25 explanatory station-announcement. By now the Martians were across the Hudson and gas was blanketing the city. The end was near. We were less than a minute from the Station Break. The organ was allowed to swirl out under the slackening fingers of its failing organist and Ray Collins, superb as the "last announcer," choked heroically to death on the roof of Broadcasting Building. The boats were all whistling for a while as the last of the refugees perished in New York Harbor. Finally, as they died away, an amateur shortwave operator was heard, from heaven knows where, weakly reaching out for human companionship across the empty world:

2 X 2L Calling CQ
2 X 2L Calling CQ
2 X 2L Calling CQ
Isn't there anyone on the air?
Isn't there anyone?

Five seconds of absolute silence. Then, shattering the reality of World's End—the Announcer's voice was heard, suave and bright:

ANNOUNCER

You are listening to the CBS presentation of Orson Welles and the Mercury Theater on the Air in an original dramatization of *The War of the Worlds,* by H. G. Wells. The performance will continue after a brief intermission.

The second part of the show was extremely well written and   26
most sensitively played—but nobody heard it. It recounted the adventures of a lone survivor, with interesting observations on the nature of human society; it described the eventual death of the Martian Invaders, slain—"after all man's defenses had failed by the humblest thing that God in his wisdom had put upon this earth"— by bacteriological action; it told of the rebuilding of a brave new world. After a stirring musical finale, Welles, in his own person, delivered a charming informal little speech about Halloween, which it happened to be.

I remember, during the playing of the final theme, the phone   27
starting to ring in the control room and a shrill voice through the receiver announcing itself as belonging to the mayor of some Midwestern city, one of the big ones. He is screaming for Welles. Choking with fury, he reports mobs in the streets of his city, women and children huddled in the churches, violence and looting. If, as he now learns, the whole thing is nothing but a crummy joke—then he, personally, is coming up to New York to punch the author of it on the nose! Orson hangs up quickly. For we are off the air now and the studio door bursts open. The following hours are a nightmare. The building is suddenly full of people and dark blue uniforms. We are hurried out of the studio, downstairs, into a back office. Here we sit incommunicado while network employees are busily collecting, destroying, or locking up all scripts and records of the broadcast. Then the press is let loose upon us, ravening for horror. How many deaths have *we* heard of? (Implying they know of thousands.) What do *we* know of the fatal stampede in a Jersey hall? (Implying it is one of many.) What traffic deaths? (The ditches must be choked with corpses.) The suicides? (Haven't you heard about the one on Riverside Drive?) It is all quite vague in my memory and quite terrible.

Hours later, instead of arresting us, they let us out a back way.   28
We scurry down to the theater like hunted animals to their hole. It is surprising to see life going on as usual in the midnight streets,

cars stopping for traffic, people walking. At the Mercury the company is . . . stoically rehearsing—falling downstairs and singing the "Carmagnole." Welles goes up on stage, where photographers, lying in wait, catch him with his eyes raised up to heaven, his arms outstretched in an attitude of crucifixion. Thus he appeared in a tabloid that morning over the caption, "I Didn't Know What I Was Doing!" The *New York Times* quoted him as saying, "I don't think we will choose anything like this again."

We were on the front page for two days. Having had to bow to   29
radio as a news source during the Munich crisis, the press was now only too eager to expose the perilous irresponsibilities of the new medium. Orson was their whipping boy. They quizzed and badgered him. Condemnatory editorials were delivered by our press-clipping bureau in bushel baskets. There was talk for a while, of criminal action.

Then gradually, after about two weeks, the excitement subsided.   30
By then it had been discovered that the casualties were not as numerous or as serious as had at first been supposed. One young woman had fallen and broken her arm running downstairs. Later the Federal Communications Commission held some hearings and passed some regulations. The Columbia Broadcasting System made a public apology. With that the official aspects of the incident were closed. . . .

Of the suits that were brought against us—amounting to over   31
three-quarters of a million dollars for damages, injuries, miscarriages, and distresses of various kinds—none was substantiated or legally proved. We did settle one claim, however, against the advice of our lawyers. It was the particularly affecting case of a man in Massachusetts, who wrote:

"I thought the best thing to do was to go away. So I took three   32
dollars twenty-five cents out of my savings and bought a ticket. After I had gone sixty miles I knew it was a play. Now I don't have money left for the shoes I was saving up for. Will you please have someone send me a pair of black shoes size 9B!"

We did.   33

RESPONSES AND IDEAS

1. Respond to this essay by telling of a time when you heard or read a frightening story (or saw a movie or TV show) that managed—for a

while—to convince you of its truth even though you knew it to be fiction. Tell what made the story so believable (the personality of the speaker, the delivery, the setting in which you heard or read the story, or the story itself).

2. Explain Houseman's concept of the relationship between literal and dramatic time (par. 20) by using examples from television programs.

3. Houseman clearly believes that Welles and his company were not morally responsible for any of the negative effects of the program, and chooses and arranges the material in the selection to support his outlook. Do you believe they were morally responsible? Why, or why not? (Note that he claims they were responsible for the other effects of the show and credits their artistry.)

PURPOSE, AUDIENCE, AND STRATEGIES

1. In which paragraph of the selection does Houseman announce that he is going to examine the causes of the show's extraordinary impact? What does he view as the main reasons for its success? Tell what role is played by the paragraphs preceding this announcement of his purpose. What sections of the essay are devoted to describing the show's effects?

2. What, if anything, did you know about the Mercury Theater on the Air broadcast of "The War of the Worlds" before reading this piece? How much? Is an extensive knowledge of the event necessary in order to understand and appreciate the selection? Indicate any sections that are particularly difficult to understand without background information. Did you know anything about Orson Welles before reading the essay? If you did, how did it change your view of him?

3. Is Houseman's purpose in this piece to tell what happened or to explain why it happened? If both, which is the primary aim? (Support your answer with evidence from the selection.)

4. Where in this essay does Houseman use patterns other than cause-and-effect? In what ways do they contribute to his discussion of causes and effects? What other purposes do they serve?

5. What strategies does Houseman use to make his account of the events believable and to encourage readers to accept his interpretation of the reasons for the show's impact?

LANGUAGE AND STYLE

1. What does Houseman's tone reveal about his attitude towards the events chronicled in the essay? Does the tone vary at different stages in the

selection? In what ways? (See Glossary: Tone.) To what extent is the tone the product of the writer's diction? Be specific. (See Glossary: Diction.)

2. How does Houseman's diction in paragraphs 9–11 emphasize the confusion and panic created by the broadcast? Describe how the syntax of the sentences in paragraphs 14 and 15 creates a sense of drama in the events Houseman is presenting. (See Glossary: Diction, Syntax.)

3. If you do not know the meaning of any of the following words, look them up in the dictionary: *transient, complacence, dominion, ethereal* (par. 1); *perceptible* (2); *enervated, credibility* (12); *ominous* (15); *retard* (16); *precarious, revulsion* (17); *aplomb, tensile* (18); *unities, purported* (20); *tedium* (21); *infallible, credulity* (22); *exhortation, formidable* (23); *incommunicado, ravening* (27); *perilous* (29); *substantiated* (31).

WRITING ACTIVITIES

1. If you have worked on a theatrical production or political campaign, helped set up a Special Olympics meet, a fund-raising drive for charity, or some similar activity, tell the story of the activity, and, following Houseman's example, concentrate on identifying the causes for its success or failure.

2. Why do some singers, movie stars, writers, or politicians succeed when many others fail? What makes some novels bestsellers and others flops? Why do a few television series last for years while others disappear after a few episodes? Write an essay exploring the causes behind a particular pair of failures or successes.

Writing Suggestions

1. Make three brief lists: one, of things you fear; another, of things that irritate you; a third, of things you like and admire. Then choose one item from each list and explain the event or factors in your life that caused this attitude. If this exercise suggests a topic for a cause-effect essay, keep writing.

2. Identify four problems facing society as a whole, or your local community or region. For each problem, specify a solution and what you hope it will achieve. In each case indicate, too, possible objections to your proposed solution. If you discover a problem and a solution worth writing about, use them as the basis for an essay.

3. Think back to an occasion when a seemingly unimportant or innocent action on your part (or on the part of someone you know) had extensive or startling results. Diagram the causes, the contributing factors, and the results in order to demonstrate the complexity of their relationships. Write about the events in an essay.

4. Choose four things that you would tell a good friend to avoid doing: for example, avoid enrolling in a particular college, taking a certain kind of job, getting married, having children, studying in a particular way, or living in an apartment with five other people. For each piece of advice list four negative effects that are good reasons for listening to what you have to say. If this exercise suggests a good approach for an essay, follow it in your writing.

ACTIVITIES

1. Using newspapers, newsmagazines, or television reports as your sources, summarize two or more contrasting explanations of the causes of some recent newsworthy event or predictions of future events. Then indicate which you find more convincing and why, paying special attention to the logic of the explanations.

2. Look at the editorial page of a local newspaper to discover how many of the editorials it contains follow a problem analysis or problem-solution format like those in this chapter. Indicate how their strategies differ, if at all, from those discussed in the introduction.

3. For a week, as you watch television and read newspapers or magazines, keep a record of deceptive practices in advertising, politics, health care, or any other aspect of life that we have come to accept as harmless. Choose the three whose effects you think are dangerous and describe each one in detail along with its consequences.

4.   Look at one chapter each from college textbooks in two very different fields—for example, music and chemistry, or engineering and anthropology. Describe the amount of space each chapter devotes to discussing causes and effects, and try to account for any differences you find in emphasis on causes and effects or on the way they are viewed.

MODELS

1.   Using Harsha and Thompson's "Our Rhythms Still Follow the African Sun" as a model, investigate a common phenomenon and offer an explanation of it. You might want to look into a common pattern of behavior among college students, office workers, or members of sports teams. Your explanation need not have the scientific basis of Harsha and Thompson's, but you should try to make it as reasonable as possible.

2.   Using the approach of Hartzel Lebed's "Who Will Take Care of the Children?" describe the causes of a problem and suggest a solution to it. You might wish to talk about day care in some other setting that Lebed describes, or a problem like student loan eligibility, drunk driving, poor services in a city or a community, or ticket sales policies for rock concerts and similar events.

3.   Drawing your inspiration from A. Alvarez's "A Test of Will," write a defense of some favorite activity of yours that other people might find dangerous, wasteful, or silly. The activity you defend need not be as serious as the one Alvarez discusses, but your strategy should involve explaining the causes of your behavior.

4.   Using Sissela Bok's methods in "Placebos," describe some other apparently harmless deception whose actual effect is the undermining of trust in an important institution or profession.

5.   Making use of some of the tactics employed by John Houseman in "The Night the Martians Landed," retell a well-known event in a way that sheds light on its causes. The event might be of historical significance, of general interest (such as the eruption of Mt. St. Helens), or the subject of curiosity (such as the story behind the making of a controversial movie).

8

ঌ DEFINITION

Identifying and Probing the Meaning

WHAT DEFINITION DOES

Definition is writing that specifies meaning, either formally, as in a dictionary—"*panatela,* noun, a long, slender cigar"—or informally, as part of the flow of writing: "When Jean came home from a summer in Europe, she was wearing a *dirndl,* an Austrian peasant dress with a red skirt, a black bodice, and a green apron."

A definition helps writers and readers agree on the meaning of a word, on the qualities of an object or emotion, on the dimensions of an idea. Writers and their audiences often start out with very different kinds of knowledge. The writer may know all about bits, bytes, and chips; the reader may find everything about computers confusing. Or they begin with very different points of view: to the author, *conservation* may mean harmful government intrusion; to most readers it may mean the preservation of valuable natural resources. As part of an essay or as the primary pattern for an entire piece of writing, definition helps bring authors and readers together, or at least within talking distance, in their understanding of an object or an idea.

A definition sets boundaries to a word or subject, indicating not only what it is but also what it is not. When a subject can be known, measured, and observed, as in Cree McCree's "Flea Market" or Roger Caras's "What's a Koala?" (both in this chapter), a definition answers questions like "What are its features? What is its history? What does it do? How is it related to similar phenomena?"

317

But when a subject is a concept, a set of values, a term, or a symbol whose meaning depends on the way people agree to use it, then a definition answers, in addition, questions like "How do people use this term? What is the history of the concept, and how has its meaning changed? How is this term or set of values different from others? What are some similar concepts, and what concepts are opposite in meaning?"

As a pattern of expression, a definition can follow one of two different strategies, either *conventional definition* or *redefinition,* each of which serves different needs. A reader in need of help turns to conventional definitions in dictionaries, handbooks of technical and scientific terms, and glossaries like the one at the end of this book (pp. 569–584). The assumption behind these definitions is that the writer knows more about a term or concept than the reader does, and that the reader, needing information, is willing to accept the definition without argument. This assumed relationship between the writer (as authority) and the reader (in search of information and understanding) fits many occasions, including the definitions that appear in textbooks, in informative magazine articles (about photography or automobile repairs for example), in travel guides ("Modified American Plan means that breakfast and dinner, but not lunch, are included in the cost of the room"), in technical manuals, or in any other kind of writing we look to for information or explanations. Even when we already know something about a subject or hold views that differ slightly from those of the author, we are generally willing to accept the authority of conventional definitions as long as they are clearly expressed and developed through examples and explanations.

When the meaning of a term or a set of values is open to discussion, as in several of the essays in this chapter (Noel Perrin's "The Androgynous Man," Susan Brownmiller's "The Contrived Postures of Femininity," and Thomas Sowell's "We're Not Really 'Equal'"), or when an argument hinges on a definition (arguments over abortion frequently revolve around a definition of the moment human life begins), then *redefinition* is the appropriate strategy. The assumption behind this strategy is that the definition of a term or concept held by readers is markedly different from the one the writer wants them to share, so the writer must play the role of persuader to get readers to accept—or think about accepting—a new perspective.

Definitions are also often classified as either *limited*, when they are only a sentence or two in length, or *extended*, when they are a paragraph long or longer. The essays in this chapter are all examples of extended definitions.

Whether the occasion calls for definition or redefinition, and whether the definition is limited or extended, writers use the same *strategies of definition* to help their readers understand a term well enough to be able to use it in speaking and writing or to enable them to grasp the implications of a concept.

One route to understanding is through *formal definition*. A formal definition places a term in the general class to which it belongs, and then presents details that show how it differs from other members of the class:

A telephoto lens
    Term
is a camera lens
    Class
that makes distant objects seem close.
    Details

A racecar driver
    Term
is a person
    Class
of exceptional courage, daring, and a touch of foolishness.
    Details

A "third world country"
    Term
is a phrase politicians often use
    Class
for an underdeveloped nation of Africa, Asia, or Latin America, aligned with neither Communist or non-Communist blocs.
    Details

Another equally important means of defining is by citing examples: To explain the term *deviant behavior*, you might cite examples of thieves, drug dealers, female impersonators, and actors in pornographic films. A definition of *star* might point to Frank Sinatra, Marilyn Monroe, Mick Jagger, Elvis Presley, Michael Jackson, and Paul Newman.

Comparisons help too, both those that identify synonyms (*naive* means innocent, unsophisticated, natural, unaffected, and artless) or that distinguish among concepts with similar, though not identical meanings—*socialism* and *communism,* for example. Similes and metaphors can be effective forms of definition, too, especially for concepts and attitudes that are difficult to grasp directly: "A transition in writing is a bridge between ideas."

The history of a term, its *etymology,* can provide valuable hints to its present meaning: *Catholic* originally meant "pertaining to the universal Christian church"; its present meaning, "of or concerning the Roman Catholic Church," retains some of the original meaning because the Roman Catholic Church claims to be the direct descendant of the ancient, undivided Christian church.

A narrative or a process analysis can also be part of a definition. A definition of *courage,* for example, might include the story of a ten-year-old saving a friend from drowning in an icy pond. A definition of *open-heart surgery* would probably include a description of the process itself.

Finally, a term or concept can be defined by negation, by indicating what it is not: "*Intelligence* is not the puzzle-solving ability that enables people to do well on multiple-choice tests and standardized exams like the SAT or ACT; nor is it the ability to remember columns of facts and figures and be able to call them up at any time whether they truly serve the needs of the occasion or not."

An extended definition can be developed through one of these strategies, particularly those like process, narration, comparison, and example, which can be patterns for entire essays. Most often, however, an extended definition consists of several strategies working together, as in this definition of *software*:

> An old-fashioned automobile that can be started only with a crank requires a person to make a series of adjustments more or less directly to the engine; in a modern car, of course, you need only turn a key and a system of electrical and mechanical devices does the rest. In the modern computer, software has developed in such a way as to fill this role of go-between. On one end you have the so-called end user who wants to be able to order up a piece of long division, say, simply by supplying two numbers to the machine and ordering it to divide them. At the other end stands the actual computer, which for all its complexity is something of a brute. It can perform only several hundred basic operations, and long division may not be one of them. The machine may have to be instructed to perform a sequence of several of its basic operations in order to accomplish a piece of long division. Software— a series of what are known as programs—translates the end user's wish into specific, functional commands for the machine.

This definition comes from Tracy Kidder's *The Soul of a New Machine* (1981), an account of the drama and excitement surrounding the creation of a new computer viewed from the perspective of the engineers who designed and built it. Though the subject is highly technical, Kidder's treatment of it is not, and this is one of the reasons many people who know little about computers begin their education by reading his book. In this passage Kidder avoids beginning with a precise formal definition of *software,* realizing, probably, that his readers will know very little about the topic and will require a much simpler approach to definition. He therefore concentrates on defining only one aspect of software, its role as a go-between. Kidder's strategy is to begin with a brief reminder of things familiar to the reader (the ignition systems in old-fashioned and in modern cars) and to use this comparison as an introduction to his real subject, software. He then defines software's role with a single term, *go-between,* an easy-to-understand synonym for *intermediary.* Following this, he explains the role at length through a single straightforward example, the long-division problem faced by a hypothetical computer. He concludes with a formal definition of software that sums up the preceding discussion.

Kidder's definition not only illustrates how strategies of definition can be combined, it also shows that the choice of strategies and the complexity of a definition should be determined more by the audience to which it is directed than by the nature of the subject.

THE PROCESS

Writers of definitions invariably start out asking themselves questions. Will my readers understand this concept, or should I define it for them in a phrase, a sentence, or a paragraph? Is this subject interesting or controversial enough to deserve an essay of its own—a definition essay? These questions identify two different occasions for definition, the first as a way of clarifying the meaning of a word or phrase used in an essay, the second as the primary pattern for an entire essay. Because these occasions call for rather different uses of the definition pattern, you are likely to follow a different writing process for each one.

As you write an essay or report, you will often find that you have introduced an expression or idea whose meaning and importance will be unclear to a majority of your readers. Occasionally you will be able to recognize these spots right away as a result of your knowledge of your audience; most often, however, you will have to rely on telltale signs like complicated or technical language or a puzzled expression on the face of a friend reading a draft of your work. The more technical the subject, the more likely the need for definition. If you read your drafts with a suspicious eye you can save yourself and your readers much misunderstanding.

Yet before you decide to add a definition to your essay, ask if the phrase or concept is essential to your meaning or adds to the impact of your writing. If not, try rewriting the passage without it. If a definition is appropriate, however, the decision you face is "How long should I make it?"

Imagine, for example, that you have been working as a stock-broker for several years and have begun sending out a monthly memorandum on the performance of the stock market to some of your regular customers. As you prepare this month's memorandum, you write, "The best way to take advantage of these developments is to buy the stock on margin." Having written this, you wonder if all your customers will know enough about margin accounts to be able to follow your advice. You have several choices. You can provide a brief definition within the sentence: "Buy on margin—that is, buy securities by borrowing part of the money required from your bro-ker." Or you can give an example: "Buy on margin—for example, put up fifty percent of the money yourself and borrow the rest from a broker." A third way is to provide a longer definition, perhaps a paragraph in length, in which you use several strategies, including negation, to show that margin accounts are not the dangerous prac-tices they were in 1929 when they contributed to the stock market crash:

> Buying on margin is no longer the risky business it was in 1929 when the small amount of capital required to buy a stock on credit ("margin") meant that many investors overextended themselves. Today the government keeps speculation in check by regulating the margin, requiring fifty, sixty, or seventy percent of the purchase price from the investor and 100 percent at times when the market is particularly volatile. Thus buying on margin is no longer a speculator's dream. It is a well-regulated strategy to be used by the serious investor who wants to add flexibility to an investment program.

Your choice of a strategy should depend, of course, upon the difficulty of the term or concept you are defining and how much readers are likely to know about the subject already.

Often as you write you will have to decide if definition is appropriate as the pattern for all or a large part of an essay. You might set out to write about the growth of special education during the last decade, for instance. Your plans will change, however, if you decide that readers know so little about special education, which serves both gifted and handicapped children, that you need to spend all of your essay, or at least the first part, answering the question, "What Is Special Education?" Sometimes, however, the pattern comes before the topic, as when college instructors make assignments like, "Write a paper that defines one of the important assumptions of political science that we have studied this semester," and "In an essay, take a fresh look at an everyday word or concept."

A subject appropriate for definition is a term or concept whose full meaning is worth exploring. Topics may come from your own interests: "What exactly does 'rock and roll' mean if people can apply it to the songs of people as different as Elvis Presley, the Beatles, Paul Anka, Donna Summers, Linda Ronstadt, Ozzy Osbourne, and Olivia Newton-John?" or from your reading: "Just what is this 'nuclear deterrence' that everyone is writing about?" They may even come from brainstorming or playing with words. Here is a list of words and definitions written down by one student, Greg Glovach, as a brainstorming activity:

squash—a tougher form of tennis
marathon—the most challenging kind of running
skydiving is parachuting for people who want extra difficulty
What's the toughest form of flying—gliding? ultralights? (no, they're easy to fly)
triathlon—now that's a really difficult sport—swimming, cycling, running!!

Notice that although squash, skydiving, and the other topics in Greg's list could have been the subject of a definition, he settled on one that his readers would probably regard as fresh and unusual and that at the same time offered plenty of material for discussion because of the variety of activities included in the sport.

Definition is also a useful pattern when a subject is the focus of much misunderstanding. Your special interest in a topic may help you realize how little most people know about it and how mistaken most of their attitudes are as a result. You may notice, for instance, that when people hear the terms *special education* and *mainstreaming*, they often think of profoundly retarded or severely handicapped students taking resources away from regular education or disrupting classes. Your definition could demonstrate just how normal special education students are in many ways. Like all other essays, a definition essay needs to have a clear purpose and a point (thesis). Your purpose may be to define by explaining each of the unfamiliar aspects of your topic. Or it may be to redefine, to encourage readers to change their views. Summarizing the point and purpose of a definition early in your writing as a tentative thesis statement can help you choose appropriate definition strategies and can guide your research. A tentative thesis statement, therefore, should specify the topic and what you want to say about it. It may even suggest ways you will go about supporting your assertions:

> The negative ways our society defines teachers these days ensure that very few people of above average ability will want to enter the profession.

> The old word for doctor was *leech*, a bloodsucker, and my own experiences and those I have read about in the news lately suggest that the term still applies accurately to many doctors.

The research you do to prepare a definition may draw on your own experience, your reading, or interviews ("What does the term *sexual harassment* mean to you?"). Or it may lead you to specialized reference works like the *Oxford English Dictionary* (which traces the meanings of a word in various periods), the *Dictionary of Slang and Unconventional English*, or the *Encyclopedia of Pop, Rock, and Soul*. Your librarian will be able to suggest many other interesting sources.

You might find it helpful to turn the various strategies of definition into questions to guide your planning and research. Here is part of the list Greg Glovach made to help him explore the meanings of *triathlon*, the word that caught his attention while he was brainstorming:

What is the history of the triathlon?
Is the triathlon like any other sport?
What does it feel like to participate in a triathlon?
What happens in a triathlon (what is the process)?
What are some examples of famous triathletes?
Are there any interesting stories about triathlons?

In finished form, a definition essay usually begins by showing why the subject is worth reading about and then indicating the author's purpose, often in the form of a thesis statement. An example, a quotation, or a summary of the way a term is used or misused can often help demonstrate the importance of the subject. The openings of the essays in this chapter illustrate other ways to begin a definition.

The organization of a definition will depend on your purpose. If you wish to survey the different meanings of a word or the ways of viewing a concept, your essay should take up each element in a different section, perhaps saving the most interesting or memorable for last. If you wish to argue for a particular interpretation, you might arrange the essay according to the different strategies of interpretation, in ascending order reflecting the strength of their support for your thesis. Many definition essays follow a variation of this pattern:

Introduction (name of thing to be defined; may include formal definition)
> Definition Strategy 1 (synonyms, examples, and so on)
> Definition Strategy 2 (synonyms, examples, and so on)
> Definition Strategies 3, 4, 5 (synonyms, examples, and so on)

Conclusion (summary)

Greg Glovach's finished essay on the triathlon followed a pattern similar to this. Here are the first two paragraphs:

> What is the toughest sport? Skydiving? Whitewater canoeing? Running the marathon? None of these sports nor any others can come near the demands placed on an athlete by the triathlon. Triathlons are endurance competitions which involve individual efforts in swimming, bicycling, and running. These competitions are the newest and most demanding events in endurance athletics. Triathletes are usually athletes who competed in one of the component sports but decided to look for a new challenge. And the triathlon certainly is challenging.

The first triathlon was a result of a dispute between two drunk friends, one a runner and one a bicyclist. In Hawaii five years ago, these two men agreed on a race to prove which was the superior athlete: a 2.4-mile ocean swim, a 112-mile bike ride, and a 26.2-mile run. The first race in February, 1978, had 20 participants. Two years later at the same race site, ABC gave the event national coverage. During the past two years this triathlon was held twice each year, but still many applicants had to be rejected.

In an earlier version of the essay, the second paragraph had concentrated on comparing the triathlon to other sports. When Greg's instructor read a draft of the essay, she commented, "This paragraph is accurate and helps develop your definition, but it isn't very interesting. Remember that a definition should help readers share your interest in a subject. If you find a word or concept interesting or fascinating, the details should help readers share your attitude." Greg's decision to recount the triathlon's unusual history not only makes his definition more interesting, it also adds variety to the ways he defines the sport.

THE PATTERN IN ACTION

Aside from the entries in dictionaries and similar works, most of the definitions you encounter are likely to be combined with other patterns of writing: for example, in a historical narrative they explain the outlook of a specific group (such as the social attitudes of the Pilgrims), in an issue analysis they explain how key terms are used by each side in a controversy, and in the description of a process they define the terms used.

Even when combined with other patterns of writing, definitions often take a special form—the stipulative definition—and on their own they take a number of forms you may want to employ in your writing.

A *stipulative definition* states the precise meaning of terms to be used in a discussion or argument. It is necessary when a term has more than one common meaning, and when considerable confusion or misunderstanding is likely to result if the writer and readers fail to agree beforehand on the meaning of the term.

The term *stipulate,* from which *stipulative* is derived, means "to specify as a condition of an agreement," thus emphasizing the necessary role such definitions play in helping readers and writers achieve understanding, perhaps even agreement. Stipulative definitions generally review the various meanings of a term or concept and then identify the meaning to be used in the present case, perhaps explaining why it is important to stick to one meaning. Most stipulative definitions come at the beginning of a discussion because the distinctions they make are necessary for proper understanding of the material that follows. Academic and technical writing often uses stipulative definitions because such writing frequently employs words in senses quite different from their everyday connotations. Stipulative definitions may even include a review of the different meanings the terms have had at one time or another for experts in the field.

Stipulative definitions are also useful at the beginning of argumentative essays because they prevent misunderstanding over terms from becoming an added source of disagreement. But when the definition itself lies at the center of an argument, a stipulative definition is inappropriate because it attempts to get people to agree ahead of time to the subject of the disagreement. A stipulative definition of the point at which life begins (at conception; at the first or second trimester) would thus be inappropriate at the start of an argumentative essay on abortion because the time at which life begins determines whether or not abortion involves the taking of human life and is in itself a matter of much controversy.

Perhaps the most common form of extended, independent definition is the *informative definition*. An informative definition focuses on a fad, trend, hobby, social phenomenon, or political movement whose impact is widespread enough to be of interest to most readers but is new enough to require definition. Magazines and newspapers are filled with articles of this type.

Informative definitions have no fixed form; yet they often begin with an indication of the reason for the subject's current importance, then move to a brief, sometimes formal definition, a discussion of the historical background, and a review of its features. Cree McCree's "Flea Market" in this chapter is a clear example of the form.

One important variation of the informative definition is the definition of an activity or hobby that is generally well-known but that the reader is learning about in detail for the first time. Essays of this sort on topics like making pottery, fly fishing, weaving, or forming a rock group often appear in magazines and newspapers or along with how-to essays in collections with titles like *The Art of Pottery,*

Weaving at Home, Tying Dry Flies, or *The Band Guide: All You Need to Know About Forming a Rock Group.*

A *redefinition* essay, in contrast, assumes that the reader already has some clear ideas about the topic and sets out to change them. Such an essay may begin as an informative definition does by creating interest in the topic and then go on to mention the ways the topic is normally viewed, following each with a reason for the superiority of the alternate view (the redefinition). Or it might review various aspects of the subject, suggesting a fresh way of looking at each. This latter strategy is similar to the one Roger Caras follows in "What's a Koala?" in this chapter. If the definition of a term or concept is a matter of controversy, a redefinition essay might open by indicating the reasons for the controversy and then present the new definition as a thesis, following it in the body of the essay with definition strategies that support the new perspective.

The essays in this chapter illustrate some of the many possible uses of the definition strategy. Cree McCree's "Flea Market" presents an informative definition of a recent social phenomenon that she insists we take seriously. Roger Caras's "What's a Koala?" redefines one of everybody's favorite animals and in the course of the definition warns us about imposing our own fantasies on wild animals. Thomas Sowell in "We're Not Really 'Equal'" calls readers to account over the often unthinking and careless way people regard the important concept of equality. Noel Perrin in "The Androgynous Man" uses definition along with several other patterns of development to explore and redefine what it means to be masculine. Susan Brownmiller in "The Contrived Postures of Femininity" uses mixed patterns to argue that so-called feminine behavior as it is currently defined is an act of submission and a form of bondage.

CREE McCREE

Cree McCree was born in 1947 in East Orange, New Jersey. She graduated from the College of Wooster in Ohio and spent a number of years as a Montessori preschool teacher in Boulder, Colorado, and as a martial arts instructor. Her writings include articles in *Omni* and *Rolling Stone* magazines and a book, *Flea Market America* (1983), based on her eight years of experience buying and selling in flea markets.

Flea Market

"Flea Market" was first published in *Psychology Today*. In this essay, Cree McCree looks beyond the inexpensive wares and the bustle of flea markets to the people who participate in them. If you have never been at a flea market, you will find her treatment of the phenomenon a good introduction. If you have been at a flea market, a country fair, or a street fair, and perhaps even sold goods at one, you will be interested in her perspective and will be able to compare your experiences with the ones she describes.

flē mär-kət n. (trans. of French Marché aux Puces, a market in Paris): usually an open-air market for secondhand articles and antiques.

Sunrise, weekend, United States: While most of the nation still sleeps, vans, pickup trucks, campers and cars crammed with every conceivable item congregate in empty parking lots, fair-grounds and drive-in movie theaters across the country. By noon, the scene overflows with thousands who have come to buy and come to browse at this crazed carnival of wonders and wares. 1

Flea markets flourish today like never before. Part of their appeal comes from a sluggish economy, for the market allows sellers to turn discards into dollars and allows buyers to pick up bargains. 2

People have traded and bartered for centuries. Whatever else the flea market may appear to be, its reason for being is the sale and exchange of goods. Whether they're aficionados of obscure collectibles or just plain bargain-hunters looking for a deal on a crescent wrench, people are drawn to the flea market by the immense scope and variety of merchandise offered. 3

329

Buying and selling activity at the flea market is like a gypsy   4
version of the stock exchange: Risks are calculated, deals transacted,
investments made. And, like the stock exchange, unpredictability
creates an air of anticipation with the beginning of each market day.
The possibility of hitting the jackpot, of finding that diamond in the
rough before anybody else does, makes shopping at flea markets a
treasure hunt.

"You find things out here you would never see anywhere else,"   5
Nell Kaufmann, co-manager of Manhattan's Canal Street flea market,
explains. "That gives the buyers as much of a chance to be creative
as the sellers. There's no challenge when you buy in a store, because
you know everything has been prepackaged."

For many buyers, the ritual of bargaining at the flea market is   6
as much a lure as the bargain itself. With savvy, you can shave the
price on something that was a good buy to begin with. It's not just
the dollar or two you save that gives that warm inner glow of
accomplishment; it's the satisfaction of playing an ancient game.

Satisfaction also comes from the immediacy of a flea-market   7
exchange. The market is "cash on the line" country—the dealer
pockets your five bucks, you carry off the toaster and that's that. You
got what you wanted, the dealer got what he wanted. In today's
world of plastic money, the flea market takes one back to a time
when life was simpler, when money had more meaning.

There's magic in a place where anything can happen, any   8
strange icon can be unearthed. The flea market allows us to be
children again, to play dress-up and try on funny hats, to embark
on an adventure of discovery and surprise. It also allows us to reclaim
relics of our past that have been swept away by time, only to reappear
again, almost miraculously, at the market.

The flea market is the American melting pot in microcosm: A   9
Chinese couple sell embroidered slippers next to a peroxide punk's
display of cat's-eye sunglasses across from the grizzled junk dealer's
hodgepodge of hubcaps, baby dolls and plastic potted-plants. Vendors may have nothing in common during their weekday lives, but,
come the weekend, this diversity becomes community.

What common denominator do they share? A belief in the Amer-   10
ican Dream, in the old Horatio Alger combination of hard work and
imagination. Many "fleas" are bootstrappers; the market offers them
the opportunity to become economically self-sufficient and to take

control of their own lives. "It's not easy money," says Canal Street's Joel Kaufmann, "but it's direct money. You can get into this with very little capital. The capital is your flesh. The bank loan is your life."

Flea markets mean freedom from the 9-to-5 world of lawyers, 11 leases, inflation and taxation; freedom to choose when, where and what you will sell; freedom to be what you want to be. Dealers adopt personas like "Jerry Junk" and "Trader Jack," and they become them, at least for the weekend.

The flea market is more than a motley crew of individualists. 12 "This is a serious enterprise," Joel Kaufmann says. "It looks like a shambles, it looks kind of half-assed, but it really isn't. The amount of labor and organization that goes into an operation like this is phenomenal. If everybody weren't so cooperative, it wouldn't work." For the market to function as a community, there must be a minimal social structure that allows for freedom of individual action.

"There used to be a lot of problems here, when one vendor's 13 property line went up immediately next to another vendor's property line," Danny, a veteran East Coast vendor, says about the Canal Street market. "The intention was you'd each give a foot and together you'd create an aisle. But it didn't work that way—there were terrible 'border fights.' Some people would have them week after week. Finally, Joel changed it and marked all the spaces with aisles in between. That got rid of the hostility and improved cooperation immensely."

Territorial security is essential for order to arise from chaos, as 14 Mike, a street merchant turned flea marketeer, says, "There's a kind of unity here you don't have among street people. They're used to having to watch out for cops, so they're very protective. They don't really look out for each other—they look out for themselves. Once you have a community like this, you begin to get the idea that it's okay to look after your neighbor, even to the point of chasing crooks and catching them."

As the season wears on, and newcomers are assimilated into 15 the community, people begin to mix in ways that go beyond mutual survival: "It's great, it's hysterical to watch a couple of punk rockers, that could slay you to look at them, selling next to an old Jewish couple from New Jersey," Nell Kaufmann says. "On the street, they would never talk. Here, they do. There's a good solid ground, and reason for, communication. It's fun to see that couple gradually become accustomed to their neighbors. They look, but they're not offended."

There's a lot of laughter at the flea market, and for many people, 16 it is the place they finally find a home. "Just to commit yourself to this, you have to have the sense of a child, a sense of imagination, a sense of 'How can I make myself better?'" says Caggie Daniels, who with her husband, Jack, runs Trader Jack's in Santa Fe, New Mexico. "At the flea market, everyone is encouraged to be an individual and to help each other out. The social potential of a structure like this is really vast. It's a shame cities aren't run like this."

COMMENTARY

Because "Flea Market" was originally written for the magazine *Psychology Today*, it reflects the magazine's emphasis on patterns of human behavior and culture. Although the author begins the selection with a dictionary definition of *flea market* and provides some indication in the opening paragraphs of the how, where, and what of flea markets, her attention soon shifts to the participants and to a definition of their relationships with each other. In paragraphs 3–8, she explains the psychological and social rewards buyers get from going to flea markets. In paragraphs 9–11, she describes the common character traits of the many outwardly different people who sell things at these gatherings. And in paragraphs 12–16 she describes how flea markets operate as self-regulating, peaceful communities that bring together people from diverse cultural backgrounds.

"Flea Market" contains little of the kind of information readers may have come to expect from informative articles on similar topics (like "Used Car Auctions," "Shopping for Antiques," or "Finding Bargains in Out-of-the-way Places"). It lacks information on where to find flea markets, how to find things to sell, and how to find bargains at a flea market. Yet the absence of such information does not weaken the essay because McCree's purpose is to define flea markets not according to the use people make of them or as economic entities but as networks of social relationships. The details she uses to help describe flea markets also emphasize their social rather than economic aspects, as do her interpretations of the examples the essay presents. In commenting on the bargains people find at flea markets, for instance, McCree points to their personal and social meaning:

"It's not just the dollar or two you save that gives that warm glow of accomplishment; it's the satisfaction of playing an ancient game" (par. 6).

When Cree McCree was interviewed during the preparation of this text, she said that she had aimed the essay at a general audience (see Glossary: Audience) and that she had guided her writing with three questions: "What makes a flea market work?" "Where does the magic come from?" and "Who makes up the community of vendors?" The essay answers these questions and presents her view of a flea market as a community well worth joining.

RESPONSES AND IDEAS

1. Respond to this essay with a brief definition of some common type of gathering that is familiar to you (a high school prom, a family picnic) or some group that meets regularly (a scout troop, a club, a church group). In your definition include the essential features of the gathering or group and indicate the ways that participants with different person-alities or values regard each other.

2. According to this essay, in what ways do people who sell things at flea markets benefit from the experience? In what ways do buyers benefit?

3. What does the author mean by the phrase, "The flea market is the American melting pot in microcosm" (par. 9)? Do you think the author agrees with the quotation at the end of the essay: "The social potential of a structure like this is really vast. It's a shame cities aren't run like this" (par. 16)? Why, or why not?

PURPOSE, AUDIENCE, AND STRATEGIES

1. Does this essay provide a detailed description of the features and op-eration of flea markets? If so, where? If not, what background infor-mation on these matters does it provide? How much does the author assume most readers know about flea markets (nothing or very little? a good deal?), and what indication of this assumption is there in the essay?

2. Is the purpose of this essay to define the flea market as a social phe-nomenon? As an economic entity? As a physical arrangement? Or in some other way? Explain. (See Glossary: Purpose.)

3. Do you think the average reader will find the roles adopted by some flea market dealers ("Jerry Junk," "Trader Jack" (par. 11)) amusing? Silly? Explain how you think most readers will respond, and indicate why you think this response is consistent or inconsistent with the way that the author wants readers to view flea markets.

4. Indicate where in the essay McCree uses each of the following strategies of definition: formal definition, comparison, example, negation. Which strategies does she use most often? Why are they appropriate to the essay's purpose?

5. Paragraphs 5, 10, and 12–16 contain quotations from flea market participants. Can readers safely assume that the author agrees with what they say? What strategies does McCree use to establish the authority of the people she quotes—or to call it into question so that readers will regard their statements critically? (See Glossary: Evidence.) At what places in the essay does the author make an important generalization through a quotation rather than in her own voice? In what ways is this strategy effective or ineffective? (See Glossary: Evaluation.)

LANGUAGE AND STYLE

1. Describe the tone of this essay? (See Glossary: Tone.) Does the author want readers to view flea markets negatively, positively, or neutrally? Explain your answer, taking note of any direct comments the author makes as well as the tone and diction. (See Glossary: Diction.)

2. Are the statements "The capital is your flesh. The bank loan is your life" (par. 10) meant to be taken literally, or are they metaphors? What, precisely, do the statements mean? For what reasons does the author begin paragraph 10 with a rhetorical question? (See Glossary: Figures of Speech.) Discuss the ways in which the dealers, the buyers, and the author regard flea markets and their wares as symbols. What specifically do they symbolize? (See Glossary: Symbol.)

3. If you do not know the meaning of any of the following words, look them up in the dictionary: *crazed* (par. 1); *aficionados* (3); *icon* (8); *microcosm, peroxide, grizzled* (9); *capital* (10); *personas* (11); *motley* (12); *assimilated* (15).

WRITING ACTIVITIES

1. *Family* is a relatively abstract term whose meanings can be explored by pointing to examples of specific families, both traditional (mother, father, two children, dog) and untraditional (college students sharing an apartment, single parents and their children sharing living quarters and expenses). Here are some other abstract terms: religion, city, social class, crime, disease, evolution, pollution, bias, greed, anger, and wisdom. Choose one of these terms, or some other, and write an extended definition that uses specific examples to explore the meaning or meanings of the term.

2. A visitor to this country from Thailand, Peru, Madagascar, or Sri Lanka might already know something about American culture from television programs, but would still have many questions like "What is baseball?"

and "What does *barbeque* mean?" Prepare an essay defining some peculiarly American phenomenon for such a visitor. (Remember, fast food, blue jeans, and similar fashions are now international, not merely American.)

&❧ ROGER CARAS

Roger Caras, a writer and naturalist, was born in 1928 in Methuen, Massachusetts. He attended Northeastern University and the University of Southern California. Besides creating numerous radio, television, and film scripts, Caras has published many articles on natural history and anthropology as well as a variety of books for adults and children. Among his most recent books are *The Private Lives of Animals* (1974), *Venomous Animals of the World* (1974), *Monarch of Deadman Bay: The Life and Death of a Kodiak Bear* (1977), and *The Forest* (1979). In all his writings, Caras tries to share the wonder and pleasure he finds in nature. At the same time he encourages readers to treat the natural world with respect, regarding it not on their terms but on its own.

What's a Koala?

"What's a Koala?" was first published in *Geo* magazine, of which Caras is a contributing editor. Throughout the essay, Caras follows a strategy of redefinition, building on his readers' probable conceptions (misconceptions, actually) about the koala in order to surprise them with his portrait of what a koala is really like. The surprise is intended in part to remind readers that koalas, like all other animals, are creatures with their own patterns of behavior and not simply products of our imaginations or the myths of our culture.

To the Australian aborigines, the Dreamtime was the time of creation. It was then that the creatures of the earth, including man, came into being. There are many legends about that mystical period, but unfortunately, the koala does not fare too well in any of them. Slow-witted though it is in life, the koala is generally depicted in myth and folklore as a trickster and a thief.

One tale tells of how the koala was forced to live among the newly created people of the earth. His hosts did not treat him well and refused to give him water in a time of drought, so the koala stole all the tribe's water and hid it at the top of a very tall tree, which he had caused to spring up from a mere bush. In another story, a koala joins forces with a starfish, a bird and another animal to steal a whale's canoe.

However illogical the notion of a canoe-owning whale might   3
seem, the koala itself, zoologically, seems hardly more logical. It is
one of the world's two favorite teddy bears. The other, of course, is
the panda, although neither the panda nor the koala is a bear at all.
In fact, unlike the panda—which is a kind of cousin twice removed
to the bears of the world—the koala doesn't even come close. It is
related to the wombat distantly, to the kangaroo even more distantly,
and to the opossum. It is a marsupial, pouch and all. But then again,
it isn't a run-of-the-mill marsupial: the typical marsupial pouch runs
transversely, across the body, while the koala's pouch opens to the
rear and extends upward and forward. That, apparently, keeps it
from getting snagged on tree limbs.

The koala, all 10 to 30 pounds and two to three feet of it (there   4
is an amazing range in size among adults), is a beast of tall trees.
Koalas live most of their lives high up in any one of 35 species of
eucalyptus, or gum tree. They subsist on eucalyptus leaves, which
they can't digest on their own. They rely on microorganisms in their
digestive tract to do it for them. They can also handle some mistletoe
leaves and some leaves from a tree known as the box.

With so particular a diet, the first koalas in captivity died because   5
no one knew what to feed them. Until recently, very little, if anything,
was known about the biology of the koala. And the knowledge we
now have has come from field studies using animals that have been
captured, marked and released. Situated on the marsupial family
tree somewhere between the opossum and the tunneling wombat
(koalas have cheek pouches to help them handle their tough, fibrous
diet, and wombats have traces of the same kind of pouch), the koalas
are a kind of zoological dead end. Their diet and their need to stay
high in their gum trees have made them so specialized that they
would be incapable of handling any marked change in their habitat
or food supply.

On occasion the koala does come down to the ground, usually   6
to shuffle over to another tree, generally taking the opportunity along
the way to lick up some gravel to aid in digestion. It is then that
koalas are most vulnerable to their foremost natural enemy, the feral
Australian dog we call the dingo. How much trouble they have with
snakes is not really known, but Australia's pythons could give them
a problem.

Koalas may be solitary, or a mature male may assemble a small   7
harem, which he guards jealously. Mating occurs every other year

from September to January, and gestation is abbreviated. (All marsupials have brief pregnancies. Even the great gray kangaroo, at 175 pounds, has a gestation period of less than 40 days.) For koalas, it is anywhere from 25 to 30 days. At birth, the single offspring weighs a barely believable one fifth of an ounce—or even a little less—and it must remain in its mother's pouch on one of her two nipples for six months if it is to have any chance at all of surviving. It is entirely dependent on its mother for at least a year. Once on its own, however, unless a dingo happens to get it during a transit between two trees, the koala is likely to live to be almost 20.

During the mating period, the increasingly bellicose male displays a surprising range of noises. (For some reason, people tend to think of koalas as virtually mute animals, except for those few that speak English on TV in Australian airline commercials.) The territorial, harem-guarding male may issue a startling guttural roar, mew like a dyspeptic cat or make a staccato sneezing sound that can be confused with the distress of a human suffering from a head cold. On rare occasions, apparently when it is in a really foul mood, the koala makes a very loud and rapid ticking noise—like a time bomb counting down. All in all, the koala has a fairly extensive, and expressive, vocabulary.   8

To add some emphasis to their noisemaking, the males discharge an oily substance from glands in their chest. This makes a mess of their fur, but it also gives pungent notice of prior claims to a tree and to breedable females. The noisy, musty belligerence of a koala during the mating season takes people by surprise; it just doesn't seem in keeping with the animal's cuddly appearance. Koalas are, in fact, less cuddly than they look. Most wild animals are.   9

The koala sleeps the day away tucked up high on its perch and then feeds for most of the night, which makes it difficult to see koalas, much less study them. White settlers were in koala country in eastern Australia for more than 10 years before they reported seeing their first specimen. In Australia today, the koala has a variety of names, including—quite pardonably—teddy bear and native bear. They are also known as bangaroos, koolewongs, narnagoons and buidelbeers. The latter four names, of course, are not likely to be used in everyday conversation outside of Australia.   10

The European discovery of the koala occurred in 1798. John Price, a servant of Captain John Hunter, the governor, went exploring with an ex-convict named James Wilson. Southwest of Sydney, they   11 encountered a koala, which Wilson likened to a South American sloth (the poor koala, it seems, has always had an identity crisis). The next explorer to report seeing a koala was a French ensign named Barrallier, who came across one in 1802 and said it was a kind of monkey. He traded some spears and axes with the natives for the "monkey's" four feet, which he sent off to his boss in a bottle of brandy. Slowly but surely, with family affiliations in a perfect muddle, the koala made its way into the European consciousness. That's when the killing started. The koala's dense gray pelt is luxuriously soft and fine, and by the early decades of this century, the animal had been hunted almost to extinction. The koala is now protected wherever it is found.

No one knows how many koalas there once were, how many 12 there should be or, indeed, how many there are today. It is hard to get much of a fix on the word *endangered,* but the International Union for the Conservation of Nature and Natural Resources (IUCN), the internationally recognized arbiter of the status of species, does not list the koala as endangered, threatened or even rare. Protection has evidently been working, and the only precarious perch that the koala may now be astride is the branch on which it sits as it sleeps away its days.

It was not always that way. As recently as 1924, nearly 2 million 13 koala skins were exported from Australia's eastern states. Three years later, 10,000 licensed trappers exported more than 600,000 pelts from Sydney alone. Public outrage at the massacre led to the enactment of protectionary measures. Today, killing a koala in Australia is considered only slightly less offensive than doing in your neighbor or spouse.

In the wild, koalas are about as inoffensive to human interests 14 as animals can be. They don't bother agricultural enterprises, and there are no reports of attacks on man. But a koala in hand is quite a different thing from one in the bush. They have well-developed claws—as their arboreal life would naturally require—and they bite with a particularly unpleasant grinding action. To look at its perennially sleepy eyes, its bulbous patent-leather nose and white-rimmed furry ears, one would not think of a koala capable of any offense at all. Still, if one has to handle a koala—and most of us never have to—it's advisable to wear gloves and lift the animal from behind, under the armpits.

The early European interest shown in the koala is not difficult 15 to understand. All the animals of Australia were oddities to Europeans who were just becoming aware of the little-known continent. Kangaroos, wombats, wallabies and the particularly dangerous snakes of the area attracted a great deal of attention. Australian animals still do, but none more affectionately than the koala. It is one of the most primitive mammals in the world and would probably make one of the least satisfactory pets (and one of the most difficult to feed). Yet each night its toy likeness is hugged to sleep by millions of children around the world. The koala that we grew up hugging is far more legend than zoological fact. The koala that exists in fact is far more interesting than its legend. It is ancient, it is secretive, and it acts in ways no one would expect it to act. Belying our first impressions and preconceived notions, the koala—the mythic trickster of the Dreamtime—is something of a trickster after all.

RESPONSES AND IDEAS

1. Respond to this essay by describing what you think are the personality and habits of a widely known though still exotic animal like a lion, tiger, wolf, moose, rhinocerous, or baboon. If one of your classmates has studied the animal you described, ask him or her to comment on the accuracy of your description. Otherwise, comment yourself on any traits in the description that you suspect come from what the animal symbolizes for you (lion = courage, for example) rather than from a real understanding of its habits.

2. Summarize those traits that make the koala seem illogical, in a zoological sense, at least (see especially pars. 3–5). What habits or traits of the koala could lead to its becoming an endangered species again?

3. What lesson(s), if any, about koalas, about the natural world, or about our attitudes towards wild animals does this essay teach? Are they stated directly, or must they be inferred from the examples and discussion? What irony is there in the contrast between the way koalas actually behave and their popularity as toys (par. 15)? (See Glossary: Irony.) What does this contrast reveal about the way humans generally view animals?

PURPOSE, AUDIENCE, AND STRATEGIES

1. At what point in the essay does it become clear that Caras intends to redefine *koala* rather than present a straightforward definition? How is this intention signalled to readers?

2. The term *marsupial* appears several times in the essay without being defined, although Caras does remind readers of marsupial characteristics in paragraph 3: "It is a marsupial, pouch and all." Is Caras correct in assuming that most readers will know what a marsupial is, or would his assumption be correct only for readers of the magazine in which the article was originally published, *Geo,* a publication that focuses on natural history and culture? Where else in the essay does Caras assume a good deal about his audience's knowledge of the natural world?

3. Why is it unlikely that readers will have given much thought to the sexual habits of koalas? In what specific ways is Caras's description of the animal's mating habits (pars. 7–9) designed to shock or surprise? What do these paragraphs contribute to the overall purpose of the essay? (See Glossary: Purpose, Unity.)

4. Which of the strategies of (re)definition (see pp. 319–320) does Caras use, and where in the essay are they used? Are they all equally effective? Which, if any, are more effective, and why? (See Glossary: Evaluation.)

5. What pattern of development does paragraph 14 follow, and how do the transitions signal this pattern? (See Glossary: Paragraph.) Describe how Caras uses transitions to create emphasis in paragraph 13. (See Glossary: Transitions.)

LANGUAGE AND STYLE

1. What is the tone of this essay, and how does it help the writer keep from irritating readers as he tries to change their attitudes about the koala? (See Glossary: Tone.) What do the touches of humor (especially in pars. 8 and 10), the diction, and the examples of curious behavior contribute to the tone?

2. Identify as many words or phrases as you can in paragraph 15 that are repeated from elsewhere in the essay and that are designed to remind readers of points covered earlier (exclude common words like "the" and "is," of course). Were these repetitions apparent to you the first time you read the essay? Is repetition of the sort paragraph 15 contains an effective strategy for a closing? (See Glossary: Closings.)

3. If you do not know what some of the following words mean, look them up in the dictionary: *aborigines* (par. 1); *zoologically, wombat, marsupial* (3); *subsist* (4); *fibrous, habitat* (5); *feral* (6); *gestation, transit* (7); *bellicose, guttural, dyspeptic* (8); *pungent, belligerence* (9); *ensign* (11); *arbiter* (12); *arboreal, bulbous* (14).

WRITING ACTIVITIES

1. The view many people have of football players, doctors, housewives, farmers, steel workers, and politicians is often far from accurate. Pre-

pare an essay in which you define (or redefine) the job of someone like a football player or politician in such a way that readers are forced to reexamine and even change their view of the people who fill these roles.

2. Some scientific concepts, like gravity, are often misunderstood; others, like evolution, are often distorted in the heat of argument. Choose a scientific concept you think readers need to understand more clearly and define it, taking care to explain any common misunderstandings or distortions.

❧ THOMAS SOWELL

Thomas Sowell was born in 1930 in Gastonia, North Carolina. Though he dropped out of high school, Sowell eventually completed his education, attending Howard and Harvard universities and The University of Chicago, from which, in 1968, he received a Ph.D. in economics. Sowell's views on politics and the economy have attracted nationwide attention in part because he is a leading black conservative but primarily because of the range and quality of his many writings. He has published twelve books, including *Pink and Brown People, and Other Controversial Essays* (1981), *Markets and Minorities* (1981), *Ethnic America* (1981), and most recently, *Civil Rights: Rhetoric or Reality* (1984).

Sowell is currently senior fellow of the Hoover Institute at Stanford University.

We're Not Really "Equal"

"We're Not Really 'Equal,'" first published in the "My Turn" column of *Newsweek* magazine, examines the assumptions underlying some current controversies and suggests that the assumptions are largely matters of definition. Sowell's interpretation of the controversies reflects his conservative outlook, and his characterization of the way others view the issues may irritate some readers, but that may well be one of the reactions Sowell is looking for.

As a teacher I have learned from sad experience that nothing so   1
bores students as being asked to define their terms systematically before discussing some exciting issue. They want to get on with it, without wasting time on petty verbal distinctions.

Much of our politics is conducted in the same spirit. We are for   2
"equality" or "the environment," or against an "arms race," and there is no time to waste on definitions and other Mickey Mouse stuff. This attitude may be all right for those for whom political crusades are a matter of personal excitement, like rooting for your favorite team and jeering the opposition. But for those who are serious about the consequences of public policy, nothing can be built without a solid foundation.

"Equality" is one of the great undefined terms underlying much   3

343

current controversy and antagonism. This one confused word might even become the rock on which our civilization is wrecked. It should be worth defining.

Equality is such an easily understood concept in mathematics 4 that we may not realize it is a bottomless pit of complexities anywhere else. That is because in mathematics we have eliminated the concreteness and complexities of real things. When we say that two plus two equals four, we either don't say two *what* or we say the same what after each number. But if we said that two apples plus two apples equals four oranges, we would be in trouble.

Yet that is what we are saying in our political reasoning. And 5 we are in trouble. Nothing is more concrete or complex than a human being. Beethoven could not play center field like Willie Mays, and Willie never tried to write a symphony. In what sense are they equal—or unequal? The common mathematical symbol for inequality points to the smaller quantity. But which is the smaller quantity—and in whose eyes—when such completely different things are involved?

When women have children and men don't, how can they be 6 either equal or unequal? Our passionate desire to reduce things to the simplicity of abstract concepts does not mean that it can be done. Those who want to cheer their team and boo the visitors may like to think that the issue is equality versus inequality. But the real issue is whether or not we are going to talk sense. Those who believe in inequality have the same confusion as those who believe in equality. The French make better champagne than the Japanese, but the Japanese make better cameras than the French. What sense does it make to add champagne to cameras to a thousand other things and come up with a grand total showing who is "superior"?

When we speak of "equal justice under law," we simply mean 7 applying the same rules to everybody. That has nothing whatsoever to do with whether everyone performs equally. A good umpire calls balls and strikes by the same rules for everyone, but one batter may get twice as many hits as another.

In recent years we have increasingly heard it argued that if 8 outcomes are unequal, then the rules must have been applied unequally. It would destroy my last illusion to discover that Willie Mays didn't really play baseball any better than anybody else, but that the umpires and sportswriters just conspired to make it look that way. Pending the uncovering of intricate plots of this magnitude, we must accept the fact that performances are very unequal in different aspects of life. And there is no way to add up these apples, oranges and grapes to get one sum total of fruit.

Anyone with the slightest familiarity with history knows that 9 rules have often been applied very unequally to different groups. (A few are ignorant or misguided enough to think that this is a peculiarity of American society.) The problem is not in seeing that unequal rules can lead to unequal outcomes. The problem is in trying to reason backward from unequal outcomes to unequal rules as the sole or main cause.

There are innumerable places around the world where those 10 who have been the victims of unequal rules have nevertheless vastly outperformed those who are favored. Almost nowhere in Southeast Asia have the Chinese minority had equal rights with the native peoples, but the average Chinese income in these countries has almost invariably been much higher than that of the general population. A very similar story could be told from the history of the Jews in many countries of Europe, North Africa and the Middle East. To a greater or lesser extent, this has also been the history of the Ibos in Nigeria, the Italians in Argentina, the Armenians in Turkey, the Japanese in the United States—and on and on.

It would be very convenient if we could infer discriminatory 11 rules whenever we found unequal outcomes. But life does not always accommodate itself to our convenience.

Those who are determined to find villains but cannot find evi- 12 dence often resort to "society" as the cause of all our troubles. What do they mean by "society" or "environment"? They act as if these terms were self-evident. But environment and society are just new confused terms introduced to save the old confused term, equality.

The American environment or society cannot explain historical 13 behavior patterns found among German-Americans if these same patterns can be found among Germans in Brazil, Australia, Ireland and elsewhere around the world. These patterns may be explained by the history of German society. But if the words "environment" or "society" refer to things that may go back a thousand years, we are no longer talking about either the causal or the moral responsibility of American society. If historic causes include such things as the peculiar geography of Africa or of southern Italy, then we are no longer talking about human responsibility at all.

This does not mean that there are no problems. There are very 14 serious social problems. But that means that serious attention will be required to solve them—beginning with defining our terms.

RESPONSES AND IDEAS

1. Respond to this essay by stating your opinion of whether preferential hiring programs designed to correct past injustices are based on appropriate or confused notions of equality. Tell how you would defend your opinion.

2. In paragraph 9, Sowell sums up his opinion about the proper application of the term *equality* in this way: "The problem is not in seeing that unequal rules lead to unequal outcomes. The problem is in trying to reason backward from unequal outcomes to unequal rules as the main cause." State in your own words the point Sowell is making, and indicate whether you think the way he states it is clear or confusing. If his expression of it is confusing, how might it be improved?

3. Do the examples of minority groups that have succeeded despite discrimination add to or undermine his argument? Explain. Do they undermine his credibility by suggesting that he is not particularly concerned with discrimination? Do they add to it by indicating that he is realistic enough to recognize the sometimes contradictory evidence that events present? Explain.

PURPOSE, AUDIENCE, AND STRATEGIES

1. Sowell claims that "In recent years we have increasingly heard it argued that if outcomes are unequal, then the rules must have been applied unequally" (par. 8). If you think this statement is accurate, cite some examples to support it. If you think Sowell has misstated or distorted the case, tell why you believe his version is inaccurate. Do you think most readers would agree with Sowell? (You may wish to poll your classmates.)

2. Would it be accurate to say that besides showing how the term *equality* has been misused and misunderstood, Sowell is arguing in favor of unequal outcomes? What evidence of this latter purpose is there in the essay? If he is not arguing for this, do you think he has any purpose in the essay other than clarifying the meaning of an important term? What other aim does he have? (See Glossary: Purpose.)

3. What attitude toward his readers does Sowell take in paragraphs 1 and 2? Where else in this essay does he adopt the same attitude? How are readers likely to feel about this attitude? Would readers be irritated by it or would they find it appropriate for the essay? Why? (See Glossary: Tone.)

4.   What sections of this essay are devoted to a discussion of causes and effects? Which paragraphs present supporting examples? What do the examples and the cause-and-effect discussion contribute to the essay?

5.   Where in the essay might Sowell have included a formal, dictionary-type definition? Why do you think he chose not to do so?

LANGUAGE AND STYLE

1.   How does the author use parallelism in paragraphs 9, 10, and 13? How does he use syntax to emphasize contrasts in paragraphs 5 and 6? (See Glossary: Syntax.)

2.   Where in this essay does Sowell use language and examples drawn from sports? In what ways is this material appropriate or inappropriate for his purpose?

3.   If you do not know the meaning of any of the following words, look them up in the dictionary: *antagonism* (par. 3); *complexities* (4); *magnitude* (8); *infer* (11).

WRITING ACTIVITIES

1.   Here are some terms that, like *equality*, are often used loosely or incorrectly: addiction, liberal, conservative, pornographic, tragic, literally, scientific, and objective. Write an essay defining one of these terms or a similar word or concept, and distinguish between its correct and incorrect usage.

2.   Choose a term or phrase like *abortion, busing, arms control, prayer in school*, or *feminism* and in an essay define its meanings for each side in a controversy in which the term is frequently used.

❧ NOEL PERRIN

Noel Perrin was born in New York in 1927. He teaches American literature at Dartmouth College and lives in Vermont, where he farms and raises beef cattle. He has written essays for *The New Yorker* and other magazines, and has published a number of books, including *Vermont: In All Weathers* (1973), and three volumes of essays, *First Person Rural* (1978), *Second Person Rural* (1980), and *Third Person Rural* (1983).

The Androgynous Man

"The Androgynous Man," first published in the *New York Times Magazine,* reflects the concern social critics have shown in recent years over the impact of sex roles on personality and behavior. In his attempt to define androgyny and redefine acceptable standards for male behavior, Perrin illustrates how definition as a pattern can deal with values and behavior as well as with words and ideas. Although this essay clearly shows the influence of feminist thought, it seems to spring equally from the concern for individuality and independence that characterizes Perrin's other writings.

The summer I was 16, I took a train from New York to Steamboat 1
Springs, Colo., where I was going to be assistant horse wrangler at a camp. The trip took three days, and since I was much too shy to talk to strangers, I had quite a lot of time for reading. I read all of "Gone With the Wind." I read all the interesting articles in a couple of magazines I had, and then I went back and read all the dull stuff. I also took all the quizzes, a thing of which magazines were even fuller then than now.

The one that held my undivided attention was called "How 2
Masculine/Feminine Are You?" It consisted of a large number of inkblots. The reader was supposed to decide which of four objects each blot most resembled. The choices might be a cloud, a steam engine, a caterpillar and a sofa.

When I finished the test, I was shocked to find that I was barely 3
masculine at all. On a scale of 1 to 10, I was about 1.2. Me, the horse wrangler? (And not just wrangler, either. That summer, I had to skin a couple of horses that died—the camp owner wanted the hides.)

The results of that test were so terrifying to me that for the first 4 time in my life I did a piece of original analysis. Having unlimited time on the train, I looked at the "masculine" answers over and over, trying to find what it was that distinguished real men from people like me—and eventually I discovered two very simple patterns. It was "masculine" to think the blots looked like man-made objects, and "feminine" to think they looked like natural objects. It was masculine to think they looked like things capable of causing harm, and feminine to think of innocent things.

Even at 16, I had the sense to see that the compilers of the test 5 were using rather limited criteria—maleness and femaleness are both more complicated than *that*—and I breathed a huge sigh of relief. I wasn't necessarily a wimp, after all.

That the test did reveal something other than the superficiality 6 of its makers I realized only many years later. What it revealed was that there is a large class of men and women both, to which I belong, who are essentially androgynous. That doesn't mean we're gay, or low in the appropriate hormones, or uncomfortable performing the jobs traditionally assigned our sexes. (A few years after that summer, I was leading troops in combat and, unfashionable as it now is to admit this, having a very good time. War is exciting. What a pity the 20th century went and spoiled it with high-tech weapons.)

What it does mean to be spiritually androgynous is a kind of 7 freedom. Men who are all-male, or he-man, or 100 percent red-blooded Americans, have a little biological set that causes them to be attracted to physical power, and probably also to dominance. Maybe even to watching football. I don't say this to criticize them. Completely masculine men are quite often wonderful people: good husbands, good (though sometimes overwhelming) fathers, good members of society. Furthermore, they are often so unself-consciously at ease in the world that other men seek to imitate them. They just aren't as free as us androgynes. They pretty nearly have to be what they are; we have a range of choices open.

The sad part is that many of us never discover that. Men who 8 are not 100 percent red-blooded Americans—say, those who are only 75 percent red-blooded—often fail to notice their freedom. They are too busy trying to copy the he-men ever to realize that men, like women, come in a wide variety of acceptable types. Why this frantic imitation? My answer is mere speculation, but not casual. I have speculated on this for a long time.

Partly they're just envious of the he-man's unconscious ease. 9
Mostly they're terrified of finding that there may be something wrong
with them deep down, some weakness at the heart. To avoid discovering that, they spend their lives acting out the role that the he-
man naturally lives. Sad.

One thing that men owe to the women's movement is that this 10
kind of failure is less common than it used to be. In releasing
themselves from the single ideal of the dependent woman, women
have more or less incidentally released a lot of men from the single
ideal of the dominant male. The one mistake the feminists have
made, I think, is in supposing that *all* men need this release, or that
the world would be a better place if all men achieved it. It would
just be duller.

So far I have been pretty vague about just what the freedom of 11
the androgynous man is. Obviously it varies with the case. In the
case I know best, my own, I can be quite specific. It has freed me
most as a parent. I am, among other things, a fairly good natural
mother. I like the nurturing role. It makes me feel good to see a child
eat—and it turns me to mush to see a 4-year-old holding a glass
with both small hands, in order to drink. I even enjoyed sewing
patches on the knees of my daughter Amy's Dr. Dentons when she
was at the crawling stage. All that pleasure I would have lost if I
had made myself stick to the notion of the paternal role that I started
with.

Or take a smaller and rather ridiculous example. I feel free to 12
kiss cats. Until recently it never occurred to me that I would want
to, though my daughters have been doing it all their lives. But my
elder daughter is now 22, and in London. Of course, I get to look
after her cat while she is gone. He's a big, handsome farm cat named
Petrushka, very unsentimental, though used from kittenhood to being
kissed on the top of the head by Elizabeth. I've gotten very fond of
him (he's the adventurous kind of cat who likes to climb hills with
you), and one night I simply felt like kissing him on the top of the
head, and did. Why did no one tell me sooner how silky cat fur is?

Then there's my relation to cars. I am completely unembarrassed 13
by my inability to diagnose even minor problems in whatever object
I happen to be driving, and don't have to make some insider's remark
to mechanics to try to establish that I, too, am a "Man With His
Machine."

The same ease extends to household maintenance. I do it, of 14 course. Service people are expensive. But for the last decade my house has functioned better than it used to because I've had the aid of a volume called "Home Repairs Any Woman Can Do," which is pitched just right for people at my technical level. As a youth, I'd as soon have touched such a book as I would have become a transvestite. Even though common sense says there is really nothing sexual whatsoever about fixing sinks.

Or take public emotion. All my life I have easily been moved by   15
certain kinds of voices. The actress Siobhan McKenna's, to take a notable case. Give her an emotional scene in a play, and within 10 words my eyes are full of tears. In boyhood, my great dread was that someone might notice. I struggled manfully, you might say, to suppress this weakness. Now, of course, I don't see it as a weakness at all, but as a kind of fulfillment. I even suspect that the true he-men feel the same way, or one kind of them does, at least, and it's only the poor imitators who have to struggle to repress themselves.

Let me come back to the inkblots, with their assumption that   16
masculine equates with machinery and science, and feminine with art and nature. I have no idea whether the right pronoun for God is He, She or It. But this I'm pretty sure of. If God could somehow be induced to take that test, God would not come out macho, and not feminismo, either, but right in the middle. Fellow androgynes, it's a nice thought.

RESPONSES AND IDEAS

1. Respond to this essay by describing any tests for masculinity or femininity you have encountered. (Tests may be in written form, like the one Perrin took, or games or jokes that supposedly identify masculine and feminine traits.)

2. Summarize Perrin's definition of the purely masculine personality. Does it differ in any way from that held by the makers of the test he describes in paragraphs 2–4?

3. The dictionary definition of *androgynous* is "having male and female characteristics in one." In what ways, if any, does Perrin's use of the term differ from the dictionary definition?

PURPOSE, AUDIENCE, AND STRATEGIES

1. Are most readers likely to be convinced by the examples Perrin gives of the advantages of androgyny? Which examples are particularly ef-

fective? Ineffective? What makes them convincing or unconvincing? (See Glossary: Evidence.)

2. State in your own words the thesis of this essay. Does the essay contain a thesis statement? In what ways other than a thesis statement does the author communicate the point of the essay? (See Glossary: Thesis.)

3. Is this essay directed primarily at men or at women? How do you know?

4. At what point in the essay does Perrin begin his definition of androgyny? Why does he wait until this point to begin?

5. Which paragraphs in the essay begin with topic sentences? What role do the topic sentences play in organizing the essay? Does Perrin use any of the topic sentences to announce his purpose or thesis? Which ones? (See Glossary: Paragraph, Topic Sentence.)

LANGUAGE AND STYLE

1. How does Perrin use the connotations of words in paragraphs 7 and 15 to help make a point? (See Glossary: Connotation.)

2. Discuss how Perrin uses sentences of varying length and structure in paragraphs 12–15 to add emphasis to what he is saying. (See Glossary: Syntax.)

3. If you do not know the meaning of any of the following words, look them up in the dictionary: *criteria, wimp* (5); *superficiality* (6); *set* (7); *nurturing* (11); *transvestite* (14); *macho, feminismo* (16).

WRITING ACTIVITIES

1. Psychologists have recently begun arguing that there are more traits to intelligence than the verbal and mathematical skills measured by IQ tests. The new definitions of intelligence take into account other skills such as visual or artistic ability, athletic ability, and musical ability. Prepare an extended definition in which you try to expand in a similar manner your readers' understanding of a concept like beauty or honesty or of an emotion like hatred or jealousy.

2. If you agree with Perrin's idea of androgyny, apply it in an essay in which you explore your own experiences or personality. If you disagree, write an essay criticizing his outlook.

ह SUSAN BROWNMILLER

Susan Brownmiller, born in 1935 in Brooklyn, New York, is a central figure in contemporary feminist thought. She has worked as a journalist and editor and contributed articles to *Ms.*, *Esquire*, and the *New York Times Magazine.* Her first book, *Against Our Will: Men, Women, and Rape* (1975), did much to gain acceptance for the view that rape is an aggressive rather than a sexual act, and the book is generally considered a classic. Her recent book, *Femininity* (1984), explores the often oppressive effect of behavior associated with femininity as a sex role.

The Contrived Postures of Femininity

Brownmiller's fresh and provocative insights into human behavior are well represented in "The Contrived Postures of Femininity," a selection from *Femininity* published as an article in *Ms.* magazine. Like most original thinkers, Brownmiller's speculations fit neatly into no particular pattern (though definition is the primary pattern in this selection), and, in addition, many of her contentions in this essay would be difficult to prove. Yet the value of exploratory writing lies in its ability to suggest new ideas and perspectives rather than to provide firm interpretations. And the redefinition of acceptable feminine behavior this selection offers is certainly provocative enough to be a subject of much discussion.

I was taught to sit with my knees close together, but I don't   1
remember if I was given a reason. Somewhere along the way I heard that boys like to look up girls' skirts and that it was our job to keep them from seeing our panties, but I didn't put much stock in this vicious slur. "Put your knees together" seemed to be a rule of good posture like "Sit up straight," and nothing more. As with other things that became entrenched in my mind as unquestionably right and feminine, when I thought about it later on I could see an aesthetic reason. The line of a skirt did seem more graceful when the knees weren't poking out in different directions. Slanting them together was the way to avoid looking slovenly in a chair. (Sitting with legs crossed became an acceptably feminine posture only after skirts were shortened in the 1920s.)

353

Bending over to pick up a piece of paper was fraught with the   2
danger of indecent exposure during the sixties miniskirt era, and
like other women who believed minis looked terrifically dashing
when we stepped along the street, I had to think twice, compose
myself, and slither down with closed knees if I dropped something.
A breed of voyeurs known as staircase watchers made their appearance during this interesting time. Slowly it dawned on me that much
of feminine movement, the inhibited gestures, the locked knees, the
nervous adjustments of the skirt, was a defensive maneuver against
an immodest, vulgar display that feminine clothing flirted with in
deliberate provocation. My feminine responsibility was to keep both
aspects, the provocative and the chaste, in careful balance, even if it
meant avoiding the beautifully designed open stairway in a certain
Fifth Avenue bookshop.

But why did I think of vulgarity when the focal point at issue—   3
I could no longer deny the obvious—was my very own crotch? And
why did I believe that if I switched to trousers, the problem would
be magically solved?

Spreading the legs is a biologically crucial, characteristically   4
female act. Not only does the female have the anatomical capacity
to stretch her legs further apart than the average male because of
the shape of her pelvis, but a generous amount of leg spread is
necessary to the act of sexual intercourse, to the assertive demand
for pleasure, and to the act of giving birth. There may have been a
time in history when this female posture was celebrated with pride
and joy—I am thinking of the Minoan frescoes on Crete where young
women are shown leaping with ease over the horns of a charging
bull (the sexual symbolism of the woman and the bull has been
remarked upon by others)—but in civilization as we know it, female
leg spread is identified with loose, wanton behavior, pornographic
imagery, promiscuity, moral laxity, immodest demeanor, and a lack
of refinement. In other words, with qualities that the feminine
woman must try to avoid, even as she must try to hint that somewhere
within her repertoire such possibilities exist.

There is nothing hidden about the male sexual organ. It is a   5
manifest presence; the legs need not spread to reveal it, nor are they
usually positioned as wide apart as the female's to accomplish the
sexual act. But while copulation and other genital activity require a
generous spread of the thighs in order for a woman to achieve her

pleasure, in the feminine code of behavior she is not supposed to take the initiative out of her own desire.

The ideology of feminine sexual passivity relies upon a pair of closed thighs more intently than it does upon speculative theories of the effects of testosterone on the libido, aggression, and the human brain. Open thighs acknowledge female sexuality as a positive, assertive force—a force that is capable of making demands to achieve satisfaction. 6

Students of Japanese history know that Samurai warriors trained their daughters in the use of weapons to give them the requisite skill to commit hara-kiri when faced with disgrace. As part of the training, girls were taught how to tie their lower limbs securely so they would not embarrass themselves and their families by inadvertently assuming an immodest position in the agony of death. Traditional Japanese etiquette pays close attention to the rules of modest posture for women. In the classic squat position for eating, men are permitted to open their knees a few inches for comfort but women are not. Men may also sit cross-legged on the floor, but women must kneel with their legs together. 7

Studies by the psychologist Albert Mehrabian show that, despite evidence of superior anatomical flexibility and grace, women are generally less relaxed than men. Mehrabian proposes that attitudes of submissiveness are conveyed through postures of tension. In his analysis of body language among high and low status males, high-ranking men are more relaxed in their gestures in the presence of subordinates. Not surprisingly, men of all ranks generally assume more relaxed postures and gestures when communicating with women. 8

Today's customary restraints on women's bodily comportment are broadly defined by fingertips and heels, a pocketbook on the shoulder, and a schooled inhibition against spreading the knees. In addition, as the French feminist Colette Guillaumin has noted, women are physically burdened by what she calls "diverse loads," the habitual signs of chief responsibility for the domestic role—children on the arm, their food and toys in hand, and a bag of groceries or shirts from the dry cleaner's hugged to the chest. Rarely does a woman experience the liberty of taking a walk with empty hands and arms swinging free at her sides. So rare is this, in fact, that many women find it physically unnerving when they do. Un- 9 accustomed to the freedom, they are beset by worries that some needed belonging, some familiar presence (a purse, a shopping bag?) has been forgotten.

Small, fluttery gestures that betray nervousness or a practiced   10
overanimation are considered girlishly feminine and cute. Toying with a strand of hair, bobbing the head, giggling when introduced, pulling the elbows in close to the body, and crossing the legs in a knee and ankle double twist are mannerisms that men studiously avoid.

Jewelry plays a subtle role in delineating masculine and feminine   11
gestures. To drum one's fingers on the table is an aggressive expression of annoyance and is conspicuously unfeminine, but to fidget with a necklace or twist a ring is a nonthreatening way of dissipating agitation. Clutching protectively at the throat is not restricted to females, but corresponding masculine gestures are to loosen the collar and adjust the necktie, actions which indicate some modicum of control.

Quaint postures that throw the body off balance, such as stand-   12
ing on one leg as if poised for flight, or leading from the hips in a debutante slouch, or that suggest a child's behavior (the stereotypic sexy secretary taking dictation while perched on the boss's knee), fall within the repertoire of femininity that is alien, awkward, and generally unthinkable as a mode of behavior for men. Reclining odalisque-style, such a shocker 30 years ago when Truman Capote posed in this manner for a book jacket, is a classic feminine tableau of eroticized passivity with an established tradition in art.

Of course, feminine movement was never intended for solo per-   13
formance. Vine-clinging, lapdog-cuddling, and birdlike perching require a strong external support. It is in order to appeal to men that the yielded autonomy and contrived manifestations of helplessness become second nature as expressions of good manners and sexual good-will. For smooth interaction between the sexes, the prevailing code of masculine action demands a yielding partner to gracefully complete the dance.

Nancy Henley, psychologist and author of *Body Politics* (Pren-   14
tice-Hall), has written, "In a way so accepted and so subtle as to be unnoticed even by its practitioners and recipients, males in couples will often literally push a woman everywhere she is to go—the arm from behind, steering around corners . . . crossing the street."

In this familiar *pas de deux,* a woman must either consent to 15
be led with a gracious display of good manners or else she must
buck and bristle at the touch of the reins. Femininity encourages the
romance of compliance, a willing exchange of motor autonomy and
physical balance for the protocols of masculine protection. Steering
and leading are prerogatives of those in command. Observational
studies of who touches whom in a given situation show that superiors
feel free to lay an intimate, guiding hand on those with inferior
status, but not the reverse. "The politics of touch," a concept of
Henley's, operates instructively in masculine-feminine relations.

Henley was the first psychologist to connect the masculine cus- 16
tom of shepherding an able-bodied woman through situations that
do not require physical guidance with other forms of manhandling
along a continuum from petty humiliation (the sly pinch, the playful
slap on the fanny) to the assaultive abuses of wife-beating and rape.
This is not to say that the husband who steers his wife to a restaurant
table with a paternal shove is no different from the rapist, but rather
to suggest that women who customarily expect to have their physical
movements directed by others are poorly prepared by their feminine
training to resist unwanted interference or violent assault. Fear of
being judged impolite has more immediate reality for many women
than the terror of physical violation.

To be helped with one's coat, to let the man do the driving, to 17
sit mute and unmoving while the man does the ordering and picks
up the check—such trained behavioral inactivity may be ladylike,
gracious, romantic and flirty, and soothing to easily ruffled masculine
feathers, but it is ultimately destructive to the sense of the functioning,
productive self. The charge that feminists have no manners is true,
for the history of manners, unfortunately for those who wish to
change the world, is an index of courtly graces addressed toward
those of the middle classes who aspire to the refinements of their
betters, embodied in the static vision of the cared-for, catered-to lady
of privilege who existed on a rarefied plane above the mundane
reality of strenuous labor. When a feminist insists on opening a door
for herself, a simple act of physical autonomy that was never an
issue for servants, field and factory workers, and women not under
the protection of men, her gesture rudely collides with chivalrous
expectations, for manly action requires manifest evidence of a helpless lady in order to demonstrate courtly respect.

The psychology of feminine movement, as we know and practice   18
its provocative airs and graces, is based on the premise that direct
acts of initiative and self-assertion are a violation of the governance
of male-female relations, if not of nature itself. In place of forthright
action we are offered a vision so exquisitely romantic and sexually
beguiling that few care to question its curious imagery of limitations:
a Venus de Milo without arms, a mermaid without legs, a Sleeping
Beauty in a state of suspended animation with her face upturned,
awaiting a kiss.

RESPONSES AND IDEAS

1. Respond to this essay by (a) offering further examples of behavior like
   that Brownmiller describes, or (b) offering examples of similarly restrictive masculine behavior, or (c) stating why you think Brownmiller's
   interpretations of feminine behavior are incorrect.

2. State in your own words the contradiction in behavior Brownmiller
   describes as a "feminine responsibility" in paragraph 2. Where else in
   the essay does she refer to this contradictory behavior?

3. What does Brownmiller identify as the causes of the restrictive, contradictory feminine behavior she describes, and where does she discuss
   the causes? What evidence does she offer to support her identification
   of causes? Is the evidence adequate, and are the causes reasonable
   ones? (See Glossary: Evidence.)

PURPOSE, AUDIENCE, AND STRATEGIES

1. How are women likely to react to the descriptions of behavior Brownmiller provides and to her explanations of it? How are men likely to
   react? On what evidence are your answers based?

2. Where in this selection does the author sum up the point(s) she is
   trying to make? Does the summary include a thesis statement, or does
   it present her thesis in some other way?

3. This selection contains a great many observations, conclusions, and
   examples. Is it a unified essay? Why, or why not? If it is unified, what
   devices does the author use to achieve unity? (See Glossary: Unity.)

4. What patterns other than definition does the author use in this essay?

5. Is paragraph 18 an effective closing for this selection? Explain your
   answer and identify any common strategies for closings that it employs.
   (See Glossary: Closings.)

LANGUAGE AND STYLE

1. Explain the metaphor(s) in the opening sentence of paragraph 15, and state whether they are appropriate and effective. (See Glossary: Figures of Speech, Evaluation.) What is meant by the phrase "romance of compliance" in the second sentence of paragraph 15? For what purpose does the author use the rhetorical questions in paragraph 3? (See Glossary: Figures of Speech.)

2. Discuss what the three images in the last sentence of the essay (par. 18) symbolize. (See Glossary: Symbol.)

3. If you do not know the meaning of any of the following words, look them up in the dictionary: *slur, aesthetic, slovenly* (par. 1); *fraught, indecent, voyeurs* (2); *anatomical, pelvis, Minoan, loose, wanton, promiscuity, laxity, demeanor, repertoire* (4); *copulation* (5); *ideology, testosterone, libido* (6); *hara-kiri* (9); *comportment, inhibition, unnerving* (9); *dissipating, modicum* (11); *debutante, odalisque* (12); pas de deux, *buck, bristle* (15).

WRITING ACTIVITIES

1. Brownmiller's writings are generally so provocative that even readers who are generally sympathetic with her point of view find much that they cannot entirely agree with. Unsympathetic readers find even more to complain about, of course. Write an essay criticizing what she has to say in "The Contrived Postures of Femininity," pointing out both what you consider to be its strengths and its weaknesses.

2. Drawing on your reading of "The Contrived Postures of Femininity" and "The Androgynous Man" (pp. 348–351) as well as on your experience, develop your own definition of masculinity, femininity, or androgyny.

Writing Suggestions

EXPLORATIONS

1. Speculate on the many different ways subjects can be defined by filling out a chart similar to the one below for five different topics:

Topic	*Can be defined as a*
Electric can opener	household appliance
Frisbee football	form of entertainment
Great-aunt	member of the family
Teenage neighbor	baby-sitter
_____	_____

    In filling out the second column of your chart, use your imagination to discover fresh but worthwhile ways of viewing each of your topics. If this exercise suggests a topic for an essay, begin working on it.

2. Define three of the following words (concepts), using for each word four different strategies of definition chosen from those described on pp. 319–320: family, marriage, success, sacrifice, cruelty, hunger, poverty, patriotism, pain, loyalty, loneliness, addiction, hope, failure, depression, struggle. If this exercise suggests a good topic for an essay, keep writing.

3. Choose a concept that different groups in our society are likely to view (define) in different ways and explain the perspective of each group and the differences in their definitions. You might examine the attitudes of most blacks and members of other minorities towards affirmative action programs and the view of whites who believe that their jobs or their chances of getting jobs are threatened by such programs. All members of a group need not agree with the definitions you present, but it should be reasonably representative. If this topic is promising, develop it into an essay.

4. Use appropriate dictionaries and other reference tools (see p. 324) to trace the changes in the meaning of a word over several centuries. Make a list of the most important meanings of the word over the years, and state the historical period in which each meaning flourished. Here are some words for a start: *leech, housewife, needle,* and *great.* To find others, simply thumb through a regular dictionary until you come across words that interest you. Then look up the words in a dictionary that traces their history, like the *Oxford English Dictionary.* If this exercise is particularly interesting to you, consider turning the information you discover into an essay.

ACTIVITIES

1. Look through two college textbooks, each from a different field, to see how they use and define technical or other unusual terms. Describe the

360

defining strategies they use, and take note of any clear differences in the way each text uses and defines words.

2. Read newspaper and magazine accounts of a current national or international controversy. Identify and define the terms central to understanding the controversy; if the argument as a whole revolves around the proper definition of terms or concepts, explain the competing definitions. Look especially for terms like *self-determination, solvency, territorial integrity,* and *deterrence.*

3. From your college textbooks or from other readings assigned for courses, select two stipulative definitions and discuss their functions within the selections from which they come.

4. Look through four informative articles from mass circulation magazines and identify the various ways, if any, they use definition. If possible, locate an article that is itself an extended definition, or in which definition is one of the primary patterns of development.

MODELS

1. Using Cree McCree's "Flea Market" as a model, write a definition of some activity or gathering in which the participants form a community. You might talk about a sports team, a service organization, or an activity similar to the holding of flea markets.

2. Borrowing strategies from Roger Caras's "What's a Koala?" redefine some common term, object, or concept in such a way that readers will see that their initial views of it are quite mistaken. Try not to anger or irritate readers; show, instead, that the new definition is preferable to the old. You might want to consider concepts like *capitalism* or *education,* terms like *revision* or *studying,* or objects like the Statue of Liberty or the Golden Gate Bridge.

3. Using Thomas Sowell's "We're Not Really 'Equal'" for guidance, define or redefine a term whose meaning you believe has been distorted in recent political discussions. Look at newspapers and television news programs to get ideas about the way terms are used in current discussion.

4. Drawing ideas from Noel Perrin's "The Androgynous Man," present your own ideas about masculine and feminine identity. Use your own experiences as a basis for your essay.

5. Using or responding to Susan Brownmiller's "The Contrived Postures of Femininity," present your own definition of common patterns of behavior and their meaning. The behavior you define can be more limited in scope than Brownmiller's, and your conclusions need not be as sweeping.

9

❧ DIVISION AND CLASSIFICATION

Examining the Parts and their Relationships

WHAT DIVISION AND CLASSIFICATION DO

Let us assume that photography has been your hobby ever since you were nine years old and got a Polaroid instant camera for your birthday. You've had pictures published in a local newspaper, and last year you even won a $250 prize in a photography contest. Yet you were still surprised and pleased when your former eleventh grade teacher called to ask you to talk to his students on the subject of photography. His only instructions were, "Try to introduce them to photography in general, not just to the correct way to load a camera or the best way to take a snapshot."

As soon as you start thinking about your presentation, however, you realize that to deal with such a broad and complicated subject and to help your audience understand its most important features, you will need to divide it into smaller parts. You begin by jotting down a list of what you think are the most significant aspects of photography along with some details you hope will be interesting and useful to high school students:

> *History*—Photography and the past (can bring in some old photos and talk about how much photography has changed since the early days)
>
> *Uses*—Photography as a hobby (taking snapshots; developing and printing your own pictures)

>   —Photography as a career (newspaper, magazine, and por-
>   trait photography, of course, but also cinematography
>   for television and movies, fashion photography, or even
>   owning a camera store)
>
> *Equipment*—What photographers use (cameras, lenses, film)
> *New Developments*—Technical changes (video recorders, com-
>   puterized cameras, trick and special-effect photography)

Having divided your presentation into manageable parts, you notice
another problem. Although you are sure you can cover the history
of photography, the new developments, and its rewards as a hobby
in from five to ten minutes each by sticking to the highlights, you
know so much about photography as a career (you're considering it
yourself) and about camera equipment as well that limiting yourself
to even a half hour on these topics will be a real struggle. Worse
yet, you realize that most of your audience will be swamped by all
the information you can provide on cameras, film, and accessories.
To arrange what you have to say in a way that will help your listeners
understand and remember it and at the same time to limit the
territory you have to cover, you decide to sort the information into
categories, as in the chart on p. 365.

By splitting the topic of careers in photography into two main
categories and by mentioning the specific jobs only briefly in the
form of examples, you can suggest that the range of career opportunities in photography is wider than most people expect—without
having to describe the opportunities in detail. By sorting equipment
into categories based on the needs of different kinds of photographers
(beginner, hobbyist, advanced) you can help your listeners focus
directly on the information they can use. You can also use one or
two pieces of equipment as representatives of each type and avoid
the temptation to bombard your audience with a catalogue of your
favorite cameras, lenses, films, and darkroom equipment.

Division and classification, then, provide ways of dealing with
large, complex, or technical subjects and of explaining them to an
audience. Yet although they often work together, as in the case of
the photography presentation, division and classification are somewhat different patterns of thought and take different forms in writing.

With *division*, also known as *analysis*, we start with a single
subject and identify its components, examining each and their relationship to each other. As a way of thinking, division enables us

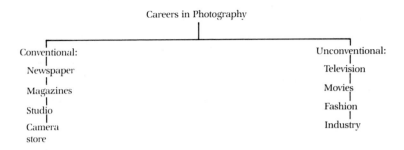

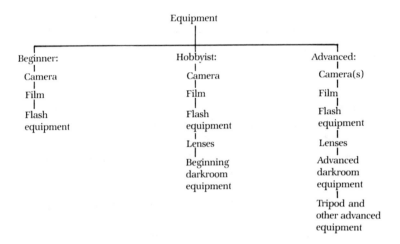

to reduce a complicated, potentially overwhelming subject to manageable segments and to examine (analyze) each one to discover its special qualities and understand its role within the larger subject. Through division we ask the questions, "What are the parts?" and "How are they related to each other and to the whole?" Division can be applied to a complex mechanism like an automobile, which consists of an engine and transmission, an electrical system, a frame and body, and an interior, all organized to provide transportation. It can be applied to an organization like a government agency, a university, or a football team; to an event like a presidential election, a war, or a recession; and to an idea or controversy like the issue of gun control, which encompasses several conflicting points of view, each consisting in turn of a variety of supporting arguments and evidence.

Most subjects can be divided in more than one way. A city government, for instance, can be divided according to the functions each unit performs (public works department, school board, recreation department, office of tax collection), or it can be divided according to the role individuals play (mayor, head of city council, finance director, city planner). The *principle of division* you choose will determine the parts of the whole that you identify and the relationship among them that you investigate. An analysis of city government focusing on the power structure, for instance, might show the extent to which the city council and the mayor must cooperate before any action can be taken, or the degree of independence the school board has in forming and implementing policy.

Process analysis (see Chapter 6) and cause-effect analysis (see Chapter 7) are both forms of division, each based on a different principle. With process analysis we examine the steps or stages necessary to bring about a certain result, such as the role players, coaches, and management must each play in order to put a professional football team on the field every Sunday afternoon. With cause-effect analysis we investigate the causes or effects of a specific incident—for example, the coaching decisions, individual player efforts, or management strategies that contributed to winning an important game.

Division need not follow a single principle, however. A subject can be divided merely to explore its many different aspects, perhaps its history, uses, required equipment, and future developments, as with the photography presentation described at the beginning of this chapter. In most cases, however, the division should reflect boundaries within the subject itself—that is, the units into which it seems to fall naturally. The one exception to this is the form of division known as *enumeration*. In enumeration some numbering system (1,2,3; a,b,c) or another arbitrary arrangement is imposed on the subject simply to make it easier to understand. A writer analyzing recent controversies over nuclear power might choose to compress six or seven topics of disagreement into three major points on the grounds that the issue is so complex readers will have trouble grasping it unless the explanation is simplified somewhat. Although enumeration is sometimes an unsatisfactory strategy because it can disguise important divisions within a subject, it can be useful as long as the writer makes sure that all essential aspects and relationships of the subject are treated thoroughly.

In division we split a subject into parts. When we classify, however, we start with many subjects and sort them into groups or classes on the basis of shared characteristics, answering the questions "What categories does it fall into?" and "What are the characteristics of each category?" Classification helps us find logical order in the welter of experiences and choices that take up so much of our lives ("What restaurant shall we go to for dinner tonight?" "I don't know. What kind of food would you like? Mexican? Italian? Barbecue? Steaks?"). It helps us discover relationships among facts and ideas so that we can share our understanding with readers.

The subjects of a classification can be people (actors, politicians, college instructors), events (wars, sports events, concerts), places (cities, universities, vacation spots), or ideas (theories of evolution, economic theories). In short, almost anything that comes in more than one version can be investigated through classification. All the elements to be classified should be related closely enough so that classification can make worthwhile distinctions among them—for instance, among the comic styles of the Marx Brothers, the Three Stooges, and Laurel and Hardy—and not merely state the obvious: that fish and lizards belong to different groups, for example, or that singing, painting, and writing a novel are different kinds of artistic endeavors.

The simplest form of classification is the *binary* (two-part) *classification,* consisting of two groups, one with a certain characteristic and one without it. Smokers and nonsmokers, politicians and non-politicians, Americans and foreigners, the musically talented and the nonmusically talented can all be separated into opposing groups through binary classification. This method is useful for emphasizing the special features of each group or pointing out their considerable differences. It is also useful in explaining conflicts or disagreements, such as the differing attitudes of people with school-age children and people without school-age children towards the size of a local school budget. Yet binary classification works only if the differences between the groups are absolute (smokers vs. nonsmokers), not when they are a matter of degree (there is, for example, no precise dividing point between light smokers and heavy smokers).

To sort out more complicated relationships (occasional, light, heavy, and compulsive smokers) we need to create categories based on one or more shared characteristics. Speakers for a stereo system, for example, can be classified on the basis of cost (inexpensive—

$100–$150 per pair; moderate—$150–$250; expensive—$250–$500) and on the quality of sound (poor, good, excellent). The *basis of classification* determines the kind of information or insight that the process will provide. A grouping based on quality of sound will tell what speakers sound the best but will not indicate whether they fall into a reasonable price range. A grouping based on both price and quality of sound will be more informative because it may help identify an inexpensive pair of speakers with an excellent, or at least a good, sound. It will also be more complicated however, because in place of three categories based on quality (poor, good, excellent) it will contain nine possible subcategories: expensive-excellent; expensive-good; expensive-poor; moderate-excellent; moderate-good, and so on. Moreover, a classification based on three features (cost, quality, appearance) would contain a possible twenty-seven subcategories, although not all the subcategories would have to be used because most expensive speakers are at least good in sound and appearance.

The categories you use in an essay, therefore, should reflect not only the nature of the things being classified but also the purpose of the essay. The number of categories should be limited, whenever possible, to avoid overwhelming your readers with multiple groups and subgroups. The same holds true for the parts into which you divide a subject; their number should not be so great that they confuse your readers rather than aid understanding.

Most often, writers use division and classification to inform or explain. Classification is, in addition, frequently combined with comparison in evaluations that place products in groups (poor, fair, good, excellent) by comparing them to a standard (see Chapter 5, Comparison). Both strategies can also be used to organize support for an argument; moreover, in explaining an idea or an activity (playing the guitar, windsurfing), a writer may at the same time try to persuade readers that it is significant or worth trying. Finally, classifications of disastrous dates, terrible landlords, eccentric friends, and the like can be a source of amusement and pleasure.

The particular combination of division and classification a writer chooses should reflect both the subject and the purpose of the writing. In the following passage from his book *Word Play* (1974), Peter Farb begins by dividing the uses of language into two broad categories—those that follow the rules and those that do not (par. 1). Then in the second paragraph, he introduces subcategories of language use and misuse by identifying each subcategory with a character in the Marx Brothers movies: Groucho, Chico, Harpo, and Margaret Dumont.

> Any transaction between two human beings—an exchange of words, silence, or a mutually intelligible gesture such as a wave of the hand—conforms to rules and conventions understood by all the members of that speech community. To have no firm rules at all is to have no language game at all. But to have the rules and to break them by lying or cheating confirms the very existence of such rules. The Marx Brothers were masters of such an anarchic attack upon the rules of language, and most of the humor in their films is derived from their assault upon the conventions of the speech community.
>
> Each brother inhabits a well-defined territory as a specialist in a different kind of language game. Groucho is the fast-talking sharpie, the dueler who employs the pointed wit of speech. Chico's habitat lies on the fringes of language. He is the speaker of a phony-Italian dialect who misconstrues both the meanings and the manners of the "foreign" American speech community in which he finds himself. Finally, the mute Harpo throws language back to the level of the beasts; instead of speech, he employs animal-like signaling systems, such as whistling or charades that substitute for words. Interacting with the verbal, dialectal, and animal systems of the three brothers is the imposing dowager Margaret Dumont, who steadfastly defends the narrow-minded rules and conventions of the American speech community.

THE PROCESS

An appropriate topic for division is anything that can be better understood by looking at its parts and their relationships. You may wish to use the pattern to explore a historical event, a painting, a song, a sport, or a movie. It can be applied to an organization like a student-run campus store, a small business owned by someone you know, or a summer camp at which you worked. And it is an especially effective means for talking about theories in political science, chemistry, business, or some other field and for addressing controversies over matters like school prayer and gun control.

Classification is a useful strategy for dealing with any group of things whose differences are worth detailed examination. Diets, exercise programs, undergraduate majors, personal computers, ways to prepare for tests, and used automobiles all come in various types, as do literary theories; careers in health care, business, or communications; and part-time or summer jobs.

To find an appropriate topic for either pattern or a combination of the two, try asking questions like these:

- Are there things that irritate or threaten me (and other people as well) that might be worth looking into through classification or division? (grading procedures in college courses; campus health or social services; government's foreign or domestic policies)
- Are there puzzling behaviors that I might understand better if I arrange them in categories or break them into parts? (overuse of alcohol, tobacco, or drugs; cheating on boyfriends or girlfriends; excessive neatness or sloppiness; workaholism or laziness)
- Are there everyday things that, if classified or separated into components, might reveal something about human nature? (study habits, sleeping habits, taste in food or friends)
- Are there choices I face, along with other people, that might be clarified through classification or division? (which movies to see, career to choose, courses to take, people or situations to avoid)

The answers to these or similar questions should suggest both a purpose and an appropriate strategy for your writing. If your purpose and subject call for classification, knowing your specific aim will help you decide on an appropriate basis for establishing categories and subcategories. You may even want to begin planning an essay by listing categories and their members in outline form. Remember, however, to stick to the principle of classification you have adopted. Classifying television programs as comedies, dramas, and shows with women in leading roles is illogical and confusing for two reasons: first, because it mixes two principles (kind of show and gender of actors) and second, because the categories overlap (both comedies and dramas can have women in leading roles). Make sure, moreover, that your classification is complete and thorough, that you have not omitted an important group or combined two categories that should be separated.

Deciding how to divide a subject poses some problems. The way a subject can be separated into parts most effectively may not be clear at first, and you will probably have to try several different approaches to find the one that works best. Still, the best place to begin is with obvious divisions. Stories and essays have a beginning, a middle, and an end. Organizations often consist of departments and committees. Most issues have two sides, a pro and a con. Writing down the different ideas you have for dividing a subject can help you spot a pattern and decide if it is the one you want to follow in your writing.

As you work on a plan for your essay following either division or classification or a combination, keep these patterns of arrangement in mind as guides:

Division Pattern:
Introduction (topic, thesis)
    Aspect (part, element) 1
    Aspect (part, element) 2
    Aspect (part, element) 3
    Aspects 4, 5, 6, 7, and so on
Conclusion (summary, final comment)

Classification Pattern:
Introduction (topic, thesis)
    Category (type, class) 1
    Category (type, class) 2
    Category (type, class) 3
    Categories 4, 5, 6, 7, and so on
Conclusion (summary, final comment)

Feel free to adapt and combine these patterns, as did the student who prepared the following informal outline for a paper by first dividing her subject into three major elements and then examining the categories within each element:

Subject: Faculty senate
Thesis: Most students don't know who is on the faculty senate or how it works, but they ought to because it is responsible for many policies that affect the academic side of their lives.
    I. Three things students should know about the faculty senate: membership, procedures, powers.   (*Division of the subject*)

II. Membership: three groups of members   (*First classification*)
   A. Faculty members (voting)
   B. Administrators (non-voting)
   C. Student representatives (non-voting)
III. Procedures: differ according to the type of meeting   (*Second classification*)
   A. Full Meetings
   B. Standing committee meetings
   C. Special committee meetings
IV. Powers   (*Third classification*)
   A. Supervise curriculum and approve new courses
   B. Determine and enforce grading standards
   C. Set academic calendar

In writing your essay, you should pay special attention to the organization, making sure your discussions of the various components or categories do not overlap in a confusing manner and that you have arranged them in a way that best supports your thesis—from least to most important, for example. To alert readers to the essay's arrangement, use terms like these:

category	type	trait	segment
sort	species	characteristic	aspect
kind	class	element	component
group	subcategory	part	feature

At the beginning of the essay let readers know the point you plan to make and the strategy you will follow so that they can better understand what you have to say and respond to it.

Your writing should provide vivid, plentiful detail to illustrate and explain the components or types you have selected and to support your thesis. Though logical structure is vital in a division or classification, the quality of detail can also determine an essay's success or failure. The following paragraphs from a student essay classifying types of smokers show how effective representative examples can be:

Cigarettes play an even larger role in the lives of the next group, habitual smokers. They cannot quit as readily as the casual smoker can because of one key factor: habit. When the phone rings, they quickly grab an ashtray and cigarettes and chat. When having a cup of coffee in the morning, they simply must have a cigarette because "the coffee won't taste as good without it." And always, without fail, a good meal is followed by a good cigarette. Habitual smokers also smoke on a regular basis—a pack or two a day, never more, never less. They become irritated when they discover they are down to their last butt and rush to buy another pack. They also play games by buying only packs instead of cartons, rationalizing that because cigarettes aren't always on hand they can't be smoking too much. They are constantly trying to cut down and tell everyone so, but never actually do, because in reality, smoking is an essential part of their lives.

The last and most extreme group consists of addicted smokers. They cannot imagine life without cigarettes. Cigarettes have become part of their lives and most of the day's actions include "lighting up." It has become almost a psychological torment for these smokers to think of a day without smoke. It has been found in some studies that people like this actually wake themselves every few hours at night to have a quick drag, and then drift back to sleep. Such rationalizations as "it helps me to relax," "it keeps my weight down," "it makes me feel comfortable," and "I just enjoy it" are the only explanations the addicted smoker offers.

Both paragraphs begin with an announcement of the category and of the principle of classification, the attachment to smoking ("habitual," "addicted"). Following this the writer presents a number of examples that describe typical actions of members of the category and that at the same time explain why such people continue to smoke despite the clear health hazards. While some of the details may be a bit exaggerated, they are for the most part vivid and effective. Moreover, they echo typical phrases used by smokers, and their humor points out accurately the absurdity of some common kinds of behavior. While many students would be tempted to use fewer examples, the number here seems about right, and they convey with impact the writer's distaste for smoking.

THE PATTERN IN ACTION

Because they help shed light on complicated topics, division and classification are often used along with other patterns in academic and technical writing. Brochures explaining the services of a hearing clinic or a women's center; studies of government or corporate organization; and textbooks on anatomy, psychology, nursing, pharmacy, and most other fields make frequent use of these strategies.

On their own, division and classification also appear in two special forms: the issue analysis and the informative report.

An *issue analysis* reports on a controversy, not taking a stand, but explaining each of the major positions on an issue. It uses division to isolate and analyze the statements and supporting evidence on each side, thereby shedding light on the disagreement. Newspaper and magazine articles on political, environmental, medical, and social controversies (the building of a nuclear reactor, national health insurance, nuclear disarmament, school prayer, hunting and fishing regulations, the proper use of caffeine, disposal of toxic chemicals) frequently take the form of an issue analysis. Likewise, reports used within corporations, government agencies, and other institutions to explore various arguments on a matter requiring a policy decision (possible responses to a lawsuit, new eligibility rules for loans or grants) use the pattern as well. And scholarly studies in all disciplines generally begin with an analysis of conflicting arguments and interpretations in the particular field the studies will address.

An issue analysis begins by identifying the controversy and the grounds for its importance, then reviews the most important arguments (statements, propositions) on each side along with the minor arguments and evidence that support them. Because an issue analysis examines one or more points of view, its possible arrangements are combinations of the comparison and division patterns (see pp. 174 and 371):

Issue Analysis Pattern 1:
Introduction (issue, thesis)
   Argument 1 (pro)
      Minor arguments
         Details and Examples
   Argument 1 (con)
      Minor arguments
         Details and Examples
   Argument 2 (pro)
      Minor arguments
         Details and Examples
   Argument 2 (con)
      Minor arguments
         Details and Examples

Arguments 3, 4, 5, (pro and con)
    (including minor arguments,
    details, and examples)
Conclusion (summary, comment)

Issue Analysis Pattern 2:
Introduction (issue, thesis)
    Argument 1 (pro)
        Minor arguments
            Details and Examples
    Argument 2 (pro)
        Minor arguments
            Details and Examples
    Arguments 3, 4, 5 (pro)
        (including minor arguments,
        details and examples)
    Argument 1 (con)
        Minor arguments
            Details and Examples
    Argument 2 (con)
        Minor arguments
            Details and Examples
    Arguments 3, 4, 5, (con)
        (including minor arguments,
        details, and examples)
Conclusion (summary, comment)

Although an issue analysis needs to be objective, it may make use of highly emotional language and examples. An issue is a subject of disagreement, and when people disagree about something important, they try to use interesting and vivid examples to support their positions. Issue analysis forces the writer to become involved in both sides of the controversy, to get inside each position in the debate in order to present it effectively. The more important the issue—nuclear disarmament, military spending, gun control, the environment—the more emotional each side is likely to be. In addition, even though your treatment of an issue has to be even-handed, you can at times permit your emotions to show. If the arguments you are analyzing appeal to the emotions, so should your treatment of them. If in the course of your analysis you decide that the arguments on one side are more fully developed or better supported, let your audience know by presenting your judgment in a concluding statement or by commenting on the quality of individual arguments. In this chapter, the essay "The Great Salt Debate" provides a model of issue analysis.

The next time you pass a drugstore, newsstand, or library, pick up several mass-circulation magazines and look at the articles they contain. At least half, if not more, are likely to be *informative reports.* Although they may vary in arrangement, subject matter, and emphasis, informative reports share two important features: (1) they make frequent use of division and classification as patterns of development, and (2) they divide a topic into some or all of the following aspects, attempting to answer questions appropriate to each one:

Significance: What is the topic and why is it worth learning about?

Background: What is the history of this topic? What are people saying about it now? What terms need to be defined in order to understand it?

Features: What are its special characteristics, capabilities? Into what categories does it fall? What is its appearance?

Good/bad: What are its strong points and weak points? How does it compare with others?

Procedures: How does it work? Where can it be gotten? How can it be done?

Applications: What is its present and future importance? How will it affect people? What should they do?

Although their overall pattern is one of division into parts, most informative reports mix several patterns. Process is used to tell how the subject works, description to present its appearance, comparison to look at its strengths and weaknesses, narrative to recount its history, and definition to clarify terms. Yet the longest section of an informative report is usually that devoted to features, and this section relies heavily on division and classification. These patterns are likely to appear also in discussions of good and bad points.

The arrangement of many informative reports follows the sequence of significance, background, features, good/bad, procedures, and applications, with the space allotted to each reflecting the nature of the subject and the emphasis the writer chooses to give it. Yet just as many informative reports cover these aspects in a different order, or drop some and substitute others, demonstrating thereby the flexibility of the pattern. In this chapter, Bernice Kanner's "Love for Sale" demonstrates how the informative report pattern can be stretched to fit a subject and uses division and classification to present much of its information.

The essays in this chapter illustrate some of the many uses to which division and classification can be put. In "Reflections on Horror Movies," Robert Brustein describes three categories of these popular entertainments and in doing so inquires into some of the reasons moviegoers find them so appealing. Malcolm Cowley, in "Vices and Pleasures: The View from 80," divides the experience of aging into parts, some pleasant, some not so pleasant. In "Cinema-types," Susan Allen Toth also looks into the movies, but her classification of films and viewers rests on a more personal basis than Brustein's, and her tastes in entertainment differ too. "The Great Salt Debate," by Janice Hopkins Tanne, presents, as the title suggests, a straightforward issue analysis of a controversy that is still unresolved. Finally, Bernice Kanner's "Love for Sale" uses a variety of patterns to report on a favorite pastime of contemporary Americans: sending greeting cards.

❧ SUSAN ALLEN TOTH

Susan Allen Toth was born in 1940 in Ames, Iowa. She attended Smith College, Berkeley, and the University of Minnesota, from which she received her Ph.D. Currently she is professor of English at Macalester College in St. Paul, Minnesota. Her short stories and articles have appeared in *Redbook, Harper's,* and *Ms.,* and her memoir of growing up in a small Iowa town, *Blooming: A Small Town Girlhood* (1981), was selected as a Notable Book of the Year by the *New York Times Books Review.* Her recent book, *Going East* (1984), is a memoir of her college years.

Cinematypes

"Cinematypes," which first appeared in *Harper's* magazine, shows how classification can be used both to organize experiences and to reveal their essential qualities. The detailed examples Toth provides not only help her specify the characteristics of each type (of film, of companion) but also give readers a chance to discover similar experiences in their own lives and to look at them from the same perspective Toth uses.

Aaron takes me only to art films. That's what I call them, anyway: strange movies with vague poetic images I don't always understand, long dreamy movies about a distant Technicolor past, even longer black-and-white movies about the general meaninglessness of life. We do not go unless at least one reputable critic has found the cinematography superb. We went to *The Devil's Eye,* and Aaron turned to me in the middle and said, "My God, this is *funny.*" I do not think he was pleased.

When Aaron and I go to the movies, we drive our cars separately and meet by the box office. Inside the theater he sits tentatively in his seat, ready to move if he can't see well, poised to leave if the film is disappointing. He leans away from me, careful not to touch the bare flesh of his arm against the bare flesh of mine. Sometimes he leans so far I am afraid he may be touching the woman on his other side. If the movie is very good, he leans forward, too, peering between the heads of the couple in front of us. The light from the screen bounces off his glasses; he gleams with intensity, sitting there on the edge of his seat, watching the screen. Once I tapped him on the arm so I could whisper a comment in his ear. He jumped.

After *Belle de Jour* Aaron said he wanted to ask me if he could 3 stay overnight. "But I can't," he shook his head mournfully before I had a chance to answer, "because I know I never sleep well in strange beds." Then he apologized for asking. "It's just that after a film like that," he said, "I feel the need to assert myself."

Pete takes me only to movies that he thinks have redeeming 4 social value. He doesn't call them "films." They tend to be about poverty, war, injustice, political corruption, struggling unions in the 1930s, and the military-industrial complex. Pete doesn't like propaganda movies, though, and he doesn't like to be too depressed, either. We stayed away from *The Sorrow and the Pity*; it would be, he said, just too much. Besides, he assured me, things are never that hopeless. So most of the movies we see are made in Hollywood. Because they are always topical, these movies offer what Pete calls "food for thought." When we saw *Coming Home*, Pete's jaw set so firmly with the first half-hour that I knew we would end up at Poppin' Fresh Pies afterward.

When Pete and I go to the movies, we take turns driving so no 5 one owes anyone else anything. We leave the car far from the theater so we don't have to pay for a parking space. If it's raining or snowing, Pete offers to let me off at the door, but I can tell he'll feel better if I go with him while he finds a spot, so we share the walk too. Inside the theater Pete will hold my hand when I get scared if I ask him. He puts my hand firmly on his knee and covers it completely with his own hand. His knee never twitches. After a while, when the scary part is past, he loosens his hand slightly and I know that is a signal to take mine away. He sits companionably close, letting his jacket just touch my sweater, but he does not infringe. He thinks I ought to know he is there if I need him.

One night, after *The China Syndrome*, I asked Pete if he wouldn't 6 like to stay for a second drink, even though it was past midnight. He thought a while about that, considering my offer from all possible angles, but finally he said no. Relationships today, he said, have a tendency to move too quickly.

Sam likes movies that are entertaining. By that he means movies 7 that Will Jones in the *Minneapolis Tribune* loved and either *Time* or *Newsweek* rather liked; also movies that do not have sappy love stories, are not musicals, do not have subtitles, and will not force him to think. He does not go to movies to think. He liked *California Suite* and *The Seduction of Joe Tynan,* though the plots, he said, could have been zippier. He saw it all coming too far in advance, and that took the fun out. He doesn't like to know what is going to happen. "I just want my brain to be tickled," he says. It is very hard for me to pick out movies for Sam.

When Sam takes me to the movies, he pays for everything. He   8
thinks that's what a man ought to do. But I buy my own popcorn, because he doesn't approve of it; the grease might smear his flannel slacks. Inside the theater, Sam makes himself comfortable. He takes off his jacket, puts one arm around me, and all during the movie he plays with my hand, stroking my palm, beating a small tattoo on my wrist. Although he watches the movie intently, his body operates on instinct. Once I inclined my head and kissed him lightly just behind his ear. He beat a faster tattoo on my wrist, quick and musical, but he didn't look away from the screen.

When Sam takes me home from the movies, he stands outside   9
my door and kisses me long and hard. He would like to come in, he says regretfully, but his steady girlfriend in Duluth wouldn't like it. When the *Tribune* gives a movie four stars, he has to save it to see with her. Otherwise her feelings might be hurt.

I go to some movies by myself. On rainy Sunday afternoons I   10
often sneak into a revival house or a college auditorium for old Technicolor musicals, *Kiss Me Kate, Seven Brides for Seven Brothers, Calamity Jane,* even, once, *The Sound of Music.* Wearing saggy jeans so I can prop my feet on the seat in front, I sit toward the rear where no one can see me. I eat large handfuls of popcorn with double butter. Once the movie starts, I feel completely at home. Howard Keel and I are old friends; I grin back at him on the screen. I know the sound tracks by heart. Sometimes when I get really carried away I hum along with Kathryn Grayson, remembering how I once thought I would fill out a formal like that. I am rather glad now I never did. Skirts whirl, feet tap, acrobatic young men perform impossible feats, and then the camera dissolves into a dream sequence I know I can comfortably follow. It is not, thank God, Bergman.

If I can't find an old musical, I settle for Hepburn and Tracy,   11
vintage Grant or Gable, on adventurous days Claudette Colbert or

James Stewart. Before I buy my ticket I make sure it will all end happily. If necessary, I ask the girl at the box office. I have never seen *Stella Dallas* or *Intermezzo.* Over the years I have developed other peccadilloes: I will, for example, see anything that is redeemed by Thelma Ritter. At the end of *Daddy Long Legs* I wait happily for the scene when Fred Clark, no longer angry, at last pours Thelma a convivial drink. They smile at each other, I smile at them, I feel they are smiling at me. In the movies I go to by myself, the men and women always like each other.

COMMENTARY

"Cinematypes" is at once a model of clear, consistent classification and an example of the way the pattern can be subtly shaped and altered to convey ideas a writer wants to emphasize. At first the classification scheme of "Cinematypes" may seem simple and straightforward, even though it has two subjects, friends and films. In the opening sentence of the paragraphs announcing the first three categories, Toth names the friend and the type of film: "Aaron . . . art films" (par. 1); "Pete . . . redeeming social values" (par. 4); and "Sam . . . entertaining" (par. 7). Although the fourth category opens by mentioning only the writer (par. 10) and does not indicate the kind of movies, it seems roughly parallel with the other categories, since, like them, it contains descriptions of a kind of movie. Yet the final sentence, "In the movies I go to by myself, the men and women always like each other" not only points up the essential difference between this category of films and the others, it comments on the relationships between the author and the men in the other categories.

The concluding sentence in the essay points towards one of the main themes of the essay, the relationship between men and women, a theme that is implicit in the description of each of the first three categories. There are other themes in the essay, too, particularly the relationship between personality and taste in films. It is interesting to note, however, that although the opening of this essay contains no thesis statement pointing to a central theme or purpose, most readers have little trouble following the essay's development or recognizing the author's main points. This is due in part to the word *types* in the title and to the announcement of a category of movies in the first sentence, "art films." Taken together, these words indicate to readers that the pattern of the essay will be classification and that one of its purposes will be to classify films. The strong parallels between the various categories in details and paragraph structure and in the linking of friends and films also convey to the reader a clear sense of purpose and pattern.

Thus even though Toth waits until the end of the essay to introduce one of her main themes, perhaps to make it seem to grow out of the experiences she has shared with the reader, the essay's clear pattern makes it easy to read and understand. In addition, it contains many subtle touches and details that make re-reading worthwhile. On a second reading, moreover, Toth's concern with the relationships between men and women becomes more apparent and adds a new dimension to the reader's perception of the essay.

RESPONSES AND IDEAS

1. Respond to this essay by briefly classifying movies or television shows you have seen or popular songs with which you are familiar, and by associating each type either with a particular kind of person or with the emotions they bring out in you.

2. Why does the author say Aaron was not pleased when he discovered that *The Devil's Eye* was funny (par. 1)? What does this reveal about Aaron's character?

3. Why does the author find it hard "to pick out movies for Sam" (par. 7)? Does she give any hint of her feelings when, after kissing her "long and hard," Sam says he cannot come in because his steady girlfriend would not like it? If so, what are her feelings? If not, why does she leave it up to the reader to guess at her feelings?

PURPOSE, AUDIENCE, AND STRATEGIES

1. Where else besides the last sentence of the essay does Toth comment more or less directly on the relationship between men and women? Where does she comment indirectly? What other purposes besides commenting on this relationship does the essay have? (See Glossary: Purpose.)

2. Describe the response you think most readers will have to Aaron, Pete, and Sam. Does your response differ in any way? If so, why?

3. Does Toth assume that her readers' experiences will enable them to understand both the types of movies and the types of friends she is describing, or does she try to present both in extensive enough detail so that most readers will be able to understand what she is talking about? Support your answer by pointing out the presence or absence of detail in each section of the essay.

4. In what specific ways does the fourth section of this essay differ from the first three? In your answer, consider matters of content, structure, and style. (See Glossary: Style.)

5. List the bases of classification Toth uses in this essay. Are they used consistently throughout the essay? If not, what is the reason (if any) for the inconsistency? Does it harm the essay in any way? Does it add to the essay's effectiveness? If so, how?

LANGUAGE AND STYLE

1. Examine the sentences Toth uses in paragraphs 1, 2, 4, 5, 7, and 8, and then describe how she uses combinations of long and short sentences to achieve emphasis in two of the paragraphs. In what ways other than length do the sentences vary in the paragraphs you have chosen, and how do these variations add emphasis? (See Glossary: Syntax, Emphasis.)

2. Compare the verbs and adverbs Toth uses to talk about each of the three men, Aaron, Sam, and Pete. What do these words reveal about each man's personality and taste and about her attitude towards each?

3. If you do not know the meaning of some of the following words, look them up in the dictionary: *Technicolor, cinematography* (par. 1); *tentatively* (2); *tattoo* (8); *peccadilloes, convivial* (11).

WRITING ACTIVITIES

1. Assume you are addressing an audience of college freshmen at an orientation, a group of people just starting to work for a corporation, a group of new councilors at a summer camp, or some similar audience. Prepare an essay using classification to tell your audience what kinds of challenges, problems, or situations they are likely to encounter and to prepare them to deal effectively with these new experiences.

2. Magazine racks in stores offer a much wider range of reading material than most people realize. Paperback books, video cassettes, and records offer similarly wide arrays of choices. Explore in an essay the major categories of magazines, books, records, cassettes, or some similar products in order to alert your audience to these many opportunities for learning and entertainment and to help guide their choices.

ଛ ROBERT BRUSTEIN

Robert Brustein was born in 1927 in New York City. He studied at
Amherst College and Columbia University from which he received
a Ph.D. Currently Director of the American Repertory Theatre in
Cambridge, Massachusetts, he has also taught at Columbia, Cornell, and Vassar. He has written *The Theatre of Revolt* (1964),
Seasons of Discontent (1965), *The Third Theatre* (1969), *Revolution as Theatre* (1971), and *Making Scenes: A Personal History of
the Turbulent Years at Yale: 1966–1979.* He regularly contributes
drama criticism to *The New Republic.*

Reflections on Horror Movies

"Reflections on Horror Movies" is taken from Brustein's book *The
Third Theatre* (1969). In this selection, Brustein classifies one of
the most enduring staples of popular entertainment: the horror
movie. Though the examples Brustein uses are all more than a
decade old, much of what he says is still applicable to today's
movies. Yet as you read, you may decide that films have changed
somewhat since the selection was written, and you may be able to
add new categories to the ones he identifies or propose modifica-
tions to his conclusions.

Although horror movies have recently been enjoying a vogue,   1
they have always been perennial supporting features among Grade
B and C fare. The popularity of the form is no doubt partly explained
by its ability to engage the spectator's feelings without making any
serious demand on his mind. In addition, however, horror movies
covertly embody certain underground assumptions about science
which reflect popular opinions.

The horror movies I am mainly concerned with I have divided   2
into three major categories: Mad Doctor, Atomic Beast and Interplanetary Monster. They do not exhaust all the types but they each
contain two essential characters, the Scientist and the Monster, towards whom the attitudes of the movies are in a revealing state of
change.

The Mad Doctor series is by far the most long lived of the three.   3
These films find their roots in certain European folk myths. Dracula
was inspired by an ancient Balkan superstition about vampires, the

Werewolf is a Middle European folk myth recorded, among other places, in the Breton *lais* of Marie de France, and even Frankenstein, though out of Mary Shelley by the Gothic tradition, has a medieval prototype in the Golem, a monster the Jews fashioned from clay and earth to free them from oppression. The spirit of these films is still medieval, combining a vulgar religiosity with folk superstitions. Superstition now, however, has been crudely transferred from magic and alchemy to creative science, itself a form of magic to the untutored mind. The devil of the Vampire and Werewolf myths, who turned human beings into baser animals, today has become a scientist, and the metamorphosis is given a technical name—it is a "regression" into an earlier state of evolution. The alchemist and devil-conjuring scholar, Dr. Faustus, gives way to Dr. Frankenstein, the research physician, while the magic circle, the tetragrammaton, and the full moon are replaced by test tubes, complicated electrical apparatus, and Bunsen burners.

Frankenstein, like Faustus, defies God by exploring areas where   4 humans are not meant to trespass. In Mary Shelley's book (it is subtitled *A Modern Prometheus*), Frankenstein is a latter-day Faustus, a superhuman creature whose aspiration embodies the expansiveness of his age. In the movies, however, Frankenstein loses his heroic quality and becomes a lunatic monomaniac, so obsessed with the value of his work that he no longer cares whether his discovery proves a boon or a curse to mankind. When the mad doctor, his eyes wild and inflamed, bends over his intricate equipment, pouring in a little of this and a little of that, the spectator is confronted with an immoral being whose mental superiority is only a measure of his madness. Like the popular image of the theoretical scientist engaged in basic research ("Basic research," says Charles Wilson, "is science's attempt to prove that grass is green"), he succeeds only in creating something badly which nature has already made well. The Frankenstein monster is a parody of man. Ghastly in appearance, clumsy in movement, criminal in behavior, imbecilic of mind, it is superior only in physical strength and resistance to destruction. The scientist has fashioned it in the face of divine disapproval (the heavens disgorge at its birth)—not to mention the disapproval of friends and frightened townspeople—and it can lead only to trouble.

For Dr. Frankenstein, however, the monster symbolizes the   5 triumph of his intellect over the blind morality of his enemies and it confirms him in the ultimate soundness of his thought ("They thought

I was mad, but this proves who is the superior being"). When it becomes clear that his countrymen are unimpressed by his achievement and regard him as a menace to society, the monster becomes the agent of his revenge. As it ravages the countryside and terrorizes the inhabitants, it embodies and expresses the scientist's own lust and violence. It is an extension of his own mad soul, come to life not in a weak and ineffectual body but in a body of formidable physical power. (In a movie like *Dr. Jekyll and Mr. Hyde,* the identity of monster and doctor is even clearer; Mr. Hyde, the monster, is the aggressive and libidinous element in the benevolent Dr. Jekyll's personality.) The rampage of the monster is the rampage of mad, unrestrained science which inevitably turns on the scientist, destroying him too. As the lava bubbles over the sinking head of the monster, the crude moral of the film frees itself from the horror and is asserted. Experimental science (and by extension knowledge itself) is superfluous, dangerous, and unlawful, for in exploring the unknown, it leads man to usurp God's creative power. Each of these films is a victory for obscurantism, flattering the spectator into believing that his intellectual inferiority is a sign that he is loved by God.

The Teen-age Monster films, a very recent phenomenon, amend   6
the assumptions of these horror movies in a startling manner. Their titles—*I Was a Teenage Werewolf, I Was a Teenage Frankenstein, Blood of Dracula,* and *Teenage Monster*—(some wit awaits one called *I Had a Teenage Monkey on My Back*)—suggest a Hollywood prank, but they are deadly serious, mixing the conventions of early horror movies with the ingredients of adolescent culture. The doctor, significantly enough, is no longer a fringe character whose madness can be inferred from the rings around his eyes and his wild hair but a respected member of society, a high-school chemistry teacher (*Blood of Dracula*) or a psychoanalyst (*Teenage Werewolf*) or a visiting lecturer from Britain (*Teenage Frankenstein*). Although he gives the appearance of benevolence—he pretends to help teen-agers with their problems—behind this facade he hides evil experimental designs. The monster, on the other hand, takes on a more fully developed personality. He is a victim who begins inauspiciously as an average, though emotionally troubled, adolescent and ends, through the influence of the doctor, as a voracious animal. The monster as teen-ager becomes the central character in the film and the teen-age audience is expected to identify and sympathize with him.

In *I Was a Teenage Werewolf,* the hero is characterized as   7
brilliant but erratic in his studies and something of a delinquent. At
the suggestion of his principal, he agrees to accept therapy from an
analyst helping maladjusted students. The analyst gets the boy under
his control and, after injecting him with a secret drug, turns him
into a werewolf. Against his will he murders a number of his con-
temporaries. When the doctor refuses to free him from this curse, he
kills him and is himself killed by the police. In death, his features
relax into the harmless countenance of an adolescent.

The crimes of the adolescent are invariably committed against   8
other youths (the doctor has it in for teen-agers) and are always
connected with those staples of juvenile culture, sex and violence.
The advertising displays show the male monsters, dressed in leather
jackets and blue jeans, bending ambiguously over the diaphanously
draped body of a luscious young girl while the female teen-age
vampire of *Blood of Dracula,* her nails long and her fangs dripping,
is herself half-dressed and lying on top of a struggling male (whether
to rape or murder him is not clear). The identification of sex and
violence is further underlined by the promotion blurbs: "In her eyes
DESIRE! in her veins—the blood of a MONSTER!" (*Blood of Dracula*);
"A Teenage Titan on a Lustful Binge that Paralyzed a Town with
Fear" (*Teenage Monster*). It is probable that these crimes are performed less reluctantly than is suggested and that the adolescent
spectator is more thrilled than appalled by this "lustful binge" which
captures the attention of the adult community. The acquisition of
power and prestige through delinquent sexual and aggressive activity
is a familiar juvenile fantasy . . ., one which we can see frequently
acted out by delinquents in our city schools. In the Teenage Monster
films, however, the hero is absolved of his aggressive and libidinous
impulses. Although he both feels and acts on them, he can attribute
the responsibility to the mad scientist who controls his behavior.
What these films seem to be saying, in their underground manner,
is that behind the harmless face of the high-school chemistry teacher
and the intellectual countenance of the psychoanalyst lies the warped
authority responsible for teen-age violence. The adolescent feels vic-
timized by society—turned into a monster by society—and if he
behaves in a delinquent manner, society and not he is to blame.
Thus, we can see one direction in which the hostility for experimental
research, explicit in the Mad Doctor films, can go—it can be transmuted into hatred of adult authority itself.

Or it can go underground, as in the Atomic Beast movies. The   9
Mad Doctor movies, in exploiting the supernatural, usually locate
their action in Europe (often a remote Bavarian village) where wild
fens, spectral castles, and ominous graveyards provide the proper
eerie background. The Atomic Beast movies depend for their effect
on the contemporary and familiar and there is a corresponding
change in locale. The monster (or "thing" as it is more often called)
appears now in a busy American city—usually Los Angeles to save
the producer money—where average men walk about in business
suits. The thing terrorizes not only the hero, the heroine, and a few
anonymous (and expendable) characters in Tyrolean costumes, but
the entire world. Furthermore, it has lost all resemblance to anything
human. It appears as a giant ant (*Them!*), a prehistoric animal
(*Beast from Twenty Thousand Fathoms*), an outsized grasshopper
(*Beginning of the End*) or a monstrous spider (*Tarantula*). Although
these films, in their deference to science fiction, seem to smile more
benignly on scientific endeavor, they are unconsciously closer to the
anti-theoretical biases of the Mad Doctor series than would first
appear.

All these films are similarly plotted, so the plot of *The Beginning*   10
of the End will serve as an example of the whole genre. The scene
opens on a pair of adolescents necking in their car off a desert road.
Their attention is caught by a weird clicking sound, the boy looks
up in horror, the girl screams, the music stings and the scene fades.
In the next scene, we learn that the car has been completely demolished and its occupants have disappeared. The police, totally baffled,
are conducting fruitless investigations when word comes that a small
town nearby has been destroyed in the same mysterious way. Enter
the young scientist hero. Examining the wreckage of the town, he
discovers a strange fluid which when analyzed proves to have been
manufactured by a giant grasshopper. The police ridicule his conclusions and are instantly attacked by a fleet of these grasshoppers,
each fifteen feet high, which wipe out the entire local force and a
few state troopers. Interrupting a perfunctory romance with the
heroine, the scientist flies to Washington to alert the nation. He
describes the potential danger to a group of bored politicians and
yawning big brass, but they remain skeptical until word comes that
the things have reached Chicago and are crushing buildings and
eating the occupants. The scientist is then put in charge of the army
and air force. Although the military men want to evacuate the city

and drop an atomic bomb on it, the scientist devises a safer method of destroying the creatures and proceeds to do so through exemplary physical courage and superior knowledge of their behavior. The movie ends on a note of foreboding: have the things been completely exterminated?

Externally, there seem to be very significant changes indeed, 11 especially in the character of the scientist. No longer fang-toothed, long-haired, and subject to delirious ravings (Bela Lugosi, John Carradine, Basil Rathbone), the doctor is now a highly admired member of society, muscular, handsome, and heroic (John Agar). He is invariably wiser, more reasonable, and more humane than the bone-headed bureaucrats and trigger-happy brass that compose the members of his "team," and he even has sexual appeal, a quality which Hollywood's eggheads have never enjoyed before. The scientist-hero, however, is not a very convincing intellectual. Although he may use technical, polysyllabic language when discussing his findings, he always yields gracefully to the admonition to "tell us in our own words, Doc" and proves that he can speak as simply as you or I; in the crisis, in fact, he is almost monosyllabic. When the chips are down, he loses his glasses (a symbol of his intellectualism) and begins to look like everyone else. The hero's intellect is part of his costume and makeup, easily shed when heroic action is demanded. That he is always called upon not only to outwit the thing but to wrestle with it as well (in order to save the heroine) indicates that he is in constant danger of tripping over the thin boundary between specialist and average Joe.

The fact remains that there is a new separation between the 12 scientist and the monster. Rather than being an extension of the doctor's evil will, the monster functions completely on its own, creating havoc through its predatory nature. We learn through charts, biological film, and the scientist's patient explanations that ants and grasshoppers are not the harmless little beasties they appear but actually voracious insects who need only the excuse of size to prey upon humanity. The doctor, rather than allying himself with the monster in its rampage against our cities, is in strong opposition to it, and reverses the pattern of the Mad Doctor films by destroying it. And yet, if the individual scientist is absolved of all responsibility for 13 the "thing," science somehow is not. These films suggest an uneasiness about science which, though subtle and unpremeditated, reflects unconscious American attitudes. These attitudes are sharpened when we examine the genesis of the thing for, though it seems to rise out of nowhere, it is invariably caused by a scientific blunder. The giant ants of *Them!*, for example, result from a nuclear explosion which caused a mutation in the species; another fission test has awakened, in *Beast from Twenty Thousand Fathoms,* a dinosaur encrusted in polar icecaps; the spider of *Tarantula* grows in size after having been injected with radioactive isotopes, and escapes during a fight in the lab between two scientists; the grasshoppers of *Beginning of the End* enlarge after crawling into some radioactive dust carelessly left about by a researcher. We are left with a puzzling substatement: science destroys the thing but scientific experimentation has created it.

I think we can explain this equivocal attitude when we acknowl-   14
edge that the thing "which is too horrible to name," which owes its birth to an atomic or nuclear explosion, which begins in a desert or frozen waste and moves from there to cities, and which promises ultimately to destroy the world, is probably a crude symbol for the bomb itself. The scientists we see represented in these films are unlike the Mad Doctors in another more fundamental respect: they are never engaged in basic research. The scientist uses his knowledge in a purely defensive manner, like a specialist working on rocket interception or a physician trying to cure a disease. The isolated theoretician who tinkers curiously in his lab (and who invented the atomic bomb) is never shown, only the practical working scientist who labors to undo the harm. The thing's destructive rampage against cities, like the rampage of the Frankenstein monster, is the result of too much cleverness, and the consquences for all the world are only too apparent.

These consequences are driven home more powerfully in movies   15
like *The Incredible Shrinking Man* and *The Amazing Colossal Man* where the audience gets the opportunity to identify closely with the victims of science's reckless experimentation. The hero of the first movie is an average man who, through contact with fallout while on his honeymoon, begins to shrink away to nothing. As he proceeds to grow smaller, he finds himself in much the same dilemma as the other heroes of the *Atomic Beast* series: he must do battle with (now) gigantic insects in order to survive. Scientists can do nothing to save him—after a while they can't even find him—so as he dwindles into an atomic particle he finally turns to God for whom "there is no zero." The inevitable sequel, *The Amazing Colossal Man,* reverses

the dilemma. The hero grows to enormous size through the premature explosion of a plutonium bomb. Size carries with it the luxury of power but the hero cannot enjoy his new stature. He feels like a freak and his body is proceeding to outgrow his brain and heart. Although the scientists labor to help him and even succeed in reducing an elephant to the size of a cat, it is too late; the hero has gone mad, demolished Las Vegas and fallen over Boulder Dam. The victimization of man by theoretical science has become, in these two movies, less of a suggestion and more of a fact.

In the Interplanetary Monster movies, Hollywood handles the 16 public's ambivalence towards science in a more obvious way, by splitting the scientist in two. Most of these movies feature both a practical scientist who wishes to destroy the invader and a theoretical scientist who wants to communicate with it. . . . In *Forbidden Planet* (a sophisticated thriller inspired in part by Shakespeare's *Tempest*), the good and evil elements in science are represented, as in *Dr. Jekyll and Mr. Hyde,* by the split personality of the scientist. He is urbane and benevolent (Walter Pidgeon plays the role) and is trying to realize an ideal community on the far-off planet he has discovered. Although he has invented a robot (Ariel) who cheerfully performs man's baser tasks, we learn that he is also responsible, though unwittingly, for a terrible invisible force (Caliban) overwhelming in its destructiveness. While he sleeps, the aggressive forces in his libido activate a dynamo he has been tinkering with which gives them enormous power to kill those the doctor unconsciously resents. Thus, Freudian psychology is evoked to endow the scientist with guilt. At the end, he accepts his guilt and sacrifices his life in order to combat the being he has created.

The Interplanetary Monster series sometimes reverses the central 17 situation of most horror films. We often find the monster controlling the scientist and forcing him to do its evil will. . . . In *The Brain from Planet Arous*, a hideous brain inhabits the mind of a nuclear physicist with the intention of controlling the universe. As the physical incarnation of the monster, the scientist is at the mercy of its will until he can free himself of its influence. The monster's intellect, like the intellect of the Mad Doctor, is invariably superior, signified graphically by its large head and small body (in the last film named it is nothing but Brain). Like the Mad Doctor, its superior intelligence is always accompanied by moral depravity and an unconscionable lust for power. If the monster is to be destroyed at all, this will not be done by matching wits with it but by finding some chink in its armor. The chink quite often is a physical imperfection: in *War of the Worlds,* the invading Martians are stopped, at the height of their victory, by their vulnerability to the disease germs of earth. Before this Achilles heel is discovered, however, the scientist is controlled to do evil, and with the monster and the doctor in collaboration again, even in this qualified sense, the wheel has come full circle.

The terror of most of these films, then, stems from the matching 18 of knowledge with power, always a source of fear for Americans—when Nietzsche's Superman enters comic book culture he loses his intellectual and spiritual qualities and becomes a muscle man. The muscle man, even with X-ray vision, poses no threat to the will, but muscle in collaboration with mind is generally thought to have a profound effect on individual destinies. The tendency to attribute everything that happens in the heavens, from flying saucers to Florida's cold wave, to science and the bomb . . . accounts for the extreme ways in which the scientist is regarded in our culture: either as a protective savior or as a destructive blunderer. It is little wonder that America exalts the physician (and the football player) and ignores the physicist. These issues, the issues of the great debate over scientific education and basic research, assert themselves crudely through the unwieldy monster and the Mad Doctor. The films suggest that the academic scientist, in exploring new areas, has laid the human race open to devastation either by human or interplanetary enemies—the doctor's madness, then, is merely a suitable way of expressing a conviction that the scientist's idle curiosity has shaken itself loose from prudence or principle. There is obviously a sensitive moral problem involved here, one which needs more articulate treatment than the covert and superstitious way it is handled in horror movies. That the problem is touched there at all is evidence of how profoundly it has stirred the American psyche.

RESPONSES AND IDEAS

1. Respond to this essay by classifying popular television shows built around a specific kind of central character (a detective or a student, for example) and comment on what attitudes in our culture the traits of the central characters reveal.

2. What does Brustein mean by this sentence, "Each of these films is a victory for obscurantism, flattering the spectator into believing that his

intellectual inferiority is a sign that he is loved by God" (par. 5)? Where does he provide evidence in the essay to support this conclusion? Does he provide enough evidence to be convincing?

3. In what ways are the portraits of scientists different in each of the categories of films? The portraits of monsters?

PURPOSE, AUDIENCE, AND STRATEGIES

1. Does Brustein think horror films are to be taken seriously as works of art? If so, how does he try to convince readers to agree with him? If not, why does he bother to discuss them?

2. Where does the writer announce the pattern this selection will follow? Does the announcement of the pattern also indicate the purpose of the selection? The thesis? If not, where are the purpose and thesis made plain to the reader? (See Glossary: Purpose, Thesis.)

3. On what bases does Brustein classify the films he discusses? Is the classification consistent? Do you believe it is complete? Why or why not? Do any of the categories overlap?

4. To what extent is it necessary to have seen the movies Brustein talks about to be able to understand his conclusions? Explain.

5. What symbols does Brustein use in paragraph 5 to represent alchemy and magic? Modern science? Are most readers likely to recognize the objects (or people) used as symbols? (If you do not recognize them, look them up in an encyclopedia.) Explain how the passage may still be effective even if readers do not recognize all the objects used as symbols. (See Glossary: Symbol.)

LANGUAGE AND STYLE

1. Examine the long sentences Brustein uses in paragraphs 4, 9, and 17 and describe the devices of syntax (including parallelism) he uses to keep them understandable. (See Glossary: Syntax.)

2. Describe the diction Brustein uses in paragraphs 4, 5, and 8 to make the examples he uses vivid and effective. To what extent, if any, is this diction in conflict with his style elsewhere in the selection? (See Glossary: Diction, Style.) Identify the allusions and metaphors in paragraph 17 and indicate what they contribute to the paragraph. (See Glossary: Allusion, Figures of Speech.)

3. If you do not know the meaning of any of the following words, look them up in the dictionary: *perennial, embody* (par. 1); *vulgar, alchemy, tetragrammaton* (par. 3); *aspiration, monomaniac, disgorge* (4); *libidinous, superfluous, obscurantism* (5); *inauspiciously, voracious* (6); *diaphanously, absolved, transmuted* (8); *fens, spectral, deference, benignly* (9); *foreboding* (10); *monosyllabic* (11); *ambivalence, endow* (16); *incarnation, graphically* (17).

WRITING ACTIVITIES

1. People collect valuable objects (paintings, fine jewelry, rare books), sentimental or nostalgic objects (old valentines, buttons and stickers from political campaigns), and objects with personal significance (beer cans, fishing lures, inexpensive china figurines). Assembling a collection is not a simple matter, however; it calls for considerable sorting and classifying. Write an essay explaining why you collect a particular sort of object and tell your readers something about the different categories that make up your collection and others like it. If you do not collect things, then report on the collections that other people assemble.

2. If you disagree with Brustein's view of horror movies, write an essay explaining why he is mistaken and offering, if you wish, another system for classifying horror movies. If you agree with Brustein's conclusions, apply his method of examining and classifying movies to some other category of films such as Westerns or musical comedies.

3. How does Brustein's way of classifying and evaluating movies differ from Susan Allen Toth's in "Cinematypes" (pp. 378–382)? Prepare an essay examining the similarities and differences in their approaches. As you write, you may want to consider which approach is better for deciding what movies to see and for understanding what we view.

🐦 MALCOLM COWLEY

Malcolm Cowley was born in 1898. He has taught at many universities and written numerous volumes of poetry, literary history, and literary criticism. He also served during the 1930s as literary editor of the *New Republic*. His books include *Exile's Return* (1934), *The Literary Situation* (1954), and *The View from Eighty* (1981).

Vices and Pleasures: The View From 80

This essay comes from the beginning of *The View from Eighty*. In it, Cowley surveys old age—and divides it into parts and subcategories, the better to share its particular qualities with his readers, most of whom have not attained the plateau he describes. Each of the subcategories he presents in this essay is illustrated with detailed examples, some humorous, some pathetic, but all effective and affecting. As you read, try to compare the categories and examples to your experience of old people.

Even before he or she is 80, the aging person may undergo   1
another identity crisis like that of adolescence. Perhaps there had also been a middle-aged crisis, the male or the female menopause, but for the rest of adult life he had taken himself for granted, with his capabilities and failings. Now, when he looks in the mirror, he asks himself, "Is this really me?"—or he avoids the mirror out of distress at what it reveals, those bags and wrinkles. In his new makeup he is called upon to play a new role in a play that must be improvised. André Gide, that long-lived man of letters, wrote in his journal, "My heart has remained so young that I have the continual feeling of playing a part, the part of the 70-year-old that I certainly am; and the infirmities and weaknesses that remind me of my age act like a prompter, reminding me of my lines when I tend to stray. Then, like the good actor I want to be, I go back into my role, and I pride myself on playing it well."

In his new role the old person will find that he is tempted by   2
new vices, that he receives new compensations (not so widely

known), and that he may possibly achieve new virtues. Chief among these is the heroic or merely obstinate refusal to surrender in the face of time. One admires the ships that go down with all flags flying and the captain on the bridge.

Among the vices of age are avarice, untidiness, and vanity, which   3
last takes the form of a craving to be loved or simply admired. Avarice is the worst of those three. Why do so many old persons, men and women alike, insist on hoarding money when they have no prospect of using it and even when they have no heirs? They eat the cheapest food, buy no clothes, and live in a single room when they could afford better lodging. It may be that they regard money as a form of power; there is a comfort in watching it accumulate while other powers are dwindling away. How often we read of an old person found dead in a hovel, on a mattress partly stuffed with bankbooks and stock certificates! The bankbook syndrome, we call it in our family, which has never succumbed.

Untidiness we call the Langley Collyer syndrome. To explain,   4
Langley Collyer was a former concert pianist who lived alone with his 70-year-old brother in a brownstone house on upper Fifth Avenue. The once fashionable neighborhood had become part of Harlem. Homer, the brother, had been an admiralty lawyer, but was now blind and partly paralyzed; Langley played for him and fed him on buns and oranges, which he thought would restore Homer's sight. He never threw away a daily paper because Homer, he said, might want to read them all. He saved other things as well and the house became filled with rubbish from roof to basement. The halls were lined on both sides with bundled newspapers, leaving narrow passageways in which Langley had devised booby traps to catch intruders.

On March 21, 1947, some unnamed person telephoned the police   5
to report that there was a dead body in the Collyer house. The police broke down the front door and found the hall impassable, then they hoisted a ladder to a second-story window. Behind it Homer was lying on the floor in a bathrobe; he had starved to death. Langley had disappeared. After some delay, the police broke into the basement, chopped a hole in the roof, and began throwing junk out of the house, top and bottom. It was 18 days before they found Langley's body, gnawed by rats. Caught in one of his own booby traps, he had died in a hallway just outside Homer's door. By that time the police

had collected, and the Department of Sanitation had hauled away, 120 tons of rubbish, including besides the newspapers, 14 grand pianos and the parts of a dismantled Model T. Ford.

Why do so many old people accumulate junk, not on the scale of Langley Collyer, but still in a dismaying fashion? Their tables are piled high with it, their bureau drawers are stuffed with it, their closet rods bend with the weight of clothes not worn for years. I suppose that the piling up is partly from lethargy and partly from the feeling that everything once useful, including their own bodies, should be preserved. Others, though not so many, have such a fear of becoming Langley Collyers that they strive to be painfully neat. Every tool they own is in its place, though it will never be used again; every scrap of paper is filed away in alphabetical order. At last their immoderate neatness becomes another vice of age, if a milder one.

The vanity of older people is an easier weakness to explain, and to condone. With less to look forward to, they yearn for recognition of what they have been: the reigning beauty, the athlete, the soldier, the scholar. It is the beauties who have the hardest time. A portrait of themselves at twenty hangs on the wall, and they try to resemble it by making an extravagant use of creams, powders, and dyes. Being young at heart, they think they are merely revealing their essential persons. The athletes find shelves for their silver trophies, which are polished once a year. Perhaps a letter sweater lies wrapped in a bureau drawer. I remember one evening when a no-longer athlete had guests for dinner and tried to find his sweater. "Oh, that old thing," his wife said. "The moths got into it and I threw it away." The athlete sulked and his guests went home early.

Often the yearning to be recognized appears in conversation as an innocent boast. Thus, a distinguished physician, retired at 94, remarks casually that a disease was named after him. A former judge bursts into chuckles as he repeats bright things that he said on the bench. Aging scholars complain in letters (or one of them does), "As I approach 70 I'm becoming avid of honors, and such things—medals, honorary degrees, etc.—are only passed around among academics on a *quid pro quo* basis (one hood capping another)." Or they say querulously, "Bill Underwood has ten honorary doctorates and I have only three. Why didn't they elect me to . . . ?" and they mention the name of some learned society. That

6

7

8

search for honors is a harmless passion, though it may lead to jealousies and deformations of character, as with Robert Frost in his later years. Still, honors cost little. Why shouldn't the very old have more than their share of them?

To be admired and praised, especially by the young, is an   9 autumnal pleasure enjoyed by the lucky ones (who are not always the most deserving). "What is more charming," Cicero observes in his famous essay *De Senectute*, "than an old age surrounded by the enthusiasm of youth! . . . Attentions which seem trivial and conventional are marks of honor—the morning call, being sought after, precedence, having people rise for you, being escorted to and from the forum. . . . What pleasures of the body can be compared to the prerogatives of influence?" But there are also pleasures of the body, or the mind, that are enjoyed by a greater number of older persons.

Those pleasures include some that younger people find hard to   10 appreciate. One of them is simply sitting still, like a snake on a sunwarmed stone, with a delicious feeling of indolence that was seldom attained in earlier years. A leaf flutters down; a cloud moves by inches across the horizon. At such moments the older person, completely relaxed, has become a part of nature—and a living part, with blood coursing through his veins. The future does not exist for him. He thinks, if he thinks at all, that life for younger persons is still a battle royal of each against each, but that now he has nothing more to win or lose. He is not so much above as outside the battle, as if he had assumed the uniform of some small neutral country, perhaps Liechtenstein or Andorra. From a distance he notes that some of the combatants, men or women, are jostling ahead—but why do they fight so hard when the most they can hope for is a longer obituary? He can watch the scrounging and gouging, he can hear the shouts of exultation, the moans of the gravely wounded, and meanwhile he feels secure; nobody will attack him from ambush.

Age has other physical compensations besides the nirvana of   11 dozing in the sun. A few of the simplest needs become a pleasure to satisfy. When an old woman in a nursing home was asked what she really liked to do, she answered in one word: "Eat." She might have been speaking for many of her fellows. Meals in a nursing home, however badly cooked, serve as climactic moments of the day. The physical essence of the pensioners is being renewed at an appointed hour; now they can go back to meditating or to watching

TV while looking forward to the next meal. They can also look forward to sleep, which has become a definite pleasure, not the mere interruption it once had been.

Here I am thinking of old persons under nursing care. Others 12 ferociously guard their independence, and some of them suffer less than one might expect from being lonely and impoverished. They can be rejoiced by visits and meetings, but they also have company inside their heads. Some of them are busiest when their hands are still. What passes through the minds of many is a stream of persons, images, phrases, and familiar tunes. For some that stream has continued since childhood, but now it is deeper; it is their present and their past combined. At times they conduct silent dialogues with a vanished friend, and these are less tiring—often more rewarding— than spoken conversations. If inner resources are lacking, old persons living alone may seek comfort and a kind of companionship in the bottle. I should judge from the gossip of various neighborhoods that the outer suburbs from Boston to San Diego are full of secretly alcoholic widows. One of those widows, an old friend, was moved from her apartment into a retirement home. She left behind her a closet in which the floor was covered wall to wall with whiskey bottles. "Oh, those empty bottles!" she explained. "They were left by a former tenant."

Not whiskey or cooking sherry but simply giving up is the 13 greatest temptation of age. It is something different from a stoical acceptance of infirmities, which is something to be admired. At 63, when he first recognized that his powers were failing, Emerson wrote one of his best poems, "Terminus":

> It is time to be old,
> To take in sail:—
> The god of bounds,
> Who sets to seas a shore,
> Came to me in his fatal rounds,
> And said: "No more!
> No farther shoot
> Thy broad ambitious branches, and thy root.
> Fancy departs: no more invent;
> Contract thy firmament
> To compass of a tent."

Emerson lived in good health to the age of 79. Within his 14 narrowed firmament, he continued working until his memory failed;

then he consented to having younger editors and collaborators. The givers-up see no reason for working. Sometimes they lie in bed all day when moving about would still be possible, if difficult. I had a friend, a distinguished poet, who surrendered in that fashion. The doctors tried to stir him to action, but he refused to leave his room. Another friend, once a successful artist, stopped painting when his eyes began to fail. His doctor made the mistake of telling him that he suffered from a fatal disease. He then lost interest in everything except the splendid Rolls-Royce, acquired in his prosperous days, that stood in the garage. Daily he wiped the dust from its hood. He couldn't drive it on the road any longer, but he used to sit in the driver's seat, start the motor, then back the Rolls out of the garage and drive it in again, back twenty feet and forward twenty feet; that was his only distraction.

I haven't the right to blame those who surrender, not being able   15 to put myself inside their minds or bodies. Often they must have compelling reasons, physical or moral. Not only do they suffer from a variety of ailments, but also they are made to feel that they no longer have a function in the community. Their families and neighbors don't ask them for advice, don't really listen when they speak, don't call on them for efforts. One notes that there are not a few recoveries from apparent senility when that situation changes. If it doesn't change, old persons may decide that efforts are useless. I sympathize with their problems, but the men and women I envy are those who accept old age as a series of challenges.

For such persons, every new infirmity is an enemy to be out-   16 witted, an obstacle to be overcome by force of will. They enjoy each little victory over themselves, and sometimes they win a major success. Renoir was one of them. He continued painting, and magnificently, for years after he was crippled by arthritis; the brush had to be strapped to his arm. "You don't need your hand to paint," he said. Goya was another of the unvanquished. At 72 he retired as an official painter of the Spanish court and decided to work only for himself. His later years were those of the famous "black paintings" in which he let his imagination run (and also of the lithographs, then a new technique). At 78 he escaped a reign of terror in Spain by fleeing to Bordeaux. He was deaf and his eyes were failing; in order to work he had to wear several pairs of spectacles, one over another, and then use a magnifying glass; but he was producing splendid work in a totally new style. At 80 he drew an ancient man propped on two sticks, with a mass of white hair and beard hiding his face and with the inscription "I am still learning."

Giovanni Papini said when he was nearly blind, "I prefer mar-   17
tyrdom to imbecility." After writing sixty books, including his famous *Life of Christ,* he was at work on two huge projects when he was stricken with a form of muscular atrophy. He lost the use of his left leg, then of his fingers, so that he couldn't hold a pen. The two big books, though never to be finished, moved forward slowly by dictation; that in itself was a triumph. Toward the end, when his voice had become incomprehensible, he spelled out a word, tapping on the table to indicate letters of the alphabet. One hopes never to be faced with the need for such heroic measures.

"Eighty years old!" the great Catholic poet Paul Claudel wrote   18
in his journal. "No eyes left, no ears, no teeth, no legs, no wind! And when all is said and done, how astonishingly well one does without them!"

RESPONSES AND IDEAS

1. Respond to this essay by listing the vices and pleasures of 18, or 27, or 35, or 48—whatever age you are.

2. In your own words, explain the "identity crisis" Cowley describes at the beginning of this essay.

3. What does the poem in paragraph 13 add to the essay? Would the essay be more or less effective if Cowley had decided not to include the poem? (See Glossary: Evaluation.)

PURPOSE, AUDIENCE, AND STRATEGIES

1. Cowley explains the experience of old age by dividing it into parts: vices, compensations, and virtues (par. 2). In which paragraphs does he examine the vices? Into what categories does he sort the vices and in which paragraph does he list these categories? Identify the examples he uses to illustrate each of these categories. Where does Cowley begin discussing the compensations (or pleasures) of old age? Into what categories does he put them? Can paragraphs 13–18 be regarded as a discussion of the virtues of old age? Why, or why not?

2. Is this essay addressed to people of any particular age? How do you know?

3. How does Cowley want his readers to react to the story of Langley Collyer? Be specific. What strategies of diction, style, and arrangement does he use to encourage this reaction?

4. How would you describe Cowley's purpose in this essay? What evidence in the text supports your answer? (See Glossary: Purpose.)

5. Which of the closing strategies does Cowley use in paragraph 18? (See Glossary: Closings.) What in particular does this closing add to the effect of the essay?

LANGUAGE AND STYLE

1. How does Cowley use sentence structure to add emphasis and impact to the story of Giovanni Papini (par. 17)? (See Glossary: Syntax.)

2. Cowley uses simile and metaphor in paragraph 10 to help describe some of the compensations of old age. Identify these figures of speech (see Glossary: Figures of Speech) and explain what they add to his description. What other strategies of diction and style does this paragraph employ to convey its point?

3. If you do not know the meaning of any of the following words, look them up in the dictionary: *obstinate* (par. 2); *succumbed* (3); *lethargy* (6); *querulously* (8); *precedence, prerogatives* (9); *indolence* (10); *nirvana, climactic* (11); *stoical* (13); *firmament* (14); *unvanquished* (16); *atropy* (17).

WRITING ACTIVITIES

1. Write an essay describing an elderly person you know whose personality and behavior display some of the characteristics Cowley identifies as part of old age. Divide your essay according to the various kinds of vices, virtues, or compensations you describe, and illustrate each trait with fully developed examples.

2. In an essay explain a job you think most readers would find interesting (stockbroker, university president, automobile dealer, magazine editor, and so on). Divide your explanation according to the various functions, rewards, or problems of the occupation, and provide as much detailed information as you can. Interviews with people holding interesting jobs can provide you with insights, facts, and examples worth sharing.

❧ JANICE HOPKINS TANNE

Janice Hopkins Tanne is a free-lance writer who has written for a variety of magazines, including *New York Magazine*.

The Great Salt Debate

"The Great Salt Debate" was first published as a magazine article. Like many arguments over food and health, the debate over salt has been going on for some time without resolution. This essay reports on both sides in the debate and attempts to clear up the misinformation that has accumulated around it. Tanne also tries to calm excessive fears that readers might have about salt in their diets—without suggesting that it is harmless.

Eat too much salt and you'll get high blood pressure. Avoid salt and you won't get it. Simple, yes—but true?

No one knows, despite what you've seen on the cover of *Time* and on television, despite a crusade by the Food and Drug Administration to reduce the amount of salt in food, despite the flurry of anti-salt paperbacks and the hype for low-salt foods. Scientists simply do not know whether eating a lot of salt causes high blood pressure, or whether avoiding salt will keep people whose blood pressure is normal now from developing high blood pressure—or hypertension—in the future. In fact, a scientific controversy is raging over the wisdom of salt restriction for everybody.

At one pole stands feisty Dr. John H. Laragh, director of the Hypertension and Cardiovascular Center at New York Hospital–Cornell Medical Center, who says, "There's no evidence that if you cut down on salt you'll prevent hypertension."

At the other pole is Dr. Arthur Hull Hayes Jr., the F.D.A. commissioner, and a hypertension expert himself, who strongly urges people to cut back on their salt intake, although he does admit, "We do not know whether increased sodium consumption *causes* hypertension."

Sodium makes up about 40 percent of table salt (the rest is chloride) and is the part of salt that the scientists are squabbling

403

about. Besides coming out of the saltshaker, sodium is invisibly present in many foods, in both bottled and tap water, and in about two dozen chemicals used in canning, preserving, or freezing food. Dairy products, spinach, and celery are naturally high in sodium; sodium compounds are added in large quantities to an improbable range of foods from diet soda to chocolate pudding; and foods such as anchovies, pickles, and soy sauce are loaded with it.

Human beings can live on diets that include only minute 6 amounts of sodium—500 milligrams a day or less, but Americans consume about eight times that amount. However, even the F.D.A.'s Dr. Hayes admits, "What we don't know is whether there is an 'ideal level' of sodium in the diet."

There's no doubt that sodium plays a role in some people's high 7 blood pressure when they already have the common form of this disease, called essential (or idiopathic) hypertension. About 20 percent of Americans will develop essential hypertension, and a third to a half of them will be helped, at least to some extent, by drastically reducing the sodium in their diets. By this analysis, only 10 percent of Americans should ever worry about their sodium intake.

This is not the same as saying that sodium *caused* the high blood 8 pressure in the first place. According to *The Medical Letter*, a respected, independent, nonprofit newsletter for physicians, "More than 80 percent of people in the U.S.A. do not become hypertensive despite lifelong consumption of a high-sodium diet; this large majority would probably gain nothing from giving up pretzels and pickles. . . . Whether the minority destined to become hypertensive would benefit from a moderate reduction in their dietary salt intake remains to be established."

So why are we in the midst of an anti-salt crusade? In large 9 part, because of various population studies done in the 1950s and '60s. Some were the work of the late Dr. Lewis K. Dahl, the man who fought for the removal of salt from baby food and suggested the populations with high salt intake also had many cases of high blood pressure. These studies have been attacked by some leaders in the profession on the grounds that the basic data may not substantiate Dr. Dahl's conclusions.

Other studies showed that primitive peoples who eat a low- 10 sodium diet do not have hypertension—facts that may or may not be related. These studies don't usually consider other factors that have been linked to low blood pressure, such as these people's high levels of exercise, their low consumption of alcohol, and the low levels of fat and high levels of potassium in their diets.

Research also showed that some primitive peoples who become 11 Westernized, changing the level of sodium in their diet, were more likely to develop hypertension. But this says nothing of the differences between living in a primitive tribal society and striving to cope with civilization in Manhattan.

None of these questions has been answered. And Dr. Dahl's 12 conclusions have been further challenged by some recent studies. Researchers in New Zealand, for instance, examined 1,200 adults and found that incidence of high blood pressure was related to increasing age and obesity, but not to the amount of sodium consumed. And an Indiana study showed that when normal individuals were loaded up with huge quantities of salt, their blood pressures did not rise into the hypertensive range. Furthermore, two new studies just reported in the highly respected British medical journal *Lancet* showed that reduction in salt intake did *not* lead to a reduction in blood pressure. Instead, the authors suggested that a reduction in fat and an increase in fiber might prevent or treat hypertension.

Various population studies of the Japanese, who consume a lot 13 more salt than Americans do, mostly in soy sauce and pickles, show that they do have a higher incidence of hypertension and strokes (but fewer heart attacks and longer life spans) than Americans. But even this apparent salt-hypertension connection is now disputed by certain Japanese researchers who think that the low level of protein in some Japanese diets, not the high level of sodium, is the link to hypertension.

Findings like these lead hypertension experts such as Dr. Frederic 14 eric C. Bartter, professor of medicine at the University of Texas, in San Antonio, to say, "There's no evidence that someone who eats a high-salt diet for years is predisposing himself to hypertension in the same way that smokers are predisposing themselves to lung cancer."

Indeed, sodium is only part of the hypertension story. Other 15 important elements in the diet are essential for normal functioning of the heart and blood vessels, including calcium, magnesium, and potassium. The roles of these chemicals and the balance among them in the diet are the subject of intense research. Dr. David A. McCarron, Director of the hypertension program at Oregon Health Sciences University, in Portland, recently published a provocative study linking a low-calcium diet to hypertension. He suggests that it doesn't make much sense to monkey with one element—sodium—until researchers understand how they all interact.

However, those people who already have high blood pressure 16 and are salt-sensitive may benefit if they reduce their salt intake to below four grams a day, preferably to below two, says Dr. Edward D. Freis, senior medical investigator at the Veterans Administration Hospital in Washington, D.C.

That means not adding any salt to food at all—when cooking 17 or at the table—as well as avoiding all naturally salty foods, and foods to which salt has been added during processing. "Modest reductions, like telling the guy not to salt his food, won't work," says Dr. Laragh.

Such diets are difficult to stay on—they're monotonous, and 18 inconvenient: no takeout foods, no canned, preserved, or prepared foods, no dairy foods, no ordinary bread or baked goods, no restaurant meals, no diet sodas, and a rigorous counting of the sodium content of all food and drink, including tap water. (New York has four to eleven parts per million, which is quite low.)

The effects of *extremely* low-salt diets (one half-gram a day) on 19 people with hypertension have been studied by a number of researchers. Dr. Bartter hospitalizes patients for a week and puts them "on a rigorous low-sodium diet, about as low as a dietitian can go without giving bizarre foods like cooked cereal mush all day. Everything tastes blah, and it's worse for those who habitually pour salt on, but any diet, unless it's just awful, can be tolerated for a week," Dr. Bartter says. About half of his hypertensive patients significantly respond, indicating that their high blood pressure can be helped by strict adherence to such a regimen.

Meanwhile, researchers are trying to devise tests to find those 20 persons with normal blood pressure who may be salt-sensitive and develop hypertension in the future. One group that is particularly suspect is the children of hypertensives. According to Dr. Norman M. Kaplan, professor of internal medicine at the University of Texas Southwestern Medical School, in Dallas, about half of them have an inherited risk and will go on to develop hypertension. But he adds, "Hypertension develops in the twenties and thirties. If you have normal blood pressure at age 45, forget about it."

Dr. James W. Woods, professor of medicine at the University of 21 North Carolina, is seeking a way to spot potential hypertension in male children of hypertensive parents. He has been looking at how sodium is transported across the membrane of red blood cells and has found that about half these boys have a faster than normal rate of sodium transport. Does it mean that these are the children who will have hypertension later in life? At the moment, it's impossible to say; 20 to 30 years of follow-up studies will be needed to find out.

Dr. Bartter is working on a different tack, with a project that monitors children's blood pressure through the day and feeds the information through a complex computer program to identify kids who, although they don't have hypertension, fall outside the normal pattern. He feels they may be at risk of getting high blood pressure. But again, there is no way to know without 20 to 30 years of follow-up studies. 22

The truth is that nobody yet knows much of anything about how salt intake affects people with normal blood pressure. But the F.D.A. and the anti-salt crusaders continue to advocate a low-sodium diet for everybody. 23

RESPONSES AND IDEAS

1. Respond to this essay by listing the foods you like that add large quantities of salt to your diet.
2. What is the cause of the "anti-salt crusade" (par. 9)?
3. Briefly state in your own words the major arguments put forth by those who think salt is harmful and those who think it is probably not harmful.

PURPOSE, AUDIENCE, AND STRATEGIES

1. What does Tanne identify as the major arguments advanced by those who think salt consumption is a serious problem and those who think it is not? Is Tanne's division and analysis of the arguments advanced by each side in the controversy easy to follow? If so, why? If not, in what ways might the essay be rearranged to make the explanation easier to follow?
2. How many paragraphs in the essay are devoted to presenting the arguments and evidence put forth by the anti-salt forces? To the position of those who believe salt may not be very dangerous? Is this proportion appropriate? Why, or why not?
3. How does the author try to convince readers that the salt controversy is worth learning about?

4.   What attitudes towards salt use does Tanne assume readers bring with them? What indications of her assumptions are there in the essay? Be specific.

5.   Does the author take a stand on the controversy? If so, what is her stand, and how does she indicate it?

LANGUAGE AND STYLE

1.   What use does the author make of transitions and parallelism to indicate the relationships between the two sides in the debate?

2.   What strategies of diction and syntax does Tanne use to emphasize the weakness of Dahl's research (pars. 10–14)? (See Glossary: Diction, Syntax.)

3.   If you do not know the meaning of some of the following words, look them up in the dictionary: *feisty* (par. 3); *milligrams* (6); *idiopathic* (7); *substantiate* (9); *provocative* (15); *regimen* (19).

WRITING ACTIVITIES

1.   People argue over the best kinds of food to eat, the proper kind of exercise, and the best route to mental well-being. The benefits of massive doses of vitamin C and the use of drugs in treating schizophrenia are two of many subjects of frequent debate. Using division and classification, examine the various arguments and evidence advanced by each side in a controversy over some matter of nutrition and health, and present them in a form that will enable readers to better understand the controversy.

2.   Prepare an essay similar in form to the one described in the preceding activity, but examine an argument over an environmental issue (like acid rain) or a disagreement over the conservation of plants and animals (like the debate over the killing of whales or baby seals).

❧ BERNICE KANNER

Throughout her career as a writer and editor, Bernice Kanner has found ways to blend her interests in advertising, marketing, and journalism. After receiving a masters degree in English Literature from the State University of New York at Binghamton, Kanner worked first in the corporate communications division of the J. Walter Thompson advertising agency and then as a senior editor of *Advertising Age*, a trade magazine for the advertising and public relations industry. She has also been marketing columnist for the *New York Daily News* and is currently a senior editor of *New York Magazine*. In her award-winning column in *New York Magazine*, "On Madison Avenue," she reports on new and unusual trends in advertising, publishing, and marketing.

Love for Sale: You Gotta Have Cards

"Love for Sale: You Gotta Have Cards" was first published as a magazine column. In this piece, Kanner examines one of the more interesting features of our culture: our fascination with greeting cards. In the course of this selection she makes use of a variety of patterns, including division and classification.

Bad news, moms, wives, girlfriends. When it comes to Valentine's Day, you're (respectively) second, third, and fourth fiddles. On that most romantic of occasions, it's American teachers who are, well, in the cards. 1

Last year, Americans exchanged 900 million valentines, 2.7 billion Christmas cards, 1.5 billion birthday cards—and 7 billion cards altogether. We sent bushels of Easter cards, Mother's and Father's Day cards, Thanksgiving cards, and cards commemorating lesser holidays as well as anniversaries, deaths, and other, less permanent departures. We dispatched cards in honor of Grandparents Day (the first Sunday after Labor Day, declared a national holiday in 1978—guess who lobbied for that?), cards that said, "Get well," "Sorry," or "Keep in touch," even cards that offered congratulations on buying a new car or sticking to a diet. 2

Last year, the self-styled "social expression" industry accounted 3 for 40 percent of all mail flowing from household to household as Americans expressed themselves to the tune of $2.5 billion. "No question, Americans are the biggest social expressers in the world," says Frank Braconi, director of research at Business Trend Analysts. "People in the habit of social expression can zip off hundreds of cards a year."

And those in the habit can choose from hundreds of thousands   4
of cards. For Valentine's Day alone, manufacturers churned out 3,000 designs, estimates Gary Smith, executive vice-president of the Greeting Card Association. Cards of endearment, once virtually the only valentines marketed, still sell the best. But now, because of all the less-than-forever relationships, there are alternatives.

"The standard formula for a successful valentine used to be that   5
it was largely red, pink, or white with hearts, flowers, or cupids," says Nancy Matheny, marketing-communications manager at Hallmark—which is to greeting cards what Campbell's is to soup. "But recent research shows a new acceptance for designs that are less cluttered with motifs and less frilly than in days past. There's an acceptance of new, offshoot colors—rich mauves and burgundies and, surprisingly, blues. Cupids especially are a little on the outs these days: It's hard to give them a contemporary treatment.

"We think the influx of working women has affected card styles,"   6
Matheny says. "People still buy sweet traditional rhymes of love. But on the whole, cards today are trendier, more sophisticated, and less flowery. Prose is gaining on poetry."

So is blankness, cards with stylized graphics on the cover—   7
contemporary cityscapes are big—and an empty page inside. Humorous and gag cards are also gaining. Hallmark has a new Lite line, which promises to be a third less serious than its regular greeting cards. "Would you be my Valentine?" asks one on the outside. Open it for the zinger: "It's a thankless job but somebody has to do it." Another sports a wooden shoe with a heart in it. Inside: "Wooden shoe like to be my Valentine?"

There's also a new crop of "activity" cards: fill-in-the-blanks,   8
crosswords, or puzzles the recipient must assemble in order to read the message. "These appeal to people who want fun but not much romantic involvement," notes Matheny. And for traditionalists, there are new, laser-cut valentines reminiscent of the fragile paper-lace ones of the nineteenth century. This Valentine's Day, the average card will fetch $1. Seven dollars will get you an electronic musical mes-

sage, $10 a perfumed card with a small vial of Revlon's Jontue tucked inside.

Most cards are designed to appeal to women, who buy at least 9 80 percent of them, including those for their husbands to send. A card's looks attract a shopper; its message sells her. And card buyers are not brand-loyal. "No one turns over a card to make sure she's buying a Hallmark," says Matheny. Nonetheless, Hallmark keeps hammering home the suggestion with its "when you care enough to send the very best" ads.

People living in the northeastern and north-central parts of the 10 country buy more cards than the national average: Southerners purchase 30 percent fewer than the norm. Heavy card consumers tend to live in their own homes, in the suburbs, come from large families, be between 35 and 54 years old, and have an average household income of $30,000. (The fascination with cards seems to taper off with higher and lower incomes.)

The "social expression" business began in the mid-1800s, when 11 literacy had become widespread and the printing press had been perfected. The industry took off in 1840, when the Penny Postage Act was passed in England. It was there, in 1843, that the first commercial Christmas card was printed.

Hallmark, the house that cards built, got its start in 1910 when 12 eighteen-year-old Joyce Hall left the small Nebraska town where he and his brothers owned a struggling gift-specialty shop and headed for Kansas City with a couple of shoe boxes full of picture postcards. Today, the company—which changed its name from Hall Brothers to Hallmark in 1954—turns out 10 million cards a day and millions of other stationery and gift items, including paper plates, napkins, and guest towels, puzzles, plaques, candles, wrapping paper, ribbon, books, toys, jewelry, and photo albums.

Card manufacturers celebrated one boom year after another until 13 the early 1970s, when the Vietnam War polarized the country, the divorce rate rose and the birthrate dropped, and a "siege mentality, a me-first attitude prevailed," says the card association's Smith. Sales slumped from about 6.5 billion to 5.7 billion. They rebounded in 1977, when "the mood of our culture changed. People recognized that they'd experienced and survived some difficult times. The retreat was over."

Because it's hard to find anyone who doesn't buy cards—per 14 capita purchases worked out to 24.9 in 1982—you might well conclude that the industry had reached the saturation point. But in fact it looks to be growing all the time. The baby-boomers are heading into middle age, a time when, apparently, people mellow, relationships matter more—and card mania strikes. The country is becoming tradition-minded again (sending cards is a traditional activity), and the population is on the move. "Ten percent of Americans relocate each year," says Ken Noble, an analyst for Paine Webber Mitchell Hutchins. "That's a ready-made market of friends to keep in contact with."

The price of cards has inched up each year, and, with 100   15 percent markups, so has the return for retailers. Thus, card boutiques are burgeoning, and a lot of other stores have begun to carry cards for the first time. In 1977, department stores accounted for 16.3 percent of all card sales; by the end of 1982, that had slipped to 9.3 percent. At the same time, sales in grocery stores zoomed from 3.4 percent to 9.8 percent of total card sales. "Most cards are impulse purchases," says Noble. "You grow this kind of market by making it available to people." And, ironically, the industry is looking forward to a boost from what has long been its major nemesis—the telephone. Phones account for 97 percent of all message transactions, says Smith, but the phone company's breakup and the toll hikes that are expected as a result may well send more people scurrying to the card racks.

The added purchases will line the pockets of Hallmark, the   16 industry leader, with 40 percent of all greeting-card sales; American Greetings, with a 26 percent share; Gibson Greeting Cards, with 10 percent; and 150 or so small companies, many of which turn out "alternative" cards, with offbeat or risqué humor, for example. Cards featuring well-known characters such as the Peanuts gang (Hallmark) and Strawberry Shortcake (American Greetings) account for between 2 and 13 percent of total sales, with sales peaking in non-holiday periods.

American Greetings, which has grown swiftly over the last few   17 years by turning out cards that are less expensive than Hallmark's— and offering free shipment to retailers and credit for unsold seasonal cards—has recently closed the price gap with its No. 1 rival, and perhaps the image gap as well. When the company first advertised on television, in 1981, it tried a soft, sentimental approach—but people thought the commercials were for Hallmark. So American Greetings has since taken the humorous route. In one spot, a man is shown chiseling HAPPY BIRTHDAY JULIUS in a stone wall when Cleopatra strolls by—and says haughtily, "Not enough warmth."

Cards generally reflect, if not the actual events of the times, the Zeitgeist. In the early 1930s, they had Depression themes. One depicted a man with patches on his clothes, wailing that the card wasn't what he'd like to send—"Ain't being poor a crime!" During World War II, cards turned patriotic. One pictured a bomber plane tied up with military-looking ribbon. In the early fifties, at the height of the Cold War, Santa was bombarded by paper airplanes; in the late fifties, he and his reindeer clung to a rocket circling the earth. In 1970, a Hallmark card reprinted the prayer of the Apollo 8 astronauts, and in the following decade, joggers and tennis nuts cropped up all over. Although most card ideas gestate for 18 to 24 months, *E.T.*-related cards were rushed onto the shelves 6 months after the movie made its debut. 18

In the fifties, the women represented on cards looked adoringly into their pipe smoking husbands' eyes. Now there are "new relationship" cards for Mom and her husband and Dad and his wife. (Though Mother's Day cards for Dad's wife address "my other mother" and "someone who's been like a mother to me," none, says Matheny, use the loaded word "stepmother.") And today, 3 percent of Hallmark's cards feature blacks or are in Spanish. 19

This is also the era of the come-on and the put-down. The Bittersweet line of cards conveys such sentiments as "Do you remember that wonderful time when . . . Oh, never mind, that wasn't you," and "You get hives from my cat . . . I get nauseous from your bull." Lyons, Ltd., another alternative-card maker, has a raft of zingers. Its best-seller: "Sometimes life is like a cactus . . . every time you turn around you meet another pr[--]k." 20

I, for one, wouldn't send such sour notes to my worst enemies. But the card people say they wouldn't make them if there were no demand. 21

RESPONSES AND IDEAS

1. Respond to this essay by listing as many other small items that you can think of that we spend as much time, money, and energy on as greeting cards.

2. What comment do the new-style cards (pars. 4–7) make on the current attitudes of society?

3. What characteristics of American society contribute to the popularity of greeting cards?

PURPOSE, AUDIENCE, AND STRATEGIES

1. Does the author seem to be aiming this essay at any particular type of reader? If so, what is her intended audience, and what features of the essay are designed to appeal to these readers?

2. How would you describe the tone of this essay? Are any readers likely to be offended by it? Explain. What does the tone add to the overall impact of the essay?

3. Which of the aspects of a topic generally covered in an informative report does this essay contain? Where in the essay does the author discuss each of these aspects? Can this essay be called an informative report? Support your answer by referring to the discussion of informative reports on pp. 376–377 and to the essay itself.

4. Where in the essay does the author use classification? Division? What other patterns does the author use?

5. Describe the strategy the author uses to begin this essay. (See Glossary: Introductions.)

LANGUAGE AND STYLE

1. The author makes use of dates and a variety of statistics throughout this essay. Do these details make the essay seem overly technical or formal? Why, or why not? What, if anything, do they contribute to the effectiveness of the essay? If you believe some of the dates or statistics could be eliminated without harming the essay, revise the passages containing them; and if you believe your version is superior to the original, indicate why.

2. What different things does Santa symbolize in paragraph 17? What other symbols are there in this paragraph, and what do they symbolize? (See Glossary: Symbol.)

3. If you do not know the meaning of either of the following words, look it up in the dictionary: *motifs* (par. 5); *Zeitgeist* (18).

WRITING ACTIVITIES

1. Prepare an informative report on a topic that interests you and that you believe will also interest most of your readers. Follow the general pattern for informative reports outlined on pp. 376–377. For subjects you may wish to turn to your hobbies, your work, or your reading. You may also need to do some research to provide all the different kinds of information usually covered in informative reports.

2. Things we often take for granted, like greeting cards, card games, high-heeled shoes, tuxedos, food processors, and typewriters may have interesting histories and surprising features. Prepare an essay in which you investigate some object or institution we depend on but pay little attention to. Use division, classification, and the strategies of the informative report (see pp. 376–377) to probe the subject and organize your essay.

3. In an essay explain why people send cards like those the author describes as *come-ons, put-downs,* and *zingers* (par. 20).

Writing Suggestions

EXPLORATIONS

1. Split into categories two topics you think most readers know very little about but might be curious about (types of Chinese or Filipino food, unusual sports, little-known marriage customs) or that they ought to know about (types of cancer, qualities that interviewers look for in hiring employees). For each topic explain briefly why readers might or should want to know about it. If either topic seems interesting, turn it into an essay.

2. A community is made up of various groups of people in a particular area. Describe the elements of a community in which you now live or have lived, and indicate some of the relationships between and among its various elements. (Hint: Companies and universities can be communities, too.) If the analysis interests you, turn it into an essay.

3. Choose two topics that might interest a variety of readers, and using the list of topics often covered in informative reports—significance, features, good/bad, procedures, applications—outline the information you would include in an essay on each topic. If one of the topics seems promising, turn the outline into an essay.

4. Choose an issue of current interest and outline the major arguments, minor arguments, and supporting evidence on each side of the controversy. Use the outline as the basis of an essay.

ACTIVITIES

1. For several days keep a notebook of observations on a topic you might use in a classification essay: kinds of college instructors, kinds of clothing, study or recreation habits of college students, behavior of clerks in stores or of gas station attendants, and so on. After you have accumulated extensive notes, divide the information you have gathered into categories and see how complete and detailed each category is. Use your notes as the basis for an essay.

2. Read a report of a recent controversy in a newsmagazine like *Time* or *Newsweek* and describe how the magazine analyzes the issue. Take special notice of any differences between its approach and the issue analysis patterns described in this chapter (p. 374–376), and try to explain the reasons, if any, for the differences.

3. Look at a magazine that provides informative articles on a variety of topics. See if any or all the articles cover the topics described in the discussion of informative reports in this chapter (see pp. 376–377). Select one or two articles that cover these topics and describe the order in which they are arranged and which, if any, are left out of the article.

4. Take notes on a television newsmagazine like *60 Minutes* or *20/20* to see how it divides an issue into parts in order to present it to viewers, or how it divides a topic into elements to make it easier to understand. Take notes on two of the show's segments, and use the notes to prepare an outline of the pattern of division employed in each of the segments.

MODELS

1. Using Susan Allen Toth's "Cinematypes" as a model, classify your friends or some other group of people according to their personalities and their activities or tastes. You might want to classify people according to the way their favorite sports or foods reflect their personalities or according to the connection between clothing or study habits and personality. Tastes in music, art, and reading can be interesting criteria, and you may want to consider classifying people from different professions—medicine, finance, and teaching, for example.

2. Borrowing strategies from Robert Brustein's "Reflections on Horror Movies," classify some other kind of movies or investigate categories of music, art, reading, or crafts. In your discussion of each category, specify what it reveals about our attitudes as a society.

3. Using Malcolm Cowley's method of division and classification in "Vices and Pleasures: The View from 80," examine and explain some other age (teens, 20s, 30s, 40s, and so on), or some other segment of life (student years, parenthood, summer vacation), giving attention to its vices, pleasures, achievements, or other distinguishing features.

4. Following Janice Hopkins Tanne's lead in "The Great Salt Debate," analyze a contemporary debate that you think your readers would benefit from examining in detail. You may want to evaluate controversies over nutrition (caffeine use; food additives); medicine (the dangers vs. the benefits of aspirin or some other drug); education (the benefits of educational enrichment before age three; mainstreaming handicapped and retarded students); or economics (free trade vs. tariff barriers to protect important industries).

5. Borrowing some ideas from Bernice Kanner, report on some other special feature of American culture (camping, motorcycling, playing frisbee) or some other product that reflects our attitudes (candy, fast food, souvenirs).

10

❧ ARGUMENT AND PERSUASION

Convincing an Audience

WHAT ARGUMENT DOES

Most writing is in some sense argumentative or persuasive. The author of a personal narrative encourages readers to accept his or her perspective on experience by re-creating events as vividly and persuasively as possible. The writer of a set of directions makes the process as interesting and clear as possible in order to get readers to try it. The student submitting a comparison-contrast paper in a college class and the professional writer preparing a cause-effect article or an informative report for a magazine want readers not only to accept as true the information presented in the essays but also to agree with their explanations or interpretations of the topic.

In some pieces of writing, however, to convince or persuade is not simply one of several aims but the dominant aim. Barbara Huttman's narrative "A Crime of Compassion" (Chapter 2), for example, is arranged primarily to support her opinion that physicians' standing orders calling for dying patients to be resuscitated are wrong. Donna Woolfolk Cross's "Sin, Suffer, and Repent" (Chapter 4) consists almost entirely of examples from soap operas, examples designed to prove her contention that soap operas are harmful because of the distorted view of reality they present. And Sissela Bok in "Placebos" (a cause-effect essay) (Chapter 7) explores the consequences of ill-advised or careless use of sugar pills and other so-called nonactive medicines to develop her thesis that placebos are a

419

420   ARGUMENT AND PERSUASION

form of lying whose use must be carefully controlled because of the
harm they can cause.

These essays and others like them can be viewed as arguments
because their purpose is to convince readers to agree with an assertion, either a statement or belief or a proposed course of action. This
assertion (often called a proposition) is generally expressed in a
thesis statement designed to direct readers' attention to the point of
argument.

Argumentative propositions are generally of three types. They
may advance a value judgment ("The racial policies of the South
African government are cruel and abhorrent"). They may propose a
specific action ("Roadblocks should be established on Friday evenings to check for drunk drivers"). Or they may state an opinion
contrary to what most people believe ("Though many people still
regard a savings account as a good investment, it is actually a very
poor one").

An argumentative assertion, as opposed to an explanatory or
informative assertion, can be recognized by the writer's evident
awareness of the opposition. An essay on how to grow an avocado
or on the various kinds of horror films, for example, does not usually
assume that a reader may have an opposing view; in contrast, argument is based on the existence of two or more conflicting points
of view and is itself an attempt to resolve or at least modify disagreements. If an assertion (proposition) does not call for debate or
does not bring to mind a reasonable or widely held opposing point
of view, then it cannot be the basis for an argument. To say "Nuclear
war is a horror" is a value judgment, but since virtually no reasonable person would be willing to assert the opposite, "Nuclear war
is a blessing," the initial judgment is really undebatable. Yet the
assertion "Nuclear war must be avoided at all costs" is clearly debatable because many people are willing to admit the propriety of
defensive nuclear war, and some even are willing to argue that
nuclear war is preferable to living under hostile military, social, or
economic systems.

Thesis statements in informative and explanatory essays may
advance value judgments, propose actions, or present interpretations,
of course; but in most cases readers are willing to accept these
statements without argument as long as the writer provides reasonable support for his or her conclusions. Yet the more controversial

the thesis, and the more it conflicts with other interpretations and explanations, the closer an informative or expository piece comes to being an argument. (Essays like "Fried Chicken" [Chapter 6] and "The Androgynous Man" [Chapter 8], for example, are explanations, although at times they come close to argument.)

Occasionally, argument is a form of writing, a pattern of development and expression as well as an aim. Argument as a pattern consists of a debatable proposition accompanied by a variety of supporting evidence and arguments, arranged in an order whose chief purpose is to secure agreement with the author's assertion. Arguments can be organized to follow logical strategies like deduction and induction as well as strategies based on appeals to emotion and imagination (see pp. 422–427).

Many essays that are argumentative in aim follow a dominant pattern of development, such as comparison, cause-effect, or definition, although they may make use of other patterns (as do "Why Don't We Complain?" in Chapter 4 [Example] and "The Contrived Postures of Femininity" in Chapter 8 [Definition].) In contrast, essays using argument as a pattern often deliberately mix strategies, making variety of support a key element of persuasion. An argument in favor of nuclear power, for example, might contain a paragraph of process analysis demonstrating the safety of nuclear power plants, then a paragraph of examples showing the damage done by pollution from other means of generating power—all arranged in an order of increasing emotional impact. And it might end with a narrative and descriptive paragraph showing what the world will be like in the future if the excessive use of fossil fuels to generate power continues, creating acid rain and, perhaps, the greenhouse effect. The essays in this chapter illustrate some of the range of argument as a form, from selections that mix many strategies of development to those that rely on only a few.

A distinction is often drawn between *argument,* meaning the use of logic and reason to gain agreement with a proposition, and *persuasion,* involving appeals to an audience's emotions, values, and prejudices to get them to endorse or undertake an action. In practice, however, successful arguments call on both reason and emotion since human judgment is compounded from both qualities. A newspaper editorial against locating a new shopping center near an established residential neighborhood might well appeal to reason by pointing to a relatively small increase in tax revenue and a large increase in the cost of producing public services, such as sewers and road maintenance. It might at the same time seek to move residents to action by appealing to their fear that the cohesiveness of their community will be disrupted and the well-being of their children endangered by the greatly increased traffic on formerly quiet residential streets. Many writers have thus begun to use the term *argument* to refer to both logical argument and persuasion or have begun to use the terms interchangeably.

Despite extensive research by scholars, it is still not entirely clear what causes readers to be persuaded by some arguments and to reject others. In part the reason may lie in the fit between a reader's beliefs and attitudes and those advanced by the writer. It is nonetheless true that most successful arguments use several different approaches to convince readers.

Chief among these approaches is the use of *logical strategies,* kinds of statements and evidence that appeal to an audience's reason and common sense. Here are some widely used logical strategies:

Consequences ("The amount of water that will be saved through this new method of irrigation and the drastically lower maintenance costs more than justify the higher start-up expenses." "If we continue to elect mayors without financial experience, our city will be bankrupt in a few years.")

Comparisons ("If the bottle bill worked in Michigan, it will work here." "Other attempts to reduce crime by increasing police protection have been only marginally successful, and there is no reason to believe the policy will work this time.")

Authority and testimony ("George Simes, an expert on health care systems in the United States, says that without a cost-containment program, medical bills are likely to grow by 300 percent over the next decade." "People who have followed this unusual combination of diet and exercise for three months report that it has helped them lose weight and aided their self-esteem.")

Examples and statistics ("The efficient operation of People Express Airlines provides further support for the policy of employee ownership of companies." "Our company's cost-cutting policy has resulted in layoffs for 30 percent of the blue-collar workers but only 2 percent of management.")

The most important logical strategies, however, are chains of reasoning, using induction and deduction. *Induction* consists of a generalization (conclusion) made on the basis of observation and evidence. While induction follows no set pattern, the process often begins with a question to be answered or a problem to be solved, moves to a collecting of evidence, and ends with a conclusion, also known as an *inference*, that is based on the evidence. Suppose, for example, the tomatoes in your garden this year are especially big and plentiful. You wonder why this is the case because you would like next year's crop to be just as successful, and you have a tentative answer (a hypothesis) in mind: the fertilizer you used this year was particularly effective. You then write down the following observations:

1. This year I planted Jones's Super Crop tomatoes and used Big Grow fertilizer; the weather was good.
2. Last year—Jones's Super Crop, store brand fertilizer, good weather. The tomato crop was average.
3. Two years ago—Hilton's Big Red Tomatoes, Big Grow fertilizer, good weather. The tomatoes were big and plentiful.
4. Three years ago—Hilton's Big Red, Big Grow fertilizer, lots of rain, which washed away the fertilizer. The tomato crop was average.

After considering the evidence, you conclude that as long as the weather is good, Big Grow fertilizer will lead to good tomatoes no matter what brand of plants you use.

Most uses of induction are more complicated than this, of course, and they call for much more detailed evidence and for consideration of alternative explanations. The movement from evidence to conclusion (known as the *inductive leap*) needs to be based on enough observations or instances so it is likely that the conclusion will apply to all other instances of the problem or situation as well. Generalizations made on the basis of inadequate, incomplete, or incorrect evidence are known as *hasty generalizations;* for the most part, the more complete the evidence and the consideration of alternative explanations, the stronger the conclusion.

When it is used in an essay as a strategy for argument, induction follows the same movement from statement of problem or issue, through consideration of evidence, to presentation of a conclusion. A writer might begin, for example, by describing a problem faced by many states and counties: whether to house mentally retarded adults in large institutions or to move them into group homes in the community. He might then offer the example of four moderately retarded adults living in group homes and show that despite some problems, they have adjusted well to life in the community. On the basis of this evidence, he could present the conclusion that for moderately retarded adults, at least, group homes provide a good solution to the problem.

Deduction, on the other hand, takes a conclusion or generally accepted principle and brings it to bear upon a new situation in order to draw a conclusion about the situation. Behind a deductive chain of reasoning lies a formal pattern called a *syllogism,* consisting of a generalization known as the "major premise," a specific statement about part of the major premise known as the "minor premise," and a conclusion derived from the relationship of the two premises:

> *Major Premise:* Searches without warrants are unconstitutional.
> *Minor Premise:* Police roadblocks to screen for drunk drivers are searches without warrants.
> *Conclusion:* Police roadblocks to screen for drunk drivers are unconstitutional.

Note that if a syllogism follows this pattern of reasoning and if both premises are true, then the conclusion must be true also. When the reasoning process is defective, however, then the syllogism is said to be invalid and the conclusion incorrect, as in this case:

> *Major Premise:* Searches without warrants are unconstitutional.
> *Minor Premise:* The police are using roadblocks to screen for drunk drivers.
> *Conclusion:* Police roadblocks that screen for drunk drivers are unconstitutional.

The problem here is that because the minor premise does not state that the roadblocks can be considered searches without warrants, we cannot conclude with any certainty that they are unconstitutional. Yet even when the reasoning in a syllogism is valid, the conclusion will be false if one of the premises is false. If the minor premise states that the roadblocks are searches without warrants yet the motor vehicle code states that licensed drivers must agree to random checks for intoxication, then the minor premise is clearly false: the warrant for a search is implied in the acceptance of a driver's license. The roadblocks, then, are constitutional.

In written form, induction seldom follows the neat order of a syllogism. Writers often choose to rearrange the premises or to imply one of the elements rather than stating it directly. In an essay, for example, you might inform (or remind) readers that federal law calls for the education of mentally retarded and handicapped children "in the least restrictive environment" and on the basis of this principle argue that the children should be placed in regular classrooms, sports programs, and extracurricular activities. In making your argument, you might feel that the second part of the syllogism will be obvious to your readers, and therefore decide to mention it only indirectly:

Major Premise: Federal law requires that mentally retarded and handicapped children be educated "in the least restrictive environment."

Minor Premise: Regular classrooms, sports programs, and extracurricular programs provide the least restrictive environment for education.

Conclusion: Mentally retarded and handicapped children should be educated in regular classrooms, sports programs, and extracurricular activities.

In using logical strategies, particularly induction and deduction, you should pay special attention to your reasoning and take care to avoid errors like the logical fallacies described on pp. 431–432.

Another approach to argument is through the use of *emotional strategies,* which draw on the values, attitudes, and emotions that play an important part in our lives and often a crucial role in making decisions. Emotional strategies are frequently directed to readers' values: to their moral outlook ("The proposed highway will destroy the homes and apartments of those people least able to defend their own interests, the old and the poor"); to their religious values ("Aid for the starving people of Africa is a reflection of our Judeo-Christian commitment to help the less fortunate"); or to other sets of attitudes ("In allowing the lake created by the dam to flood these three towns, we will be destroying a small but valuable example of early nineteenth-century American culture").

Response to language can also be the basis for emotional appeals. The connotations of words (*withered, cool, hot, gay, liberal, conservative, rotten, unstable*) can shape readers' reactions as can figures of speech (simile, metaphor, allusion—see Glossary: Figures of Speech) and descriptive detail: "Unless we act soon, the throngs of starving children with distended bellies, collapsed cheeks, reedlike arms, and starving eyes will double and triple again in size as the famine spreads."

Appeals to values and emotion certainly have an important place in argument; yet they can be misused, too, as in ads suggesting that family and personal happiness depend on the purchase of a refrigerator, a car, or a bed that turns into a chair.

Another important persuasive strategy is the *ethical appeal,* which refers to the impression a writer makes on readers. Writers who appear trustworthy, fair, and careful are more likely to have their arguments accepted than those who sound careless, excessively opinionated, and devious. How does a writer convey the first set of impressions rather than the second? By adopting a moderate, reasonable tone; by presenting facts, figures, quotations, and other evidence accurately; and by acknowledging and refuting opposing arguments fairly and without hostility.

Imaginative strategies seldom receive much attention in discussions of argument, but they can play important roles. Imaginative strategies ask readers to adopt a fresh perspective towards the issues in question, to consider, for a moment or two, "what if." The writer hopes this new perspective will encourage readers to respond sympathetically to logical and emotional appeals. The chief devices for imaginative strategies are figurative language, analogy, and narrative. By describing the Detroit automobile industry figuratively, that is, metaphorically, as "the engine that drives our country's economic prosperity," a writer hopes to get a positive reception for his arguments for government policies aiding the industry. In a well-known analogy, Anne and Paul Ehrlich compare government and industry leaders who pay attention to growth but not the environment to people spending their time popping the rivets out of an airplane on which we all have to fly. This analogy encourages readers to view economic growth in a less positive light than they would normally. Likewise, a narrative told from the perspective of a skid-row homeless person might be an effective way to gain sympathy for people most readers would probably prefer to ignore, and could set the stage for an argument in favor of community houses to provide food and shelter for indigents.

All four strategies—logical, emotional, ethical, and imaginative—have a place in argument, as this paragraph demonstrates:

> Four and a half billion years ago, the earth was formed. Perhaps a half billion years after that, life arose on the planet. For the next four billion years, life became steadily more complex, more varied, and more ingenious, until, around a million years ago, it produced mankind—the most complex and ingenious species of them all. Only six or seven thousand years ago—a period that is to the history of the earth as less than a minute is to a year—civilization emerged, enabling us to build up a human world, and to add to the marvels of evolution marvels of our own: marvels of art, of science, of social organization, of spiritual attainment. But, as we built higher and higher, the evolutionary foundation beneath our feet became more and more shaky, and now, in spite of all we have learned and achieved—or, rather, because of it—we hold this entire terrestrial creation hostage to nuclear destruction, threatening to hurl it back into the inanimate darkness from which it came. And this threat of self-destruction and planetary destruction is not something that we will pose one day in the future, if we fail to take certain precautions; it is here now, hanging over the heads of all of us at every moment. The machinery of destruction is complete, poised on a hair trigger, waiting for the "button" to be "pushed" by some misguided or deranged human being or for some faulty computer chip to send out the instruction to fire (Jonathan Schell, *The Fate of the Earth*, 1982).

THE PROCESS

An argumentative essay calls for many of the same writing skills that other essays do, but it also calls for some special approaches that are the subject of this section: deciding on an assertion, analyzing the audience, selecting evidence, checking the logic. Some ways of organizing argument essays, along with a sample student essay, are discussed in the next section, "The Pattern In Action."

Deciding on an Assertion   Strong feelings about an issue are a good starting point for an argumentative essay because they give you a reason for writing and will constantly remind you of the essay's purpose: to get readers to accept your opinion or the course of action you propose. If you are writing your essay as a direct response to a situation, perhaps as an editorial for a campus newspaper protesting recent actions of the police, then your feelings have already given direction to your work, and you simply need to be careful not to let them overwhelm your ability to speak reasonably with readers who look at that matter in a different light.

If, however, you have been assigned an argumentative essay for a class, you can use feelings as a guide. Look for something that troubles you (lack of security in campus housing, lack of computer training in high schools, the amount of money the government spends on military or domestic programs), or for something you oppose or support (school prayer, bilingual education, new drop/add procedures for courses). Consider a change in policy you think would be worthwhile (a bottle bill, changes in hunting or fishing regulations, new parking policies, revisions of traffic laws).

Once you have selected a topic and recognized your attitude towards it, you should begin developing an assertion around which to build your essay. The assertion should be specific enough to guide your research and planning and perhaps even to use as a thesis statement in your finished essay. If your assertion is too broad and vague, it will probably be hard to defend in specific terms ("Solar power is an excellent idea"—Will you argue for the use of solar power for heating homes or offices? For generating power? For running small appliances? For passive solar heating? For solar power cells?). If it is too bland, it will fail to interest readers ("We need to pay more attention to the amount of junk food in our diets"). If your assertion is a statement of fact ("Imports have taken over a significant proportion of the American car market"), it will not call for defense at all.

You may find that the best way to arrive at a specific, arguable assertion is to divide your topic into parts and limit yourself to talking about only one part, even though you are interested in more than one. If your essay is to be short, under five pages in length, you probably will be unable to cover effectively more than one aspect of a broad topic. Under the topic *gun control*, for example, you should probably select only one of these parts:

    gun registration
    handgun bans
    education vs. regulation
    Saturday night specials
    laws against using guns to commit a crime
    banning of hollow-tipped bullets

Longer essays, too (those of from five to twenty pages), are generally most effective when the issue being argued is divided into parts. The temptation to tackle all parts of a broad topic is one you should resist; after all, if you can convince your audience to agree with you about the registration of handguns, they may also begin to change their minds about related issues. If you try to get readers to agree with a sweeping assertion, you may simply stiffen their resistance to your arguments.

Analyzing the Audience   Since the primary purpose of an argument is to get readers to agree with an assertion, your choice of evidence, arrangement, emphasis, and style for an argumentative essay should take into account the assumptions and attitudes your readers will bring with them. While you cannot possibly know exactly what your readers will be thinking, you can anticipate some general responses.

If you are writing to an audience of people whose attitudes are familiar to you (classmates, fellow workers, people who live in your community), you can probably anticipate their attitudes and their possible objections to your assertion. If you are writing to a more general audience whose characteristics you know little about, you can still anticipate several different groups among the members of your audience and choose strategies to answer their concerns:

1. People who already agree with you or are inclined to agree with you and are looking for a clear statement of arguments and evidence to confirm their outlook.
2. People who know little about the issue and its importance or who have not yet made up their minds and would like a detailed discussion of the issue, the arguments, and the evidence.
3. People who are inclined to disagree with you but who might be persuaded to change their minds by an essay that provides plentiful, carefully developed evidence and that answers their objections.

If you think one of these groups is likely to predominate in your audience, you can choose strategies accordingly, perhaps spending some time dealing with possible objections to your proposition, placing emphasis on the importance of the issue and the need to take a stand, or choosing emotional language that will confirm your readers' beliefs and move them to action.

Selecting Evidence   Some assertions can be effectively supported through evidence from personal experience. If you are arguing that the quality of care in a local hospital is poor, then your experiences and those of other former patients that you interview would certainly be relevant. Personal experience and data gathered from reading would be a good mixture if you plan to argue in favor of a new and unusual-sounding diet for losing weight or for a way to improve the quality of your town's schools. Arguments proposing new patent regulations governing high-technology products or taking a stand on the continuation of affirmative action hiring in business and government would have to rely almost entirely on information, expert testimony, and statistics you collect through your research on a topic.

The logical, emotional, and imaginative strategies for argument (pp. 422–427) can also be turned into questions to help you discover supporting evidence. The actual questions you use will depend on your assertion, audience, and specific purpose, of course, but here are some examples:

> What are some good or bad consequences of this policy?
> What do the experts say about solutions to the problem?
> What religious or moral values support my position on this issue?
> Are there any analogies that might help readers understand my
>   perspective?

Opposing arguments can actually be a form of support if you acknowledge and refute them effectively (see Glossary: Refutation). Indeed, if you do not acknowledge an opposing attitude,· your reader—who may hold this view—will find your essay unconvincing. Your reading and your analysis of the audience for your essay should help you select the major arguments against your point of view. By acknowledging the opposition in your essay, you get a chance to point out its weaknesses in contrast with the strength of your position, and if your refutation is fair and moderate in tone, you may add to the willingness of readers to trust and accept what you have to say elsewhere in the essay.

Checking the Logic   As you write or revise an argumentative essay, check to see that the evidence on which your conclusions are based is accurate and complete and that your reasoning is sound.

If the facts, examples, and statistics you cite are inaccurate or incomplete, the conclusions you base on them will be questionable. Make a special effort, then, to report the evidence just as it appears in your sources. If you base your conclusion on very little evidence, it may be premature, and you should think about doing further research to see whether other evidence supports your point of view. Finally, if you cite only that evidence that supports your proposition and fail to acknowledge evidence that contradicts it, you open yourself to charges of dishonesty.

Although it is seldom possible to arrive at absolute proof in argument—the issues of value and action that most arguments address are not subject to mathematical certainty—it is possible with care to avoid errors in reasoning like the following *logical fallacies.*

> *Post hoc ergo propter hoc* ("After this therefore because of this"). If one thing happens after another, the first event did not necessarily cause the second. In arguing without detailed evidence that a drop in traffic fatalities is the result of new drunk-driving laws, you may well be falling into this error unless you can show that other possible explanations (lowered speed limits, a seat-belt campaign, severe weather) are not responsible for the decrease.
>
> *Begging the question.* When a writer assumes the truth of something that still needs to be proven, he is "begging the question." To begin an essay by arguing that "The impractical and unfair law raising the drinking age in this state should be repealed" is to assume, without offering proof, that the law is neither practical nor fair.
>
> *Ignoring the question.* To ignore the question is to shift attention away from the issue to a loosely related or even unrelated matter: "This new proposal for government support of research in high-technology fields is suspect because it is being advanced by people who in the past have opposed government support for industry." (This argument draws

attention away from the quality of the present proposal.)
The *ad hominem* ("toward the person") argument is a
similar problem; it shifts to personal attack instead of
addressing the issue at hand.

THE PATTERN IN ACTION

Argument essays take many different forms, with the individual
arrangement often depending on the audience and the occasion.
Arguments designed to influence public policy, such as a proposal
for a new town swimming pool, an elementary school, a library
addition, or rerouting a major thoroughfare generally have to (1)
prove a need for the project, (2) show that it can be accomplished
in a reasonable time at a modest cost, and (3) demonstrate that it
will actually fulfill the needs it is supposed to meet. Handbooks of
business and technical writing describe the many kinds of argumentative writing used frequently in financial and industrial organizations and in technical fields. Entire textbooks and college courses
are often devoted to studying the forms and strategies of argument.

Despite the wide range of possible arrangements, the structure
of many argumentative essays remains relatively simple, a variation
on a basic pattern that is itself similar to the thesis-and-support essay
(see Chapter 4, pp. 124–126). In essays of this sort, the writer states
an assertion (proposition) and supports it with evidence and reasoning. The functions of each part of the pattern are as follows:

Introduction (including title): Describes the issue and indicates
        why it is timely or significant; indicates the writer's stand
        on the controversy or proposes a course of action, usually
        doing so in the form of a thesis statement to which the
        rest of the essay refers either directly or indirectly.

Body: Provides a variety of supporting evidence and reasoning;
        uses various patterns of development to present the evi-
        dence (including comparison, cause-effect, classification,
        narrative, and the other patterns discussed in this text);
        makes frequent direct or indirect references to the essay's
        thesis in order to demonstrate how the evidence and
        reasoning support it; acknowledges and refutes opposing
        points of view.

Conclusion: Sums up, restates, and reinforces the thesis and the evidence presented in the essay.

Within this framework a writer is free to choose various strategies for presenting supporting evidence, and the framework itself can be stretched and adapted in a variety of ways as long as the basic structure of assertion followed by support is maintained.

The following essay, written by a student but printed as an editorial in newspapers nationwide, illustrates how the pattern can be used in a short essay. As the discussion following the essay indicates, however, the strategies the writer uses are not the only ones or necessarily the best ones he could have chosen.

Electronic Encyclopedia Salesmen?

Howard Ullman

Many computer companies have spent considerable sums on advertisements that build parental computer guilt: the idea that children will fail in school and life if they don't have home computers. This is a clever and deceptive play to public fears and is nothing more than a high-tech version of encyclopedia sales.   1

In reality, most people in the future won't need to be computer-literate—in the sense of knowing computer languages and programming. Computer science will be taught as it is now, as an option.   2

The trend in computer science is toward simplification, with the goal of making computers as easy to use as calculators. People will need to know how to use computers, but not how computers work. Thus, computer manufacturers engage in a deliberate falsification in basing selling appeals on the premise that the job market of tomorrow will require programming skills.   3

While computers are not and probably never will be the educational wonders that their makers would like us to believe, they do make wonderful tools. They provide us with powerful abilities to calculate, write and sort and file faster and more efficiently. As we all know, computers will be used as tools in the job market and schools of tomorrow.   4

It is precisely in education, however, that we must look carefully at computers' limitations. There are three ways to use computers in school. The first is called computer-assisted instruction, in which the computer asks students questions, scores their responses and presents them explanatory text or graphics. This is useful in drills, a necessary but small part of learning.   5

What is lacking in computer-assisted instruction is imagination. Computers cannot examine students' thinking: how they approach a problem and think it through. Machines can only judge right and   6 wrong, true or false. This is precisely the approach that has turned off many students by making school a place to earn grades rather than a place of excitement, fun and learning.

The second educational use of computers is in teaching computer   7
languages, for which there is obviously no substitute for a computer. Proponents note that studying computer languages helps students to think logically—but so does study in the liberal arts. The rewards of studying the liberal arts are certainly richer than those of computer languages, although perhaps not in a monetary sense.

Computers can be used to extend students' abilities, especially in   8
research and writing. But what good is such a tool to students lacking basic math and reading skills? Giving a word processor to an elementary school student is in some ways like giving a first grader a calculator for his math problems. Students should master the central concept of a discipline before turning to computers. They should not use computers to attain that mastery.

Computers have a place in education as tools, but they are not a   9
form of social insurance against incompetence and woolly thinking. In the long run, the nation and computer manufacturers will profit most if students can be taught to think. There is no technological short-cut to that goal.

One way to understand and evaluate this argumentative essay (or any other kind of essay) is to examine each of its major parts: title, introduction, body, and conclusion.

Title   Most parents remember when encyclopedias were advertised in much the same way computers are today—as essential parts of a child's education, a claim that proved to be untrue. The title therefore raises an interesting question: Are computer salespeople making the same kinds of false claims encyclopedia sellers did? But if this essay were addressed to the author's classmates it would probably have little impact since few of them are likely to have had any experience with encyclopedia sellers.

Introduction   The opening paragraph sums up the issue briefly and states what appears to be a thesis: The sales tactics used for computers are a "clever and deceptive play to public fears." The focus of this statement is actually too broad for the essay, however. Beyond stating that the advertisements are wrong in linking success in school and life to home computers, Ullman argues that the claims made for the computers are intentionally false—a strong accusation and one for which no proof is offered in the essay. He repeats the assertion in paragraph 3, this time in the form of a conclusion, "Thus . . . ," but again without support.

The real thesis of the essay—the one it does support—is the assertion that "most people in the future won't need to be computer-literate" (par. 2).

Body The body of the essay supports the assertion that knowledge of computers will be unnecessary in getting and holding jobs (pars. 3–4) and in school (pars. 5–9). Ullman's point in discussing each of the three ways computers can be used in education is that these uses are quite limited and clearly do not demand computer literacy. He offers evidence to support this conclusion and refutes opposing arguments. But while the first two ways are clearly highlighted as first (par. 5) and second (par. 7), there is no corresponding numbering to indicate where the third begins. Moreover, the writer fails to remind readers in any clear way of the thesis these examples are supporting; nor are the examples arranged in ascending order of importance, building up to a conclusion restating the thesis.

Conclusion In the conclusion, Ullman restates the point of his thesis and reflects briefly on the implications of his argument.

"Electronic Encyclopedia Salesmen?" illustrates some of the ways the basic pattern can be adapted to the needs of a specific argument, but there are many others. All the patterns of development covered in this text can be used to provide support for a thesis, including example, narrative, comparison, definition, and cause-effect.

In addition, the supporting evidence in an essay can be arranged in a number of ways, three of which are ascending order, refutation-proof, and con-pro. *Ascending order* is the method that places the strongest, most emotionally powerful, or complex evidence at the end of an essay, where it will have the greatest effect. For instance, an argument in favor of banning smoking in offices might start by citing the discomfort that smoking creates for nonsmokers, then point out that the average number of sick days is greater in offices where smoking is permitted, and end by showing that life expectancy for nonsmokers is sharply reduced when they inhale smoke-filled air on a regular basis.

Refutation-proof is the strategy of presenting and refuting opposing arguments near the beginning of the essay, then going on to build a case for the author's point of view. An argument following this pattern might begin by acknowledging that smokers have a right to their habit as long as it does not harm others and then go on to argue that smoking in offices harms the peace of mind, efficiency, and physical health of smokers and nonsmokers alike.

Con-pro first presents then refutes opposing arguments one by one, continuing until all the positive evidence has been presented and all the opposing arguments have been refuted. This strategy can be especially effective when many opposing arguments must be dealt with. Following this pattern, a writer arguing against smoking in offices could take up and refute opposing arguments in this way:

1. Smokers have a right to enjoy their habits (opposing argument)—they do not, however, have the right to impose their habit on others in the same room (refutation).
2. Smokers will work more efficiently if they are allowed to smoke while working (opposing argument)—productivity as a whole drops when smoking is allowed because both smokers and non-smokers take more sick days (refutation).
3. Smokers harm only themselves (opposing argument)—non-smokers who breathe smoke-filled air on a regular basis are subject to the same serious physical ailments, including lung cancer and emphysema, as smokers (refutation).

The essays in this chapter illustrate other possible arrangements for argument. Ellen Goodman's "Honor Society Hypocrisy" has a two-part structure based on deduction and definition. Michal Kaufman's "Facing Violence" uses numerous examples and anecdotes, many of which are arranged in patterns of comparison and contrast. H. L. Mencken's "The Penalty of Death" sets out to reverse many of his readers' most cherished assumptions in an idiosyncratic argument for the death penalty as a form of revenge. Barbara Parker advances and defends an idea many readers are likely to find surprising: Censorship is alive and well in this country. Russell Baker uses narrative and other patterns of development to argue that the present criminal justice system is bogging down in trivial matters. And Edward Abbey combines comparison and problem-solution (cause-effect) to argue that projects designed to make the wilderness more accessible to the average citizen actually make it less accessible and even destroy it.

❧ ELLEN GOODMAN

For biographical information on Ellen Goodman, see p. 194.

Honor Society Hypocrisy

"Honor Society Hypocrisy" was published as a newspaper editorial soon after the events it recounts. Like most good arguments, it addresses a specific situation and at the same time touches on broader issues of concern to most readers.

If they ever give a college board test for students of hypocrisy, I am sure that the teenagers of Marion Center, Pa., will score way up in the 700s. Teenagers are always the great hypocrisy spotters in our culture. But in the past few months, they've had a lot of extra practice in this small rural town. 1

The central characters of the case that has put Marion Center on the sociological map include 17-year-old Arlene Pfeiffer, her five-month-old daughter, Jessica, the school board and the National Honor Society. 2

Arlene, a high school senior, was class president for three years, student council president last year and a member of the honor society since tenth grade. But in August, she gave birth to Jessica and decided to keep her. In November, Arlene was kicked out of the honor society by her high school. In January the school board agreed to her removal. Now Arlene is taking her case to the Human Relations Commission and the Equal Employment Opportunity Commission. 3

What is at issue is not her grades—they have remained high—but two other qualities the honor society demands: "leadership and character." The question is whether an unwed mother had lost her "character," whether she would "lead" others in the wrong direction. 4

It is easy to follow the trail of hypocrisy in this move against Arlene, easy as a multiple choice questionnaire. To begin with, the school didn't strip Arlene of her honor society epaulets because she had sex but because she "got caught." About 37 percent of 16-year-old teenagers in this country have had intercourse. Arlene was judged to have less character than those who didn't get pregnant. 5

Then too, if Arlene had not had her baby, she would surely have   6
kept her membership. A little less than half of the teen pregnancies
end in abortion. So she was judged to have less character than a
girl who chose abortion.

Perhaps it would even have been alright if Arlene had given her   7
baby up for adoption. Of if she had married. No one, for that matter,
had ever questioned the character of an unwed teenage father.

Indeed, it is difficult to identify exactly what part of Arlene's   8
behavior—sex, pregnancy, motherhood, singleness, none of the
above—the school wants to punish. This speaks to the confusion of
the adults in this situation.

It may well be that these adults—teachers and board members—   9
are suffering from simple hypocrisy. Surely the teenagers in town see
it that way. But there may also be a more deeply rooted ambivalence
that centers around the word "leadership."

A generation ago, unwed pregnancy produced a shotgun mar-   10
riage, an illegal abortion, or a six-month stay out of town. A decade
ago, a pregnant teenager could be barred altogether from school.

Now those of us who shepherd kids through the high-risk years   11
know that early parenthood is still the surest, most direct route to a
diminished future. But we are told that some of the young mothers
who have kept their babies were inspired by fairy tales of Hollywood
love-children. Many of us now share an underlying anxiety that if
we make unwed motherhood appear acceptable, we may make it
more possible, and then more likely. If we pin a medal on Arlene
Pfeiffer, does she become a role model?

"They said," recalls Arlene Pfeiffer, "that by 'leadership' I might   12
lead others to do it—to get pregnant. But I don't go around saying
'stand in line and get pregnant.'" Nor do girls follow the leader into
pregnancy.

For all our anxiety, we have no evidence to prove that lifting a   13
sanction produces a bumper crop of babies. On the contrary, we
know that teenagers don't get pregnant because they want to. Study
after study after study has concluded that they simply take chances.

The saga of Arlene Pfeiffer, who mothers by night and gathers   14
honor grades by day, who lives at home with parental support and
child care, is an exception. If we are afraid of lauding her success,
it is largely because of our own failures. We've done a poor job of
discouraging early sexual activity. A poor job at getting teenagers to

take more responsibility. A poor job at communicating the real handicaps of early childbearing.

As for Arlene, she is pursuing fairness through all the flak of   15 hypocrisy and ambivalence in Marion Center, Pa. I think she's giving the adults a lesson in "character" and "leadership."

COMMENTARY

The subject of Goodman's argument is an emotional one, and her charge of hypocrisy is also designed to evoke a strong emotional reaction against the people who removed Arlene Pfeiffer from the honor society. Yet the substance of this argument and its arrangement are decidedly logical. She clearly wants to make her readers feel angry—even indignant—about the events in Marion Center, yet Goodman wishes to do so only through a demonstration that makes use of the logical strategies of definition, deduction, and expert testimony.

In paragraphs 1–3, the author summarizes the controversy and asserts her belief that the actions of the National Honor Society and the school board were hypocritical. In paragraph 4, she introduces the claim of the honor society that Pfeiffer was correctly barred from the society because she failed to demonstrate "leadership and character." This argument is a form of deduction based on definition: Since Pfeiffer's behavior does not fit the definition of behavior appropriate to the honor society, she cannot be a member of it. In the rest of the essay, Goodman sets out to show that since this position is clearly illogical, the only way the honor society could have banned Pfeiffer is by ignoring the logic of its position—in short, by hypocrisy.

In paragraphs 5–8, Goodman addresses the question of *character* by pointing out the contradictions in reasoning involved in the judgment that Arlene Pfeiffer has lost her character. The kind of tight, witty reasoning the author displays in these paragraphs is a pleasure to observe. In addition, it encourages readers to examine their own all-too-easy moral assumptions.

In paragraphs 9–12, Goodman turns to the question of *leadership*. Her path here is a little less clear than in the preceding section since she attempts to prove not that Pfeiffer displayed the good leadership qualities required of honor society members but simply that she did not provide bad leadership. Goodman does, however, manage to demonstrate through testimony from Pfeiffer and from studies of teenage pregnancy (pars. 12, 13) that Pfeiffer took no active role in promoting pregnancy and that her pregnancy itself cannot be regarded as a form of leadership.

Goodman's argument is a good one, but it is not airtight—no argument ever is. Perhaps the chief limitation is the lack of a refutation, of a chance to examine at length the arguments that can be made in favor of the expulsion. It would be interesting, too, to know how people in Marion Center would respond to what Goodman says.

RESPONSES AND IDEAS

1. Respond to this essay by describing a situation in which you or some person or group of people you know judged a person's character in the same way Arlene Pfeiffer's character was judged.

2. Explore the implications of this comment: "No one, for that matter, had ever questioned the character of an unwed teenage father" (par. 7). Does this comment detract from the unity of the essay, or is it related directly to her argument? Explain. What does the comment add to the essay? (See Glossary: Unity.)

3. What are the "fairy tales of Hollywood love-children" to which Goodman refers (par. 11), and why would they inspire unwed teenage mothers to keep their babies?

PURPOSE, AUDIENCE, AND STRATEGIES

1. What attitudes towards teenage pregnancy does Goodman assume her readers have? What evidence of her assumption is there in the essay?

2. Why would Goodman bother to talk in her nationally syndicated newspaper column about the expulsion of a student from a high school honor society? What larger purpose might she have in mind than defending Arlene Pfeiffer?

3. What groups of readers are likely to be offended by Goodman's argument? Does she take any steps to avoid offending them?

4. Describe the strategy Goodman uses to close this essay. Is it effective? (See Glossary: Closings.)

5. How do the transitions between paragraphs in this essay help clarify the stages in the argument? (See Glossary: Transitions.)

LANGUAGE AND STYLE

1. Name several places in this essay where Goodman relies on connotations of important words to reinforce her argument.

2. Describe how Goodman uses repetition and sentence structure to provide emphasis and emotional impact in paragraph 14. To what extent is the effectiveness of this paragraph dependent also on its diction? (See Glossary: Style, Emphasis, Diction.) To what extent is the emotional impact of the points she makes in paragraph 14 justified by the evidence presented earlier in the essay?

3. If you do not know the meaning of any of the following words, look them up in the dictionary: *hypocrisy* (par. 1); *sociological* (2); *epaulets* (5); *ambivalence* (9); *lauding* (14).

WRITING ACTIVITIES

1. Write the strongest refutation you can of Goodman's argument. You need not in fact disagree with Goodman, but try to present the best possible opposing case.

2. Most people would agree that government officials and similar public figures should follow a higher standard of behavior than the average citizen. For instance, we expect our elected representatives to avoid both obvious conflict of interest and the appearance of impropriety in their business dealings. Yet some people argue that our expectations may be unrealistically high. Choose a public figure whose business or social dealings have been in the news and argue whether his or her actions were proper or whether media treatment of the person was fair, excessive, or even slanted.

❧ MICHAEL T. KAUFMAN

Michael T. Kaufman was born in Paris in 1938 and grew up in the United States. He attended the Bronx High School of Science in New York City and studied at the City College of New York and Columbia University. He has worked as a reporter and feature writer for the *New York Times* and has served as *Times* bureau chief in Ottawa and, currently, Warsaw. He has received many awards for his work as a feature writer and is the author of a children's book, *Roof Tops and Alleys* (1974) and a collection of feature articles, *In Their Own Good Time* (1973).

Facing Violence

"Facing Violence" was first published in the *New York Times Magazine.* In it Kaufman takes a fresh approach to the question of making children aware of the violence that permeates the world, but his focus is not limited to children and violence. He looks at the complicated relationship between violence on television and our attitudes towards death and dying.

Almost 20 years ago, when my oldest son was very young, I tried to shield the boy from violence and aggression, these alleged attributes of manliness. My wife and I had agreed to raise our children in an atmosphere of nonviolence, without playthings that simulated weapons. Then my uncle came to visit us from Israel. My uncle, unlike his wife and children, had survived Auschwitz, and he was surprised that my son had no toy guns. I tried to explain, but, asserting the moral authority of a war victim and survivor, he took my son off to Macy's to buy the biggest, noisiest toy machine gun he could find. My uncle said that if people do not go bang bang when they are young they go bang bang when they grow up.

Since then, we have lived in Africa and in Asia and I have seen and heard bang bang. I am not sure I fully understand what my uncle meant, but I no longer think that exposure to the symbols of death and violence causes little boys to grow up ethically impaired. In fact, now that I am living in North American civilization, where enormous energies are spent rendering death and violence either fictional or abstract, I think the greatest moral pitfall is not that we witness too much bang bang, but that, for the most part, we perceive it vicariously. We shield ourselves from real death and pain while paying to see these same things, sanitized and stylized, in the movies.

This idea crystallized in my mind after a conversation I had a short while ago with Jack Troake, a thoughtful man who, like his father, grandfather and great-grandfather, makes his living by fishing from his home port of Twillingate, Newfoundland. Like his ancestors and neighbors, he also used to spend the icebound winter months hunting gray skin seals, but he does so no longer. The market for seal pelts in Europe and the United States has been destroyed because of protests launched abroad by animal-rights groups. The original protests were against the clubbing of baby white-furred seal pups, a hunt that Jack Troake never joined. Then the outcry spread to include all seals. Last year, a British supermarket chain declared it would no longer stock Canadian fish because of someone's belief that some fishermen either now hunt seals or once did.

As we sat on Mr. Troake's radar-equipped boat watching his sons mend nets, he made it clear that he was flabbergasted and insulted by what he assumed to be the view of some foreigners that he and his neighbors were barbarians. "Look old boy, there's no doubt about it, I make my living killing things. We kill mackerel and cod and we used to kill seals. Now, there seems to be a bunch of people who do not like that. I imagine them sitting eating lamb chops and steak and chicken, thinking they all come neatly wrapped in plastic from some food factory. I wonder whether they have ever seen anything die or anything born, except on television and in the movies. But, to tell you the truth, old boy, I really feel sorry for those people who are so upset about this old Christian."

Me too. I left Twillingate, and in a motel that night I watched the footage from Beirut. As I remember now, it contained what have become the current visual clichés of violence. Men firing bazookas around a corner at something. Smoke and rubble. Women with shopping bags walking fast across a street. Adolescent gunmen smiling into the camera from the backs of trucks. It conveyed a sense of destruction, but it stopped short of being horrible. I knew the images were authentic, but they did not seem real. They blurred into an already crowded memory bank of two-dimensional violence: Dirty Harry, the A Team, Beirut, Belfast, El Salvador, car crashes. And I thought how I, bombarded with such pictures of death, had, two years ago, backed away from the real drama of death when it touched me as something more than a witness. I had sent my own mother to die in a nursing home, among death specialists. I did not hold her as her life ebbed. Later, I consoled myself with the thought that this is what people do in a technological culture, and that, anyway, the room was clean and the doctors said she did not suffer greatly.

I recall how we used to hear that the images of the Vietnam   6
War, shown on television, sensitized the nation. Perhaps. I can recall the naked little girl running from napalm, and the man being shot by a police official in Saigon. But everything else has been jumbled in memory, and what remains are mostly recollections of what I now think of as my skin-deep shock and my pious responses. There were too many images. The only people I hear talking about Vietnam now are the ones who were there.

What I do remember is the first dead man I ever saw, a man   7
shot and bleeding on dirty stairs in New York. I remember victims of massacres in Zaire and Rhodesia, and I can recall where each of those bodies lay. I remember an Afghan freedom fighter in a hospital in Peshawar, his leg lost in a land-mine explosion. He had his rifle with him, and his 7-year-old son was on his bed touching the man's stump. The father was talking about returning to fight Soviet forces; he hoped that his son would continue the fight. For that small boy, perhaps, the moment was indeed too much bang bang, but I am no longer sure.

As for little boys playing with toy guns, I don't think it matters   8
much, one way or the other. What does matter, it seems to me, is that at some time in their formative years, maybe in high school, our children should bear witness to the everyday violence they could see, say, in an emergency ward of a big city hospital. I know it sounds extreme, but maybe our children could learn something valuable if they were taken for a day or two to visit a police station or an old-age home. It might serve as an antidote for the unreal violence on all our screens.

What would be learned, I think, is that, up close and in three   9
dimensions, the dead, the dying and the suffering are always to some extent "us." On the screens they always seem to be "them." I don't understand it, really, any more than my uncle's view of bang bang, but I know that as long as men die and men kill it is wrong to turn away too much. Also, I am certain that I would prefer to be judged

by the hunter Jack Troake than by anyone who would judge him harshly.

RESPONSES AND IDEAS

1. Respond to this essay by describing your response to violence on television news programs. Does the violence on television seem real to you? Has it made you accept violence more readily?

2. Where is the thesis sentence in this essay? Is the thesis stated in more than one place and in more than one way? If so, where is it communicated to readers? (See Glossary: Thesis.)

3. Explain why Kaufman says in the last sentence that he "would prefer to be judged by the hunter Jack Troake" (par. 9).

PURPOSE, AUDIENCE, AND STRATEGIES

1. Are the strategies of argument in this essay primarily logical or primarily emotional? Support your response with direct reference to the essay. Identify the major strategies. For the emotional strategies, state the basis of their effect on the audience.

2. In paragraph 8 Kaufman proposes a solution. Is this solution consistent with the essay's thesis, or does it disrupt the unity of the essay? Is there enough evidence in the essay to support the proposed solution? (See Glossary: Unity.)

3. Is paragraph 6 clearly related to the rest of the essay? Would the essay be harmed in any way if it were dropped? Explain.

4. Why is the anecdote with which Kaufman opens the essay surprising? How is it related to the essay's thesis?

5. What pattern of development does the author use in paragraphs 3–4 to support his argument? In paragraph 5?

LANGUAGE AND STYLE

1. Identify the allusions in paragraph 5. What images do they bring to mind, and are these images effective in furthering the purpose of the essay? (See Glossary: Figures of Speech.)

2. The phrase "bang bang" brings to mind, among other things, children's play acting with toy guns. What other connotations, if any, does it have? (See Glossary: Connotation.) What meanings does it have in paragraphs 1, 2, and 9? Is the author's use of the phrase in these paragraphs effective? In what ways? Does it add a silly, childish tone to the essay? Why, or why not? Why do you think Kaufman avoided using the term in paragraphs 5–7?

WRITING ACTIVITIES

1. State and defend your opinion about the extent to which what we see on television, in movies, or read about in books affects our actions and values.

2. If you believe that acts of violence and other negative examples on television or in books need to be limited because of their impact on young children and on some adults as well, propose and defend in an essay whatever form of censorship you think appropriate. Before you write your essay, however, read Barbara Parker's "Am r ca s D l g nt C ns rs," pp. 452–454.

H. L. MENCKEN

H. L. Mencken (1880–1956) was born in Baltimore, Maryland, where he worked for many years as a reporter, columnist, and editor. In the 1920s he edited the magazine *American Mercury* and built a reputation as a writer, a reputation based on his caustic, witty style as well as his attacks on hypocrisy and pomposity in American society.

Mencken's newspaper pieces and his essays have been reprinted in numerous collections. He is also well known for three volumes of autobiography, *Happy Days* (1940), *Newspaper Days* (1941), and *Heathen Days* (1943), and a study of lasting scholarly importance, *The American Language* (first published in 1919 and extensively revised several times before his death).

The Penalty of Death

Although this essay was first published in 1926, Mencken's biting wit and incisive arguments are still fresh and bracing. Even readers who disagree with him will probably find that his writing has made them re-examine their own values.

Of the arguments against capital punishment that issue from uplifters, two are commonly heard most often, to wit:

1. That hanging a man (or frying him or gassing him) is a dreadful business, degrading to those who have to do it and revolting to those who have to witness it.
2. That it is useless, for it does not deter others from the same crime.

The first of these arguments, it seems to me, is plainly too weak to need serious refutation. All it says, in brief, is that the work of the hangman is unpleasant. Granted. But suppose it is? It may be quite necessary to society for all that. There are, indeed, many other jobs that are unpleasant, and yet no one thinks of abolishing them—that of the plumber, that of the soldier, that of the garbage-man, that of the priest hearing confessions, that of the sand-hog, and so on. Moreover, what evidence is there that any actual hangman complains

447

of his work? I have heard none. On the contrary, I have known many who delighted in their ancient art, and practiced it proudly.

In the second argument of the abolitionists there is rather more force, but even here, I believe, the ground under them is shaky. Their fundamental error consists in assuming that the whole aim of punishing criminals is to deter other (potential) criminals—that we hang or electrocute A simply in order to so alarm B that he will not kill C. This, I believe, is an assumption which confuses a part with the whole. Deterrence, obviously, is *one* of the aims of punishment, but it is surely not the only one. On the contrary, there are at least a half dozen, and some are probably quite as important. At least one of them, practically considered, is *more* important. Commonly, it is described as revenge, but revenge is really not the word for it. I borrow a better term from the late Aristotle: *katharsis*. *Katharsis*, so used, means a salubrious discharge of emotions, a healthy letting off of steam. A school-boy, disliking his teacher, deposits a tack upon the pedagogical chair; the teacher jumps and the boy laughs. This is *katharsis*. What I contend is that one of the prime objects of all judicial punishments is to afford the same grateful relief (*a*) to the immediate victims of the criminal punished, and (*b*) to the general body of moral and timorous men.

These persons, and particularly the first group, are concerned only indirectly with deterring other criminals. The thing they crave primarily is the satisfaction of seeing the criminal actually before them suffer as he made them suffer. What they want is the peace of mind that goes with the feeling that accounts are squared. Until they get that satisfaction they are in a state of emotional tension, and hence unhappy. The instant they get it they are comfortable. I do not argue that this yearning is noble; I simply argue that it is almost universal among human beings. In the face of injuries that are unimportant and can be borne without damage it may yield to higher impulses; that is to say, it may yield to what is called Christian charity. But when the injury is serious Christianity is adjourned, and even saints reach for their sidearms. It is plainly asking too much of human nature to expect it to conquer so natural an impulse. A keeps a store and has a bookkeeper, B. B steals $700, employs it in playing at dice or bingo, and is cleaned out. What is A to do? Let B go? If he does so he will be unable to sleep at night. The sense of injury, of injustice, of frustration will haunt him like pruritus. So he turns B over to the police, and they hustle B to prison. Therefore A can sleep. More, he has pleasant dreams. He pictures B chained to the wall of a dungeon a hundred feet underground, devoured by rats and scorpions. It is so agreeable that it makes him forget his $700. He has got his *katharsis.*

The same thing precisely takes place on a larger scale when there is a crime which destroys a whole community's sense of security. Every law-abiding citizen feels menaced and frustrated until the criminals have been struck down—until the communal capacity to get even with them, and more than even, has been dramatically demonstrated. Here, manifestly, the business of deterring others is no more than an afterthought. The main thing is to destroy the concrete scoundrels whose act has alarmed everyone, and thus made everyone unhappy. Until they are brought to book that unhappiness continues; when the law has been executed upon them there is a sigh of relief. In other words, there is *katharsis.*

I know of no public demand for the death penalty for ordinary crimes, even for ordinary homicides. Its infliction would shock all men of normal decency of feeling. But for crimes involving the deliberate and inexcusable taking of human life, by men openly defiant of all civilized order—for such crimes it seems, to nine men out of ten, a just and proper punishment. Any lesser penalty leaves them feeling that the criminal has got the better of society—that he is free to add insult to injury by laughing. That feeling can be dissipated only by a recourse to *katharsis,* the invention of the aforesaid Aristotle. It is more effectively and economically achieved, as human nature now is, by wafting the criminal to realms of bliss.

The real objection to capital punishment doesn't lie against the actual extermination of the condemned, but against our brutal American habit of putting it off so long. After all, every one of us must die soon or late, and a murderer, it must be assumed, is one who makes that sad fact the cornerstone of his metaphysic. But it is one thing to die, and quite another thing to lie for long months and even years under the shadow of death. No sane man would choose such a finish. All of us, despite the Prayer Book, long for a swift and unexpected end. Unhappily, a murderer, under the irrational American system, is tortured for what, to him, must seem a whole series of eternities. For months on end he sits in prison while his lawyers carry on their idiotic buffoonery with writs, injunctions, mandamuses, and appeals. In order to get his money (or that of his friends) they have to feed him with hope. Now and then, by the imbecility of a judge or some trick of juridic science, they actually justify it. But let us say that, his money all gone, they finally throw up their hands. Their client is now ready for the rope or the chair. But he must still wait for months before it fetches him.

That wait, I believe, is horribly cruel. I have seen more than one   8
man sitting in the death-house, and I don't want to see any more. Worse, it is wholly useless. Why should he wait at all? Why not hang him the day after the last court dissipates his last hope? Why torture him as not even cannibals would torture their victims? The common answer is that he must have time to make his peace with God. But how long does that take? It may be accomplished, I believe, in two hours quite as comfortably as in two years. There are, indeed, no temporal limitations upon God. He could forgive a whole herd of murderers in a millionth of a second. More, it has been done.

RESPONSES AND IDEAS

1. Respond to this essay by exploring in a paragraph your own attitudes towards capital punishment; take into account the possibility that under certain conditions you might feel a need for revenge.

2. What is the difference between *katharsis* and revenge as Mencken explains it? Is this a real difference, or does Mencken simply use it to make his argument more acceptable? Explain.

3. What is Mencken's view of Christian charity in paragraph 4? Is his view accurate? Why or why not?

PURPOSE, AUDIENCE, AND STRATEGIES

1. What objections to his position does Mencken assume his audience will raise, and where does he acknowledge these objections?

2. In paragraph 8, Mencken says that a condemned prisoner may "make his peace with God" "in two hours quite as comfortably as in two years." What evidence is there here or elsewhere in the essay that he is less concerned with the actual time it may take the prisoner to ask for forgiveness than he is with attacking what he sees as the silly, and in this case cruel, rituals of formal religion? What closing strategy does Mencken use in paragraph 8? Is it effective? (See Glossary: Closings.)

3. What purposes other than arguing in favor of the death penalty does Mencken have in this essay? Be specific.

4. What does Mencken gain or lose by opening the essay with a refutation? What strategies of refutation does he use? (See Glossary: Refutation.)

5.   Explain how the arguments and evidence in this essay fit into an ascending order, a refutation-proof or con-pro arrangement, or into some combination of these.

LANGUAGE AND STYLE

1.   Where in this essay does Mencken use rhetorical questions, and for what purposes does he use them? (See Glossary: Figures of Speech.)
2.   Discuss how effective the example at the end of paragraph 4 would be if it did not include hyperbole (obvious exaggeration): ". . . B chained to the wall of a dungeon a hundred feet underground, devoured by rats and scorpions."
3.   If you do not know the meaning of any of the following words, look them up in the dictionary: *sand-hog* (par. 2): *salubrious, pedagogical, timorous* (3); *pruritus* (4); *wafting* (6); *mandamuses, juridic* (7).

WRITING ACTIVITIES

1.   On the basis of the attitudes he displays in this essay, try to imagine how Mencken might have responded in present-day debates over warfare, arms reduction, and nuclear disarmament. Take his likely responses into account as you prepare your own essay taking a stand on one aspect of any of these broad issues.
2.   Since Mencken's time, sociologists, psychologists, moral philosophers, and criminologists have spent much time examining the question of capital punishment. Argue your own position on capital punishment making whatever use you can of their research. You will not have time to read all that has been written on the subject, of course, but you should be able to find some articles or books that summarize the most important findings both for and against capital punishment.

❧ BARBARA PARKER

Barbara Parker is director of the Freedom-to-Learn project of People for the American Way, a citizens' group that defends the First Amendment, the constitutional guarantee of freedom of religion, of speech, of the press, and of assembly.

AM R CA S   D L G NT   C NS RS

If you were to say, "contrary to what most people believe, there is extensive censorship in this country," many people would disagree and remind you of the guarantee of free speech in the constitution. In this essay, first printed as a newspaper editorial, Barbara Parker makes just such an argument. Whether or not you accept her assertion about the seriousness of the problem, the evidence she presents is clearly thought-provoking and disturbing.

Last year was a banner one for America's censors. In 48 of the 50 states, there were attempts to remove, alter or restrict textbooks, library books, teaching materials and courses that don't match the censor's view of the world.

It is clear from this that censorship is not a small-town, Midwestern, or Southern phenomenon. National censorship data confirm that attempts to restrict reading materials occur as often in California or New York as they do in Iowa or Mississippi. In fact, there are usually more censorship attempts in metropolitan areas than in small, rural towns. Big city school systems and libraries offer a greater diversity of books and ideas, which makes it easier for people to find material they don't like.

In New York State, more than 20 percent of the school superintendents who responded to a recent survey reported censorship attempts in their districts during the past three years. Teaching materials removed from New York's school systems included "The Catcher in the Rye," Norma Klein's "It's O.K. If You Don't Love Me" and a high school health text.

Just as censorship knows no geographic boundaries, neither is it confined to one end of the political spectrum. Whether from the right or the left, the censors have in common an attitude that shows little regard for the reader's ability to arrive at his own conclusions.

By and large, however, scattered attempts by women's groups   5
and minorities to remove books because they are "racist," "sexist"
or "anti-Semitic" are rarely successful, in part because of the prevailing wisdom that holds that to inhibit discussion of discrimination
and intolerance only perpetuates them.

On the other hand, attempts by ultra-fundamentalists to ban   6
textbooks and literature that probes past and present social problems
are becoming increasingly successful. The shibboleth invented by
the far right—"secular humanism"—has been used effectively to
label any book or teaching material that isn't God-centered as inevitably man-centered and, therefore, unacceptable.

The charge of "secular humanism" has been used to ban books   7
and courses that explore the theory of evolution, the controversy over
Vietnam, the Watergate experience and current national problems
such as poverty, teenage pregnancy, unemployment, drug use, the
arms race and shifting roles in the American family.

Anyone who's not convinced about who the winners are in the   8
current struggle needs only to look at a sampling of censors' victories
over the past several years:

—In 1981, Laidlaw Brothers, a division of Doubleday, bowed to   9
demands of the "scientific creationists" and deleted the word "evolution" from its only high school biology textbook. The publisher
said that the word was omitted "to avoid the publicity that would
surround a controversy."

—Last year, in Folsom, Calif., 146 volumes of "The American   10
Heritage Dictionary" were banished to a storage room—before being
returned to the publisher—because of 13 "inappropriate" words.
(The same dictionary has been banned from use in Texas classrooms
as well as in others in towns in Ohio, Indiana, Alaska and Missouri.)

—In 1982, members of Phyllis Schlafly's Eagle Forum succeeded   11
in eliminating all required reading lists from the high school English
curriculum in St. David, Ariz. Targets of the campaign: "Of Mice
and Men," "Lord of the Flies" and classics by Poe, Hawthorne,
Stevenson and Hemingway.

—In February 1983, the Alabama state school superintendent   12
said that he would write a letter to all of the state's local school
districts urging them to be cautious when—or if—they assign 10
books in literature classes. The "questionable" material included "Of
Mice and Men," Ibsen's "A Doll's House," "The Diary of Anne Frank"
and Langston Hughes's poem "Harlem." The works were labeled

"sad, bizarre, hostile, depressing, and discouraging" by four members of the state textbook committee.

—In Fremont, Ohio, after complaints that a passage in James   13
Baldwin's "If Beale Street Could Talk" was "sexually explicit," a
compromise was reached: The book now is being taught with eight
pages torn out of each edition.

Censorship today is more than just an ugly word. It's a fright-   14
ening and increasingly powerful political phenomenon. If it continues to go unreported and unchallenged, its effects will be even more
far-reaching than the chill it casts on public school classrooms and
libraries. What is at stake in censorship struggles is more than the
freedom to learn. Our tradition as a pluralistic democracy begins in
local communities—and in the public schools.

RESPONSES AND IDEAS

1. Respond to this essay by describing your feelings about one or more of
   the instances of censorship Parker describes.

2. Does Parker explain why right-wing groups have had more success as
   censors than have women and minorities? What is her explanation? Is
   it satisfactory?

3. What is "secular humanism" (pars. 6–7)?

PURPOSE, AUDIENCE, AND STRATEGIES

1. Describe the attitudes towards censorship Parker seems to believe most
   readers hold, and state where in the essay she assumes such attitudes
   in constructing her argument.

2. Does it surprise you that there were so many attempts at censorship in
   New York State? Why? Did the writer intend to surprise her readers?
   For what purpose?

3. Among the books Parker cites as targets of censorship are John Steinbeck's *Of Mice and Men,* Henrik Ibsen's *A Doll's House, The Diary of Anne Frank,* and *The American Heritage Dictionary.* What was your
   reaction when you learned that people were trying to censor works like
   these? Do you think that most other readers of the essay would have
   the same reaction? Why do you think Parker chose these works and
   the others she mentions in the essay as examples of the kind of writing
   that has attracted the attention of censors? In what ways might your
   reactions to her arguments have changed if she had used magazines
   like *Playgirl, Playboy,* and *Penthouse* as examples?

4. Why does Parker let the evidence speak for itself in paragraphs 9–13?
   Is this strategy effective? (See Glossary: Evaluation.) What evidence does

the author use to prove that censorship is widespread? Is the evidence sufficient, or is her reasoning flawed in some way?

LANGUAGE AND STYLE

1. Where in the essay does Parker use emotional strategies to support her point of view (see pp. 425–426)? To what extent do these emotional strategies rely on language (diction) for their effectiveness? (See Glossary: Diction.)

2. Focusing on two paragraphs from the essay, demonstrate how the author uses the connotations of words to reinforce her point of view. (See Glossary: Connotation). Look up the word *shibboleth* in the dictionary. Why is it appropriate to use this word to describe the actions of religion-oriented groups?

3. If you do not know the meaning of some of the following words, look them up in the dictionary: *spectrum* (par. 4); *inhibit* (5); *shibboleth* (6); *pluralistic* (14).

WRITING ACTIVITIES

1. Though most people believe in the fundamental rights of freedom of speech and expression, they are also willing to agree to limits on these rights. Most people, for example, agree that children should not be allowed to view sexually explicit movies and that magazines and newspapers can be sued for libel if they print malicious lies. It is often difficult, however, to draw the line between what should be censored and what should be available to everyone. In an essay of your own, argue why children should or should not be permitted to see violent or sexually explicit movies or to read certain magazines or books. To strengthen your argument, use as examples specific movies or reading material that are probably familiar to your readers.

2. Parker has only negative things to say about the values and outlooks of the groups behind the censorship efforts she reports. Do some research of your own on activities like those described in the essay, concentrating, if possible, on recent events. In an essay, report on the arguments and evidence the would-be censors use to justify their efforts. If as a result of your research you find yourself sympathetic with their point of view, prepare an essay defending them against attacks like those Parker makes in her essay.

❧ RUSSELL BAKER

Russell Baker was born in 1925 in Virginia. He began his career as a journalist with the *Baltimore Sun* in 1947 and went to work for the *New York Times* in 1954. As a reporter for the *Times* he covered the White House, Congress, and national politics. Since 1967 he has written the "Observer" and "Sunday Observer" columns in the *Times*. In 1972 he was awarded the George Polk Award for Distinguished Commentary. *Growing Up*, Baker's memoir of his childhood, was published in 1982. Among his other books are *All Things Considered* (1965), *So This Is Depravity* (1980), and *The Rescue of Miss Yaskell and Other Pipe Dreams* (1983).

Chicken Caper

In his "Sunday Observer" column Russell Baker often makes wry observations based on his experiences. His subject here is a minor incident that reveals a not-so-minor problem. His approach to argument, while seemingly informal, actually involves a carefully laid-out comparison pattern, narrative examples, and cause-effect reasoning.

1   Here are the bare bones—I am tempted to say the bare chicken bones—of the case:

2   A young woman enters a fried-chicken establishment carrying a $10 bill to purchase a small quantity of the house specialty. A young man, whom she knows casually, enters behind her. There is a brief contretemps, the young woman exits to find a policeman, finds two and tells them the young man has snatched her chicken money. The policemen arrest him. He is charged with feloniously stealing the chicken money by forcibly removing it from the young woman's hand.

3   Such is the entire case. As a police reporter 35 years ago, I saw justice done in hundreds of such affairs, and it was done with dispatch and efficiency. The cops haled the accused man immediately to police court, where a magistrate listened to both sides of the story. If he believed the woman, he checked with the cops to discover if the young man was a consistently bad actor.

4   If he was, the magistrate might send him to the hoosegow for

30 days. If he wasn't, the magistrate might give him a brief sentence, suspend it and talk to him like a Dutch uncle, warning him that another offense would cost him 30 years in stir. Next case!

But stay. Not so swiftly. The course of justice, as I recently 5 discovered at some cost to my digestion and wallet, has become more complex since I last idled in police courts. This very case, the case of the snatched chicken money, came to trial in New York recently while my wife was on jury duty.

Sworn to secrecy by the court, she could not reveal the nature 6 of the crime until the case was settled, but confided that the jury selection had taken three days and said the case was apparently complex, since the judge had advised jurors to bring pajamas, tooth-brushes and other equipment necessary to survive a long bout of jury deadlock.

Naturally, I assumed the case must involve a complicated em- 7 bezzling scheme, a corporate conspiracy to defraud the public, or homicide, so I was not amazed when a genial bailiff phoned at 8 P.M. on the third day of the trial to inform me that the jury had been locked up for the night in a hotel and that I must make my own dinner.

Never mind the menu. My wife and I have a marriage contract 8 which obliges me to stay occupied full time at typewriters and commits her to mastery of the culinary arts. When compelled to carry her share of the duty, I produce a meal that would make a sword swallower gag.

Previous experience had prepared me for a sleep fraught with 9 nightmare, and I was not disappointed. The following day, aware that it might be weeks before she could again turn her hand to hollandaise and crab gumbo and determined not to suffer another night of agony, I proposed a restaurant visit with two friends.

Sure enough, the bailiff phoned again to report that the jury had 10 dined and was resuming its deliberations. The restaurant dinner—this was New York, remember—cost me $50. All right, I had a drink. Maybe two.

My wife had just arrived home when I returned at 11 P.M. At 11 last I would hear the details of this case so sinuous that it required three days for jury selection, two days for the testimony and two days of jury deliberation.

In precise detail, she related the story of the snatched chicken 12 money. She is a woman who likes to have her little joke, so when she finished I said, "Very witty, and now tell me the real story. Was it a kidnapping?"

"She said this young man took her chicken money. That was the   13
case," she said.

"Surely there is more to it. When did it happen?"   14

"Eleven months ago," she said.   15

"But when I was a kid reporter they tried that kind of case two   16
hours after it happened and the judge settled it in 90 seconds."

"Don't blame me because you're getting old," she said.   17

I don't want to be one of those cranks who hate to see an accused 18
man enjoy his day in court, but this incident has shaken my faith in
American justice. Faced with a case that could be disposed of within
24 hours, it had taken 11 months to bring it to trial, three days to
pick a jury, two days to record the evidence and two days for the
jury to reach a verdict, which turned out to be "petty larceny."

Besides tying up a judge and a courtroom for an entire week,   19
the trial of this $10 chicken caper had cost the state the price of two
lunches, two dinners and a breakfast for each of 12 jurors, plus the
price of housing them for a night in a hotel, not to mention the eight
hours of nightmare and $50 food bill it cost at least one juror's
spouse.

It would have made more sense if the state had offered the young 20
woman a $20 bribe and a free box of fried chicken to abandon her
complaint. Still, maybe it was worth it for the pleasure it gave my
wife, who likes her little joke. She now boasts that, having been
locked up for a night by order of the court, she has spent more time
in custody than most New York muggers.

RESPONSES AND IDEAS

1. Respond to this essay by arguing briefly why the "system" Baker de-
    scribes in paragraphs 3–4 was or was not a good one.

2. In a paragraph of your own, state briefly why you think the process
    Baker describes in paragraphs 3 and 4 was a just or unjust way of
    dealing with minor crimes.

PURPOSE, AUDIENCE, AND STRATEGIES

1. This essay contains a good deal of humor. Why should readers take
    seriously Baker's conclusions about our system of justice? What, if

anything, does the humor contribute to the effectiveness of the argument?

2. What effect does Baker's talk about having to take responsibility for his meals (pars. 8–10) have on the strength of the argument? By what logic, if any, is it linked to the rest of the argument?

3. In view of the humor in the essay, will most readers think Baker's statement in paragraph 18 is meant to be taken as a serious statement of what he believes? Why? What is his tone in paragraph 18? In the essay as a whole? (See Glossary: Tone.)

4. What strategies does Baker use to make himself appear trustworthy and fair-minded? Does he succeed? (See p. 426, ethical appeal.)

5. Identify the various patterns of development Baker uses in this essay. Explain which logical strategies he uses.

LANGUAGE AND STYLE

1. What differences in diction are there between paragraph 2 and paragraphs 3 and 4? What does the contrast reveal about the point he wants to make? (See Glossary: Diction.) Why might the last sentence in the essay be considered ironic? Paradoxical? Or is it meant to be taken literally? (See Glossary: Irony, Figures of Speech.) Why does this sentence make an effective closing? (See Glossary: Closings.)

2. Do you think Baker really has a "marriage contract" (par. 8)? If not, why does he use the term here?

3. If you do not know the meaning of some of the following words, look them up in the dictionary: *contretemps, feloniously* (par. 2); *haled* (3); *hoosegow* (4); *idled* (5); *culinary* (8); *hollandaise, gumbo* (9).

WRITING ACTIVITIES

1. If you or an acquaintance has had an experience that confirms or contradicts Baker's conclusions, build an argumentative essay of your own around it. Feel free, however, to use evidence and arguments from other sources as well.

2. Many controversies revolve around whether we have extended our rights and freedoms so far that they are disrupting society (as Baker seems to be arguing) or whether we should expand them to new areas such as a right to health care and to decent employment. In an essay of your own, argue whether we should restrict a specific right or freedom or whether we should expand in some way the privileges guaranteed to all citizens.

Edward Abbey was born in Pennsylvania in 1927 and attended the University of New Mexico. An essayist and a novelist who worked for a number of years as a park ranger and forest fire lookout, Abbey writes about the American West, particularly about the desert. One of his persistent concerns is the encroachment of civilization on wilderness and the destruction it brings to the beauty and solitude of the desert and the canyonlands. Abbey's essays have appeared in *GEO, National Geographic, Rolling Stone, Harper's, Running, Backpacker Magazine,* and many other periodicals. His books include *The Monkey Wrench Gang* (1975, a novel) and collections of his essays and journals: *Desert Solitaire* (1968), *The Journey Home: Some Words in Defense of the American West* (1977), *Abbey's Road* (1979), *Down the River* (1982), and *Beyond the Wall* (1984).

The Damnation of a Canyon

In "The Damnation of a Canyon," an essay from *Beyond the Wall,* Abbey argues against the creation of recreational lakes behind power dams. At the center of the essay is a comparison of the present Lake Powell formed by the Glen Canyon Dam with Glen Canyon before the dam was built. Glen Canyon is not, however, so much the subject of the essay as it is a means by which Abbey presents his argument about the uses and preservation of wilderness. In addition to comparison, Abbey uses several other strategies to involve readers in the argument and persuade them to accept his point of view and consider his proposals for undoing the harm caused by unwise development.

There was a time when, in my search for essences, I concluded 1 that the canyonland country has no heart. I was wrong. The canyonlands did have a heart, a living heart, and that heart was Glen Canyon and the golden, flowing Colorado River.

In the summer of 1959 a friend and I made a float trip in little 2 rubber rafts down through the length of Glen Canyon, starting at Hite and getting off the river near Gunsight Butte—The Crossing of the Fathers. In this voyage of some 150 miles and ten days our only motive power, and all that we needed, was the current of the Colorado River.

    In the summer and fall of 1967 I worked as a seasonal park   3
ranger at the new Glen Canyon National Recreation Area. During
my five-month tour of duty I worked at the main marina and headquarters area called Wahweap, at Bullfrog Basin toward the upper
end of the reservoir, and finally at Lee's Ferry downriver from Glen
Canyon Dam. In a number of powerboat tours I was privileged to
see almost all of our nation's newest, biggest and most impressive
"recreational facility."

    Having thus seen Glen Canyon both before and after what we   4
may fairly call its damnation, I feel that I am in a position to evaluate
the transformation of the region caused by construction of the dam.
I have had the unique opportunity to observe firsthand some of the
differences between the environment of a free river and a power-
plant reservoir.

    One should admit at the outset to a certain bias. Indeed I am a   5
"butterfly chaser, googly eyed bleeding heart and wild conservative."
I take a dim view of dams; I find it hard to learn to love cement; I
am poorly impressed by concrete aggregates and statistics in the
cubic tons. But in this weakness I am not alone, for I belong to that
ever-growing number of Americans, probably a good majority now,
who have become aware that a fully industrialized, thoroughly ur-
banized, elegantly computerized social system is not suitable for
human habitation. Great for machines, yes. But unfit for people.

    Lake Powell, formed by Glen Canyon Dam, is not a lake. It is a   6
reservoir, with a constantly fluctuating water level—more like a
bathtub that is never drained than a true lake. As at Hoover (or
Boulder) Dam, the sole practical function of this impounded water
is to drive the turbines that generate electricity in the powerhouse at
the base of the dam. Recreational benefits were of secondary importance in the minds of those who conceived and built this dam. As a
result the volume of water in the reservoir is continually being
increased or decreased according to the requirements of the Basin
States Compact and the power-grid system of which Glen Canyon
Dam is a component.

    The rising and falling water level entails various consequences.   7
One of the most obvious, well known to all who have seen Lake
Mead, is the "bathtub ring" left on the canyon walls after each
drawdown of water, or what rangers at Glen Canyon call the Bathtub Formation. This phenomenon is perhaps of no more than aesthetic importance; yet it is sufficient to dispel any illusion one might

have, in contemplating the scene, that you are looking upon a natural lake.

Of much more significance is the fact that plant life, because of   8
the unstable water line, cannot establish itself on the shores of the reservoir. When the water is low, plant life dies of thirst; when high, it is drowned. Much of the shoreline of the reservoir consists of near-perpendicular sandstone bluffs, where very little flora ever did or ever could subsist, but the remainder includes bays, coves, sloping hills and the many side canyons, where the original plant life has been drowned and new plant life cannot get a foothold. And of course where there is little or no plant life there is little or no animal life.

The utter barrenness of the reservoir shoreline recalls by contrast   9
the aspect of things before the dam, when Glen Canyon formed the course of the untamed Colorado. Then we had a wild and flowing river lined by boulder-strewn shores, sandy beaches, thickets of tamarisk and willow, and glades of cottonwoods.

The thickets teemed with songbirds: vireos, warblers, mocking-   10
birds and thrushes. On the open beaches were killdeer, sandpipers, herons, ibises, egrets. Living in grottoes in the canyon walls were swallows, swifts, hawks, wrens and owls. Beaver were common if not abundant: not an evening would pass, in drifting down the river, that we did not see them or at least hear the whack of their flat tails on the water. Above the river shores were the great recessed alcoves where water seeped from the sandstone, nourishing the semitropical hanging gardens of orchid, ivy and columbine, with their associated swarms of insects and birdlife.

Up most of the side canyons, before damnation, there were   11
springs, sometimes flowing streams, waterfalls and plunge pools— the kind of marvels you can now find only in such small-scale remnants of Glen Canyon as the Escalante area. In the rich flora of these laterals the larger mammals—mule deer, coyote, bobcat, ring-tailed cat, gray fox, kit fox, skunk, badger and others—found a home. When the river was dammed almost all of these things were lost. Crowded out—or drowned and buried under mud.

The difference between the present reservoir, with its silent sterile   12
shores and debris-choked side canyons, and the original Glen Canyon, is the difference between death and life. Glen Canyon was alive. Lake Powell is a graveyard.

For those who may think I exaggerate the contrast between the   13
former river canyon and the present man-made impoundment, I
suggest a trip on Lake Powell followed immediately by another boat
trip on the river below the dam. Take a boat from Lee's Ferry up
the river to within sight of the dam, then shut off the motor and
allow yourself the rare delight of a quiet, effortless drifting down the
stream. In that twelve-mile stretch of living green, singing birds,
flowing water and untarnished canyon walls—sights and sounds a
million years older and infinitely lovelier than the roar of motorboats—you will rediscover a small and imperfect sampling of the
kind of experience that was taken away from everybody when the
oligarchs and politicians condemned our river for purposes of their
own.

The effects of Glen Canyon Dam also extend downstream, caus-   14
ing changes in the character and ecology of Marble Gorge and Grand
Canyon. Because the annual spring floods are now a thing of the
past, the shores are becoming overgrown with brush, the rapids are
getting worse where the river no longer has enough force to carry
away the boulders washed down from the lateral canyons, and the
beaches are disappearing, losing sand that is not replaced.

Lake Powell, though not a lake, may well be as its defenders   15
assert the most beautiful reservoir in the world. Certainly it has a
photogenic backdrop of buttes and mesas projecting above the ex-
pansive surface of stagnant waters where the speedboats, houseboats
and cabin cruisers ply. But it is no longer a wilderness. It is no
longer a place of natural life. It is no longer Glen Canyon.

The defenders of the dam argue that the recreational benefits   16
available on the surface of the reservoir outweigh the loss of Indian
ruins, historical sites, wildlife and wilderness adventure. Relying on
the familiar quantitative logic of business and bureaucracy, they
assert that whereas only a few thousand citizens ever ventured down
the river through Glen Canyon, now millions can—or will—enjoy
the motorized boating and hatchery fishing available on the reservoir.
They will also argue that the rising waters behind the dam have
made such places as Rainbow Bridge accessible by powerboat. Formerly you could get there only by walking (six miles).

This argument appeals to the wheelchair ethos of the wealthy,   17
upper-middle-class American slob. If Rainbow Bridge is worth
seeing at all, then by God it should be easily, readily, immediately

available to everybody with the money to buy a big powerboat. Why should a trip to such a place be the privilege only of those who are willing to walk six miles? Or if Pikes Peak is worth getting to, then why not build a highway to the top of it so that anyone can get there? Anytime? Without effort? Or as my old man would say, "By Christ, one man's just as good as another—if not a damn sight better."

Or as ex-Commissioner Floyd Dominy of the U.S. Bureau of   18
Reclamation pointed out poetically in his handsomely engraved and illustrated brochure *Lake Powell: Jewel of the Colorado* (produced by the U.S. Government Printing Office at our expense): "There's something about a lake which brings us a little closer to God." In this case, Lake Powell, about five hundred feet closer. Eh, Floyd?

It is quite true that the flooding of Glen Canyon has opened up   19
to the motorboat explorer parts of side canyons that formerly could be reached only by people able to walk. But the sum total of terrain visible to the eye and touchable by hand and foot has been greatly diminished, not increased. Because of the dam the river is gone, the inner canyon is gone, the best parts of the numerous side canyons are gone—all hidden beneath hundreds of feet of polluted water, accumulating silt, and mounting tons of trash. This portion of Glen Canyon—and who can estimate how many cubic miles were lost?— *is no longer accessible to anybody.* (Except scuba divers.) And this, do not forget, was the most valuable part of Glen Canyon, richest in scenery, archaeology, history, flora and fauna.

Not only has the heart of Glen Canyon been buried, but many   20
of the side canyons above the fluctuating waterline are now rendered more difficult, not easier, to get into. This because the debris brought down into them by desert storms, no longer carried away by the river, must unavoidably build up in the area where flood meets reservoir. Narrow Canyon, for example, at the head of the impounded waters, is already beginning to silt up and to amass huge quantities of driftwood, some of it floating on the surface, some of it half afloat beneath the surface. Anyone who has tried to pilot a motorboat through a raft of half-sunken logs and bloated dead cows will have his own thoughts on the accessibility of these waters.

Hite Marina, at the mouth of Narrow Canyon, will probably   21
have to be abandoned within twenty or thirty years. After that it will be the turn of Bullfrog Marina. And then Rainbow Bridge Marina.

And eventually, inevitably, whether it takes ten centuries or only one, Wahweap. Lake Powell, like Lake Mead, is foredoomed sooner or later to become a solid mass of mud, and its dam a waterfall. Assuming, of course, that either one stands that long.

Second, the question of costs. It is often stated that the dam and 22 its reservoir have opened up to the many what was formerly restricted to the few, implying in this case that what was once expensive has now been made cheap. Exactly the opposite is true.

Before the dam, a float trip down the river through Glen Canyon 23 would cost you a minimum of seven days' time, well within anyone's vacation allotment, and a capital outlay of about forty dollars—the prevailing price of a two-man rubber boat with oars, available at any army-navy store. A life jacket might be useful but not required, for there were no dangerous rapids in the 150 miles of Glen Canyon. As the name implies, this stretch of the river was in fact so easy and gentle that the trip could be and was made by all sorts of amateurs: by Boy Scouts, Camp Fire Girls, stenographers, schoolteachers, students, little old ladies in inner tubes. Guides, professional boatmen, giant pontoons, outboard motors, radios, rescue equipment were not needed. The Glen Canyon float trip was an adventure anyone could enjoy, on his own, for a cost less than that of spending two days and nights in a Page motel. Even food was there, in the water: the channel catfish were easier to catch and a lot better eating than the striped bass and rainbow trout dumped by the ton into the reservoir these days. And one other thing: at the end of the float trip you still owned your boat, usable for many more such casual and carefree expeditions.

What is the situation now? Float trips are no longer possible. 24 The only way left for the exploration of the reservoir and what remains of Glen Canyon demands the use of a powerboat. Here you have three options: (1) buy your own boat and engine, the necessary auxiliary equipment, the fuel to keep it moving, the parts and repairs to keep it running, the permits and licenses required for legal operation, the trailer to transport it; (2) rent a boat; or (3) go on a commercial excursion boat, packed in with other sightseers, following a preplanned itinerary. This kind of play is only for the affluent.

The inescapable conclusion is that no matter how one attempts 25 to calculate the cost in dollars and cents, a float trip down Glen Canyon was much cheaper than a powerboat tour of the reservoir.

Being less expensive, as well as safer and easier, the float trip was an adventure open to far more people than will ever be able to afford motorboat excursions in the area now.

What about the "human impact" of motorized use of the Glen   26
Canyon impoundment? We can visualize the floor of the reservoir gradually accumulating not only silt, mud, waterlogged trees and drowned cattle but also the usual debris that is left behind when the urban, industrial style of recreation is carried into the open country. There is also the problem of human wastes. The waters of the wild river were good to drink, but nobody in his senses would drink from Lake Powell. Eventually, as is already sometimes the case at Lake Mead, the stagnant waters will become too foul even for swimming. The trouble is that while some boats have what are called "self-contained" heads, the majority do not; most sewage is disposed of by simply pumping it into the water. It will take a while, but long before it becomes a solid mass of mud Lake Powell ("Jewel of the Colorado") will enjoy a passing fame as the biggest sewage lagoon in the American Southwest. Most tourists will never be able to afford a boat trip on this reservoir, but everybody within fifty miles will be able to smell it.

All of the foregoing would be nothing but a futile exercise in   27
nostalgia (so much water over the dam) if I had nothing constructive and concrete to offer. But I do. As alternate methods of power generation are developed, such as solar, and as the nation establishes a way of life adapted to actual resources and basic needs, so that the demand for electrical power begins to diminish, we can shut down the Glen Canyon power plant, open the diversion tunnels, and drain the reservoir.

This will no doubt expose a drear and hideous scene: immense   28
mud flats and whole plateaus of sodden garbage strewn with dead trees, sunken boats, the skeletons of long-forgotten, decomposing water-skiers. But to those who find the prospect too appalling, I say give nature a little time. In five years, at most in ten, the sun and wind and storms will cleanse and sterilize the repellent mess. The inevitable floods will soon remove all that does not belong within the canyons. Fresh green willow, box elder and redbud will reappear; and the ancient drowned cottonwoods (noble monuments to themselves) will be replaced by young of their own kind. With the renewal of plant life will come the insects, the birds, the lizards and snakes, the mammals. Within a generation—thirty years—I predict

the river and canyons will bear a decent resemblance to their former selves. Within the lifetime of our children Glen Canyon and the living river, heart of the canyonlands, will be restored to us. The wilderness will again belong to God, the people and the wild things that call it home.

RESPONSES AND IDEAS

1. Respond to this essay by describing a place where you believe development, including the construction of dams, buildings, or trails, has been either harmful or beneficial. Or explain briefly why you think the way Abbey presents his arguments makes them seem either particularly convincing or unconvincing.

2. What answer do you think Abbey would give to the question he raises in paragraph 17: "Why should a trip to such a place be the privilege only of those who are willing to walk six miles"? What answer do you think most people would give?

3. Does the author really expect that "Within the lifetime of our children Glen Canyon and the living river, heart of the canyonlands, will be restored to us. The wilderness will again belong to God, the people and the wild things that call it home" (par. 28)?

PURPOSE, AUDIENCE, AND STRATEGIES

1. Where in the essay does Abbey refer directly to the attitudes readers are likely to bring with them to the essay or to what he considers their probable response to his arguments? Do these direct references strengthen or weaken the essay?

2. To what values of the audience does he appeal as support for his argument? Are the strategies used in this essay primarily logical or emotional? What proportion of the essay is given over to each of the four kinds of strategies—logical, emotional, ethical, and imaginative?

3. Where does Abbey announce his purpose and the primary pattern of development the essay will follow? Could these be announced in another, more effective manner? If so, revise the passage to improve it. In what way can the title be viewed as an announcement of the essay's thesis? In what other ways does Abbey communicate his point of view to readers? (See Glossary: Purpose, Thesis.)

4. Where in the essay does the author refute opposing points of view? What are the opposing views, and how does he refute them? (See Glossary: Refutation.)

5. What is the relationship in this essay between comparison and problem-solution (cause-effect) as patterns of development? What other patterns

does the author use to develop and present support for his point of view?

LANGUAGE AND STYLE

1. What impact are paragraphs 9–12 likely to have on readers? Describe the resources of diction and syntax Abbey draws on to achieve this effect. (See Glossary: Diction, Syntax.) What role do these paragraphs play in the overall development of the essay?

2. Abbey's style in this essay is sometimes quite formal (pars. 6 and 16, for example) and at other times very informal ("Eh, Floyd?"—par. 18, and par. 17). For what purposes does Abbey adopt a formal style? An informal style? (See Glossary: Style.)

3. If you do not know the meaning of any of the following words, look them up in the dictionary: *motive* (par. 2); *aggregates* (5); *alcoves* (10); *impoundment* (13); *buttes, mesas* (15); *quantitative* (16); *heads* (26).

WRITING ACTIVITIES

1. Write an essay arguing that more wilderness land should be turned into parks and developed for camping and recreation. Take into account the objections to this policy that Abbey raises in his essay.

2. Development in populated areas often destroys historic or architecturally important buildings or districts. Prepare an essay arguing against a particular development project or in favor of preserving a particular building or district. If, on the other hand, you know of a project that would improve the appearance of a neighborhood or the quality of life for its residents, argue in favor of it.

Writing Suggestions

EXPLORATIONS

1. Make a list of five issues that worry, irritate, or anger you in each of these categories: environmental problems, political controversies, social problems, local issues. From each category choose one topic that might be developed into a good argument essay and describe the controversy briefly, stating the major points of view including your own. If one of these topics is particularly interesting to you, develop it into an essay.

2. Choose an issue like capital punishment, handgun control, or nuclear power on which you have some strong opinions, and prepare a list of arguments and supporting opinions that someone arguing the opposing point of view could use. As you prepare the list, be as sympathetic as you can to the point of view you have adopted for this exercise, and try to make the arguments and evidence you choose as strong as possible.

3. Take three broad subjects of disagreement—gun control, nuclear disarmament, health care, for example—and for each one identify five more limited topics suitable for a short (3–5 page) argumentative essay. Then take one of the limited topics from each subject and construct two possible thesis statements for use in an essay. The thesis statements should be quite different in content and in outlook (or even exact opposites), not simply variations of the same idea. If you wish, use one of the thesis statements as the basis for an essay.

4. For three of the thesis statements you constructed for the preceding exercise, explain briefly two logical strategies that might be used for support, two emotional strategies, and one imaginative strategy. Be specific about the content of each of the strategies. If you wish, use the strategies you have selected in an essay.

ACTIVITIES

1. Look at the editorial pages of a national newspaper like the *New York Times,* the *Washington Post,* the *Los Angeles Times,* or the *Wall Street Journal,* or at an opinion magazine like the *New Republic,* the *National Review,* or the *Nation.* Among the articles and columns you find, locate those that can be classified as arguments. Then state whether they make a value judgment, propose an action, advance an unusual opinion, or combine these purposes.

2. Choose three of the arguments you selected in the preceding exercise. Study them in order to discover the patterns of development each uses. For two of the arguments list the basic patterns of development they use (that is, the patterns of development covered in the chapters of this text) as well as the logical, emotional, ethical, and imaginative strategies that they employ.

3.   Choose a national issue like nuclear disarmament, or a local issue like changes in the property tax structure or plans for building a new high school, for which you are aware of two or more distinct points of view. Briefly write out the major arguments on each side, then interview several people about the issue, asking them to explain their stands and to respond to and refute each of the major arguments made by the opposition. Take notes on their responses to the opposition, and afterwards write up a description of each response along with an evaluation of its success in refuting the opposing point of view.

4.   Listen to a news interview or debate program on television or radio, and take notes on the various strategies the speakers use to support their arguments and to attack opposing points of view. Then turn your notes into a list summarizing the strategies used in the program, adding a brief note on the effectiveness with which the participants used the various strategies of argument.

MODELS

1.   Using Ellen Goodman's approach in "Honor Society Hypocrisy," argue against actions recently taken by some organization or institution. You might want to attack a hospital that turns away patients who are seriously ill but cannot demonstrate their ability to pay the costs of care; you might want to argue against the actions of some charity or local government in deciding that an individual or a group of people is ineligible for benefits of some sort.

2.   Borrowing the approach of Michael Kaufman's "Facing Violence," write an essay in which you argue that the best way to get people to avoid something is to show them its effects in a direct manner. You might take excessive TV viewing, drug use, smoking, or some similar topic as the subject of your essay.

3.   Taking H. L. Mencken's "The Penalty of Death" as your guide, argue in favor of physical roughness in sports, of danger in activities like auto racing and mountain climbing, or of the killing in sports like hunting and fishing on the ground that they represent the working out of basic human drives and emotions that society incorrectly and unjustly tries to ignore.

4.   Following many of the strategies in Barbara Parker's "Am r ca s D l g nt C ns rs," argue that rights most of us take for granted as part of our democratic society are constantly being violated, often by pressure groups intent on advancing their own interests. As a topic you might use freedom of expression, the right to worship, the right to associate with other people in groups with a political aim, or the right to private property, among others.

5.   Using Russell Baker's "The Chicken Caper" as a model, argue against some policy or practice, from knowledge based on personal experience

or the experiences of someone you know well. Feel free to argue in favor of present practices or government policies as well as against them. You may wish to make the object of your protest as narrow as a policy against drinking beer in a state park or as broad as a major element in American foreign policy.

6. Using some of the same strategies that Edward Abbey employs in "The Damnation of a Canyon," argue against (or for) a policy or project by comparing its probable effect to the present situation. Or argue that the policy should be reversed or the project undone because of its disastrous effects.

11

~ WRITERS ON WRITING

Student writers often assume that professionals have learned the correct way to write, and as a result they are surprised to discover that successful authors work in many different ways. Each magazine article, newspaper column, novel, nonfiction book, or scholarly essay makes its own special demands on a writer. Besides, writers themselves are individuals, as diverse in the ways they compose as they are in personality and outlook. Some writers can work almost anywhere—on an airplane, in the busy city room of a newspaper, at home surrounded by noisy children and barking dogs. Others require a quiet room, a special pen with a favorite color of ink, or a certain kind of writing paper. A few writers make detailed outlines before drafting an essay. Many others start with scribbled notes and write a hurried first draft, which they then patiently revise until the essay is in final form. As William Zinsser puts it in one of the essays in this chapter,

> Writing is a deeply personal process, full of mystery and surprise. No two people go about it in exactly the same way. We all have little devices to get us started, or to keep us going, or to remind us of what we think we want to say, and what works for one person may not work for anyone else. The main thing is to get something written—to get the words out of our heads.

Their work habits may differ greatly, yet successful writers have all developed the same essential skills. They know how to probe memories and experiences for the details that make writing vivid and interesting, and they are good at drawing ideas and information from what they read. From their reading and writing experiences they have assembled a ready stock of essay patterns, paragraph strategies, and sentence structures to draw on as they compose, and they are able to adapt these devices to the needs of varied subjects, audiences, and purposes for writing. They are aware of readers' interests and attitudes, and they make careful, often extensive revision a regular part of their writing.

Not all writers who have worked hard to acquire these skills are aware enough of what happens as they compose to be able to share their knowledge, but those who are—like the writers of the essays in this chapter—can provide good advice for student writers. Four of the essays presented here are the work of writers who are also teachers of writing and who have directed their essays to beginning writers. The fifth, Eudora Welty's "Listening," was originally part of a series of lectures in which the author shared some of the experiences that led to her development as a writer. Two of the essays, Sylvan Barnet's "Writing and Reading: Some Concrete Observations" and Mike Rose's "Writing Around Rules," were written especially for this collection and address issues raised elsewhere in the text, sometimes agreeing with the editor's outlook but just as often presenting another point of view or a complementary one. All the essays are addressed to students and to other people interested in writing, and they contain detailed practical advice for sharpening the habits of mind that lead to good writing. In addition, each essay looks at reading and its many relationships to writing. Taken as a group, the essays suggest that reading is not one process but many, with each kind of reading contributing to what we can gain from encountering another person's words and ideas (or from looking over our own) and each adding something to our own writing.

In "Listening," Eudora Welty talks about the childhood experiences that helped shape her awareness of the world and foster the skills she would use later to create the smaller worlds of her short stories and novels. The essay itself provides excellent examples of the ways a writer can probe memories and bring back vivid details, happenings, and characters to share with readers. Welty also identifies two kinds of reading—that which looks for information and ideas to bring away from the reading and that which seeks merely to participate in the reality created by the writer—a distinction central to an understanding of purpose in both writing and reading.

Sylvan Barnet's "Writing and Reading: Some Concrete Observations" offers good advice on a number of topics—responding to assignments, using patterns in writing, making reading a springboard for writing—and comments on several of the essays in this text. Most important, the essay talks about how reading can be a creative, enlightening experience and shows how such reading turns almost inevitably into further writing. Like most good writers, Barnet provides detailed examples for his audience, but he also goes beyond this to call attention to many of the strategies he uses in his writing, thus making the entire essay a commentary on the ways we can shape expression.

In "The Maker's Eye: Revising Your Own Manuscripts," Donald Murray talks about the need to redraft and revise a piece of writing until it not only says what the writer wants it to but does so in a way that readers will be able to understand readily. The reading that accompanies revision is critical reading, the ability to see one's own work not as a writer does but from a reader's perspective. Murray suggests several ways to develop the skill of critical reading. His primary focus is on revision, however, and his essay is filled with detailed advice for revising words, sentences, paragraphs, and whole essays.

In an essay written especially for this book, Mike Rose draws on his detailed studies of student writers to show how the rules we learn in composition classes can sometimes make writing more difficult. He suggests ways to use rules creatively and constructively as aids to writing rather than as barriers. Rose points out that as we write, we read our own work to see if we are satisfied by it and to see if it is consistent with the rest of what we have written. He uses examples from his own and his students' writing to show that the doubts and worries that flood in as we read our own sentences are often self-defeating unless we learn how to control them and make them work for us.

William Zinsser's "Writing with a Word Processor: One Man's Method" is as much about writing in general as it is about the ways a word processor shapes the act of writing. Zinsser's suggestions for revising, for cutting extra words, and for rereading one's own work to see that it makes a unified whole can be used with or without a word processor. In addition, his awareness of the ways other people are likely to respond to his work gives some valuable hints about the way all of us go about reading essays.

The essays in this chapter, then, speak with many voices about writing and reading, reflecting the many ways we go about creating and responding to texts. The advice from these essayists is often provocative, sometimes contradictory, but always stimulating and helpful.

❧ EUDORA WELTY

Eudora Welty was born in 1909 in Jackson, Mississippi. She attended Mississippi State College for Women, the University of Wisconsin, and Columbia University School of Business. She spent some time working for radio stations and newspapers but soon began concentrating on writing fiction. Among her publications are *A Curtain of Green* (1941, a collection of short stories), and the novels *Ponder Heart* (1954), *Losing Battles* (1970), and *The Optimist's Daughter* (1972). The focus of most of her writing is Southern society and the people that make it up, yet her fiction has attracted a broad audience. Among the honors she has received are a Pulitzer Prize, the American Book Award for fiction, and a Gold Medal for the Novel from the American Academy and Institute of Arts and Letters (awarded for her achievements in fiction writing). In addition to novels and stories, Miss Welty has published *The Eye of the Story: Selected Essays and Reviews* (1977) and *One Writer's Beginnings* (1984), a memoir of the experiences that helped shape her outlook as a writer (first delivered as the William E. Massey Sr. Lectures in the History of American Civilization at Harvard University). The following piece, "Listening" (editor's title), is excerpted from the opening chapter of *One Writer's Beginnings*.

Listening

In our house on North Congress Street in Jackson, Mississippi, 1
where I was born, the oldest of three children, in 1909, we grew up
to the striking of clocks. There was a mission-style oak grandfather
clock standing in the hall, which sent its gong-like strokes through
the livingroom, diningroom, kitchen, and pantry, and up the sounding board of the stairwell. Through the night, it could find its way
into our ears; sometimes, even on the sleeping porch, midnight could
wake us up. My parent's bedroom had a smaller striking clock that
answered it. Though the kitchen clock did nothing but show the
time, the diningroom clock was a cuckoo clock with weights on long
chains, on one of which my baby brother, after climbing on a chair
to the top of the china closet, once succeeded in suspending the cat
for a moment. I don't know whether or not my father's Ohio family,
in having been Swiss back in the 1700s before the first three Welty
brothers came to America, had anything to do with this; but we all

of us have been time-minded all our lives. This was good at least
for a future fiction writer, being able to learn so penetratingly, and
almost first of all, about chronology. It was one of a good many
things I learned almost without knowing it; it would be there when
I needed it.

My father loved all instruments that would instruct and fascinate.   2
His place to keep things was the drawer in the "library table" where
lying on top of his folded maps was a telescope with brass extensions,
to find the moon and the Big Dipper after supper in our front yard,
and to keep appointments with eclipses. There was a folding Kodak
that was brought out for Christmas, birthdays, and trips. In the back
of the drawer you could find a magnifying glass, a kaleidoscope,
and a gyroscope kept in a black buckram box, which he would set
dancing for us on a string pulled tight. He had also supplied himself
with an assortment of puzzles composed of metal rings and inter-
secting links and keys chained together, impossible for the rest of us,
however patiently shown, to take apart; he had an almost childlike
love of the ingenious.

In time, a barometer was added to our diningroom wall; but   3
we didn't really need it. My father had the country boy's accurate
knowledge of the weather and its skies. He went out and stood on
our front steps first thing in the morning and took a look at it and
a sniff. He was a pretty good weather prophet.

"Well, I'm *not*," my mother would say with enormous self-   4
satisfaction.

He told us children what to do if we were lost in a strange   5
country. "Look for where the sky is brightest along the horizon," he
said. "That reflects the nearest river. Strike out for a river and you
will find habitation." Eventualities were much on his mind. In his
care for us children he cautioned us to take measures against such
things as being struck by lightning. He drew us all away from the
windows during the severe electrical storms that are common where
we live. My mother stood apart, scoffing at caution as a character
failing. "Why, I always loved a storm! High winds never bothered
me in West Virginia! Just listen at that! I wasn't a bit afraid of a little
lightning and thunder! I'd go out on the mountain and spread my
arms wide and *run* in a good big storm!"

So I developed a strong meteorological sensibility. In years ahead   6
when I wrote stories, atmosphere took its influential role from the
start. Commotion in the weather and the inner feelings aroused by

such a hovering disturbance emerged connected in dramatic form. (I tried a tornado first, in a story called "The Winds.")

From our earliest Christmas times, Santa Claus brought us toys   7
that instruct boys and girls (separately) how to build things—stone blocks cut to the castle-building style, Tinker Toys, and Erector sets. Daddy made for us himself elaborate kites that needed to be taken miles out of town to a pasture long enough (and my father was not afraid of horses and cows watching) for him to run with and get up on a long cord to which my mother held the spindle, and then we children were given it to hold, tugging like something alive at our hands. They were beautiful, sound, shapely box kites, smelling delicately of office glue for their entire short lives. And of course, as soon as the boys attained anywhere near the right age, there was an electric train, the engine with its pea-sized working headlight, its line of cars, tracks equipped with switches, semaphores, its station, its bridges, and its tunnel, which blocked off all other traffic in the upstairs hall. Even from downstairs, and through the cries of excited children, the elegant rush and click of the train could be heard through the ceiling, running around and around its figure eight.

All of this, but especially the train, represents my father's fondest   8
beliefs—in progress, in the future. With these gifts, he was preparing his children.

And so was my mother with her different gifts.   9

I learned from the age of two or three that any room in our   10
house, at any time of day, was there to read in, or to be read to. My mother read to me. She'd read to me in the big bedroom in the mornings, when we were in her rocker together, which ticked in rhythm as we rocked, as though we had a cricket accompanying the story. She'd read to me in the diningroom on winter afternoons in front of the coal fire, with our cuckoo clock ending the story with "Cuckoo," and at night when I'd got in my own bed. I must have given her no peace. Sometimes she read to me in the kitchen while she sat churning, and the churning sobbed along with *any* story. It was my ambition to have her read to me while *I* churned; once she granted my wish, but she read off my story before I brought her butter. She was an expressive reader. When she was reading "Puss in Boots," for instance, it was impossible not to know that she distrusted *all* cats.

It had been startling and disappointing to me to find out that   11
story books had been written by *people,* that books were not natural

wonders, coming up of themselves like grass. Yet regardless of where they came from, I cannot remember a time when I was not in love with them—with the books themselves, cover and binding and the paper they were printed on, with their smell and their weight and with their possession in my arms, captured and carried off to myself. Still illiterate, I was ready for them, committed to all the reading I could give them.

Neither of my parents had come from homes that could afford 12 to buy many books, but though it must have been something of a strain on his salary, as the youngest officer in a young insurance company, my father was all the while carefully selecting and ordering away for what he and Mother thought we children should grow up with. They bought first for the future.

Besides the bookcase in the livingroom, which was always called 13 "the library," there were the encyclopedia tables and dictionary stand under windows in our diningroom. Here to help us grow up arguing around the diningroom table were the Unabridged Webster, the Columbia Encyclopedia, Compton's Pictured Encyclopedia, the Lincoln Library of Information, and later the Book of Knowledge. And the year we moved into our new house, there was room to celebrate it with the new 1925 edition of the Britannica, which my father, his face always deliberately turned toward the future, was of course disposed to think better than any previous edition.

In "the library," inside the mission-style bookcase with its three 14 diamond-latticed glass doors, with my father's Morris chair and the glass-shaded lamp on its table beside it, were books I could soon begin on—and I did, reading them all alike and as they came, straight down their rows, top shelf to bottom. There was the set of Stoddard's Lectures, in all its late nineteenth-century vocabulary and vignettes of peasant life and quaint beliefs and customs, with matching halftone illustrations: Vesuvius erupting, Venice by moonlight, gypsies glimpsed by their campfires. I didn't know then the clue they were to my father's longing to see the rest of the world. I read straight through his other love-from-afar: the Victrola Book of the Opera, with opera after opera in synopsis, with portraits in costume of Melba, Caruso, Galli-Curci, and Geraldine Farrar, some of whose voices we could listen to on our Red Seal records.

My mother read secondarily for information; she sank as a 15 hedonist into novels. She read Dickens in the spirit in which she would have eloped with him. The novels of her girlhood that had stayed on in her imagination, besides those of Dickens and Scott and Robert Louis Stevenson, were *Jane Eyre, Trilby, The Woman in White, Green Mansions, King Solomon's Mines.* Marie Corelli's name would crop up but I understood she had gone out of favor with my mother, who had only kept *Ardath* out of loyalty. In time she absorbed herself in Galsworthy, Edith Wharton, above all in Thomas Mann of the *Joseph* volumes.

St. Elmo was not in our house; I saw it often in other houses. 16 This wildly popular Southern novel is where all the Edna Earles in our population started coming from. They're all named for the heroine, who succeeded in bringing a dissolute, sinning roué and atheist of a lover (St. Elmo) to his knees. My mother was able to forgo it. But she remembered the classic advice given to rose growers on how to water their bushes long enough: "Take a chair and *St. Elmo.*"

To both my parents I owe my early acquaintance with a beloved 17 Mark Twain. There was a full set of Mark Twain and a short set of Ring Lardner in our bookcase, and those were the volumes that in time united us all, parents and children.

Reading everything that stood before me was how I came upon 18 a worn old book without a back that had belonged to my father as a child. It was called *Sanford and Merton.* Is there anyone left who recognizes it, I wonder? It is the famous moral tale written by Thomas Day in the 1780s, but of him no mention is made on the title page of *this* book; here it is *Sanford and Merton in Words of One Syllable* by Mary Godolphin. Here are the rich boy and the poor boy and Mr. Barlow, their teacher and interlocutor, in long discourses alternating with dramatic scenes—danger and rescue allotted to the rich and the poor respectively. It may have only words of one syllable, but one of them is "quoth." It ends with not one but two morals, both engraved on rings: "Do what you ought, come what may," and "If we would be great, we must first learn to be good."

This book was lacking its front cover, the back held on by strips 19 of pasted paper, now turned golden, in several layers, and the pages stained, flecked, and tattered around the edges; its garish illustrations had come unattached but were preserved, laid in. I had the feeling even in my heedless childhood that this was the only book my father as a little boy had had of his own. He had held onto it, and might have gone to sleep on its coverless face: he had lost his mother when he was seven. My father had never made any mention to his own children of the book, but he had brought it along with him from Ohio to our house and shelved it in our bookcase.

My mother had brought from West Virginia that set of Dickens;   20 those books looked sad, too—they had been through fire and water before I was born, she told me, and there they were, lined up—as I later realized, waiting for *me*.

I was presented, from as early as I can remember, with books   21 of my own, which appeared on my birthday and Christmas morning. Indeed, my parents could not give me books enough. They must have sacrificed to give me on my sixth or seventh birthday—it was after I became a reader for myself—the ten-volume set of Our Wonder World. These were beautifully made, heavy books I would lie down with on the floor in front of the diningroom hearth, and more often than the rest volume 5, *Every Child's Story Book*, was under my eyes. There were the fairy tales—Grimm, Andersen, the English, the French, "Ali Baba and the Forty Thieves"; and there was Aesop and Reynard the Fox; there were the myths and legends, Robin Hood, King Arthur, and St. George and the Dragon, even the history of Joan of Arc; a whack of *Pilgrim's Progress* and a long piece of *Gulliver*. They all carried their classic illustrations. I located myself in these pages and could go straight to the stories and pictures I loved; very often "The Yellow Dwarf" was first choice, with Walter Crane's Yellow Dwarf in full color making his terrifying appearance flanked by turkeys. Now that volume is as worn and backless and hanging apart as my father's poor *Sanford and Merton*. The precious page with Edward Lear's "Jumblies" on it has been in danger of slipping out for all these years. One measure of my love for Our Wonder World was that for a long time I wondered if I would go through fire and water for it as my mother had done for Charles Dickens; and the only comfort was to think I could ask my mother to do it for me.

I believe I'm the only child I know of who grew up with this   22 treasure in the house. I used to ask others, "Did you have Our Wonder World?" I'd have to tell them The Book of Knowledge could not hold a candle to it.

I live in gratitude to my parents for initiating me—and as early   23 as I begged for it, without keeping me waiting—into knowledge of the word, into reading and spelling, by way of the alphabet. They taught it to me at home in time for me to begin to read before starting to school. I believe the alphabet is no longer considered an essential piece of equipment for traveling through life. In my day it was the keystone to knowledge. You learned the alphabet as you learned to count to ten, as you learned "Now I lay me" and the Lord's Prayer and your father's and mother's name and address and telephone number, all in case you were lost.

My love for the alphabet, which endures, grew out of reciting it 24 but, before that, out of seeing the letters on the page. In my own story books, before I could read them for myself, I fell in love with various winding, enchanted-looking initials drawn by Walter Crane at the heads of fairy tales. In "Once upon a time," an "O" had a rabbit running it as a treadmill, his feet upon flowers. When the day came, years later, for me to see the Book of Kells, all the wizardry of letter, initial, and word swept over me a thousand times over, and the illumination, the gold, seemed a part of the word's beauty and holiness that had been there from the start.

❧ SYLVAN BARNET

Sylvan Barnet was born in New York City in 1926. After studying at New York University (B.A.) and Harvard (Ph.D.), he began teaching at Tufts University. During his career at Tufts, he was professor of English, chairperson of the English Department, and director of the freshman English program. Professor Barnet's interest in literature (especially drama), in the teaching of writing, and in art are reflected in his many publications. Besides numerous scholarly articles on literature, he has written a *Short Guide to Shakespeare* (1974) and *A Short Guide to Writing About Literature* (1985). He is also general editor of the Signet Classic Shakespeare and co-editor (with Morton Berman and William Burto) of *An Introduction to Literature* (1985). As a consultant he has helped shape many well-known writing texts and has shared his insights with students through the *Practical Guide to Writing* (1983) and *The Little, Brown Reader* (1983), both with Marcia Stubbs, as well as *Literature for Composition* (with Morton Berman and William Burto, 1983). His publications on art include *Zen Ink Painting* (with William Burto, 1983) and *A Short Guide to Writing About Art* (1985). He is currently at work on a history of Japanese painting.

Writing and Reading: Some Concrete Observations

When Bob Schwegler asked me to contribute an essay to this book, he tried to make the job easy: "Just write something about how you write. You know, something about writing about your reading." But as every student knows, the hardest essay to write is one that is not on a clearly defined topic. Anyone can write something fairly decent—if called upon to write on, say, "Why I Favor [or Don't Favor] Capital Punishment" or on "What's Wrong with Our Freshman Registration Procedure." One either does a little research, or one looks into one's heart, and writes—probably roughing out an outline, and then moving to a first draft. Of course in such cases the real work begins with revising, that is, with shaping one's first draft, which usually means clarifying the organization, getting the one right word instead of using three wrong words, supporting generalizations with effective details, and so on. Still, these things can usually be done fairly easily if one keeps in view the assigned topic.

But to be on one's own, to flounder around while trying to narrow a broad subject into a focused topic, that is to be in a condition that an existentialist philosopher called "dreadful freedom." And so my first point about writing, or, more specifically about writing about reading, is this: Hope that your instructor does the hard part for you and assigns a fairly precise topic, such as "Analyze the Methods of Persuasion used in 'The Declaration of Independence.'"

My second point is this: if a topic has been assigned, write on   2
it. My third point requires a bit more work: study the patterns that Schwegler discusses, take to heart his point that writers usually employ several patterns in a single essay, and see which ones will help you to write clearly and interestingly. It is a fact that these patterns will not only help you to present material clearly but will also help to generate ideas that you didn't have, or didn't know you had before you started to write. Patterns can serve you somewhat as rhyme can serve a poet: the need for a rhyme forces the poet to think of words with particular sounds, and one of these words may generate an unexpected but valuable idea. Robert Frost said that he often went into a poem, rather like an explorer, to see how he could get out. When he began the last stanza of "Stopping by Woods on a Snowy Evening" with "The woods are lovely, dark and deep," he may not have known what was coming next, and he may have said to himself, "'Deep,' 'sheep—no, there are no sheep out at this time,' 'reap—no, that's the wrong season,' 'keep—yes, that's it:

> But I have promises to keep.'"

And then, "'Heap,' 'peep,' 'sleep—yes, sleep:

> And miles to go before I sleep,
> And miles to go before I sleep.'"

Similarly, if in a history course you are comparing two battles, or in an education course two kinds of tests, or in an art course two pictures, jotting down something about one and, so to speak, looking for the rhyme in the other will probably force you to see something in the second, something you may have overlooked up to that point. When you are going to write about something you are reading, you will encounter unfamiliar ideas, and these will stimulate your own thoughts, which may be slightly different or on the other hand radically different from what you are reading. You have two duties to the author: one is to read sympathetically, listening to what the author has to say; but the other is to read (and re-read) critically, testing the author's assertions and reflecting on your own experience.

We all need to be stimulated to think, and one of the reasons   3
that we read anything (I am now getting down to my topic) is that we want to understand better, to see better. We read in order to become educated. Now, one of the emphases in this book, and it is an entirely proper one, is that we read in order to learn how to write. That is, as I have already suggested, we want to write clearly and interestingly—partly for reasons that are utilitarian. We want to get good grades on our papers in history courses, we want to write letters of application that will land us jobs, and, once we are on the job, we want to write reports that will keep us in our jobs or will perhaps gain us promotions. But surely our chief motive for reading, and for learning to write, is that we want to live thoughtful lives. We want to see the complexities of life, and we want to respond to them justly, thoughtfully, to the fullest extent of our powers. Perhaps the most memorable statement of a reader's experience is that of John Keats, in "On First Looking Into Chapman's Homer." In this sonnet Keats says he had heard people praise the work of the Greek poet Homer, but Homer was to him a closed book. One day, however, he read George Chapman's translation, and the scales fell from his eyes:

> Then felt I like some watcher of the skies
> When a new planet swims into his ken.

Reading a book, then, can be an *experience*, quite as much as putting in a day's work, falling ill, winning a lottery, or getting married. So we read, at least partly, in order to gain experiences, to know more (which also means to feel more) of life than we are likely to encounter in our otherwise relatively confined existence. We want to know (and Homer can tell us) what it feels like to be shipwrecked, or to win (or lose) a battle. We also want to know things that are more commonplace: what it feels like to walk through a decaying city, how an American of Mexican descent feels about growing apart from the culture of his parents, how it feels to take possession of some new piece of property. On this last point, about possessing property, I have in mind E. M. Forster's delightful essay, "My Wood" (pp. 527–530). With his title Forster playfully misleads us: we probably expect an essay that is chiefly a description of scenery, but it turns out that the emphasis is as much on the "My" as on the "Wood" because Forster is really writing about the effect of ownership, that is, about what the wood does to him. First of all, he says, "It makes me feel heavy." "Property produces men of weight, and it was a man of weight who failed to get into the kingdom of Heaven." Second, the wood makes him "feel it ought to be larger," and he gives a delightful example. A bird alights in his wood. Ah, it is *his* bird. But then the bird flies over a hedge and into Mrs. Henessy's wood, whereupon the bird becomes Mrs. Henessy's bird, and this bothers Forster. Forster is, of course, talking about greed—and we recognize the feeling. The shoe fits; it pinches, but we recognize it as ours, our own rather nasty feeling. We probably had not quite thought of possessions—of *our* possessions—this way. Forster has gently, good-naturedly, but firmly taught us something about ourselves, though of course he has not been so rude as to say that he is talking about us. He claims only to be talking about himself, but we are learning about what it is to be a human being. Forster goes on to set forth two additional points about the effect of owning something, but I need not go into them here. If you haven't read his short essay, I imagine that you will soon do so.

From Forster you can learn the virtue of simple enumeration: 4 he is not ashamed to say, "In the first place," "In the second place," "In the third place," and even "And this brings us to our fourth and last point." Seeing an esteemed author making every effort to be clear may be a help to the student-writer who might otherwise feel that such clarity "is too obvious" or "lacks style." Notice, by the way, that Forster tells us that his fourth point is his final point. He is letting the reader know that the journey is nearly over, so the reader won't feel, after reading a few more sentences, that the essay ends abruptly. Things of this sort you will learn by reading Schwegler's comments and by reading the essays in this book, and you should not hesitate to make these devices your own.

But what about writing *about* reading? You may, of course, be 5 asked to write an analysis of Forster's organization, or of his tone, and by doing so you will probably gain a closer understanding both of the subject of Forster's essay and of the art of writing than you would gain merely by reading his essay. Or you may be asked to write on a topic related to the subject of your reading. Writing about reading offers the opportunity to think for ourselves, with a little help from our friends the masters. Thus, after reading Forster's essay you may want to write about the effect, on you, of owning a stereo set, a car, or a cat. As you think about this, you may find yourself taking on Forster as a sparring-partner: you find that owning X or Y gives you quite a different set of sensations from those Forster described. Forster may be the godfather of your essay, and you owe him thanks for helping you to get started, but your essay will be your own work, and by writing it you will have clarified, at least for a while, one aspect of your own life—and perhaps of your reader's too, for if your essay is honest, if you search your mind and don't simply say that owning a pet teaches one to be responsible, your essay will probably touch on universal but neglected feelings. Or, triggered by Forster, you may find yourself thinking about describing (in concrete terms, as he does) some abstraction, such as education, love, the police system, or public libraries. You will examine your experience, which (remember Keats) includes your feelings, and you will talk about one or the other of these things concretely.

Speaking of concrete, I want to mention that Edward Abbey's "The Damnation of a Canyon" [pp. 460–467] irked me when I read in its fifth paragraph, "I find it hard to learn to love cement." Abbey is a skillful writer, an effective persuader, and I can enjoy his wry understatement when he says, "I take a dim view of dams; I find it hard to learn to love concrete." Nice alliteration in "dim" and "dam," and in "learn" and "love," but somehow there popped into my mind a big new building—part shops, part offices—in my neighborhood. It is made of poured concrete and glass, and when it was going up we all grumbled that it was a monstrosity. But when the windows got put in, and when tenants moved in and we could see people moving about at their jobs, it became quite attractive. The pale gray concrete provided a handsome framework for the colorful dresses, shirts, and furniture inside. And then another image came into my mind, Margaret Bourke-White's great photograph [p. 489] of the Fort Peck Dam in Montana, a picture which adorned the cover of the first issue of *Life*, in 1936. I don't know what the ecological effect of the dam has been—it was one of a chain of dams built in the Columbia River basin as part of Roosevelt's New Deal—but I do know that the dam, and others like it, was of enormous assistance in helping the country recover from the Depression, in giving employment and a sense of purpose to a dispirited generation. It may be, of course, that the long-range costs have far outweighed the short-term benefits. That could be the subject of a very interesting

6

LIFE

NOVEMBER 23, 1936 10 CENTS

research paper. One thing I do know, however, is that Bourke-White's photograph helps us to see the dam the way Roosevelt, the engineers, the farmers, and the laborers saw it, indeed the way the whole nation saw it, as a great and beautiful achievement. Abbey emphasizes the beauty of nature, and it will be tragic if we ever lose sight of this beauty, but nature is not the whole of our lives, and Bourke-White with equal propriety emphasizes the beauty of engineering, the beauty of what must be regarded as a heroic achievement inspired by high ideals and made real by great mental and physical skills. These dams, rich in human aspiration and accomplishment, are America's pyramids, America's castles, America's cathedrals. And so I am moved to say that although Abbey's essay is both a valuable example of persuasive writing and an inherently interesting piece, it is not the last word about dams or about cement. Admittedly, though cement can have a range of hues, from pale gray to buff, rose, and dark gray, it is not immediately beautiful, but that fact is only an argument on behalf of why we, as thoughtful people, should look more closely at it—what it is, what we have done with it, and what it has done for us. It is easy enough to disparage cement; it is harder to be fair to it, but we can try—perhaps in an essay of five hundred words.

At the risk of violating the sound principle that an essay should   7
have a clear organization, I want to tack on an ending. (My strategy in the previous sentence is transparent but I think adequate: I am forestalling an objection to my writing by calling attention to the fault. Abbey himself does this, in his fifth paragraph, when he admits "at the outset to a certain bias.") My point in the previous paragraph is not that Abbey's essay is unconvincing or uninteresting. Quite the contrary. From it a reader can learn a lot about tampering with nature, and a lot about effective persuasive writing. Notice, for example, this neat comparison: "Lake Powell, formed by Glen Canyon Dam, is not a lake. It is a reservoir, with a constantly fluctuating water level—more like a bathtub that is never drained than a true lake." A bathtub that is never drained: that's beautiful writing. I cannot imagine a more persuasive way of making us feel that Lake Powell is, well, icky. Or consider Abbey's use of concrete (he'll pardon the expression) images, for instance when he writes: "Then we had a wild and flowing river lined by boulder-strewn shores, sandy beaches, thickets of tamarisk and willow, and glades of cottonwood." It happens that I don't know a tamarisk from a cotton-wood

(I must find out about these), but the passage convinces me that *he* knows, and that he has a right to speak about the lake and its environs.

The final lesson, then, is simply this: from reading we learn. One of the first things we learn is that if we want our own writing to be taken seriously we have to convince the reader, as Abbey does, that we know what we are talking about. One of the second things we learn is this: if we are grateful to writers for what they teach us about the world, we are also grateful to them for prodding us to take issue with them, for helping us to develop our own ideas in essays that take off from what we have read.

❧ DONALD M. MURRAY

Donald M. Murray was born in Boston in 1924 and educated at the University of New Hampshire and Boston University. He worked as a newspaper reporter, rewrite man, and editorial writer, winning the Pulitzer Prize (at age 29) for editorials in the *Boston Herald.* Murray also worked as a contributing editor for *Time,* and while on the staff of the *Boston Globe,* he became the newspaper's first writing coach. In 1963, Murray began teaching at the University of New Hampshire, becoming, in due course, English Department chairperson and director of both freshman and advanced composition programs. His writings include magazine articles, poetry, short stories, a novel (*The Man Who Had Everything,* 1964), and both adult and juvenile nonfiction. Murray's advice for writers and teachers has appeared in several dozen scholarly articles and in *A Writer Teaches Writing* (a text for writing teachers, 1968), *Learning by Teaching* (a collection of essays, 1984), *Write to Learn* (a college freshman text, 1984), and *Writing for Your Readers: Notes on the Writer's Craft from the "Boston Globe"* (1983). The following essay was first published in *The Writer* in 1973 and later extensively revised.

The Maker's Eye: Revising Your Own Manuscripts

When students complete a first draft, they consider the job of 1 writing done—and their teachers too often agree. When professional writers complete a first draft, they usually feel that they are at the start of the writing process. When a draft is completed, the job of writing can begin.

That difference in attitude is the difference between amateur and 2 professional, inexperience and experience, journeyman and craftsman. Peter F. Drucker, the prolific business writer, calls his first draft "the zero draft"—after that he can start counting. Most writers share the feeling that the first draft, and all of those which follow, are opportunities to discover what they have to say and how best they can say it.

To produce a progression of drafts, each of which says more 3 and says it more clearly, the writer has to develop a special kind of reading skill. In school we are taught to decode what appears on

492

the page as finished writing. Writers, however, face a different category of possibility and responsibility when they read their own drafts. To them the words on the page are never finished. Each can be changed and rearranged, can set off a chain reaction of confusion or clarified meaning. This is a different kind of reading, which is possibly more difficult and certainly more exciting.

Writers must learn to be their own best enemy. They must accept 4 the criticism of others and be suspicious of it; they must accept the praise of others and be even more suspicious of it. Writers cannot depend on others. They must detach themselves from their own pages so that they can apply both their caring and their craft to their own work.

Such detachment is not easy. Science fiction writer Ray Bradbury 5 supposedly puts each manuscript away for a year to the day and then rereads it as a stranger. Not many writers have the discipline or the time to do this. We must read when our judgment may be at its worst, when we are close to the euphoric moment of creation.

Then the writer, counsels novelist Nancy Hale, "should be critical 6 of everything that seems to him most delightful in his style. He should excise what he most admires, because he wouldn't thus admire it if he weren't . . . in a sense protecting it from criticism." John Ciardi, the poet, adds, "The last act of the writing must be to become one's own reader. It is, I suppose, a schizophrenic process, to begin passionately and to end critically, to begin hot and to end cold; and, more important, to be passion-hot and critic-cold at the same time."

Most people think that the principal problem is that writers are 7 too proud of what they have written. Actually, a greater problem for most professional writers is one shared by the majority of students. They are overly critical, think everything is dreadful, tear up page after page, never complete a draft, see the task as hopeless.

The writer must learn to read critically but constructively to cut 8 what is bad, to reveal what is good. Eleanor Estes, the children's book author, explains: "The writer must survey his work critically, coolly, as though he were a stranger to it. He must be willing to prune, expertly and hard-heartedly. At the end of each revision, a manuscript may look . . . worked over, torn apart, pinned together, added to, deleted from, words changed and words changed back. Yet the book must maintain its original freshness and spontaneity."

Most readers underestimate the amount of rewriting it usually 9 takes to produce spontaneous reading. This is a great disadvantage to the student writer, who sees only a finished product and never watches the craftsman who takes the necessary step back, studies the work carefully, returns to the task, steps back, returns, steps back, again and again. Anthony Burgess, one of the most prolific writers in the English-speaking world, admits, "I might revise a page twenty times." Roald Dahl, the popular children's writer, states, "By the time I'm nearing the end of a story, the first part will have been reread and altered and corrected at least 150 times. . . . Good writing is essentially rewriting. I am positive of this."

Rewriting isn't virtuous. It isn't something that ought to be done. 10 It is simply something that most writers find they have to do to discover what they have to say and how to say it. It is a condition of the writer's life.

There are, however, a few writers who do little formal rewriting, 11 primarily because they have the capacity and experience to create and review a large number of invisible drafts in their minds before they approach the page. And some writers slowly produce finished pages, performing all the tasks of revision simultaneously, page by page, rather than draft by draft. But it is still possible to see the sequence followed by most writers most of the time in rereading their own work.

Most writers scan their drafts first, reading as quickly as possible 12 to catch the larger problems of subject and form, then move in closer and closer as they read and write, reread and rewrite.

The first thing writers look for in their drafts is *information.* 13 They know that a good piece of writing is built from specific, accurate, and interesting information. The writer must have an abundance of information from which to construct a readable piece of writing.

Next writers look for *meaning* in the information. The specifics 14 must build to a pattern of significance. Each piece of specific information must carry the reader toward meaning.

Writers reading their own drafts are aware of *audience.* They 15 put themselves in the reader's situation and make sure that they deliver information which a reader wants to know or needs to know in a manner which is easily digested. Writers try to be sure that they anticipate and answer the questions a critical reader will ask when reading the piece of writing.

Writers make sure that the *form* is appropriate to the subject 16 and the audience. Form, or genre, is the vehicle which carries meaning to the reader, but form cannot be selected until the writer has adequate information to discover its significance and an audience which needs or wants that meaning.

Once writers are sure the form is appropriate, they must then look at the *structure,* the order of what they have written. Good writing is built on a solid framework of logic, argument, narrative, or motivation which runs through the entire piece of writing and holds it together. This is the time when many writers find it most effective to outline as a way of visualizing the hidden spine by which the piece of writing is supported. 17

The element on which writers may spend a majority of their time is *development.* Each section of a piece of writing must be adequately developed. It must give readers enough information so that they are satisfied. How much information is enough? That's as difficult as asking how much garlic belongs in a salad. It must be done to taste, but most beginning writers underdevelop, underestimating the reader's hunger for information. 18

As writers solve development problems, they often have to consider questions of *dimension.* There must be a pleasing and effective proportion among all the parts of the piece of writing. There is a continual process of subtracting and adding to keep the piece of writing in balance. 19

Finally, writers have to listen to their own voice. *Voice* is the force which drives a piece of writing forward. It is an expression of the writer's authority and concern. It is what is between the words on the page, what glues the piece of writing together. A good piece of writing is always marked by a consistent, individual voice. 20

As writers read and reread, write and rewrite, they move closer and closer to the page until they are doing line-by-line editing. Writers read their own pages with infinite care. Each sentence, each line, each clause, each phrase, each word, each mark of punctuation, each section of white space between the type has to contribute to the clarification of meaning. 21

Slowly the writer moves from word to word, looking through language to see the subject. As a word is changed, cut, or added, as a construction is rearranged, all the words used before that moment and all those that follow that moment must be considered and reconsidered. 22

Writers often read aloud at this stage of the editing process, muttering or whispering to themselves, calling on the ear's experi- 23 ence with language. Does this sound right—or that? Writers edit, shifting back and forth from eye to page to ear to page. I find I must do this careful editing in short runs, no more than fifteen or twenty minutes at a stretch, or I become too kind with myself. I begin to see what I hope is on the page, not what actually is on the page.

This sounds tedious if you haven't done it, but actually it is fun.   24 Making something right is immensely satisfying, for writers begin to learn what they are writing about by writing. Language leads them to meaning, and there is the joy of discovery, of understanding, of making meaning clear as the writer employs the technical skills of language.

Words have double meanings, even triple and quadruple mean-   25 ings. Each word has its own potential for connotation and denotation. And when writers rub one word against the other, they are often rewarded with a sudden insight, an unexpected clarification.

The maker's eye moves back and forth from word to phrase to   26 sentence to paragraph to sentence to phrase to word. The maker's eye sees the need for variety and balance, for a firmer structure, for a more appropriate form. It peers into the interior of the paragraph, looking for coherence, unity, and emphasis, which make meaning clear.

I learned something about this process when my first bifocals   27 were prescribed. I had ordered a larger section of the reading portion of the glass because of my work, but even so, I could not contain my eyes within this new limit of vision. And I still find myself taking off my glasses and bending my nose towards the page, for my eyes unconsciously flick back and forth across the page, back to another page, forward to still another, as I try to see each evolving line in relation to every other line.

When does this process end? Most writers agree with the great   28 Russian writer Tolstoy, who said, "I scarcely ever reread my published writings, if by chance I come across a page, it always strikes me: all this must be rewritten; this is how I should have written it."

The maker's eye is never satisfied, for each word has the potential   29 to ignite new meaning. This article has been twice written all the way through the writing process, and it was published four years ago. Now it is to be republished in a book. The editors make a few small suggestions, and then I read it with my maker's eye. Now it has been re-edited, re-revised, re-read, re-re-edited, for each piece of writing to the writer is full of potential and alternatives.

A piece of writing is never finished. It is delivered to a deadline, 30 torn out of the typewriter on demand, sent off with a sense of accomplishment and shame and pride and frustration. If only there were a couple more days, time for just another run at it, perhaps then . . .

🐚 MIKE ROSE

Mike Rose was born in Los Angeles in 1944. He studied at Loyola University of Los Angeles (B.A.) and the University of Southern California (M.S.) before receiving an M.A. and Ph.D. from the University of California at Los Angeles. He is currently director of the Freshman Writing Program at UCLA, where he has also taught in the English Department and coordinated the Freshman Summer Program and the Freshman Preparatory Program. Rose has written extensively on the cognitive processes that shape writing, on educational administration, and on academic tutoring and counseling. His scholarly articles have appeared in a variety of journals, including *College Composition and Communication* and *College English*. He is the author of a book, *Writer's Block: The Cognitive Dimension* (1983) and editor of another, *When a Writer Can't Write: Studies in Writer's Block and Other Composing Process Problems* (1984). In addition to his scholarly writing, Rose is also a published poet whose work has appeared in numerous small magazines. The piece that follows was written especially for this book.

Writing Around Rules

I

Here's Liz, a junior English major, at work on a paper for a 1 college course: she has been given a two-page case study and must analyze it using the ideas contained in a second, brief handout. She has about one hour to complete her assignment. As she reads and rereads the handouts, she scribbles notes to herself in the margins. Liz is doing what most effective writers would do with such materials: paraphrasing the main points in the passages, making connections among them, recording associations to other pertinent knowledge. But a closer look at these interpretive notes reveals something unusual: Liz seems to be editing them as she goes along, cleaning them up as though they were final copy. In one of her notes she jots down the phrase "is saying that not having creative work is the. . . ." She stops, thinks for a moment, and changes "is the" to "causes." (Later on, explaining this change, she'll comment that "you're not supposed to have passive verbs.") She then replaces "is saying" with "says," apparently following her directive about passive voice, but later changes it again, noting that "says" is "too collo-quial." Liz pauses after this editing and looks up—she has forgotten what she initially was trying to capture in her writing. "That happens a lot," she says.

Liz was one of the many college students I studied over a two-and-one-half-year period (*Writer's Block: The Cognitive Dimension*). The purpose of my study was to try to gain insight into what causes some young writers to compose with relative fluency and what leads others to experience more than their fair share of blocks, dead-ends, conflicts, and the frustrations of the blank page. What I uncovered was a whole array of problems that I would label as being primarily *cognitive* rather than primarily *emotional* in nature. That is, many students were engaging in self-defeating composing behaviors not because they had some deep-seated fear of revealing their thoughts or of being evaluated or because of some long-standing aversion to writing, but rather because they had somehow learned a number of rules, planning strategies, or assumptions about writing that limited rather than enhanced their composing. We saw Liz lose her train of thought by adhering too rigidly to stylistic rules when she should have been scribbling ideas freely in order to discover material for her essay. Let me offer two further vignettes that illustrate some of the other cognitive difficulties I uncovered.

Tyrrell, also a junior English major, says he doesn't like to sketch out any sort of plan or draft of what he's going to write. He'll think about his topic, but his pen usually won't touch paper until he begins writing the one, and only, draft he'll produce. As he writes, he pauses frequently and at length to make all sorts of decisions about words, ideas, and rhetorical effects. In short, he plans his work as he goes along. There's nothing inherently wrong with writing this way, but where difficult assignments involving complex materials are con-cerned, it helps to sketch out a few ideas, some direction, a loose organizational structure before beginning to write. When a co-worker and I studied Tyrrell's composing, we noted the stylistic flourishes in his essay, but also its lack of direction. As my colleague noted, "[His] essay bogs down in description and in unexplained abstractions." Perhaps the essay would have had more direction if Tyrrell had roughed out a few ideas before composing his one and only draft. Why didn't he do so? Consider his comment on planning:

> [Planning] is certainly not spontaneous and a lot of the times it's not even really what you feel because it becomes very mechanical. It's

almost like—at least I feel—it's diabolical, you know, because . . . it'll sacrifice truth and real feelings that you have.

Tyrrell assumes that sketching out a plan before writing somehow violates the spontaneity of composing: to plan dooms one to write mechanical, unemotional prose. Yet, while too much planning may sometimes make the actual writing a joyless task, it is also true that most good writing is achieved through some kind of prefiguring, most often involving pen and paper. Such planning does not necessarily subvert spontaneity; in fact, since it reduces the load on the writer's immediate memory, it might actually free one to be more spontaneous, to follow the lead of new ideas as they emerge. Tyrrell's assumption, then, is inaccurate. By recognizing only this one path to spontaneity, he is probably limiting his effectiveness as a writer and, ironically, may be reducing his opportunities to be spontaneous.

Gary is an honors senior in biochemistry. When I observed him,   4
he spent over half of his writing time meticulously analyzing each sentence of the assignment's reading passage on one of the handouts. He understood the passage and the assignment well enough but wanted to make sure the passage was sufficiently broken down to be of use when he composed his essay. As Gary conducted this minute analysis, he wrote dozens and dozens of words and phrases across the handouts. He then summarized these words and phrases in a list of six items. He *then* tried to condense all six items into a thesis sentence:

> I have concepts . . . and my task here is to say what is being said about all of those all at once.

Gary's method was, in this case, self-defeating. He worked in too precise a fashion, generating an unwieldy amount of preliminary material, which he didn't seem to be able to rank or thin out—and he was unable to focus his thinking in a single thesis sentence. Gary's interpretive and planning strategies were inappropriately elaborate, and they were inflexible. It was not surprising that when Gary's hour was up, he had managed to write only three disconnected sentences. Not really an essay at all.

But what about the students who weren't stymied, who wrote   5
with relative fluency? They too talked of rules and assumptions and displayed planning strategies. The interesting thing, though, is that their rules were more flexible; that is, a rule seemed to include conditions under which it ought and ought not to be used. The rules

weren't absolutes, but rather statements about what one might do in certain writing situations. Their assumptions, as well, were not absolute and they tended to enhance composing, opening up rather than restricting possibilities. And their planning strategies tended to be flexible and appropriate to the task. Fluent writers had their rules, strategies, and assumptions, but they were of a different kind from those of the blocked writers.

What to do? One is tempted to urge the blocked writers to clear 6 their minds of troubling rules, plans, and assumptions. In a few cases, that might not be such a bad idea. But what about Liz's preoccupation with passive constructions? Some degree of concern about casting one's language in the active voice is a good thing. And Gary's precise strategies? It would be hard to imagine good academic writing that isn't preceded by careful analysis of one's materials. Writers need the order and the guidance that rules, strategies, and assumptions provide. The answer to Liz's, Tyrrell's, and Gary's problems, then, lies in altering their approaches to make them more conditional, adaptive, and flexible. Let me explain further. For the sake of convenience, I'll focus on rules, though what I'll say has application to the assumptions we develop and the planning strategies we learn.

II

Writing is a phenomenally complex learned activity. To write in 7 a way that others can understand we must employ a large and complicated body of conventions. We learn from our parents or earliest teachers that script, in English, goes left to right straight across the page. We learn about letter formation, spelling, sentence structure, and so on. Some of this information we absorb more or less unconsciously through reading, and some of it we learn formally as guidelines, as directives . . . as rules.

And there are all kinds of rules. Some tell us how to format our 8 writing (for example, when to capitalize, how to paragraph, how to footnote). There are grammar rules (for example, "Make a pronoun agree in number with its antecedent"). There are preferences concerning style that are often stated as rules ("Avoid passive voice"). There are usage rules (*"That* always introduces restrictive clauses; *which* can introduce both restrictive and nonrestrictive clauses"). There are rules that tell us how to compose ("Before you begin writing, decide on your thesis and write it down in a single declarative sentence"). The list goes on and on. Some of these rules make sense; others are confusing, questionable, or contradictory. Fortunately, we assimilate a good deal of the information they contain gradually by reading other writers, by writing ourselves, or by simply being around print. Therefore, we can confirm or alter or reject them from experience.

But all too often the rules are turned into absolutes. And that's   9
where the trouble begins. Most rules about writing should not be expressed (in textbooks), stored (in our minds), or enacted (on the page) as absolutes, as mathematical, unvarying directives. True, a few rules apply in virtually all situations (for example, certain formatting rules or capitalization rules). But most rules do not. Writing rules, like any rules about language, have a history and have a time and place. They are highly context-bound.

Should you always, as some textbooks suggest, place your thesis   10
sentence at the beginning of your first paragraph or, as others suggest, work up to it and place it at the end of the paragraph? Well, the answer is that both injunctions are right . . . and wrong. Students writing essay exams would be well-advised to demonstrate their knowledge and direct the reader's attention as soon as possible. But the writer who wants to evoke a mood might offer a series of facts and events that gradually lead up to a thesis sentence. The writing situation, the rhetorical purpose, and the nature of the material one is working with will provide the answer. A single-edged rule cannot.

How about our use of language, usage rules? Certainly there's   11
a right and a wrong here? Again, not quite. First of all, there's a time in one's writing to worry about such things. Concern yourself with questions of usage too early in your composing and you'll end up like Liz, worryimg about the minutiae of language while your thought fades to a wisp. Second, the social consequences of following or ignoring such rules vary widely depending on whether you're writing formal or informal prose. Third, usage rules themselves have an evolutionary history: we aren't obliged to follow some of the rules that turn-of-the-century writers had to deal with, and our rules will alter and even disappear as the English language moves on in time. No, there are no absolutes here either.

Well, how about some of the general, commonsense rules about   12
the very act of writing itself? Certainly, rules like "Think before you write" ought to be followed? Again, a qualification is in order. While

it certainly is good advice to think through ideas before we record them for others to see, many people, in fact, use writing as a way of thinking. They make major decisions *as* they write. There are times when it's best to put a piece of writing aside and ponder, but there are also times when one ought to keep pen in hand and attempt to resolve a conceptual tangle by sketching out what comes to mind. Both approaches are legitimate.

I'll stop here. I hope I've shown that it's difficult to make hard 13 and fast statements about the structure, the language, or the composing of an essay. Unfortunately, there's a strong push in our culture to make absolute statements about writing, especially where issues of style and usage are concerned. But I hope by now the reader of this essay believes that most rules about writing—about how to do it, about how it should be structured, about what words to use— are not absolute, and should be taught and enacted in a flexible, context-dependent way. Given certain conditions, you follow them; given other conditions you modify or suspend them. A teacher may insist that a young writer follow a particular dictum in order to learn a pattern, but there must come a time when the teacher extends the lesson and explains when the dictum is and isn't appropriate.

Because I've relied on the writing of college students for my 14 illustrations, it might seem that my assertions—particularly about the connection between inflexible rules and blocking—apply only to young, developing writers. Not so. A professional writer's sense of self is intimately involved in his or her work, so, to be sure, the blocks and resistances such writers experience are often related to emotional factors. But the cognitive dimension we've seen with collegiate writers is present as well. The rules that trip up the professional writer may be different, but the fundamental processes and problems can be quite similar. Let me illustrate this point by coming closer to home and offering an illustration from my own writing, the composition of a poem.

III

Here's the background. My father has been dead for many years 15 now, but he is still very much present in my dreams. In one recent dream, I was standing by his bedside; he was comatose. The dream then shifted—as dreams often do—and I was outside watching him tinker at a workbench. When I woke, I knew I had the central image

of a poem, a short elegy. Here is what finally emerged, five or so
revisions later:

> The last we knew
> doctors were explaining "aneurysm."
> Father lay in the next room, asleep.
> We were surprised, then,
> to find him at his workbench,
> white oleander at his back
> rustling night music in direct sun.
>
> He set the vise
> on a bar of red metal
> and with thin flame
> pared it into petals.
> He cupped them, whispering.
> Slipping dowels through his fingers
> he made a fist, hard,
> opened it,
> and handed us two shining roses.
>
> We place them by him
> asleep in the next room.

I was happy with the poem—with its images, its compression.   16
But I knew that the abrupt shifts in time and place could confuse
readers unless they knew that the poem is a dream vision. Now, I
didn't want to wreck the poem's compression or interrupt the reader's movement through the events of the poem by intruding into the
lines themselves, by grabbing a reader by the collar and yelling,
"Hey! This is a dream. Get it?" I knew that I had to do whatever I
was going to do in the title; the reader had to be clued in before the
poem began. At this point, I blocked. And for reasons not unlike
those that tripped up the students I had observed. Titles, to my mind,
did certain things, fit certain conventions that I had either read or
heard or somehow absorbed from years and years of reading other
people's poems: Titles should add something to a poem, not just
state the obvious. Titles should be evocative. Titles take up one line.
Titles are direct and declarative. The words in a title should be in
one sentence. So went the list. Some of these rules I recall learning
from mentors. Others I acquired somehow, somewhere. Some of the
rules made sense. Others were nonsense. And some—like the injunctions to be evocative and to be direct—potentially conflicted. I
tried titles like "The Dream Answer" and junked them quickly as

clichés and as . . . well . . . just stupid. Days passed. And more days. I was stuck. I was working with a whole set of notions about titles that placed certain boundaries on what I could invent and what I would consider acceptable. All writers work within boundaries, but these were proving to be too restrictive.

One afternoon I was talking to my friend Bonnie Verburg—a   17
fine writer—about my dilemma. She thought for a while and went to get a poem of her own: a dream poem. We made some comparisons and talked about the effects we were trying to get by keeping the dissociated structure of the dream. Then she asked why I didn't try a title that itself was dream-like, that is, that compressed disparate words or ideas or events together. Something clicked. I wasn't sure I was following exactly what Bonnie was asking of me, but I saw that I *could* have a title different from the kind dictated by my various directives and assumptions. The poem's title came quickly:

Dream
My Father's Flowers

Bonnie, in effect, had provided a new direction that I hadn't   18
seen as a possibility. My experience with her made it clear that some of my rules about titles were limiting rather than guiding my thinking. In solving the problem before me, I rejected some rules and recast others into more flexible directives, directives with some play in them that might now lead to the composing of effective titles for what I hope are reams of future poems.

* WILLIAM ZINSSER

William Zinsser was born in 1922 in New York City. After attending Princeton University he worked on the *New York Herald Tribune* as a feature writer, drama and film critic, and editorial writer, and then as a columnist for *Look* and *Life* magazines. In 1970 he began teaching expository writing at Yale University, an experience that led to a textbook, *On Writing Well: An Informal Guide to Writing Non-Fiction* (1976). Since 1979, Zinsser has been executive editor of the Book-of-the-Month Club and has continued to write for magazines. His books include *Any Old Place With You* (1957), *Seen Any Good Movies Lately?* (1958), *The City Dwellers* (1962), *The Haircut Papers* (1964), *Pop Goes America* (1966), *The Lunacy Boom* (1970), and, most recently, *Writing with a Word Processor* (1983). The selection that follows is a chapter from *Writing with a Word Processor*.

The Act of Writing: One Man's Method

Writing is a deeply personal process, full of mystery and surprise. 1 No two people go about it in exactly the same way. We all have little devices to get us started, or to keep us going, or to remind us of what we think we want to say, and what works for one person may not work for anyone else. The main thing is to get something written—to get the words out of our heads. There is no "right" method. Any method that will do the job is the right method for you.

It helps to remember that writing is hard. Most non-writers 2 don't know this; they think that writing is a natural function, like breathing, that ought to come easy, and they're puzzled when it doesn't. If you find that writing is hard, it's because it *is* hard. It's one of the hardest things that people do. Among other reasons, it's hard because it requires thinking. You won't write clearly unless you keep forcing yourself to think clearly. There's no escaping the question that has to be constantly asked: What do I want to say next?

So painful is this task that writers go to remarkable lengths to 3 postpone their daily labor. They sharpen their pencils and change their typewriter ribbon and go out to the store to buy more paper. Now these sacred rituals, as [the computer manuals] would say, have been obsoleted.

When I began writing this book on my word processor I didn't   4
have any idea what would happen. Would I be able to write anything
at all? Would it be any good? I was bringing to the machine what I
assumed were wholly different ways of thinking about writing. The
units massed in front of me looked cold and sterile. Their steady
hum reminded me that they were waiting. They seemed to be waiting
for information, not for writing. Maybe what I wrote would also be
cold and sterile.

I was particularly worried about the absence of paper. I knew   5
that I would only be able to see as many lines as the screen would
hold—twenty lines. How could I review what I had already written?
How could I get a sense of continuity and flow? With paper it was
always possible to flick through the preceding pages to see where I
was coming from—and where I ought to be going. Without paper I
would have no such periodic fix. Would this be a major hardship?

The only way to find out was to find out. I took a last look at   6
my unsharpened pencils and went to work.

My particular hang-up as a writer is that I have to get every   7
paragraph as nearly right as possible before I go on to the next
paragraph. I'm somewhat like a bricklayer: I build very slowly, not
adding a new row until I feel that the foundation is solid enough to
hold up the house. I'm the exact opposite of the writer who dashes
off his entire first draft, not caring how sloppy it looks or how badly
it's written. His only objective at this early stage is to let his creative
motor run the full course at full speed; repairs can always be made
later. I envy this writer and would like to have his metabolism. But
I'm stuck with the one I've got.

I also care how my writing looks while I'm writing it. The visual   8
arrangement is important to me: the shape of the words, of the
sentences, of the paragraphs, of the page. I don't like sentences that
are dense with long words, or paragraphs that never end. As I write
I want to see the design that my piece will have when the reader
sees it in type, and I want that design to have a rhythm and a pace
that will invite the reader to keep reading. O.K., so I'm a nut. But
I'm not alone; the visual component is important to a large number
of people who write.

One hang-up we visual people share is that our copy must be   9
neat. My lifelong writing method, for instance, has gone like this. I
put a piece of paper in the typewriter and write the first paragraph.
Then I take the paper out and edit what I've written. I mark it up

horribly, crossing words out and scribbling new ones in the space between the lines. By this time the paragraph has lost its nature and shape for me as a piece of writing. It's a mishmash of typing and handwriting and arrows and balloons and other directional symbols. So I type a clean copy, incorporating the changes, and then I take that piece of paper out of the typewriter and edit it. It's better, but not much better. I go over it with my pencil again, making more changes, which again make it too messy for me to read critically, so I go back to the typewriter for round three. And round four. Not until I'm reasonably satisfied do I proceed to the next paragraph.

This can get pretty tedious, and I have often thought that there must be a better way. Now there is. The word processor is God's gift, or at least science's gift, to the tinkerers and the refiners and the neatness freaks. For me it was obviously the perfect new toy. I began playing on page 1—editing, cutting and revising—and have been on a rewriting high ever since. The burden of the years has been lifted.

Mostly I've been cutting. I would guess that I've cut at least as many words out of this book as the number that remain. Probably half of those words were eliminated because I saw that they were unnecessary—the sentence worked fine without them. This is where the word processor can improve your writing to an extent that you will hardly believe. Learn to recognize what is clutter and to use the DELETE key to prune it out.

How will you know clutter when you see it? Here's a device I used when I was teaching writing at Yale that my students found helpful; it may be a help here. I would put brackets around every component in a student's paper that I didn't think was doing some kind of work. Often it was only one word—for example, the useless preposition that gets appended to so many verbs (order up, free up), or the adverb whose meaning is already in the verb (blare loudly, clench tightly), or the adjective that tells us what we already know (smooth marble, green grass). The brackets might surround the little qualifiers that dilute a writer's authority (a bit, sort of, in a sense), or the countless phrases in which the writer explains what he is about to explain (it might be pointed out, I'm tempted to say). Often my brackets would surround an entire sentence—the sentence that essentially repeats what the previous sentence has said, or tells the reader something that is implicit, or adds a detail that is irrelevant. Most people's writing is littered with phrases that do no new work whatever. Most first drafts, in fact, can be cut by fifty percent without losing anything organic. (Try it; it's a good exercise.)

By bracketing these extra words, instead of crossing them out, I 13
was saying to the student: "I may be wrong, but I think this can go and the meaning of the sentence won't be affected in any way. But *you* decide: read the sentence without the bracketed material and see if it works." In the first half of the term, the students' papers were festooned with my brackets. Whole paragraphs got bracketed. But gradually the students learned to put mental brackets around their many different kinds of clutter, and by the end of the term I was returning papers to them that had hardly any brackets, or none. It was always a satisfying moment. Today many of those students are professional writers. "I still see your brackets," they tell me. "They're following me through life."

You can develop the same eye. Writing is clear and strong to 14
the extent that it has no superfluous parts. (So is art and music and dance and typography and design.) You will really enjoy writing on a word processor when you see your sentences growing in strength, literally before your eyes, as you get rid of the fat. Be thankful for everything that you can throw away.

I was struck by how many phrases and sentences I wrote in this 15
book that I later found I didn't need. Many of them hammered home a point that didn't need hammering because it had already been made. This kind of overwriting happens in almost everybody's first draft, and it's perfectly natural—the act of putting down our thoughts makes us garrulous. Luckily, the act of editing follows the act of writing, and this is where the word processor will bail you out. It intercedes at the point where the game can be won or lost. With its help I cut hundreds of unnecessary words and didn't replace them.

Hundreds of others were discarded because I later thought of a 16
better word—one that caught more precisely or more vividly what I was trying to express. Here, again, a word processor encourages you to play. The English language is rich in words that convey an exact shade of meaning. Don't get stuck with a word that's merely good if you can find one that takes the reader by surprise with its color or aptness or quirkiness. Root around in your dictionary of synonyms and find words that are fresh. Throw them up on the screen and see how they look.

Also learn to play with whole sentences. If a sentence strikes 17
you as awkward or ponderous, move your cursor to the space after

the period and write a new sentence that you think is better. Maybe you can make it shorter. Or clearer. Maybe you can make it livelier by turning it into a question or otherwise altering its rhythm. Change the passive verbs into active verbs. (Passive verbs are the death of clarity and vigor.) Try writing two or three new versions of the awkward sentence and then compare them, or write a fourth version that combines the best elements of all three. Sentences come in an infinite variety of shapes and sizes. Find one that pleases you. If it's clear, and if it pleases you and expresses who you are, trust it to please other people. Then delete all the versions that aren't as good. Your shiny new sentence will jump into position and the rest of the paragraph will rearrange itself as quickly and neatly as if you had never pulled it apart.

Another goal that the word processor will help you to achieve   18
is unity. No matter how carefully you write each sentence as you assemble a piece of writing, the final product is bound to have some ragged edges. Is the tone consistent throughout? And the point of view? And the pronoun? And the tense? How about the transitions? Do they pull the reader along, or is the piece jerky and disjointed? A good piece of writing should be harmonious from beginning to end in the voice of the writer and the flow of its logic. But the harmony usually requires some last-minute patching.

I've been writing this book by the bricklayer method, slowly and   19
carefully. That's all very well as far as it goes—at the end of every chapter the individual bricks may look fine. But what about the wall? The only way to check your piece for unity is to go over it one more time from start to finish, preferably reading it aloud. See if you have executed all the decisions that you made before you started writing. . . .

I mention this [in part] because word processors are going to   20
be widely used by people who need to impart technical information: matters of operating procedure in business and banking, science and technology, medicine and health, education and government and dozens of other specialized fields. The information will only be helpful if readers can grasp it quickly and easily. If it's muddy they will get discouraged or angry, or both, and will stop reading.

You can avoid this dreaded fate for your message, whatever it   21
is, by making sure that every sentence is a logical sequel to the one that preceded it. One way to approach this goal is to keep your sentences short. A major reason why technical prose becomes so

tangled is that the writer tries to make one sentence do too many jobs. It's a natural hazard of the first draft. But the solution is simple: see that every sentence contains only one thought. The reader can accommodate only one idea at a time. Help him by giving him only one idea at a time. Let him understand A before you proceed to B.

In writing this book I was eager to explain the procedures that 22 I had learned about how word processors work, and I would frequently lump several points together in one sentence. Later, editing what I had written, I asked myself if the procedure would be clear to someone who was puzzling through it for the first time—someone who hadn't struggled to figure the procedure out. Often I felt that it wouldn't be clear. I was giving the reader too much. He was being asked to picture himself taking various steps that were single and sequential, and that's how he deserved to get them.

I therefore divided all troublesome long sentences into two short 23 sentences, or even three. It always gave me great pleasure. Not only is it the fastest way for a writer to get out of a quagmire that there seems to be no getting out of; I also like short sentences for their own sake. There's almost no more beautiful sight than a simple declarative sentence. This book is full of simple declarative sentences that have no punctuation and that carry one simple thought. Without a word processor I wouldn't have chopped as many of them down to their proper size, or done it with so little effort. This is one of the main clarifying jobs that your machine can help you to perform, especially if your writing requires you to guide the reader into territory that is new and bewildering.

Not all my experiences, of course, were rosy. The machine had 24 disadvantages as well as blessings. Often, for instance, I missed not being able to see more than twenty lines at a time—to review what I had written earlier. If I wanted to see more lines I had to "scroll" them back into view.

But even this wasn't as painful as I had thought it would be. I 25 found that I could hold in my head the gist of what I had written and didn't need to keep looking at it. Was this need, in fact, still another writer's hang-up that I could shed? To some extent it was. I discovered, as I had at so many other points in this journey, that various crutches I had always assumed I needed were really not necessary. I made a decision to just throw them away and found that I could still function. The only real hardship occurred when a paragraph broke at the bottom of the screen. This meant that the first lines of the paragraph were on one page and the rest were on the next page, and I had to keep flicking the two pages back and forth to read what I was writing. But again, it wasn't fatal. I learned to live with it and soon took it for granted as an occupational hazard.

The story that I've told in this chapter is personal and idiosyn- 26 cratic: how the word processor helped one writer to write one book. In many of its details it's everybody's story. All writers have different methods and psychological needs. . . .

❧ FURTHER READINGS

*An Anthology of Styles
and Strategies*

CLASSIC ESSAYS

੨**JONATHAN SWIFT**

Jonathan Swift (1667–1745) was born and raised in Dublin, Ireland, by English parents and attended Trinity College, Dublin. After spending time in England and being ordained an Anglican priest, he returned to Dublin as dean of St. Patrick's Cathedral. Swift is best known for his satiric writings, including *Gulliver's Travels* (1726), *A Tale of a Tub* (1704), and *The Battle of the Books* (1704). In his satires, as in his other writings, Swift attacks social injustice and the corruption of religion and learning. "A Modest Proposal" is directed at English insensitivity toward the sufferings of the Irish people and England's mistreatment of Ireland. As you read "A Modest Proposal," remember that the speaker in the essay, the "I," is not Swift but a fictional character whose attitudes and values differ greatly from those of the author.

A Modest Proposal
For Preventing the Children of Poor People in Ireland from Being a Burden to Their Parents or Country, and for Making Them Beneficial to the Public

It is a melancholy object to those who walk through this great 1 town[1] or travel in the country, when they see the streets, the roads, and cabin doors, crowded with beggars of the female sex, followed by three, four, or six children, all in rags and importuning every passenger for an alms. These mothers, instead of being able to work for their honest livelihood, are forced to employ all their time in strolling to beg sustenance for their helpless infants, who, as they grow up, either turn thieves for want of work, or leave their dear native country to fight for the Pretender in Spain, or sell themselves to the Barbadoes.[2]

I think it is agreed by all parties that this prodigious number of 2 children in the arms, or on the backs, or at the heels of their mothers, and frequently of their fathers, is in the present deplorable state of the kingdom a very great additional grievance; and therefore whoever

1. Dublin.
2. That is, agree to work for a number of years in exchange for transportation to a colony.

could find out a fair, cheap, and easy method of making these children sound, useful members of the commonwealth would deserve so well of the public as to have his statue set up for a preserver of the nation.

But my intention is very far from being confined to provide only 3 for the children of professed beggars; it is of a much greater extent, and shall take in the whole number of infants at a certain age who are born of parents in effect as little able to support them as those who demand our charity in the streets.

As to my own part, having turned my thoughts for many years 4 upon this important subject, and maturely weighed the several schemes of other projectors, I have always found them grossly mistaken in their computation. It is true, a child just dropped from its dam may be supported by her milk for a solar year, with little other nourishment; at most not above the value of two shillings, which the mother may certainly get, or the value in scraps, by her lawful occupation of begging; and it is exactly at one year old that I propose to provide for them in such a manner as instead of being a charge upon their parents or the parish, or wanting food and raiment for the rest of their lives, they shall on the contrary contribute to the feeding, and partly to the clothing, of many thousands.

There is likewise another great advantage in my scheme, that it 5 will prevent those voluntary abortions, and that horrid practice of women murdering their bastard children, alas, too frequent among us, sacrificing the poor innocent babes, I doubt, more to avoid the expense than the shame, which would move tears and pity in the most savage and inhuman breast.

The number of souls in this kingdom being usually reckoned 6 one million and a half, of these I calculate there may be about two hundred thousand couples whose wives are breeders; from which number I subtract thirty thousand couples who are able to maintain their own children, although I apprehend there cannot be so many under the present distress of the kingdom; but this being granted, there will remain an hundred and seventy thousand breeders. I again subtract fifty thousand for those women who miscarry, or whose children die by accident or disease within the year. There only remain an hundred and twenty thousand children of poor parents annually born. The question therefore is, how this number shall be reared and provided for, which, as I have already said, under the present situation of affairs, is utterly impossible by all the methods hitherto proposed. For we can neither employ them in handicraft nor agriculture; we neither build houses (I mean in the country) nor cultivate land. They can very seldom pick up livelihood by stealing till they arrive at six years old, except where they are of towardly parts; although I confess they learn the rudiments much earlier, during which time they can however be looked upon only as probationers, as I have been informed by a principal gentleman in the county of Cavan, who protested to me that he never knew above one or two instances under the age of six, even in a part of the kingdom so renowned for the quickest proficiency in that art.

I am assured by our merchants that a boy or a girl before twelve   7
years old is no salable commodity; and even when they come to this age, they will not yield above three pounds, or three pounds and half a crown at most on the Exchange; which cannot turn to account either to the parents or the kingdom, the charge of nutriment and rags having been at least four times that value.

I shall now therefore humbly propose my own thoughts, which   8
I hope will not be liable to the least objection.

I have been assured by a very knowing American of my ac-   9
quaintance in London, that a young healthy child well nursed is at a year old a most delicious, nourishing, and wholesome food, whether stewed, roasted, baked, or boiled; and I make no doubt that it will equally serve in fricassee or a ragout.

I do therefore humbly offer it to public consideration that of the   10
hundred and twenty thousand children, already computed, twenty thousand may be reserved for breed, whereof only one fourth part to be males, which is more than we allow to sheep, black cattle, or swine; and my reason is that these children are seldom the fruits of marriage, a circumstance not much regarded by our savages, therefore one male will be sufficient to serve four females. That the remaining hundred thousand may at a year old be offered in sale to the persons of quality and fortune through the kingdom, always advising the mother to let them suck plentifully in the last month, so as to render them plump and fat for a good table. A child will make two dishes at an entertainment for friends; and when the family dines alone, the fore or hind quarter will make a reasonable dish, and seasoned with a little pepper or salt will be very good boiled on the fourth day, especially in winter.

I have reckoned upon a medium that a child just born will   11 weigh twelve pounds, and in a solar year if tolerably nursed increaseth to twenty-eight pounds.

I grant this food will be somewhat dear, and therefore very 12 proper for landlords, who, as they have already devoured most of the parents, seem to have the best title to the children.

Infant's flesh will be in season throughout the year, but more 13 plentiful in March, and a little before and after. For we are told by a grave author, an eminent French physician,[3] that fish being a prolific diet, there are more children born in Roman Catholic countries about nine months after Lent, than at any other season; therefore, reckoning a year after Lent, the markets will be more glutted than usual, because the number of popish infants is at least three to one in this kingdom; and therefore it will have one other collateral advantage, by lessening the number of Papists among us.

I have already computed the charge of nursing a beggar's child 14 (in which list I reckon all cottagers, laborers, and four fifths of the farmers) to be about two shillings per annum, rags included; and I believe no gentleman would repine to give ten shillings for the carcass of a good fat child, which, as I have said, will make four dishes of excellent nutritive meat, when he hath only some particular friend or his own family to dine with him. Thus the squire will learn to be a good landlord, and grow popular among the tenants; the mother will have eight shillings net profit, and be fit for work till she produces another child.

Those who are more thrifty (as I must confess the times require) 15 may flay the carcass; the skin of which artificially dressed will make admirable gloves for ladies, and summer boots for fine gentlemen.

As to our city of Dublin, shambles may be appointed for this 16 purpose in the most convenient parts of it, and butchers we may be assured will not be wanting; although I rather recommend buying the children alive, and dressing them hot from the knife as we do roasting pigs.

A very worthy person, a true lover of his country, and whose 17 virtues I highly esteem, was lately pleased in discoursing on this matter to offer a refinement upon my scheme. He said that many gentlemen of his kingdom, having of late destroyed their deer, he conceived that the want of venison might be well supplied by the

3. François Rabelais.

bodies of young lads and maidens, not exceeding fourteen years of age nor under twelve, so great a number of both sexes in every county being now ready to starve for want of work and service; and these to be disposed of by their parents, if alive, or otherwise by their nearest relations. But with due deference to so excellent a friend and so deserving a patriot, I cannot be altogether in his sentiments; for as to the males, my American acquaintance assured me from frequent experience that their flesh was generally tough and lean, like that of our schoolboys, by continual exercise, and their taste disagreeable; and to fatten them would not answer the charge. Then as to the females, it would, I think with humble submission, be a loss to the public, because they soon would become breeders themselves; and besides, it is not improbable that some scrupulous people might be apt to censure such a practice (although indeed very unjustly) as a little bordering upon cruelty; which, I confess, hath always been with me the strongest objection against any project, how well soever intended.

But in order to justify my friend, he confessed that this expedient   18 was put into his head by the famous Psalmanazar, a native of the island Formosa, who came from thence to London above twenty years ago, and in conversation told my friend that in his country when any young person happened to be put to death, the executioner sold the carcass to the persons of quality as a prime dainty; and that in his time the body of a plump girl of fifteen, who was crucified for an attempt to poison the emperor, was sold to his Imperial Majesty's prime minister of state, and other great mandarins of the court, in joints from the gibbet, at four hundred crowns. Neither indeed can I deny that if the same use were made of several plump young girls in this town, who without one single groat to their fortunes cannot stir abroad without a chair, and appear at the playhouse and assemblies in foreign fineries which they never will pay for, the kingdom would not be the worse.

Some persons of a desponding spirit are in great concern about   19 that vast number of poor people who are aged, diseased, or maimed, and I have been desired to employ my thoughts what course may be taken to ease the nation of so grievous an encumbrance. But I am not in the least pain upon that matter, because it is very well known that they are every day dying and rotting by cold and famine, and filth and vermin, as fast as can be reasonably expected. And as to the younger laborers, they are now in almost as hopeful a condition. They cannot get work, and consequently pine away for want of nourishment to a degree that if any time they are accidentally hired to common labor, they have not strength to perform it; and thus the country and themselves are happily delivered from the evils to come.

I have too long digressed, and therefore shall return to my 20 subject. I think the advantages by the proposal which I have made are obvious and many, as well as of the highest importance.

For first, as I have already observed, it would greatly lessen the 21 number of Papists, with whom we are yearly overrun, being the principal breeders of the nation as well as our most dangerous enemies; and who stay at home on purpose to deliver the kingdom to the Pretender, hoping to take their advantage by the absence of so many good Protestants, who have chosen rather to leave their country than to stay at home and pay tithes against their conscience to an Episcopal curate.

Secondly, the poorer tenants will have something valuable of 22 their own, which by law may be made liable to distress, and help to pay their landlord's rent, their corn and cattle being already seized and money a thing unknown.

Thirdly, whereas the maintenance of an hundred thousand chil- 23 dren, from two years old and upwards, cannot be computed at less than ten shillings a piece per annum, the nation's stock will be thereby increased fifty thousand pounds per annum, besides the profit of a new dish introduced to the tables of all gentlemen of fortune in the kingdom who have any refinement in taste. And the money will circulate among ourselves, the goods being entirely of our own growth and manufacture.

Fourthly, the constant breeders, besides the gain of eight shillings 24 sterling per annum by the sale of their children, will be rid of the charge for maintaining them after the first year.

Fifthly, this food would likewise bring great custom to taverns, 25 where the vintners will certainly be so prudent as to procure the best receipts for dressing it to perfection, and consequently have their houses frequented by all the fine gentlemen, who justly value themselves upon their knowledge in good eating; and a skillful cook, who understands how to oblige his guests, will contrive to make it as expensive as they please.

Sixthly, this would be a great inducement to marriage, which 26 all wise nations have either encouraged by rewards or enforced by laws and penalties. It would increase the care and tenderness of mothers toward their children, when they were sure of a settlement for life to the poor babes, provided in some sort by the public, to their annual profit instead of expense. We should see an honest emulation among the married women, which of them could bring the fattest child to the market. Men would become as fond of their wives during the time of pregnancy as they are now of their mares in foal, their cows in calf, or sows when they are ready to farrow; nor offer to beat or kick them (as is too frequent a practice) for fear of a miscarriage.

Many other advantages might be enumerated. For instance, the 27 addition of some thousand carcasses in our exportation of barreled beef, the propagation of swine's flesh, and improvements in the art of making good bacon, so much wanted among us by the great destruction of pigs, too frequent at our tables, which are no way comparable in taste or magnificence to a well-grown, fat, yearling child, which roasted whole will make a considerable figure at a lord mayor's feast or any other public entertainment. But this and many others I omit, being studious of brevity.

Supposing that one thousand families in this city would be 28 constant customers for infants' flesh, besides others who might have it at merry meetings, particularly weddings and christenings, I compute that Dublin would take off annually about twenty thousand carcasses, and the rest of the kingdom (where probably they will be sold somewhat cheaper) the remaining eighty thousand.

I can think of no one objection that will possibly be raised against 29 this proposal, unless it should be urged that the number of people will be thereby much lessened in the kingdom. This I freely own, and it was indeed one principal design in offering it to the world. I desire the reader will observe, that I calculate my remedy for this one individual kingdom of Ireland and for no other that ever was, is, or I think ever can be upon earth. Therefore, let no man talk to me of other expedients: of taxing our absentees at five shillings a pound: of using neither clothes nor household furniture except what is of our own growth and manufacture: of utterly rejecting the materials and instruments that promote foreign luxury: of curing the expensiveness of pride, vanity, idleness, and gaming in our women: of introducing a vein of parsimony, prudence, and temperance: of learning to love our country, in the want of which we differ even from Laplanders and the inhabitants of Topinamboo[4]: of quitting our animosities and factions, nor acting any longer like the Jews, who were murdering one another at the very moment their city was taken: of being a little cautious not to sell our country and conscience for nothing: of teaching landlords to have at least one degree of mercy toward their tenants: lastly, of putting a spirit of honesty, industry, and skill into our shopkeepers; who, if a resolution could now be taken to buy only our native goods, would immediately unite to cheat and exact upon us in the price, the measure, and the goodness, nor could ever yet be brought to make one fair proposal of just dealing, though often and earnestly invited to it.[5]

Therefore, I repeat, let no man talk to me of these and the like 30 expedients, till he hath at least some glimpse of hope that there will ever be some hearty and sincere attempt to put them in practice.

But as to myself, having been wearied out for many years with 31 offering vain, idle, visionary thoughts, and at length utterly despairing of success, I fortunately fell upon this proposal, which, as it is wholly new, so it hath something solid and real, of no expense and little trouble, full in our own power, and whereby we can incur no danger in disobliging England. For this kind of commodity will not bear exportation, the flesh being of too tender a consistence to admit a long continuance in salt, although perhaps I could name a country which would be glad to eat up our whole nation without it.

After all, I am not so violently bent upon my own opinion as to 32 reject any offer proposed by wise men, which shall be found equally innocent, cheap, easy, and effectual. But before something of that kind shall be advanced in contradiction to my scheme, and offering a better, I desire the author or authors will be pleased maturely to consider two points. First, as things now stand, how they will be able to find food and raiment for an hundred thousand useless mouths and backs. And secondly, there being a round million of creatures in human figure throughout this kingdom, whose sole subsistence put into a common stock would leave them in debt two millions of pounds sterling, adding those who are beggars by profession to the bulk of farmers, cottagers, and laborers, with their wives and children who are beggars in effect; I desire those politicians who dislike my overture, and may perhaps be so bold to attempt an

4. A district in Brazil.
5. These are proposals Swift had already made in other works.

answer, that they will first ask the parents of these mortals whether they would not at this day think it a great happiness to have been sold for food at a year old in this manner I prescribe, and thereby have avoided such a perpetual scene of misfortunes as they have since gone through by the oppression of landlords, the impossibility of paying rent without money or trade, the want of common sustenance, with neither house nor clothes to cover them from the inclemencies of the weather, and the most inevitable prospect of entailing the like or greater miseries upon their breed forever.

I profess, in the sincerity of my heart, that I have not the least 33 personal interest in endeavoring to promote this necessary work, having no other motive than the public good of my country, by advancing our trade, providing for infants, relieving the poor, and giving some pleasure to the rich. I have no children by which I can propose to get a single penny; the youngest being nine years old, and my wife past childbearing.

❧ THOMAS JEFFERSON

Thomas Jefferson (1743–1826) was born near Charlottesville, Virginia, and attended the College of William and Mary. A delegate to the Continental Congress in 1775 and governor of Virginia, he had vast influence in the shaping of the new republic. After the war, he served as secretary of state under Washington, as vice president, and as the third president of the United States. Jefferson wrote "The Declaration of Independence" in mid-June 1776. The Continental Congress, meeting in Philadelphia, amended the document, and it was approved on July 4, 1776. The document still reflects Jefferson's thought and style of writing, however, and is widely considered a model of reasoning and expression.

The Declaration of Independence

When in the course of human events, it becomes necessary for one people to dissolve the political bands which have connected them with another, and to assume among the Powers of the earth, the separate and equal station to which the Laws of Nature and of Nature's God entitle them, a decent respect to the opinions of mankind requires that they should declare the causes which impel them to the separation. 1

We hold these truths to be self-evident, that all men are created equal, that they are endowed by their Creator with certain unalienable Rights, that among these are Life, Liberty and the pursuit of Happiness. That to secure these rights, Governments are instituted among Men, deriving their just powers from the consent of the governed. That whenever any Form of Government becomes destructive of these ends, it is the Right of the People to alter or to abolish it, and to institute a new Government, laying its foundation on such principles and organizing its powers in such form, as to them shall seem most likely to effect their Safety and Happiness. Prudence, indeed, will dictate that Governments long established should not be changed for light and transient causes; and accordingly all experience hath shown that mankind are more disposed to suffer, while evils are sufferable, than to right themselves by abolishing the forms to which they are accustomed. But when a long train of abuses and usurpations pursuing invariably the same Object evinces a design to 2 reduce them under absolute Despotism, it is their right, it is their duty, to throw off such government, and to provide new Guards for their future security. Such has been the patient sufferance of these Colonies; and such is now the necessity which constrains them to alter their former Systems of Government. The history of the present King of Great Britain is a history of repeated injuries and usurpations, all having in direct object the establishment of an absolute Tyranny over these States. To prove this, let Facts be submitted to a candid world.

3 He has refused his assent to Laws, the most wholesome and necessary for the public good.

4 He has forbidden his Governors to pass Laws of immediate and pressing importance, unless suspended in their operation till his Assent should be obtained; and when so suspended, he has utterly neglected to attend to them.

5 He has refused to pass other Laws for the accommodation of large districts of people, unless those people would relinquish the right of Representation in the Legislature, a right inestimable to them and formidable to tyrants only.

6 He has called together legislative bodies at places unusual, uncomfortable, and distant from the depository of their Public Records, for the sole purpose of fatiguing them into compliance with his measures.

7 He has dissolved Representative Houses repeatedly, for opposing with manly firmness his invasions on the rights of the people.

8 He has refused for a long time, after such dissolutions, to cause others to be elected; whereby the Legislative Powers, incapable of Annihilation, have returned to the People at large for their exercise; the State remaining in the mean time exposed to all dangers of invasion from without, and convulsions within.

9 He has endeavored to prevent the population of these States; for that purpose obstructing the Laws of Naturalization of Foreigners; refusing to pass others to encourage their migration hither, and raising the conditions of new Appropriations of Lands.

10 He has obstructed the Administration of Justice, by refusing his Assent to Laws for establishing Judiciary Powers.

11 He has made Judges dependent on his Will alone, for the tenure of their offices, and the amount and payment of their salaries.

12 He has erected a multitude of New Offices, and sent hither swarms of Officers to harass our People, and eat out their substance.

He has kept among us, in time of peace, Standing Armies without 13 the consent of our Legislature.

He has affected to render the Military independent of and su- 14 perior to the Civil Power.

He has combined with others to subject us to jurisdictions foreign 15 to our constitution, and unacknowledged by our laws; giving his Assent to their acts of pretended Legislation:

For quartering large bodies of armed troops among us: 16

For protecting them, by a mock Trial, from Punishment for any 17 Murders which they should commit on the Inhabitants of these States:

For cutting off our Trade with all parts of the world: 18

For imposing Taxes on us without our Consent: 19

For depriving us in many cases, of the benefits of Trial by Jury: 20

For transporting us beyond Seas to be tried for pretended offen- 21 ses:

For abolishing the free System of English Laws in a Neighbour- 22 ing Province, establishing therein an Arbitrary government, and enlarging its boundaries so as to render it at once an example and fit instrument for introducing the same absolute rule into these Colonies:

For taking away our Charters, abolishing our most valuable 23 Laws, and altering fundamentally the Forms of our Governments:

For suspending our own Legislatures, and declaring themselves 24 invested with Power to legislate for us in all cases whatsoever.

He has abdicated Government here, by declaring us out of his 25 Protection and waging War against us.

He has plundered our seas, ravaged our Coasts, burnt our towns 26 and destroyed the Lives of our people.

He is at this time transporting large Armies of foreign Mercen- 27 aries to compleat the works of death, desolation and tyranny, already begun with circumstances of Cruelty & perfidy scarcely paralleled in the most barbarous ages, and totally unworthy the Head of a civilized nation.

He has constrained our fellow Citizens taken Captive on the high 28 Seas to bear Arms against their Country, to become the executioners of their friends and Brethren, or to fall themselves by their Hands.

He has excited domestic insurrections amongst us, and has 29 endeavored to bring on the inhabitants of our frontiers, the merciless Indian Savages, whose known rule of warfare, is an undistinguished destruction of all ages, sexes and conditions.

In every stage of these Oppressions We Have Petitioned for   30
Redress in the most humble terms: Our repeated petitions have been
answered only by repeated injury. A Prince, whose character is thus
marked by every act which may define a Tyrant, is unfit to be the
ruler of a free People.

Nor have We been wanting in attention to our British brethren.   31
We have warned them from time to time of attempts by their legislature to extend an unwarrantable jurisdiction over us. We have
reminded them of the circumstances of our emigration and settlement
here. We have appealed to their native justice and magnanimity and
we have conjured them by the ties of our common kindred to disavow
these usurpations, which would inevitably interrupt our connections
and correspondence. They too have been deaf to the voice of justice
and of consanguinity. We must, therefore, acquiesce in the necessity,
which denounces our Separation, and hold them, as we hold the
rest of mankind, Enemies in War, in Peace Friends.

We, therefore, the Representatives of the United States of Amer-   32
ica, in General Congress, Assembled, appealing to the Supreme Judge
of the world for the rectitude of our intentions, do, in the Name, and
by Authority of the good People of these Colonies, solemnly publish
and declare, That these United Colonies are, and of Right ought to
be, Free and Independent States; that they are Absolved from all
Allegiance to the British Crown, and that all political connection
between them and the State of Great Britain, is and ought to be
totally dissolved; and that as Free and Independent States, they have
full power to levy War, conclude Peace, contract Alliances, establish
Commerce, and to do all other Acts and Things which Independent
States may of right do. And for the support of this Declaration, with
a firm reliance on the protection of Divine Providence, we mutually
pledge to each other our lives, our Fortunes and our sacred Honor.

❧ E. M. FORSTER

E[dward] M[organ] Forster (1879–1970) was a British novelist and essayist. He was born in London and attended King's College, Cambridge. After spending some time in Greece, Italy, and India, he returned to England, where he spent the rest of his life. His novels include *Where Angels Fear to Tread* (1905), *The Longest Journey* (1907), *A Room with a View* (1908), *Howards End* (1910), *Maurice* (published after his death), and *A Passage to India* (1924) (mentioned in the opening of the essay below). Forster also published a volume of literary criticism, *Aspects of the Novel* (1927) and two collections of essays, *Two Cheers for Democracy* (1951) and *Abinger Harvest* (1936), from which the following essay is taken.

My Wood

A few years ago I wrote a book which dealt in part with the difficulties of the English in India. Feeling that they would have had no difficulties in India themselves, the Americans read the book freely. The more they read it the better it made them feel, and a cheque to the author was the result. I bought a wood with the cheque. It is not a large wood—it contains scarcely any trees, and it is intersected, blast it, by a public footpath. Still, it is the first property that I have owned, so it is right that other people should participate in my shame, and should ask themselves, in accents that will vary in horror, this very important question: What is the effect of property upon the character? Don't let's touch economics; the effect of private ownership upon the community as a whole is another question—a more important question, perhaps, but another one. Let's keep to psychology. If you own things, what's their effect on you? What's the effect on me of my wood?

In the first place, it makes me feel heavy. Property does have this effect. Property produces men of weight, and it was a man of weight who failed to get into the Kingdom of Heaven. He was not wicked, that unfortunate millionaire in the parable, he was only stout; he stuck out in front, not to mention behind, and as he wedged himself this way and that in the crystalline entrance and bruised his well-fed flanks, he saw beneath him a comparatively slim camel passing through the eye of a needle and being woven into the robe

of God. The Gospels all through couple stoutness and slowness. They
point out what is perfectly obvious, yet seldom realized: that if you
have a lot of things you cannot move about a lot, that furniture
requires dusting, dusters require servants, servants require insurance
stamps, and the whole tangle of them makes you think twice before
you accept an invitation to dinner or go for a bathe in the Jordan.
Sometimes the Gospels proceed further and say with Tolstoy that
property is sinful; they approach the difficult ground of asceticism
here, where I cannot follow them. But as to the immediate effects of
property on people, they just show straightforward logic. It produces
men of weight. Men of weight cannot, by definition, move like the
lightning from the East unto the West, and the ascent of a fourteen-
stone[1] bishop into a pulpit is thus the exact antithesis of the coming
of the Son of Man. My wood makes me feel heavy.

In the second place, it makes me feel it ought to be larger.   3

The other day I heard a twig snap in it. I was annoyed at first,   4
for I thought that someone was blackberrying, and depreciating the
value of the undergrowth. On coming nearer, I saw it was not a
man who had trodden on the twig and snapped it, but a bird, and
I felt pleased. My bird. The bird was not equally pleased. Ignoring
the relation between us, it took fright as soon as it saw the shape of
my face, and flew straight over the boundary hedge into a field, the
property of Mrs. Henessy, where it sat down with a loud squawk. It
had become Mrs. Henessy's bird. Something seemed grossly amiss
here, something that would not have occurred had the wood been
larger. I could not afford to buy Mrs. Henessy out, I dared not murder
her, and limitations of this sort beset me on every side. Ahab did not
want that vineyard—he only needed it to round off his property,
preparatory to plotting a new curve—and all the land around my
wood has become necessary to me in order to round off the wood.
A boundary protects. But—poor little thing—the boundary ought in
its turn to be protected. Noises on the edge of it. Children throw
stones. A little more, and then a little more, until we reach the sea.
Happy Canute! Happier Alexander! And after all, why should even
the world be the limit of possession? A rocket containing a Union
Jack, will, it is hoped, be shortly fired at the moon. Mars. Sirius.
Beyond which . . . But these immensities ended by saddening me. I
could not suppose that my wood was the destined nucleus of uni-

---

1. 196-pound. (Editor's note)

versal dominion—it is so very small and contains no mineral wealth beyond the blackberries. Nor was I comforted when Mrs. Henessy's bird took alarm for the second time and flew clean away from us all, under the belief that it belonged to itself.

In the third place, property makes its owner feel that he ought 5
to do something to it. Yet he isn't sure what. A restlessness comes over him, a vague sense that he has a personality to express—the same sense which, without any vagueness, leads the artist to an act of creation. Sometimes I think I will cut down such trees as remain in the wood, at other times I want to fill up the gaps between them with new trees. Both impulses are pretentious and empty. They are not honest movements towards money-making or beauty. They spring from a foolish desire to express myself and from an inability to enjoy what I have got. Creation, property, enjoyment form a sinister trinity in the human mind. Creation and enjoyment are both very very good, yet they are often unattainable without a material basis, and at such moments property pushes itself in as a substitute, saying, "Accept me instead—I'm good enough for all three." It is not enough. It is, as Shakespeare said of lust, "The expense of spirit in a waste of shame": it is "Before, a joy proposed; behind, a dream." Yet we don't know how to shun it. It is forced on us by our economic system as the alternative to starvation. It is also forced on us by an internal defect in the soul, by the feeling that in property may lie the germs of self-development and of exquisite or heroic deeds. Our life on earth is, and ought to be, material and carnal. But we have not yet learned to manage our materialism and carnality properly; they are still entangled with the desire for ownership, where (in the words of Dante) "Possession is one with loss."

And this brings us to our fourth and final point: the blackberries. 6

Blackberries are not plentiful in this meagre grove, but they are 7
easily seen from the public footpath which traverses it, and all too easily gathered. Foxgloves, too—people will pull up the foxgloves, and ladies of an educational tendency even grub for toadstools to show them on the Monday in class. Other ladies, less educated, roll down the bracken in the arms of their gentlemen friends. There is paper, there are tins. Pray, does my wood belong to me or doesn't it? And, if it does, should I not own it best by allowing no one else to walk there? There is a wood near Lyme Regis, also cursed by a public footpath, where the owner has not hesitated on this point. He has built high stone walls each side of the path, and has spanned it

by bridges, so that the public circulate like termites while he gorges on the blackberries unseen. He really does own his wood, this able chap. Dives in Hell did pretty well, but the gulf dividing him from Lazarus could be traversed by vision, and nothing traverses it here.[2] And perhaps I shall come to this in time. I shall wall in and fence out until I really taste the sweets of property. Enormously stout, endlessly avaricious, pseudo-creative, intensely selfish, I shall weave upon my forehead the quadruple crown of possession until those nasty Bolshies come and take it off again and thrust me aside into the outer darkness.

---

2. Parable of the rich man (often referred to as Dives) who ignored the poor beggar lying at his door (Lazarus) only to end up in Hell, from where he could see Lazarus in heaven (Luke 16:19–26). (Editor's note)

❧ GEORGE ORWELL

Eric Blair, who used the pen name George Orwell, was born in 1903 in Motihari, India. He was educated at Eton in England, but he then decided to join the Indian Imperial Police in Burma, where he served from 1922 to 1927. He returned to Europe, worked at various jobs, and wrote, producing his first book, *Down and Out in Paris and London* (1933) and his first novel, *Burmese Days* (1935). During the Spanish Civil War, Orwell fought on the Republican side, and during World War II he worked as a newspaper correspondent. His attitudes towards government oppression and the dangers of totalitarian rule are made plain in the novels *Animal Farm* (1945) and *Nineteen Eighty-Four* (1949), the latter published just before his death in 1950. Orwell's essays were collected in *Critical Essays* (1946), *Shooting an Elephant and Other Essays* (1950), and *Such, Such Were the Joys* (1953). Orwell's views of the relationships among politics, language, and thought are carefully laid out in "Politics and the English Language," one of his most famous essays.

Politics and the English Language

Most people who bother with the matter at all would admit that   1
the English language is in a bad way, but it is generally assumed that we cannot by conscious action do anything about it. Our civilization is decadent and our language—so the argument runs—must inevitably share in the general collapse. It follows that any struggle against the abuse of language is a sentimental archaism, like preferring candles to electric light or hansom cabs to aeroplanes. Underneath this lies the half-conscious belief that language is a natural growth and not an instrument which we shape for our own purpose.

Now, it is clear that the decline of a language must ultimately   2
have political and economic causes: it is not due simply to the bad influence of this or that individual writer. But an effect can become a cause, reinforcing the original cause and producing the same effect in an intensified form, and so on indefinitely. A man may take to drink because he feels himself to be a failure, and then fail all the more completely because he drinks. It is rather the same thing that is happening to the English language. It becomes ugly and inaccurate because our thoughts are foolish, but the slovenliness of our language

makes it easier for us to have foolish thoughts. The point is that the process is reversible. Modern English, especially written English, is full of bad habits which spread by imitation and which can be avoided if one is willing to take the necessary trouble. If one gets rid of these habits one can think more clearly, and to think clearly is a necessary first step towards political regeneration: so that the fight against bad English is not frivolous and it is not the exclusive concern of professional writers. I will come back to this presently, and I hope that by that time the meaning of what I have said here will have become clearer. Meanwhile, here are five specimens of the English language as it is now habitually written.

These five passages have not been picked out because they are   3 especially bad—I could have quoted far worse if I had chosen—but because they illustrate various of the mental vices from which we now suffer. They are a little below the average, but are fairly representative samples. I number them so that I can refer back to them when necessary:

(1) I am not, indeed, sure whether it is not true to say that the Milton who once seemed not unlike a seventeenth-century Shelley had not become, out of an experience ever more bitter in each year, more alien [*sic*] to the founder of that Jesuit sect which nothing could induce him to tolerate.

Professor Harold Laski (Essay in *Freedom of Expression*)

(2) Above all, we cannot play ducks and drakes with a native battery of idioms which prescribes such egregious collocations of vocables as the Basic *put up with* for *tolerate* or *put at a loss* for *bewilder*.

Professor Lancelot Hogben (*Interglossa*)

(3) On the one side we have the free personality: by definition it is not neurotic, for it has neither conflict nor dream. Its desires, such as they are, are transparent, for they are just what institutional approval keeps in the forefront of consciousness; another institutional pattern would alter their number and intensity; there is little in them that is natural, irreducible, or culturally dangerous. But *on the other side,* the social bond itself is nothing but the mutual reflection of these self-secure integrities. Recall the definition of love. Is not this the very picture of a small academic? Where is there a place in this hall of mirrors for either personality or fraternity?

Essay on psychology in *Politics* (New York)

(4) All the "best people" from the gentlemen's clubs, and all the frantic fascist captains, united in common hatred of Socialism and bestial horror of the rising tide of the mass revolutionary movement,

have turned to acts of provocation, to foul incendiarism, to medieval legends of poisoned wells, to legalize their own destruction of proletarian organizations, and rouse the agitated petty-bourgeoisie to chauvinistic fervor on behalf of the fight against the revolutionary way out of the crisis.

Communist pamphlet

(5) If a new spirit *is* to be infused into this old country, there is one thorny and contentious reform which must be tackled, and that is the humanization and galvanization of the B.B.C. Timidity here will bespeak cancer and atrophy of the soul. The heart of Britain may be sound and of strong beat, for instance, but the British lion's roar at present is like that of Bottom in Shakespeare's *Midsummer Night's Dream*—as gentle as any sucking dove. A virile new Britain cannot continue indefinitely to be traduced in the eyes or rather ears, of the world by the effete languors of Langham Place, brazenly masquerading as "standard English." When the Voice of Britain is heard at nine o'clock, better far and infinitely less ludicrous to hear aitches honestly dropped than the present priggish, inflated, inhibited, school-ma'amish arch braying of blameless bashful mewing maidens!

Letter in Tribune

Each of these passages has faults of its own, but, quite apart   4
from avoidable ugliness, two qualities are common to all of them. The first is staleness of imagery; the other is lack of precision. The writer either has a meaning and cannot express it, or he inadvertently says something else, or he is almost indifferent as to whether his words mean anything or not. The mixture of vagueness and sheer incompetence is the most marked characteristic of modern English prose, and especially of any kind of political writing. As soon as certain topics are raised, the concrete melts into the abstract and no one seems to think of turns of speech that are not hackneyed: prose consists less and less of *words* chosen for the sake of their meaning, and more and more of *phrases* tacked together like the sections of a prefabricated henhouse. I list below, with notes and examples, various of the tricks by means of which the work of prose-construction is habitually dodged:

DYING METAPHORS

A newly invented metaphor assists thought by evoking a visual   5
image, while on the other hand a metaphor which is technically "dead" (e.g., *iron resolution*) has in effect reverted to being an ordinary word and can generally be used without loss of vividness.

But in between these two classes there is a huge dump of worn-out metaphors which have lost all evocative power and are merely used because they save people the trouble of inventing phrases for themselves. Examples are: *ring the changes on, take up the cudgels for, toe the line, ride roughshod over, stand shoulder to shoulder with, play into the hands of, no axe to grind, grist to the mill, fishing in troubled waters, on the order of the day, Achilles' heel, swan song, hotbed.* Many of these are used without knowledge of their meaning (what is a "rift", for instance?), and incompatible metaphors are frequently mixed, a sure sign that the writer is not interested in what he is saying. Some metaphors now current have been twisted out of their original meaning without those who use them even being aware of the fact. For example, *toe the line* is sometimes written *tow the line*. Another example is *the hammer and the anvil*, now always used with the implication that the anvil gets the worst of it. In real life it is always the anvil that breaks the hammer, never the other way about: a writer who stopped to think what he was saying would be aware of this, and would avoid perverting the original phrase.

OPERATORS OR VERBAL FALSE LIMBS

These save the trouble of picking out appropriate verbs and   6
nouns, and at the same time pad each sentence with extra syllables which give it an appearance of symmetry. Characteristic phrases are: *render inoperative, militate against, make contact with, be subjected to, give rise to, give grounds for, have the effect of, play a leading part (role) in, make itself felt, take effect, exhibit a tendency to, serve the purpose of, etc., etc.* The keynote is the elimination of simple verbs. Instead of being a single word, such as *break, stop, spoil, mend, kill,* a verb becomes a *phrase,* made up of a noun or adjective tacked on to some general-purpose verb such as *prove, serve, form, play, render.* In addition, the passive voice is wherever possible used in preference to the active, and noun constructions are used instead of gerunds (*by examination of* instead of *by examining*). The range of verbs is further cut down by means of the *-ize* and *de-* formation, and the banal statements are given an appearance of profundity by means of the *not un-* formation. Simple conjunctions and prepositions are replaced by such phrases as *with respect to, having regard to, the fact that, by dint of, in view of, in the interests of, on the hypothesis that;* and the ends of sentences are saved from anticlimax

by such resounding common places as *greatly to be desired, cannot be left out of account, a development to be expected in the near future, deserving of serious consideration, brought to a satisfactory conclusion,* and so on and so forth.

PRETENTIOUS DICTION

Words like *phenomenon, element, individual* (as noun), *objec-*   7
tive, categorical, effective, virtual, basic, primary, promote, consti-
tute, exhibit, exploit, utilize, eliminate, liquidate, are used to dress
up simple statements and give an air of scientific impartiality to
biased judgments. Adjectives like *epoch-making, epic, historic, un-*
forgettable, triumphant, age-old, inevitable, inexorable, veritable,
are used to dignify the sordid processes of international politics,
while writing that aims at glorifying war usually takes on an archaic
color, its characteristic words being: *realm, throne, chariot, mailed*
fist, trident, sword, shield, buckler, banner, jackboot, clarion. Foreign words and expressions such as *cul de sac, ancien régime, deus*
ex machina, mutatis mutandis, status quo, gleichshaltung, weltan-
schauung, are used to give an air of culture and elegance. Except
for the useful abbreviations *i.e., e.g.,* and *etc.,* there is no real need
for any of the hundreds of foreign phrases now current in English.
Bad writers, and especially scientific, political and sociological writers, are nearly always haunted by the notion that Latin or Greek
words are grander than Saxon ones, and unnecessary words like
expedite, ameliorate, predict, extraneous, deracinated, clandestine,
subaqueous and hundreds of others constantly gain ground from
their Anglo-Saxon opposite numbers.[1] The jargon peculiar to Marxist
writing (*hyena, hangman, cannibal, petty bourgeois, these gentry,*
lacquey, flunkey, mad dog, White Guard, etc.) consists largely of
words and phrases translated from Russian, German, or French; but
the normal way of coining a new word is to use a Latin or Greek
root with the appropriate affix and, where necessary, the *-ize* formation. It is often easier to make up words of this kind (*deregion-*
alize, impermissible, extramarital, nonfragmentatory and so forth)

1. An interesting illustration of this is the way in which the English flower names which were in use till very recently are being ousted by Greek ones, *snapdragon* becoming *antirrhinum, forget-me-not* becoming *myosotis,* etc. It is hard to see any practical reason for this change of fashion: it is probably due to an instinctive turning-away from the more homely word and a vague feeling that the Greek word is scientific.

than to think up the English words that will cover one's meaning.
The result, in general, is an increase in slovenliness and vagueness.

MEANINGLESS WORDS

In certain kinds of writing, particularly in art criticism and   8
literary criticism, it is normal to come across long passages which
are almost completely lacking in meaning.[2] Words like *romantic,
plastic, values, human, dead, sentimental, natural, vitality,* as used
in art criticism, are strictly meaningless in the sense that they not
only do not point to any discoverable object, but are hardly ever
expected to do so by the reader. When one critic writes, "The outstanding feature of Mr. X's work is its living quality," while another
writes, "The immediately striking thing about Mr. X's work is its
peculiar deadness," the reader accepts this as a simple difference of
opinion. If words like *black* and *white* were involved, instead of the
jargon words *dead* and *living,* he would see at once that language
was being used in an improper way. Many political words are
similarly abused. The word *Fascism* has now no meaning except in
so far as it signifies "something not desirable." The words *democracy,
socialism, freedom, patriotic, realistic, justice,* have each of them
several different meanings which cannot be reconciled with one
another. In the case of a word like *democracy,* not only is there no
agreed definition, but the attempt to make one is resisted from all
sides. It is almost universally felt that when we call a country democratic we are praising it: consequently the defenders of every kind
of régime claim that it is a democracy, and fear that they might have
to stop using the word if it were tied down to any one meaning.
Words of this kind are often used in a consciously dishonest way.
That is, the person who uses them has his own private definition,
but allows his hearer to think he means something quite different.
Statements like *Marshal Pétain was a true patriot, The Soviet Press
is the freest in the world, The Catholic Church is opposed to per-
secution,* are almost always made with intent to deceive. Other words
used in variable meanings, in most cases more or less dishonestly,

2. Example: "Comfort's catholicity of perception and image, strangely Whitman-
esque in range, almost the exact opposite in aesthetic compulsion, continues to evoke
that trembling atmospheric accumulative hinting at a cruel, an inexorably serene
timelessness . . . Wrey Gardiner scores by aiming at simple bull's-eyes with precision.
Only they are not so simple, and through this contented sadness runs more than the
surface bitter-sweet of resignation." (*Poetry Quarterly.*)

are: *class, totalitarian, science, progressive, reactionary, bourgeois, equality.*

Now that I have made this catalogue of swindles and perversions, let me give another example of the kind of writing that they lead to. This time it must of its nature be an imaginary one. I am going to translate a passage of good English into modern English of the worst sort. Here is a well-known verse from *Ecclesiastes:*

> I returned and saw under the sun, that the race is not to the swift, nor the battle to the strong, neither yet bread to the wise, nor yet riches to men of understanding, nor yet favour to men of skill; but time and chance happeneth to them all.

Here it is in modern English:

> Objective consideration of contemporary phenomena compels the conclusion that success or failure in competitive activities exhibits no tendency to be commensurate with innate capacity, but that a considerable element of the unpredictable must invariably be taken into account.

This is a parody, but not a very gross one. Exhibit (3), above, for instance, contains several patches of the same kind of English. It will be seen that I have not made a full translation. The beginning and ending of the sentence follow the original meaning fairly closely, but in the middle the concrete illustrations—race, battle, bread—dissolve into the vague phrase "success or failure in competitive activities." This had to be so, because no modern writer of the kind I am discussing—no one capable of using phrases like "objective consideration of contemporary phenomena"—would ever tabulate his thoughts in that precise and detailed way. The whole tendency of modern prose is away from concreteness. Now analyze these two sentences a little more closely. The first contains forty-nine words but only sixty syllables, and all its words are those of everyday life. The second contains thirty-eight words of ninety syllables: eighteen of its words are from Latin roots, and one from Greek. The first sentence contains six vivid images, and only one phrase ("time and chance") that could be called vague. The second contains not a single fresh, arresting phrase, and in spite of its ninety syllables it gives only a shortened version of the meaning contained in the first. Yet without a doubt it is the second kind of sentence that is gaining ground in modern English. I do not want to exaggerate. This kind of writing is not yet universal, and outcrops of simplicity will occur

here and there in the worst-written page. Still, if you or I were told
to write a few lines on the uncertainty of human fortunes, we should
probably come much nearer to my imaginary sentence than to the
one from *Ecclesiastes*.

As I have tried to show, modern writing at its worst does not   11
consist in picking out words for the sake of their meaning and
inventing images in order to make the meaning clearer. It consists
in gumming together long strips of words which have already been
set in order by someone else, and making the results presentable by
sheer humbug. The attraction of this way of writing is that it is easy.
It is easier—even quicker once you have the habit—to say *In my
opinion it is a not unjustifiable assumption that* than to say *I think*.
If you use ready-made phrases, you not only don't have to hunt about
for words; you also don't have to bother with the rhythms of your
sentences, since these phrases are generally so arranged as to be
more or less euphonious. When you are composing in a hurry—
when you are dictating to a stenographer, for instance, or making a
public speech—it is natural to fall into a pretentious, Latinized style.
Tags like *a consideration which we should do well to bear in mind*
or *a conclusion to which all of us would readily assent* will save
many a sentence from coming down with a bump. By using stale
metaphors, similes and idioms, you save much mental effort, at the
cost of leaving your meaning vague, not only for your reader but for
yourself. This is the significance of mixed metaphors. The sole aim
of a metaphor is to call up a visual image. When these images
clash—as in *The Fascist octopus has sung its swan song, the jackboot is thrown into the melting pot*—it can be taken as certain that
the writer is not seeing a mental image of the objects he is naming;
in other words he is not really thinking. Look again at the examples
I gave at the beginning of this essay. Professor Laski (1) uses five
negatives in fifty-three words. One of these is superfluous, making
nonsense of the whole passage, and in addition there is the slip *alien*
for *akin*, making further nonsense, and several avoidable pieces of
clumsiness which increase the general vagueness. Professor Hogben
(2) plays ducks and drakes with a battery which is able to write
prescriptions, and, while disapproving of the everyday phrase *put
up with*, is unwilling to look *egregious* up in the dictionary and see
what it means. (3), if one takes an uncharitable attitude towards it,
is simply meaningless: probably one could work out its intended
meaning by reading the whole of the article in which it occurs. In

(4), the writer knows more or less what he wants to say, but an accumulation of stale phrases chokes him like tea leaves blocking a sink. In (5), words and meaning have almost parted company. People who write in this manner usually have a general emotional meaning—they dislike one thing and want to express solidarity with another—but they are not interested in the detail of what they are saying. A scrupulous writer, in every sentence that he writes, will ask himself at least four questions, thus: What am I trying to say? What words will express it? What image or idiom will make it clearer? Is this image fresh enough to have an effect? And he will probably ask himself two more: Could I put it more shortly? Have I said anything that is avoidably ugly? But you are not obliged to go to all this trouble. You can shirk it by simply throwing your mind open and letting the ready-made phrases come crowding in. They will construct your sentences for you—even think your thoughts for you, to a certain extent—and at need they will perform the important service of partially concealing your meaning even from yourself. It is at this point that the special connection between politics and the debasement of language becomes clear.

In our times it is broadly true that political writing is bad writing. 12 Where it is not true, it will generally be found that the writer is some kind of rebel, expressing his private opinions and not a "party line." Orthodoxy, of whatever color, seems to demand a lifeless, imitative style. The political dialects to be found in pamphlets, leading articles, manifestos, White Papers and the speeches of under-secretaries do, of course, vary from party to party, but they are all alike in that one almost never finds in them a fresh, vivid, home-made turn of speech. When one watches some tired hack on the platform mechanically repeating the familiar phrases—*bestial atrocities, iron heel, blood-stained tryanny, free peoples of the world, stand shoulder to shoulder*—one often has a curious feeling that one is not watching a live human being but some kind of dummy, a feeling which suddenly becomes stronger at moments when the light catches the speaker's spectacles and turns them into blank discs which seem to have no eyes behind them. And this is not altogether fanciful. A speaker who uses that kind of phraseology has gone some distance towards turning himself into a machine. The appropriate noises are coming out of his larynx, but his brain is not involved as it would be if he were choosing his words from himself. If the speech he is making is one that he is accustomed to make over and over again, he may be almost unconscious of what he is saying, as one is when one utters the responses in church. And this reduced state of consciousness, if not indispensable, is at any rate favorable to political conformity.

In our time, political speech and writing are largely the defense   13 of the indefensible. Things like the continuance of British rule in India, the Russian purges and deportations, the dropping of the atom bombs on Japan, can indeed be defended, but only by arguments which are too brutal for most people to face, and which do not square with the professed aims of political parties. Thus political language has to consist largely of euphemism, question-begging and sheer cloudy vagueness. Defenseless villages are bombarded from the air, the inhabitants driven out into the countryside, the cattle machine-gunned, the huts set on fire with incendiary bullets: this is called *pacification*. Millions of peasants are robbed of their farms and sent trudging along the roads with no more than they can carry: this is called *transfer of population* or *rectification of frontiers*. People are imprisoned for years without trial, or shot in the back of the neck or sent to die of scurvy in Arctic lumber camps: this is called *elimination of unreliable elements.* Such phraseology is needed if one wants to name things without calling up mental pictures of them. Consider for instance some comfortable English professor defending Russian totalitarianism. He cannot say outright, "I believe in killing off your opponents when you can get good results by doing so." Probably, therefore, he will say something like this:

"While freely conceding that the Soviet régime exhibits certain   14 features which the humanitarian may be inclined to deplore, we must, I think, agree that a certain curtailment of the right to political opposition is an unavoidable concomitant of transitional periods, and that the rigors which the Russian people have been called upon to undergo have been amply justified in the sphere of concrete achievement."

The inflated style is itself a kind of euphemism. A mass of Latin   15 words falls upon the facts like soft snow, blurring the outlines and covering up all the details. The great enemy of clear language is insincerity. When there is a gap between one's real and one's declared aims, one turns as it were instinctively to long words and exhausted idioms, like a cuttlefish squirting out ink. In our age there is no such thing as "keeping out of politics." All issues are political issues, and politics itself is a mass of lies, evasions, folly, hatred and schizophrenia. When the general atmosphere is bad, language must suffer. I should expect to find—this is a guess which I have not sufficient knowledge to verify—that the German, Russian and Italian languages have all deteriorated in the last ten or fifteen years, as a result of dictatorship.

But if thought corrupts language, language can also corrupt 16 thought. A bad usage can spread by tradition and imitation, even among people who should and do know better. The debased language that I have been discussing is in some ways very convenient. Phrases like *a not unjustifiable assumption, leaves much to be desired, would serve no good purpose, a consideration which we should do well to bear in mind,* are a continuous temptation, a packet of aspirins always at one's elbow. Look back through this essay, and for certain you will find that I have again and again committed the very faults I am protesting against. By this morning's post I have received a pamphlet dealing with conditions in Germany. The author tells me that he "felt impelled" to write it. I open it at random, and here is almost the first sentence that I see: "(The Allies) have an opportunity not only of achieving a radical transformation of Germany's social and political structure in such a way as to avoid a nationalistic reaction in Germany itself, but at the same time of laying the foundations of a co-operative and unified Europe." You see, he "feels impelled" to write—feels, presumably, that he has something new to say—and yet his words, like cavalry horses answering the bugle, group themselves automatically into the familiar dreary pattern. This invasion of one's mind by ready-made phrases (*lay the foundations, achieve a radical transformation*) can only be prevented if one is constantly on guard against them, and every such phrase anaesthetizes a portion of one's brain.

I said earlier that the decadence of our language is probably 17 curable. Those who deny this would argue, if they produced an argument at all, that language merely reflects existing social conditions, and that we cannot influence its development by any direct tinkering with words and constructions. So far as the general tone or spirit of a language goes, this may be true, but it is not true in detail. Silly words and expressions have often disappeared, not through any evolutionary process but owing to the conscious action of a minority. Two recent examples were *explore every avenue* and *leave no stone unturned,* which were killed by the jeers of a few journalists. There is a long list of flyblown metaphors which could similarly be got rid of if enough people would interest themselves in the job; and it should also be possible to laugh the *not un-* formation out of existence,[3] to reduce the amount of Latin and Greek in the average sentence, to drive out foreign phrases and strayed scientific words, and, in general, to make pretentiousness unfashionable. But all these are minor points. The defense of the English language implies more than this, and perhaps it is best to start by saying what it does *not* imply.

To begin with it has nothing to do with archaism, with the salvaging of obsolete words and turns of speech, or with the setting up of a "standard English" which must never be departed from. On the contrary, it is especially concerned with the scrapping of every word or idiom which has outworn its usefulness. It has nothing to do with correct grammar and syntax, which are of no importance so long as one makes one's meaning clear, or with the avoidance of Americanisms, or with having what is called a "good prose style." On the other hand, it is not concerned with fake simplicity and the attempt to make written English colloquial. Nor does it even imply in every case preferring the Saxon word to the Latin one, though it does imply using the fewest and shortest words that will cover one's meaning. What is above all needed is to let the meaning choose the word, and not the other way about. In prose, the worst thing one can do with words is to surrender to them. When you think of a concrete object, you think wordlessly, and then, if you want to describe the thing you have been visualizing you probably hunt about till you find the exact words that seem to fit. When you think of something abstract, you are more inclined to use words from the start, and unless you make a conscious effort to prevent it, the existing dialect will come rushing in and do the job for you, at the expense of blurring or even changing your meaning. Probably it is better to put off using words as long as possible and get one's meaning as clear as one can through pictures or sensations. Afterwards one can choose—not simply *accept*—the phrases that will best cover the meaning, and then switch round and decide what impression one's words are likely to make on another person. This last effort of the mind cuts out all stale or mixed images, all prefabricated phrases, needless repetitions, and humbug and vagueness generally. But one can often be in doubt about the effect of a word or a phrase, and

3. One can cure oneself of the *not un-* formation by memorizing this sentence: *A not unblack dog was chasing a not unsmall rabbit across a not ungreen field.*

one needs rules that one can rely on when instinct fails. I think the following rules will cover most cases:

    (i) Never use a metaphor, simile or other figure of speech which you are used to seeing in print.

    (ii) Never use a long word where a short one will do.

    (iii) If it is possible to cut a word out, always cut it out.

    (iv) Never use the passive where you can use the active.

    (v) Never use a foreign phrase, a scientific word or jargon word if you can think of an everyday English equivalent.

    (vi) Break any of these rules sooner than say anything outright barbarous.

These rules sound elementary, and so they are, but they demand a deep change in attitude in anyone who has grown used to writing in the style now fashionable. One could keep all of them and still write bad English, but one could not write the kind of stuff that I quoted in those five specimens at the beginning of this article.

I have not here been considering the literary use of language, 19 but merely language as an instrument for expressing and not for concealing or preventing thought. Stuart Chase and others have come near to claiming that all abstract words are meaningless, and have used this as a pretext for advocating a kind of political quietism. Since you don't know what Fascism is, how can you struggle against Fascism? One need not swallow such absurdities as this, but one ought to recognize that the present political chaos is connected with the decay of language, and that one can probably bring about some improvement by starting at the verbal end. If you simplify your English, you are freed from the worst follies of orthodoxy. You cannot speak any of the necessary dialects, and when you make a stupid remark, its stupidity will be obvious, even to yourself. Political language—and with variations this is true of all political parties, from Conservatives to Anarchists—is designed to make lies sound truthful and murder respectable, and to give an appearance of solidity to pure wind. One cannot change this all in a moment, but one can at least change one's own habits, and from time to time one can even, if one jeers loudly enough, send some worn-out and useless phrase— some *jackboot, Achilles' heel, hotbed, melting pot, acid test, veritable inferno* or other lump of verbal refuse—into the dustbin where it belongs.

CONTEMPORARY ESSAYS

❧JOHN MCPHEE

John McPhee was born in 1931 in Princeton, New Jersey. He received a B.A. from Princeton University and also attended Cambridge University in England. McPhee began his writing career by working for *Time* magazine, but now he writes regularly for the *New Yorker*. One remarkable feature of McPhee's work is its range. In his seventeen books he has investigated the history and popularity of oranges in *Oranges* (1967), the pine barrens of central New Jersey in *The Pine Barrens* (1968), the state of Alaska in *Coming into the Country* (1977), the headmaster of a prep school in *The Headmaster* (1966), the Scottish highlands in *The Crofter and the Laird* (1969), the geology of North America in *Basin and Range* (1981) and *In Suspect Terrain* (1983), and the Swiss army in *La Place de la Concorde de la Suisse* (1984). In his writing, McPhee weaves facts, ideas, and commentary into tight and often surprising forms that hold a subject up to inspection from many angles. "The Search for Marvin Gardens" mixes several levels of reality to comment on the decaying resort town of Atlantic City. The essay was written in 1972, however, and since that time hotels and gambling casinos have begun to reshape the town and the lives of its residents.

The Search for Marvin Gardens

Go. I roll the dice—a six and a two. Through the air I move my token, the flatiron, to Vermont Avenue, where dog packs range.

The dogs are moving (some are limping) through ruins, rubble, fire damage, open garbage. Doorways are gone. Lath is visible in the crumbling walls of the buildings. The street sparkles with shattered glass. I have never seen, anywhere, so many broken windows. A sign—"Slow, Children at Play"—has been bent backward by an automobile. At the lighthouse, the dogs turn up Pacific and disappear. George Meade, Army engineer, built the lighthouse—brick upon brick, six hundred thousand bricks, to reach up high enough to throw a beam twenty miles over the sea. Meade, seven years later, saved the Union at Gettysburg.

I buy Vermont Avenue for $100. My opponent is a tall, shadowy figure, across from me, but I know him well, and I know his game

1

2

3

like a favorite tune. If he can, he will always go for the quick kill. And when it is foolish to go for the quick kill he will be foolish. On the whole, though, he is a master assessor of percentages. It is a mistake to underestimate him. His eleven carries his top hat to St. Charles Place, which he buys for $140.

The sidewalks of St. Charles Place have been cracked to shards by through-growing weeds. There are no buildings. Mansions, hotels once stood here. A few street lamps now drop cones of light on broken glass and vacant space behind a chain-link fence that some great machine has in places bent to the ground. Five plane trees— in full summer leaf, flecking the light—are all that live on St. Charles Place.   4

Block upon block, gradually, we are cancelling each other out— in the blues, the lavenders, the oranges, the greens. My opponent follows a plan of his own devising. I use the Hornblower & Weeks opening and the Zuricher defense. The first game draws tight, will soon finish. In 1971, a group of people in Racine, Wisconsin, played for seven hundred and sixty-eight hours. A game begun a month later in Danville, California, lasted eight hundred and twenty hours. These are official records, and they stun us. We have been playing for eight minutes. It amazes us that Monopoly is thought of as a long game. It is possible to play to a complete, absolute, and final con-clusion in less than fifteen minutes, all within the rules as written. My opponent and I have done so thousands of times. No wonder we are sitting across from each other now in this best-of-seven series for the international singles championship of the world.   5

On Illinois Avenue, three men lean out from second-story win-dows. A girl is coming down the street. She wears dungarees and a bright-red shirt, has ample breasts and a Hadendoan Afro, a black halo, two feet in diameter. Ice rattles in the glasses in the hands of the men.   6

"Hey, sister!"   7

"Come on up!"   8

She looks up, looks from one to another to the other, looks them flat in the eye.   9

"What for?" she says, and she walks on.   10

I buy Illinois for $240. It solidifies my chances, for I already   11
own Kentucky and Indiana. My opponent pales. If he had landed
first on Illinois, the game would have been over then and there, for
he has houses built on Boardwalk and Park Place, we share the
railroads equally, and we have cancelled each other everywhere else.
We never trade.

In 1852, R. B. Osborne, an immigrant Englishman, civil engi-   12
neer, surveyed the route of a railroad line that would run from
Camden to Absecon Island, in New Jersey, traversing the state from
the Delaware River to the barrier beaches of the sea. He then sketched
in the plan of a "bathing village" that would surround the eastern
terminus of the line. His pen flew glibly, framing and naming spa-
cious avenues parallel to the shore—Mediterranean, Baltic, Oriental,
Ventnor—and narrower transsecting avenues: North Carolina, Pennsylvania, Vermont, Connecticut, States, Virginia, Tennessee, New
York, Kentucky, Indiana, Illinois. The place as a whole had no name,
so when he had completed the plan Osborne wrote in large letters
over the ocean, "Atlantic City." No one ever challenged the name, or
the names of Osborne's streets. Monopoly was invented in the early
nineteen-thirties by Charles B. Darrow, but Darrow was only trans-
literating what Osborne had created. The railroads, crucial to any
player, were the making of Atlantic City. After the rails were down,
houses and hotels burgeoned from Mediterranean and Baltic to New
York and Kentucky. Properties—building lots—sold for as little as
six dollars apiece and as much as a thousand dollars. The original
investors in the railroads and the real estate called themselves the
Camden & Atlantic Land Company. Reverently, I repeat their names:
Dwight Bell, William Coffin, John DaCosta, Daniel Deal, William
Fleming, Andrew Hay, Joseph Porter, Jonathan Pitney, Samuel Rich-
ards—founders, fathers, forerunners, archetypical masters of the
quick kill.

My opponent and I are now in a deep situation of classical   13
Monopoly. The torsion is almost perfect—Boardwalk and Park Place
versus the brilliant reds. His cash position is weak, though, and if I
escape him now he may fade. I land on Luxury Tax, contiguous to
but in sanctuary from his power. I have four houses on Indiana. He
lands there. He concedes.

Indiana Avenue was the address of the Brighton Hotel, gone   14
now. The Brighton was exclusive—a word that no longer has retail
value in the city. If you arrived by automobile and tried to register
at the Brighton, you were sent away. Brighton-class people came in
private railroad cars. Brighton-class people had other private railroad cars for their horses—dawn rides on the firm sand at water's
edge, skirts flying. Colonel Anthony J. Drexel Biddle—the sort of
name that would constrict throats in Philadelphia—lived, much of
the year, in the Brighton.

Colonel Sanders' fried chicken is on Kentucky Avenue. So is   15
Clifton's Club Harlem, with the Sepia Revue and the Sepia Follies,
featuring the Honey Bees, the Fashions, and the Lords.

My opponent and I, many years ago, played 2,428 games of   16
Monopoly in a single season. He was then a recent graduate of the
Harvard Law School, and he was working for a downtown firm,
looking up law. Two people we knew—one from Chase Manhattan,
the other from Morgan, Stanley—tried to get into the game, but after
a few rounds we found that they were not in the conversation and
we sent them home. Monopoly should always be *mano a mano*
anyway. My opponent won 1,199 games, and so did I. Thirty were
ties. He was called into the Army, and we stopped just there. Now,
in Game 2 of the series, I go immediately to jail, and again to jail
while my opponent seines property. He is dumbfoundingly lucky. He
wins in twelve minutes.

Visiting hours are daily, eleven to two; Sunday, eleven to one;   17
evenings, six to nine. "NO MINORS, NO FOOD, Immediate Family Only
Allowed in Jail." All this above a blue steel door in a blue cement
wall in the windowless interior of the basement of the city hall. The
desk sergeant sits opposite the door to the jail. In a cigar box in front
of him are pills in every color, a banquet of fruit salad an inch and
a half deep—leapers, co-pilots, footballs, truck drivers, peanuts, blue
angels, yellow jackets, redbirds, rainbows. Near the desk are two
soldiers, waiting to go through the blue door. They are about eighteen
years old. One of them is trying hard to light a cigarette. His wrists
are in steel cuffs. A military policeman waits, too. He is a year or so
older than the soldiers, taller, studious in appearance, gentle, fat.

On a bench against a wall sits a good-looking girl in slacks. The blue door rattles, swings heavily open. A turnkey stands in the doorway. "Don't you guys kill yourselves back there now," says the sergeant to the soldiers.

"One kid, he overdosed himself about ten and a half hours ago," says the M.P. 18

The M.P., the soldiers, the turnkey, and the girl on the bench 19 are white. The sergeant is black. "If you take off the handcuffs, take off the belts," says the sergeant to the M.P. "I don't want them hanging themselves back there." The door shuts and its tumblers move. When it opens again, five minutes later, a young white man in sandals and dungarees and a blue polo shirt emerges. His hair is in a ponytail. He has no beard. He grins at the good-looking girl. She rises, joins him. The sergeant hands him a manila envelope. From it he removes his belt and a small notebook. He borrows a pencil, makes an entry in the notebook. He is out of jail, free. What did he do? He offended Atlantic City in some way. He spent a night in the jail. In the nineteen-thirties, men visiting Atlantic City went to jail, directly to jail, did not pass Go, for appearing in topless bathing suits on the beach. A city statute requiring all men to wear full-length bathing suits was not seriously challenged until 1937, and the first year in which a man could legally go bare-chested on the beach was 1940.

Game 3. After seventeen minutes, I am ready to begin construc- 20 tion on overpriced and sluggish Pacific, North Carolina, and Pennsylvania. Nothing else being open, opponent concedes.

The physical profile of streets perpendicular to the shore is 21 something like a playground slide. It begins in the high skyline of Boardwalk hotels, plummets into warrens of "side-avenue" motels, crosses Pacific, slopes through church missions, convalescent homes, burlesque houses, rooming houses, and liquor stores, crosses Atlantic, and runs level through the bombed-out ghetto as far—Baltic, Mediterranean—as the eye can see. North Carolina Avenue, for example, is flanked at its beach end by the Chalfonte and the Haddon Hall (908 rooms, air-conditioned), where, according to one biographer, John Philip Sousa (1854–1932) first played when he was twenty-two, insisting, even then, that everyone call him by his entire name. Behind these big hotels, motels—Barbizon, Catalina—crouch.

Between Pacific and Atlantic is an occasional house from 1910—
wooden porch, wooden mullions, old yellow paint—and two
churches, a package store, a strip show, a dealer in fruits and
vegetables. Then, beyond Atlantic Avenue, North Carolina moves on
into the vast ghetto, the bulk of the city, and it looks like Metz in
1919, Cologne in 1944. Nothing has actually exploded. It is not bomb
damage. It is deep and complex decay. Roofs are off. Bricks are
scattered in the street. People sit on porches, six deep, at nine on a
Monday morning. When they go off to wait in unemployment lines,
they wait sometimes two hours. Between Mediterranean and Baltic
runs a chain-link fence, enclosing rubble. A patrol car sits idling by
the curb. In the back seat is a German shepherd. A sign on the fence
says, "Beware of Bad Dogs."

Mediterranean and Baltic are the principal avenues of the ghetto.   22
Dogs are everywhere. A pack of seven passes me. Block after block,
there are three-story brick row houses. Whole segments of them are
abandoned, a thousand broken windows. Some parts are intact,
occupied. A mattress lies in the street, soaking in a pool of water.
Wet stuffing is coming out of the mattress. A postman is having a
rye and a beer in the Plantation Bar at nine-fifteen in the morning.
I ask him idly if he knows where Marvin Gardens is. He does not.
"HOOKED AND NEED HELP? CONTACT N.A.R.C.O." "REVIVAL NOW GOING
ON, CONDUCTED BY REVEREND H. HENDERSON OF TEXAS." These are
signboards on Mediterranean and Baltic. The second one is upside
down and leans against a boarded-up window of the Faith Temple
Church of God in Christ. There is an old peeling poster on a ware-
house wall showing a figure in an electric chair. "The Black Panther
Manifesto" is the title of the poster, and its message is, or was, that
"the fascists have already decided in advance to murder Chairman
Bobby Seale in the electric chair." I pass an old woman who carries
a bucket. She wears blue sneakers, worn through. Her feet spill out.
She wears red socks, rolled at the knees. A white handkerchief,
spread over her head, is knotted at the corners. Does she know
where Marvin Gardens is? "I sure don't know," she says, setting
down the bucket. "I sure don't know. I've heard of it somewhere,
but I just can't say where." I walk on, through a block of shattered
glass. The glass crunches underfoot like coarse sand. I remember
when I first came here—a long train ride from Trenton, long ago,
games of poker in the train—to play basketball against Atlantic City.
We were half black, they were all black. We scored forty points, they

scored eighty or something like it. What I remember most is that they had glass backboards—glittering, pendent, expensive glass backboards, a rarity then in high schools, even in colleges, the only ones we played on all year.

I turn on Pennsylvania, and start back toward the sea. The 23 windows of the Hotel Astoria, on Pennsylvania near Baltic, are boarded up. A sheet of unpainted plywood is the door, and in it is a triangular peephole that now frames an eye. The plywood door opens. A man answers my question. Rooms there are six, seven, and ten dollars a week. I thank him for the information and move on, emerging from the ghetto at the Catholic Daughters of America Women's Guest House, between Atlantic and Pacific. Between Pacific and the Boardwalk are the blinking vacancy signs of the Aristocrat and Colton Manor motels. Pennsylvania terminates at the Sheraton-Seaside—thirty-two dollars a day, ocean corner. I take a walk on the Boardwalk and into the Holiday Inn (twenty-three stories). A guest is registering. "You reserved for Wednesday, and this is Monday," the clerk tells him. "But that's all right. We have *plenty* of rooms." The clerk is very young, female, and has soft brown hair that hangs below her waist. Her superior kicks her.

He is a middle-aged man with red spiderwebs in his face. He 24 is jacketed and tied. He takes her aside. "Don't say 'plenty,'" he says. "Say 'You are fortunate, sir. We have room available.'"

The face of the young woman turns sour. "We have all the rooms 25 you need," she says to the customer, and, to her superior, "How's that?"

Game 4. My opponent's luck has become abrasive. He has 26 Boardwalk and Park Place, and has sealed the board.

Darrow was a plumber. He was, specifically, a radiator repair- 27 man who lived in Germantown, Pennsylvania. His first Monopoly board was a sheet of linoleum. On it he placed houses and hotels that he had carved from blocks of wood. The game he thus invented was brilliantly conceived, for it was an uncannily exact reflection of the business milieu at large. In its depth, range, and subtlety, in its luck-skill ratio, in its sense of infrastructure and socio-economic parameters, in its philosophical characteristics, it reached to the profundity of the financial community. It was as scientific as the stock market. It suggested the manner and means through which an underdeveloped world had been developed. It was chess at Wall Street level. "Advance token to the nearest Railroad and pay owner twice the rental to which he is otherwise entitled. If Railroad is unowned, you may buy it from the Bank. Get out of Jail, free. Advance token to nearest Utility. If unowned, you may buy it from Bank. If owned, throw dice and pay owner a total ten times the amount thrown. You are assessed for street repairs: $40 per house, $115 per hotel. Pay poor tax of $15. Go to Jail. Go directly to Jail. Do not pass Go. Do not collect $200."

The turnkey opens the blue door. The turnkey is known to the 28 inmates as Sidney K. Above his desk are ten closed-circuit-TV screens—assorted viewpoints of the jail. There are three cellblocks— men, women, juvenile boys. Six days is the average stay. Showers twice a week. The steel doors and the equipment that operates them were made in San Antonio. The prisoners sleep on bunks of butcher block. There are no mattresses. There are three prisoners to a cell. In winter, it is cold in here. Prisoners burn newspapers to keep warm. Cell corners are black with smudge. The jail is three years old. The men's block echoes with chatter. The man in the cell nearest Sidney K. is pacing. His shirt is covered with broad stains of blood. The block for juvenile boys is, by contrast, utterly silent—empty corridor, empty cells. There is only one prisoner. He is small and black and appears to be thirteen. He says he is sixteen and that he has been alone in here for three days.

"Why are you here? What did you do?" 29

"I hit a jitney driver." 30

The series stands at three all. We have split the fifth and sixth 31 games. We are scrambling for property. Around the board we fairly fly. We move so fast because we do our own banking and search our own deeds. My opponent grows tense.

Ventnor Avenue, a street of delicatessens and doctors' offices, is 32 leafy with plane trees and hydrangeas, the city flower. Water Works is on the mainland. The water comes over in submarine pipes. Electric Company gets power from across the state, on the Delaware River, in Deepwater. States Avenue, now a wasteland like St. Charles, once had gardens running down the middle of the street, a horse-drawn trolley, private homes. States Avenue was as exclusive as the Brighton. Only an apartment house, a small motel, and the All Wars Memorial Building—monadnocks spaced widely apart—stand along States Avenue now. Pawnshops, convalescent homes, and the Paradise Soul Saving Station are on Virginia Avenue. The soul-saving station is pink, orange, and yellow. In the windows flanking the door of the Virginia Money Loan Office are Nikons, Polaroids, Yashicas, Sony TVs, Underwood typewriters, Singer sewing machines, and pictures of Christ. On the far side of town, beside a single track and locked up most of the time, is the new railroad station, a small hut made of glazed firebrick, all that is left of the lines that built the city. An authentic phrenologist works on New York Avenue close to Frank's Extra Dry Bar and a church where the sermon today is "Death in the Pot." The church is of pink brick, has blue and amber windows and two red doors. St. James Place, narrow and twisting, is lined with boarding houses that have wooden porches on each of three stories, suggesting a New Orleans made of salt-bleached pine. In a vacant lot on Tennessee is a white Ford station wagon stripped to the chassis. The windows are smashed. A plastic Clorox bottle sits on the driver's seat. The wind has pressed newspaper against the chain-link fence around the lot. Atlantic Avenue, the city's principal thoroughfare, could be seventeen American Main Streets placed end to end—discount vitamins and Vienna Corset shops, movie theatres, shoe stores, and funeral homes. The Boardwalk is made of yellow pine and Douglas fir, soaked in pentachlorophenol. Down-beach, it reaches far beyond the city. Signs everywhere—on windows, lampposts, trash baskets—proclaim "Bienvenue Canadiens!" The salt air is full of Canadian French. In the Claridge Hotel, on Park Place, I ask a clerk if she knows where Marvin Gardens is. She says, "Is it a floral shop?" I ask a cabdriver, parked outside. He says, "Never heard of it." Park Place is one block long, Pacific to Boardwalk. On the roof of the Claridge is the Solarium, the highest point in town—panoramic view of the ocean, the bay, the saltwater ghetto. I look down at the rooftops of the side-avenue motels and into swimming pools. There are hundreds of people around the rooftop pools, sunbathing, reading—many more people than are on the beach. Walls, windows, and a block of sky are all that is visible from these pools—no sand, no sea. The pools are craters, and with the people around them they are countersunk into the motels.

The seventh, and final, game is ten minutes old and I have hotels 33
on Oriental, Vermont, and Connecticut. I have Tennessee and
St. James. I have North Carolina and Pacific. I have Boardwalk,
Atlantic, Ventnor, Illinois, Indiana. My fingers are forming a "V." I
have mortgaged most of these properties in order to pay for others,
and I have mortgaged the others to pay for the hotels. I have seven
dollars. I will pay off the mortgages and build my reserves with
income from the three hotels. My cash position may be low, but I
feel like a rocket in an underground silo. Meanwhile, if I could just
go to jail for a time I could pause there, wait there, until my opponent, in his inescapable rounds, pays the rates of my hotels. Jail, at
times, is the strategic place to be. I roll boxcars from the Reading
and move the flatiron to Community Chest. "Go to Jail. Go directly
to Jail."

The prisoners, of course, have no pens and no pencils. They 34
take paper napkins, roll them tight as crayons, char the ends with
matches, and write on the walls. The things they write are not
entirely idiomatic; for example, "In God We Trust." All is in carbon.
Time is required in the writing. "Only humanity could know of such
pain." "God So Loved the World." "There is no greater pain than
life itself." In the women's block now, there are six blacks, giggling,
and a white asleep in red shoes. She is drunk. The others are pushers,
prostitutes, an auto thief, a burglar caught with pistol in purse. A
sixteen-year-old accused of murder was in here last week. These
words are written on the wall of a now empty cell: "Laying here I
see two bunks about six inches thick, not counting the one I'm laying
on, which is hard as brick. No cushion for my back. No pillow for
my head. Just a couple scratchy blankets which is best to use it's
said. I wake up in the morning so shivery and cold, waiting and
waiting till I am told the food is coming. It's on its way. It's not
worth waiting for, but I eat it anyway. I know one thing when they
set me free I'm gonna be good if it kills me."

How many years must a game be played to produce an Anthony 35
J. Drexel Biddle and chestnut geldings on the beach? About half a
century was the original answer, from the first railroad to Biddle at
his peak. Biddle, at his peak, hit an Atlantic City streetcar conductor
with his fist, laid him out with one punch. This increased Biddle's
legend. He did not go to jail. While John Philip Sousa led his band

along the Boardwalk playing "The Stars and Stripes Forever" and
Jack Dempsey ran up and down in training for his fight with Gene
Tunney, the city crossed the high curve of its parabola. Al Capone
held conventions here—upstairs with his sleeves rolled, apportioning
among his lieutenant governors the states of the Eastern seaboard.
The natural history of an American resort proceeds from Indians to
French Canadians via Biddles and Capones. French Canadians,
whatever they may be at home, are Visigoths here. Bienvenue Visigoths!

My opponent plods along incredibly well. He has got his fourth   36
railroad, and patiently, unbelievably, he has picked up my potential
winners until he has blocked me everywhere but Marvin Gardens.
He has avoided, in the fifty-dollar zoning, my increasingly petty
hotels. His cash flow swells. His railroads are costing me two
hundred dollars a minute. He is building hotels on States, Virginia,
and St. Charles. He has temporarily reversed the current. With the
yellow monopolies and my blue monopolies, I could probably defeat
his lavenders and his railroads. I have Atlantic and Ventnor. I need
Marvin Gardens. My only hope is Marvin Gardens.

There is a plaque at Boardwalk and Park Place, and on it in   37
relief is the leonine profile of a man who looks like an officer in a
metropolitan bank—"Charles B. Darrow, 1889–1967, inventor of the
game of Monopoly." "Darrow," I address him, aloud. "Where is
Marvin Gardens?" There is, of course, no answer. Bronze, impassive,
Darrow looks south down the Boardwalk. "Mr. Darrow, please,
where is Marvin Gardens?" Nothing. Not a sign. He just looks south
down the Boardwalk.

My opponent accepts the trophy with his natural ease, and I   38
make, from notes, remarks that are even less graceful than his.

Marvin Gardens is the one color-block Monopoly property that   39
is not in Atlantic City. It is a suburb within a suburb, secluded. It is
a planned compound of seventy-two handsome houses set on cur-
vilinear private streets under yews and cedars, poplars and willows.
The compound was built around 1920, in Margate, New Jersey, and
consists of solid buildings of stucco, brick, and wood, with slate
roofs, tile roofs, multimullioned porches, Giraldic towers, and Span-

ish grilles. Marvin Gardens, the ultimate outwash of Monopoly, is a citadel and sanctuary of the middle class. "We're heavily patrolled by police here. We don't take no chances. Me? I'm living here nine years. I paid seventeen thousand dollars and I've been offered thirty. Number one, I don't want to move. Number two, I don't need the money. I have four bedrooms, two and a half baths, front den, back den. No basement. The Atlantic is down there. Six feet down and you float. A lot of people have a hard time finding this place. People that lived in Atlantic City all their life don't know how to find it. They don't know where the hell they're going. They just know it's south, down the Boardwalk."

✿ ANNIE DILLARD

Annie Dillard was born in 1945 in Pittsburgh, Pennsylvania. She earned a B.A. and M.A. at Hollins College and lived for several years in the Roanoke Valley of Virginia—an experience that formed the basis for her book, *Pilgrim at Tinker Creek* (1974), which was awarded the Pulitzer Prize for general nonfiction. Dillard has taught at Western Washington State University and is currently on the faculty of Wesleyan University. In addition to *Pilgrim at Tinker Creek*, she has published a volume of poetry, *Tickets for a Prayer Wheel* (1974); two collections of essays, *Holy the Firm* (1978) and *Teaching a Stone to Talk* (1982); and a book of literary criticism, *Living by Fiction* (1982). "In the Jungle" is typical of Dillard's writing in its mixing of vividly re-created scenes and events combined with meditations on the cosmic implications of personal experience.

In the Jungle

Like any out-of-the-way place, the Napo River in the Ecuadorian   1
jungle seems real enough when you are there, even central. Out of
the way of *what?* I was sitting on a stump at the edge of a bankside
palm-thatch village, in the middle of the night, on the headwaters
of the Amazon. Out of the way of human life, tenderness, or the
glance of heaven?

A nightjar in a deep-leaved shadow called three long notes, and   2
hushed. The men with me talked softly in clumps: three North
Americans, four Ecuadorians who were showing us the jungle. We
were holding cool drinks and idly watching a hand-sized tarantula
seize moths that came to the lone bulb on the generator shed beside
us.

It was February, the middle of summer. Green fireflies spattered   3
lights across the air and illumined for seconds, now here, now there,
the pale trunks of enormous, solitary trees. Beneath us the brown
Napo River was rising, in all silence; it coiled up the sandy bank
and tangled its foam in vines that trailed from the forest and roots
that looped the shore.

Each breath of night smelled sweet, more moistened and sweet   4
than any kitchen, or garden, or cradle. Each star in Orion seemed
to tremble and stir with my breath. All at once, in the thatch house

across the clearing behind us, one of the village's Jesuit priests began playing an alto recorder, playing a wordless song, lyric, in a minor key, that twined over the village clearing, that caught in the big trees' canopies, muted our talk on the bankside, and wandered over the river, dissolving downstream.

This will do, I thought. This will do, for a weekend, or a season, or a home.

5

Later that night I loosed my hair from its braids and combed it smooth—not for myself, but so the village girls could play with it in the morning.

6

We had disembarked at the village that afternoon, and I had slumped on some shaded steps, wishing I knew some Spanish or some Quechua so I could speak with the ring of little girls who were alternately staring at me and smiling at their toes. I spoke anyway, and fooled with my hair, which they were obviously dying to get their hands on, and laughed, and soon they were all braiding my hair, all five of them, all fifty fingers, all my hair, even my bangs. And then they took it apart and did it again, laughing, and teaching me Spanish nouns, and meeting my eyes and each other's with open delight, while their small brothers in blue jeans climbed down from the trees and began kicking a volleyball around with one of the North American men.

7

Now, as I combed my hair in the little tent, another of the men, a free-lance writer from Manhattan, was talking quietly. He was telling us the tale of his life, describing his work in Hollywood, his apartment in Manhattan, his house in Paris. . . . "It makes me wonder," he said, "what I'm doing in a tent under a tree in the village of Pompeya, on the Napo River, in the jungle of Ecuador." After a pause he added, "It makes me wonder why I'm going *back*."

8

The point of going somewhere like the Napo River in Ecuador is not to see the most spectacular anything. It is simply to see what is there. We are here on the planet only once, and might as well get a feel for the place. We might as well get a feel for the fringes and hollows in which life is lived, for the Amazon basin, which covers half a continent, and for the life that—there, like anywhere else—is always and necessarily lived in detail: on the tributaries, in the riverside villages, sucking this particular white-fleshed guava in this particular pattern of shade.

9

What is there is interesting. The Napo River itself is wide (I   10
mean wider than the Mississippi at Davenport) and brown, opaque,
and smeared with floating foam and logs and branches from the
jungle. White egrets hunch on shoreline deadfalls and parrots in
flocks dart in and out of the light. Under the water in the river,
unseen, are anacondas—which are reputed to take a few village
toddlers every year—and water boas, stingrays, crocodiles, mana-
tees, and sweet-meated fish.

Low water bares gray strips of sandbar on which the natives   11
build tiny palm-thatch shelters, arched, the size of pup tents, for
overnight fishing trips. You see these extraordinarily clean people
(who bathe twice a day in the river, and whose straight black hair
is always freshly washed) paddling down the river in dugout canoes,
hugging the banks.

Some of the Indians of this region, earlier in the century, used   12
to sleep naked in hammocks. The nights are cold. Gordon Mac-
Creach, an American explorer in these Amazon tributaries, reported
that he was startled to hear the Indians get up at three in the
morning. He was even more startled, night after night, to hear them
walk down to the river slowly, half asleep, and bathe in the water.
Only later did he learn what they were doing: they were getting
warm. The cold woke them; they warmed their skins in the river,
which was always ninety degrees; then they returned to their hammocks and slept through the rest of the night.

The riverbanks are low, and from the river you see an unbroken   13
wall of dark forest in every direction, from the Andes to the Atlantic.
You get a taste for looking at trees: trees hung with the swinging
nests of yellow troupials, trees from which ant nests the size of grain
sacks hang like black goiters, trees from which seven-colored tana-
gers flutter, coral trees, teak, balsa and breadfruit, enormous emer-
gent silk-cotton trees, and the pale-barked *samona* palms.

When you are inside the jungle, away from the river, the trees   14
vault out of sight. It is hard to remember to look up the long trunks
and see the fans, strips, fronds, and sprays of glossy leaves. Inside
the jungle you are more likely to notice the snarl of climbers and
creepers round the trees' boles, the flowering bromeliads and epi-
phytes in every bough's crook, and the fantastic silk-cotton tree trunks
thirty or forty feet across, trunks buttressed in flanges of wood whose
curves can make three high walls of a room—a shady, loamy-aired
room where you would gladly live, or die. Butterflies, iridescent

blue, striped, or clear-winged, thread the jungle paths at eye level. And at your feet is a swath of ants bearing triangular bits of green leaf. The ants with their leaves look like a wide fleet of sailing dinghies—but they don't quit. In either direction they wobble over the jungle floor as far as the eye can see. I followed them off the path as far as I dared, and never saw an end to ants or to those luffing chips of green they bore.

Unseen in the jungle, but present, are tapirs, jaguars, many species of snake and lizard, ocelots, armadillos, marmosets, howler monkeys, toucans and macaws and a hundred other birds, deer, bats, peccaries, capybaras, agoutis, and sloths. Also present in this jungle, but variously distant, are Texaco derricks and pipelines, and some of the wildest Indians in the world, blowgun-using Indians, who killed missionaries in 1956 and ate them.

Long lakes shine in the jungle. We traveled one of these in dugout canoes, canoes with two inches of freeboard, canoes paddled with machete-hewn oars chopped from buttresses of silk-cotton trees, or poled in the shallows with peeled cane or bamboo. Our part-Indian guide had cleared the path to the lake the day before; when we walked the path we saw where he had impaled the lopped head of a boa, open-mouthed, on a pointed stick by the canoes, for decoration.

The lake was wonderful. Herons, egrets, and ibises plodded the sawgrass shores, kingfishers and cuckoos clattered from sunlight to shade, great turkeylike birds fussed in dead branches, and hawks lolled overhead. There was all the time in the world. A turtle slid into the water. The boy in the bow of my canoe slapped stones at birds with a simple sling, a rubber thong and leather pad. He aimed brilliantly at moving targets, always, and always missed; the birds were out of range. He stuffed his sling back in his shirt. I looked around.

The lake and river waters are as opaque as rain-forest leaves; they are veils, blinds, painted screens. You see things only by their effects. I saw the shoreline water roil and the sawgrass heave above a thrashing *paichi,* an enormous black fish of these waters; one had been caught the previous week weighing 430 pounds. Piranha fish live in the lakes, and electric eels. I dangled my fingers in the water, figuring it would be worth it.

We would eat chicken that night in the village, and rice, yucca, onions, beets, and heaps of fruit. The sun would ring down, pulling darkness after it like a curtain. Twilight is short, and the unseen birds of twilight wistful, uncanny, catching the heart. The two nuns in their dazzling white habits—the beautiful-boned young nun and the warm-faced old—would glide to the open cane-and-thatch schoolroom in darkness, and start the children singing. The children would sing in piping Spanish, highpitched and pure; they would sing "Nearer My God to Thee" in Quechua, very fast. (To reciprocate, we sang for them "Old MacDonald Had a Farm"; I thought they might recognize the animal sounds. Of course they thought we were out of our minds.) As the children became excited by their own singing, they left their log benches and swarmed around the nuns, hopping, smiling at us, everyone smiling, the nuns' faces bursting in their cowls, and the clear-voiced children still singing, and the palm-leafed roofing stirred.

The Napo River: it is not out of the way. It is *in* the way, catching 20
sunlight the way a cup catches poured water; it is a bowl of sweet air, a basin of greenness, and of grace, and, it would seem, of peace.

❧ RICHARD RODRIGUEZ

Richard Rodriguez was born in San Francisco in 1944 to Mexican-American parents. Although he did not learn to speak English until he attended grammar school, Rodriguez eventually received a Ph.D. in English literature from the University of California at Berkeley, having also attended Stanford University, Columbia University, and the Warburg Institute in London. Rodriguez now works as a writer and lecturer. His articles have appeared in *Saturday Review, College English, Change,* the *American Scholar,* and *Harper's.* His prize-winning memoir, *Hunger of Memory* (1982), records the many conflicts in language and culture he experienced growing up in an immigrant family in America. "Does America Still Exist?" was written for *Harper's* as part of a group of articles commissioned by the magazine in response to the question, "Does America still exist?" In the essay, Rodriguez defines and explores America in terms of its diversity as well as its special identity. The structure and style of his writing reflect the diversity of his subject.

Does America Still Exist?

For the children of immigrant parents the knowledge comes easier. America exists everywhere in the city—on billboards, frankly in the smell of French fries and popcorn. It exists in the pace: traffic lights, the assertions of neon, the mysterious bong-bong-bong through the atriums of department stores. America exists as the voice of the crowd, a menacing sound—the high nasal accent of American English. 1

When I was a boy in Sacramento (California, the fifties), people would ask me, "Where you from?" I was born in this country, but I knew the question meant to decipher my darkness, my looks. 2

My mother once instructed me to say, "I am an American of Mexican descent." By the time I was nine or ten, I wanted to say, but dared not reply, "I am an American." 3

Immigrants come to America and, against hostility or mere loneliness, they recreate a homeland in the parlor, tacking up postcards or calendars of some impossible blue—lake or sea or sky. Children of immigrant parents are supposed to perch on a hyphen between two countries. Relatives assume the achievement as much 4

as anyone. Relatives are, in any case, surprised when the child begins
losing old ways. One day at the family picnic the boy wanders away
from their spiced food and faceless stories to watch other boys play
baseball in the distance.

There is sorrow in the American memory, guilty sorrow for   5
having left something behind—Portugal, China, Norway. The American story is the story of immigrant children and of their children—
children no longer able to speak to grandparents. The memory of
exile becomes inarticulate as it passes from generation to generation,
along with wedding rings and pocket watches—like some mute stone
in a wad of old lace. Europe. Asia. Eden.

But, it needs to be said, if this is a country where one stops   6
being Vietnamese or Italian, this is a country where one begins to
be an American. America exists as a culture and a grin, a faith and
a shrug. It is clasped in a handshake, called by a first name.

As much as the country is joined in a common culture, however,   7
Americans are reluctant to celebrate the process of assimilation. We
pledge allegiance to diversity. America was born Protestant and bred
Puritan, and the notion of community we share is derived from a
seventeenth-century faith. Presidents and the pages of ninth-grade
civics readers yet proclaim the orthodoxy: We are gathered together—but as individuals, with separate pasts, distinct destinies.
Our society is as paradoxical as a Puritan congregation: We stand
together, alone.

Americans have traditionally defined themselves by what they   8
refused to include. As often, however, Americans have struggled,
turned in good conscience at last to assert the great Protestant virtue
of tolerance. Despite outbreaks of nativist frenzy, America has remained an immigrant country, open and true to itself.

Against pious emblems of rural America—soda fountain, Elks   9
hall, Protestant church, and now shopping mall—stands the cold-
hearted city, crowded with races and ambitions, curious laughter,
much that is odd. Nevertheless, it is the city that has most truly
represented America. In the city, however, the millions of singular
lives have had no richer notion of wholeness to describe them than
the idea of pluralism.

"Where you from?" the American asks the immigrant. "Mexico,"   10
the boy learns to say.

Mexico, the country of my blood ancestors, offers formal contrast   11
to the American achievement. If the United States was formed by

Protestant individualism, Mexico was shaped by a medieval Catholic dream of one world. The Spanish journeyed to Mexico to plunder, and they may have gone, in God's name, with an arrogance peculiar to those who intend to convert. But through the conversion, the Indian converted the Spaniard. A new race was born, the *mestizo*, wedding European to Indian. José Vasconcelos, the Mexican philosopher, has celebrated this New World creation, proclaiming it the "cosmic race."

Centuries later, in a San Francisco restaurant, a Mexican-American lawyer of my acquaintance says, in English, over *salade niçoise*, that he does not intend to assimilate into gringo society. His claim is echoed by a chorus of others (Italian-Americans, Greeks, Asians) in this era of ethnic pride. The melting pot has been retired, clanking, into the museum of quaint disgrace, alongside Aunt Jemima and the Katzenjammer Kids. But resistance to assimilation is characteristically American. It only makes clear how inevitable the process of assimilation actually is. 12

For generations, this has been the pattern. Immigrant parents have sent their children to school (simply, they thought) to acquire the "skills" to survive in the city. The child returned home with a voice his parents barely recognized or understood, couldn't trust, and didn't like. 13

In Eastern cities—Philadelphia, New York, Boston, Baltimore—class after class gathered immigrant children to women (usually women) who stood in front of rooms full of children, changing children. So also for me in the 1950s. Irish-Catholic nuns. California. The old story. The hyphen tipped to the right, away from Mexico and toward a confusing but true American identity. 14

I speak now in the chromium American accent of my grammar school classmates—Billy Reckers, Mike Bradley, Carol Schmidt, Kathy O'Grady. . . . I believe I became like my classmates, became German, Polish, and (like my teachers) Irish. And because assimilation is always reciprocal, my classmates got something of me. (I mean sad eyes; belief in the Indian Virgin; a taste for sugar skulls on the Feast of the Dead.) In the blending, we became what our parents could never have been, and we carried America one revolution further. 15

"Does America still exist?" Americans have been asking the question for so long that to ask it again only proves our continuous link. But perhaps the question deserves to be asked with urgency 16 now. Since the black civil rights movement of the 1960s, our tenuous notion of a shared public life has deteriorated notably.

The struggle of black men and women did not eradicate racism, 17 but it became the great moment in the life of America's conscience. Water hoses, bulldogs, blood—the images, rendered black, white, rectangular, passed into living rooms.

It is hard to look at a photograph of a crowd taken, say, in 1890 18 or in 1930 and not notice the absence of blacks. (It becomes an impertinence to wonder if America *still* exists.)

In the sixties, other groups of Americans learned to champion 19 their rights by analogy to the black civil rights movement. But the heroic vision faded. Dr. Martin Luther King Jr. had spoken with Pauline eloquence of a nation that would unite Christian and Jew, old and young, rich and poor. Within a decade, the struggles of the 1960s were reduced to a bureaucratic competition for little more than pieces of a representational pie. The quest for a portion of power became an end in itself. The metaphor for the American city of the 1970s was a committee: one black, one woman, one person under thirty . .

If the small town had sinned against America by too neatly 20 defining who could be an American, the city's sin was a romantic secession. One noticed the romanticism in the antiwar movement— certain demonstrators who demonstrated a lack of tact or desire to persuade and seemed content to play secular protestants. One noticed the romanticism in the competition among members of "minority groups" to claim the status of Primary Victim. To Americans unconfident of their common identity, minority standing became a way of asserting individuality. Middle-class Americans—men and women clearly not the primary victims of social oppression—brandished their suffering with exuberance.

The dream of a single society probably died with *The Ed Sullivan* 21 *Show*. The reality of America persists. Teenagers pass through bigcity high schools banded in racial groups, their collars turned up to a uniform shrug. But then they graduate to jobs at the phone company or in banks, where they end up working alongside people unlike themselves. Typists and tellers walk out together at lunchtime.

It is easier for us as Americans to believe the obvious fact of our 22 separateness—easier to imagine the black and white Americas prophesied by the Kerner report (broken glass, street fires)—than to recognize the reality of a city street at lunchtime. Americans are wedded by proximity to a common culture. The panhandler at one corner is related to the pamphleteer at the next who is related to the banker who is kin to the Chinese old man wearing an MIT sweat-shirt. In any true national history, Thomas Jefferson begets Martin Luther King Jr. who begets the Gray Panthers. It is because we lack a vision of ourselves entire—the city street is crowded and we are each preoccupied with finding our own way home—that we lack an appropriate hymn.

Under my window now passes a little white girl softly rehearsing 23 to herself a Motown obbligato.

GLOSSARY

Useful Terms and Concepts

Abstract and *Concrete*   *Abstract* words point to ideas, attributes, states of mind, or conditions we cannot perceive through the senses: freedom, honor, capitalism, frustration, hatred, charity. *Concrete* words point to things we can perceive with our senses: pine tree, gravel, moth, brick wall, lilac scent, crackling, hot, slimy. Concrete examples enliven readers' perception of a subject and help writers convey abstract concepts in a specific way. Good writing usually mingles abstract and concrete language in order to convey general ideas and illustrate them in a vivid and precise manner. (See *General* and *Specific.*)

Allusion   A brief reference to a person, event, place, saying, movie, song, or literary work is an allusion. Allusions allow the writer to compress much meaning into a few words: "This candidate could be another John F. Kennedy [or Harry Truman]"; "Their relationship was like a story line out of 'General Hospital' or 'All My Children'"; "Neil Simon is not a Shakespeare, but his work is entertaining." An allusion calls up in readers' minds the events, ideas, and emotions associated with the original subject and uses them to enrich the piece of writing containing the allusion. Thus when the popular song says two lovers are "just like Romeo and Juliet," the songwriter wants the audience to see in the characters he has created the same overwhelming passion that drove Shakespeare's young lovers.

    An allusion works only when readers can recognize it. To use allusions effectively, therefore, writers need to be aware of how much their readers are likely to know. Most readers, for example, will understand an allusion to *Star Wars* or to famous generals like Caesar, Napoleon, Grant, and MacArthur; few will recognize a play like *The Country Wife,* a novel like *The Way We Live Now,* or a historical event like the siege of La Rochelle.

Analogy   An analogy is a comparison of two generally unlike things, for example, a government or society and a family. It may be used to illustrate and explain, to explore new ideas, or to suggest a fresh perspective on events and issues. (See Chapter 5, Comparison.)

Anecdote   A brief narrative of a single incident, often drawn from personal experience and used to illustrate or support a point, is called an anecdote.

Argument   To argue or persuade is one of the primary aims of writing. Others are to amuse, to inform, to explain, to explore, or to create an imaginative (literary) experience. As a form of writing, argument consists of an assertion (proposition) combined with a variety of supporting evidence; the assertion may set forth a value judgment, propose an action, or state a conclusion likely to arouse considerable opposition. (See Chapter 10, Argument and Persuasion.)

Arrangement   The order in which an essay presents details, statements, and ideas is frequently referred to as its arrangement or structure. An essay may be arranged or structured according to one of the basic *patterns of development* covered in this text (narration, description, example, comparison, process, cause and effect, definition, division, classification, or argument). It may be arranged according to a logical pattern like *induction* or *deduction* (see Chapter 10, Argument and Persuasion) or according to a pattern of emphasis, moving, for example, from the least important ideas to the most important or vice versa. Or an essay may be arranged in response to the demands of a specific subject, purpose, or audience.

Audience   A writer's audience consists of all the intended or probable readers of an essay. Audiences may be *general,* consisting of people whose tastes, attitudes, and abilities the writer can know only in a broad sense (all educated readers, the average American), or they may be *limited,* consisting of people whose characteristics the writer may know in more detail (students at a particular college, residents of a city or state, football players, liberals). The decisions a writer makes about content and strategy should take into account the attitudes, level of knowledge, and reading skill of the probable audience. Responding to the needs and outlook of a general audience can be difficult for many student writers; examining the estimates of this audience revealed through the writing decisions of professional authors can provide some guidance, however.

Brainstorming and *Clustering*   Brainstorming and clustering are techniques for discovering and arranging possible subjects and materials for a piece of writing. In *brainstorming* writers let their minds play freely over a broad subject area and write down topics, ideas, and details in brief form in whatever order they come to mind. Brainstorming may be done by individual writers or by groups of people such as a committee or the students in a composition course. In *clustering* the writer identifies groups of ideas or details in a list generated through brainstorming and uses these to suggest ways of developing and arranging an essay. (See also *Freewriting.*)

Cause and Effect   Cause and effect is a pattern of thinking and writing that concentrates on identifying and exploring the sources of an event, idea, or decision and on speculating about its possible and probable consequences. (See Chapter 7, Cause and Effect.)

Classification   The act of grouping things according to shared characteristics is classification; it is also a pattern of development in writing that emphasizes the sorting of a subject into categories and subcategories. (See Chapter 9, Division and Classification.)

Cliché   Any expression that has become so worn through excessive use that it no longer conveys a fresh perception or adds liveliness to writing is a cliché. *As dead as a doornail, read him like a book, blind as a bat, fits like a glove, made to measure, run out of steam, in a family way,* and *through hell and high water* are all clichés.

Closings   The closing of an essay should bring what the writer has to say to a logical end, giving the readers a sense of the essay's completeness and purpose. If readers carry away with them a feeling that what the writer wanted to say is somehow unfinished, or if the ending leaves open some questions about the essay's purpose and thesis, then all the work the writer has done elsewhere in the essay may be undermined. Closing strategies that seriously weaken an essay include (1) stopping abruptly without any attempt to tie together the various elements of the essay, (2) ending on a minor point or an extra thought that seems left over from the body of the essay, (3) apologizing for the content or style of an essay (a strategy that destroys any authority the author gained through effective writing in the rest of the essay), and (4) bringing up an entirely new idea in the closing, or introducing a qualification that contradicts much of what was said earlier. Effective conclusions often make use of one or more of the following strategies, depending on the subject, the author's purpose, and the nature of the audience:

1. A restatement of the main point of the essay, one that incorporates any significant points made in the course of the essay; a statement of the essay's main point, if for some reason the writer has waited until the conclusion to announce it directly.
2. A summary of the most important ideas and information presented in the essay, generally given in brief enough form so that readers will be able to remember it easily (often combined with another closing strategy to avoid overly obvious repetition of points that have already been made clearly and effectively).
3. An indication of the topic's significance, its broad applications to readers' lives, or its implications.
4. A prediction based on the information or ideas presented in the selection.
5. A proposal that readers take or support a specific action or policy, usually one that has been discussed thoroughly in the selection or that grows logically out of the discussion.
6. An echo of the introduction, either in word choice, phrasing, content, or ideas.
7. A presentation of the essay's most important point or example, if it is clearly the climax of the essay, if in effect it sums up what has been said before, and if adding anything after it might weaken its effectiveness and that of the entire essay.
8. A quotation, an anecdote, an example, a witty or memorable remark—in short, any special device that drives home the point of the essay.
9. Word signals like *finally, in conclusion,* and *thus,* combined with one of the other strategies mentioned here.

Clustering   See *Brainstorming* and *Clustering.*

Coherence   When a reader can follow the development of a thought or a subject in a clear and orderly way from sentence to sentence, from paragraph to paragraph, and from the beginning of an essay to the end, the writing is said to have coherence. Coherent writing comes from the logical arrangement and development of ideas and segments of a topic, from transitions that guide readers from one section of an essay to the next, from repetition of key ideas, and from direct statements, including summaries and thesis statements that alert readers to the arrangement of a selection. (See also *Transitions*, *Thesis*.)

Colloquial Language   Colloquial language consists of words and phrases characteristic of informal conversation. Contractions (*I've*, *they're*), shortened words (*TV*, *psych*, *bio*, *ad*, *auto*), and informal expressions ("go broke," "That car's a lemon") are typical of colloquial language. Although such words and phrases are appropriate for conversation and for those places in a formal essay where the writer needs to add a touch of informality, they are inappropriate in most formal writing like research reports, term papers, and opinions about a serious controversy. (See also *Diction*.)

Comparison and *Contrast*   Comparison and contrast are patterns of thought and expression that explore the similarities and differences between two or more subjects. The term *comparison* is often used to refer to both patterns. (See Chapter 5, Comparison.)

Conclusions   See *Closings*.

Concrete   See *Abstract* and *Concrete*.

Connotation and *Denotation*   The *denotation* of a word is its literal dictionary definition. The *connotation* of a word consists of the various associations it arouses in a reader's mind, or the suggestions it conveys as a result of the way it is commonly used in a culture. Connotations may be the result of personal experience. Hong Kong, for example, is (literally) a city (and a territory) on the coast of China; for people familiar with banking and finance, however, it may connote a certain free-wheeling type of capitalism. For many of us, it will bring to mind either cheaply produced electronics products and toys (because of our experience as consumers) or a sense of exotic adventure (because of the television shows and movies we have seen that were set in Hong Kong). Often clusters of words with similar denotations have different connotations: *love*—suggests an intense feeling not easily controlled; *affection* suggests a feeling of warm regard, milder and more controlled than *love*; *devotion* suggests dedication, attachment, and stability, with less variability than *love* and more strength than *affection*; *fondness* suggests a strong but not necessarily stable attraction to a person or thing; *infatuation* suggests an intense and generally brief attachment to a person or thing, and is usually taken to be a sign that good judgment has been abandoned.

Credibility   *Credibility* is a term referring to the extent to which readers consider an author believable or reliable; that is, an honest, authoritative, and accurate source of information or a trustworthy, fair, and competent source of opinions and arguments. A writer builds credibility by mastery of detail, by effective presentation of ideas and evidence, by recognition of the audience's needs and assumptions, and by projection of character through tone and language.

Cue Words   See *Transitions.*

Deduction   Deductive reasoning moves from general instances to a specific conclusion. (See Chapter 10, Argument and Persuasion, for a detailed discussion.)

Definition   A definition explains the meaning of a word or concept. An extended definition may be the pattern of development for an entire essay. (See Chapter 8, Definition.)

Denotation   See *Connotation* and *Denotation.*

Description   This is a pattern of thought and expression that uses detail from the senses to present the features of scene, person, or feeling. (See Chapter 3, Description.)

Diction   The words that a writer chooses to make meaning clear and to give emphasis are generally referred to as *diction.* Diction can be concrete or abstract, clichéd or fresh, and formal or informal. It can depend on choice of words for their connotation or denotation and on figures of speech. (See *Connotation* and *Denotation, Figures of Speech.*) *Formal diction* uses words and grammatical constructions typical of formal speeches, business and technical reports, most non-fiction books, and many newspapers and magazines. Most of the essays in this text make consistent use of formal diction. *Colloquial diction,* in contrast, makes use of contractions and informal expressions. It is used widely in conversation and sometimes in less serious books, magazines, and newspapers. (See *Colloquial Language.*) *Slang* consists of short-lived words and expressions used by a relatively small group and probably not understood by readers in general.

Division Division, also known as *analysis,* is a method of thought and expression that calls for dividing a subject into its parts or components. (See Chapter 9, Division and Classification.)

Effect See *Cause and Effect.*

Emphasis Writers can use a number of devices to stress the importance of details, ideas, and other elements of an essay. Most devices of emphasis are actually ways of attracting and holding the reader's attention. Commonly used devices include:

> *Proportion*—giving more space to major points than to minor ones.
>
> *Position*—locating the most important ideas and information in the most emphatic positions, usually at the end of an essay, paragraph, or sentence, or at the beginning.
>
> *Repetition*—repeating key words or phrases at important points to provide emphasis, as in a sentence that comes at the beginning of a paragraph and echos a thesis statement. To avoid turning emphasis into boring repetition, writers often repeat ideas by using synonyms: dangerous effects, serious consequences, threatening implications.
>
> *Direct Statement*—commenting openly on the significance: "The most important argument in favor of increased government control is. . . ." This strategy is often effective, but if it is overused, readers will begin to ignore the signals.
>
> *Mechanical devices*—italics (indicated with underlining), capital letters, lists, diagrams, and exclamation points. These can add emphasis, but they work best when combined with one of the other devices of emphasis, and they can easily be overused.

Essay An essay is a short, nonfiction prose composition written to communicate a central theme, assertion, or point of view on a subject. Essays often draw on the writer's personal experience and convey personal response and insight, but they may be objective in content and approach as well.

Evaluation Evaluation of a whole essay or some part means judging its success in carrying out the author's purpose and in serving the needs of readers. An explanation or evidence that supports the writer's thesis but is so complex that only a few readers can understand it must thus be considered only partially successful. In evaluating an essay, try to base your judgment on the response most readers are likely to have; even if you find a topic personally uninteresting, you may judge the essay successful if most readers are likely to find it very interesting.

Evidence   Evidence consists of the facts, statistics, examples, arguments (chains of reasoning), and testimony that support an assertion or a thesis. (See also *Support.*)

Example   An example is a specific instance of a general principle. As a pattern of thought and expression (also called *exemplification*) it links specific instances to general statements (generalizations). (See Chapter 4, Example; see also *Generalization.*)

Exposition   Exposition is one of the primary aims of writing. It means both to inform and to explain. Most of the essays in this book are expository in aim.

Fallacies   See *Logical Fallacies.*

Figures of Speech   Figures of speech are extensions of language beyond its literal meanings to achieve special emphasis or insight. They include the following:

> *Simile*—a comparison of two unlike things, using *like* or *as*: "He's as attentive to her as a cat chasing a mouse or a tiger stalking a gazelle." "She looks like someone who just spilled wine on the hostess at a formal party."
>
> *Metaphor*—a comparison that equates two things: "The moon's a balloon"; "My desk is a pigsty."
>
> *Personification*—the attribution of human qualities to inanimate objects, animals, or abstractions: "The stones of the altar speak of the human blood that was shed in this place"; "The trees shivered and sighed as the storm came closer"; "The mud grabbed at our legs as we began walking across the bog."
>
> *Hyperbole*—obvious exaggeration: "The roaches covered every square inch of the apartment."
>
> *Understatement*—obvious downplaying: "As the stove caught on fire, she said to her husband, 'I think we've got a small problem here.'"

> *Rhetorical Question*—a question that requires no answer; used to begin a discussion, to call attention to the writer's point of view, or to add emphasis, for example, "Are we to believe such preposterous claims?"
>
> *Paradox*—an apparently contradictory statement that is actually true: "The more you earn, the less you have."

Focus   Writers limit the subject matter of an essay so that it can be covered in depth, or restrict conclusions to one aspect of a subject in order to be able to provide adequate support for those interpretations in the space available. The focus a writer chooses depends on the subject, the purpose, and the needs and attitudes of the audience.

Focus Statement   During the composing or revising of an essay, writers often prepare a brief statement of their purpose, point of view, primary emphasis, thesis, or specific topic in order to clarify their intentions and guide the writing or revising process. Such focus statements are an aid to composing and appear in a finished essay only if they can help guide the reader's attention to the most important features of the essay.

Freewriting   Freewriting is a technique for discovering possible subjects for writing or for starting to write on a particular topic. Freewriting calls for nonstop writing for a period of time (ten or fifteen minutes, for example) and the recording of whatever thoughts enter the writer's mind, whether directly related to the topic or not. The ideas and details that emerge through freewriting often provide a fresh perspective on a subject or suggest original material the writer can develop in an essay.

General and *Specific*   General words identify a broad class or category: cars, cats, sociological theories, shoes. Specific words refer to members of the category or class: a Pontiac, Mike the tomcat, symbolic interactionism, Saucony running shoes. *General* and *specific* are relative terms often viewed as part of a ladder of abstraction running from the most general to the least: ground vehicles, cars, Pontiacs, a 1985 Pontiac, a 1985 Pontiac 6000ES, *my* 1985 Pontiac 6000ES. Specific words are generally more vivid and interesting than general words. (See *Abstract* and *Concrete*.)

Generalization   A broad statement covering all the members of a class but based on knowledge of only a few (a representative sample). A generalization is the product of induction (see Chapter 10, Argument and Persuasion). Generalizations (general statements) are often linked to examples or illustrations (see Chapter 4, Example; see also *Example.*)

Hyperbole   See *Figures of Speech.*

Illustration   Illustration is the technique of providing an example to support or explain a general statement or an idea. (See *Example*; see also Chapter 4, Example.)

Induction   Inductive reasoning moves from particulars to a general conclusion. (See Chapter 10, Argument and Persuasion for a detailed discussion.)

Introductions   An introduction to an essay may range in length from a sentence or two to several paragraphs. Its task is to announce the subject and the essay's focus, to tell why readers ought to be interested in the topic, to indicate the pattern the essay will follow, to make clear the essay's purpose and the writer's point of view (or thesis), and to set the tone (see *Tone*) for the essay. While a writer may choose to move one of these functions to some other part of the essay, or to omit one entirely for special effect, an essay that predicts at least the main outlines of an essay's pattern and purpose is essential for effective, critical reading (see Chapter 1, Reading and Writing). The following are some effective strategies for introductions:

1. Explain the significance of the subject, showing why it is worth knowing about, or explore the sources and importance of any controversy surrounding it.
2. Give background information to bring the reader up to date and provide a context for the discussion in the essay.
3. State the central theme (thesis) of the essay, letting readers know why it is important to them.
4. Outline the issue or problem the essay will address, stressing its importance to individual readers and the society at large.
5. Make an unusual or intriguing statement, or present some startling statistics or facts to get the audience's attention and direct it to the significant aspects of the subject you plan to discuss.
6. Begin with an example or anecdote that introduces an issue the essay will address or that suggests its main theme (thesis).
7. Open with a quotation or a question that reveals the main concern of the essay.

8. Begin with a broad survey of the subject and then focus on the topic that will be covered in the essay.

9. Present a quotation or a summary of some point of view the essay will argue against, or open with a vivid comparison or contrast that points to the central theme (thesis) of the essay.

Irony   *Verbal irony* involves a discrepancy between what is said and what is meant ("Another test—how wonderful!"). It can range from mild *understatement* ("98 degrees and 96 percent humidity is a bit uncomfortable") to cutting *sarcasm* ("Thanks for not telling me about the test so I wouldn't worry about it"). *Irony of situation* is the term used for a contrast between what is expected to happen and what actually happens: A man puts out what he thinks is poison for raccoons, only to discover that they thrive on it.

Logical Fallacies   See Chapter 10, Argument and Persuasion, pp. 431–432.

Metaphor   See *Figures of Speech.*

Narrative   A pattern of thought and expression that focuses on what happened. (See Chapter 2, Narrative.)

Objective and *Subjective*   *Objective* writing presents ideas and information in an unemotional manner. *Subjective* writing reports the author's feelings and attitudes along with ideas and information. Most good writing mixes both approaches.

Outline   An outline may be the plan a writer develops in order to guide composition of the first draft of an essay or the overview of a completed draft the writer uses to review its structure and coverage of the topic. An *informal outline* may consist merely of jotted notes or may be an organized list of the major points and supporting evidence to be covered in an essay. A *formal outline* uses a system of numbers and letters to present in the order they will be covered (or are covered in a completed draft) all the divisions and subdivisions of the topic along with the generalizations and details that convey the author's point of view. A *topic outline* uses single words or brief phrases for each entry; a *sentence outline* uses complete sentences.

Paradox   See *Figures of Speech.*

Paragraph   A paragraph is a cluster of sentences set off by an indentation. Paragraphs can be used to break up long stretches of prose and make reading easier. They can be used to highlight ideas and information. And they can be used to indicate stages in the development of an essay and logical relationships among ideas. The last function is by far the most important. Most paragraphs in essays, like the ones in this book, consist of sentences designed to illustrate or support a single point—which in turn supports, develops, or illustrates the main theme (thesis) or themes of the essay. The point of a paragraph is often announced explicitly in a *topic sentence*; it may, however, be implied.

Brief paragraphs are sometimes used in essays as transitions from one part of a discussion to another. (See also *Topic Sentence.*)

Parallelism   The use of similar grammatical forms to emphasize similarities or contrasts between ideas is parallelism. Parts of sentences can be parallel: "Stone walls do not a prison make, nor iron bars a cage." Sentence pairs may contain parallel elements: "Odysseus is true to the values of his society and submits to the fate laid out for him. Huck Finn rejects the values of his society and rebels against the plans society has made for him." Entire paragraphs may have parallel elements as well. Parallel elements make sentences presenting complicated information easier to read and understand, and they help a writer emphasize relationships among ideas. Parallelism can also add greatly to the rhythm and sound and therefore the pleasure of prose.

Pattern of Development   See *Arrangement.*

Personification   See *Figures of Speech.*

Persuasion   See *Argument*; see also Chapter 10, Argument and Persuasion.

Point of View   In argumentative and explanatory writing, *point of view* refers to the author's opinion on an issue, interpretation of a subject, or thesis. In other kinds of writing, however, *point of view* can refer to a physical or mental perspective the author takes on a subject. It can also refer to the pronoun used to identify that perspective: *I* or *we* (first-person point of view), *you* (second-person), or *he, she, it,* or *they* (third-person).

Process   Process, also known as *process analysis,* is a pattern of thought and expression by which one examines the steps or stages that bring about a specific result. (See Chapter 6, Process.)

Purpose Purpose is the writer's reason for writing and the goal the essay is designed to achieve. All essays have one or more *general* purposes: to explain, to amuse, to explore, to argue or persuade, to create an imaginative (literary) experience. They also have *specific* purposes: to help readers cook steak without destroying the flavor, to convince readers to buy personal computers, to help readers evaluate the differences between three inexpensive subcompact cars. Purpose and thesis (main idea, theme) often overlap. The thesis is the particular opinion or interpretation the author sets forward in the essay; the purpose is to get readers to agree with the thesis or act on it. When purpose and thesis act together to determine the choices a writer makes and shape an essay, it is said to be *unified*. (See *Thesis, Unity.*)

Qualification Qualification is the use of phrases like *usually, generally, in many cases,* or *seldom* to limit or modify broad statements so that they more accurately represent or interpret facts and evidence or so that they make an author's interpretations more precise.

Refutation In argumentative writing the refutation of opposing arguments provides support for an assertion by showing that the writer's position is superior to that advanced by the opposition. A refutation provides a brief summary of the opposing point of view along with a discussion of its inadequacies. There are three commonly used strategies for refutation: (1) pointing out weaknesses in the evidence on which the opposing arguments are based, (2) pointing out errors in logic in the opposing arguments, and (3) questioning the relevance of opposing arguments to the specific issue being discussed. Refutations need to be moderate in tone and accurate in their representation of the opposition; otherwise, readers may feel that the writer has been unfair, and they may judge his or her arguments more harshly.

Rhetorical Question See *Figures of Speech.*

Sentence Structure See *Syntax.*

Setting The place, time, and circumstances in which the actions or events being recounted take place. Setting is important not only in narrative and descriptive essays, but in any form of writing in which events play an important role, including patterns such as process, cause and effect, and argument.

Simile   See *Figures of Speech.*

Slang   See *Diction.*

Specific and *General*   See *General* and *Specific.*

Structure   See *Arrangement.*

Style   Style is the manner in which things are expressed in contrast to what is expressed. A writer's style or the style of an essay is made up of word choice (*diction*), *syntax* (sentence structure), *emphasis,* and arrangement of ideas and information.

Support   Support, or supporting evidence, consists of the details and statements an author uses either to convince readers to accept the truth of an argumentative or interpretive assertion or to explain the implications of an informative generalization. Support can take a variety of forms, including (1) facts and figures such as statistical or numerical data, (2) anecdotes or extended narrative examples (see *Anecdote*), (3) quotations from participants in an event or from authorities on a subject, (4) explanations following any of a number of patterns (for example, detailed accounts of a process or cause-effect relationship; comparisons to similar situations or ideas).

Syllogism   This refers to the formal pattern that underlies deductive reasoning. (See Chapter 10, Argument and Persuasion, pp. 424–425, for a detailed explanation and examples.)

Symbol   A symbol is a person, object, or place that represents something other than itself: Clasped hands symbolize friendship or marriage; a cross symbolizes Christianity; the Gateway Arch symbolizes St. Louis and the beginning of the pioneers' journey to the West; chevrons symbolize rank in the armed forces.

Syntax   Syntax means the arrangement of words and phrases within a sentence. *Sentence structure* is another name for syntax. Of most interest to readers of essays and writers are the *sentence types* or *syntactic patterns.* A basic sentence consists of a subject, verb, and complements (direct and indirect objects, subject complement, prepositional phrases). In a *periodic sentence,* phrases and clauses are added to the beginning of a basic sentence. In a *cumulative sentence,* phrases and clauses are added to the end. Effective writing uses a variety of sentence types and structures to provide interest and to give appropriate emphasis to ideas and information. (See also *Parallelism.*)

Thesis The thesis is the central idea of an essay, the assertion, interpretation, idea, or theme it is designed to convey. All the elements in an essay should work effectively and clearly towards conveying the thesis. In an explanatory or argumentative essay, the parts of the essay should support the thesis so that readers will come to acknowledge its accuracy or truth. Often the thesis is made explicit in a single sentence known as a *thesis statement.* A thesis statement serves as a guide to readers, and if it comes at the beginning of an essay, as is often the case, it announces the goal of the essay and provides readers with a standard against which to measure the author's success in supporting and developing the central idea. The terms *main theme, central theme, point of view,* and *main idea* are often used interchangeably with *thesis.* In argument, *thesis, assertion,* and *proposition* are terms with similar meanings.

Thesis Statement See *Thesis.*

Tone Tone is the writer's attitude towards the subject and towards the audience, made plain through choice of words, sentence structure, selection and arrangement of detail, and direct statement. Tone in writing is similar to tone in speaking, and may range from sympathetic, kind, and mild through amused, irritated, and agitated to angry, disgusted, and ecstatic.

Topic Sentence A topic sentence is a statement of the main point or purpose of a paragraph. Topic sentences often appear near the beginning of a paragraph either as generalizations that the rest of the paragraph will support or as indications of the pattern of development the paragraph will follow (comparison, for instance, or classification). Topic sentences may also appear elsewhere in a paragraph—at the end, for instance, as the point towards which the entire paragraph builds. The main point of a paragraph may also be implicit rather than directly stated in a topic sentence.

Transitions Transitions are the devices that link ideas, sentences, and paragraphs in an essay, enabling readers to move smoothly from one to the next and to understand their various relationships. One useful way to view transitions is as cuing devices (*cue words* or *phrases*) alerting readers to an essay's arrangement, to the relationships among its parts, or to a point the author wishes to emphasize. Most transitions fall into these categories:

1. Repetition of a key phrase or word, repetition of synonymous terms, or use of a string of pronouns referring to an important subject or idea.
2. Sentences or paragraphs that act as bridges, referring to what goes before and what follows and indicating their relationship.
3. Parallel elements that stress similarities or contrasts among ideas.
4. Standard transitional expressions, including these:
   Time—*next, then, soon, after, meanwhile, along with*
   Place—*beyond, next to, across from, near*
   Result—*consequently, therefore, thus, hence, as a result*
   Comparison—*likewise, similarly, also, in the same way*
   Contrast—*nonetheless, however, still, yet, but, on the other hand, in contrast*
   Addition—*first, second, third, also, then, furthermore, moreover, finally*
   Miscellaneous—*for instance, for example, indeed*
5. Transitional expressions appropriate for a specific pattern of development (see pp. 176, 218, 272, 372).

Understatement   See *Figures of Speech.*

Unity   A unified essay is one in which all elements—sentences, words, paragraphs, ideas, information—work together to accomplish the purpose and develop the thesis. In a unified essay, purpose and thesis are closely related, and they serve as organizing points for the entire work. (See *Thesis, Purpose.*)

Acknowledgments *(continued)*

Russell Baker, "Chicken Caper." Copyright © 1984 by The New York Times Company. Reprinted by permission.

Sylvan Barnet, "Writing and Reading: Some Concrete Observations." Copyright © 1985 by Sylvan Barnet. Used by permission of the author.

Ira Berkow, "At Nineteen, Thomas Makes His Decision," *The New York Times*, April 25, 1981. Copyright © 1981 by The New York Times Company. Reprinted by permission.

Sissela Bok, "Placebos." From *Lying: Moral Choice in Public and Private Life* by Sissela Bok. Copyright © 1978 by Sissela Bok. Reprinted by permission of Pantheon Books, a Division of Random House, Inc.

Robert P. Boyle, excerpt from "A Rain of Death on the Striper" is reprinted courtesy of *Sports Illustrated*. © 1984 Time Inc.

Robert H. Brody, "Competing with Cool," *Esquire*, January 1984. Reprinted by permission of the author.

Susan Brownmiller, "The Contrived Postures of Femininity." From *Femininity* by Susan Brownmiller. Copyright © 1983 by Susan Brownmiller. Reprinted by permission of Linden Press, a division of Simon & Schuster, Inc.

Robert Brustein, "Reflections on Horror Movies." From *The Third Theatre* by Robert Brustein. Copyright © 1969 by Robert Brustein. Reprinted by permission of Alfred A. Knopf, Inc.

William F. Buckley, Jr., "Why Don't We Complain?" Reprinted by permission of Wallace & Sheil Agency, Inc. Copyright © 1960, 1963 by William F. Buckley, Jr. First published in *Esquire*.

Fox Butterfield, "Foreign Devils." Copyright © 1982 by Fox Butterfield. Reprinted by permission of Times Books/The New York Times Book Co., Inc. from *China: Alive in the Bitter Sea* by Fox Butterfield.

Roger Caras, "What's a Koala?" Copyright © 1983 by Roger Caras. First appeared in *Geo* Magazine, May 1983. Reprinted by permission of International Creative Management.

Bruce Catton, "Grant and Lee: A Study in Contrasts." From *The American Story*, Earl Schenck Miers, editor. © 1956 by Broadcast Music, Inc. Reprinted by permission.

Malcolm Cowley, "Vices and Pleasures: The View from 80." From *The View from 80* by Malcolm Cowley. Copyright © 1976, 1978, 1980 by Malcolm Cowley. Reprinted by permission of Viking Penguin Inc.

Donna Woolfolk Cross, "Sin, Suffer, and Repent." Reprinted by permission of Coward-McCann from *Mediaspeak* by Donna Woolfolk Cross. Copyright © 1983 by Donna Woolfolk Cross.

Sharon Curtin, "Garbage Man." From *Nobody Ever Died of Old Age* by Sharon R. Curtin. Copyright © 1972 by Sharon R. Curtin. By permission of Little, Brown and Company in association with the Atlantic Monthly Press.

Annie Dillard, "In the Jungle." From *Teaching a Stone to Talk: Expeditions and Encounters* (pp. 53–59) by Annie Dillard. Copyright © 1982 by Annie Dillard. Reprinted by permission of Harper & Row, Publishers, Inc.

Loren Eiseley, "The Angry Winter." Copyright © 1968 by Loren Eiseley. Reprinted from "The Angry Winter" in his volume *The Unexpected Universe* by permission of Harcourt Brace Jovanovich, Inc.

E. M. Forster, "My Wood." From *Abinger Harvest*, copyright 1936, 1946 by Edward Morgan Forster. Reprinted by permission of Harcourt Brace Jovanovich, Inc., and Edward Arnold (Publishers) Ltd.

Robert Frost, lines from "Stopping by Woods on a Snowy Evening." From *The Poetry of Robert Frost* edited by Edward Connery Lathem. Copyright 1923, © 1969

ESSAYS ARRANGED
BY THEME

589

SOCIETY AND SOCIAL CHANGE

EXPLAINING HUMAN BEHAVIOR

DEATH AND DYING

HEALTH AND FOOD

WRITING, READING, AND LANGUAGE

EDUCATION, THINKING, AND LEARNING

ROOTS

INDEX

To the Student:

Part of our job as educational publishers is to try to improve the textbooks we publish. Thus, when revising, we take into account the experience of both instructors and students with the previous edition. At some time your instructor will be asked to comment extensively on *Patterns in Action*, but right now we want to hear from you. After all, though your instructor assigned this book, you are the one who paid for it.

Please help us by completing this questionnaire and returning it to College English, Little, Brown and Company, 34 Beacon Street, Boston, Massachusetts 02106.

School _____ Course title _____

Instructor's name _____

Other books assigned _____

	Liked best			Liked least		Didn't read
Curtin, *Garbage Man*	5	4	3	2	1	_____
Eiseley, *The Angry Winter*	5	4	3	2	1	_____
Huttman, *A Crime of Compassion*	5	4	3	2	1	_____
Berkow, *At Nineteen, Thomas Makes His Decision*	5	4	3	2	1	_____
Walker, *Beauty: When the Other Dancer Is the Self*	5	4	3	2	1	_____
Haines, *The Yard*	5	4	3	2	1	_____
Lee, *Mayakovsky Square*	5	4	3	2	1	_____
Malcolm, *Dad*	5	4	3	2	1	_____
Arlen, *Ode to Thanksgiving*	5	4	3	2	1	_____
White, *Once More to the Lake*	5	4	3	2	1	_____
Thomas, *Clever Animals*	5	4	3	2	1	_____
Butterfield, *Foreign Devils*	5	4	3	2	1	_____
Cross, *Sin, Suffer, and Repent*	5	4	3	2	1	_____
Buckley, *Why Don't We Complain?*	5	4	3	2	1	_____
Jastrow, *Brains and Computers*	5	4	3	2	1	_____
Catton, *Grant and Lee: A Study in Contrasts*	5	4	3	2	1	_____
Goodman, *The Challenge to Keep Family Together*	5	4	3	2	1	_____
Lopez, *My Horse*	5	4	3	2	1	_____
Vilas, *Fried Chicken*	5	4	3	2	1	_____
Woodroffe, *Staging Concerts*	5	4	3	2	1	_____
Petrunkevitch, *The Spider and the Wasp*	5	4	3	2	1	_____
Brody, *Competing with Cool*	5	4	3	2	1	_____
Swain, *Avocados*	5	4	3	2	1	_____
Harsha and Thompson, *Our Rhythms Still Follow the African Sun*	5	4	3	2	1	_____
Lebed, *Who Will Take Care of the Children?*	5	4	3	2	1	_____
Alvarez, *A Test of Will*	5	4	3	2	1	_____
Bok, *Placebos*	5	4	3	2	1	_____
Houseman, *The Night the Martians Landed*	5	4	3	2	1	_____
McCree, *Flea Market*	5	4	3	2	1	_____
Caras, *What's a Koala?*	5	4	3	2	1	_____
Sowell, *We're Not Really "Equal"*	5	4	3	2	1	_____
Perrin, *The Androgynous Man*	5	4	3	2	1	_____

	Liked best				Liked least	Didn't read
Brownmiller, *The Contrived Postures of Femininity*	5	4	3	2	1	_____
Toth, *Cinematypes*	5	4	3	2	1	_____
Brustein, *Reflections on Horror Movies*	5	4	3	2	1	_____
Cowley, *Vices and Pleasures: The View from 80*	5	4	3	2	1	_____
Tanne, *The Great Salt Debate*	5	4	3	2	1	_____
Kanner, *Love for Sale: You Gotta Have Cards*	5	4	3	2	1	_____
Ullman, *Electronic Encyclopedia Salesmen?*	5	4	3	2	1	_____
Goodman, *Honor Society Hypocrisy*	5	4	3	2	1	_____
Kaufman, *Facing Violence*	5	4	3	2	1	_____
Mencken, *The Penalty of Death*	5	4	3	2	1	_____
Parker, *Am r ca s D l g nt C ns rs*	5	4	3	2	1	_____
Baker, *Chicken Caper*	5	4	3	2	1	_____
Abbey, *The Damnation of a Canyon*	5	4	3	2	1	_____
Welty, *Listening*	5	4	3	2	1	_____
Barnet, *Writing and Reading*	5	4	3	2	1	_____
Murray, *The Maker's Eye*	5	4	3	2	1	_____
Rose, *Writing Around Rules*	5	4	3	2	1	_____
Zinsser, *The Act of Writing: One Man's Method*	5	4	3	2	1	_____
Swift, *A Modest Proposal*	5	4	3	2	1	_____
Jefferson, *The Declaration of Independence*	5	4	3	2	1	_____
Forster, *My Wood*	5	4	3	2	1	_____
Orwell, *Politics and the English Language*	5	4	3	2	1	_____
McPhee, *The Search for Marvin Gardens*	5	4	3	2	1	_____
Dillard, *In the Jungle*	5	4	3	2	1	_____
Rodriguez, *Does America Still Exist?*	5	4	3	2	1	_____

1. Are there any authors not included whom you would like to see represented? _____

2. Was the introductory material in each chapter useful? _____
   How might it be improved? _____

3. Were the questions following each selection useful? _____
   How might they be improved? _____

4. Were the questions following each chapter useful? _____
   How might they be improved? _____
   _____

5. Will you keep this book for your library? _____

6. Please add any comments or suggestions. _____
   _____
   _____

7. May we quote you in our promotional efforts for this book?
   _____ yes _____ no

Date _____ Signature _____

Mailing address _____